The International Thesaurus of Musical Terms

Containing Synonyms and Other Related Terms
In English, Italian, French, German, Spanish, Latin and Greek

With Special Attention to Historical and Liturgical Terms

By

Ted Grudzinski

First Edition

Copyright 2006 © by Ted Grudzinski. All rights reserved.

Manufactured in the United States of America

Celebrity Profiles Publishing
P.O. Box 344
Stonybrook, NY 11790
(631) 862-8555
(631) 862-0139 FAX
www.richardgrudens.com

BIOGRAPHY

Author of the recent best seller Winequest - The Wine Dictionary, Ted Grudzinski was born and raised in Brooklyn, New York and is a graduate of the prestigious Brooklyn Technnical High School, where he majored in art. He holds degrees in music from both Queens College in New York and the University of California at Berkeley.

Grudzinski taught high school music classes in Nassau County, Long Island, New York, retiring in 1993 to his "gentleman's farm" deep in Virginia's Shenandoah Valley where he is hard at work on a collection of some 35,000 American and foreign idioms to be published in 2007.

Grudzinski continues to transcribe, compose and arrange music for school, church and professional use, including the words and music for a new musical play.

Ted, a brother of celebrity author Richard Grudens, author of the recent biographies Bing Crosby - Crooner of the Century and When Jolson was King, is a gourmet cook and loves organic gardening.

His most avid interest, however, is researching and tasting wines, an interest that dates back to the late 1970s. He has been tasting, collecting and even selling wines ever since.

INTRODUCTION

This is a the first time a complete English-language **thesaurus of musical terms** has been undertaken in this country. It is a serious attempt at providing synonyms and other closely related terms for each musical term in up to seven languages. In most cases English, Italian, French, German and Spanish equivalents are listed, as many that are commonly known or that are, or were regularly in use. Latin and Greek terms are also included, especially in early music and liturgical entries, and several other foreign terms occur as well. Meanings that are in **boldface** are not given separate entries, since the meanings are cognates that would otherwise appear close by, thereby saving considerable duplication and space. An asterisk (*) placed before a term indicates where to find the fullest list of synonyms for that term, and also where to find lists of related terms. In this way a great deal of repetition is avoided. This is not meant to be an exhaustive representation of every music term that ever existed, but rather a serious beginning of a new process in musical lexicography.

Many obscure, technical, ethnic, and less important terms, esp. in the pop music field, have not been included in this volume, and many foreign equivalents have been, regrettably, difficult to obtain. Regrettable also are the numerous errors that have proven to be even more elusive. Highly detailed technical terms and organ terms have been kept down to a minimum. However, Liturgy, historical, and Spanish terms have been given very strong representation.

.

For the most part terms are cross-indexed, although not every translation or synonym will have a separate entry, but most will. Terms that have numerous synonyms which have numerous translations of each synonym might produce enormous lists; therefore, it seemed wise to relegate translations of a synonym to each individual term. A typical case would be **backround music.** A synonym would be **light music**, but the translations of **light music** would be found only under **light music.** There will ocasionally be exceptions to this and other rules. The point is to make this book useful, logical and practical.

Please bear in mind that this is NOT a DICTIONARY - it is a THESAURUS - that is, a book of word lists; therefore, definitions as such are not included in this book Sometimes, however, a brief meaning will be given in order to clarify the term (when there is not a clear term in use). In addition to synonyms for each term, other related words are included that might be of interest to the reader. You will find that most of the synonyms listed under the main entry will have their own proper entry; however, explanatory words may not always receive a separate entry, depending on common usage and convenience. In addition, it should be noted that parts of speech are not always in agreement in some entries, and the same can be said for number (singular and plural)

It is my earnest wish that this volume will be useful, interesting, colorful, entertaining, informative, easy and fun to use. Suggestions, corrections and additions will be greatly appreciated.

Ted Grudzinski, Churchville, VA, April, 2006

Abbreviations used in this book

Byz. – Byzantine	**Jap.** - Japan
c. – century (date)	**Lat.** – Latin
E. – English (in special cases)	**n.** – noun
e.g. – for example	**org.** – organ
esp. – especially	**Pol.** – Polish
etc. – and so on	**Port.** – Portuguese
Fr. – French	**Prov.** – Provençal (Occitan)
G. – German	**Rus.** – Russian
Gr. – Greek	**S. Amer.** – South American
Heb. – Hebrew	**Sp.** – Spanish
Hung. - Hungarian	**Uk.** - Ukraine
Ind. - India	**vb.** – verb
instr. – instrument	**vs.** - versus (as opposed to: antonym)
It. – Italian	

A

AAB form
*bar (G.)
stollen (G.)
formes fixes (Fr.)
lai (Fr.)
Abgesang (G.)
Leich (G.)
song
aria
folk song
Minnesinger
Troubadour (Fr.)
Trouvère (Fr.)

ABA form
* three-part form
da capo form
tripartite form
song form
ternary form
arch form
bow form
Bogenform (G.)

A instrument
clarinet
horn

B flat instrument
saxophone (soprano, tenor and bass)
clarinet (soprano, bass and contrabass)
trumpet

C instrument
strings
bassoon
trumpet
oboe

trombone
flute
harp
guitar
lute
keyboards

E instrument
horn
French horn

E flat instrument
saxophone (sopranino, alto, and baritone)

F instrument
horn
French horn
English horn

G instrument
alto flute
bass flute
horn

à 2 (Fr., It.)
.* unison

2. divisi

a battuta (It.)
a tempo (It.)
primo tempo (It.)
first tempo
* in tempo

2.* in time
in strict time
in tempo
a tempo (It.)
en mesure (Fr.)
a compás (Sp.)
im Takt (G.)
im Zeitmass (G.)

a bene placito (It.)

*freely
ad libitum (Lat.)
a capriccio (It.)
a piacere (It.)
beneplacito (It.)
libre (Fr.)
à plaisir (Fr.)
à votre gré (Fr.)
au caprice (Fr.)
nach Belieben (G.)
nach Gefallen (G.)
a placer (Sp.)
a voluntad (Sp.)
a capricho (Sp.)

a bocca chiuso (It.)
to hum
to trill
canticchiare (It.)
furberia del canto (It.)
chantonner (Fr.)
avec bouche fermée (Fr.)
fredonner (Fr.)
trällern (G.)
Brummstimmen (G.)
canturrear (Sp.
canticar (Sp.))

a cap(p)ella (It.)
*unaccompanied
Palestrina style
without accompaniment
alla Palestrina (It.)
stile antico (It.)
stile osservato (It.)
sans instruments (Fr.)
style de chapelle (Fr.)
à la Palestrienne (Fr.)
im Kapellstil (G.)
Palestrina-Stil (G.)
música vocal (Sp.)
a capilla (Sp.)

2. 2/2 meter
cut time
alla breve (It.)

a cuatro manos (Sp.)
  four-handed (piano)
  a quattro mani (It.)
  à quatre mains (Fr.)
  vierhändig (G.)

à deux (Fr.)
  a due (It.)
  a dos (Sp.)
  zu Zweit (G.)
  in Zwei (G.)
  * in two
  .together
  * unison
  à 2

 2. divisi
  separately
  * in two

a fior di labbra (It.)
  softly sung
  very lightly sung
  au bout des lèvres (Fr.)
  gehaucht (G.)
  piano (It.)
  con la boca chico (Sp.)

a forma aperta (It.)
  through-composed
  progressive composition
  open form
  durchkomponiert (G.)
  de forme ouverte (Fr.)
  compuesto de principio a fin
(Sp.)

à go-go (Fr.)
  *night club
  dance club
  night spot
  cabaret
  discothèque
  cocktail lounge

a grado a grado (It.)

little by little
gradually
step by step
by degrees
di grado (It.)
per gradi (It.)
poco a poco (It., Sp.)
poi a poi (It.)
peu à peu (Fr.)
petit à petit (Fr.)
nach und nach (G.)
de grado en grado (Sp.)
por grado (Sp.)

à l'allemande (Fr,)
  in the German style
  in the style of an allemande,
landler or waltz
  alla tedesca (It.)
  a la alemana (Sp.)

à l'octave (Fr.)
  at the octave
  all' ottava (It.)
  in der Oktave (G.)
  a la octava (Sp.)

à la (Fr.)
  * in the manner of
  in the style of
  alla (It.)
  all' (It.)
  a la (Sp.)

à la blanche (Fr.)
  *cut time
  double time
  quick time
  march time
  alla breve (It.)
  a cappella (It.)
  in halben Noten (G.)
  a la breve (Sp.)

à la boiteuse (Fr.)
  *syncopated

off-beat
boiteux (Fr.)
contra-tempo (It.)
alla zoppa (It.)
synkopierung (G.)
cojeando (Sp.)

à la fin (Fr.)
  al fine (It.)
  to the end
  bis zu Ende (G.)
  hasta el fin (Sp.)

à la hausse (Fr.)
  at the frog
  *down-bow
  al tallone (It.)
  arco/arcata in giù (It.)
  au talon (Fr.)
  tiré (Fr.)
  am Frosch (G.)
  Abstrich (G.)
  al talón (Sp.)
  tirado (Sp.)

vs. de la pointe (Fr.)
  up-bow
  arco in su (It.)

à la hongroise (Fr.)
  *gypsy style
  alla zingara (It.)
  à la tzigane (Fr.)
  nach Art der Zigeuner (G.)
  al estilo cingaro (Sp.)

a la manera di (It.)
  in the style of
  after (a composer)
  alla (It.)
  à la manière de (Fr.)
  à la (Fr.)
  nach Art der (G.)
  a la manera de (Sp.)

à la même (Fr.)

same tempo
  *a tempo (It.)
  tempo primo (It.)
  *l'istesso tempo (It.)
  medesimo tempo (It.)
  le même mouvement (Fr.)
  dasselbe Zeitmass (G.)
  die gleiche Geschwindigkeit (G.)
  el mismo tiempo/movimiento (Sp.)

à la mesure (Fr.)
  *a tempo (It.)
  a battuta (It.)
  en mesure (Fr.)
  im Zeitmass (G.)
  im Takt (G.)
  a tiempo (Sp.)
  a compás (Sp.)
  in tempo

à la Palestrienne (Fr.)
  Palestrina style
  unaccompanied
  a cappella (It.)
  alla Palestrina
  stile antico (It.)
  stile osservato (It.)
  style de chapelle (Fr.)
  im Kapellstil (G.)
  Palestrina-Stil (G.)
  a capilla (Sp.)
  música vocal (Sp.)

à la Turque (Fr.)
  Turkish military style
  janissary music
  alla Turca (It.)
  musique Turque (Fr.)
  *chapeau Chinois (Fr.)
  nach Turkischer Art (G.)
  a la turca (Sp.)
  al estilo Turca (Sp.)

a memoria (It.)
  memorized
  from memory
  by heart
  by rote
  par coeur (Fr.)
  auswendig (G.)
  de memoria (Sp.)

à part (Fr.)
  *aside
  whispered
  stage whisper
  very *soft
  sotto voce (It.)
  in disparte (It.)
  beiseite (G.)
  für Sich (G.)
  a parte (Sp.)
  de coté (Fr.)
  à mi-voix (Fr.)

a piacere (It.)
  *freely
  ad libitum (Lat.)
  a bene placito (It.)
  a capriccio (It.)
  au caprice (Fr.)
  à plaisir (Fr.)
  libre (Fr.)
  nach Gefallen (G.
  a placer (Sp.)

à plusiers voix (Fr.)
  multi-voiced
  polyphonic
  a più voci (It.)
  vielstimmig (G.)
  a muchas voces (Sp.)
  a varias voces (Sp.)

a poco a poco (It., Sp.)
  little by little
  gradually
  by degrees
  step by step
  *poco a poco (It., Sp.)

  peu à peu (Fr.)
  petit à petit (Fr.)
  nach und nach (G.)

à premier vue (Fr.)
  at first sight
  *at sight
  a prima vista (It.)
  a primera vista (Sp.)
  à vue (Fr.)
  vom Blatt (G.)

a punta d'arco (It.)
  with the point of the bow
  arco in su (It.)
  de la pointe (Fr.)
  avec le pointe de l'archet (Fr.)
  mit der Spitze (G.)
  Anstrich (G.)
  Aufstrich (G.)
  a la punta del arco (Sp.)
  *up-bow

vs. al tallone (It.)
  downbow

à quatre mains (Fr.)
  piano/organ duet
  a quattro mani (It.)
  a cuatro manas (Sp.)
  vierhändig (G.)

a rovescio (It.)
  contrary motion
  opposite motion
  inversion
  al rovescio (It.)
  mouvement contraire (Fr.)
  movimiento contrario (Sp.)
  Gegenbewegung (G.)

à sa place (Fr.)
  as written
  as it stands
  at pitch
  ad locum (Lat.)

loco (It.)
come stà (It.)
comme il est écrit (Fr.)
am Orte (G.)
wie geschrieben steht (G.)
wie es dasteht (G.)
a su puesto (Sp.)
como está (Sp.)

a sovoz (Sp.)
*aside
in a low voice
under one's breath
pianissimo (It.)
sotto voce (It.)
mezza voce (It.)
à part (Fr.)
à mi-voix (Fr.)
beiseite (G.)
mit halbe Stimme (G.)
cuchicheado (Sp.)
a parte (Sp.)

a tempo (It.)
same tempo
back to the original tempo
first tempo
tempo one
l'istesso tempo (It.)
tempo primo (It.)
à la même (Fr.)
premier mouvement (Fr.)
le même mouvement (Fr.)
die gleiche Geschwindigkeit
(G.)
erstes Tempo/Zeitmass (G.)
dasselbe Zeitmass (G.)
mismo movimiento (Sp.)
primero tiempo (Sp.)
primero movimiento (Sp.)
movimiento anterior (Sp.)

  2. in time
in tempo
a battuta (It.)
en mesure (Fr.)

à la mesure (Fr.)
mesuré (Fr.)
a compás (Sp.)
a tiempo (Sp.)
im Zeitmass (G.)
im Takt (G.)

a una voce (It.)
*solo
monody
monophonic
homophonic
une voix seule (Fr.)
einstimmig (G.)
für eine Stimmig (G.)
a una voz (Sp.)

à volonté (Fr.)
* freely
ad libitum (Lat.)
a voluntad (Sp.)
à votre gré (Fr.)

à vue (Fr.)
* at sight
at first sight
à premier vue (Fr.)

ab (G.)
off (organ stop or mute)
cancel
découpler (Fr.)
auflösen (G.)

vs. auf, an

ab initio (Lat.)
da capo (It.)
from the beginning
from the top
dal principio (It.)
au début (Fr.)
vom Anfang (G.)
von Vorn (G.)
desde el principio (Sp.)
reprise

recapitulation
D.C.

abandonné (Fr.)
with abandon
free
unrestrained
avec abandon Fr.)
con abbandono (It.)
mit Hingabe (G.)
Hingebung (G.)
con abandono (Sp.)

abbassamento (It.)
lowering, esp. of one hand
under another, in piano playing

abbassare (It.)
to flat a note, etc.
bemolisar (It.)
bémoliser (Fr.)
abaisser (Fr.)
baisser (Fr.)
erniedrigen (G.)
senken (G.)
abemolar (Sp.)
bajar, rebajar (Sp.)

vs. alzare (It.)
diesare (It.)
raise, sharp

abbattimento (It.)
*downbeat
first beat of the measure
strong beat
thesis (Gr.)
crusis (Lat.)
frappé (Fr.)

vs. anacrusi (It., Sp.)

abbellimenti (It.)
embellishments
*ornaments
divisions

4

grace notes
fioretti (It.)
fregiaturi (It.)
agréments (Fr.)
ornements (Fr.)
Verzierungen (G.)
adornos (Sp.)

abbellire (It.)
embellish
ornament
embroider
adornare (It.)
embellir (Fr.)
verzieren (G.)
adornar (Sp.)

Abc-diren (G.)
*solmization
sol-fa
A-b-c musikalische
Gesangübung (G.)
solfeggio (It.)
solfège (Fr.)
solfeo (Sp.)
tonic solfa

abdämpfen (G.)
to *mute
dampen
muffle
dämpfen (G.)
assourdir (Fr.)
smorzare (It.)
apagar (Sp.)

Abendandacht (G.)
Vespers
Evensong
prayer service
*Divine Office
canonical hour
Vesperae (Lat.)
vespro (It.)
vêpres (Fr.)
Vesper (G.)

Visperas (Sp.)

Abendmahl (G.)
communion service
Eucharist
agape feast
Holy Communion
*mass
Lord's Supper
love feast
*liturgy
Divine Service
Agende (G.)
Kirchenordnung (G.)
Kirchenamt (G.)

Abendmusik (G.)
evening music
evening song
serenata (It.)
*serenade
nocturne
Abendlied (G.)
Nachtmusik (G.)

vs. Morgenständchen (G.)

abertura acústica (Sp.)
soundhole
*rose, rose hole
F-hole
occhi (It.)
foro di resonanza (It.)
ouïe (Fr.)
Schalloch (G.)
oído (Sp.)

Abgesang (G.)
In medieval music:
cauda (Lat.), ending section of
a lai
bar form
lai

vs. Stollen, pedes

abgestossen (G.)
*detatched
*staccato
détaché (Fr.)
piqué (Fr.)
destacado (Sp.)
no ligado (Sp.)

abierto (Sp.)
first ending
apertum (Lat.)
prima volta (It.)
aperto (It.)
ouvert (Fr.)
offen (G.)

Ablösen (G.)
finger substitution
diteggiatura cambiata (It.)
changer le doigté (Fr.)
cambiar la digitación (Sp.)

Abnehmen(d), Abnehmung (G.)
*diminuendo
*decrescendo (It.)
get softer
decay
fade out
die away
morendo (It.)
calando (It.)
en perdant le son (Fr.)
Sterbend (G.)
expirando (Sp.)

vs. anschwellend (G.)
crescendo (It.)

Abreissung (G.)
interrupted melody
hiatus
abruptio (Lat.)
break
caesura
pause
*fermata (It., E.)

hocket
railroad tracks

Absatz (G.)
    section
    part (of a piece)
    fragment
    excerpt
    parte (It., Sp.)
    partie (Fr.)
    Satz (G.)
    Teil (G.)

2. melodic *phrase

Abschlag (G.)
    *downbeat
    strong beat
    crusis (Lat.)
    thesis (Gr., Lat.)
    abbattimento (It.)
    frappé (Fr.)
    Abtakt (G.)

vs. Auftakt (G.)

 2. cut-off (conducting)
    taglio (It.)
    coupé (Fr.)

abschreiben (G.)
    plagiarize
    steal
    quote
    borrow
    imitate
    parody
    plagiare (It.)
    plagier (Fr.)
    plagiar (Sp.)

abschwellen (G.)
    *decrescendo (It.)
    softer
    diminuendo (It.)

vs. wachsend (G.)

absetzen (G.)
    *detatched
    staccato (It.)
    détaché (Fr.)

vs. gebunden (G.)
    legato (It.)

absolute music
    abstract music
    pure music
    musique pure (Fr.)
    musica assoluta (It.)
    música absoluta (Sp.)
    absolute Musik (G.)
    música pura (I., Sp.)

vs. *program music

absolute pitch
    true pitch
    *perfect pitch
    orecchio assoluto (It.)
    oreille absolue (Fr.)
    absolutes Gehör (G.)
    oïdo absoluto (Sp.)

vs. relative pitch

Abstand (G.)
    *interval (pitch)
    tonal distance
    diastema (Gr.)
    intervallum (Lat.)
    intervallo (It.)
    intervalle (Fr.)
    intervalo (Sp.)

abstimmen (G.)
    to *tune
    adjust the pitch
    accordare (It.)
    accorder (Fr.)
    einstimmen (G.)

stimmen (G.)
akkordieren (G.)
acordar (Sp.)

abstossen (G.)
    to detatch
    play staccato

2. remove a stop (organ)

Abstrich (G.)
    *down-bow
    arco in giù (It.)
    tiré (Fr.)
    tirado (Sp.)

vs. Aufstrich (G.)

Abstufung (G.)
    nuance (E., Fr.)
    shading
    inflection
    sfumatura (It.)
    graduare (It.)
    matizado (Sp.)

Abweichung (G.)
    a variant
    *variation

Abzug (G.)
    *ornament
    *appoggiatura
    non-harmonic tone
    grace note

acachatura (Sp.)
    *acciaccatura (It.)
    *mordent

academy of music
    *concert hall
    recital hall
    opera house
    symphonic hall
    philharmonic hall

music hall

2. conservatory of music
   lyceum
   *music school
   conservatoire (Fr.)
   schola cantorum (Lat.)
   Konservatorium (G.)
   liceo (It.)
   institute
   conservatorio (It., Sp.)
   académie de musique (Fr.)
   accademia musicale (It.)
   Hochschule für Musik (G.)
   Musikakademie (G.)
   escuela de música (Sp.)
   scuola di música (It.)

accademia (It.)
   concert
   *performance
   recital
   rendition
   program
   presentation

2. music society
   philharmonic society
   *academy of music

accelerando, accelerato (It.)
   gradually *faster
   stringendo (It.)
   stretto (It.)
   en serrant (Fr.)
   en serrant le mouvement (Fr.)

vs. ritardando (It.)
   allargando (It.)
   rallentando (It.)

accent (E., Fr.)
   a *stress
   accento (It.)
   Accent (G.)
   Betonung (G.)

acento (Sp.)
sforzando (It.)
sforzato (It.)
rinforzato (It.)
fortepiano (It.)
forzando, forzato (It.)

2. metrical accent
   agogic accent
   tonic accent
   dynamic accent

accentor (E.)
   lead singer (choir)
   *cantor
   hazan, chazzan (Heb.)

accentuation
   declamation
   text underlay
   *stress

accentus (Lat.)
   chanting or intoning by the
priest at the altar, or simple chant.

   vs, concentus, sung by the
choir. or elaborate chant.

accentus ecclesiastici (Lat.)
   formulae for the seven
different modal inflections for
intoning the psalms in plainsong.
   *intonation
   incipit
   psalm-tone
   modes
   ecclesiastical modes

acciaccatura (It.)
   grace note
   ornament
   appoggiatura (short)
   *mordent
   pincé étouffé (Fr.)
   crushed note

appoggiatura brève (Fr.)
kürzer Vorschlag (G.)
Quetschung (G.)
Zusammenschlag (G.)
acachatura (Sp.)
apoyatura breve (Sp.)

accidental
   altered tone
   non-harmonic tone
   chromatic tone/sign
   sharp, flat, etc.
   half-step
   accidente (It.)
   accident (Fr.)
   altération (Fr.)
   signe accidentel (Fr.)
   Vorzeichen (G.)
   Versetzungszeichen (G.)
   accidente (Sp.)

acción (Sp.)
   *action (piano)
   mechanism

accolade (E., Fr.)
   *brace
   bracket
   staves
   grappa (It.)
   graffa (It.)
   Akkolade (G.)
   Klammer (G.)
   corchete (Sp.)

accompaniment
   backround
   backup
   support
   assist
   accompagnamento (It.)
   accompagnement (Fr.)
   Begleitung (G.)
   acompañamiento (Sp.)
   music minus one
   split track

karaoke
recorded accompaniment

accompanist
backup
support
accompagnatore (It.)
accompagnateur (Fr.)
Begleiter (G.)
acompañante (Sp.)
.
accompany
accompagnare (It.)
accompagner (Fr.)
begleiten (G.)
acompañar (Sp.)

accoppiamento (It.)
*coupler (organ)
accouplement (Fr.)
tirasse (Fr.)
Koppel(pedal) (G.)
Pedalkoppel (G.)
enganche al pedalero (Sp.)
acoplamiento (Sp.)

accord (Fr.)
a *chord
triad
harmony
accordo (It.)
Akkord (G.)
acorde (Sp.)
cluster
homophonic
Dreiklang (G.)

2. accordatura (It.)

accord brisé (Fr.)
broken chord
accordo arpeggiato (It.)
accord arpégé (Fr.)
gebrochener Akkord (G.)
acorde arpegiado (Sp.)

vs. accord plaqué (Fr.)

accord de septième de dominante (Fr.)
*dominant seventh chord
accordo di settima di dominante (It.)
Dominantsept(imen)akkord (G.)
acorde de séptima de dominante (Sp.)

accord de sixte (Fr.)
sixth-chord
six-three chord
first inversion chord/triad
chord of the sixth
accordo di sesta (It.)
erste Umkehrung (G.)
Sextakkord (G.)
acorde sexta (Sp.)
acorde sexta y tercera (Sp.)

accord de sixte augmentée (Fr.)
*augmented sixth-chord
sesta eccedente (It.)
sesta aumentata (It.)
übermässige Sexte (G.)
sexta aumentada (Sp.)

accord de sixte Napolitaine (Fr.)
Neapolitan sixth chord
accordo di sesta Napoletana (It.)
sesta Napoletana (It.)
Neapolitanischer Sextakkord (G.)
acorde de sexta Napoletana (Sp.)

accord parfait (Fr.)
common chord
accòrdo perfetto (It.)
acorde perfecto (Sp.)
Dreiklang (G.)

accord plaqué (Fr.)
solid chord
unbroken chord
non-arpeggio (It.)
simultaneous
concento (It.)
accordo incollato (It.)
accordo sovrapposto (It.)
acorde apoyado (Sp.)
platter Akkord (G.)
Akkord anschlagen (G.)

vs. arpeggio (It.)
accord brisé (Fr.)
broken chord

accord renversé (Fr.)
inverted chord
first inversion
second inversion
third inversion

accord substitué (Fr.)
substitute chord
jazz chord
accordo sostituito (It.)
Substitutklang (G.)
stellvertretender Akkord (G.)
acorde sustituido (Sp.)

accordamento (It.)
* consonance

accordando (It.)
in tune
tuned

accordare (It.)
to *tune
adjust the pitch
intonare (It.)
accorder (Fr.)
stimmen (G.)
einstimmen (G.)
afinar (Sp.)
acordar (Sp.)

accordatura (It.)
 tuning
 tuning scheme of string
instruments
 cordatura (It.)
 l'accord (Fr.)
 Stimmung (G.)
 acorde (Sp.)
 scordatura (It.)

accordion
 concertina
 squeezebox
 hand harmonica
 keyboard
 piano accordion
 fisarmonica (It.)
 armonica a manticino (It.)
 organetto (It.)
 soufflet (Fr.)
 accordéon (Fr.)
 accordéon à boutons/à
clavier **(Fr.)**
 Handharmonika (G.)
 Accordeon (G.)
 Akkordeon (G.)
 Ziehharmonika (G.)
 Schifferklavier (G.)
 Quetsche (G.)
 Quetschkommode (G.)
 Konzertina (G.)
 fuelle (Sp.)
 bandoneón (Sp.)
 accordeón (Sp.)

accordo (It.)
 a *chord
 triad
 harmony
 accord (Fr.)
 Akkord (G.)
 acorde (Sp.)

2. bass viol with 12-15 strings
 lyre, bass lyre
 Barbary lyre

 lira (It.)
 lirone (It.)
 archiviola di lira (It.)
 lira di braccio (It.)
 lira tedesca (It.)

accordo di quarto e sesta (It.)
 six-four chord
 second inversion
 accord de sixte et quarte
(Fr.)
 Quartsextakkord (G.)
 acorde de sexta-cuarta (Sp.)
 acorde de sexta y cuarta
(Sp.)

accordoir (Fr.)
 tuning key
 tuning cone or horn (organ)
 accordatoio (It.)
 clef d'accordeur (Fr.)
 Stimmhammer (G.)
 afinador (Sp.)

accouplement (Fr.)
 *coupler, pedal coupler
(organ)
 accoppiamento (It.)
 acoplamiento (Sp.)
 Koppel, Koppelpedal (G.)
 Pedalkoppel (G.)
 enganche al pedalero (Sp.)

accrescimento (It.)
 *augmentation (fugal theme)
 augmentationem (Lat.)
 aumentazione (It.)

vs. diminuzione (It.)

accusé (Fr.)
 emphasized
 prominent
 brought out
 con enfasi (It.)
 risaltato (It.)

 enfatico (It.)
 avec emphase (Fr.)
 mis en relief (Fr.)
 emphatique (Fr.)
 en dehors (Fr.)
 betont (G.)
 mit Emphase (G.)
 hervorgehoben (G.)
 nachdrucklich (G.)
 con énfasis (Sp.)
 enfático (Sp.)
 resaltado (Sp.)

acento (Sp.)
 stress
 *accent

acetabulum, -a (Lat.)
 cymbals
 cinelli (It.)
 piatti (It.)
 cymbales (Fr.)
 Becken (G.)

Achte (G.)
 octave (E., Fr.)
 ottava (It.)
 Oktave (G.)
 octava (Sp.)

Achtel, Achtelnote (G.)
 eighth note
 quaver
 croma (It.)
 croche (Fr.)
 corchea (Sp.)
 unca (Lat.)
 semiminim (Lat.)
 hooked note

Achtelpause (G.)
 eighth rest
 quaver rest
 pausa di croma (It.)
 demi-soupir (Fr.)
 silencio de corchea (Sp.)

acid rock
    hard rock
    heavy metal
    *rock and roll
    pop music

acorde (Sp.)
    chord
    triad
    accordo (It.)
    accord (Fr.)
    Akkord (G.)
    Dreiklang (G.)

2. tuning scheme
    accordatura (It.)
    cordatura (It.)
    l'accord (Fr.)
    Stimmung (G.)
    scordatura (It.)

acorde apoyado (Sp.)
    solid chord
    not arpeggiated
    accordo incollato (It.)
    accord plaqué (Fr.)
    platter Akkord (G.)
    Akkord anschlagen (G.)

acorde pivote (Sp.)
    pivotal chord
    common chord
    secondary dominant
    interdominant
    modulation
    Zwischendominante (G.)

acoustic bass
    string bass
    bass fiddle
    bull fiddle
    stand up bass
    upright bass
    double bass
    contrabass
    *bass

    bass viol
    contrabbasso (It.)
    Kontrabass (G.)
    contrebasse (Fr.)
    octobasse (Fr.)
    contrabajo (Sp.)

vs. electric bass
    bass guitar

2. resultant tone (organ)
    resultant bass
    combination tone

acoustic guitar
    classical guitar
    folk guitar
    Spanish guitar
    vihuela (Sp.)

vs. electric guitar

acoustical ceiling
    acoustical tiles/walls
    anechoic chamber
    dead room
    echoless

acoustical feedback
    feedback
    microphone squeal
    reazione (It.)
    réaction (Fr.)
    Rukkoppelung (G.)
    Reakion (G.)
    reacción (Sp.)

acoustics
    sound
    vibration
    frequency
    pitch
    acoustique (Fr.)
    Akustik (G.)
    acústica (It., Sp.)
    science of sound

2. characteristics of sound

act
    scene
    actus (Lat.)
    acte (Fr.)
    atto (It.)
    Akt (G.)
    Aufzug (G.)
    acto (Sp.)

act-tune
    *entr'acte
    curtain tune/music
    interlude
    act music (17c.)
    scene change music
    intermezzo (It.)
    intermède (Fr.)
    divertissement (Fr.)
    Zwischenspiel (G.)
    intermedio (Sp.)

action
    mechanism (of piano)
    meccanica (It.)
    mécanique (Fr.)
    Mechanik (G.)
    mecanismo (Sp.)
    acción (Sp.)

2. (of organ)
    trasmissione (It.)
    traction (Fr.)
    Traktur (G.)
    tracción (Sp.)

active tone/chord
    dissonant tone/chord
    unstable tone/chord

vs. inactive tone/chord

acuta (Lat.)
    *mixture (organ)
    high mixture (3-5 ranks)

acute mixture
compound stop
cymbale (Fr.)
Scharf (G.)
mutation stop

acuto (It.)
shrill
loud
aigu (Fr.)
scharf (G.)
hoch (G.)
agudo (Sp.)

ad-lib
*improvise
impromptu
extempore
play by ear
fake it
jam
read charts
follow lead sheets

ad libitum (Lat.)
a bene placito (It.)
*freely
ad placitum (Lat.)
a piacere (It.)
libre (Fr.)

vs. obligato (It.)

ad locum (Lat.)
at (that) pitch
as written
as it stands
loco (It.)
come stà (It.)
à sa place (Fr.)
comme il est écrit (Fr.)
am Orte (G.)
wie es dasteht (G.)
wie geschrieben steht (G.)
a su puesto (Sp.)
como está (Sp.)

ad longum (Lat.)
in equal values (medieval church music)
*free rhythm
Gregorian chant
chant style

adagietto (It.)
*slow
not as slow as adagio

2. a short, slow piece

adagio (It.)
*slow, slowly
lento (It., Sp.)
largo (It.)
adagietto (It.)
lent, lentement (Fr.)
langsam (G.)
despacio (Sp.)
lentamente (Sp.)

vs. allegro (It.)
presto (It.)

2. a slow piece or movement

adapt
*arrange
edit
transcribe
elaborate
improvise
extemporize
adapter (Fr.)
adattare (It.)
adaptar (Sp.)

added sixth
triad plus a sixth
sixte ajouté (Fr.)

additamenta (It.)
solo verse

solo phrase answered by a refrain (13th c. Fr. song)

addolorato (It.)
plaintive
sad, sadly
doleful
lagnoso (It.)
plaintif (Fr.)
klagend (G.)
schmerzlich (G.)
lamentoso (It., Sp.)
doloroso (It., Sp.)

adiastematic
staffless (neumes)
nondiastematic
in campo aperto (Lat., open field)
cheironomic
oratorical
cantillation
ekphonetic
ecphonetic

vs. diastematic

addition (E., Fr.)
*dot (added to a note or rest)
punctum (Lat.)
punto, puntato (It.)
point (Fr.)
Punkt (G.)
puntado, puntillo (Sp.)

adornar (Sp.)
embellish
ornamented
embroider
adornare (It.)
verzieren (G.)
abbellire (It.)
embellir (Fr.)
melismatic
ornate

adorno (Sp.)
  grace note
  *ornament (E.)
  ornement (Fr.)
  agrément (Fr.)
  abbellimento (It.)
  adornamento (It.)
  fioretto (It.)
  fregiatura (It.)
  Verzierung (G.)

Aeolian
  wind-like sound
  eolio (It., Sp.)
  éolien (Fr.)
  aolisch (G.)
  Aeolian harp
  wind harp
  zither

2. mode nine,. a-a'

Aeolian harp
  wind harp
  zither
  arpa eolia (It., Sp.)
  harpe éoline (Fr.)
  Äolsharfe (G.)
  Windharfe (G.)
  Geisterharfe (G.)
  Wetterharfe (G.)

Aeolian mode (mode 9, A-A)
  natural minor scale
  minor scale
  hypodorian mode

aeoline, aeolina
  *harmonium
  aeolodicon
  aeolodion
  aeolsklavier
  melicordion

2. mouth organ
  *harmonica

aeoline
  soft reed stop (organ)
  soft string stop

Aequalstimmen (G.)
  equal voices
  voces aequales (Lat.)
  voci pari (It.)
  voci eguales (It.)
  voix égales (Fr.)
  gleiche Stimmen (G.)
  voces iguales (Sp.)
  men's voices
  women's voices
  treble voices
  close harmony
  barbershop harmony
  enge Harmonie (G.)
  enge Lage (G.)

vs. gemischte Stimmen (G.)

2. eight-foot pitch (organ pipes)

aer (Lat., Gr.)
  *song (16 c.)
  air
  tune
  melody
  *aria

aerophone(s)
  wind instrument
  brass and woodwinds
  fiati (It.)
  strumenti a fiato (It.)
  instruments à vent (Fr.)
  Blasinstrumente (G.)
  instrumentos de viento (Sp.)

2. reed instrument
  *harmonium
  accordion
  harmonica

aeuia (Lat.)
  *alleluia (shorthand)
  aevia (lat.)
  euouae (Lat.)
  evovae (Lat.)
  proper of the mass

affannato, affannoso (It.)
  agitated
  *agitato (It.)
  affrettando (It.)
  essouflé (Fr.)
  atemlos (G.)
  anheloso (Sp.)

affettuoso, affetto, con affezione (It.)
  *tenderly
  with feeling
  con affetto (It.)
  con affezione (It.)
  affectueux (Fr.)
  innig (G.)
  herzlich (G.)
  carinoso (Sp.)

affinalis (Lat.)
  final (chant)
  close
  *cadence
  confinalis (Lat.)
  finalis (Lat.)

affrettando, affrettato (It.)
  hurrying
  agitated
  *agitato (It.)
  affannato (It.)
  en pressant (Fr.)
  eilend (G.)
  apresurando (Sp.)

afinador (Sp.)
  tuning key/hammer
  tuning fork
  accordatoio (It.)

forchetta d'accordo (It.)
accordoir (Fr.)
fourchette tonique (Fr.)
clef d'accordeur (Fr.)
Stimmhammer (G.)
Gabelton (G.)
Stimmgabel (G.)

afinar (Sp.)
*tune (up)
set the pitch
intonare (It.)
accordare (It.)
accorder (Fr.)
einstimmen (G.)
stimmen (G.)

Afro-Cuban music
Latin-American jazz/pop
South-American music
latin disco
salsa music
musica sudamericana (It.)
musique d'Amérique latine (Fr.)
musique latino-Américaine (Fr.)
lateinamerikanische Musik (G.)
música tropical (Sp.)
música latinoamericana (Sp.)
mambo
cha-cha-cha
rumba
bolero
tango
conga

after-beat
ending of a trill
trill
Nachschlag (G.)
terminaison (Fr.)
note de complément (Fr.)

after-dance
second dance of a pair
Nachtanz (G.)
Proportz, Proportio (G.)
tripla (It.)
rotta (It.)
proporzione (It.)
segunda danza (Sp.)

Agende (G.)
*liturgy
service
Divine Service
liturgia (Lat., It., Sp)
liturgie (Fr.)
Liturgie (G.)
Kirchenordnung (G.)
Kirchenamt (G.)
Gottesdienst (G.)
Abendmahl (G.)
ritual, rite
rubrics
worship service
*Mass
eucharist
Holy Communion
Lord' Supper
agape feast
love feast

agent
representative
booking agent
manager
impresario

agitato (It.)
agitated
agité (Fr.)
aufgeregt (G.)
agitado (Sp.)
affannato (It.)
affrettando (It.)

2. *concerto
*concitato

Agnus Dei (Lat.)
Lamb of God
mass movement
ordinary of the mass

agogic accent
duration accent
agógica (It., Sp.)
agogique (Fr.)
agogik (G.)

vs. tonic, metrical accents

agrément (Fr.)
*ornament
grace note
embellishment
adornamento (It.)
fioretto (It.)
fregiatura (It.)
ornamento (It.)
abbellimento (It.)
ornement (Fr.)
Verzierung (G.)
adorno (Sp.)

agudo (Sp.)
shrill
loud
deafening
ear-splitting
acuto (It.)
forte, fortissimo (It.)
aigu (Fr.)
scharf (G.)
hoch (G.)

agujero (Sp.)
fingerhole
buco (It.)
foro (It.)
trou (Fr.)
Fingerloch (G.)
Griffloch (G.)
Tonloch (G.)
orificio (Sp.)

Aida trumpet
    long, straight trumpet
    trompette thébaine (Fr.)
    Aïdatrompete (G.)
    Fanfarentrompete (G.)
    Heroldstrompete (G.)
    state trumpet
    herald's trumpet
    Alphorn, Alpenhorn (G.)
    ceremonial trumpet
    buisine (Fr.)
    buccina (Lat., medieval)
    tuba (Lat., ancient Rome)
    natural trumpet
    chamade (Fr.)

air, ayre
    *song
    *aria
    melody
    tune
    art song
    folk song
    popular song

air à boire (Fr.)
    *drinking song
    tavern song
    vinata, vinetto (It.)
    brindisi (It.)
    chanson à boire (Fr.)
    Trinklied (G.)
    canción baquica (Sp.)
    carmina burana Lat.,
medieval)

air de cour (Fr. 16-17c.)
    short, strophic song
    *song
    air
    chanson (Fr.)
    canzona, canzonetta (It.)
    Lied (G.)
    canción (Sp.)

aius Trishagion (Gr.)

the *Sanctus (Gallican,
Mozarabic)
    cherubic hymn
    song of the angels
    ter sanctus (Lat.)
    trisagion (Gr.)
    kadosh (H.)
    kedusha (H.)

Akademie (G.)
    *music school
    conservatory
    lyceum
    *academy of music

Akathistos (Gr.)
    Marian hymn (Byzantine)
    hymn to the Blessed Virgin
Mary

Akkolade (G.)
    brace
    bracket
    accolade (E., Fr.)
    graffa, grappa (It.)
    Klammer (G.)
    corchete (Sp.)

Akkord (G.)
    a *chord
    triad
    harmony

2. a set of instruments
    chest (of viols, e.g.)
    consort
    Stimmwerk (G.)

Akkord anschlagen (G.)
    simultaneous
    solid chord
    unbroken chord
    concento (It.)
    accord plaqué (Fr.)
    accordo incollato (It.)
    acorde apoyado (Sp.)

platter Akkord (G.)

vs. arpeggiando (It.)
    gebrochener Akkord (G.)

Akkordeon (G.)
    *accordian
    squeezebox
    fisarmonica (It.)
    accordéon (Fr.)
    Zieharmonika (G.)
    bandoneón (Sp.)
    accordeón (Sp.)

Akkordpassage (G.)
    *arpeggio (It.)
    batterie (Fr.)
    bariolage (Fr.)
    broken chords

akkordieren (G.)
    to *tune
    accordare (It.)
    accorder (Fr.)

Akkordzither (G.)
    *autoharp
    zither

Akolouthia (Gr.)
    *anthology
    Byzantine
    Papadike (Gr.)
    collection

Akt (G.)
    *act
    scene
    actus (Lat.)
    atto (It.)
    acte (Fr.)
    Aufzug (G.)
    acto (Sp.)

Akustik (G.)
    *acoustics

science of sound

al estilo cingaro (Sp.)
  *gypsy style

al fine (It.)
  to the end
  end
  à la fin (Fr.)
  bis zu Ende (G.)
  hasta el fin (Sp.)

al paño (Sp.)
  *backstage
  behind the scenes
  in the wings
  offstage
  fra le quinte (It.)
  dans les coulisses (Fr.)
  hinter der Szene (G.)
  bastidores (Sp.)
  paño (Sp.)

al rovescio (It.)
  a rovescio (It.)
  *contrary motion
  opposite motion
  inversion
  oblique motion

al segno (It.)
  to the sign
  au signe (Fr.)
  bis zu Zeichen (G.)
  al signo (Sp.)
  dal segno (It.)

al talón (Sp.)
  at the frog
  *down-bow
  al tallone (It.)
  arco in giù (It.)
  au talon (Fr.)
  à la hausse (Fr.)
  am Frosch (G.)

vs. con la punta (Sp.)
  a la punta del arco (Sp.)

alabado (Sp.)
  hymn of praise
  akathistos (Gr.)
  alabanza (Sp.)
  Lobgesang (G.)

alba
  song
  morning song
  matin song
  serenade
  dawn song
  (medieval France)
  Troubadour song
  Trouvère song
  aubade (Fr.)
  mattinata (It.)
  Tagelied (G.)
  albada (Sp.)
  albata (It.)
  Wächterlied (G.)

Alberti bass
  broken chords
  *arpeggio (It.)
  tremolo
  batterie (Fr.)
  bariolage (Fr.)
  Brillenbässe (G.)
  Albertischer Bass (G.)

alborada (Sp.)
  *reveille
  wake-up call
  dawn song/music
  matin song
  mattinata (It.)
  aubade (Fr.)

vs. serenada (Sp.)

album (recording)
  song set

LP record
CD recording

vs. a single

album-leaf
  short piece
  foglio d'album (It.)
  pagina d'album (It.)
  feuillet d'album (Fr.)
  hoja de album (Sp.)
  Albumblatt (G.)

aleatory, aleatoric music
  chance music
  indeterminacy music
  dice music
  pitch aggregate
  tone clusters
  atonal
  musica aleatoria (It.)
  musique aléatoire (Fr.)
  aleatorische Musik (G.)
  música aleatoria (Sp.)

alegre (Sp.)
  fast
  allegro (It.)
  vif, vite (Fr.)
  rapide (Fr.)
  lebhaft (G.)
  schnell (G.)
  rasch (G.)
  pronto (Sp.)
  veloz (Sp.)
  presto (It.)

alia modo (Lat.)
  variation
  variant
  alternate version

aliquot tone(s)
  harmonics
  armonichi (It.)
  harmoniques (Fr.)

aliquotes (Fr.)
Aliquottöne (G.)
alicuotes (Sp.)
armonicos (Sp.)
partials
overtones
chord of nature
open note
open tone
natural tone
flageolet tone

aliquot strings
sympathetic strings
corda simpatica (It.)
corda di risonanza (It.)
corde sympathetique (Fr.)
corde de résonance (Fr.)
Resonanzsaite (G.)
cuerda de resonancia (Sp.)
cuerda simpático (Sp.)
viola d'amore (It.)
sitar

Aliquostimmen (G.)
mutation stops (organ)
partials
harmonics
overtones
mixtures
fourniture (Fr.)
Scharff (G.)
cornet (Fr.)
cymbale

all' (It.)
in the manner of
in the style of
à la (Fr.)
alla (It.)
nach Art der (G.)

all' ongarese (It.)
* gypsy style
à la hongroise (Fr.)

all' ottava (It.)
at the octave
à l'octave (Fr.)
in der Oktave (G.)
a la octava (Sp.)
all' unisono (It.)
at the unison or octave
colla voce (It.)

alla (It.)
in the manner of
in the style of
after (composer's name)
à la (Fr.)
a la maniera di (It.)
à la manière de (Fr.)
nach Art der (G.)
a la manera de (Sp.)

alla breve (It.)
*cut time
double time
quick time
march time
half-note is a beat
à la blanche (Fr.)
a la breve (Sp.)
in halben Noten (G.)
a cappella (It.)
duple meter
C-barré (Fr.)
C-barred

vs. common time

alla marcia (It.)
march style
military style
quick time
double time
*cut time
alla breve (It.)

alla mente (It.)
impromptu
improvised

off the cuff
on the spot
ad-libbing
faking it
jamming
playing by ear

alla Palestrina (It.)
Palestrina style
unaccompanied
a cappella (It.)
stile antico (It.)
stile osservato (It.)
style de chapelle (Fr.)
à la Palestrienne (Fr.)
im Kapellstil (G.)
Palestrina-Stil (G.)
a capilla (Sp.)
música vocal (Sp.)

alla Polacca (It.)
like a polonaise
Polish style

alla punta d'arco/dell'arco (It.)
with the point or tip of the bow
avec le pointe de l'archet (Fr.)
an der Bogenspitze (G.)
con la punta (Sp.)
*up-bow

vs. al tallone (It.)

alla tedesca (It.)
in the German style
à l'allemande (Fr.)
a la alemana (Sp.)
nach Deutcher Art

2. in the style of an allemande,
landler or waltz

alla Turca (It., Sp.)
in the style of Turkish military
band
Janissary music

à la turque (Fr.)
nach Türkischer Art (G.)

alla zingara (It.)
in the *gypsy style
à la tzigane (Fr.)
nach Art der Zigeuner (G.)
al estilo cingaro (Sp.)
all' ongarese (It.)
à la hongroise (Fr.)

alla zoppa (It.)
*syncopated
off-beat
Scotch snap
stile Lombardo (It.)
Lombard rhythm
reversed dotting
inverted dotting
dotted rhythm
limping
boiteux (Fr.)
hinkend (G.)
cojeando (Sp.)

allant, en allant (Fr.)
going
*andante (It.)

allargando (It.)
broader
*slower
ritardando (It.)
rallentando (It.)
ritenuto (It.)

Alle(s) (G.)
all
everyone
omnes, omnia (Lat.)
tutti (It.)
tous (Fr.)
todos (Sp.)

alle Saiten (G.)
release soft pedal

tutte corde (It.)
senza sordini (It.)
mutes off
remove mutes
*ohne Dämpfer (G.)
toutes les cordes (Fr.)
todas las cuerdas (Sp.)
sin sordina (Sp.)

allegramente (It.)
lively
briskly
animated
allègrement (Fr.)
munter (G.)
con alegria (Sp.)
animato (It.)

allegretto (It.)
not as fast as allegro
moving along
*fast
allegro (It.)

allegro (It.)
*fast
lively
brisk
quick
up tempo
veloce (It.)
presto (It.)
vif, vite (Fr.)
rapide (Fr.)
rasch (G.)
lebhaft (G.)
schnell (G.)
alegro (Sp.)
pronto (Sp.)
veloz (Sp.)

allegro form
*sonata-allegro form
symphony form
first movement form

alleluia, alleluja, halleluia, allelujah (Heb.)
*refrain
respond
chorus
Laudes (Gallican and Mozarabic)
Post Epistolam (Ambrosian)

allemande (Fr., G.)
German dance (16-18 c.)
alman(d) (old English)
almain, almayne (old English)
allemanda (It.)
tedesca (It.)
Teutschertanz (G.)
Ländler (G.)

allentando, allentamento (It.)
*slowing down
allargando (It.)
rallentando (It.)
ritenuto (It.)
allonger (Fr.)

allgemeiner Bass (G.)
*figured bass
continuo
basso continuo (It.)
thoroughbass

alma (Sp.)
sound post
anima (It.)
âme (Fr.)
Seele (G.)
Stimmstock (G.)

2. languid (on organ pipe)
languette
tongue (for tuning)
anima (It.)
biseau (Fr.)
Kern (G.)
bisel (Sp.)

alma mater (Lat.)
  school anthem or hymn
  *hymn

almain (Old Eng.)
  *allemande (Fr., G.)
  alman(d)
  almayne

almérie (Fr.)
  *lute (17 c.)

Alpenglocke (G.)
  cowbell
  campanaccio (It.)
  sonnaille (Fr.)
  cloche de vache (Fr.)
  Kuhglocke (G.)
  Kuhschelle (G.)
  cencerro (Sp.)

Alphorn (G., Eng.)
  alpine horn
  cor des Alpes (Fr.)
  corno delle Alpi (It.)
  cuerno alpino (Sp.)
  long, straight trmpet
  ceremonial trumpet
  *Aida trumpet
  buisine, busine, buzine,
  buysine (O.Fr.)
  tuba (Lat., Roman)
  buccina Lat,. Roman)
  state trumpet
  natural trumpet

Alt (G.)
  *alto voice
  countertenor
  contralto

alta (Sp.)
  altadanza (Sp.)
  salterello (It.)
  passo brabante (It.)
  pas de Brabant (Fr.)

altar bells
  sanctus bells
  campanelli della messa (It.)
  clochettes pour la messe (Fr.)
  Messglöckchen (G.)
  Messklingeln (G.)
  pellet bells
  *bells

altavoz (Sp.)
  loudspeaker
  PA system
  altoparlante (It.)
  Lautsprecher (G.)
  hautparleur (Fr.)

alte Musik (G.)
  early music
  ancient music
  historical music
  musica antiqua (Lat.)
  Ars Antiqua (Lat.)
  ars vetus (Lat.)
  musica antico (It.)
  stile antico (It.)
  musique ancienne (Fr.)
  música antigua (Sp.)

alteration
  chromatic alteration
  alteratio (Lat.)
  alterato (It.)
  altéré (Fr.)
  altération (Fr.)

2. augmentation (16c. notation)

altered chord
  chromatically changed

altered time
  stolen time
  borrowed time
  *rubato (It.)
  tempo rubato (It.)
  verrucktes Zeitmass (G.)

gestohlenes Zeitmass (G.)

altered tone
  chromatic tone
  accidental
  half-step
  sharps and flats

alternatim mass (15-18 c.)
  organ mass (organ verses and
sung plainsong alternate)
  organ hymn
  organ verse
  verso, versetto (It.)
  verset (Fr.)
  Versett, Versetl (G.)
  versillo (Sp.)
  antiphonal

alternativo (It.)
  B section of a minuet or
scherzo, etc.
  trio section
  middle section
  contrasting section
  alternative
  alternativement (Fr.)
  Überleitung (G.)
  release
  channel
  bridge

Althorn (G.)
  tenor horn
  alto saxhorn
  ballad horn
  mellophone
  baritone
  *baritone horn
  flicorno contralto (It.)
  saxhorn tenor
  bugle contralto (Sp.)

alto (voice)
  contralto
  countertenor

falsetto
falsettista (It.)
fausset (Fr.)
Falsett (G.)
Fistelstimme (G.)
alto-tenor
cambiata
altista (It.)
haute-contre (Fr.)
Alt (G.)
Altistin (G.)
Altstimme (G.)
Kontraalt (G.)
Kontratenor (G.)
altus (Lat.)
alti naturali (Lat., It.)

alto (Fr., It.)
*viola
quinte (Fr.)
cinquième (Fr.)
basse de violon (Fr.)
taille de violon (Fr.)
violon-ténor (Fr.)
Bratsche (G.)
Altviole (G.)
Altgeige (G.)
Tenorgeige (G.)
alta viola (It.)
alto-viola (Fr.)
tenor violin

alto clarinet
*basset horn
tenor clarinet
clarone (It.)
cor de basset (Fr.)
Bassethorn (G.)
corno di bassetto (It.)

alto clef
viola clef
C-clef
chiave di contralto (It.)
chiave di do (It.)
clef d'alto (Fr.)

clef d'ut (Fr.)
C-Schlüssel (G.)
Alt-Schlüssel (G.)
llave de do (Sp.)
clave de contralto (Sp.)
clave de viola (Sp.)

alto flute (in G)
*bass flute
Altflöte (G.)
flautone (It.)
flûte alto (Fr.)
flauta baja (Sp.)

alto horn, alto saxhorn
*althorn
ballad horn
tenor horn
baritone (horn)

alto-tenor
*changing voice
cambiata

altra volta (It., 18 c.)
*encore
again
bis (Lat.)
ancore (It.)
noch einmal (G.)
otra vez (Sp.)

Altviole (G.)
tenor violin
Altgeige (G.)
basse de violon (Fr.)
taille de violon (Fr.)
cinquième (Fr.)
*alto (It., Fr.)
*viola

alzare (It.)
to *raise
to sharp
hausser (Fr.)
erhöhen (G.)

alzar (Sp.)

vs. to lower, flat
abbassare (It.)

alzati (It.)
remove mutes
mute(s) off
*ohne Dämpfer (G.)

am Frosch (G.)
at the frog
*down bow
al tallone (It.)
à la hausse (Fr.)
au talon (Fr.)
Abstrich (G.)
al talón (Sp.)

vs. Aufstrich (G.)

am Griffbrett (G.)
bow on the fingerboard
sul tasto (It.)
sulla tastiera (It.)
flautando, flautato (It.)
sur la touche (Fr.)
sobre el batidor (Sp.)

am Orte (G.)
as written
at pitch
as it stands
ad locum (Lat.)
loco (It.)
come stà (It.)
à sa place (Fr.)
comme il écrit (Fr.)
wie geschrieben steht (G.)
wie es dasteht (G.)
an seinem platz (G.)
a su puesto (Sp.)
como está (Sp.)

am Rand
rim shot (drum)

sul bordo (It.)
sur le bord (Fr.)
sobre el borde (Sp.)

am Steg (G.)
near, or at the bridge
sul ponticello (It.)
au chevalet (Fr.)
près du chevalet (Fr.)
sobre el puentecillo (Sp.)

amateur voice horn
*ballad horn
*althorn
alto saxhorn
vocal horn

ambiance
*echo
reverb
surround-sound
live room

ambitus (Lat., Fr., E.)
range
* compass
tessitura
gamut
estensione (It.)
ambito (It., Sp.)
Umfang (G.)
Raum (G.)
Ausdehnung (G.)
diapason (Fr.)
étendue (Fr.)

Amboss (G.)
anvil
incudine (It.)
enclume (Fr.)
yunque (Sp.)

Ambrosian chant
Milanese chant
Mediolanensis (Lat.)
plainsong/plainchant

*chant
liturgical chant
cantus planus (Lat.)
Gallican chant
Mozarabic chant
Gregorian chant

Ambrosian Hymn
hymnus Ambrosianus (Lat.)
Te Deum (Lat.)

âme (Fr.)
sound post
anima (It.)
Stimmstock (G.)
Seele (G.)
alma (Sp.)

amen cadence
*plagal cadence
church cadence
cadenza plagale (It.)
cadence plagale (Fr.)
Kirchenschluss (G.)
plagale Kadenz (G.)
cadencia plagal (Sp.)

amener (Fr.)
dance movement in triple time
branle à mener (Fr.)

American organ
reed organ
pump organ
parlor organ
harmonium
melodeon

ammezzato (It.)
mezzanine
*balcony
gallery
entresol (Fr.)
Mezzanin (G.)
mezanina (Sp.)
entresuelo (Sp.)

amoroso (It., Sp.)
*tenderly
warmly
tendrement (Fr.)
liebevoll (G.)

amplitude (Eng., Fr.)
loudness
volume
gain
*dynamics
ampiezza (It.)
Amplitude (G.)
amplitud (Sp.)

an der Bogenspitze (G.)
with the point or tip of the bow
*up-bow
arco in su (It.)
alla punta d'arco/dell'arco (It.)
avec le pointe de l'archet (Fr.)
con la punta (Sp.)

vs. am Frosch (G.)

anabole (Gr., 16 c.)
*prelude
voluntary
proemium (Lat.)

anacaria (It.)
small kettledrums
*timpani

anacrusis (Lat.)
*upbeat
arsis (Gr.)
arsi (It.)
pick-up
élévation (Fr.)
levé (Fr.)
anacrouse (Fr.)
anacrusi (It., Sp.)
Anakrusis (G.)
Auftakt (G.)
Hebung (G.)

vs. crusis (Lat.)

analog(ue) recording
    electronic recording

vs. digital

analytical notes
    program notes
    liner notes

anapest (12-13 c.)
    fourth rhythmic mode
    reversed dactyl

anchamente (Sp.)
    broadly
    *slow
    largo (It.)

anche (Fr.)
    *reed
    reed instrument
    reed organ pipe
    ancia (It.)
    Zunge (G.)
    caña (Sp.)
    lengüeta (Sp.)

anche double (Fr.)
    double reed
    ancia doppia (It.)
    Doppelrohrblatt (G.)

ancora (It.)
    *encore
    repeat
    bis (Lat., Fr., G.)
    altra volta (It.)
    noch einmal (G.)
    otra vez (Sp.)

andamento (It.)
    subject
    theme
    soggetto (It.)

episode (fugue)

andante (It.)
    going
    moderato (It.)
    andantino (It.)
    moderate tempo
    en allant (Fr.)
    allant (Fr.)
    gehend (G.)
    andando (Sp.)

andantino (It.)
    moderate tempo
    less slow than andante

Änderungsabsatz (G.)
    *half-cadence
    semi-cadence
    imperfect cadence
    half-close
    cadenza sospesa (It.)
    cadenza imperfetta (It.)
    demi-cadence (Fr.)
    cadence suspendue (Fr.)
    Halbschluss (G.)
    semicadencia (Sp.)
    cadencia suspendida (Sp.)

anechoic chamber
    dead room
    echoless
    acoustic ceiling, wall, tiles
    sound absorbent
    soundproof
    insonorizzato ((It.)
    isolato acusticamente (It.)
    sourd (Fr.)
    insonorisé (Fr.)
    Schalltot (G.)
    insonoro (Sp.)
    antisonoro (Sp.)

angel lute
    archlute
    theorbo

*lute
angelica (It.)
angélique (Fr.)

angelic hymn
    Gloria in Excelsis Deo (Lat.)
    Hymn of the angels
    hymnus angelicus (Lat.)
    doxology
    hymn to the Trinity
    Greater Doxology
    cherubim song

anglaise, anglois (18 c. Fr.)
    country dance in duple time
    contredanse (Fr.)
    Française (G.)
    Écossaise (Fr.)

Anglican chant
    harmonized chant
    falsobordone (It.)
    fabordón (Sp.)
    homophonic
    fauxbourdon (Fr.)
    faburden (15 c. Eng.)

Anhang (G.)
    *coda
    codetta (It.)
    tag
    Koda (G.)
    cola (Sp.)
    partie finale (Fr.)

anheloso (Sp.)
    *agitated
    agitato (It.)

anhemitonic
    whole-tone scale
    pentatonic scale
    oriental scale

anima (It.)
    sound post

âme (Fr.)
Seele (G.)
Stimmstock (G.)
alma (Sp.)

2. languid (organ pipe)
languette
tongue for tuning
biseau (Fr.)
Kern (G.)
bisel (Sp.)
alma (Sp.)

animato, animando (It.)
animated
spirited
spirituoso (It.)
con spirito)It.)
animé (Fr.)
belebt (G.)
lebhaft (G.)
animado (Sp.)
lively
con moto (It.)
vivace (It.)
munter (G.)

anmutig (G.)
gracious, graceful
grazioso (It.)
gracieux, gracieuse (Fr.)
gracioso (Sp.)

Ansatz (G.)
embouchure (Fr.)
lip
imboccatura (It.)
Mundloch (G.)
embocadura (Sp.)
boquilla (Sp.)

2. attack
attacca (It.)
attaque (Fr.)
ataca (Sp.)

Anschlag (G.)
touch (esp. piano)
tocco (It.)
toucher Fr.)
tacto (Sp.)

2. double appoggiatura (It.)
ornament
appoggiatura (It.)

anschwellen(d) (G.)
getting louder
louder
*crescendo (It.)

anstimmen (G.)
*intone
strike up
intonare (It.)
entonner (Fr.)
entonar (Sp.)

Anstrich (G.)
*up-bow
arcata in su (It.)
poussé (Fr.)
arcada hacia arriba (Sp.)
Hinstrich, Hinaufstrich (G.)
Aufstrich (G.)

answer
respond
responsory
responsorium (Lat.)
reply
imitation
consequent
réponse (Fr.)
replique (Fr.)
riposta (It.)
respuesta (Sp.)
conseguènte (It.)
consecuente (Sp.)
Antwort (G.)
Gefährte (G.)
comes (Lat.)

real and tonal answers

vs. subject, principal

ante-communion (Anglican)
Mass of the Catecumens
fore-mass
Liturgy of the Word

antecedent
*subject (of a fugue)
question
dux (Lat.)
phrase
antecedente (It.)
proposta (It.)
guida (It.)
theme (Fr.)
Führer (G.)
period

vs. consequent

2. first lead voice of a canon

anteludium (Lat.)
*prelude
introduction
voluntary
intonazione (It.)
overture
intermezzo

vs. postlude

anthem
antiphon
motet
sacred piece
hymn
chorus
sacred song
canticle
sequence
national anthem/hymn
alma mater (Lat.)

inno (It.)
antienne (Fr.)
hymne (Fr.)
Hymne (G.)
Lobgesang (G.)
himno (Sp.)
paean (Gr.)
lauda (It.)
theody
introit
verse anthem (with solo
verses)
full anthem (choir)
Tudor church music
Cathedral music

anthology
collection
repertoire
repertory
assortment
sampling
edition
album
cantionale (Lat.)
corpus (Lat.)
codex (Lat., E., Fr.)
manuscript collection
anthologium (Lat.)
raccolta (It.)
recueil (Fr.)
repertorio (It., Sp.)
antologia (It., Sp.)
anthologie (Fr.)
Sammelwerk (G.)
Sammeldruck (G.)
Denkmäler (G.)
Sammlung (G.)
Gesangbuch (G.)
chansonnier (Fr.)
collezione (It.)
colección (Sp.)
cancionero (Sp.)
fake book
florigelium (Lat.)
enchiriadis (Gr.)

enchiridion (Gr.)
Akolouthia (Gr.)
Papadike (Gr.)

anticipation (Eng., Fr.)
upbeat
ornament
repeated note
Nachschlag (G.)
Antizipation (G.)
Vorausnahme (G.)
anticipazione (It.)
cercar la nota (It.)
anticipación (Sp.)

antiphon
anthem
*refrain
respond
chorus
psalm
psallenda (Ambrosian)
antifona (It., Sp.)
antienne (Fr.)
Antiphonie (G.)
antiphona, -on (Gr.)

antiphonal choirs
polychoral
multiple choirs
double chorus
divided choirs
binaural
stereophonic
echo chorus
responsorial
dialogue, musical
call and response
cori spezzati (It.)
coro spezzato (It.)
Doppelchor (G.)
Apsidenchöre (G.)
cori battente (It., 16 c.)
double choeur (Fr.)
coro separado (Sp.)
coro dividido (Sp.)

policoral (Sp.)
cantoris
decani
choirwise

2. chant collection
antiphonary
antiphoner
antiphonale (Lat.)
liber antiphonalius (Lat.)
antiphonarium (Lat.)
antiphonaire (Fr.)
office
Divine Office
Monastic Office
Breviary
prayer services
morning, evening prayer
canonical hours
liturgical chants
antifonario (It., Sp.)
antiphonaire (Fr,)
Antiphonar (G.)
antifonal (Sp.)

vs.*missal
mass
Gradual
Graduale (L.)

antiphonal organ
nave organ
*echo organ

antiphonia (Gr.)
octave interval
ottava (It.)
octave (Fr.)
Oktav (G.)
octava (Sp.)

antique cymbals
crotales (Fr.)
*crotalum (Lat.)
cymbals antiques (Fr.)
finger cymbals

Fingerzimbeln (G.)
castenets
clappers

antisonoro (Sp.)
soundproof
dead room
anechoic chamber
insonorizzato (It.)
isolato acusticamente (It.)
sourd (Fr.)
insonorisé (Fr.)
shalltot (G.)
insonoro (Sp.)

antistrophe (Gr.)
*refrain
chorus
respond
ode
epode (Gr.)
epistrophe (Gr.)

Antwort (G.)
*answer (fugue)
comes (Lat.)
consequent
riposta (It.)
réponse (Fr.)
respuesta (Sp.)

anvil
enclume (Fr.)
incùdine (It.)
Amboss (G.)
yunque (Sp.)

anwachsend (G.)
*crescendo (It.)

Äolsharfe (G.)
*Aeolian harp
Windharfe (G.)

apagador (Sp.)
damper

*mute
sordino (It.)
sourdine (Fr.)
étouffoir (Fr.)
Dämpfer (G.)
sordina (Sp.)
una corde (It.)

apagar (Sp.)
to mute
dampen
muffle
smorzare (It.)
assourdir (Fr.)
abdämpfen (G.)
dämpfen (G.)

aperto (It.)
open (bell of horn)
loud pedal

vs. stopped
chiuso (It.)

2. ouvert (14c. Fr.)
apertum (Lat.)
first ending
prima volta (It.)

vs.clos (Fr.)
clausum (Lat.)
secunda volta (It.)

Apollo club
glee club (men's)
male chorus
choral society
Orphéon (Fr.)
Liedertafel (G.)
Liederkranz (G.)
Männergesangverein (G.)

apostrophe
breath mark
break
breathing sign

comma

apotheosis
*lament
lamentation
apothéose (Fr.)
requiem
déploration (Fr.)
elegy
plaint
dirge
Klage(G.)

apotome (Gr.)
*half-step
half-tone
semitone
minor second
degree
limma (Gr.)
diesis (Gr.)

apoyatura breve (Sp.)
*mordent
*acciaccatura (It.)

Appalachian dulcimer
dulcimer
folk zither
mountain zither
tamborin à cordes (Fr.)
Scheitholt (G.)
Hummel, Humle (G.)

appareil à vent (Fr.)
wind machine
eolifono (It.)
éoliphone (Fr.)
machine à vent (Fr.)
Windmaschine (G.)
máquina de viento (Sp.)

appassionato (It.)
impassioned
*emotional
expressive

appearance
*performance
engagement
concert
recital
gig
debut
premiere

appeau (Fr.)
bird-call (organ)
richiamo per ucelli (It.)
cri d'oiseau (Fr.)
Vogelsang, Vogelgesang (G.)
Vogelpfeife (G.)
reclamo (Sp.)

applause
clapping
accolades
cheers
approval
appreciation
ovation
kudos
bravo (It.)
adulation
claque
applauso (It.)
applaudissement (Fr.)
Beifall (G.)
aplauso (Sp.)

applicatio (It.)
fingering
application (Fr.)
Applikatur (G.)
Fingersatz (G.)
aplicación (Sp.)
digitazione (It.)
doigté (Fr.)
digitación (Sp.)

applied music
practical music
performance music

vs. theory

appoggiatura (It.)
ornament
grace note
non-harmonic tone
leaning note
suspension
dissonance
backfall
forefall
acciaccatura (It.)
coulé (Fr.)
Nachschlag (G.)
Abzug (G.)
Accent (G.)
Accent fallend (G.)
Steigend (G.)
cheute, chute (Fr.)
port-de-voix (Fr.)
appogiature (Fr.)
Vorschlag (G.)
apoyatura (Sp.)

appogiature brève (Fr.)
*mordent
*acciaccatura
crushed note

Apsidenchöre (G.)
double chorus
divided choirs
*antiphonal choirs
stereophonic
cori spezzati (It.)

apuntador, -ora (Sp.)
prompter
teleprompter
cue cards
suggeritore (It.)
souffleur, -euse (Fr.)
Souffleur (G.)
*prompt box

Aquitanian notation

chant notation
Gregorian notation
square notes/notation
neumes
quadratic notation
notazione quadrata (It.)
notation carrée (Fr.)
Quadratnotation (G.)
notación cuadrada (Sp.)

arabesque (Eng., Fr.)
lyrical piece
*fancy
instrumental
impromptu
arabesca (It.)
Arabeske (G.)
arabesco (Sp.)

aragonaise (Fr.)
Spanish dance in triple time
aragonesa (Sp.)
jota (Sp.)
Jota aragonesa (G.)

arch form
ABA form
*three-part form
ternary form
tripartite form
bow form

arch-top guitar
jazz guitar
rhythm guitar

vs. flat-top guitar

archet (Fr.)
bow
fiddlestick
fiddle bow
arco (It., Sp.)
archetto (It.)
Bogen (G.)

archiviola di lira (It.)
  bass lyre
  lira (It.)
  lirone (It.)
  accordo (It.)
  lira da braccio (It.)
  lira da gamba (It.)
  lira tedesca (It.)

archlute
  lute, large
  theorbo
  bass lute
  chitarrone (It.)
  archiluth (Fr.)
  Erzlaute (G.)
  arciliuto (It.)
  archilaúd (Sp.)
  angelica(It.)
  angélique (Fr.)
  tiorba (It., Sp.)
  Theorbe (G.)
  théorbe (Fr.)
  oud (Arab.)
  pandoura, pandura (Gr.)
  trichordon (Gr.)

arco, archetto (It.)
  a bow
  archet (Fr.)
  Bogen (G.)
  arco (Sp.)

 2. bow (after playing pizzicato)
  bowed
  bogenführung (G.)

arco in giù (It.)
  *down-bow
  arcata in giù (It.)
  tiré (Fr.)
  Abstrich (G.)
  arco por bajo (Sp.)

arco in su (It.)
  *up-bow

arcata in su (It.)
  poussé (Fr.)
  Anstrich (G.)
  Aufstrich (G.)
  Hinaufstrich (G.)
  arco por arriba (Sp.)
  arcada hacia arriba (Sp.)

Aretinian syllables
  sol-fa syllables
  *solmization
  Aretinische Silben (G.)
  fasola
  tonic sol-fa

aria (It.)
  solo song (esp. operatic)
  arioso (It.)
  arietta (It.)
  ariette (Fr.)
  Arie (G.)
  air
  melody
  mélodie
  cavatina (It.)
  cabaletta (It.)
  *song
  *art song

aria d'imitazione (It.)
  descriptive music
  program music
  word painting
  tone poem

Armgeige (G.)
  *viola da braccio (It.)
  viola

armonia (It.)
  harmony
  chords
  harmonie (Fr.)
  Harmonie (G.)
  armonía (Sp.)

armonía de las esferas celestes (Sp.)
  harmony of the spheres
  music of the spheres
  celestial harmony
  musica mundana (Lat.)
  l'armonia delle esferas celeste (It.)
  musique des spheres célestes (Fr.)
  Sphärenmusik (G.)
  música de las esferas celestes (Sp.)

armonía por cuartes (Sp.)
  quartal harmony
  armonia quartale (It.)
  armonia per quarte (It.)
  harmonie par quartes (Fr.)
  Quartenharmonik (G.)

armonica (It., Sp.)
  glass harmonica
  musical glasses
  verrillon (Fr.)
  Glassspiel (G.)
  Hamonika (G.)
  copólogo (Sp.)
  armonica a calici (It.)
  armonica a vetro (It.)
  harmonica de verres (Fr.)
  harmonica de Franklin (Fr.)

 2. harmonica
  aeoline
  mouth organ
  French harp
  Mundharmonika (G.)
  armonica a bocca (It.)

armonica a manticino (It.)
  *accordion
  concertina

armonica de madera (Sp.)
  *xylophone

straw fiddle
sticcato (It.)
gigelira (It.)
organo di legno (It.)
orgue de bois (Fr.)
échelettes (Fr.)
*claquebois (Fr.)
Strohfiedel (G.)
Xylophon (G.)
xilófono (Sp.)

armónicos (Sp.)
*harmonics
overtones
armonichi (It.)
harmoniques (Fr.)
aliquotes (Fr.)
Aliquottöne (G.)
alicuotes (Sp.)
aliquot tones
partials
natural tones
flageolet tones

armonio (It., Sp.)
harmonium
reed organ
pump organ
parlor organ
American organ
armonium (It.)
orgue expressif (Fr.)
Harmonium (G.)
Expressivorgel (G.)

armure (Fr.)
*key signature
armature (Fr.)
signes accidentels (Fr.)
armatura di chiave (It.)
Vorzeichnung (G.)
Tonartvorzeichnung (G.)
armadura (Sp.)

2. action
mechanism

arpa (It., Sp.)
harp
harpe (Fr.)
Harfe (G.)
arpanetta (It.)
arpa doppia (It.)
Spitzharfe (G.)

arpa eolia (It.)
*Aeolian harp
harpe éoline/eolienne (Fr.)
Äolsharfe (G.)
Windharfe (G.)
arpa eolia (Sp.)

arpanetta (It.)
double zither
Spitzharfe (G.)
arpa doppia (It.)
arpanette (Fr.)

arpeggio (It.)
broken shords
rolled chords
arpeggiated
Alberti bass
Brillenbass (G.)
arpeggiando (It.)
battimento (It.)
batterie (Fr.)
brisé (Fr.)
battery (Old Eng.)
crackle (Old Eng.)
strumming
arpège, arpègement, arpégé (Fr.)
harpège, etc. (Fr.)
Akkordpassage (G.)
Rauscher (G.18c.)
Brechung (G.)
gebrochener Akkord (G.)
rasgado, rasgueado (Sp.)
arpegio (Sp.)

vs. plaqué (Fr.)

arpicordo (It.)
*harpsichord
chekker
cembalo (It.)
clavicembalo (It.)
clavecin (Fr.)
épinette (Fr.)
Klavizimbel (G.)
Kielflügel (G.)
clave, clavicordio (Sp.)

arraché (Fr.)
*pizzicato (strong, forceful)
plucking strings

arrange(ment) (E., Fr.)
adapt(ation)
edit(ion)
transcribe, transcription
reduction
paraphrase
elaboration
version
variation (E., Fr.)
variazione (It.)
Veränderung (G.)
variación (Sp.)
abridgement
parody mass
contrafactum (Lat.)
model after
setting
scoring
arranger (Fr.)
adapter Fr.)
adattare (It.)
riduzione (It.)
arrangiare (It.)
réduction (Fr.)
traduzione (It.)
Auszug (G.)
bearbeiten, -ung (G.)
einrichten (G.)
adaptar (Sp.)
arreglar (Sp.)

arrullo (Sp.)
 cradle song
 lullaby
 ninnananna (It.)
 ninnerella (It.)
 berceuse (Fr.)
 dodinette, dodo, dodino (Fr.)
 Wiegenlied (G.)
 Schlummerlied (G.)
 Ständchen (G.)
 nana (Sp.)
 canción de cuna (Sp.)

Ars Antiqua (Lat.)
 Gothic music
 Medieval music
 stile antico (It.)
 prima prattica (It. 17c.)
 Palestrina style
 old style
 ancient style
 ars vetus (Lat.)

vs. Ars Nova (Lat.)

Ars Nova (Lat., 14 c.)
 new music
 modern music
 contemporary music
 Nuove Musiche (It. 17 c.)
 seconda prattica (It. 17c.)
 avant-garde (Fr.)

vs. Ars Antiqua

arsis (Gr., Lat.)
 *up-beat
 pick-up
 weak beat
 arsi (It.)
 anacrusis (Lat.)
 anacrusi (It., Sp.)
 anacrouse (Fr.)
 levé (Fr.)
 élévation (Fr.)
 Auftakt (G.)

Hebung (G.)

vs. thesis (Gr., Lat.)
 downbeat

art music
 classical music
 serious music
 high-brow music
 long-haired music
 art song
 concert music

vs. popular music
 folk music

art song
 Lied, Lieder (G.)
 Kunstlied (G.)
 solo *song
 melody
 concert song/aria
 chamber music
 mélodie (Fr.)
 chanson (Fr.)
 *aria
 air

articulation
 attack
 tonguing (wind instruments)
 phrasing
 bowing
 chiff (organ)
 articolare (It.)
 articuler (Fr.)
 deutlich Aussprechen (G.)
 articular (Sp.)

2. pronunciation of text
 declamation

articulation double (Fr.)
 flutter-tonguing
 frullato, frulando (It.)
 double coup de langue (Fr.)

Flatterzunge (G.)
 tripe articulación (Sp.)
 raspberry
 French kiss

artiste
 chanteuse (Fr.)
 singer
 diva
 *performer
 artist
 concert artist
 rectalist

as written
 loco (It.)
 ad locum (Lat.)
 as it stands
 at (that) pitch
 come stà (It.)
 à sa place (Fr.)
 comme il écrit (Fr.)
 am Orte (G.)
 wie geschrieben steht (G.)
 wie es dasteht (G.)
 a su puesto (Sp.)
 como está (Sp.)

aside
 very soft
 whispered
 under one's breath
 stage whisper
 sotto voce (It.)
 mezza voce (It.)
 in disparte (It.)
 fra se (It.)
 à part (Fr.)
 de côté (Fr.)
 en aparté (Fr.)
 für sich (G.)
 beiseite (G.)
 à mi-voix (Fr.)
 mit halbe Stimme (G.)
 a parte (Sp.)
 bisbigliato (It.)

chuchoté (Fr.)
geflüstert (G.)
cuchicheado (Sp.)
a parte (Sp.)
a sovoz (Sp.)
quedo (Sp.)

assai (It.)
enough/rather/very
assez (Fr.)
très (Fr.)
beaucoup (Fr.)
sehr/ziemlich (G.)
mucho/bastante/muy (Sp.)
molto (It.)
viel (G.)

assist
backup
backround
*accompaniment

assistant conductor
concertmaster
concertmistress
violino primo (It.)
chef d'attaque (Fr.)

associazione corale (It.)
choral society
community chorus
chorale
civic chorus
symphonic choir
philharmonic chorus
societá di coro (It.)
société chorale (Fr.)
Gesangverein (G.)
Singakademie (G.)
orfeón (Sp.)

assourdir (Fr.)
dampen
mute
deaden
smorzare (It.)

assourdir (Fr.)
abdämpfen (G.)
dämpfen (G.)
apagar (Sp.)

at sight
at first sight
sight-read
prima vista (It.)
à vue (Fr.)
vom Blatt (G.)
a primera vista (Sp.)

at the frog
*down-bow
arco in giù (It.)
al tallone (It.)
à la hausse (Fr.)
tiré (Fr.)
am Frosch (G.)
Abstrich (G.)
al talón (Sp.)
au talon (Fr.)
tirado (Sp.)

vs. with the point of the bow

atabal (Sp.)
kettledrum
*timpani
atabale (Fr.)
double drum
timbale (Fr.)
Pauke (G.)
Kesselpauke (G.)

Atempause (G.)
breath mark/pause
comma
respiro (It.)
virgula (It.)
virgule (Fr.)
suspension de respiration (Fr.)
Komma (G.)
Atemzeichen (G.)
respiración (Sp.)

coma (Sp.)

atemlos (G.)
*agitated
agitato (It.)

atonal (Eng., Fr., G., Sp.)
twelve-tone music
serial music
dodecaphonic
polytonal
atonale (It.)

vs. tonal music

atril (Sp.)
music stand
music desk
leggio (It.)
pupitre (Fr.)
Notenständer (G.)
podio (Sp.)
podium

attacca (It.)
begin
attack
hit it!
attaque (Fr.)
commence sufficant (Fr.)
greife an (G.)
beginne (G.)
es folg (G.)
ataca (Sp.)
segue(It.)
suit, suivez (Fr.)
enchaînez (Fr.)
sigue (Sp.)

2. articulate
chiff (Organ)

atto (It.)
*act
scene
actus (Lat.)

acte (Fr.)
Akt (G.)
Aufzug (G.)
acto (Sp.)

au bout des lèvres (Fr.)
*softly
piano (It.)
a fior di labbra (It.)
gehaucht (G.)
fast unvernehmlich (G.)
con la boca chico (Sp.)

au caprice (Fr.)
ad libitum (Lat.)
a bene placito (It.)
a piacere (It.)
*freely
libre (Fr.)
a capriccio (It.)
a capricho (Sp.)

au chevalet (Fr.)
at/on/near the bridge
sul ponticello (It.)
près du chevalet (Fr.)
am Steg (G.)
sobre el puentecillo (Sp.)

au début (Fr.)
from (to) the beginning
repeat
*da capo (It.)
D. C. (It.)
dal principio (It.)
von Vorn (G.)
desde el principio (Sp.)

au dehors (Fr.)
emphasize
bring out
lead voice
melody
Hervorgehoben (G.)

au movement (Fr.)

in time
*a tempo (It.)
en mesure (Fr.)
im Zeitmass (G.)
im Takt (G.)
a compás (Sp.)

au signe (Fr.)
to/from the sign
al segno (It.)
dal segno (It.)
vom Zeichen
du signe (Fr.)
desde el signo (Sp.)

au talon (Fr.)
with the frog/nut of the bow
at the frog
*down-bow
al tallone (It.)
à la hausse (Fr.)
am Frosch (G.)
al talón (Sp.)

vs. de la pointe (Fr.)

aubade (Fr.)
matin song
morning song
mattinata (It.)
alba (Prov.)
Morgenständchen (G.)
alborada (Sp.)
dawn song

vs. serenade
nocturne

auctoralis (Lat.)
authentic (modes)
*church mode
ecclesiastical mode
medieval mode

vs. plagal
plagius, plagalis (Lat.)

audible (E., Fr.)
perceptible (E., Fr., Sp.)
percettibile (It.)
hörbar (G.)

vs. inaudible

audience
listeners
spectators
fans
the public
the house
concertgoers
congregation

audio
sound
sound reproduction
stereo
high-fi
high fidelity
recording/playback

audio tape
recording tape
magnetic tape
cassette
audio cassette
reel-to-reel tape

audition (Eng., Fr.)
tryout
hearing
screen test
audizione (It.)
Vorspiel (G.)
audición (Sp.)

auditorium
*concert hall
music hall
recital hall
concert stage
performance center
symphony hall

opera house
theatre
playhouse
lyric theatre
hippodrome
stadium
arena
ampitheater

Aufbau (G.)
form
plan
structure
forma (It., Sp.)
fattura (It.)
forme (Fr.)
facture (Fr.)
dessin (Fr.)
Faktur (G.)
Gestalt (G.)

Aufführung (G.)
*performance
recital
concert
rendition
presentation

Aufführungspraxis (G.)
applied music
practical music
performance practice
prassi d'esecuzione (It.)
pratico d'esecuzione (It.)
pratique de l'exécution (Fr.)
práctica de ejecución (Sp.)

Aufführungsrecht (G.)
performing rights
rights
diritti d'esecuzione (It.)
droits d'exécution (Fr.)
derechos de ejecución (Sp.)

Aufgabe (G.)
exercise

drill
study
*étude (Fr., E.)
lesson
practice piece
exercitium (Lat.)
studio (It.)
esercizio (It.)
exercice (Fr.)
Übung (G.)
estudio (Sp.)
ejercicio (Sp.)

aufgeregt (G.)
*agitato
excited

Auflage (G.)
*edition (E., Fr.)
edizione (It.)
tirage (Fr.)
edición (Sp.)
Ausgabe (G.)

auflösen (G.)
cancel (organ stop)
off
découpler (Fr.)
ab (G.)

Auflösungszeichen (G.)
natural sign
cancel sign
quadro, bequadro (It.)
bécarre (Fr.)
naturel (Fr.)
Quadrat, B-Quadrat (G.)
becuadro (Sp.)

Aufnahme (G.)
*recording
sound reproduction
registrazione (It.)
enregistrement (Fr.)
registro (Sp.)

aufnehmen (G.)
to record
to tape, tape-record
registrare (It.)
enregister (Fr.)
registrar (Sp.)

Aufsatzbogen (G.)
*crook (brass instr.)
shank
extension
corpo di ricambio (It.)
ritorto (It.)
corps de rechange (Fr.)
Tonbogen (G.)
tonillo (Sp.)
cuerpo de recambio (Sp.)

Aufstrich (G.)
*up-bow
with the point of the bow
arco/arcata in su (It.)
a punta d'arco (It.)
poussé (Fr.)
de la pointe (Fr.)
mit der Spitze (G.)
Anstrich (G.)
Hinaufstrich (G.)
arcada hacia arriba (Sp.)
con la punta (Sp.)

vs. Abstrich (G.)
downbow

Auftakt (G.)
*upbeat
anacrusis (Lat.)
arsis (Gr., Lat.)
arsi (It.)
anacrusi (It., Sp.)
levé (Fr.)
élévation (Fr.)
Hebung (G.)
pickup

vs. Abtakt (G.)

Niederschlag (G.)

Aufzug (G.)
  *act of a drama
  atto (It.)
  acte (Fr.)
  Akt (G.)
  acto (Sp.)
  actus (Lat.)

Augenmusik (G.)
  eye-music
  *program music
  música de ojo (Sp.)

augmentation (Eng., Fr.)
  *cantus firmus (Lat.)
  augmentationem (Lat.)
  elongation
  prolongation
  extended
  slow
  drone
  organum
  tenor
  aumentazione (It.)
  Vergrösserung (G.)
  Verüngerung (G.)
  aumentación (Sp.)
  chant melody
  canon

vs. diminution

augmented (interval, chord)
  raised
  sharped
  aumentatio (It.)
  eccedente (It.)
  augmenté (Fr.)
  übermässig (G.)
  hochalteriert (G.)
  aumentado (Sp.)

vs. diminished

augmented fourth
  *tritone
  diabolus in musica (Lat.)
  mi contra fa (Lat.)
  hemidiapente (Gr.)
  diminished fifth
  false fifth
  devil's interval
  tetratone, three whole-steps

augmented sixth (chord)
  pentatone, five whole-tones
  French sixth
  German sixth
  Italian sixth
  Neapolitan sixth
  sesta eccedente (It.)
  sesta aumentata (It.)
  accord de sixte augmentée (Fr.)
  übermässige Sexte (G.)
  sexta aumentada (Sp.)

aulos (Gr.)
  oboe
  shawm
  chalumeau (Fr.)
  diaulos (Gr.)
  tibia (Lat.)
  reed
  double-reed
  syrinx
  kalamos (Gr.)
  panpipe

aural
  sound
  acoustical
  hearing

Ausarbeitung (G.)
  *development (section)

Ausdehnung (G.)
  range
  tessitura

ambitus (Lat., Fr., E.)
  ambito (It., Sp.)
  *compass
  estensione (It.)
  étendue (Fr.)
  diapason (Fr.)
  Umfang (G.)
  Raum (G.)

Ausdruck (G.)
  expression (E., Fr.)
  feeling
  expresión (Sp.)
  esspressione (It.)

Ausdrucksvoll (G.)
  *with expression, feeling, emotion
  espressivo (It.)
  expressif (Fr.)
  expresivo (Sp.)

Ausführung (G.)
  execution
  performance
  delivery
  esecuzione (It.)
  exécution (Fr.)
  ejecución (Sp.)

ausgedehnt (G.)
  broadly
  *slow
  largo (It.)
  lento (It.)

vs. schnell (G.)

aushalten (G.)
  sustain, sustained
  sostenuto (It.)
  soutenu (Fr.)
  ausgehalten (G.)
  getragen (G.)
  sostenido (Sp.)

Auslöser, Auslösung (G.)
escapement (piano)
release, key release
hopper
grasshopper
scappamento (It.)
échappement (Fr.)
escape, escapatoria (Sp.)
*double escapement

Aussenstimme (G.)
outer voice/part
parte estrema (It.)
partie extrême (Fr.)
voz extrema (Sp.)
parte extrema (Sp.)

vs. Mittelstimme (G.)
Innenstimme (G.)

Aussetzung (G.)
realization (of figured bass)
filling in
arrangement
realizzazione (It.)
réalisation (Fr.)
realización (Sp.)

Ausstattungsstück (G.)
*revue (E., Fr.)
vaudeville
minstrel show
floor show
variety show
follies
*medley
potpourri (E., Fr.)
rivista (It.)
revista (Sp.)

Ausstreifen (G.)
strumming
thrumming
broken chords
arpeggiating
strappata (It.)

grattant (Fr.)
Durchstreichen (G.)
rasgueado (Sp.)

Auswahl (G.)
selection
piece
movement
excerpt
extract
scelta (It.)
selezione (It.)
sélection (Fr.)
choix (Fr.)
Satz (G.)
Auszug (G.)
Ausschnitt (G.)
selección (Sp.)

Ausweichung (G.)
modulation
*change of key
transition
modulazione (It.)
Modulation (G., Fr.)
modulación (Sp.)
key change/shift

auswendig (G.)
memorized
from memory
by heart
by rote
a memoria (It.)
par coeur (Fr.)
de memoria (Sp.)

Auszug (G.)
*arrangement
edition

2. *excerpt
extract
Ausschnitt (G.)
estratto (It.)
extrait (Fr.)

extracto (Sp.)

authentic cadence
full cadence
*perfect cadence
full close
final cadence
cadenza perfetta (It.)
cadence authentique (Fr.)
cadence parfaite (Fr.)
Ganzschluss (G.)
authentische Kadenz (G.)
vollkommene Kadenz (G.)
cadencia perfecta (Sp.)

authentic instrument(s)
period instruments
historical instruments
original instruments
old instruments
early music
instruments originaux (Fr.)
Originalinstrumenten (G.)

authentic mode
church mode
ecclesiastical mode
medieval mode
minor mode/scale
auctoralis (Lat.)

vs. plagal mode

auto (Sp.)
*liturgical drama
azione sacra (It.)
auto sacramental (Sp.)
misterio (Sp.)
religious play
miracle (Fr.)
mystère (Fr.)
moralité (Fr.)
geistliche Spiel (G.)
miracle play
mystery play
morality play

magi play
sacra rappresentazione (It.)

autograph (score)
manuscript
original score
Urtext (G.)
manoscritto (It.)
manuscrit (Fr.)
Handschrift (G.)
manuscrito (Sp.)

autoharp
zither
dulcimer
cetra ad accordi (It.)
autoarpa (It.)
cithare d'amateur (Fr.)
Akkordzither (G.)
Tischharfe (G.)
auto-arpa (Sp.)

automatisches Klavier (G.)
player piano
mechanical piano
automatic piano
pianola (It.)
planchette (Fr.)
piano mécanique (Fr.)
autopiano (Sp.)
piano automático (Sp.)
piano mecánico (Sp.)
piano rolls
nickelodeon
juke-box

auxiliary tone/note
non-harmonic tone
neighbor note/tone
embellishment
ornament
mordent
inverted mordent
trill
broderie (Fr.)
Hilfsnote (G.)

Nebennote (G.)
appoggiatura (It.)
nota ausiliare (It.)
note secondaire (Fr.)
note auxiliaire (Fr.)
nota auxiliar (Sp.)

avanera (It.)
habanera (E., Sp.)
havanaise (Fr.)
Spanischer Tanz (G.)

avant-garde (Eng., Fr.)
modern music
contemporary music
experimental music
nuove musiche (It.)
musicum novum (Lat.)
ars nova (Lat., 14c.)
new music
manneristic music
new age
new wave

vs. musique ancienne (Fr.)

avec abandon (Fr.)
unrestrained
with abandon
*free
con abbandono (It.)
abandonné (Fr.)
mit Hingabe (G.)
con abandono (Sp.)

avec bouche fermée (Fr.)
to trill
to hum
fredonner (Fr.)
chantonner (Fr.)
a bocca chiusa (It.)
canticchiare (It.)
furberia del canto (It.)
trällern (G.)
Brummstimmen (G.)
canturrear (Sp.)

canticar (Sp.)

avec emphase (Fr.)
*emphasized
*accusé (Fr.)
en déhors (Fr.)
mise en relief (Fr.)
enfatico (It.)
con enfasi (It.)
betont (G.)
mit Emphase (G.)
hervorgehoben (G.)
resaltado (Sp.)

avec feu (Fr.)
with fire
con fuoco (It.)
mit Feuer (G.)
con fuego (Sp.)

avec force (Fr.)
forcefully
con forza (It.)
mit Kraft (G.)
con fuerza (Sp.)

avec l'archet (Fr.)
bowed, not plucked
with the bow
non-pizzicato
coll'arco (It.)
mit dem Bogen (G.)
nicht Pizzikato (G.)
con el arco (Sp.)

avec le bois (Fr.)
*col legno (It.)
with the wood of the bow
avec le dos (Fr.)
mit der Bogenstange (G.)
mit der Stange (G.)
mit dem Holz (G.)
mit dem Bogen schlagen (G.)
con la madera (Sp.)
con le varilla (Sp.)

avec le point de l'archet (Fr.)
  with the point of the bow
  alla punta d'arco (It.)
  an der Bogenspitze (G.)
  mit der Spitze (G.)
  con la punta (Sp.)
  up-bow

vs. au talon (Fr.)
  downbow

avec sourdine (Fr.)
  with damper/mute
  en sourdain (Fr.)
  con sordina (It., Sp.)
  mit Dämpfer (G.)
  una corda (It.)
  une corde (Fr.)
  eine Saiten (G.)
  una cuerda (Sp.)

avoided cadence
  *deceptive cadence
  half-cadence
  semi-cadence
  suspended cadence
  interrupted cadence
  surprise cadence
  cadenza evitata (It.)
  cadence évitée (Fr.,)
  Trugkadenz (G.)
  Halbschluss (G.)
  Trugschluss (G.)
  cadencia evitada (Sp.)
  cadencia interrumpida (Sp.)

ayre (old English)
  *song
  art song
  folk song
  popular song
  air
  *aria, arietta (It.)
  canzona, canzonetta (It.)
  ariette (Fr.)
  chansonette (Fr.)

air de cour (Fr.)
Liedchen (G.)

azione sacra (It.)
  oratorio (staged)
  religious play
  miracle play
  morality play
  mystery play
  magi play
  Nativity play
  sepulcrum play
  tomb play
  Krippenspiel (G.)
  *liturgical drama
  azione teatrale (It.)
  rappresentazione sacra (16c. It.)
  sepolcro (It.)
  opera
  dramma per musica (It.)
  drame lyrique (Fr.)
  miracle (Fr.)
  moralité (Fr.)
  mystère (Fr.)
  geistliche Spiel (G.)
  Mysterien (G.)
  auto sacramental (Sp.)
  misterio (Sp.)

B

B cancellatum (Lat.)
  B quadratum (Lat.)
  B quadrum (Lat.)
  natural sign
  cancel sign
  bequadro (It.)
  bécarre (Fr.)
  Quadrat (G.)
  becuadro (Sp.)
  B natural
  B durum (Lat., G.)
  B-Quadrat (G.)

B molle (G.)
  flat sign
  B flat
  bémol (Fr.)
  bemolle (It.)
  bemol (Sp.)
  B rotundum (Lat.)

B section
  middle section
  bridge
  alternative
  alternativo (It.)
  alternativement (Fr.)
  Überleitung (G.)
  trio section
  release
  channel
  trio section
  contrasting section

baby grand
  *grand piano
  semi-grand
  parlor grand
  boudoir grand

drawing-room grand
Stutzflügel (G.)
Salonflügel (G.)
horizontal piano
pianoforte a mezza
coda (It.)
  piano à queue mignon (Fr.)
  piano de boudoir (Fr.)
  grand piano de concert (Fr.)
  piano de media cola (Sp.)
  gran cola (Sp.)

vs. upright piano

bacchanal
  drinking song
  tavern song
  bacchanalian song
  dithyramb
  brindisi (It.)
  baccanale (It.)
  canto bacchico (It.)
  chanson bacchique (Fr.)
  chanson à boire (Fr.)
  Trinklied (G.)
  Bacchanal (G.)
  bacanal (Sp.)
  canción de taberna (Sp.)
  canción báquica (Sp.)

bacchetta da tamburo (It.)
  *drumstick
  mallet
  hammer
  baguette de tambour (Fr.)
  Trommelschlegel (G.)
  Schlegel (G.)
  baqueta (Sp.)
  macillo (Sp.)
  palillo de tambor (Sp.)

Bach trumpet
  baroque trumpet
  *trumpet (in D)
  piccolo trumpet
  clarion

clarino (It.)
clairon (Fr.)

backdrop
  drop
  curtain
  traveler
  scrim
  cyclorama
  telone (It.)
  siparia, siparietto (It.)
  rideau (Fr.)
  Vorhang (G.)
  Bühnenvorhang (G.)
  telón (Sp.)

backfall
  *appoggiatura
  forefall
  *ornament
  relish
  trill
  mordent

backround, backup
  *accompaniment
  assist

backround music
  light music
  mood music
  elevator music
  lift music
  easy listening
  salon music
  drawing-room music
  light classics
  dentist music
  dinner music
  table music
  banquet music
  cocktail music
  café music
  Muzak
  furniture music
  musique d'ameublement (Fr.)

musica di fondo (It.)
musica leggiera (It.)
musica da tavola (It.)
musique de table (Fr.)
musique légère (Fr.)
leichte Musik (G.)
musique de fond (Fr.)
musique d'ascenseur (Fr.)
musique de supermarché (Fr.)
música de fondo (Sp.)
musichetto (It.)
musiquette (Fr.)
musiquillo (Sp.)
música de mesa (Sp.)
Hintergrundmusik (G.)
Unterhaltungsmusik (G.)
Tafelmusik (G.)
*incidental music

backstage
offstage
behind the scenes
in the wings
retroscèna (It.)
fra le quinte (It.)
dans les coulisses (Fr.)
en coulisse (Fr.)
Hinterbühne (G.)
hinter der Szene (G.)
hinter den Kulissen (G.)
bastidores (Sp.)
entre bastidores (Sp.)
paño, al paño (Sp.)

badinage, badinerie (Fr.)
duple, fast dance (18 c.)
galop
polka
can-can

bagatelle (Fr.)
trifle
character piece
short piece
fancy
caprice

boutade (Fr.)
fantasie

bagpipe
musette (Fr.)
musetta (It.)
Dudelsack (G.)
piva (It.)
gaita (Sp.)
sampogna, zampogna (It.)
cornemuse (Fr.)
cornamusa (It., Sp.)
Sackpfeife (G.)
chanter (Fr.)
droner (Fr.)
chevrette, cabrette (Fr.)
biniou (Fr.)
sordellina (It.)
ceramella (It.)
surdelina (It.)
Schäferpfeiff (G.)
Hummel (G.)
Hümmelchen (G.)
Dudey (G.)

baguette (Fr.)
stick
*baton
drumstick
bacchetta (It.)
Schlegel (G.)
baqueta (Sp.)
Schlegel (G.)

2. bow
arco (It., Sp.)
archet (Fr.)
Bogen (G.)

baile, bailete, -o (Sp.)
*dance
ball
danza (It., Sp.)
Tanz (G.)
danse (Fr.)
bal (Fr.)

Ballett (G.)
ballo (It.)

baisser (Fr.)
to lower (pitch)
to flat, flatten
abaisser (Fr.)
abbassare (It.)
senken (G.)
erniedrigen (G.)
bemolisar (It.)
bémoliser (Fr.)
abemolar (Sp.)
bajar, rebajar (Sp.)

vs. hausser (Fr.)

bajo bufo (Sp.)
basso buffo (It.)
comic bass/baritone
basse bouffe (Fr.)
Bassbuffo (G.)
buffo bass
character baritone/bass

bajo continuo (Sp.)
*figured bass
basso continuo (It.)
thoroughbass
Generalbass (G.)

bajo de organo (Sp.)
drone
*pedal point
pedal note
organ point
burden
bourdon (Fr.)

bajo fundamental (Sp.)
fundamental bass
root bass
basso fondamentale (It.)
basse fondamentale (Fr.)
Grundbass (G.)

bajo obstinado (Sp.)
 *basso ostinato
 ground bass
 chaconne
 passacaglia
 pes

bajón (Sp.)
 *bassoon

bal, ballo, balletto (It.)
 *ballet
 dance
 masque
 ball

balais, balais de jazz (Fr.)
 brushes
 wire/steel brushes
 spazzole (It.)
 Rute (G.)
 Besen, Jazzbesen (G.)
 escobillas (Sp.)

balalaika (Eng., Fr., G.)
 balalaica (It., Sp.)
 domra, dombra (Rus.)
 bandura
 *guitar
 lute

balancella (It.)
 characteristic piece
 (rocking of a boat, gondola)
 * barcarole
 barcarolle (Fr.)
 balancelle (Fr.)
 barcarola (It.)

balancement (Fr.)
 tremolo (It.)
 *vibrato
 close shake
 tremolando (It.)
 trillo (It.)
 vibré (Fr.)

 flatté, flaté (Fr.)
 Bebung (G.)

balcony
 gallery
 *mezzanine
 dress circle
 loges
 loggia
 boxes, box seats
 bleachers
 peanut gallery
 standing room
 il paradiso (It.)
 upper circle
 choir loft
 galleria (It.)
 loggione (It.)
balconata (It.)
balcon (Fr.)
 galerie (Fr.)
 poulailles (Fr.)
 corbeille (Fr.)
 Galerie (G.)
balcón (Sp.)
 paraiso (Sp.)
 galería (Sp.)

Balg (G.)
 *bellows (of an organ)
 mantici (It.)
 soufflet (Fr.)
 fuelle (Sp.)
 Gebläse (G.)
 air supply

Balken (G.)
 beam (on notes)
 hook
 cross-bar
 flag
 ligatura (It.)
 stanghetta (It.)
 tratto d'unione (It.)
 barre de liaison (Fr.)
 barre horizontale (Fr.)

 barre transversale (Fr.)
 Querbalken (G.)
 Notenbalken (G.)
 Balkenverbindung (G.)
 barra de compás (Sp.)
 travesaño (Sp.)

ballad
 *song
 folk ballad
 popular ballad
 folk song
 spinning song
 chanson de toile (Fr.)
 chanson de geste (Fr.)
 Spinnenlied (G.)

ballad horn
 *althorn
 alto saxhorn
 baritone (horn)
 vocal horn
 amateur voice horn
 mellophone
 voice/vocal horn
 tromba de vocal (Sp.)

ballad opera
 folk opera
 English opera
 operetta
 musical
 opéra comique (Fr.)
 Spieloper (G.)
 Singspiel (G.)
 light opera
 jig(g)
 entertainment

vs. grand opera

ballad singer
 folk singer
 balladeer
 bard
 poet

38

singer
vocalist
*minstrel
Troubadour
gleeman
scop
goliard
ministerialis (Lat.)
menestrello (It.)
ménéstrier (Fr.)
Spielmann (G.)
ministril (Sp.)

ballade
medieval song (14c., Fr.)
art song
canzo
bar
*song
forme fixe (Fr.)
chanson (Fr.)
Trouvère (Fr.)
Troubadour

2. Lied (G.)
art song
ballad

3. instrumental piece
piano piece

ballata (It.)
song (14c.)
villancico (Sp.)
virelai (Fr.)
ripresa (It. refrain)
piedi (It.)
volta (It.)

ballet
*dance
masque
ball
theatrical dance
ballet de cour (Fr.)
opéra-ballet (Fr.)

ballo (It. 17c.)
bal (It.)

ballet(t) (17c. Eng.)
part-song
madrigal
glee
catch
balletto (It.)
Ballett (G.)
bailete, -o (Sp.)

balletto (It.)
part-song
ballet
madrigal

2. dance movement
suite (17-18c.)

a ballet (dance)
ball (social dance)
bal (Fr.)
ballo (It.)

ballroom
dance hall
dance club
night club
discotheque
dance palace

band
ensemble
orchestra
combo
banda (It., Sp.)
bande (Fr.)
Kapelle (G.)
concert band
jazz band
marching band
big band
swing band
dance band
stage band

military band
brass band
wind band
string band
fiddle band
jug band
steel band

2. track (on a disk)
pista (It.. Sp.)
traccia (It.)
piste (Fr.)
Spur, Tonspur (G.)

band leader
*conductor
bandmaster
batonist
chef d'orchestre (Fr.)
Dirigent (G.)
maestro (It.)
capobanda (It.)

band music
wind music
music for brass
military band music
Harmoniemusik (G.)

banda (It., Sp.)
fanfare
*call
flourish
tantara
trumpet call
chamade (Fr.)
chiamata (It.)

banda de sonido (Sp.)
sound track (film)
sound stripe
film recording
collona sonora (It.)
colonne sonore (Fr.)
bande sonore (Fr.)
Tonspur (G.)

pista sonora (Sp.)

banda Turca (It.)
 *Janissary music
 Turkish crescent
 cappello cinese (It.)
 *chapeau Chinois (Fr.)
 Halbmond (G.)
 Schellenbaum (G.)
 chinesco (Sp.)

bandola (Sp.)
 *guitar (small)
 vihuela (Sp.)
 bandurria (Sp.)

bandoneon (Sp.)
 *accordion
 concertina

bandora, bandore (Eng.)
 bass guitar (16c.)
 lute
 archlute
 pandora
 orpharion

bandstand
 band shell
 bandwagon
 stage
 platform
 palco della banda (It.)
 palco dell'orchestra (It.)
 carro della banda musicale (It.)
 kiosque à musique (Fr.)
 Musikpavillon (G.)
 Konzertpavillon (G.)
 quiosco de música (Sp.)
 plataforma con concha
acústica (Sp.)

bandstration
 scoring for band
 *orchestration
 instrumentation

bandura, bandoura (Uk.)
 balalaika
 bass guitar
 guitar
 archlute

banjo
 tenor banjo
 *guitar
 lute
 mandolin
 ukulele
 banjo-ukulele
 banger
 bangio (It.)

banquet music
 table music
 dinner music
 café music
 cocktail music
 *backround music
 Tafelmusik (G.)
 musica da tavola (It.)
 musique de table (Fr.)
 música de mesa (Sp.)

baqueta (Sp.)
 drumstick
 mallet
 hammer
 bacchetta da tamburo (It.)
 baguette de tsmbour (Fr.)
 mailloche (Fr.)
 Trommelschlegel (G.)
 palillo de tambor (Sp.)

baqueta de dos cabezas (Sp.)
 two-headed drumstick
 battente doppio (It.)
 mazzuolo a doppia testa (It.)
 mailloche double (Fr.)
 mailloche à double tête (Fr.)
 tampon (Fr.)
 Doppelschlegel (G.)
 zweikopfiger Schlegel (G.)

bar
 measure
 metrical
 mensural
 meter
 mesure (Fr.)
 misura (It.)
 Takt (G.)
 battuta (It.)
 barra (Sp.)

2. bar line
 double bar
 barre (Fr.)
 Taktstrich (G.)
 barra (It., Sp.)
 sbarra (It.)
 linea divisoria (Sp.)
 stranghetta (It.)
 barra de compás (Sp.)
 Mensurstrich (G.)

3. bar form (12c.)
 AAB form
 Minnesinger (G.)
 Meistersinger (G.)
 Stollen (G.)
 Leich (G.)
 lai (Fr.)
 canzo (12c. Fr.)
 Troubadour
 Trouvère
 formes fixes (Fr.)
 ballade (Fr.)

barbada (Sp.)
 chin rest
 mentoniera (It.)
 mentonnière (Fr.)
 Kinnhalter (G.)
 mentonera (Sp.)

Barbary lyre
 *lyre
 accordo (It.)

barbershop harmony
close harmony
equal voices
voci pari (It.)
voix égales (Fr.)
voces iguales (Sp.)
gleiche Gesangstimmen (G.)
Aequalstimmen (G.)
enge Harmonie (G.)
enge Lage (G.)
men's voices

Barbitos, Barbiton (Gr.)
lyre (ancient Gr.)
harp

barcarole
boat song
gondola song
barcarolle (Fr.)
barcarola (It., Sp.)
Barkarole (G.)
balancella (It.)

bard
*minstrel
poet
balladeer
*singer
vocalist
performer
jongleur (Fr.)
goliard
scop
troubadour
ménéstrier (14c. Fr.)
ménestrel (Fr.)
bardo (It., Sp.)
barde (Fr.)
Barde (G.)

bariolage (Fr.)
ondeggiando (It.)
ondulé (Fr.)
broken "chords"
alternating notes (strings)

baritone (voice)
lyric bass
high bass
baritenor
bass 1
first bass
baritenor
baritono (It., Sp.)
baryton (Fr.)
Bariton (G.)
basse chantante (Fr.)
basse-taille (Fr.)
bass-baritone
basso cantante (It.)
basse noble (Fr.)

baritone
baritone horn
saxhorn
euphonium
tenor tuba
*althorn

baritone clef
bass clef on third line
F-clef
chiava di fa (It.)

baritone horn
saxhorn
*althorn
baritone
tuba
tenor tuba
saxhorn
*euphonium
bugle contralto (Sp.)
bass à pistons (Fr.)
Baryton (G.)
Barytonhorn (G.)

baritone oboe
heckelphone
basset oboe
bass/baritone oboe
basse de musette (Fr.)

Musettenbass (G.)

baroque (Eng., Fr.)
17-18c. music
rococo
barocco (It.)
Barock (G.)
barroco (Sp.)
nuovo musiche (It.)

baroque trumpet
Bach trumpet
piccolo trumpet
trumpet in D
clarion
clarino (It.)
clairon (Fr.)
hohe Trompete (G.)
Clarintrompete (G.)

barré (Fr.)
grand-barré (Fr.)
capotasto (Eng., It.)
capo
capodastre (Fr.)
Kapodaster (G.)
Saitenfessel (G.)
ceduela (Sp.)
ceja, cejilla (Sp.)

barre de liaison (Fr.)
beam
cross-bar
barre horizontale (Fr.)
barre transversale (Fr.)
tratto d'unione (It.)
barra de compás (Sp.)
Notenbalken
Balken (G.)
Querbalken (G.)
travesaño (Sp.)
ligatura (It.)
stanghetta (It.)

barrel organ
hand organ

street organ
street piano
barrel piano
*hurdy-gurdy
organetto (It.)
organo a manovella (It.)
organo di Barberia (It.)
orgue à cilindre (Fr.)
orgue à manivelle (Fr.)
orgue de Barbarie (Fr.)
Drehorgel (G.)
Leierkasten (G.)
organillo (Sp.)
calliope
Orgelwalze (G.)
organ

barrelhouse
jazz style
boogie-woogie
stride piano
stomping
pop music

baryton (G.)
viola da gamba (It.)
bass viol
cello
viola bastarda (It.)
viola di bordone (It.)

barzelletta (It.)
frottola (It.)
madrigal
part-song
ballata (It.)
canzona (It.)

bas-dessus (Fr.)
mezzo, mezzo-soprano
alto voice
second soprano
second dessus (Fr.)
Mittelsopran (G.)
Mezzosopran (G.)

basilica
*cathedral
duomo (It.)
Dom (G.)
seo (Sp.)

Baskische Trommel (G.)
*tambourine
tambour de Basque (Fr.)
tambour (Fr.)
tamburino (It.)
Tamborin (G.)
Schellentrommel (G.)

bass
low instrument, voice
basso (It.)
basso profundo (It.)
basso cantante (It.)
basso buffo (It.)
basse (Fr.)
Bass (G.)
bajo (Sp.)
baritone
bass-baritone

2. string bass
bass viol
consort viol
double bass
contrabass
bass fiddle
bull fiddle
acoustic bass
octobasse (Fr.)
octo-bass
basse gigantique (Fr.)
stand up bass
washtub bass
upright bass
doghouse bass
bass guitar
electric bass
contrabasso (It.)
contrebasse (Fr.)
Kontrabass (G.)

contrabajo (Sp.)
violone (It., Fr.)
violonar (Fr.)
violonaro (It.)
basse-contre de violon (Fr.)
basse des Italiens (Fr.)

bass clarinet
clarone (It.)
clarinetto basso (It.)
clarinette basse (Fr.)
Bassklarinette (G.)

bass clef
F clef
baritone clef
chiave di fa (It.)
chiave di basso (It.)
clef de fa (Fr.)
F-Schlüssel (G.)
Bassschlüssel (G.)
llave de fa (Sp.)
clave de fa (Sp.)
clave grave (Sp.)

bass cornett
serpent
serpentone (It.)
serpentón (Sp.)

bass drum
gran cassa (It.)
cassa grande (It.)
gran tamburo (It.)
grosse caisse (Fr.)
gros-tambour (Fr.)
grosse Trommel (G.)
bombo (Sp.)

2. tympani
kettledrum(s)

bass flute
alto flute
*flute
flautone (It.)

flute alto (Fr.)
Altflöte (G.)
flauto baja (Sp.)

bass guitar
electric bass
acoustic bass guitar

bass horn
serpent
keyed horn
Russian bassoon
basson russe (Fr.)
serpent droit (Fr.)
Basshorn (G.)
cor basse (Fr.)
corno basso (It.)

2. tuba
sousaphone

bass lute
theorbo
*archlute
chittarrone (It.)

bass lyre
lira (It.)
lirone (It.)
accordo (It.)
archiviola di lira (It.)
lira da braccio (It.)
lira da gamba (It.)
lira tedesca (It.)

bass oboe
heckelphone
baritone oboe
basset oboe
basse de musette (Fr.)
Musettenbass (G.)

bass trombone
cimbasso (It.)
tuba

bass trumpet
*trombone
sackbut
Posaune (G.)

bass tuba
helicon
tuba

bass viol
*bass
bass fiddle
string bass
contrabass
double bass
basse-contre (Fr.)
basse-contre de viole (Fr.)
double bass viol

2.*viola da gamba

basse à pistons (Fr.)
*euphonium
tenor tuba
flicorno basso (It.)
Baryton (G.)
Barytonhorn (G.)
bombardino (Sp.)

basse bouffe (Fr.)
comic bass/baritone
buffo bass
basso buffo (It.)
basso comico (It.)
Bassbuffo (G.)
bajo bufo (Sp.)
character bass/baritone

basse-chantante (Fr.)
lyric bass (singer)
*baritone
high bass
bass 1
first bass
basse noble (Fr.)
basso cantante (It.)

basse chiffrée (Fr.)
*figured bass
*basso continuo (It.)
thoroughbass
continuo
bezifferter Bass (G.)

basse continue (Fr.)
*figured bass
continuo
*basso continuo (It.)
Generalbass (G.)
allgemeiner Bass (G.)

basse contrainte (Fr.)
*basso ostinato
gezwungener Bass (G.)

basse danse (Fr.)
court dance (15c.)
minuet
*branle (Fr.)
bassadanza (It.)
saltarello (tedesco) (It.)
piva (It.)
calata (It.)
cascarda (It.)
gagliarda (It.)
tordiglione (It.)
quaternaria (It.)
pas de Brabant (Fr.)
galliarde (Fr.)
to(u)rdion (Fr.)
Hoftanz (G., 16c.)
Nachtanz (G., 16c.)
baxa (Sp.)

basse de musette (Fr.)
heckelphone
bass/baritone oboe
basset oboe
Musettenbass (G.)

basse de violon (Fr.)
*viola
*alto

alta viola (It.)
Bratsche (G.)
Altviole (G.)

basse d'harmonie (Fr.)
ophicleide
oficleide (It.)
ophicléide (Fr.)
Ophikleide (G.)
figle (Sp.)
key(ed) bugle
Kent bugle
Royal Kent bugle
bugle à clés (Fr.)
Klappenhorn (G.)
serpent
tuba

basse fondamentale (Fr.)
root (of a chord)
do
tonic
ut (Lat.)

2. first overtone/harmonic
fundamental bass
*fundamental note/tone
radical bass
suono fondamentale (It.)
Basston (G.)
Grundton (G.)
sonido fundamental (Sp.)

basse gigantique (Fr.)
octobasse (Fr.)
octo-bass
large bass fiddle
*bass

basse-taille (Fr.)
*baritone voice
lyric bass
Bassbariton (G.)
basse noble (Fr.)
basse chantante (Fr.)

2. *cello
baryton (G.)
Halbbass (G.)
basso di camera (It.)

basset horn
clarinet
alto clarinet
tenor clarinet
clarone (It.)
cor de basset (Fr.)
Bassetthorn (G.)
corno di bassetto (It.)
clarinete alto (Sp.)

basset oboe
heckelphone
baritone oboe
basse de musette (Fr.)
Musettenbass (G.)

bassetto (It.)
small doublebass
*cello
bassetto di mano (It.)
Bassett, Bassettl, Bassl (G.)
Halbbass (G.)
basso di camera (It.)
Kammerbass (G.)

bassin (Fr.)
cup (brass mouthpiece)
tazza (It.)
Kessel (G.)
taza (Sp.)
Mundstück (G.)
embouchure (Fr.)
bocchino (It.)
imboccatura (It.)
embocadura (Sp.)
boquilla (Sp.)

bassist
bass player
bass singer

Basslaute (G.)
bass lute
*archlute
theorbo
chitarrone (It.)

basso cantante (It.)
*baritone
bass-baritone
lyric bass

basso continuo (It.)
*figured bass
continuo
thoroughbass
basso generale (It.)
basso figurato (It.)
basso cifrato (It.)
basso numerato (It.)
Generalbass (G.)
bezifferter Bass (G.)
allgemeiner Bass (G.)
basse continue (Fr.)
basse chiffrée (Fr.)
basse figurée (Fr.)
bajo continuo (Sp.)
basso seguente (It.)

basso di camera (It.)
small doublebass
bassetto (It.)
Kammerbass (G.)
Halbbass (G.)
Bassett, Bassettl, Bassl (G.)
*cello

basso ostinato (It.)
ground bass
ostinato bass
chaconne
passacaglia
pes
basse obstinée (Fr.)
basse constrainte (Fr.)
bajo obstinado (Sp.)

folia
variations

basso profundo (It.)
low bass
second bass

basson russe (Fr.)
Russian bassoon
*bass horn
serpent
bassoon

bassoon
fagotto (It.)
basson (Fr.)
Fagott (G.)
fagote (Sp.)
bajon (Sp.)
sarrusophone
bombard
bombardon
curtal
Dulzian (G.)

Bassschlüssel (G.)
bass clef
baritone clef
*F clef
chiave di fa (It.)
clef de fa (Fr.)
clave de fa (Sp.)
clave grave (Sp.)

basta el fin (Sp.)
*al fine (It.)
à la fin (Fr.)
bis zu Ende (G.)

bastante (Sp.)
very
*assai (It.)
très (Fr.)
sehr (G.)

bastidores (Sp.)

*backstage
in the wings
offstage
behind the scenes
retroscena (It.)
en coulisse (Fr.)
Hinterbühne (G.)

bâteau-théatre (Fr.)
showboat
road show
showmobile
touring company
buque teatro (Sp.)

batidor (Sp.)
fingerboard
fretboard
tastiera (It.)
touche (Fr.)
Griffbret (G.)

batintín (Sp.)
gong
Chinese gong
tam-tam
kettle gong
tambour de bronze (Fr.)
Kesselgong (G.)
tantán (Sp.)

baton
stick
baguette (Fr.)
bâton de mesure (Fr.)
bacchetta di direttore (It.)
Taktstock, Taktstab (G.)
baqueta (Sp.)
batuta (Sp.)
Schlegel (G.)

bâton (Fr.)
vertical or slanting bars
multiple-measure rest sign

bâton de reprise (Fr.)

repeat sign
segno di repetizione (It.)
signe de répétition (Fr.)
Wiederholungszeichen (G.)
signo de repetición (Sp.)

batonist, batoneer
conductor
bandleader
chef d'orchestre (Fr.)
Dirigent (G.)
choir director
choral director
maestro (It.)

battement (Fr.)
ornament
trill
mordent
neighbor note
vibrato

2. acoustical beats

battement de tambour (Fr.)
drum-beat
ruff, ruffle
drag
flam, flourish
paradiddle
rub-a-dub
roll
colpo di tamburo (It.)
batterie (Fr.)
Trommelschlag (G.)
tantarán, tantarantán (Sp.)
redoble (Sp.)

battente (It.)
*drumstick
mallet
hammer
bacchetto (It.)
baguette (Fr.)
mailloche (Fr.)
Schlegel (G.)

palillo (Sp.)
baqueta (Sp.)

battente doppio (It.)
two-headed drumstick
mazzuolo a doppia testa (It.)
mailloche double (Fr.)
tampon (Fr.)
mailloche à double tête (Fr.)
Doppelschlegel (G.)
zweikopfiger Schlegel (G.)
baqueta de dos cabezas (Sp.)

batterie (Fr.)
broken chord
repeated notes (fast)
*arpeggio (It.)
battery
crackle
Brechung (G.)
battimento (It.)
Rauscher (G.)
Schwärmer (G.)
trillo (It.)

2. percussion ensemble

3. drum roll

4. striking of strings (guitar)

battuta (It.)
a *beat
a *bar
mesure (Fr.)
Takt (G.)
Schlag (G.)
compás (Sp.)
barra (Sp.)

battuta composta (It.)
compound meter
mesure composée (Fr.)
divisio (14c. It.)
zusammengesetzte Takt (G.)
compás compuesto (Sp.)

batuque (Port.)
samba
dance
bossa nova (Port.)
carioca (Port.)
maxixe (Port.)

Bauernleier (G.)
*hurdy-gurdy
street piano,organ
barrel organ/piano
hand organ

baxa (Sp.)
*basse-danse (Fr.)
court dance (15c.)
bassadanza (It.)
piva (It.)
saltarello (It.)
Hoftanz (G.)
Nachtanz (G.)
minuet

baxoncillo (Sp.)
*open diapason (organ)
principal
prestant
foundation stop
montre (Fr.)

bazoo
kazoo
mirliton
eunuch flute
toy instrument

beak(ed) flute
*recorder
English flute
whistle flute
end-blown flute
flûte à bec (Fr.)
Schnabelflöte (G.)

beam
cross-bar

hook
note
tratto d'unione (It.)
stanghetta (It.)
barre transversale (Fr.)
Notenbalken (G.)
Balken (G.)
Querbalken (G.)
barra de compás (Sp.)
travesaño (Sp.)

Bearbeitung (G.)
*arrangement
adaptation
transcription
*edition

beat (n.)
pulse
time
metrical accent
count
tactus (Lat.)
tempus (Lat.)
battuta (It.)
temps (Fr.)
Schlag (G.)
Takt (G.)
Zählzeit (G.)
tiempo (Sp.)
Taktschlag (G.)
Taktteil (G.)
battement de mesure (Fr.)

2. stroke, strike
colpo (It.)
coup (Fr.)
Schlag (G.)
batido (Sp.)
golpe (Sp.)

beat (vb)
strike
battere (It.)
battre (Fr.)
schlagen (G.)

pegar (Sp.)

beat (17c. E.)
  ornament
  appoggiatura (It.)
  trill
  mordent

beat time
  conduct
  direct
  lead
  wave a stick
  count time
  battere il tempo (It.)
  battre la mesure (Fr.)
  taktieren (G.)
  dirigere (It.)
  diriger (Fr.)
  dirigieren (G.)
  dirigir (Sp.)

beats (n.)
  detuned
  *celeste (organ)
  unda maris (organ)
  out of tune
  off-key
  off-pitch

bebization
  sol-fa
  *solmization
  solfeggio

bebop
  jazz
  bop
  swing
  pop music
  cool jazz

Bebung (G.)
  *vibrato (clavichord)
  tremolo
  *balancement (Fr.)

vibré (Fr.)
trillo (It.)
close shake

bec (Fr.)
  *mouthpiece
  bocchino (It.)
  becco (It.)
  embouchure (Fr.)
  Mundstück (G.)
  Schnabel (G.)
  pico (Sp.)
  boquilla (Sp.)
  embocadura (Sp.)

pick
plectrum
plettro (It.)
plectre (Fr.)
médiator (Fr.)
Plektrum (G.)
pua (Sp.)

bécarre (Fr.)
  natural sign
  cancel sign
  bequadro (It.)
  Auflösungszeichen (G.)
  becuadro (Sp.)
  B quadratum (Lat.)
  Quadrat (G.)

Becher (G.)
  *bell (of horn, e.g.)
  campana (It., Sp.)
  pavillon (Fr.)
  padiglione (It.)
  Stürze (G.)
  Schallbecher (G.)
  Schalltrichter (G.)
  pabellón (Sp.)

Becken (G.)
  *cymbals
  crash cymbals
  piatti (It.)

cinelli (It.)
cymbales (Fr.)
platillos (Sp.)
cimbalos (Sp.)
Schallbecken (G.)

bedeckt (G.)
  damped
  muted
  muffled
  covered
  velato (It.)
  coperto (It.)
  couvert (Fr.)
  cubierto (Sp.)
  gedämpft (G.)
  sourd (Fr.)

beffroi (Fr.)
  gong
  tam-tam

2. tocsin (E., Fr.)
  alarm bell

begleiten (G.)
  *accompany
  assist

Begleiter(in) (G.)
  *accompanist

Begleitung (G.)
  *accompaniment

béguine (Fr.)
  dance
  bolero (Sp.)
  rumba (Sp.)
  rhumba (Sp.)

behind the scenes
  *backstage
  in the wings
  retroscena (It.)
  dans la coulisse (Fr.)

hinter den Szene (G.)
bastidores (Sp.)

Beifall (G.)
  *applause
  accolades
  adulation
  applauso (It.)
  applaudissement (Fr.)
  aplauso (Sp.)
  claque (Fr.)

beiseite (G.)
  *aside
  very soft
  stage whisper
  in disparte (It.)
  sotto voce (It.)
  a parte (Sp.)
  à part (Fr.)

Beisser (G.)
  *mordent
  ornament
  *acciaccatura (It.)
  grace note
  neighbor note
  trill

Beitöne (G.)
  overtones
  *harmonics
  partials

bel
  loudness
  decibel (E., It., Sp.)
  amplitude
  gain
  volume
  sound level
  décibel (Fr.)
  Dezibel (G.)
  decibelio (Sp.)

bel canto (It.)

beautiful song/singing
singing style
lyrical
opera
grand opera
opera seria (It.)

belebt (G.)
  *animato, animando (It.)
  lively
  spirited
  animated
  con moto (It.)
  vivace (It.)
  con spirito (It.)
  spirit(u)oso (It.)
  animé (Fr.)
  munter (G.)
  lebhaft (G.)
  animando (Sp.)

belfry
  bell tower
  steeple
  campanile (E., It.)
  campanaria (It.)
  carillon
  clocher (Fr.)
  Glockenstube (G.)
  Glockenturm (G.)
  campanario (Sp.)

bell(s)
  carillon
  churchbells
  chimes
  chime-bells
  cathedral chimes
  tubular bells
  cowbells
  campanelli (It.)
  jeu de timbres (Fr.)
  nolettes (Fr.)
  juego de timbres (Sp.)
  campanólogo (Sp.)
  campane tubolari (It.)

Röhrenglocken (G.)
cloches tubulaires (Fr.)
glockenspiel (E., G.)
Lyra (G.)
handbells
clochettes (Fr.)
orchestra bells
celesta
céleste (Fr.)
cloche (Fr.)
campana (It., Sp.)
squilla (It.)
cimbalo (Sp.)
Glocke (G.)
sanctus bells
altar bells
sleighbells
jingle bells
harness bells
bubboli (It.)
sonaglio, sonagliera (It.)
grelots (Fr.)
nolettes (Fr.)
sonnettes, sonnailles (Fr.)
Schellen (G.)
Schellengeläute (G.)
Rollschellen (G.)
Schalenglöckchen (G.)
cascabeles (Sp.)
cencerro (Sp.)
pellet bells
Tintinnabulum (Lat., G.)
tintinnabolo (It.)
nolae (Lat.)
campanae (Lat.)
cascavellus (Lat.)
cimbelstern (org.)
Cymbelstern (G.)
Zimbelstern (G.)
tocsin (E., Fr.)
beffroi (Fr.)
alarm bell
tower bells

2. flair of horn
  padiglione (It.)

campana (Lat., It., Sp.)
Becher (G.)
Schallbecher (G.)
Stürze (G.)
bonnet (Fr.)
pavillon (Fr.)
pabellón (Sp.)
Schallstück (G.)
Schalltrichter (G.)

bell choir
handbells
bell ringers
carilloneurs (Fr.)

bell down (horn)
posizione normale (I.)
position naturelle (Fr.)
natürlich (G.)
normalmente (Sp.)

bell harp
psaltery (use plectra)
zither
fairy bells
box zither
cithare sur caisse (Fr.)
Kastenzither (G.)
lyre
dulcimer
harp
salterio (It., Sp.)
psalterion (Fr.)
Psalten (G.)

bell in the air
raise the bell (of a horn)
campana in alto (It.)
padiglioni in alto (It.)
pavillon en l'air (Fr.)
Stürze hoch (G.)
Schalltrichter hoch (G.)
pabellón al aire (Sp.)

bell lyre
*glockenspiel

bell lyra
lyra glockenspiel
strumento d'acciaio (It.)
Stahlspiel (G.)
Lyra (G.)

bell-piano
*glockenspiel
orchestra bells
celesta

bell ringer
carilloneur (Fr.)
campanist
campanista (It.)
campanaio (It.)
Glockenspieler (G.)
campanero (Sp.)

bell tree
Turkish crescent
Chinese crescent
Janissary music
jingling Johnny
banda Turca (It.)
*chapeau Chinois (Fr.)
Halbmond (G.)
Schellenbaum (G.)
sombrero Chino (Sp.)

bellows
soffietto (It.)
soufflet (Fr.)
Balg (G.)
fuelle (Sp.)
mantice (It.)
Gebläse (G.)
*wind chest
wind supply

belly
body of a violin, etc.
table (E., Fr.)
soundboard
tavola armonica (It.)
table d'harmonie (Fr.)

Decke (G.)
Resonanztafel (G.)
tapa, tabla de armonia (Sp.)

2. soundboard
piano armonico (It.)
table d'harmonie (Fr.)
Resonanzboden (G.)
caja armónica (Sp.)

belt (vb.)
sing out loud
* chest voice
full voice
low voice
belting voice

bémoliser (Fr.)
flatten a note, etc.
abbassare (It.)
bemolisar (It.)
erniedrigen (G.)
abemolar (Sp.)

vs. diéser (Fr.)

bemolle (It.)
flat sign
bémol (Fr.)
Bemol (G.)
bemol (Sp.)
B rotundum (Lat.)

vs. diesis (It.)

ben marcato (It.)
well-marked
accented

bend, bender
tone bender
pitch bender
vibrato
wow
slide
portamento (It.)

glissando (It.)
port de voix (Fr.)
scoop

beneplacito (It.)
  *freely
  ad libitum (Lat.)
  a bene placito (It.)
  a capriccio (It.)
  a piacere (It.)
  au caprice (Fr.)
  a capricho (Sp.)

Benzinfass (G.)
  steel drum (tuned)
  percussion instr.
  tamburo di latte (It.)
  tamburo d'acciaio (It.)
  tambour d'acier (Fr.)
  Stahltrommel (G.)
  Calypsotrommel (G.)
  tambor metálico (Sp.)

bequadro (It.)
  natural sign
  cancel sign
  quadro (It.)
  bécarre (Fr.)
  becuadro (Sp.)
  Auflösungszeichen (G.)
  Quadrat (G.)
  B-Quadrat (G.)
  B quadratum (Lat.)

berceuse (Fr.)
  lullaby
  cradle song
  ninnananna (It.)
  ninnerella (It.)
  dodinette, dodo, dodino (Fr.)
  Wiegenlied (G.)
  Schlummerlied (G.)
  Ständchen (G.)
  canción de cuna (Sp.)
  nana (Sp.)
  arrullo (Sp.)

bergamasca (It.)
  dance, song (16c,)

  2. chaconne (Fr.)
  ground bass
  passacaglia (It.)
  folia
  variations
  *basso ostinato

bergerette (Fr., 18c.)
  pastoral song
  song
  brunette (Fr.)

  2. 15c. rondeau (Fr.)
  virelai (Fr.)
  forme fixe (Fr.)

Besen, Jazzbesen (G.)
  brushes
  wire/steel brushes
  spazzole (It.)
  balais de jazz (Fr.)
  Rute (G.)
  escobillas (Sp.)

Besetzung (G.)
  setting
  scoring
  *arranged

betont (G.)
  accented
  stressed
  emphasized
  *accusé (Fr.)
  en dehors (Fr.)
  lead part

betrübt (G.)
  plaintive
  *sadly
  doloroso (It.)
  tristement (Fr.)
  tristamente (Sp.)

Bettlorleier (G.)
  *hurdy-gurdy
  street piano
  barrel organ
  organistrum (Lat.)
  lira tedesca (It.)
  chifonie (Fr.)
  vielle (Fr.)
  Bauernleier (G.)
  cifonia (Sp.)

bewegt (G.)
  animated
  quick
  *fast
  lively
  rapid
  mosso (It.)
  animato (It.)
  animé (Fr.)
  animado (Sp.)
  movido (Sp.)

Bezifferter Bass (G.)
  *figured bass
  basso continuo (It.)
  basso cifrato (It.)
  thoroughbass
  Generalbass (G.)
  basse continue (Fr.)
  bajo continuo (Sp.)

bianca (It.)
  half note
  minum (Lat.)
  blanche (Fr.)
  Halbe (G.)
  blanca (Sp.)

bible organ
  *portative organ
  positive organ
  chamber organ
  cabinet organ
  portable organ
  regal

bicinium (Lat.)
  duet
  duo
  diphona (Gr.)
  tricinium
  trio

big band
  dance band
  stage band
  swing band
  40's band
  dixieland band
  jazz band

binary form
  two-part form
  AB form
  bipartite form
  bipartito (It.)
  biparti (Fr.)
  binario (It., Sp.)
  binaire (Fr.)
  zweiteilige Form (G.)
  bipartido (Sp.)
  bar form
  Stollen (G.)
  canzo (Fr.)
  ballade (Fr.)
  vers (Fr.)
  Troubadour (Fr.)
  Trouvère (Fr.)
  formes fixes (Fr.)
  Minnesinger (G.)
  Meistersinger (G.)

binary measure
  common time
  common measure
  duple meter
  2/4, 2/2, 4/4 time
  cut-time
  ordinary time
  ritmo binario (It.)
  tempo binario (It.)
  mesure binaire (Fr.)

rythme binaire (Fr.)
Vierertakt (G.)
Viervierteltakt (G.)
Zweiertakt (G.)
tempo ordinario (It.)
mouvement ordinaire (Fr.)
movimiento ordinario (Sp.)
compás binario (Sp.)

binaural, bi-naural
  stereo
  stereophonic
  dual-channel
  diotic

vs. monaural

bind
  slur
  ligature
  neume
  legato sign
  legatura (It.)
  liaison (Fr.)
  Bindung (G.)
  Bindebogen (G.)
  ligadura (Sp.)

2. tie
  legatura di valore (It.)
  signe de tenue (Fr.)
  Haltebogen (G.)
  ligadura de valor (Sp.)

biniou (Fr.)
  *bagpipe
  musette (Fr.)
  piva (It.)
  Dudelsack (G.)
  Sackpfeife (G.)
  cornemuse (Fr.)
  cornamusa (Lat., It., Sp.)
  gaita (Sp.)

bird-call
  merula (Lat.)

richiamo per ucelli (It.)
Vogelsang, Vogelgesang (G.)
Vogelpfeife (G.)
cri d'oiseau (Fr.)
appeau (Fr.)
chant des oiseau (Fr.)
reclamo (Sp.)

bird organ
  organetto (It.)
  *barrel-organ
  serinette (Fr.)
  Vogelorgel (G.)

birimbao (Sp.)
  *Jew's harp
  crembalum (Lat.)
  scacciapensieri (It.)
  rebube (Fr.)
  Maultrommel (G.)

bis (Fr., It.)
  twice
  repeat
  reprise
  encore
  altra volta (It.)
  noch Einmal (G.)
  Zugabe (G.)
  otra vez (Sp.)

bis zum Ende (G.)
  *al fine (It.)
  à la fin (Fr.)
  hasta el fin (Sp.)

bis zum Zeichen (G.)
  al segno (It.)
  d'al segno (It.)
  au signe (Fr.)
  al signo (Sp.)
  to the sign

bisbigliando, -ato (It.)
  tremolo (harp)
  harp tremolo

2. whispered
chuchoté (Fr.)
geflüstert (G.)
cuchicheado (Sp.)
*aside
stage whisper
sotto voce (It.)
very soft

bischero (It.)
tuning peg/pin
pirolo (It.)
caviglia (It.)
cheville (Fr.)
Wirbel (G.)
Stimmnagel (G.)
clavija (Sp.)

biscroma (It.)
thirty-second note/rest
demi-semiquaver
triple-croche (Fr.)
Zweiunddreissigstel (Pause)
(G.)
trentaduesimo (It.)
pausa di biscroma (It.)
huitième de soupir (Fr.)
silencio de fusa (Sp.)
fusa (Sp.)

bisdiapason (Lat.)
double octave
fifteenth
superoctave

biseau (Fr.)
languid (organ pipe)
tuning tongue
languette
anima (It.)
Kern (G.)
alma (Sp.)
bisel (Sp.)

bit part
minor role

supporting role
walk-on
extra
super
supernumerary
comprimario/a (It.)
Statist (G.)

bitonal
polytonal
atonal
dodecaphonic
twelve-tone music

biucolo (It.)
*bugle
bugle-horn
cor bugleret (Fr.)
Bügelhorn (G.)

black key(s)
accidentals
sharps and flats
tasto nero (It.)
tasto del diesis (It.)
touche noire (Fr.)
touche dièse (Fr.)
touche supérieure (Fr.)
feintes (Fr.)
Halbtontaste (G.)
Obertasten (G.)
schwarze Obertasten (G.)
tecla negra (Sp.)
sostenido (Sp.)

vs. white key(s)

blanca (Sp.)
half-note
minum
blanche (Fr.)
Halbe (G.)
bianca (It.)

blaring
loud

ear-splitting
deafening
forte, fortissimo (It.)
fort, fortement (Fr.)
laut (G.)
stark (G.)
fuerte (Sp.)

blasen (G.)
blow (a wind instr.)
play
sound
soffiare (It.)
souffler (Fr.)
soplar (Sp.)

Bläser (G.)
wind player
instrumentalist

Blasinstrumente (G.)
wind instruments
aerophones
fiati (It.)
strumenti a fiato (It.)
instruments à vent (Fr.)
instrumentos de viento (Sp.)

Blatt (G.)
reed
Rohrblatt (G.)
ancia (It.)
anche (Fr.)
lengüeta (Sp.)
caña (Sp.)
tibia (Lat.)
aulos (Gr.)

Blattspiel (G.)
sight-reading
at first sight
a prima vista (It.)
à livre ouvert (Fr.)
vom Blatt (G.)
à vue (Fr.)
a primera vista (Sp.)

bleachers
  *balcony
  peanut gallery
  gallery
  paradiso (It.)
  dress circle
  loges

Blechinstrument (G.)
  brass instrument
  ottoni, d'ottone (It.)
  cuivres (Fr.)
  metales (Sp.)

blind octaves
  two-handed octaves

bloc de bois (Fr.)
  wood block
  *Chinese wood-block
  cassa di legno (It.)
  caisse Chinoise (Fr.)
  Holzblock (G.)
  Holzblocktrommel (G.)
  caja China (Sp.)
  cassettina (It.)
  blochetto (It.)
  clog box
  tap box
  Chinese temple blocks
  Korean temple blocks

Blockflöte (G.)
  *recorder
  English flute
  vertical flute
  beak flute
  whistle flute
  duct flute
  flauto a becco (It.)
  flauto diritto (It.)
  flûte à bec (Fr.)
  flauta de pico (Sp.)
  Schnabelflöte (G.)
  ocarina

vs. Querflöte (G.)

blow (vb.)
  sound
  play
  soffiare (It.)
  souffler (Fr.)
  blasen (G.)
  soplar (Sp.)

blower (organ)
  *bellows
  wind supply
  tiramantici (It.)
  souffleur (Fr.)
  Kalkant (G.)
  Balgentreter (G.)
  Gebläse (G.)
  soffietto (It.)
  soufflet (Fr.)
  fuelle (Sp.)

blue note
  flatted third or seventh
  jazz note

bluegrass music
  country music
  mountain music
  folk music
  traditional music
  old-time music
  string band

blues
  jazz
  pop
  ragtime
  barrelhouse
  Dixieland
  boogie-woogie
  stride piano
  torch song

bluette (Fr.)
  short, light piece

morceau (Fr.)
bagatelle (Fr.)
album-leaf

Blumen (G.)
  grace notes
  ornaments
  *ornamentation
  fioritura (It.)
  fioritures (Fr.)
  floreos (Sp.)
  glosas (Sp.)

boat song
  barcarole
  barcarola (It., Sp.)
  barcarolle (Fr.)
  Barkarole (G.)
  gondoliera (It.)
  sea shanty
  work song

bob
  burden
  burthen
  *refrain
  chorus

bobby-sox music
  *pop music
  bubblegum music
  teeny-bop music
  rock 'n' roll

bobization
  *solmization
  sol-fa
  tonic sol-fa
  bocedization
  jamization
  solfeggio (It.)
  solfège (Fr.)
  Abc-diren (G.)
  solfeo (Sp.)
  fasola
  shaped-note

buckwheat notes
damenization
scale
note-reading

bocca chiusa (It.)
  * humming
  bouche fermée (Fr.)
  geschlossener Mund (G.)
  Brummstimme (G.)
  Summstimme (G.)
  boca chiusa (Sp.)

bocchino (It.)
  mouthpiece
  embouchure (Fr.)
  Mundstück (G.)
  boquilla (Sp.)
  embocadura (Sp.)
  imboccatura (It.)
  Schnabel (G.)
  bec (Fr.)
  becco (It.)

Bockstriller (G., 18c.)
  tremolo
  vibrato
  chevrotement (Fr.)
  goat's trill
  trillo caprino (It.)
  trino de cabra (Sp.)
  Geisstriller (G.)

body (of insrument)
  belly
  table
  corpo (It.)
  corps (Fr.)
  coffre (Fr.)
  Resonanztafel (G.)
  Korpus, Körper (G.)
  Corpus (G.)
  tavola armonica (It.)
  tabla/tapa de armonia (Sp.)
  table d'harmonie (Fr.)
  Decke (G.)

Boethian notation
  letter notation (6c.)
  Daseian notation
  Odoistic/Oddonic notation
  Guidonian notation/hand
  music notation

Bogen (G.)
  bow
  fiddle bow
  fiddlestick
  arco (It., Sp.)
  archetto (It.)
  archet (Fr.).

2. *slur
  tie
  ligature

Bogenform (G.)
  bow form
  arch form
  song form
  da capo form
  ABA form
  *three-part form
  ternary form
  tripartite form

Bogenhaare (G.)
  hair(s) of a bow
  crini (It.)
  crins (Fr.)
  crines (Sp.)
  cuerdas del arco (Sp.)

Bohrung (G.)
  bore (of a wind instr.)
  fori, foratura (It.)
  perce (Fr.)
  perforación (Sp.)
  cylindrical bore
  conical bore

boîte à musique (Fr.)
  music box

carillon à musique (Fr.)
Spieldose (G.)
caja de música (Sp.)
scatola musicale (It.)
scatola armonica (It.)

boîte de nuit (Fr.)
  night club
  night spot
  cabaret
  supper club
  disco
  dance club
  locale notturno (It.)
  ritrovo notturno (It.)
  Nachtklub, Nachtlokal (G.)
  café-cantante (Sp.)

boîte expressive (Fr.)
  swell-box (organ)
  under expression
  cassa d'organo (It.)
  cassa espressiva (It.)
  Schwellwerk (G.)
  Schwellkasten (G.)
  caja de expresión (Sp.)
  caja expresiva (Sp.)

boiteux (Fr.)
  *syncopated
  Scotch snap
  off-beat
  alla zoppa (It.)
  cojeando (Sp.)

bolero (Sp.)
  dance
  rumba, rhumba (Sp.)
  béguine (Fr.)

bomba (Sp.)
  slide (of a trombone)
  tiro (It.)
  pompa (It.)
  coulisse (Fr.)
  Kulisse (G.)

Scheide (G.)
Stimmzug (G.)
corredera (Sp.)

bombard
  *bassoon
  shawm
  bombardo (It.)
  bombarde (Fr.)
  Fagott (G.)
  fagotto (It.)
  Pommer (G.)

2. organ reed stop
  Posaune (G.)

bombarde (Fr.)
  third manual (organ)

bombardino (Sp.)
  *euphonium
  tenor tuba
  basse à pistons (Fr.)
  Baryton (G.)
  Barytonhorn (G.)
  flicorno basso (It.)

bombardon (G.)
  bass bombard
  ophicleide
  tuba
  helicon
  sousaphone

2. organ reed stop

bombo (Sp.)
  *bass drum
  gran cassa (It.)
  cassa grande (It.)
  gran tamburo (It.)
  grosse caisse (Fr.)
  gros-tambour (Fr.)
  grosse Trommel (G.)

bones

Brettchenklapper (G.)
clappers
rhythm sticks
rattle
*maraca
claves (Sp., E., Fr., It.)
Klangstäbe (G.)
castanets
spoons

bongo (drums)
  drums
  tom-toms
  conga drums
  pair of drums
  Bongo-Trommel (G.)

boogie-woogie
  jazz
  barrelhouse
  ragtime
  stride piano
  Dixieland

book (of a musical)
  script
  libretto (opera)
  lyrics
  livret (Fr.)
  Textbuch (G.)
  Libretto (G.)
  libreto, -a, -e (Sp.)
  play
  screenplay (movie)

booking
  gig
  engagement
  run
  performance
  job playing, singing, etc.
  club date
  tour
  season
  concert
  recital

contract

booking agent
  agent
  manager
  impresario
  representative

bop
  bebop
  jazz
  cool jazz

boquilla (Sp.)
  embouchure (Fr.)
  embocadura (Sp.)
  mouthpiece
  bec (Fr.)
  bocchino (It.)
  Mundstück (G.)

bord (Fr.)
  rim (of a drum)
  orlo (It.)
  Rand (G.)
  borde (Sp.)

bordoniera (It.)
  snare (of a drum)
  timbre (Fr.)
  Trommelsaite (G.)
  Schnarrsaite (G.)
  bordón (Sp.)

Bordun (G.)
  *bourdon (Fr.)
  bordune (Fr.)
  bordone (It.)
  drone
  drone bass
  pedal point
  organ point

bore (wind instr.)
  tube
  cylindrical bore

conical bore
  perce (Fr.)
  Bohrung (G.)

bore. borea, boree
  *bourée (Fr.)

borrowed material
  quoted material
  parody
  satire
  take-off
  spoof
  *parody mass/motet
  pirated material
  plagiarism
  modeled on

bossa-nova (Port.)
  dance
  samba (Port.)
  carioca (Port.)
  jazz
  cool jazz
  Brazil
  batuque (Port.)
  maxixe (Port.)

bottoni dei registri (organ It.)
  draw-knobs
  draw-stops
  stop tabs
  boutons de registres (Fr.)
  registre (Fr.)
  Registerzüge (G.)
  Züge (G.)
  Registerknöpfe (G.)
  botones de los registros (Sp.)
  botones tiradores (Sp.)
  plancas de los registros (Sp.)

bouché (Fr.)
  muted
  stopped (horns)
  chiuso (It.)
  suono chiuso (It.)

étouffé (Fr.)
gestopft (G.)
gedackt, gedeckt (G.)
tappato (It.)
sonido cerrado (Sp.)
tapado (Sp.)

bouche fermée (Fr.)
  *humming
  bocca chiuso (It.)
  geschlossener Mund (G.)
  Brummstimme (G.)
  Summstimme (G.)
  boca chiusa (Sp.)

boudoir grand (piano)
  *baby grand
  parlor grand
  semi-grand
  *grand piano
  drawing-room grand
  pianoforte a coda (It.)
  piano de boudoir (Fr.)
  grand piano de concert (Fr.)
  Stutzflügel (G.)
  Salonflügel (G.)
  gran cola (Sp.)
  piano de media cola (Sp.)

bounce
  swing
  jazz
  jive
  rhythm
  big band

bounced (bow)
  staccato bowing
  spiccato (It.)
  saltando (It.)
  sautillé (Fr.)
  jeté (Fr.)
  Springbogen (G.)
  saltado (Sp.)

bourdon (organ)

Gedackt (G.)
stopped flute

bourdon (Fr.)
  drone
  burden
  burdo (Lat.)
  bordone (It.)
  *pedal point
  organ point
  sympathetic strings
  *bagpipe
  hurdy-gurdy
  trumpet marine
  viola d'amore
  organum
  cantus firmus (Lat.)

2. lowest bell
  great bell
  lowest string

bourée (Fr.)
  fast duple dance
  borry (Eng.)
  boree (Eng.)
  bore (It.)
  rigaudon
  gavotte
  suite

bout d'archet (Fr.)
  tip of the bow
  point of the bow
  punta d'arco (It., Sp.)
  Spitze (G.)

vs. talon (Fr.)
  hausse (Fr.)

boutade (Fr.)
  dance
  fantasie
  caprice
  character piece
  program music

capriccio (It.)
pièce charactéristique (Fr.)
Charakterstück (G.)
bagatelle

bouton de combinaison (Fr.)
piston
combination stop/piston
pre-sets
Kollektivzug (G.)
toe stud/piston
thumb piston
pistoncini (It.)
Druckknopf (G.)
pédale de combinaison (Fr.)

bouzouki (Gr.)
*guitar
*lute

bow, bowed
arco (It., Sp.)
archetto (It.)
archet (Fr.)
Bogen (G.)
strings (instr.)

bowed harp (Welsh)
crwth
crowd, crouth
*crotta (It.)

bowing
phrasing
tongueing
shaping
expression
*articulation
attack

box seats
loges
*balcony
mezzanine
dress circle
loggia

box zither
*bell harp
fairy bells
cithare sur caisse (Fr.)
Kastenzither (G.)

boyau (Fr.)
gut string
catgut string
budello (It.)
minugia (It.)
Darmsaite (G.)
nylon string

vs. steel string

boychoir
Knabenchor (G.)
maîtrise d'enfants (Fr.)
coro di ragazzi (It.)
putti (It.)
escolanía (Sp.)

brace
  bracket
graffa, grappa (It.)
accolade (E., Fr.)
Klammer (G.)
Akkolade (G.)
corchete (Sp.)

branle (Fr.)
basse danse (Fr.)
bransle (Fr.)
brando (It.)
farandole
cotillion
brangill (Eng.)
brall, brawl (Eng.)
hay, haye (Eng.)

brano (It.)
piece
*composition
concert piece
excerpt

pezzo (It.)
morceau (Fr.)
Stück (G.)
opus
obra (Sp.)

brass (insrument)
trumpets
cornet
bugle
trombone
horns
tuba
cuivres (Fr.)
Blechinstrumente (G.)
ottoni (It.)
metales (Sp.)

brass band
*band
military band
marching band
wind band
symphonic band

Bratsche (G.)
*viola
alto (Fr., It.)
tenor violin
alta viola (It.)
basse de violon (Fr.)
quinte (Fr.)

Brautlied (G.)
wedding song
bridal song
epithalamium (E., Lat.)
epithalamy
canto nuziale (It.)
chanson de noce (Fr.)
canto nupcial (Sp.)

bravo (It.)
well-done
*applause
brava

bravissimo
claque

bravura
virtuoso
florid
cadenza
spirit
boldness

break
register change
passo, passagio (It.)
cavalletto (It.)
passage (Fr.)
Passage (G.)
paso, pasaje (Sp.)

2. pause
*caesura
hiatus
railroad tracks
*breath mark
abruptio (Lat.)
Abreissung (G.)

3. solo passage (jazz)
riff
lick

breakdown
fast dance
juba

breaking (17c.)
ornamenting
divisions
florid

breath mark
comma
apostrophe
breathing sign
break
railroad tracks
pause

hiatus
abruptio (Lat.)
Abreissung (G.)
caesura
cesura (It., Sp.)
césure (Fr.)
Zäsur (G.)

Brechung (G.)
*broken chord
*arpeggio
Alberti bass
batterie (Fr.)
bariolage (Fr.)

vs. platter Akkord (G.)
solid chord

breit (G.)
broad
*slow
largo (It.)
lento (It.)
large, largement (Fr.)
lentement (Fr.)
langsam (G.)
amplio (Sp.)
ancho (Sp.)

Brettchenklapper (G.)
*bones
clappers
castanets
claves

breve (It., Fr. Eng.)
whole note
double note
double whole note
square note
neume
quadrat(um) (Lat.)
brevis (Lat., G.)
Doppelganze (G.)
carrée (Fr.)
quarré (Fr.)

Doppeltaktnote (G.)
cuadrada (Sp.)

breviary
*office
monastic office
breviarium (Lat.)
day hours
canonical hours
officium (Lat.)
divine office
morning and evening prayer

bridal song
*wedding song
nuptual song
epithalamium (Lat., E.)
canto nuziale (It.)
chanson de noce (Fr.)
Brautlied (G.)
canto nupcial (Sp.)

bridge
ponticello (It.)
scagnello (It.)
Steg (G.)
chevalet (Fr.)
puente (Sp.)
cavalletto (It.)

2. B-section
release
channel
trio section
*alternativo (It.)
Rückführung (G.)
Rückgang (G.)

3. transition
episode
modulation
key change
transizione (It.)
ponte (It.)
pont (Fr.)
Übergang (G.)

Überleitung (G.)
transición (Sp.)
puente (Sp.)

brillante (It., Fr.)
bright
showy

Brillenbässe (G.)
Alberti bass
tremolo
broken chords
*arpeggio (It.)
batterie (Fr.)
bariolage (Fr.)
Brechung (G.)

brindisi (It.)
drinking song
tavern song
*bacchanal
vinata, vinetta (It.)
chanson à boire (Fr.)
air à boire (Fr.)
Trinklied (G.)
canción báquica (Sp.)
carmina burana (Lat.)

brisé (Fr.)
detatched
*staccato (It.)

2. *turn (!8c.)
doublé (Fr.)
ornament

3. *arpeggio

Brisser (G.)
*mordent
grace note
ornament
trill
neighbor-note (lower)
shake
acciaccatura (It.)

tiret (Fr.)
pincé, pincement (Fr.)
Pralltriller (G.)
mordiente (Sp.)

broadcast, telecast
transmission
radio broadcast
on the air
over the airways
wireless
cable
satellite
trasmissione (It.)
radiodiffusione (It.)
Rundfunk (G.)
Sendung (G.)
radiodiffusion (Fr.)
emission (Fr.)
emissión (Sp.)
radiodifusión (Sp.)

broad(ly)
big
largo (It.)
largamente (It.)
largo (It.)
largement (Fr.)
ausgedehnt (G.)
breit (G.)
anchamente (Sp.)
*slow

broadside ballad
* ballad
folk song
song
strophic

Broadway musical
musical comedy
musical play
operetta
Singspiel (G.)
vaudeville
revue

variety show
follies
floor show
masque

broderie (Fr.)
*ornamentation
grace notes
embellishments
melismatic
coloratura(It.)
fioritura (It.)

2. auxiliary tone
neighbor note/tone
échappée (Fr.)
escape note/tone

broken cadence
*deceptive cadence
interrupted cadence
cadence interrompue (Fr.)

broken chord
*arpeggio (It.)
rolled chord
Alberti bass
Brillenbässe (G.)
batterie (Fr.)
bariolage (Fr.)
Brechung (G.)
gebrochener Akkord (G.)
harpégé (Fr.)
harpeggiato (It.)

vs. solid chord

broken consort
mixed consort
ensemble
chamber orchestra
company of musicians
band
combo

vs. whole consort

broken note
    curtailed note
    staccato (It.)
    *hocket
    truncated note
    crackle
    truncatio vocis (Lat.)
    coup sec (Fr.)
    détaché (Fr.)
    tactée (Fr.)
    son coupé (Fr.)
    silence d'articulation (Fr.)
    troncatio (It.)

broken octave
    short octave (keyboard)
    partial octave
    incomplete stop
    partial stop
    mi re ut (It.)
    octave courte (Fr.)
    kurze Oktave (G.)
    octava corta (Sp.)

2. walking bass
    murky (18c.)
    murky bass
    boogie-woogie
    jazz

Bronx cheer
    raspberry
    *flutter-tongueing
    French kiss

Bruchstück (G.)
    fragment (E., Fr.)
    Fragment (G.)
    frammento (It., Sp.)
    excerpt
    selection

Brummeisen (G.)
    *Jew's harp
    cymbalum orale (Lat.)
    rebube (Fr.)

ribeba (It.)
Maultrommel (G.)
birimbao (Sp.)

Brummstimmen (G.)
    humming
    a bocca chiusa (It.)
    à bouche fermée (Fr.)
    boca chiusa (Sp.)
    Summstimme (G.)

brunette (Fr.)
    song
    pastoral song (17-18c.)
    love song
    bergerette (Fr.)

brushes (percussion)
    wire brushes
    steel brushes
    spazzole (It.)
    balais (de jazz) (Fr.)
    Besen (G.)
    Jazzbesen (G.)
    Rute (G.)
    escobillas (Sp.)

Bruststimme (G.)
    *chest voice
    full voice
    low voice
    belting voice
    registro di petto (It.)
    voce di petto (It.)
    voix de poitrine (Fr.)
Brustregister (G.)
    voz de pecho (Sp.)

vs. Kopfstimme (G.)
    head voice

Brustwerke (G.)
    swell division (organ)
    under expression
    organo d'espressione (It.)
    clavier de récit (Fr.)

Brustpositiv (G.)
    Oberwerk (G.)
    Schwellwerk (G.)

vs. Hauptwerk (G.)
    great organ

bubblegum music
    pop music
    teeny-bop music
    rock-n-roll
    bobby-sox music

bubboli (It.)
    *bells
    pellet bells
    jingle bells
    sleighbells
    harness bells
    Sanctus bells
    altar bells
    sonagli, sonagliera (It.)
    grelots (Fr.)
    sonnettes, sonnailles (Fr.)
    Rollschellen (G.)
    Schellengeläute (G.)
    cascabeles (Sp.)

buca del suggeritore (It.)
    prompt-box
    prompter's box
    stage right
    prompt side
    teleprompter
    cue cards
    trou de souffleur (Fr.)
    Souffleurkasten (G.)
    concha del apuntador (Sp.)

buca dell'orchestra (It.)
    orchestra pit
    fossa orchestrale (It.)
    fosse d'orchestre (Fr.)
    Orchestergraben (G.)
    foso de orquesta (Sp.)
    foso orquestrale (Sp.)

buccina (Lat.)
  *Aida trumpet
  state trumpet
  ceremonial trumpet
  natural trumpet
  straight trumpet
  salpinx (Gr.)
  lituus (Lat.)
  tuba (Lat.)
  buisine (Fr.)
  Alpenhorn (G.)

bûche (Fr.)
  zither
  cimbalom, cembalom
  épinette des Vosges (Fr.)
  bûche de Flandres (Fr.)
  Hackbrett (G.)
  Hummel, Humle (G.)
  dulcimer
  hammered dulcimer

buckwheat notes
  shaped notes
  character notes
  patent notes
  dunce notes
  fasola
  *solmization
  music-reading
  sol-fa
  solfeggio (It.)

buco (It.)
  fingerhole
  foro (It.)
  trou (Fr.)
  Fingerloch (G.)
  Tonloch (G.)
  Griffloch (G.)
  agujero (Sp.)
  orificio (Sp.)

budello (It.)
  gut string
  catgut

boyau (Fr.)
  minugia (It.)
  Darmsaite (G.)
  nylon string

vs. steel string

buff stop (harpsichord)
  *mute
  lute stop
  harp stop
  jeu de luth (Fr.)
  jeu de harpe (Fr.)
  Lautenzug (G.)
  Nasalzug (G.)
  una corda (It.)
  étouffoir (Fr.)

buffet (Fr.)
  organ case
  casework
  domus organaria (Lat.)
  Gehäuse (G.)
  Orgelkasten (G.)
  cassa dell'organo (It.)

buffo role
  *comic role
  character part
  servetta (It.)
  basso buffo (It.)
  tenore buffo (It.)
  trial (Fr.)
  dugazon (Fr.)
  soubrette (Fr.)
  ingénue (Fr.)
  tiple cómico (Sp.)

bugle (horn)
  keyed bugle
  bugle-horn
  cornet
  trumpet
  tromba (It.)
  clairon (Fr.)
  clairon à clefs (Fr.)

biucolo (It.)
  Hiefhorn (G.)
  Hifthorn (G.)
  Bügelhorn (G.)
  Flügelhorn (G.)
  cor bugler (Fr.)
  cor bugleret (Fr.)
  Signalhorn (G.)
  Jagdhorn (G.)
  Jagdsignal (G.)
  regent's bugle
  Kent bugle
  Royal Kent bugle

bugle à clés (Fr.)
  key bugle
  Kent bugle
  Royal Kent bugle
  Regent's bugle
  key/keyed bugle
  ophicleide
  clairon à clefs (Fr.)
  Klappenhorn (G.)
  cornet
  trumpet

bugle call
  call
  signal call
  military call
  reveille
  taps
  Hornsignal (G.)
  chiamata (It. 17c.)
  chamade (Fr. 17c.)
  chasse (Fr.)
  caccia (It.)
  toque de corneta (Sp.)

bugle contralto (Sp.)
  *baritone horn
  *althorn

Bühne (G.)
  stage
  platform

bandwagon
scena (It.)
scène (Fr.)
escena, escenario (Sp.)
tablado (Sp.)

Bühnenvorhang (G.)
*curtain
drop, backdrop
rideau (Fr.)
telone (It.)
Vorhang (G.)
sipario, siparietto (It.)

Bühnenmusik (G.)
* incidental music
dramatic music
stage music
film music
underscore
backround music
musica di scena (It.)
musique de scène (Fr.)
Schauspielmusik (G.)
música de escena (Sp.)

buisine, busine, buzine, buysine (Fr.)
*Aida trumpet
state trumpet
herald trumpet
straight trumpet
lituus (Lat.)
salpinx (Gr.)
buccina (Lat.)
tuba (Lat.)
natural trumpet
Alpenhorn (G.)

bull fiddle
*bass
doublebass
string bass
contrabass
stand-up bass
upright bass

acoustic bass
washtub bass
doghouse bass
bass viol
violone (It., Fr.)

Bund (G.)
fret
half-step
touche (Fr.)
tasto (It.)
touchette (Fr.)
traste (Sp.)

buque teatro (Sp.)
showboat
road show
touring company
traveling show
showmobile
bâteau-théatre (Fr.)

burden
*refrain
chorus
burthen
bob

2. drone
bourdon (Fr.)
burdo (Lat.)
organum
*cantus firmus (Lat.)

Burgundian cadence
Landini cadence
double leading-tone cadence
lydian cadence
medieval cadence

burla, burlesca (It.)
musical joke
musikallischer Spass (G.)
Burleske (G.)
burlesque (Eng., Fr.)
humoresque

Humoreske (G.)
playful piece
bagatelle
scherzo (It.)
capriccio (It.)
caprice (Fr., E.)

burial service
*funeral (service, mass)
memorial service/mass
exequies
memorial service
requiem (Lat.)
Missa de profunctis (Lat.)
Missa pro defunctis (Lat.)
messa da requiem (It.)
messe des morts (Fr.)
Totenmasse (G.)
misa de muertos (Sp.)

burletta (It.)
vaudeville
burlesque
musical comedy
Broadway musical
operetta
light opera
minstrel show
variety show
revue
follies
Singspiel (G.)
masque
cabaret
floor show

burrasca (It.)
storm music
descriptive music
*program music
tone poem
tone painting

Busaune (G.)
*trombone (E., It., Fr.)
bass trumpet

sackbut
slide trombone
valve trombone
Posaune (G.)

by degrees
    gradually
    litle by little
    step by step
    poco a poco (It., Sp.)
    a grado a grado (It.)
    poi a poi (It.)
    di grado (It.)
    per gradi (It.)
    peu à peu (Fr.)
    petit à petit (Fr.)
    nach und nach (G.)
    por grado (Sp.)
    de grado en grado (Sp.)

vs. subito (It.)

by heart
    memorized
    from memory
    by ear
    by rote
    a memoria (It.)
    par coeur (Fr.)
    auswendig (G.)
    de memoria (Sp.)

Byzantine chant
    Eastern chant
    Orthodox Church
    plainsong
    *chant
    Gregorian chant
    plainsong
    plainchant

C

C-barré (Fr.)
*cut time
double time
quick time
twice as fast
march time
alla breve (It.)
a cappella (It.)
doppio movimento (It.)
tagliato (It.)
à la blanche (Fr.)
in halben Noten (G.)
a la breve (Sp.)
doble movimiento (Sp.)
C-barred

C-clef
alto clef
viola clef
tenor clef
soprano clef
chiave di do (It.)
chiave di contralto (It.)
clef d'ut (Fr.)
clef d'alto (Fr.)
C-Schlüssel (G.)
Altschlüssel (G.)
llave de do (Sp.)
clave de do (Sp.)
clave de contralto (Sp.)
clave de viola (Sp.)

C-instrument
non-transposing instrument
pitched in C
concert pitch

vs. transposing instrument

cabaletta (It.)
*song
aria
cavatina (It.)
cavatinetta (It.)
rondo

cabaret
night club
night spot
supper club
cocktail lounge
dance club
discothèque (Fr.)
boîte de nuit (Fr.)
locale notturno (It.)
ritrovo notturno (It.)
Nachtlokal (G.)
Nachtklub (G.)
café-cantante (Sp.)

cabeza de las notas (Sp.)
note head
capocchia (It.)
testina (It.)
tête de la note (Fr.)
Notenkopf (G.)
punto de las notas (Sp.)

cabinet organ
positiv
portative
small, portable *organ
reed organ
continuo organ

cabinet piano
spinet
console piano
*upright piano
vertical piano
studio piano
upright grand
pianoforte verticale (It.)
piano droit (Fr.)
Klavier (G.)
piano vertical (Sp.)

vs. grand piano

cable
television
satellite TV
radio
*broadcast
over the airways
on the air

cabrette (Fr.)
*bagpipe
musette (Fr.)
Dudelsack (G.)
gaita (Sp.)
cornemuse (Fr.)

caccia (It. 14c.)
catch
chace, chasse (Fr.)
canon
round
caça (Sp.)
descriptive music
program music
hunting song
*call
bugle call
madrigal

cachucha (Sp.)
dance, in triple time
fandango
bolero

cacophony
discord
dissonance
noise
clash
jarring sounds
*shivaree
mock serenade
charivari (Fr.)

cacofonia (It., Sp.)
cacophonie (Fr.)
Kakophonie (G.)
Missklang (G.)
Dutch concert
*callithumpian concert
cal(l)ithump, callathump
cat's concert/music

cadence (E., Fr.)
harmonic close
close
ending
first, second ending
ouvert, clos (Fr.)
clausula (Lat.)
point of rest
pause
repose
harmonic resolution
phrase ending
caesura
cadentia (Lat.)
cadenza (It.)
cadencia (Sp.)
Kadenz (G.)
Schluss (G.)
Landini cadence
Burgundian cadence
double leading-tone cadence
Corelli clash
plagal cadence
amen cadence
authentic cadence
half cadence
semi-cadence
imperfect cadence
deceptive cadence
Phrygian cadence

2. rhythm
tempo

3.*trill (17c. Fr.)

cadence authentique (Fr.)

authentic cadence
full cadence
full close
*perfect cadence
cadenza perfetta (It.)
cadence parfaite (Fr.)
Ganzschluss (G.)
cadencia perfecta (Sp.)

cadence interrompue (Fr.)
*deceptive cadence
cadenza evitata (It.)
cadenza d'inganno (It.)
cadenza coperta (It.)
cadence évitée (Fr.)
cadence par surprise (Fr.)
cadence trompeuse (Fr.)
Trugschluss (G.)
cadencia coperta (Sp.)
cadencia evitada
(Sp.)
cadencia interrumpida (Sp.)
cadencia por engaño (Sp.)

cadence plagale (Fr.)
*plagal cadence
amen cadence
cadenza plagale (It.)
cadencia plagal (Sp.)
Kirchenschluss (G.)
Plagalschluss (G.)
plagale Kadenz (G.)

cadence suspendue (Fr.)
* half cadence
semi-cadence
imperfect cadence
*deceptive cadence
cadencia suspendida (Sp.)
cadenza imperfetta (It.)
cadenza sospesa (It.)
cadence imparfaite (Fr.)
Halbschluss (G.)
hängende Kadenz (G.)
cadence trompeuse (Fr.)

cadent
ornament
grace note
anticipation note
backfall
Nachschlag (G.)

cadenza (It.)
close
harmonic close
pause
*cadence
cadencia (Sp.)

2. cadenza
bariolage (Fr.)
Kadenz (G.)
virtuoso
improvise
concerto

caesura
rest
pause
cadence
railroad tracks
G.P.
general pause
grand pause
cesura (It., Sp.)
vuoto (It.)
pause generale (It.)
pause générale (Fr.)
césure (Fr.)
Zäsur (G.)
Generalpause (G.)
*fermata (E., It.)

café-cantante (Sp.)
*night club
night spot
cabaret
supper club
disco
dance club
ritrovo notturno (It.)

locale notturno (It.)
boîte de nuit (Fr.)
Nachtklub (G.)
Nachtlokal (G.)

café music
dinner music
light music
salon music
cocktail music
dinner music
table music
elevator music
dentist music
*backround music

caisse (Fr.)
drum
cassa (It.)
tamburo (It.)
tambour (Fr.)
Trommel (G.l)
tambor (Sp.)
caja (Sp.)
tympanum (Lat.)

caisse Chinoise (Fr.)
*Chinese(wood)block
bloc de bois (Fr.)
cassettina (It.)
Holzblock (G.)
Holzblocktrommel (G.)
blochetto (It.)
caja china (Sp.)
temple blocks
clog box
tap box
cassa di legno (It.)
Korean temple blocks

caisse clair (Fr.)
*snare drum
side drum
military drum
cassa chiara (It.)
tamburo militare (It.)

tamburo piccolo (It.)
caisse militaire (Fr.)
petit tambour (Fr.)
kleine Trommel (G.)
Militärtrommel (G.)
tambor militar pequeño(Sp.)

caisse de résonance (Fr.)
sound box
sound chest
resonance chamber
cassa di resonanza (It.)
Resonanzboden (G.)
caja de resonancia (Sp.)

caisse roulante (Fr.)
tenor drum
caisse sourde (Fr.)
cassa rullante (It.)
tamburo rullante (It.)
tamburo da rollo (It.)
Wirbeltrommel (G.)
redoblante (Sp.)
Rührtrommel (G.)
Rolltrommel (G.)

caja armónica (Sp.)
soundboard
belly
table
piano armonico (It.)
tavola armonico (It.)
table d'harmonie (Fr.)
Resonanzboden (G.)

caja de expresión (Sp.)
swell-box (organ)
under expression
cassa d'organo (It.)
organo espressivo (It.)
cassa espressiva (It.)
boîte expressive (Fr.)
Schwellkasten G.)
caja expresiva (Sp.)

caja de música (Sp.)

*music box
boite à musique (Fr.)
Spieldose (G.)
carillon à musique (Fr.)
scatola musicale (It.)
scatola armonica (It.)

caja del órgano (Sp.)
console (organ, E., Fr.)
consolle (It.)
Spieltisch (G.)

cakewalk
dance
ragtime
jazz

calamus (Lat.)
reed pipe
*shawm
oboe
chalumeau (Fr.)
Shalmei (G.)
tibia (Lat.)
syrinx
aulos (Gr.)
diaulos (Gr.)
kalamos (Gr.)
calamellus (Lat.)
ciaramella (It.)
panpipe

calando (It.)
fade
dying away
decay
diminuendo (It.)
*decrescendo (It.)
morendo (It.)
smorzando (It.)
perdendosi (It.)
smorendo (It.)

calata (It.)
dance (15c.)
*basse danse (Fr.)

court dance
minuet
saltarello (It.)
Hoftanz (G.)
pas de Brabant (Fr.)
piva (It.)
baxa (Sp.)

calderón (Sp.)
hold
*fermata (It., Sp.)
point d'orgue (Fr.)
couronne (Fr.)
punto d'organo (It.)
Orgelpunkt (G.)
Fermate (G.)
Krone (G.)

calenda
calypso
song of Trinidad
kalinda
carnival song

call
bugle call
signal call
reveille
taps
Hornsignal (G.)
chasse (Fr.)
*caccia (It.)
chiamata (It., 17c.)
chamade (Fr., 17c.)

call and response
antiphonal
responsorial
dialogue
refrain
chorus
litany
Wechselgesang (G.)
joc-parti, jeu-parti (Fr.)
partimen (Fr.)
tenso, tenson (Fr.)

cállate (Sp.)
tacet (Lat.)
do not play (a movement)
silent for a long time
tace, taci (It.)
se taire (Fr.)
ne pas jouer (Fr.)
schweigen (G.)
callarse (Sp.)

calliope
organ
* barrel organ
steam organ
street organ
organo a vapore (It.)
orgue à vapeur (Fr.)
Dampforgel (G.)
órgano de vapor (Sp.)

callithumpian concert
cacophony
shivaree
cal(l)ithump, callathump
mock serenade
racket, din
catawauling
cat's concert
scampata (It.)
charivari (Fr.)
Katzenmusik (G.)
Lärm (G.)
chiasso (It.)
scampanata (It.)
musica di gatti (It.)
cencerrada (Sp.)
horning
Dutch concert

calmato (It.)
calme (Fr.)
ruhig (G.)
calmo (It., Sp.)
calmly

calypso
song of Trinidad
calenda
kalinda
carnival music

Calypsotrommel (G.)
steel drum (tuned)
tamburo di latta (It.)
tamburo d'acciaio (It.)
tambour d'acier (Fr.)
Stahltrommel (G.)
Benzinfass (G.)
tambor metálico (Sp.)

cambiar la digitación (Sp.)
finger substitution
diteggiatura cambiata (It.)
changer le doigté (Fr.)
ablösen (G.)

cambiata (It.)
nota cambiata (It.)
changing note
escape note
non-harmonic tone
note de rechange (Fr.)
échappée (Fr.)
Wechselnote (G.)
nota cambiada (Sp.)
ornament

2. *changing voice
alto-tenor
voice-change

campana (It., Lat., Sp.)
*bell
cloche (Fr.)
Glocke (G.)

2. flair of a horn
padiglione (It.)
pavillon (Fr.)
Schallbecher (G.)

campanaccio (It.)
  cowbell
  cloche de vache (Fr.)
  sonnaille (Fr.)
  Kuhglocke (G.)
  Kuhschelle (G.)
  Alpenglocke (G.)
  cencerro (Sp.)

campanas tubulares (Sp.)
  tubular bells
  chimes
  orchestral chimes
  *bells
  campane tubolari (It.)
  cloches tubulaires (Fr.)
  Röhrenglocken (G.)
  Glocken (G.)
  campanólogo (Sp.)

campana in alto (It.)
  bell in the air
  raise the bell
  pavillon en l'air (Fr.)
  padiglioni in alto (It.)
  Stürze hoch (G.)
  Schalltrichter hoch (G.)
  pabellón al aire (Sp.)

vs. posizione normale (It.)

campanear (Sp.)
  peal
  ring
  toll
  chime
  play
  suonare (It.)
  scampanare (It.)
  sonner (Fr.)
  schallen (G.)
  läuten (G.)
  resonar (Sp.)

campanelli (It.)
  *bells

glockenspiel
bell lyre
Stahlspiel (G.)
carillon (Fr., It.)
jeu de timbres (Fr.)
campanelle (Fr.)
campanette (It.)
campanólogo (Sp.)
carillón (Sp.)

campanelli della messa (It.)
  altar bells
  Sanctus bells
  clochettes pour la messe (Fr.)
  Messglöckchen (G.)
  Messklingeln (G.)
  pellet bells
  sleighbells
  jingle bells
  *bells

campanile (E., It.)
  bell tower
  * belfry
  carillon
  clocher (Fr.)
  campanario (Sp.)
  steeple bells
  tower bells

campanist
  bell-ringer
  carilloneur (Fr.)
  campanista (It.)
  campanaio (It.)
  Glockenspieler (G.)
  campanero (Sp.)

campo aperto (Lat.)
  nondiastematic
  adiastematic
  neumes
  staffless neumes
  oratorical
  cheironomic
  chant

notation

caña (Sp.)
  reed
  ancia (It.)
  anche (Fr.)
  Rohr, Rohrblatt (G.)

canard (Fr.)
  mistake
  wrong note
  false note
  sour note
  clinker
  stecca (It.)
  falsa nota (It.)
  fausse note (Fr.)
  falsche Note (G.)
  Misston (G.)
  gallipavo (Sp.)

canarie (Fr. 17c.)
  dance (fast triple)
  gigue
  giga (It.)
  jig
  canary
  canario (It., Sp.)

canary
  singer (female)
  pop singer
  songstress
  chanteuse (Fr.)
  artiste
  vocalist

cancan (Fr.)
  dance, fast duple
  galop
  vaudeville
  polka
  quadrille
  quadriglia (It.)

cancel (organ)

take off all stops
découpler (Fr.)
ab (G.)
auflösen (G.)

cancel sign
natural sign
B cancellatum (Lat.)
B quadratum/quadrum (Lat.)
bequadro (It.)
bécarre (Fr.)
Auflösungszeichen (G.)
Quadrat (G.)
becuadro (Sp.)

canción (Sp.)
* song
tune
melody
chanson (Fr.)
Lied (G.)
air
aria
canto (It.)

canción báquica (Sp.)
drinking song
tavern song
*bacchanal
brindisi (It.)
chanson à boire (Fr.)
Trinklied (G.)
vinata, vinetta (It.)
air à boire (Fr.)
carmina burana (Lat.)

canción de cuna
cradle song
lullaby
ninna nanna (It.)
ninnerella (It.)
berceuse (Fr.)
dodinette, dodo, dodino (Fr.)
Wiegenlied (G.)
Schlummerlied (G.)
Ständchen (G.)

nana (Sp.)
arrullo (Sp.)

canción de mayo (Sp.)
May song
maggiolata (It.)
chanson de mai (Fr.)
Mailied (G.)
spring song

canción de moda (Sp.)
hit song
pop song
top 10, 20, 40
chanson à la mode (Fr.)
chanson à succès (Fr.)
Schlager (G.)
canción en boga (Sp.)

canción de primavera (Sp.)
spring song
may song
canto di primavera (It.)
canzona della primavera (It.)
reverdie (Fr. Trouvère)
Frühlingslied (G.)

canción gitana/tzigana (Sp.)
gypsy song
canzone gitana (It.)
chant tzigane/gitan (Fr.)
Zigeunerlied (G.)
canto gitano (Sp.)
tzigana (Sp.)

cancionero (Sp.)
songbook
*anthology
song collection
repertory
repertoire
canzoniere (It.)
chansonnier (Fr.)
Liederbuch (G.)

canna d'anima (It.)

flue pipe (organ)
labial
canna labiale (It.)
tuyau à bouche (Fr.)
Labialpfeife (G.)
tubo de boca (Sp.)

vs. reed pipe

canna d'organo (It.)
organ pipe
tuyau d'orgue (Fr.)
Orgelpfeife (G.)
tubo (Sp.)
caño (Sp.)

canne di facciata (It.)
dummy pipes (organ)
display pipes
facade, façade
montre (Fr.)
Füllpfeifen (G.)
Prospektpfeifen (G.)
Stummepfeifen (G.)

canned music
recorded music
elevator music
dentist music
karaoke music
Muzak
*backround music
* light music
music minus one
split track

vs. live music

canon (E., Fr., Sp.)
catch
round
rota
glee
troll
fugue
imitation

subject

2. crab canon
   retrograde canon
   mirror canon
   canon by retrograde
inversion
   imitatio per motum
retrogradum (Lat.)
   imitatio recurrens (Lat.)
   canon cancrizans (Lat.)
   canon per recto et retro
(Lat.)
   canone a ritroso (It.)
   canone retrogrado (It.)
   canone cancrizzante (It.)
   canone al rovescio (It.)
   canon à l'écrevisse (Fr.)
   canon récurrent (Fr.)
   canon inverse (Fr.)
   canon contraire (Fr.)
   canon renversable (Fr.)
   canon rétrograde
(Fr.)
   alla riversa (It.)
   imitazione al rovescio (It.)
   Krebskanon (G.)
   Krebsgang (G.)
   Spiegelkanon (G.)
   Umkehrungskanon (G.)

   enigmatic canon
   canone enigmatico (It.)
   Rätselkanon (G.)
   canon énigmatique (Fr.)

   canone ((It.)
   Kanon (G.)
   chace, chasse (Fr.)
   caccia (It.)
   Radel (G.)
   motet
   Mass
   fuga
   ricercare (It.)
   strict canon

free canon

canone perpetuo (It., Sp.)
   perpetual canon
   circular canon
   infinite canon
   canon perpétuel (Fr.)
   unendlicher Kanon (G.)

canonical hours
   office
   daily office
   monastic office
   *Divine Office
   hours of the day
   horae canonicae (Lat.)
   Opus Dei (Lat.)
   officium Divinum (Lat.)
   breviary
   *antiphonal
   antiphonary
   antiphoner
   antiphonale (Lat.)
   antiphonarium (Lat.)
   morning and evening prayer
   evensong
   officium (Lat.)
   day hours
   Little Hours
   prime
   terce
   sext
   none
   vespers
   matins
   lauds
   vigils
   night office
   compline
   rhymed office

canso, canzo
   song
   *bar form
   Troubadour song
   Trouvère song

*ballade (Fr.)
formes fixes (Fr.)

can't carry a tune (in a bucket)
   monotone
   sing off-key, off-pitch
   out of tune
   tone-deaf
   amusia

cantabile (It.)
   lyrical
   song-like
   melodious
   cantando (It.)
   chantant (Fr.)
   singbar (G.)
   cantable (Sp.)

cantante (It., Sp.)
   *singer
   vocalist
   chorister
   songster
   cantore (It.)
   chanteur, chanteuse (Fr.)
   Sänger, Sängerin (G.)

cantar (Sp.)
   song
   *melody
   canto (It., Sp.)
   chanson (Fr.)
   Lied (G.)
   Gesang (G.)

2. to sing
   cantare (It.)
   chanter (Fr.)
   singen (G.)

cantare (It.)
   to sing
   vocalize
   croon
   warble

chanter (Fr.)
singen (G.)
cantar (Sp.)

cantarella (It.)
chanterelle (Fr.)
cantino (It.)
E-string (violin)
cantarela (Sp.)
Sangsaite (G.)
Quintsaite (G.)
prima (Sp.)
tiple (Sp.)

cantata (It., E., Sp.)
oratorio
ode
Passion
Crucifixion
rappresentazione (It.)
pasticcio (It.)
cantate (Fr.)
Kantate (G.)
cantada (Sp.)

cantata da camera (It.)
chamber cantata
secular cantata
Kammerkantate (G.)
weltliche Kantate (G.)
cantata profana (It.)
cantate de chambre (Fr.)
cantate profane (Fr.)
cantada de camera (Sp.)

cantata da chiesa (It.)
sacred cantata
church cantata
Kirchenkantate (G.)
geistliche Kantate (G.)
cantate d'église (Fr.)
cantata de inglesia (Sp.)

cantatorium (Lat.)
graduale (Lat.)
gradual

alleluia
tract
tractus (Lat.)
chant collection
mass
* anthology

cantatrice (It., Fr.)
opera singer (female)
diva
divette (Fr.)
prima donna (It.)
cantatore (It.)
Sängerin (G.)
cantatriz (Sp.)
vocal artist
soloist

cante hondo/jondo (Sp.)
flamenco
deep song
Phrygian mode
seguidilla (Sp.)
soleá (Sp.)
canto hondo/jondo (Sp.)

canti carnascialeschi (It.)
carnival songs (15-16c.)
part-songs
carmina burana (Lat.)

canticchiare (It.)
to hum
to trill
a bocca chiusa (It.)
furberia del canto (It.)
fredonner (Fr.)
avec bouche fermée (Fr.)
chantonner (Fr.)
trällern (G.)
Brummstimmen (G.)
canturrear (Sp.)
canticar (Sp.)

canticle
*song

hymn
anthem
sequence
psalm
chant
canticum (Lat.)
cantico (It.)
cántico (Sp.)
cantique (Fr.)
Lobgesang (G.)
ode
paean
Päan (G.)
lauda (It.)
theody
Office

Canticle of Anna
Exultavit cor meum (Lat.)
Song of Hannah

Canticle of Canticles
Song of Songs
Song of Solomon
Canticum Canticorum (Lat.)
Cantique des Cantiques (Fr.)
Lied der Lieder (G.)
Hohelied (G.)
Cantico dei Cantici (It.)
Cantar de los Cantares (Sp.)

Canticle of Habakkuk
Domine audivi (Lat.)

Canticle of Hezekiah
Ego dixi (Lat.)
canticum Ezechiae (Lat.)

Canticle of Isaiah
Confitebor tibi, Domine (Lat.)

Canticle of Mary
Magnificat (Lat.)
Song of Mary
Canticle of the Virgin

Canticle of the Blessed Virgin
Office
Vespers
Evening Prayer

Canticle(s) of Moses
Song of Moses
Cantemus Domino (Lat.)
Audite caeli (Lat.)
Moses' and
Miriam's song

Canticle of Simeon
Song of Simeon
Nunc Dimittis (Lat.)
canticum Simeonis (Lat.)
Evening Prayer
Compline
Vespers
Office

Canticle of the Sun
hymn of St. Francis of Assisi
Cantico del Sole (It.)
Cantico della Creature (It.)

Canticle of the Three Children
Song of the Three Children
Benedicite (Lat.)
Canticle of the Three Young Men
Office
Lauds

Canticle of Zachary
Song of Zechariah
canticum Zachariae (Lat.)
Benedictus Dominus Deus
Israel (Lat.)
Office
Lauds

cántico de Navidad (Sp.)
Christmas carol
chant de noël (Fr.)

cantique de noël (Fr.)
Weinachtslied (G.)
villancico (Sp.)
Quempas (G.)
canzone di natale (It.)

cantiga (Sp., 13c.)
*song
monophonic
Virgin Mary
spiritual songs
zajal (Sp.)
villancico (Sp.)
virelai (Fr.)

cantilena (Lat., It.)
*song
melody
chant
cradle song
lullaby
Kantilene (G.)
cantilène (Fr.)

15c. song (melody in soprano part)
treble-dominated
discant
discantus (Lat.)
deschant (Fr.)
chanson (Fr.)

cantilena Romanum (Lat.)
Gregorian chant
Roman chant
plainsong
plainchant
*chant
cantus planus (Lat.)
canto liturgico (It.)
canto gregoriano (Sp.)
chant Grégorien (Fr.)

cantillation
Hebrew chant
Jewish chant

cantor

cantino (It.)
e-string (violin)
highest string
chanterelle (Fr.)
cantarella (It.)
cantarela (Sp.)
Sangsaite (G.)
Quintsaite (G.)
prima (Sp.)
tiple (Sp.)

cantio (Lat.)
*song
hymn
chant
monophonic (medieval)
monody

cantio sacra (Lat.)
motet
sacred song
canzoni spirituali (It.)
chanson spirituelle (Fr.)
geistliche Lieder (G.)
cantiones ecclesiasticae (Lat.

cantionale (Lat., G.)
collection of hymns, chorales
hymnal
hymnbook
songbook
repertory
*anthology

cantique (Fr.)
song
sacred song
*canticle

cantique de noël (Fr.)
Christmas carol
chant de noël (Fr.)
*carol
cántico de Navidad (Sp.)

Weinachtslied (G.)
villancico (Sp.)
Quempas (G.)
canzone di Natale (It.)
natalizio (It.)

canto (It., Sp.)
*song
melody
tune
air
chant
cantio (Lat.)
chanson (Fr.)
Lied (G.)
Gesang (G.)

canto di primavera (It.)
spring song
may song/carol
canzona della primavera (It.)
reverdie (Fr. Trouvère)
Frülingslied (G.)
canción de primavera (Sp.)

canto fermo (It.)
*cantus firmus (Lat.)
cantus prius factus (Lat.)
tenor
mass
motet

canto figurato (It.)
figural music
mensural music
polyphonic music
musica figurata (Lat.)
*cantus figuralis (Lat.)
Figuralgesang (G.)
Figuralmusik (G.)
canto de órgano (Sp.)

canto folklórico (Sp.)
folksong, folk music
ethnic folk music
canto folcloristico (It.)

canto popolare (It.)
chant folklorique (Fr.)
Volkslied (G.)

canto fúnebre (Sp.)
*funeral song
requiem
*lament
trenodia (It.)
treno (Sp.)
endecha (Sp.)

canto gitano (Sp.)
gypsy song
canzone gitana (It.)
chant tzigana/gitan (Fr.)
Zigeunerlied (G.)
tzigana (Sp.)
canción gitana/tzigana (Sp.)

canto llano (Sp.)
plainsong
*chant
plainchant
Gregorian chant

canto nuziale (It.)
*wedding song
nuptual song
bridal song
epithalamy
epithalamium (Lat., E.)
chanson de noce (Fr.)
Brautlied (G.)
canto nupcial (Sp.)

cantor (E., Sp.)
chanter
leader of song
singer (solo)
soloist
accentus (Lat.)
primicerius (Lat.)
primicerio (It., Sp.)
accentor (E.)
precentor

succentor
chazzan (Heb.)
hazan (Heb.)
cantore (It.)
chantre (Fr.)
Vorsänger (G.)
Kantor (G.)
Primicerius (G.)

cantore (It.)
*singer
choir-singer
chorister
*choirboy
cantor
chorus singer

cantoria (It.)
choir
chancel
choir gallery
balcony

cantoris (Lat.)
of the cantor
precentor
left/north side of choir
gospel side
chancel choir
choir

vs. decani
epistle side
south/right side

canturrear (Sp.)
to trill
to hum
canticchiare (It.)
a bocca chiusa (It.)
chantonner (Fr.)
fredonner (Fr.)
avec bouche fermée (Fr.)
trällern (G.)
Brummstimmen (G.)

cantus (Lat.)
  *song
  tune
  melody
  *chant

2. *soprano part
  superius (Lat.)
  discant
  discantus (Lat.)
  highest voice-part
  dessus (Fr.)
  erste Stimme (G.)

3. tract (Ambrosian)
  tractus (Lat.)
  chant (Mass)

cantus choralis (Lat.)
  *chant
  plainsong
  Gregorian chant
  cantus planus (Lat.)
  canto liturgico (It.)
  canto llano (Sp.)
  Gregorianische Choral (G.)

cantus compositus (Lat.)
  written music
  unadorned chant
  res facta (Lat. 15c.)
  chose faite (Fr.)

cantus coronatus (Lat.)
  cantus fractus (Lat.)
  contrapunctus diminutus (Lat.)
  divisions
  embellishment

2. prize song
  crowned song
  competition song
  contest
  puy (Fr.)
  chanson couronnée (Fr.)
  gekröntes Lied (G.)

Preislied (G.)
Meistersinger
Troubadour song
Trouvère song

cantus durus (Lat.)
  hard song
  hexachord
  hexachordum durum (Lat.)

cantus figuralis, figuratus (Lat.)
  figured melody
  measured melody
  pricked melody
  mensural notation
  metrical music
  cantus indentatus (Lat.)
  cantus mensuratus (Lat.)
  polyphonic music
  musica figurate (It.)
  canto figurato (It.)
  canto de órgano (Sp.)
  Figuralgesang (G.)
  Figuralmusik (G.)

cantus firmus (Lat.)
  chant melody
  tenor
  augmentation
  drone
  organum (Lat.)
  In Nomine (Lat., 16-17c.)
  In Seculum (Lat., 12c.)
  Felix Namque (Lat., 16c.)
  canto fermo (It.)
  cantus prius factus (Lat.)

cantus gemellus (Lat.)
  gymel, gimel, gemel
  semel
  parallel thirds
  duo
  duet

cantus gestualis (Lat.)
  epic songs

narrative songs
chanson de geste (Fr.)
chanson de toile (Fr.)
chanson d'histoire (Fr.)

cantus mollis (Lat.)
  soft song
  hexachordum molle (Lat.)

cantus naturalis (Lat.)
  natural song
  hexachordum naturale (Lat.)

canzo, canso
  chanson (Fr.)
  song (troubadour)
  vers (Fr.)
  bar form
  AAB form
  Stollen (G.)
  formes fixes (Fr.)
  ballade (Fr.)

canzona, canzone (It.)
  instrumental piece
  canzona da sonare (It.)
  ricercare (It.)
  ricercar

2. song
  part-song
  madrigal
  balletto (It.)
  villanella (It.)
  frottola (It.)
  capitolo (It.)
  barzelletta (It.)
  canzonetta (It.)
  chanson (16c.)

canzonaccia (It.)
  street song
  vulgar song
  popular song
  pont-neuf (Fr.)
  Gassenhauer (G.)

canzone della tela (It.)
chanson de toile (Fr.)
chanson de geste (Fr.)
canción de tela (Sp.)
cantus gestualis (Lat.)
epic song
ballad

canzone di Natale (It.)
Christmas carol/song
natalizio (It.)
chant de noël (Fr.)
cantique de noël (Fr.)
villancico (Sp.)
Weinachtslied (G.)
Quempas (G.)
cántico de Navidad (Sp.)
zajal, zejel (Sp.)

canzonet
song
villanella (It.)
canzonetta (It.)
part-song
madrigal
balletto (It.)
chanson (Fr.)
canzonette (Fr.)
frottola (It.)

canzoniere (It.)
song book
song collection
hymnal
*anthology
fake book
repertoire
repertory
chansonnier (Fr.)
Liederbuch (G.)
cancionero (Sp.)
libro de cantos (Sp.)

Capellmeister (G.)
Kapellmeister
choirmaster

*choir director

capo
bar (on guitar)
transposer
capotasto (It.)
capo di tasto (It.)
barré (Fr.)
grand-barré (Fr.)
capodastre (Fr.)
Kapodaster (G.)
Saitenfessel (G.)
ceduela (Sp.)
ceja, cejilla (Sp.)

2. nut (string instr.)

capo d'orchestra (It.)
*conductor
batonist
orchestra leader
chef d'orchestre (Fr.)
Dirigent (G.)
director de orquestra (Sp.)

capobanda (It.)
bandleader
bandmaster
director
*conductor
maestro

capocchia (It.)
note head
testina (It.)
tête de la note (Fr.)
Notenkopf (G.)
cabeza de las notas (Sp.)
punto de las notas (Sp.)

capolavoro (It.)
masterpiece/masterwork
major work
opus magnus (Lat.)
chef d'oeuvre (Fr.)
Meisterwerk (G.)

obra maestra (Sp.)

capotasto (It.)
*capo (guitar)
transposer

2. thumb position (on 'cello)
position du pouce (Fr.)
démanché, démanchement
(Fr.)
Daumenaufsatz (G.)
posición del pulgar (Sp.)

cappella (It., Lat.)
chapel
church
chapelle (Fr.)
Kapelle (G.)
capilla (Sp.)
sanctuary

2. tutti (It. 17c.)
ripieno (It.)
full orchestra/chorus
coro pieno/ripieno (It.)
grand choeur (Fr.)
grosser Chor (G.)
Tuttichor (G.)

vs.*concertino (It.)

cappello cinese (It.)
Chinese crescent
Turkish crescent
jingling Johnny
Chinese pavilion
*chapeau Chinois (Fr.)

capriccio (It., Fr.)
fantasia
fanciful instrumental piece
caprice (Fr.)
character piece
characteristic piece
boutade (Fr.)
bagatelle

*program music
rhapsody
romance
romanza (It.)

2. study
*etude
invention
lesson

caprioccioso (It.)
   * freely
   capricious(ly)
   at will
   libre (Fr.)
   a capriccio (It.)
   a bene placido (It.)
   ad libitum (It.)
   a piacere (It.)
   a placer (Sp.)
   a voluntad (Sp.)
   nach Belieben (G.)
   nach Gefallen (G.)
   impromptu

caracteristica (Sp.)
   theme song/music
   signature song/music
   sigla melodica (It.)
   indicatif musicale (Fr.)
   idée fixe (Fr.)
   Leitmotiv (G.)
   Kennmelodie (G.)

caramillo (Sp.)
   *shawm
   calamus (Lat.)
   kalamos (Gr.)
   ciaramello, -a (It.)
   Schalmei (G.)
   chalumeau Fr.)

caricature
   *parody
   satire
   take-off

carillon (Fr., E.)
   *bells, tuned
   chimes
   churchbells
   Glockenklavier (G.)
   Glöckchenspiel (G.)

2. campanile
   bell tower
   belfry

carillon à musique (Fr.)
   music box
   boite à musique (Fr.)
   Spieldose (G.)
   scatola musicale (It.)
   scatola armonica (It.)
   caja de música (Sp.)

carillonneur (Fr.)
   bell-ringer
   campanist
   campanaio (It.)
   campanista (It.)
   Glockenspieler (G.)
   campanero (Sp.)

carioca (Port.)
   dance
   samba (Port.)
   bossa-nova (Port.)
   batuque (Port.)
   maxixe (Port.)
   cool jazz
   Brazil

carmen, carmina (Lat.)
   *song
   chanson (Fr.)
   part-song
   carmina burana (Lat.)
   drinking songs
   tavern songs
   love songs
   goliard songs
   jongleurs

Troubadour
Trouvère
Minnesinger
Meistersinger

carnival songs
   canti carnascialeschi (It.)
   Florence, 16c
   carmina burana (Lat.)
   calypso
   calenda
   Kalinda.

carol
   English Christmas songs, 15c.
   macaronic carol
   nowell
   natalizio (It.)
   noël (Fr.)
   Weihnachtslied (G.)
   canzone di Natale (It.)
   chant de noël (Fr.)
   cantique de noël (Fr.)
   villancico (Sp., 16c.)
   cántico de Navidad (Sp.)
   Quempas (G., 16c.)
   zajal, zejel (Sp.)

2. circle dance (12-13c.)
   round dance
   carole (Fr.)
   carola (It.)

carraca (Sp.)
   *rattle
   ratchet
   raganella (It.)
   hochet (Fr.)
   crécelle (Fr.)
   sonajero (Sp.)
   Knarre (G.)
   Rassel (G.)
   Ratsche (G.)
   matraca (Sp.)
   maraca
   rain stick

carré (Fr.)
   breve (It., Fr., E.)
   double whole note
   brevis (Lat., G.)
   Doppelganze (G.)

carro della banda musicale (It.)
   band shell
   bandstand
   bandwagon
   stage
   platform
   palco della banda (It.)
   palco dell'orchestra (It.)
   kiosque à musique (Fr.)
   Musikpavillon (G.)
   Konzertpavillon (G.)
   platforma con concha acústica (Sp.)
   quiosco de música (Sp.)

carry a tune
   sing (in tune)
   on pitch

vs. monotone
   tone-deaf

carta da musica (It.)
   manuscript paper
   *staff paper
   music paper
   carta pentagrammato (It.)
   carta rigata (It.)
   papier à musique (Fr.)
   liniertes Papier (G.)
   Notenpapier (G.)
   pautada (Sp.)
   papel de música (Sp.)

cascabeles (Sp.)
   *bells
   jingle bells
   sleighbells
   harness bells
   pellet bells

Sanctus bells
Schellen (G.)
Rollschellen (G.)
Schalenglöckchen (G.)
Cimbelstern (organ)
Zimbelstern (G.)
Cymbelstern (G.)
Tintinnabulum (Lat., G.)
Glockenspiel (G.)
nolae (Lat.)
cascavellus (Lat.)
   tintinnabolo (It.)
   campanae (Lat.)

cascarda (It. 16c.)
   court dance
   gagliarda (It.)
   galliard
   saltarello

cassa (It.)
   *drum
   tabor
   tambour (Fr.)
   tamburo (It.)
   tambor (Sp.)
   caja (Sp.)
   Trommel (G.)
   caisse (Fr.)
   tympanum (Lat.)

cassa dell'organo (It.)
   organ case
   casework
   buffet (Fr.)
   Gehäuse (G.)
   Orgelkasten (G.)
   domus organaria (Lat.)

cassa di legno (It.)
   *Chinese wood-block
   caisse Chinoise (Fr.)
   bloc de bois (Fr.)
   Holzblock (G.)
   Holzblocktrommel (G.)
   caja China (Sp.)

blochetto (It.)
cassettina (It.)
   clog box
   tap box
   temple blocks
   Korean temple blocks

cassa di resonanza (It.)
   sound box/chest
   resonance chamber
   caisse de résonance (Fr.)
   Resonanzboden (G.)
   caja de resonancia (Sp.)

cassa d'organo (It.)
   swell-box (organ)
   cassa espressiva (It.)
   boîte expressive (Fr.)
   Schwellkasten (G.)
   caja de expresión (Sp.)
   caja expresiva (Sp.)

cassa grande (It.)
   bass drum
   gran cassa (It.)
   gran tamburo (It.)
   tamburo grande (It.)
   tamburone (It.)
   grosse caisse (Fr.)
   gros-tambour (Fr.)
   grosse Trommel (G.)
   bombo (Sp.)

cassa rullante (It.)
   tenor drum
   tamburo rullante (It.)
   tamburo da rollo (It.)
   caisse roulante (Fr.)
   redoblante (Sp.)
   Rührtrommel (G.)
   Rolltrommel (G.)

cassation
   serenade
   divertimento (It.)
   cassatio (It.)

cassazione (It.)
Kassation (G.)
sérénade (Fr.)
suite

cassette (tape)
audio cassette
portable recorded tape
reel-to-reel tape

castanets
clappers
bones
claves (Sp.)
castagnettes (Fr.)
nacchere (It.)
Kastagnetten (G.)
postizas (Sp.)
castañuelas (Sp.)
castañetas (Sp.)
spoons
maraca(s)
rattle

castrato
male singer
male soprano
male alto
countertenor
eunuch
evirato (It.)
sopranista (It.)
tenorino (It.)
castrat (Fr.)
Kastrat (G.)
castrado (Sp.)

catawauling
mock serenade
shivaree
Dutch concert
*callithumpian concert
cat's music
musica di gatti (It.)
charivari (Fr.)
scampanata (It.)

Katzenmusik (G.)

catch
round
*canon
glee
madrigal
rota
caccia (It.)
chasse (Fr.)
Radel (G.)
troll

catgut string
gut string
budello (It.)
boyau (Fr.)
minugia (It.)
Darmsaite (G.)

vs. nylon string
steel string

cathedral
church
basilica
cattedrale (It.)
cathédrale (Fr.)
duomo (It.)
Dom (G.)
catedral (Sp.)
seo (Sp.)

cathedral chimes
chimes
tubular chimes
*bells
church bells

cathedral choir
church choir
liturgical choir
Domchor (G.)

cathedral music
Tudor church music

Anglican music
Anglican chant
Episcopal music
musique de cathédrale (Fr.)
música de las catedrales (Sp.)
música catedralícia (Sp.)
Kirchenmusik (G.)
choral music
verse anthem
full anthem
Great Service
short service

cauda (Lat.)
Abgesang (G.)
bar form
lai (Fr.)
Leich (G.)
Troubadour song

2. note stem
ligature
tail, hook
codetta (It.)
crochet de la note (Fr.)
Fahne, Fähnchen (G.)
Notenfahne (G.)
rabillo (Sp.)
gancho (Sp.)

3. coda
codetta (It.)
tag
envoi, envoy (Fr.)
conductus section
neupme (13c. Lat.)
exitus (Lat.)

cavaletto (It.)
bridge (violin)
ponticello(It.)
chevalet (Fr.)
Steg (G.)
puente (Sp.)

2. break (in the voice)

register change
passo, passagio (It.)
passage (Fr.)
Passage (G.)
paso, pasaje (Sp.)

cavalry horn
*helicon
bass tuba
sousaphone

cavata, cavatina (It.)
aria, arioso (It.)
air
Arie (G.)
cabaletta (It.)
Lied (G.)
Weise (G.)
chanson (Fr.)
canción (Sp.)
solo*song

caviglia (It.)
tuning peg/pin
bischero (It.)
pirolo (It.)
cheville (Fr.)
Wirbel (G.)
Stimmnagel (G.)
clavija (Sp.)

cebell, cibell (17c.)
* gavotte
rigaudon
bourrée (Fr.)
suite

cedendo (It.)
* slowing down
ritardando (It.)
rallentando (It.)
céder, cédez (Fr.)

ceduela (Sp.)
*capo
barré (Fr.)

ceja, cejilla (Sp.)

2. nut (at the end of the
fingerboard)
saddle
sella (It.)
sillet (Fr.)
Sattel (G.)

celesta
*bells
carillon
glockenspiel
orchestral bells
keyboard bells

celestial harmony
music of the spheres
harmony of the spheres
musica mundana (Lat.)
l'aronia delle sfere/celeste (It.)
musique des spheres célestes
(Fr.)
Sphärenmusik (G.)
armonía de las esferas celestes
(Sp.)
música de las esferas celestes
(Sp.)

céleste (organ stop)
detuned
voix céleste (Fr.)
jeu céleste (Fr.)
jeu d'anges (Fr.)
vox angelica (Lat.)
voce angelica (It.)
vox coelestis (Lat.)
unda maris (Lat.)
Engelstimme (G.)
voz angelica (Sp.)
vox humana (Lat.)

cello
violoncello
viola da gamba (It.)
baritone

baryton (G.)
cellone (It.)
viola da spalla (It.)
viola di bordone (It.)
basse-taille (Fr.)
Bassett (G.)
bassetto (It.)
Bassettl, Bassl (G.)
Halbbass (G.)
basso di camera (It.)
Kammerbass (G.)

Celtic harp
Irish harp
clarsach
folk harp
Troubadour harp
*harp

vs. pedal harp
concert harp

cembali (It.)
*cymbals
crash cymbals
acetabulum (Lat.)
piatti (It.)
cinelli (It.)
cymbales (Fr.)
Becken (G.)
Schallbecken (G.)
cimbalos (Sp.)
platillos (Sp.)

cembalo (It., G.)
clavicembalo (It.)
*harpsichord
arpicordo (It.)
clavecin (Fr., Sp.)
clavier (E., Fr., G.)
Kielflügel (G.)
clavichord
clavicordio (Sp.)
cimbalo (It.)
virginal(s)
keyboard

cembalo verticale (It.)
   clavicytherium (Lat.)
   upright harpsichord
   clavecin vertical (Fr.)
   claviciterio (It.)
   claveciterio (Sp.)
   Klavizitherium (G.)

cembalom
   cimbalom
   dulcimer (medieval)
   psaltery
   hammered dulcimer
   Hackbrett (G.)

cencerrada (Sp.)
   *shivaree
   noise, din
   racket
   charivari (Fr.)
   Dutch concert
   Callithumpian concert
   cat's concert
   Katzenmusik (G.)
   scampanata (It.)
   musica di gatti (It.)
   chiassa (It.)
   Lärm (G.)

cencerreo (Sp.)
   strumming
   thrumming
   twanging
   strimpellio (It.)
   tapotage (Fr.)
   geklimper (G.)
   zangarreo (Sp.)
   rasgueado (Sp.)

cencerro (Sp.)
   *bell
   cowbell
   Kuhglocke (G.)
   Kuhschelle (G.)
   Alpenglocken (G.)
   cloche de vache (Fr.)

campanaccio (It.)
   sonnaille (Fr.)

cennamella (It.)
   *shawm
   chalumeau (Fr.)
   Shalmei (G.)
   caramillo (Sp.)
   bagpipe
   zampogna (It.)

cent
   interval
   microtone
   *comma
   schisma
   centitone

cento, centonization
   fragments
   motive, motivic
   quodlibet
   potpourri
   medley
   olio
   olla potrida (Sp.)
   pasticcio (It.)
   pastiche (Fr.)
   Flickwerk, Flickoper (G.)
   cento (Lat.)
   centone (It.)
   centon (Fr.)
   centón (Sp.)
   commatic chants
   through-composed

ceramella (It.)
   *bagpipe
   piva (It.)
   musette (Fr.)
   Dudelsack (G.)
   gaita (Sp.)

cercar la nota (It.)
   *anticipation
   passing tone

grace note

ceremonial trumpet
   state trumpet
   long trumpet
   *Aida trumpet
   herald trumpet

ceremony
   rite, ritual
   *liturgy
   religious service
   rubrics
   ordo (Lat.)
   cerimonia (It.)
   cérémonie (Fr.)
   Zeremonie, -iell (G.)
   ceremonia (Sp.)

cervelas, cervelat (Fr.)
   *racket(t) (E., Fr., Sp.)
   sausage bassoon
   bassoon
   cervellato (It.)
   rochetta (It.)
   Rackett, Rankett (G.)
   Ranket-Fagott (G.)
   Stockfagott (G.)
   Wurstfagott (G.)
   cervelas (Sp.)
   clarinet

cesura (It., Sp.)
   caesura
   césure (Fr.)
   Zäsur (G.)
   Fermate (G.)
   railroad tracks
   vuoto (It.)
   misura vuota (It.)
   empty measure/bar
   grand pause
   general pause
   G.P.
   hold
   fermata (It.)

pausa generale (It.)
pause générale (Fr.)

cetera, cetra (It.)
  *zither
  citare (Fr.)
  citara (Sp.)
  cetra da tavolo (It.)

 2. cittern
  cither
  cistre (Fr.)
  Cister (G.)
  Schlagzither (G.)
  cedar (Sp.)
  cistro, citola (Sp.)
  citara punteada (Sp.)
  tympanón (Sp.)
  *cithara (Lat.)
  kithara (Gr.)
  lyre

cetra ad accordi (It.)
  autoharp
  zither
  Tischharfe (G.)
  Akkordzither (G.)

chace, chasse (Fr.)
  caccia (It.)
  round
  canon
  part-song
  catch

cha cha cha (Sp.)
  *latin dance
  rumba
  mambo
  conga

chaconne (Fr.)
  ciaccona (It.)
  ruggiero (It.)
  chacona (Sp.)
  chacony (17c. E.)

ground bass
ostinato bass
strophic bass
strophic variations
basso ostinato (It.)
passacaglia
folia (It.)
pes
variations

chair organ
  *choir organ/division
  Rückpositiv (G.)
  positif (Fr.)
  positif de dos (Fr.)
  Positiv im Stuhl (G.)
  Chororgel (G.)
  órgano de silla (Sp.)

chalumeau (Fr.)
  shawm
  pipe
  chanter (of a bagpipe)
  oboe
  clarinet
  kalamos (Gr.)
  calamus (Lat.)
  cennamella (It.)
  Schalmei (G.)
  caramillo (Sp.)
  tiple (Sp.)

 2. tin whistle
  tin flute
  toy flute
  zufolo (It.)
  scialumo (It.)
  pipeau (Fr.)
  pipette (Fr.)
  Hirtenpfeife (G.)
  pipa, pipitaña (Sp.)

 3. low register (clarinet))
  play an octave lower

 3. organ stop – hautbois

chamade (Fr.)
  state trumpet (organ)
  en chamade (Fr.)
  horizontal display pipes

 2. call of the hunt
  *bugle call
  fanfare
  flourish
  caccia (It.)
  Hornsignal (G.)
  chace, chasse (Fr.)

chamber choir
  semi-chorus
  madrigal singers
  madrigal choir
  choral ensemble
  concertino (It.)
  favoriti (It.)
  coro favorito (It.)
  demi-choeur (Fr.)
  petit-choeur (Fr.)
  Kammerchor (G.)
  coro de cámara (Sp.)
  vocal ensemble
  echo choir

chamber music
  musica da camera (It.)
  Kammermusik (G.)
  musique de chambre (Fr.)
  musica de camara (Sp.)
  salon music
  ensemble music

vs. symphonic music

chamber opera
  small-scale opera
  opera da camera (It.)
  opéra de chambre (Fr.)
  Kammeroper (G.)

vs. grand opera

chamber orchestra
  orchestra da camera (It.)
  orchestre de chambre (Fr.)
  Kammerorchester (G.)
  orquesta de camara (Sp.)
  sinfonietta
  small orchesatra
  string orchestra

chamber organ
  portative organ
  positive organ
  cabinet organ
  reed organ
  regal
  organo reale (It.)
  régale (Fr.)
  Regal (G.)
  realejo (Sp.)
  Bible regal
  book regal
  bible-organ

chamber pitch
  Kammerton (G.)
  ton de chambre (Fr.)
  corista di camera (It.)
  tonalidad de cámera (Sp.)

chamber sonata
  sonata da camera (It.)
  trio sonata
  solo sonata

chamber symphony
  modern work for small
orchestra
  Kammersymphonie (G.)
  small orchestra

chamois horn
  goathorn
  recorder
  Gemshorn (G., organ)
  cor de chamois (Fr.)
  gamuza (Sp.)

chance music
  aleatory music
  indeterminacy
  dice music
  atonal music
  tone clusters
  pitch aggregate

chancel
  choir
  choir stalls
  cantoris
  decani
  choir gallery
  sanctuary

chancel choir
  church choir
  chapel choir
  cathedral choir
  cantoris
  decani
  Kantorei (G.)
  Domchor (G.)
  schola (Lat.)
  schola cantorum (Lat.)

change(s)
  bell-ringing
  variations
  carillon

change (of) key
  modulation
  key change
  key shift
  transition
  modulazione (It.)
  modulacion (Sp.)
  modulieren (G.)
  moduler (Fr.)
  modulare (It.)
  modular (Sp.)
  Ausweichung (G.)

change-ringing

bell ringing
peal ringing
carillon

changer le doigté (Fr.)
  finger substitution
  diteggiatura cambiata (It.)
  ablösen (G.)
  cambiar la digitación (Sp.)

changing note, tone, chord
  passing tone
  non-harmonic tone
  cambiata
  escape note
  nota cambiata (It.)
  note changée (Fr.)
  échappée (Fr.)
  Wechselnote (G.)
  note cambiada (Sp.)

changing voice
  cambiata
  alto-tenor
  mutazione della voce (It.)
  mue de la voix (Fr.)
  Veränderung der
Knabenstimme zur
Männerstimme (G.)
  Stimmbruch (G.)
  Stimmwechsel (G.)
  mudanza de la voz (Sp.)

channel
  release
  bridge
  B section
  middle section
  alternative
  alternativo (It.)
  pont (Fr.)
  alternativement (Fr.)
  Übergang (G.)

  2. band on a disk
  track

cut
    pista (It., Sp.)
    traccia (It.)
    piste (Fr.)
    Spur, Tonspur (G.)

chanson (Fr.)
    *song
    melody
    part-song
    glee
    chansonette (Fr.)
    canzona (It.)
    Lied (G.)
    carmen (Lat.)

chanson à boire (Fr.)
    drinking song
    tavern song
    bacchanal
    brindisi (It.)
    air à boire (Fr.)
    canción baquica (Sp.)
    vinata, vinetto (It.)
    carmina burana (Lat.)

chanson à la mode (Fr.)
    hit song
    pop song
    top 10, 20, 40
    chanson à succès (Fr.)
    Schlager (G.)
    canción de moda (Sp.)
    canción en boga (Sp.)

chanson-avec-des-refrains (Fr.)
    Troubadour song
    multiple refrains

chanson balladée (Fr.)
    *song (14c.)
    virelai (14c. Fr.)
    ballade (Fr.)
    forme fixe (Fr.)
    ballata (It.)
    villancico (Sp.)

refrain
    piedi (It.)
    ripresa (It.)
    volta (It.)
    bergerette (Fr.)

chanson couronée (Fr.)
    crowned song
    prize song
    contest song
    cantus coronatus (Lat.)
    Trouvère song
    puy (Fr.)
    gekröntes Lied (G.)
    Preislied (G.)
    Meistersinger

chanson de geste (Fr.)
    medieval song
    narrative song
    epic song
    ballad
    cantus gestualis (Lat.)
    chanson de toile (Fr.)
    chanson d'histoire (Fr.)
    chanson de croisade (Fr.)
    Troubadour
    Trouvère
    spinning song
    laisse (Fr.)

chanson de mai (Fr.)
    spring song
    May song
    maggialata (It.)
    reverdie (Fr.)
    Mailied (G.)
    canción de mayo (Sp.)

chanson de noce (Fr.)
    bridal song
    *wedding song
    epithalamium (Lat., E.)
    canto nuziale (It.)
    Brautlied (G.)
    canto nupcial (Sp.)

chanson mesurée (Fr.)
    vers mesuré (16c.Fr.)
    musique mesurée (Fr.)

chanson pieuse (Fr.)
    Troubadour song
    song of piety
    religious song

chansonnier (Fr.)
    song collection
    *anthology
    cancionero
    repertoire

chant
    *song
    *hymn
    psalm
    canticle
    plainsong
    plainchant
    liturgical chant/song
    cantus planus (Lat.)
    cantus choralis (Lat.)
    cantus Romanus (Lat.)
    musica plana (Lat.)
    musica piana (It.)
    Gregorian chant
    cantilena Romana (Lat., Sp.)
    chant d'église (Fr.)
    chant Grégorien (Fr.)
    chant Romain (Fr.)
    Choral (G.)
    Gregorianischer Gesang (G.)
    canto Gregoriano (It., Sp.)
    cantico (It., Sp.)
    Ambrosian chant
    Gallican chant
    Mozarabic chant
    Anglican chant

chant (Fr.)
    *song
    melody
    tune

Gesang (G.)
Lied (G.)
canto (It., Sp.)
chanson (Fr.)
chant
vocal music

chant collection
*anthology
anthiphonale (Lat.)
antiphonal
graduale (Lat.)
gradual
Liber Usualis (Lat.)
kyriale (Lat.)
offertoriale (Lat.)
processionale (Lat.)

chant de noël (Fr.)
Christmas carol/song
noel, nowell
canzone di Natale (It.)
natalizio (It.)
cantique de noël (Fr.)
noé, nouel (Fr.)
Quempas (G.)
Weinachtslied (G.)
cántico de Navidad (Sp.)
villancico (Sp.)
zajal, zejel (Sp.)
kolenda, koleda (Pol.)

chant notation
square notation
Gregorian notation
neumes
square notes
quadratic notation
Aquitanian notation
nota Romana (It.)
nota/notazione quadrata (It.)
note/notation carée (Fr.)
Quadratnotenschrift (G.)
Quadratnotation (G.)
notación cuadrada (Sp.)
notación Gregoriana (Sp.)

chant tzigane/gitan (Fr.)
gypsy song
canzone gitana (It.)
Zigeunerlied (G.)
tzigana (Sp.)
canto gitano (Sp.)
canción gitana/tzigana (Sp.)

chanter
pipe
bagpipe
chaunter
scialumo (It.)
pipeau (Fr.)
pipette (Fr.)
Melodiepfeife (G.)
pipa, pipitaña (Sp.)

chanter (Fr.)
to sing
singen (G.)
cantare (It.)
cantar (Sp.)
intone
to chant
warble
trill
lilt
croon
vocalise

chanterelle (Fr.)
e-string
highest string
cantino (It.)
Sangsaite (G.)
prima (Sp.)
tiple (Sp.)
Quinsaite (G.)
soprana corda (It.)

chantey, chanty
*shanty
sea song
sailor's song
boat song

worksong

chanteuse (Fr.)
chanteur (Fr.)
* singer
songstress
Sängerin (G.)
song stylist
vocalist
artiste
performer

chantonner (Fr.)
to hum
to trill
fredonner (Fr.)
canticchiare (It.)
a bocca chiusa (It.)
furberia del canto (It.)
avec bouche fermée (Fr.)
trällern (G.)
canturrear (Sp.)
canticar (Sp.)

chantre (Fr.)
*cantor (E., Sp.)
cantore (It.)
Kantor (G.)
song leader

chapeau (Fr.)
*tie
bind
slur
portato (It.)
legatura (It.)
légatoure (Fr.)
liaison (Fr.)
Haltebogen (G.)
Bindebogen (G.)
ligadura (Sp.)

chapeau Chinois (Fr.)
Chinese pavilion
Chinese crescent
Chinese hat

Turkish crescent/pavilion
jingling Johnny
bell tree
Janissary music
banda Turca (It.)
padiglione cinese (It.)
cappello cinese (It.)
mezzaluna (It.)
pavillon Chinois (Fr.)
Schellenbaum (G.)
Halbmond (G.)
Chinesco (Sp.)
sombrero Chino (Sp.)

chapel
chapelle (Fr.)
cappella (Lat., It.)
Kapelle (G.)
capilla (Sp.)
*church
house of worship
sanctuary

chapel choir
chancel choir
church choir
Kantorei (G.)
schola (Lat.)
scola cantorum (Lat.)

character notation/notes
shape notes
patent notes
buckwheat notes
dunce notes
fasola
*solmization
tonic sol-fa
solfeggio

character piece
*program music
descriptive music
tone poem
pièce charactéristique (Fr.)
Charakterstück (G.)

*fancy
fantasy
bagatelle
caprice
romance
romanza (It.)

charanga (Sp.)
*fanfare
flourish
bugle call
fanfara (It.)
squillo di tromba (It.)
banda (It., Sp.)
sonnerie (Fr.)
military band
Tusch (G.)
sonada (Sp.)
fanfarria (Sp.)

charivari (Fr.)
shivaree
cat's music
Katzenmusik (G.)
Lärm (G.)
scampanata (It.)
chiasso (It.)
noise
cacaphony
cal(l)ithump, callathump
*callithumpian concert
Dutch concert

Charleston-Maschine (G.)
choke cymbals
sock cymbals
hi-hat, high-hat
Charleston (It.)
hi-hat pédal (Fr.)
cymbales choquées (Fr.)
pedal del bombo de jazz (Sp.)

chart(s)
lead sheet
fake book
songs

improvise
harmonize
condensed score
short score

chef d'attaque (Fr.)
concertmaster
section leader
Konzertmeister (G.)
primo violino (It.)
violino primo (It.)
Primgeiger (G.)
Vorgeiger (G.)
concertino (Sp.)
assistant conductor
concertmistress

chef de choeur (Fr.)
choirmaster
*choir director
chef de la maîtrise (Fr.)
Kapellmeister (G.)
maestro di capela (It.)

chef d'oeuvre (Fr.)
masterpiece/masterwork
major work
opus magnus (Lat.)
capolavoro (It.)
Meisterwerk (G.)
obra maestra (Sp.)

chef d'orchestre (Fr.)
conductor
director
batonist
orchestra leader
Dirigent (G.)
direttore d'orchestra (It.)
director de orquestra (Sp.)
maestro (It.)

cheironomic neumes
staffless
in campo aperto (Lat.)
adiastematic

oratorical
nondiastematic
notation

cheironomy
directing a choir
conducting
hand movements
chant directing

chekker (14-16c.)
keyboard instr.
*clavichord
eschaquier, échiquier (Fr.)
escacherium (Lat.)
scacarum (Lat.)
Schachtbrett (G.)
escaque, esaquier, exaquier
(Sp.)

chelys (Gr.)
lyra
lyre
lira
viol
psaltery
kithara (Gr.)
cythara (Lat.)

cherub choir
children's choir (young)
treble choir
equal voices
coro di ragazzi (It.)
coro di fanciulli (It.)
choeur d'enfants (Fr.)
Kinderchor (G.)
coro de niños (Sp.)
coro infantil (Sp.)
escolanía (Sp.)

cherubic hymn
song of the angels
offertory (Byzantine)
aius Trishagion (Gr.)
trisagion (Gr.)

Sanctus (Lat.)
Holy, Holy, Holy
Kadosh (H.)
Kedusha (H.)
ter sanctus (Lat.)
Hymn of Victory (Byz.)
Triumphant Hymn
epiniciom (Gr.)

cherubim song
doxology
Hymn of the Angels
Hymnus Angelicus (Lat.)
angelic hymn
Gloria in excelsis (Lat.)
trinitarian hymn
Gloria Patri (Lat.)

chest of viols
set of six viols
whole consort
consort of viols
string ensemble
Akkord (G.)
Stimmwerk (G.)

chest voice
full voice
low voice
chest register
chest tone
belting tone
belt it out
voce di petto (It.)
voix de gorge (Fr.)
voix de poitrine (Fr.)
registro di petto (It.)
Bruststimme (G.)
voz de pecho (Sp.)

chevalet (Fr.)
bridge (of instr.)
ponticello (It.)
scagnello (It.)
Steg (G.)
puente (Sp.)

cavaletto (It.)

Chevé system
sol-fa
*solmization
solfeggio (It.)
sight-reading
solfège (Fr.)
fasola

cheville (Fr.)
peg (of string instr.)
tuning peg/pin
bischero (It.)
caviglia (It.)
pirolo, pirone (It.)
Wirbel (G.)
Stimmnagel (G.)
clavija (Sp.)

chevrette (Fr. 13c.)
*bagpipe
musette (Fr.)
piva (It.)
Dudelsack (G.)
gaita (Sp.)

chevrotement (Fr.)
goat's trill
tremolo
*vibrato
Bockstriller (G.)
trillo caprino (It.)
trino de cabra (Sp.)
Geisstriller (G.)

chiamata (It.)
fanfare
flourish
*call
battle call
chamade (Fr.)
banda (Sp.)

chiarenzana (It.)
dance

Italian sixth
Neopolitan sixth
augmented sixth chord

chorda (Lat., Gr.)
string
note
tone

chordal (melody)
skips
arpeggiated
arpeggiando (It.)
broken chords

vs. scale melody

chordophone
string(ed) instrument
stromento a corda (It.)
instrument à cordes (Fr.)
Saiteninstrumente (G.)
Streichinstrumente (G.)
instrumento de cuerdo (Sp.)

Chororgel (G.)
*choir organ
petit orgue (Fr.)
chair organ
positif (Fr.)
positif de dos (Fr.)
organo di coro (It.)
órgano de silla (Sp.)
órgano de coro (Sp.)

Chorton (G.)
choir pitch
organ pitch
church pitch
tuono chorista (It.)
corista di coro (It.)
ton de chapelle (Fr.)
ton de choeur (Fr.)
Kapellton (G.)

chorus

*choir
chorale
choral society
coro (It., Sp.)
choeur (Fr.)
Chor (G.)

2. *refrain
respond
antiphon
tutti (It.)
all

vs. verse
vs. solo

chorus girl
show girl

chorus master
*choir director
maestro
conductor

chorus reed
choral bass
choral principal
pedal flute
Chorbass (G.)
Prinzipalbass (G.)

chose faite (Fr.)
res facta (Lat.)
cantus compositus (Lat.)
written music
unadorned chant

Christmas carol
canzona di natale (It.)
natalizio (It.)
chant de noël (Fr.)
cantique de noël (Fr.)
Quempas (G.)
Weinachtslied (G.)
villancico (Sp.)
cántico de Navidad (Sp.)

zéjel (Sp.)
kolenda, koleda (Pol.)

chromatic
half-steps
altered tones
non-harmonic tones
accidentals
sharps and flats
hemitonic
twelve tones
cromatico (It., Sp.)
chromatisch (G.)
chromatique (Fr.)
semitonique (Fr.)

vs. diatonic, pentatonic

chronista (Lat.)
narrator
evangelist
historicus (Lat.)
evangelium (Lat.)
narratore (It.)
testo (It.)
narrateur (Fr.)
récitant (Fr.)
Erzähler (G.)
narrador (Sp.)

chrotta (Fr.)
crwth, crowth, crowd
lyre
harp
crotta (It.)
Chrotta (G.)
rota (Sp.)

chuchoté (Fr.)
whispered
*aside
very soft
stage whisper
under one's breath
bisbigliato (It.)
cuchicheado (Sp.)

geflüstert (G.)

church
chiesa (It.)
église (Fr.)
Kirche (G.)
iglesia (Sp.)
*chapel
sanctuary
basilica
cathedral
Dom (G.)
duomo (It.)
catedral (Sp.)
cathédrale (Fr.)

church bells
steeple bells
tower bells
carillon
chimes
*bells

church cadence
plagal cadence
amen cadence
cadenza plagale (It.)
cadence plagale (Fr.)
Kirchenschluss (G.)
plagale Kadenz (G.)
Plagalschluss (G.)
cadencia plagal (Sp.)

church mode
authentic mode
ecclesiastical mode
modo ecclesiastico (It.)
Kirchentonart (G.)
mode ecclesiastique (Fr.)
modo eclesiástico (Sp.)
scale, diatonic scale

church music
sacred music
religious music
liturgical music

ecclesiastic music
musica da chiesa (It.)
Kirchenmusik (G.)
musique d'église (Fr.)
música de iglesia (Sp.)
cathedral music

vs. secular music

chute, cheute (Fr.)
ornamental tone
passing tone
ornament
appoggiatura
anticipation

ciaccona (It.)
*chaconne (Fr.)
ground bass
ostinato bass
basso ostinato (It.)
passacaglia
folia
pes
variations
chacona (Sp.)
chacony (17c. E.)

ciaramello (It.)
oboe
*shawm
calamellus (Lat.)
*calamus (Lat.)
kalamos (Gr.)
chalumeau (Fr.)
Shalmei (G.)

cibell, cebell (17c.)
*gavotte
rigaudon
bourée
suite

ciclo di canzoni (It.)
song cycle
cycle de lieder (Fr.)

cycle de mélodies (Fr.)
Liederzyklus (G.)
Liederkreis (G.)
ciclo de canciones (Sp.)

cicuta (Lat.)
flute
*pan-pipes
pipes of Pan

cilindro (It., Sp.)
piano-roll
player-piano roll
cylindre (Fr.)
rouleau (Fr.)
Walze (G.)
rollo (Sp.)

cimbala (Sp.)
*mixture (org.)
compound stop
lleno (Sp.)

cimbales sobre palillos (Sp.)
sizzle cymbals
rivet cymbals
piatti chiodati (It.)
cymbales sur tiges (Fr.)
Sizzle-Becken (G.)
Nietenbecken (G.)
Zischbecken (G.)

cimbalini (It.)
finger cymbals
*crotales (Fr.)
cymbales antiques (Fr.)
Fingerzimbeln (G.)
cymbales digitales (It.)
cimbalillos digitales (Sp.)

cimbalo (Sp.)
cymbal
piatto (It.)
cymbale (Fr.)
platillo (Sp.)

2. small bell
   *bell

cimbalo (It.)
   *cymbal
   crash cymbal

2. cembalo (It., G.)
   *harpsichord

3. *tambourine
   timbrel
cimbalino (It.)
cimbaletto (It.)
   tamburino (It.)
   Handtrommel (G.)
   Schellentrommel (G.)
   panderete (Sp.)
   tambour de Basque (Fr.)

cimbalom, cembalom
   dulcimer (Hung.)
   hammered dulcimer
   Hackbrett (G.)
   tympanon (Fr.)
   zimbalon
   zither
   psaltery
   autoharp

cimbasso (It.)
   bass trombone
   tuba
   *ophicleide
   serpent
   bass horn

cimbel (organ)
   *mixture
   compound stop
   Zimbel (G.)
   Cimbale (G.)
   Scharff (G.)
   cornet (Fr.)

cinelli (It.)

cymbals
crash cymbals
piatti (It.)
Becken (G.)
cymbales (Fr.)
cimbalos (Sp.)
platillos (Sp.)

cinema organ
   theatre organ
   unit organ
   unified organ
   extension organ
   organo da teatro (It.)
   organo da cinematografo (It.)
   orgue de cinéma (Fr.)
   Kinoorgel (G.)
   Multiplexorgel (G.)
   órgano de cine (Sp.)

cinfonia (Sp.)
   *hurdy-gurdy
   chifonie (Fr.)
   barrel-organ
   stampella (It.)

cinque-pace (E.)
   old dance
   cinque-passi (It.)
   cinq pas (Fr.)
   galliard
   saltarello
   sinkapass, sink-a pace
   sink apart

cinquième (Fr.)
   tenor violin
   viola
   basse de violon (Fr.)
   taille de violon (Fr.)
   quinte de violon (Fr.)
   quinte (Fr.)
   Tenorgeige (G.)
   Altgeige (G.)
   Altviole (G.)
   violon-ténor (Fr.)

alto (It., Fr.)
Bratsche (G.)
alta-viola (It.)
alto-viola (Fr.)

2. fifth (interval)
   quinta (It., Sp.)
   quinte (F.)
   Quinte (G.)

circle of fifths
   Quintenzirkel (G.)
   circolo delle quinte (It.)
   ciclo de las quintas (Sp.)
   cycle des quintes (Fr.)

circolo mezzo (It.)
   *turn
   ornament
   Doppelschlag (G.)
   tour de gosier (Fr.)
   gruppetto (It.)

circular canon
   perpetual canon
   infinite canon
   *canon
   canone perpetuo (It., Sp.)
   canon perpétuel (Fr.)
   unendlicher Kanon (G.)

2. *perpetual motion
   moto perpetuo (It.)
   perpetuum mobile (Lat.)
   mouvement perpétuel (Fr.)
   movimento perpetuo (It.)

cithara (Lat.)
   Kithara (Gr.)
   lyre
   harp
   psaltery
   lira (Lat.)
   lyra (Gr.)
   cruit
   rotta

2. **cittern**
   citole
   cistre (Fr.)
   Cister (G.)
   *cetera, cetra (It.)
   cither
   zither

cithare sur caisse (Fr.)
   *bell harp
   box zither
   fairy bells
   Kastenzither (G.)

civic auditorium
   *concert hall
   civic center
   performing arts center
   recital hall
   symphonic hall
   philharmonic hall

civic chorus/choir
   *choral society
   community chorus
   oratorio society
   symphonic chorus
   philharmonic chorus
   associazione corale (It.)
   société chorale (Fr.)
   Gesangverein (G.)
   orfeón (Sp.)

clacchista (It.)
   claque
   applause
   bravos
   claqueur (Fr.)

clairon (Fr.)
   * bugle
   keyed bugle
   clairon à clefs (Fr.)
   Kent bugle
   Royal Kent bugle
   Regent's bugle

Klappenhorn (G.)
ophicleide
cornet
trumpet

2. **clarin trumpet**
   clarino (It.)
   tromba (It.)
   Jagdhorn (G.)

clambake (jazz)
   jam session
   improvisation
   hootnanny

clappers
   rhythm sticks
   *bones
   castanets
   spoons
   *claves (Sp., E., Fr., It.)
   Klangstäbe (G.)

claquebois (Fr.)
   xylophone
   straw fiddle
   gigelira (It.)
   sticcado pastorale (It.)
   sticcato (It.)
   organo di legno (It.)
   xilofono (It.)
   patouille (Fr.)
   harmonica de bois (Fr.)
   orgue de paille (Fr.)
   échelettes (Fr.)
   régale de bois (Fr.)
   régale de percussion (Fr.)
   Xylophon (G.)
   Strohfiedel (G.)
   xilófono (Sp.)
   xilórgano (Sp.)
   armonica de madera (Sp.)
   marimba
   vibraharp
   vibraphone
   vibes

clarinet
   licorice stick
   basset horn
   *chalumeau (Fr.)
   clarinetto (It.)
   clarinette (Fr.)
   Klarinette (G.)
   clarinete (Sp.)

clarinete alto (Sp.)
   * basset horn
   clarinet
   cor de basset (Fr.)
   corno di bassetto (It.)
   Bassetthorn (G.)

clarinette basse (Fr.)
   bass clarinet
   basset horn
   clarinetto basso (It.)
   clarone (It.)

clarino (It.)
   trumpet in D
   Bach trumpet
   baroque trumpet
   piccolo trumpet
   clarion

clarsach, clarseach, clarseth (Gael.)
   Irish harp
   Celtic harp
   folk harp
   Troubadour harp

vs. pedal harp
   concert harp

clash
   *dissonance
   cross-relation
   mistake
   wrong note

classical guitar

acoustic guitar
folk guitar
Spanish guitar
flat-top guitar

vs. electric guitar

classical music
long-haired music
high-brow music
serious music
the classics
great music
art music
concert music

vs. popular, folk music

2. classical period (1750-1830)
neo-classical music

classical pitch
international pitch
low pitch
French pitch
diapason normal (Fr.)
Normalton (G.)
Franzton (G.)
diapasön normal (Sp.)
diapasön de bajo (Sp.)

clausola sostituta (It.)
substitute clausula
discant section
organum
clausule substitué (Fr.)
Ersatzklausel (G.)
clausula sustitutiva (Sp.)

clausula (Lat.)
organum section
discant section
Klausel (G.)
clausola (It.)
clausule (Fr.)

2. *cadence
close
ending

clave (Sp.)
*harpsichord
clavicordio (Sp.)

2. key
tonality
*scale
scala (It.)
gamme (Fr.)
Skala (G.)
Tonleiter (G.)
escala (Sp.)
gama (Sp.)

3. clef (E., Fr.)
clavis (Lat.)
chiava (It.)
Schlüssel (G.)

clave aguda (Sp.)
*G-clef
chiave di sol (It.)
clef d'ut (Fr.)
G-Schlüssel (G.)

clave de baja (Sp.)
*F-clef
chiave di fa (It.)
clef de fa (Fr.)
F-Schlüssel (G.)
clave de grave (Sp.)

clave de do (Sp.)
*C-clef
chiave di do (It.)
clef d'alto (Fr.)
C-Schlüssel (G.)
clave de contralto (Sp.)

clave paralela (Sp.)
parallel key (same tonic)
tono parallelo (It., Sp.)

mode parallèle Fr.)
Paralleltonart (G.)

clave relativa (Sp.)
relative minor/major
same key signature
tono relativo (It., Sp.)
mode relatif (Fr.)
verwandte Tonart (G.)

clavecin (Fr., Sp.)
cembalo (G.)
clavicembalum (Lat.)
clavicembalo (It. Sp.)
*harpsichord
Kielflügel (G.)
virginal(s)
clavichord

clavecin-luth (Fr.)
lute harpsichord
Lautenwerk (G.)
Lautenklavier (G.)

clavecin oculaire (Fr.)
color organ
tastiera per luce (It.)

claves (E., Sp., It., Fr.)
rhythm sticks
baguettes de percussion (Fr.)
Klangstäbe (G.)
Schlaghölzer (G.)
*castanets
clappers
bones
spoons

clavichord
Klavichord (G.)
Klavier (G.)
Clavier (G.)
clavicordo (It.)
clavicorde (Fr.)
doucemelle (Fr.)
dulce melos (Lat.)

clavicordio (Sp.)
*chekker
eschaquier (Fr.)
eschaque (Sp.)
escacherium (Lat.)
Schachtbrett (G.)

clavicylinder
*glass harmonica
*hurdy-gurdy

clavicytherium (Lat.)
upright harpsichord
vertical harpsichord
clavecin vertical (Fr.)
claviciterio (It.)
cembalo verticale (It.)
claveciterio (Sp.)
Klavizitherium (G.)

clavier (G., Fr., E.)
keyboard
manual (organ)
manuel (Fr.)
pedalboard (organ)
Klaviatur G.)
claviatur (G.)
tastatura (It.)
teclado (Sp.)

clavier d'écho (Fr.)
echo organ
gallery organ
nave organ
antiphonal organ
organo d'eco (It.)
Echoklavier (G.)
Fernwerk (G.)

clavier de pédales (Fr.)
pedalboard
pedal division
pedal keyboard
pédaliere (Fr.)
pedaliera (It.)
Pedalklavier (G.)

Pedalklaviatur (G.)
pedalero (Sp.)

clavier de récit (Fr.)
swell division/manual
under expression
organo d'espressione (It.)
Schweller (G.)
Schwellwerk (G.)
recitativo (Sp.)

clavier des bombardes (Fr.)
solo organ
bombard organ
organo d'assolo (It.)
Soloklavier (G.)
teclado de las bombardas (Sp.)
Oberwerk (G.)

clavier-übung (G.)
keyboard study
*etude
practice piece

clavija (Sp.)
peg
tuning peg/pin
bischero (It.)
caviglia (It.)
pirolo, pirone (It.)
cheville (Fr.)
Wirbel (G.)
Stimmnagel (G.)

clavijero (Sp.)
pin block (piano)
sommier de chevilles (Fr.)
Stimmstock (G.)

clef, cleff (E., Fr.)
pitch indicator
cliff
key
chiave (It.)
clavis (Lat.)
clé (Fr.)

clave (Sp.)
llave (Sp.)
Schlüssel (G.)

2. *key
tonality
tonal center
scale
mode, modality
tonalita (It.)
tonalité (Fr.)
Tonart (G.)
Tonalität (G.)
tonalidad (Sp.)

3. digital
Klappe (G.)
tasto (It.)
touche (Fr.)
Taste (G.)
tecla (Sp.)

clef d'accordeur (Fr.)
tuning key
accordatoio (It.)
accordoir (Fr.)
Stimmhammer (G.)
afinador (Sp.)

clef de do (Fr.)
*C-clef
viola clef
chiave di do (It.)
chiave di contralto (It.)
clef d'ut (Fr.)
clef d'alto (Fr.)
C-Schlüssel (G.)
Altschlüssel (G.)
llave de do (Sp.)
clave de contralto (Sp.)

clef de fa (Fr.)
*F-clef
bass clef
chiave di basso (It.)
F-Schlüssel (G.)

Bassschlüssel (G.)
llave de fa (Sp.)
clave de bajo (Sp.)
clave grave (Sp.)

clef de sol (Fr.)
*G-clef
violin clef
treble clef
soprano clef
chiave di sol (It.)
chiave del canto (It.)
chiave di violino (It.)
clef de violon (Fr.)
G-Schlüssel (G.)
llave de sol (Sp.)
clave de sol (Sp.)

clinker
mistake
wrong note
false note
sour note
discord
dissonance
cacaphony
stecca (It.)
falsa nota (It.)
canard (Fr.)
fausse note (Fr.)
falsche Note (G.)
Missklang, Misston (G.)
gallipavo (Sp.)

cloche (Fr.)
*bell
campana (It., Sp.)
Glocke (G.)

cloche de vache (Fr.)
cowbell
campanaccio (It.)
sonnaille (Fr.)
Kuhschelle (G.)
Kuhglocke (G.)
Alpenglocke (G.)

clocher (Fr.)
bell tower
belfry
campanile (E., It.)
steeple
campanario (Sp.)
Glockenturm (G.)
Glockenstube (G.)
campanaria (It.)
carillon

cloches (Fr.)
*bells
glockenspiel
orchestra bells
Glocken (G.)

cloches tubulaires (Fr.)
tubular bells
chimes
campane tubolari (It.)
Röhrenglocken (G.)
campanólogo (Sp.)
campanas tubulares (Sp.)

clochettes (Fr.)
*glockenspiel
jeu de timbres (Fr.)
campanette (It.)
campanólogo (Sp.)
bell lyre
carillon (Fr.)

handbells
campanelli (It.)
sonnettes (Fr.)
Handglöckchen (G.)

clochettes pour la messe (Fr.)
altar bells
Sanctus bells
campanelli della messa (It.)
Messglöckchen (G.)
Messklingeln (G.)
Schellen (G.)
pellet bells

jingle bells
sleighbells
*bells

clog box
tap box
wood block
*Chinese (wood) block
cassettina (It.)
blochetto (It.)
bloc de bois (Fr.)
caisse Chinoise (Fr.)
Holzblock (G.)
Holzblocktrommel (G.)
caja China (Sp.)
temple blocks
Korean temple blocks

clos (Fr.)
second ending
seconda volta (It.)
chiuso (It.)

vs. first ending
ouvert (Fr.)
aperto (It.)

close (E., Fr.)
cadence
ending
Schluss (G.)
Kadenz (G.)
cadenza (It.)
cadencia (Sp.)
fine (It.)
fin (Fr.)
differentia (Lat.)

close harmony
barbershop harmony
equal voices
voci pari (It.)
voix égales (Fr.)
enge Harmonie (G.)
enge Lage (G.)
gleiche Stimmen (G.)

Aequalstimmen (G.)
voces iguales (Sp.)

close score
compact scoring

vs. open score

close shake
shake
Bebung (clavichord)
vibrato
tremolo
balancement (Fr.)
trillo (It.)
vibré (Fr.)
flatté, flaté (Fr.)

clôture (Fr.)
postlude
voluntary
Nachspiel (G.)
Postludium (Lat., G.)
postludio (It., Sp.)

club date
gig
booking
performance
job playing/singing
engagement
run
season
tour

cluster
tone cluster
pitch aggregate
aleatory
Tonballung (G.)

coach
teacher
tutor
ripetitore (It.)
maestro sostituto (It.)

Korrepetitor (G.)
répétiteur (Fr.)
repetidor (Sp.)
maestro concertador (Sp.)

cobla (Sp.)
*band
mariachi (Sp., Mex.)
ensemble
combo

cocktail lounge
night club
night spot
cabaret
locale notturno (It.)
ritrovo notturno (It.)
discothèque (Fr.)
boîte de nuit (Fr.)
Nachtlokal, Nachtklub (G.)
café-cantante (Sp.)

cocktail music
light music
dinner music
Musak
easy listening
light music
elevator music
backround music
salon music

coda
tag
cauda (Lat.)
codetta (It.)
envoi, envoy (Fr.)
epilogue
partie finale (Fr.)
Koda (G.)
Anhang (G.)
Schlussgruppe (G.)
cola (Sp.)
neupme (Lat.)
exitus (Lat.)

codetta (It.)
flag
hook
tail
crochet de la note (Fr.)
Fahne, Fähnchen (G.)
Notenfahne (G.)
Notenfähnchen (G.)
rabillo (Sp.)
gancho (Sp.)

codex (Lat., E., Fr.)
manuscript
collection of ancient music
*anthology
codice (It.)
Kodex (G.)
códice (Sp.)

Coena Domini (Lat.)
Holy Thursday
Maundy Thursday
Last Supper
eucharist
giovedi santo (It.)
jeudi saint (Fr.)
Gründonnerstag (G.)
jueves santo (Sp.)
jueves del mandato (Sp.)

cog rattle
rattle
ratchet
rain stick
crécelle (Fr.)
hochet (Fr.)
raganella (It.)
Rassel (G.)
Knarre (G.)
Ratsche (G.)
sonajero (Sp.)
maraca

cojeando (Sp.)
*syncopated
off-beat

jazzy
Scotch snap
contrattempo (It.)
contre-temps (Fr.)
alla zoppa (It.)
Synkope (G.)

col legno (It.)
use the wood of the bow
with the wood
avec le bois (Fr.)
avec le dos (Fr.)
mit der Stange (G.)
mit dem Holz (G.)
mit dem Bogen schlagen (G.)
mit der Bogenstange (G.)
con la madera (Sp.)
con la varilla (Sp.)

colascione (It.)
*lute
pandoura
colachon (Fr.)
colachón (Sp.)
Langhalslaute (G.)
theorbo
*archlute
chitarrone (It.)
oud (Arab.)

colección (Sp.)
*anthology
collection
repertoire

coll'arco (It.)
with the bow
bowed, not plucked
aves l'archet (Fr.)
mit dem Bogen (G.)
nicht Pizzikato (G.)
con el arco (Sp.)

coll'ottava (It.)
add the octave note
in octaves

con ottava (It.)
mit der Oktav (G.)
à l'octave
con la octava (Sp.)

colla parte (It.)
with the leading part
avec la partie principal (Fr.)
mit der Hauptstimme (G.)
con la parte principal (Sp.)

colla punta dell'arco (It.)
with the point or tip of the bow
*up-bow
avec le point de l'archet (Fr.)
an der Bogenspitz (G.)
con la punta (Sp.)

vs. al tallone (It.)

colla voce (It.)
follow the singer
col canto (It.)
avec la voix (Fr.)
avec le chant (Fr.)
mit der Stimme (G.)
con la voz (Sp.)

collect
prayer
litany
suffrages
oratio (Lat.)
oremus (Lat.)
orazione (It.)
colletta (It.)
collecte (Fr.)
Tagesgebet (G.)
colecta (Sp.)

collection
*anthology
collezione (It.)
colección (Sp.)
Sammlung (G.)
edition

critical edition
Denkmäler

collegium musicum (Lat.)
early music ensemble
consort
band
Renaissance band

colonne sonore (Fr.)
sound track
sound stripe
film recording
collona sonora (It.)
bande sonore (Fr.)
Tonspur (G.)
banda de sonido (Sp.)
pista sonora (Sp.)

colophony
rosin, resin (for a bow)
colofonia (It., Sp.)
colophane (Fr.)
Kolophon, Kolophonium (G.)
Geigenharz (G.)
resina (Sp.)

color
tone
tone color
timbre (E., Fr., Sp.)
timbro (It.)
character
style
sound
Tonfarbe (G.)
Klangfarbe (G.)

color, coloration
embellishment
ornamentation
florid

color (Lat.)
isorhythm (14-15 c.)
mensural notation device

talea (Lat.)
hemiola
sesquialtera (Lat.)
amiola (It.)
hémiola (Fr.)
Hemiole (G.)

color organ
clavecin oculaire (Fr.)
tastiera per luce (It.)

coloratura (It.)
embellishment
ornamentation
divisions
runs
figurations
florid
melismatic
fioritura (It.)
Blumen (G.)
fioritures (Fr.)
floreos (Sp.)
roulade (Fr.)
gorgia (It.)
glosas (Sp.)
colorature (Fr.)
broderie (Fr.)
Koloratur (G.)
adornamento (It.)
adorno (Sp.)
passaggio (It.)
passage work
diminutio (Lat.)

coloratura soprano
high and light soprano voice
soprano legg(i)ero (It.)
soprano di coloratura (It.)
soprano sfogato (It.)
soprano léger (Fr.)
Koloratursopran (G.)
tiple ligero (Sp.)
soprano ligero (Sp.)

colpo di lingua (It.)

tonguing
coup de langue (Fr.)
Zungenstoss (G.)
Zungenschlag (G.)
golpe de lengua (Sp.)

colpo di tamburo (It.)
drumbeat
paradiddle
ruff,ruffle
drag
flam
rub-a-dub
batterie (Fr.)
battement de tambour (Fr.)
Tromellschlag (G.)
redoble (Sp.)
tantarán, tantarantán (Sp.)

combination stop (organ)
piston
coupler
pre-sets
unione (It.)
copula (Lat.)
Koppel (G.)
accopplement (Fr.)
accoppiamento (It.)
acoplamiento (Sp.)

combination tone
resultant tone
difference/differential tone
summation tone
Tartini's tone
suono/tono addizionale (It.)
suono d'addizione (It.)
tono combinato (It.)
son combiné (Fr.)
son additionell (Fr.)
suono di combinazione (It.)
terzo suono (It.)
sonido de combinación (Sp.)
sonido adicional (Sp.)
Kombinationston (G.)
Summationston (G.)

acoustic bass (organ)

combo
dance band (small)
ensemble
jazz group
trio, quartet, quintet
company of musicians
consort

come prima (It.)
same
as before
repeat
reprise
simile (It.)
comme avant (Fr.)
wie vorher (G.)
como antes (Sp.)

come sopra (It.)
as above
repeat
wie oben (G.)
comme plus haut (Fr.)
como arriba (Sp.)

come sta (It.)
as written
tel quel (Fr.)
comme il est écrit (Fr.)
como está (Sp.)
nach Vorschrift (G.)

comedia musical (Sp.)
musical comedy
*musical, Broadway musical
olio
revue
operetta
light opera
comic opera
minstrel show
vaudeville
follies
variety show

showboat
masque
jigg
revista (It.)
burletta (Fr.)
Spieloper (G.)
Singspiel (G.)
zarzuela (Sp.)

comes (Lat.)
consequent
*answer
riposta (It.)
réponse (Fr.)
Antwort (G.)
respuesta (Sp.)

vs. dux (Lat.)

comic baritone
character baritone
basso buffo (It.)
basse bouffe (Fr.)
Bassbuffo (G.)
bajo bufo (Sp.)

comic opera
operetta
light opera
vaudeville
opera buffa (It.)
Singspiel (G.)
masque
komische Oper (G.)
opéra bouffe (Fr.)
opéra comique (Fr.)
opera bufa (Sp.)
musical (play)
musical comedy
revue
follies
tonadilla (Sp.)
zarzuela (Sp.)
sainete (Sp.)
Spielopera (G.)

vs. grand opera

comic role
character part
buffo (It.)
basso buffo (It.)
tenore buffo (It.)
comic baritone
bajo bufo (Sp.)
Bassobuffo (G.)
soubrette
ingenue
servetta (It.)
tiple cómico (Sp.)
basse bouffe (Fr.)
trial (Fr.)

comma (E., It., Fr.)
breathing sign
apostrophe
breath mark
respiro (It.)
signo di respirazione (It.)
virgula (It.)
virgule (Fr.)
signe de repiration (Fr.)
Atemzeichen (G.)
Atempause (G.)
Komma (G.)
coma (Sp.)
respiración (Sp.)

2. interval
microtone
quarter-tone
cent
centitone
schisma
diascisma
didymic comma
syntonic comma
Pythagorean comma
limma (Gr.)
diesis (Gr.)
comma maxima (Lat.)
Komma (G.)

coma (Sp.)

commatic (chants)
through-composed
centonization
dialogue
call-and-response

commiato (It.)
envoi, envoy (Fr.)
tornada (Prov.)
coda
tag

common chord
major triad, root position
accord parfait (Fr.)
accòrdo perfetto (It.)
accordo perfecto (Sp.)
Dreiklang (G.)

2. pivotal chord
modulating chord
interdominant
secondary dominant
Zwischendominante (G.)
acorde pivote (Sp.)

common measure
common time
ordinary time
*duple meter
*binary measure
four/four
tempo ordinario (It.)
passo ordinario (It.)
mouvement ordinaire (Fr.)
Vierertakt (G.)
Viervierteltakt (G.)
Zweiertakt (G.)
compás binario (Sp.)
movimiento ordinario (Sp.)

vs. cut time

common metal (organ)

organ metal
pipe metal
tin metal
plain metal
spotted metal

common of the mass
ordinary of the mass
ordinarium missae (Lat.)

vs. proper of the mass

common of the saints
music for Saints feasts
commune sanctorum (Lat.)
proprium sanctorum (Lat.)
proper of the Saints

common tone
pivot tone

communion (chant)
communion antiphon
confractorium (Lat.
Ambrosian)
trecanum (Lat.Gallican)
transitorium (Lat. Ambrosian)
proper of the mass

communion service
*mass
missa (Lat.)
eucharist service
Holy Communion
Lord's Supper
liturgy
love feast
agape
Abendmahl (G.)
Agende (G.)
Kirchenordnung (G.)
Kirchenamt (G.)

community chorus/choir
choral society
oratorio society

chorale
civic chorus
symphonic chorus
philharmonic choir
associazione corale (It.)
societá di coro (It.)
société chorale (Fr.)
Gesangverein (G.)
Singakademie (G.)
orfeón (Sp.)

community sing
sing-in
sing-along
hootenanny
jamboree
jam session

compact disc
CD
CD-rom
DVD
digital versatile disc
digital video disc
record
recording
phonograph record
platter
cylinder record
shellac record
vinyl record
LP
78
45
extended play
long-playing record
audio tape
cassette tape
reel-to-reel tape
wire recording
recorded music
canned music

company of musicians
consort
band

ensemble
combo
collegium musicum (Lat.)

compás (Sp.)
*bar
measure
beat
barra (Sp.)

compás compuesto (Sp.)
compound time/meter
battuta composta (It.)
divisio (14c. It.)
zusammengesetzte Takt (G.)
mesure composée (Fr.)

compás de cinco tiempos (Sp.)
5-4 time
quintuple meter/time
Cretic meter
misura a cinque tempos (It.)
quinario (It.)
mesure à cinque temps (Fr.)
Fünfertakt (G.)

compás de tres tiempo (Sp.)
triple meter
perfect time
three-quarter time
waltz time
tempus ternarium (Lat.)
tempus perfectum (Lat.)
tempo ternario (It.)
mesure ternaire (Fr.)
Dreiertakt (G.)
ungerader Takt (G.)
compás ternario (Sp.)

compass
range
tessitura (It.)
gamut (Lat.)
diapason (Fr.)
étendue (Fr.)
tessiture (Fr.)

ambitus (Lat., Fr., E.)
ambito (It., Sp.)
Umfang (G.)
Raum (G.)
Lage (G.)
Ausdehnung (G.)
estensione (It.)
extensión (Sp.)
tesitura (Sp.)

competition
contest
concorso (It.)
Wettbewerb (G.)
concours (Fr.)
concurso (Sp.)

complainte (Fr.)
*lament
lamentation
elegy
planctus (Lat.)
Klagelied (G.)
threnody
lamento (It., Sp.)
dirge

compline
night song/prayer
completorium (Lat.)
compieta (It.)
complies (Fr.)
Komplet (G.)
completas (Sp.)
office
*Divine Office
canonical hours

compose
write music
set to music
comporre (It.)
composer (Fr.)
Komponieren (G.)
componer (Sp.)

composer
writer of music
Komponist (G.)
Tonkünstler (G.)
compositore (It.)
compositeur (Fr.)
compositor (Sp.)

composition
piece (of music)
selection
set piece
number
morceau (Fr.)
pièce (Fr.)
pezzo (It.)
brano (It.)
opera (It.)
opus
obra (Sp.)
concert piece
composizione (It.)
composición (Sp.)
Komposition (G.)
Concertstück (G.)
Konzertstück (G.)
concertante (It., Sp.)
concertant (Fr.)
excerpt
work
oeuvre (Fr.)
Werk (G.)
Stück (G.)
pieza (Sp.)
trozo (Sp.)

compound interval
larger than an octave
zusammengesetzte Intervalle
(G.)

vs. simple interval

compound meter
battuta composta (It.)
mesure composée (Fr.)

divisio (14c. It.)
zusammengesetzte Takt (G.)
compás compuesto (Sp.)

vs. simple meter

compound stop (organ)
*mixture
Mixtur (G.)
fourniture (Fr.)
mistura (It.)
registro composta (It.)
Kornett (G.)
cornet (Fr.)
Scharf(f) (G.)
Cimbale (G.)
sesquialtera (Lat.)

comprimario/a (It.)
supporting role
secondary role
minor role
ruolo secondario (It.)
rôle secondaire (Fr.)
Nebenrolle (G.)
papel secundario (Sp.)

comptez (Fr.)
count time
beat time
keep time
contano (It.)
cuenten (Sp.)
zählen Sie (G.)

**compuesto de principio a fin
(Sp.)**
through-composed
progressive composition
open form
a forma aperta (It.)
de forme ouverte (Fr.)
durchkomponiert (G.)

computerized recording
*digital

compact disc (CD, CD-Rom)
DVD

vs. analog

con abandono (Sp.)
  unrestrained
  with abandon
  *free
  con abbandono (It.)
  mit Hingabe (G.)
  avec abandon (Fr.)

con affetto (It.)
  tenderly
  with feeling

con alcuna licenza (It.)
  *freely

con alegria (Sp.)
  lively
  animated
  munter (G.)
  animato (It.)

con amore (It.)
  tenderly
  ardently
  affectionately

con brio (It.)
  spirited
  with vigor

con el arco (Sp.)
  with the bow
  bowed, not plucked
  coll'arco (It.)
  avec l'archet (Fr.)
  mit dem Bogen (G.)
  nicht Pizzikato (G.)

con espressione (It.)
  with expression
  with feeling

expressif (Fr.)
gefühlvoll (G.)
espressivo (It.)
expresivo (Sp.)
mit Gefühl (G.)

con forza (It.)
  forcefully
  avec force (Fr.)
  mit Kraft (G.)
  con fuerza (Sp.)

con fuoco (It.)
  with fire
  avec feu (Fr.)
  mit Feuer (G.)
  con fuego (Sp.)

con la boca chico (Sp.)
  softly
  piano (It.)
  a fior di labbra (It.)
  au bout des lèvres (Fr.)
  gehaucht (G.)

con la madera (Sp.)
  *col legno (It.)
  with the wood of the bow
  avec le bois (Fr.)
  mit der Bogenstange (G.)
  con la varilla (Sp.)

con la punta (Sp.)
  with the tip/point of the bow
  *up-bow
  alla punta d'arco (It.)
  an der Bogenspitze (G.)
  avec le point de l'archet (Fr.)

con moto (It.)
  spirited
  *animato (It.)
  animé (Fr.)
  munter (G.)
  lebhaft (G.)
  con spirito (It.)

animado (Sp.)

con ottava (It.)
  add the octave note
  coll'ottava (It.)
  à l'octave (Fr.)
  mit der Oktav (G.)
  con la octava (Sp.)

con sordina (It., Sp.)
  with damper/mute
  avec sourdine (Fr.)
  en sourdain (Fr.)
  una corda (It.)
  une corde (Fr.)
  mit Dämpfer (G.)
  eine Saiten (G.)
  una cuerda (Sp.)

concave pedals
  radiating pedalboard
  fan-shaped pedals
  fächerörmiges Pedal (G.)

concento (It.)
  simultaneous
  non arpeggio
  Zusammenklang (G.)
  accord plaqué (Fr.)
  accordo incollato (It.)
  acorde apoyado (Sp.)
  platter Akkord (G.)
  Akkord anschlagen (G.)

vs. arpeggio (It.)

2. concord
  harmony

3. **concentus (Lat.)**
  ornate chant style

vs. accentus (Lat.)

concert (E., Fr.)
  musical performance

recital
  musicale
  rendition
  execution
  concerto (It.)
  concierto (Sp.)
  Konzert (G.)

concert artist
  recitalist
  performer
  soloist
  diva
  virtuoso
  musician
  vocalist
  instrumentalist
  concertista (It., Sp.)
  concertiste (Fr.)
  Konzertgeber (G.)
  Konzerist (G.)

concert band
  symphonic band
  brass band
  military band
  *band

concert flute
  cross flute
  *flute
  transverse flute
  Konzertflöte (G.)

concert grand
  grand piano
  baby grand
  parlor grand
  square piano
  pianoforte a coda (It.)
  piano à queue (Fr.)
  Flügel, Salonflügel (G.)
  piano de cola (Sp.)

vs. upright piano

concert hall
  recital hall
  music hall
  auditorium
  theatre
  performing arts center
  opera house
  academy of music
  symphonic hall
  philharmonic hall
  hippodrome
  sala da concerto (It.)
  salle de concert (Fr.)
  Konzertsaal (G.)
  salón de concierto (Sp.)

concert harp
  pedal harp
  chromatic harp
  Trittharfe (G.)
  Pedalharfe (G.)

vs. Irish/celtic harp

concert music
  classical music
  long-haired music
  high-brow music
  serious music
  art music
  great music
  the classics

vs. pop music
  folk music

concert pitch
  philharmonic pitch
  international pitch
  high pitch
  diapasón alto (Sp.)
  diapasón de concierto (Sp.)

2. at pitch
  true pitch
  absolute pitch

  non-transposing note

concertante (It.)
  virtuoso
  brillante (It.)

2. 18c. concerto for soli
  concerto grosso
  concertone

3. 17c. large choral, soli,
orchestral groups

concertato (It. 17c.)
  dramatic contrasts style
  concerto (It.)
  concerted
  concerté (Fr.)
  Konzertiert (G.)
  concertado (Sp.)

concertgoer(s)
  audience
  listeners
  the public
  fans

concertina
  *accordion
  bandoneon
  squeezebox
  hand harmonica
  Konzertina (G.)
  Schifferklavier (G.)

concertino (It.)
  solo group in a concerto grosso
  coro concertino (It.)
  coro principale (It.)
  coro concertato (It.)
  soli (It.)
  favoriti (It.)

vs. ripieno
  cappella (It.)
  tutti (It.)

2. short concerto
  Konzertstück (G.)

concertino (Sp.)
  *concertmaster
  chef d'attaque
  Konzertmeister (G.)

concertize
  perform
  play, sing
  make music
  harmonize
  give recitals
  conduct
  direct
  lead

concertmaster/-mistress
  assistant conductor
  section leader
  first chair
  principal violin
  violino primo (It.)
  chef d'attaque (Fr.)
  Konzertmeister (G.)
  Primgeiger (G.)
  Vorgeiger (G.)
  concertino (Sp.)

concerto (It. 17c.)
  tutti (It.)
  ripieno (It.)
  full orchestra

vs. concertino (It.)

concerto
  solo and orchestra
  Konzert (G.)
  concertone
  concierto (Sp.)

concerto da camera (It.)
  chamber concerto
  concerto grosso (It.)

concerto di chiesa (It.)
  church concerto
  concerto grosso (It.)
concerto ecclesiastici (vocal, It.)
  solo motet with organ
  concerto spirituale (It.)
  concert spirituel (Fr.)
  geistliches Konzert (G.)
  concierto spiritual (Sp.)

concerto grosso (It.)
  concerto with several soloists
  church concerto
  concerto di chiesa (It.)
  double concerto
  triple concerto
  grand concerto (Fr.)
  grosses Konzert (G.)
  Konzertierende Sinfonie (G.)
  gran concierto (Sp.)

concertstück (G.)
  concert piece
  concerto
  Konzertstück (G.)

concha del apuntador (Sp.)
  prompt box
  prompter's box
  prompt side
  stage right
  *prompter
  teleprompter
  cue cards
  buca del suggeritore (It.)
  trou de souffleur (Fr.)
  Souffleurkasten (G.)

concitato (It.)
  agitated
  agité (Fr.)
  agitado (Sp.)
  agitirt (G.)

2. stile concitato (17c. It.)

war madrigals
*program music
descriptive music
word painting
tone poem

conclusión (Sp.)
  finale (E., It.)
  concluding movement
  last movement
  mouvement final (Fr.)
  dernier mouvement (Fr.)
  Finalsatz (G.)
  Schlussstück (G.)
  Schlusssatz (G.)
  final (Sp.)
  movimiento final (Sp.)
  último movimiento (Sp.)

concord
  *consonance
  harmony
  harmonious
  concordant

vs. discord

concrete music
  musique concrète (Fr.)
  electronic music
  computer music
  musica concreta (It.)
  Konkrete Musik (G.)
  música concreta (Sp.)

condensed score
  piano score
  piano-vocal score
  short score
  close score
  conductor's part
  reduction
  lead sheet
  charts
  fake book
  partitura ridotta (It.)

partition réduite (Fr.)
Partiturauszug (G.)

vs. full score

condotta delle voci (It.)
*voice-leading
part-leading
conduite des voix (Fr.)
Stimmführung (G.)
conducción de las voces (Sp.)
dirigiendo la voz (Sp.)

conduct (vb.)
direct
lead
dirigere (It.)
diriger (Fr.)
dirigieren (G.)
dirigir (Sp.)
leiten (G.)

conductor
music director
*orchestra leader
bandleader
*choir director
choirmaster
batonist, batoneer
maestro (It.)
maestro di cappella (It.)
chef d'orchestre (Fr.)
Dirigent (G.)
Leiter (G.)
Kapellmeister (G.)
Capellmeister (G.)
direttore d'orchestra (It.)
capo d'orchestra (It.)
director de orquestre (Sp.)

conductus (Lat. 12-13c.)
medieval latin song
discant
discantus (Lat.)

confinalis (Lat., chant)

affinalis (Lat.)
finalis (Lat,)
final
*cadence
close
ending

conflicting signatures
partial signatures
key signatures
musica ficta (Lat.)

confractorium (Lat.)
communion chant (Ambrosian, Gallican, Mozarabic rites)
transitorium (Lat. Ambrosian)
fraction anthem
Proper of the mass
trecanum (Gallican)

conga (Sp.)
carnival dance
line-dance
mambo
calypso
Afro-Cuban jazz
Latin-American music
samba (Braz.)

2. hand drum(s)

congregation
audience
listeners
churchgoers
parisheners
worshippers
the faithful
followers

conjunct motion
stepwise motion
melodic
scale notes
congiunto (It.)
conjoint (Fr.)

schrittweise (G.)
conjunto (Sp.)
di grado (It.)
par degré (Fr.)
per grado (Sp.)
Stufenweise (G.)

vs. disjunct motion

conjuncta (Lat., 14c.)
musica ficta (Lat.)
falsa musica (Lat.)
chromatic notes

consecutive fifths
hidden fifths
covered fifths
horn fifths
parallel fifths
Hornquinten (G.)
Hornsatz (G.)
Ohrenquinten (G.)
verdeckte Quinten (G.)

consequent
answer
comes (Lat.)
second voice entering
imitation
consequenza (It.)
Gefährte (G.)
conseguente (It.)
réponse (Fr.)

vs. antecedent
dux (Lat.)

conservatory
music school
academy of music
lyceum
institute
conservatorio (It., Sp.)
conservatoire (Fr.)
Konservatorium (G.)
liceo (It.)

académie de musique (Fr.)
accademia musicale (It.)
Hochschule für Musik (G.)
schola cantorum (Lat.)
scuola di musica (It.)
escuela de música (Sp.)

console (organ, E., Fr.)
  consolle (It.)
  Spieltisch (G.)
  consola (Sp.)
  caja del órgano (Sp.)

console piano
  upright piano
  spinet piano
  cabinet piano
  upright grand
  cottage piano
  studio upright
  couched harp

vs. grand piano

consonant (E., Fr.)
  resolved
  at rest
  stable
  consonante (It., Sp.)
  accordant (Fr.)
  Konsonant (G.)

vs. dissonant

consonance (E., Fr.)
  consonanza (It.)
  consonne (Fr.)
  Konsonanz (G.)
  accord (Fr.)
  consonancia (Sp.)

vs. dissonance

consort
  ensemble
  band

combo
collegium musicum (Lat.)
broken consort
full consort
early music ensemble

2. chest (of viols; recorders)
  set of like instruments

consort viol
  *bass
  bass viol
  double bass
  contrabass

contano (It.)
  count time
  keep time
  beat time
  comptez (Fr.)
  cuenten (Sp.)
  zählen Sie (G.)

contemporary music
  modern music
  new music
  avant-garde
  new wave
  new age
  musica contemporanea (It.)
  musique contemporaine (Fr.)
  zeitgenössische Musik (G.)
  música contemporánea (Sp.)

continuo
  *figured bass
  thoroughbass
  basso continuo (It.)
  basso seguente (It.)
  Generalbass (G.)
  basse continue (Fr.)
  basse chifrée (Fr.)
  bajo continuo (Sp.)
  bajo cifrado (Sp.)
  basso cifrato (It.)
  bezifferter Bass (G.)

contrabass
  double bass
  *bass
  bass fiddle
  bull fiddle
  stand-up bass
  upright bass
  washtub bass
  bass viol
  contrabajo (Sp.)
  Kontrabass (G.)
  contrebasse (Fr.)
  octobasse (Fr)
  violone (It.. Fr.)

contrabass clarinet
  double clarinet
  pedal clarinet
  Kontrabassklarinette (G.)

contrabassoon
  double bassoon
  contrafagotto (It.)
  contrebasson (Fr.)
  Kontrafagott (G.)
  contrafagot (Sp.)
  fagottone (It.)

contradance
  Schottisch
  contredanse (Fr.)
  écossaise (Fr.)
  Kontertanz (G.)
  German polka
  anglaise (Fr.)
  française (Fr.)

contrafactum (Lat.)
  clausula (Lat.)
  parody
  arrangement
  adaptation
  parody mass

contralto (It., E., Sp.)
  alto

countertenor
mezzo-soprano
altista (It.)
haute-contre (Fr.)
Alt (G.)
Altistin (G.)
Altstimme (G.)
Kontraalt (G.)
altus (Lat.)

contrappunto doppio (It.)
*double counterpoint
invertible counterpoint
convertible counterpoint
double contrepoint (Fr.)
doppelter Kontrapunkt (G.)
doble contrapunto (Sp.)

contrapuntal
polyphonic
imitative
counterpoint
polyrhythmic
prick song (E. 16-17 c.)
contrappunto (It.)
contrapunctus (Lat.)
contrepoint (Fr.)
contrapunto (Sp.)
Kontrapunkt (G.)

contrary motion
opposite motion
oblique motion
inversion
motus contrarius (Lat.)
a rovescio (It.)
al rovescio (It.)
moto contrario (It.)
Gegenbewegung (G.)
mouvement contraire (Fr.)
movimiento contrario (Sp.)

vs. parallel motion

contrasoggetto (It.)
*counter-subject

second theme
contresujet (Fr.)
contrasujeto (Sp.)
Kontresubjekt (G.)
Gegensatz (G.)
Gegenthema (G.)

contrattempo (It.)
*syncopation
off-beat
jazzy
Scotch snap
contra-tempo (It.)
contre-temps (Fr.)
Kontra-tempo (G.)
contra-tempo (Sp.)
alla zoppa (It.)
boiteux (Fr.)
Synkope (G.)
syncopé (Fr.)

contratenor (Lat.)
tenor
countertenor
male alto
falsetto
contratenore (It.)
alti naturalis (It.)
haute-contre (Fr.)
Kontraalt (G.)
contralto (Sp.)

contrepoint (Fr.)
counterpoint
polyphony
contrappunto (It.)
Kontrapunkt (G.)
contrapunto (Sp.)

conversio (Lat.)
inversion (E., Fr.)
inversión (Sp.)
rivolto (It.)
rovescio (It.)
Umkehrung (G.)

convertible counterpoint
invertible counterpoint
double counterpoint
contrappunto doppio (It.)
contrepoint double (Fr.)
doppelter Kontrapunkt (G.)
doble contrapunto (Sp.)

cool jazz
jazz
bop
be-bop

vs. swing
hot jazz

coperto (It.)
muffled
muted
damped
covered
velato (It.)
couvert (Fr.)
sourd (Fr.)
bedeckt (G.)
gedämpft (G.)
cubierto (Sp.)

vs. aperto (It.)

copla (Sp.)
stanza
couplet
verse

copólogo (Sp.)
glass harmonica
harmonica
musical glasses
armonica a vetro (It.)
armonica a calici (It.)
verrillon (Fr.)
harmonica de verres Fr.)
harmonica de Franklin (G.)
Glasspiel (G.)
Harmonika (G.)

copula (Lat.)
organum section
discant
discantus (Lat.)
déchant (Fr.)
conductus (Lat.)
Diskant (G.)

cor (Fr.)
horn
French horn
corno (It.)
Horn (G.)
Waldhorn (G.)
trompa (Sp.)
valve horn
corno ventile (It.)
corno a macchina (It.)
cor-à-pistons (Fr.)
cor chromatique (Fr.)
cuerno (Sp.)
trompa de pistón (Sp.)
Ventilhorn (G.)

cor anglais (Fr.)
English horn
oboe
taille (Fr.)
oboe da caccia (It.)
tenor hautboy (E.)
corno Inglese (It.)
Englischhorn (G.)
corno, corno ingles (Sp.)

cor bugler (Fr.)
*bugle
bugle-horn
cor bugleret (Fr.)
Signalhorn (G.)
Bügelhorn (G.)

cor de basset (Fr.)
*basset horn
clarinet
alto clarinet
corno di bassetto (It.)

cor de chamois (Fr.)
Gemshorn (organ stop)
chamois horn
goathorn
recorder
gamuza (Sp.)

cor de chasse (Fr.)
hunting horn
French horn
natural horn
corno da caccia (It.)
trompe de chasse (Fr.)
cor à main (Fr.)
Jagdhorn (G.)
Waldhorn (G.)
Naturhorn (G.)
trompa de caza (Sp.)
cuerno de caza (Sp.)

cor de nuit (Fr.)
Nachthorn (G.)
soft horn stop (organ)

cor de signal (Fr.)
signal horn
bugle-horn
*bugle
Signalhorn (G.)

cor des Alpes (Fr.)
*Alphorn
corno delle Alpi (It.)
corno alpino (Sp.)
straight trumpet
tuba (Lat.)

corale (It.)
choral
chorus
chorale
choral ensemble
Chor (G.)
Choral (G.)
Gesangverein (G.)
coral (Sp.)

corant(o) (E.)
*courante (Fr., E., G.)
corrente (It.)
corranda (Sp.)
corriente (Sp.)
sarabande

corbeille (Fr.)
dress circle
*balcony
mezzanine
prima galleria (It.)
premier balcon (Fr.)
erster Rang (G.)
balcón (Sp.)

corchea (Sp.)
eighth note
quaver
croche (Fr.)
croma (It.)
Achtel (G.)

corchete (Sp.)
brace
bracket
graffa, grappa (It.)
accolade (E., Fr.)
Akkolade (G.)
Klammer (G.)
staves

corda (It.)
string
wire
corde (Fr.)
Saite (G.)
cuerda (Sp.)

corda d'acciaio (It.)
steel string
metal string
corde d'acier (Fr.)
corde métallique (Fr.)
Stahlsaite (G.)
cuerda de alambre (Sp.)

cuerda métalica (Sp.)

corda doppia (It.)
double-stop
double corde (Fr.)
Doppelgriff (G.)
dobla cuerda (Sp.)

corda simpatica (It.)
sympathetic string(s)
aliquot string
corda di risonanzia (It.)
corde sympathetique (Fr.)
corde de résonance (Fr.)
Resonanzsaite (G.)
cuerda de resonancia (Sp.)
cuerda simpático (Sp.)

corda vuota (It.)
open string
open note
open tone
corde à vide (Fr.)
corde à jour (Fr.)
leere Saite (G.)
offene Saite (G.)
cuerda al aire (Sp.)

cordatura (It.)
tuning
accordatura (It.)
l'accord (Fr.)
Stimmung (G.)
acorde (Sp.)

corde vocali (It.)
vocal cords
vocal folds
voice-box
cordes vocales (Fr.)
Stimmbänder (G.)
cuerdas vocales (Sp.)

Corelli clash
*cadence
dissonance

cori spezzati (It.)
double chorus
*antiphonal choirs
divided choir
polychoral
Doppelchor (G.)

corista (It., Sp.)
chorister
*choirboy
choral/choir singer
choriste (Fr.)
Chorist, Choristin (G.)

2. *tuning fork
pitch-pipe
fourchette tonique (Fr.)
Stimmgabel (G.)

corista di camera (It.)
chamber pitch
ton de chambre (Fr.)
Kammerton (G.)
tonalidad de cámera (Sp.)

corista di coro (It.)
choir pitch
church pitch
organ pitch
tuono chorista (It.)
ton de choeur (Fr.)
ton de chapelle (Fr.)
Kapellton (G.)
Chorton (G.)

cork opera
minstrel show
vaudeville
variety show
revue
follies
entertainment

cormorne (Fr.)
crumhorn
Krummhorn (G.)

storto (It.)
piva torta (It.)
cromorne (Fr.)
orlo (Sp.)
tournebout (Fr.)
cornamuto torto (It.)
cornamuda tuerta (Sp.)

cornemuse (Fr.)
*bagpipe
cornamusa (It.)
musette (Fr.)
gaita (Sp.)
Dudelsack (G.)
Sackpfeife (G.)

cornet (E., Fr.)
trumpet
bugle
cornopean
cornetta (It.)
cornetin (Sp.)
corneta (Sp.)
cornetta a pistoni (It.)
cornet-à-pistons (Fr.)
Kornett (G.)
Ventilkornett (G.)

2. reed stop on organ
cornetino

cornet (Fr.)
compound organ stop
*mixture
overtones
Aliquostimmen (G.)
fourniture (Fr.)
Scharff (G.)
Cimbale (G.)
sesquialtera (Lat.)

cornett
Zink (G.)
cornet à bouquin (Fr.)
cornetto (It.)
cromorne (Fr.)

corneta (Sp.)
lyzarden (early E.)
lituus (Lat.)

corno (It., Sp.)
horn
French horn
natural horn
hunting horn
cor (Fr.)
Horn (G.)
Waldhorn (G.)
cuerno (Sp.)

corno Alpino (Sp.)
straight trumpet
*Alphorn
cor des Alpes (Fr.)
corno delle Alpi (It.)

corno da caccia (It.)
hunting horn
French horn
natural horn
hand horn
cor de chasse (Fr.)
cor à main (Fr.)
trompe de chasse (Fr.)
Jagdhorn (G.)
Waldhorn (G.)
Handhorn (G.)
Naturhorn (G.)
cuerno de caza (Sp.)
trompa de caza (Sp.)

corno di bassetto (It.)
*basset horn
clarinet
cor de basset (Fr.)
Bassetthorn (G.)
clarinete alto (Sp.)

corno inglese (It.)
English horn
cor anglais (Fr.)
Englisch(es) Horn (G.)

oboe da caccia (It.)
oboe d'amore (It.)
corno, corno inglés (Sp.)
alto oboe

coro (It., Sp.)
chorus
choir
choeur (Fr.)
Chor (G.)

2. *course (of strings)

coro concertato (It. 17c.)
ensemble
soli (It.)
*favoriti (It.)
concertina (It.)
coro concertino (It.)
semi-chorus

vs. cappella (It.)
coro ripieno (It.)

coro de niños (Sp.)
children's choir
treble choir
cherub choir
equal voices
coro di fanciulli (It.)
choeur d'enfants (Fr.)
Kinderchor (G.)
coro infantil (Sp.)
escolanía (Sp.)

coro misto (It.)
mixed chorus
choeur mixte (Fr.)
choeur à voix mixtes (Fr.)
gemischter Chor (G.)
gemischte Stimmen (G.)

coro ripieno (It.)
cappella (It.)
ripieno (It.)
full chorus

tutti (It.)
grand-choeur (Fr.)
coro pieno (It.)
grosser Chor (G.)

vs. coro concertino (It.)
favoriti (It.)

coro spezzato (It.)
antiphonal choirs
coro battente (It.)
split choir
double chorus
polychoral
double choeur (Fr.)

corona (It.)
*fermata (It., Sp.)
hold
point d'orgue (Fr.)
punto d'organo (It.)
punto coronato (It.)
punto de organo (Sp.)
couronne (Fr.)
Fermate (G.)
Krone (G.)
Orgelpunkt (G.)

coronach
*lament (Scottish)
dirge
elegy
funeral
requiem
apotheosis
plaint
threnody
planctus (Lat.)
lamento (It.)
tombeau (Fr.)
Klage (G.)

corps de rechange (Fr.)
crook (brass instr.)
shank
extension

tuning slide
pezzo di reserva (It.)
corpo di ricambio (It.)
ritorto (It.)
Stimmbogen (G.)
Tonbogen (G.)
Aufsatzbogen (G.)
tonillo (Sp.)
cuerpo de recambio (Sp.)

corpus (Lat.)
collection
*anthology
repertoire
repertory
sampling
edition

corredera (Sp.)
slide (of a trombone)
tiro (It.)
pompa (It.)
coulisse (Fr.)
Kulisse (G.)
Scheide (G.)
Stimmzug (G.)
bomba (Sp.)

corrente (It.)
courante (Fr., E., G.)
coranto (It.)
corranda (Sp.)
corriente (Sp.)
sarabande

corte (Sp.)
cut
delete
taglio (It.)
Schnitt (G.)
Einschnitt (G.)
incise (Fr.)
coupure (Fr.)
inciso (It., Sp.)
vide, vi---de (Lat.)

cortina musical (Sp.)
theme song
signature song
Leitmotiv (G.)
idée fixe (Fr.)

cotillion
cotillon (Fr.)
quadrille (Fr.)
Kotillon (G.)
square dance
dance

cottage organ
portable organ
parlor organ
reed organ
portative organ
portatif

cottage piano
upright
spinet
console piano
studio piano
pianette
pianino (It.)
piano droit (Fr.)
couched harp

coulé (Fr.)
*appoggiatura
Nachschlag (G.)
ornament
grace note
backfall
apoyatura (Sp.)

2. slide (ornament)
   coulade (Fr.)
   fusée (Fr.)
   Schleifer (G.)

2. slurred
   * legato (It.)
   Schleifer (G.)

ligado (Sp.)

coulée (Fr.)
notes inégales (Fr.)
unequal eighth-notes
pointé (Fr.)
puntato (It.)
puntado (Sp.)
Punktiert (G.)

vs. coups égaux (Fr.)

couler (Fr.)
slur
lourer (Fr.)
binden (G.)
legato (It.)

2. slide
   scoop
   glissando (It.)
   portamento (It.)
   Schleifen (G.)

3. notes inégales (Fr.)
   unequal eighth-notes

couler les tierces (Fr.)
fill in the third
passing notes
non-harmonic tones
Nachschlag (G.)

coulisse (Fr.)
slide of trombone
Zug (G.)
tiro (It.)
vara (Sp.)

count
a *beat
a pulse
metrical unit
tactus (Lat.)
battuta (It.)
temps (Fr.)

Takt (G.)
tiempo (Sp.)

count
keep time
beat time
conduct
contano (It.)
comptez (Fr.)
zählen Sie (G.)
cuenten (Sp.)

countermelody
descant
countersubject
double fugue

counterpoint
polyphony
polyrhythm
contrapuntal
imitation
contrappunto (It.)
contrapunctus (Lat.)
contrepoint (Fr.)
Kontrapunkt (G.)
contrapunto (Sp.)

countersubject
countermelody
fugue
imitation
contrasoggetto (It.)
contre-sujet (Fr.)
Kontrasubjekt (G.)
Gegensatz (G.)
Gegenthema (G.)
contrasujeto (Sp.)

countertenor
male alto
contratenor (Lat.)
haute-contre (Fr.)
alti naturali (It.)
Männeraltist (G.)
Kontraalt (G.)

Alt'Stimme (G.)

countertenor clef
alto clef
C clef

country cries
street cries
madrigal
London street cries
cries of London
cris de Paris (Fr.)
cris de la rue (Fr.)
musique de la rue (Fr.)

country music
mountain music
folk music
old-time music
bluegrass music
hillbilly music
western music
cowboy music
ethnic folk music

coup de glotte (Fr.)
glottal stop
glottal attack
glottal catch
glottale (It.)
occlusiva glottale (It.)
Glottisschlag (G.)
Kehlschlag (G.)
Kehlverschlusslaut (G.)
Knacklaut (G.)
Stimmritzenverschlusslaut (G.)

coup de langue (Fr.)
tonguing
colpo di lingua (It.)
Zungenschlag (G.)
Zungenstoss (G.)
golpe de lengua (Sp.)
articulation

coupé (Fr.)

cut-off (conducting)
Abschlag (G.)
taglio (It.)

coupler
piston
combination
unione (It.)
accoppiamento (It.)
accouplement (Fr.)
copula (Lat.)
Koppel (G.)
Koppelung (G.)
acoplamiento (Sp.)

couplet (Fr.)
episode in a rondo
transition
bridge passage

2. pair of lines of poetry
distich
verse
strophe
couplet
strofa (It.)
Strophe (G.)
copla (Sp.)

3. solo verses in operetta
stanza of humorous song
copla (Sp.)

4. duplet
two eighth-notes in the time of
three eighths
duolet (Fr.)
duina (It.)
Duole (G.)
dosillo (Dp.)

coupure (Fr.)
*cut
deletion
taglio (It.)
Schnitt (G.)

corte (Sp.)

courante (Fr., E., G.)
baroque dance
corrente (It.)
corant(o) (E.)
corranda (Sp.)
corriete (Sp.)
sarabande
rant
jig

couronne (Fr.)
*fermata (It.)
hold
corona (It.)
punto d'organo (It.)
point d'orgue (Fr.)
Krone (G.)
Orgelpunkt (G.)
punto coronato (It.)
punto de organo (Sp.)
calderón (Sp.)
Fermate (G.)

course (string instr.)
set of 1-3 strings at unison or
octave pitch on lute, guitar,
mandolin, etc.
coro (It., Sp.)
cours (Fr.)
choeur (Fr.)
jeu (Fr.)
ordre (Fr.)
Chor (G.)
Saitenchor (G.)
orden (Sp.)
double course
triple course (piano)
octave course
12-string guitar

courtaut, courtaud
*curtal
bassoon
Kortholt (G.)

sordone (It.)
sourdine (Fr.)
Sordun (G.)
basson (Fr.)
Dulzian (G.)
dolzaine (Fr.)
fagotto (It.)
bajón (Sp.)

couvert (Fr.)
covered
muted
damped
coperto (It.)
velato (It.)
bedeckt (G.)
cubierto (Sp.)
sourd (Fr.)
gedämpft (G.)

vs. ouvert (Fr.)

covered fifths, octaves
hidden fifths
consecutive fifths
parallel fifths
horn fifths
Hornquinten (G.)
Hornsatz (G.)
Ohrenquinten (G.)
verdeckte Quinten (G.)

cowbell(s)
campanaccio (It.)
squilla (It.)
cloches de vache (Fr.)
sonnaille (Fr.)
Alpenglocken (G.)
Kuhglocken (G.)
Kuhschelle (G.)
cencerros (Sp.)

crab canon
*canon
retrograde canon
mirror canon

canon by inversion
canon cancrizans (Lat.)
recte et retro (Lat.)
canone retrogrado (It.)
al rovescio (It.)
à l'écrevisse (Fr.)
canon rétrograde (Fr.)
Spiegelkanon (G.)
Krebsgang (G.)
Krebskanon (G.)
canon cancrizante (Sp.)
canon retrogrado (Sp.)

crackle
*arpeggiando (It.)
broken chords
battery
batterie (Fr.)
en batterie (Fr.)
battimento (It.)
Brechung (G.)
Rauscher (G.)
Schwärmer (G.)

cracovienne (E., Fr.)
polka
krakowiak (E., It.)
cracoviana (It., Sp.)
cracoviac (Fr.)
krakauer Tanz (G.)
Krakowiak (G.)

cradle song
lullaby
slumber song
serenade
berceuse (Fr.)
dodinette, dodo, dodino (Fr.)
Wiegenlied (G.)
Ständchen (G.)
Schlummerlied (G.)
ninnerella (It.)
ninna nanna (It.)
canción de cuna (Sp.)
nana (Sp.)
arrullo (Sp.)

crash cymbals
  cymbals
  piatti (It.)
  cinelli (It.)
  cymbales (Fr.)
  Becken (G.)
  platillos (Sp.)
  cimbalos (Sp.)

crécelle (Fr.)
  rattle
  raganella (It.)
  hochet (Fr.)
  Rassel (G.)
  Ratsche (G.)
  Knarre (G.)
  Schnarre (G.)
  sonajero (Sp.)
  carraca (Sp.)
  matraca (Sp.)
  maraca
  Gefässrassel (G.)
  Kürbisrassel (G.)
  rainstick

credo (Lat.)
  creed
  Ordinary of the mass
  Nicene creed (said at mass:
  Credo in unum Deo)
  Apostle's creed (Credo in
  Deum patrem)
  Patrem omnipotentem (Lat.)
  Athanasian creed (Quicumque
  vult)
  Symbolum apostolicum
  (Mozarabic)

crembalum (Lat.)
  cymbalum orale (Lat.)
  *Jew's harp
  Jew's trump
  scacciapensieri (It.)
  guimbarde (Fr.)
  Maultrommel (G.)
  birimbao (Sp.)

crescendo (It.)
  getting louder
  en augmentant (Fr.)
  anschwellen(d) (G.)
  zunehmen(d) (G.)
  Zunahme (G.)
  Wachsen(d) (G.)
  creciendo (Sp.)

vs. diminuendo (It.)

crescendo pedal (organ)
  swell pedal
  crescendo rotativo (It.)
  rouleau crescendo (Fr.)
  Crescendowalze (G.)
  Walze (G.)
  Kollektivschweller (G.)
  Crescendozug (G.)
  Rollschweller (G.)
  Registerrad, -walze (G.)
  rodillo del crescendo (Sp.)

Cretic meter
  5-4 time
  quintuple meter/time
  misura a cinque tempi (It.)
  quinario (It.)
  mesure à cinq temps (Fr.)
  Fünfertakt (G.)
  compás de cinco tiempos (Sp.)

cri d'oiseau (Fr.)
  bird-call (organ)
  richiamo per ucelli (It.)
  appeau (Fr.)
  Vogelsang, Vogelgesang (G.)
  Vogelpfeife (G.)
  reclamo (Sp.)

crini (It.)
  hair(s) of a bow
  crins (Fr.)
  Bogenhaare (G.)
  crines (Sp.)
  cuerdas del arco (Sp.)

cries of London
  madrigal
  London street cries
  country cries
  cris de Paris (Fr.)
  cris de la rue (Fr.)
  musique de la rue (Fr.)

croche (Fr.)
  *eighth-note
  quaver
  croma (It.)
  ottavo (It.)
  Achtel (G.)
  corchea (Sp.)

crochet de la note (Fr.)
  flag
  hook
  tail
  codetta (It.)
  Fahne, Fähnchen (G.)
  Notenfahne (G.)
  rabillo (Sp.)
  gancho (Sp.)

cromatico (It., Sp.)
  *chromatic
  half-steps
  sharps and flats
  hemitonic
  chromatique (Fr.)
  semitonique (Fr.)
  chromatisch (G.)

vs. diatonico (It.)

cromorno (It., Sp.)
  *crumhorn
  lituus (Lat.)
  Krummhorn (G.)
  cromorne (Fr.)
  *oboe

crook
  shank

extension
pezzo di reserva (It.)
corpo di ricambio (It.)
corps de rechange (Fr.)
Stimmbogen (G.)
Tonbogen (G.)
Aufsatzbogen (G.)
tonillo (Sp.)
ritorto (It.)
cuerpo de recambio (Sp.)

croon, crooning
sing slow pop song
song style
ballad style

crooner
*singer
vocalist
songster
song stylist
artiste
songbird
chanteuse
canary

cross-bar
beam
hook
flag
ligatura (It.)
tratto d'unione (It.)
stanghetta (It.)
barre de liaison (Fr.)
barre horizontale (Fr.)
barre transversale (Fr.)
Querbalken (G.)
Balkenverbindung (G.)
Notenbalken (G.)
barra de compás (Sp.)
travesaño (Sp.)

cross flute
transverse flute
concert flute
German flute

*flute
Querflöte (G.)
Kreuzflöte (G.)
flauto traverso (It.)
flûte traversière (Fr.)
flûte allemande (Fr.)
flûte à six trous (Fr.)
flauta traversa (Sp.)
flauta alemana (Sp.)

vs. recorder

cross-relation
false relation
clash
discord
dissonance
falsa relazione (It.)
Querstand (G.)
fausse relation (Fr.)
falsa relación (Sp.)

cross rhythm
polyrhythm
counterpoint
Gegenrhythmus (G.)

crossing (of parts, voices, hands)
incrosciemento (It.)
croisement (Fr.)
Kreuzung (G.)
Übergreifen (G.)
cruzamiento (Sp.)

crossover
fusion
third stream
jazz blended with rock or classical

crotales (Fr.)
antique cymbals
cymbales antiques (Fr.)
finger cymbals
cimbalini (It.)

cimbaletto (It.)
cimbali antichi (It.)
Fingercymbeln (G.)
kleine Tanzbecken (G.)
cimbalillos digitales (Sp.)

crotalum, crotala (Lat.)
crotali (It.)
crotales (Fr., E.)
crotales antiques (Fr.)
Krotalon (G., Gr.)
crótalo (Sp.)
castagnettes (Fr.)
clappers
castanets

crotchet
quarter-note
nera (It,)
quarto (It.)
semiminima (It.)
noire (Fr.)
Viertel (G.)
schwarze Note (G.)
negra (Sp.)
semínima (Sp.)

crotta (It.)
crwth, crowd
lyre (Welsh)
bowed harp
chrotta, **crouth (Fr.)**
Chrotta (G.)
Rotta, Rotte (G.)
rota (Sp.)

crowd (in a Passion)
the multitude, mob
turba (Lat.)
synagoga (Lat.)

crowned song
prize song
contest song
cantus coronatus (Lat.)
chanson couronée (Fr.)

puy (Fr.)
Trouvère song
gekröntes Lied (G.)
Preislied (G.)
Meistersinger

Crucifixion
cantata
oratorio
Passion
Seven last words of Christ

crumhorn
oboe
double-reed
cromorno (It., Sp.)
cromorne (Fr.)
Krummhorn (G.)
tournebout (Fr.)
storto (It.)
piva torto (It.)
orlo (Sp.)
lituus (Lat., post-classical)

crushed note
*acciaccatura (It.)
grace note
ornament

crusis (Lat.)
*downbeat
thesis
accent
strong beat
abbattimento (It.)
frappé (Fr.)
Abschlag (G.)

vs. anacrusis (Lat.)

csardas, *czardas
Hungarian dance
gypsy dance

cuadrada (Sp.)
breve (It., Fr., E., Sp.)

whole note
double whole note
brevis (Lat.)
Doppelganze (G.)
carrée (Fr.)
quarrée (Fr.)

cuadrilla (Sp.)
quadrille (E., Fr.)
square dance
galop
polka
cancan
quadriglia (It.)
Quadrille (G.)

cuarta (Sp.)
fourth (interval)
Quarta (It.)
quarte (Fr.)
Quart(e) (G.)
diatesseron (Gr.)

cuarteto con piano (Sp.)
piano quartet
quartetto con pianoforte (It.)
quatuor avec piano (Fr.)
Klavierquartett (G.)

cuarteto de cuerdas (Sp.)
string quartet
quartetto d'archi (It.)
quatuor à cordes (Fr.)
Streichquartett (G.)

cuarto de tono (Sp.)
quarter-tone
demi-semitone
quarto di tono (It.)
quart de ton (Fr.)
Viertelton (G.)
microtone

cuatrillo (Sp.)
quadruplet
quartina (It.)

quartolet (Fr.)
Quartole (G.)

cubierto (Sp.)
covered
muted
*coperto (It.)
couvert (Fr.)
bedeckt (G.)

cue, cue cards
*prompt, prompter
teleprompter
prompt box
prompt side
stage right wings

cue, cue notes
signal to play or speak
small notes of other parts
direction
rubric
lead-in
notina (It.)
petite note (Fr.)
Stichnoten (G.)
guías (Sp.)

2. *custos (Lat.)
guide
direct
index
tractulus (Lat.)

cuenten (Sp.)
count time
beat time
contano (It.)
comptez (Fr.)
zählen

cuerda (Sp.)
string
wire
corda (It.)
corde (Fr.)

Saite (G.)

cuerda al aire (Sp.)
*open string
unstopped
open note
corda vuota (It.)
corde à jour (Fr.)
offene Saite (G.)

cuerda de alambre (Sp.)
steel string
metal string
corda d'acciaio (It.)
corde d'acier (Fr.)
corde métallique (Fr.)
Stahlsaite (G.)
cuerda metálica (Sp.)

cuerda de resonancia (Sp.)
sympathetic string
aliquot string
corda simpatico (It.)
corda di risonanza (It.)
corde sympathique (Fr.)
corde de résonance (Fr.)
Resonanzsaite (G.)
cuerda simpático (Sp.)

cuerdas vocales (Sp.)
vocal cords
vocal folds
voice-box
corde vocali (It.)
cordes vocales (Fr.)
Stimmbänder (G.)

cuerno, cuerna (Sp.)
horn
French horn
cor (Fr.)
corno (It.)
Horn (G.)

cuerno alpino (Sp.)
*Alphorn (G., E.)

cor des Alpes (Fr.)

cuerno de caza (Sp.)
horn
natural horn
French horn
hand horn
hunting horn
corno da caccia (It.)
cor de chasse (Fr.)
cor à main (Fr.)
trompe de chasse (Fr.)
Jagdhorn (G.)
Naturhorn (G.)
Waldhorn (G.)
Handhorn (G.)
trompa de caza (Sp.)

cuerpo de recambio (Sp.)
shank (brass instr.)
crook
extension
tuning slide
ritorto (It.)
corpo di ricambio (It.)
corps de rechange (Fr.)
Aufsatzbogen (G.)
Tonbogen (G.)
Stimmbogen (G.)
tonillo (Sp.)

cup (brass instr.)
mouthpiece
Kessel (G.)
Mundstück (G.)
embouchure (Fr.)
imboccatura (It.)
embocadura (Sp.)

curtain
drop
backdrop
traveler
scrim
cyclorama
sipario (It.)

siparietto (It.)
telone (It.)
rideau (Fr.)
Vorhang (G.)
Bühnenvorhang (G.)
telón (Sp.)

curtain call
bows
applause
claque (Fr.)

curtain music
scene-change music
traveling music
intermezzo (It.)
interludio (It.)
interludium (Lat.)
interlude
act-tune
curtain tune
entr'acte (Fr.)
entreacto (Sp.)
intermède (Fr.)
intermedio (Sp.)
Zwischenaktmusik (G.)
Zwischenspiel (G.)

curtain raiser
curtain warmer
intermedium (Lat.)
opening act

curtal (E.)
bassoon
fagotto (It.)
basson (Fr.)
fagot (Fr.)
douçaine (Fr.)
Dulzian (G.)
Fagott (G.)
bajón (Sp.)
fagot(e) (Sp.)
chirimia (Sp.)
Kortholt (G.)
Kurzholz (G.)

Kurzpfeife (G.)
courtaut (E.)
sordone (It.)
sourdine (Fr.)
Sordun (G.)
dolzaine (Fr.)
dolzaina (It.)
dulzaina (Sp.)
dulceuse (E.16c.)

custos (Lat., E.)
a guide (plainsong)
a direct
cue note
index
guida (It.)
mostra (It., Sp.)
guidon (Fr.)
Kustos (G.)
tractulus (Lat.)

cut
delete
strike out
deletion
abridgement
taglio (It.)
inciso (It., Sp.)
coupure (Fr.)
incise (Fr.)
Schnitt (G.)
Einschnitt (G.)
corte (Sp.)
vide, vi---de (Lat.)

2. band (on a disk)
track
channel
pista (It., Sp.)
traccia (It.)
piste (Fr.)
Spur, Tonspur (G.)

cut-off (conducting)
taglio (It.)
Abschlag (G.)

coupé (Fr.)
gesto de cortar (Sp.)

cut time
alla breve (It.)
half-note is a beat
double time
quick time
twice as fast
march time
duple meter
c-barred
c-barré (Fr.)
à la blanche (Fr.)
double mouvement (Fr.)
a cappella (It.)
doppio movimento (It.)
tagliato (It.)
in halben Noten (G.)
doppelte Bewegung (G.)
doble movimiento (Sp.)
a la breve (Sp.)

vs. common time/meter

cycle
vibration
* frequency
hertz
sound wave
pitch

2. series of songs, etc.
song cycle
suite
set
group
Mass
madrigal comedy
idée fixe (Fr.)
Leitmotiv (G.)
*Liederkreis (G.)
motto cycle

cycle de lieder (Fr.)
song cycle

song suite
ciclo di canzoni (It.)
cycle de mélodies (Fr.)
Liederkreis (G.)
Liederzyklus (G.)
ciclo de canciones (Sp.)

cycle des quintes (Fr.)
circle of fifths
circolo delle quinte (It.)
Quintenzirkel (G.)
ciclo de las quintas (Sp.)

cylinder (recording)
recording
record
phonograph record
gramophone record
platter
disc
Schallplatte (G.)
disque (Fr.)
disco (It., Sp.)

cylindre (Fr.)
piston (E., Fr.)
valve
pistone (It.)
Ventil (G.)
Pumpventil (G.)
pistón (Sp.)
valvula de pistón (Sp.)

2. piano-roll
player-piano roll
cilindro (It., Sp.)
rouleau (Fr.)
Walze (G.)
rollo (Sp.)

cymbal (organ)
*mixture
compound stop
cimbalo (It., Sp.)
cymbale (Fr.)

cymbales antiques (Fr.)
  *antique cymbals
  crotalum, crotala (Lat.)
  crotales (Fr.)
  crotali (It.)
  Krotalon (G.)
  cimbalini (It.)
  castanets
  clappers
  bones
  spoons

cymbales choquées (Fr.)
  choke cymbals
  hi-hat, high-hat
  sock cymbals
  Charleston (It.)
  hi-hat pédal (Fr.)
  Charlestonmaschine (G.)
  pedal del bombo de jazz (Sp.)

cymbales sur tiges (Fr.)
  sizzle cymbals
  rivet cymbales
  piatti chiodati (It.)
  Sizzle-Becken (G.)
  Nietenbecken (G.)
  Zischbecken (G.)
  cimbales sobre palillos (Sp.)

cymbals
  crash cymbals
  piatti (It.)
  *crotalum (Lat., G.)
  crotales (Fr.)
  cinelli (It.)
  cembali (It.)
  cymbales (Fr.)
  Becken (G.)
  Schallbecken (G.)
  cimbalos (Sp.)
  platillos (Sp.)
  acetabulum (Lat.)
  hi-hat
  high-hat
  choke cymbals

ride cymbals
sizzle cymbals

cymbalum (Lat.)
  small bells
  *bells
  pellet bells
  jingle bells
  harness bells
  altar bells
  nolae (Lat.)
  tintinnabula (Lat.)
  campanae (Lat.)

cymbalum orale (Lat.)
  crembalum (Lat.)
  *Jew's harp
  spassapensieri (It.)
  guimbarde (Fr.)
  Judenharfe (G.)
  birimbao (Sp.)

Cymbelstern (organ, G.)
  tinkling bells
  Zimbelstern (G.)
  Cimbelstern (G.)
  tintinnabulum (Lat., G.)
  tintinnabolo (It.)
  horologium (Lat.)
  cascabeles (Sp.)

cythara Lat.)
  Kithara (Gr.)
  *cithara (Lat.)
  lyra, lyre
  psaltery

czardas, csardas
  Hungarian dance
  danza Ungharesa (It.)
  danse Hongroise (Fr.)
  Ungarischer Volktanz (G.)
  danza Hungara (Sp.)

D

d'accord (Fr.)
in tune
accordando It.)
in tono (It.)
intonato (It.)
essere intonato (It.)
rein singen/spielen (G.)
templado (Sp.)
armoniosamente (Sp.)

da capo (It.)
from the beginning
from the top
D.C.
ab initio (Lat.)
dal principio (It.)
au début (Fr.)
vom Anfang (G.)
von Vorn (G.)
desde el principio (Sp.)
reprise
recapitulation

da capo aria
ABA form
song form
ternary form
tripartite form
three-part form
arch form

daily hours/office
office
*Divine Office
monastic office
opus Dei (Lat.)
day hours
hours of prayer
morning/evening prayer
breviary

antiphonary

dal segno (It.)
from the sign
du signe (Fr.)
vom Zeichen (G.)
desde el signo (Sp.)

dal segno al fine (It.)
from the sign to the end
du signe à la fin (Fr.)
vom Zeichen bis zum Schluss
(G.)
desde el signo hasta el fin (Sp.)

damenization
*solmization
solfa
solfeggio (It.)
bebization
bobization
jamization

damper
mute
sordino (It.)
smorzo (It.)
sourdine (Fr.)
étouffoir (Fr.)
Dämpfer (G.)
sordina (Sp.)
apagador (Sp.)
sotto voce (It.)
soft pedal (piano)
una corda (It.)
une corde (Fr.)
eine Saite (G.)
una cuerda (Sp.)
buff stop (harpsichord)
lute stop (harpsichord)

damper pedal
loud pedal
right pedal
sustaining pedal
sostenuto pedal

pedale destra (It.)
pedale del forte (It.)
pedale di risonanza (It.)
pédale droite (Fr.)
pédale forte (Fr.)
pédale grande (Fr.)
pédale de résonance (Fr.)
*prolongement (Fr.)
Gross-Pedal (G.)
rechte Pedal (G.)
Dämpfer Pedal (G.)
Sustain-Pedal (G.)
Haltepedal (G.)
Tonhaltungspedal (G.)
Fortepedal (G.)
pedal fuerte (Sp.)
pedal de resonancia (Sp.)

Dämpfer weg/ab (G.)
mute(s) off
*remove mutes
senza sordini (It.)
sans sourdine(s) (Fr.)
alle Saiten (G.)
Dämpfer abheben/
abnehmen/absetzen (G.)
*ohne Dämpfer (G.)
toutes les cordes (Fr.)
tutti corde (It.)
todas las cuerdas (Sp.)
sin sordina (Sp.)

Dampforgel (G.)
calliope
steam organ/piano
orgue à vapeur (Fr.)
órgano de vapor (Sp.)

dance (n.)
ball
ballet
danse (Fr.)
ballo (It.)
bal (Fr.)
danza (It., Sp.)
Ball (G.)

Tanz (G.)
baile (Sp.)

folk dance
line dance
round dance
square dance
contradance
country dance
reel
cotillion
masquerade ball
social dance

dance (vb.)
cut a rug
danzare (It.)
ballare (It.)
danser (Fr.)
tanzen (G.)
danzar (Sp.)
ballar (Sp.)

dance band
big band
swing band
combo
jazz band
cobla (Sp.)

dance club
*night club
discotheque
dance hall
dance palace
ballroom
cabaret

dans les coulisses (Fr.)
in the wings
behind the scenes
*backstage
fra le quinte (It.)
Hinterbühne (G.)
entre bastidores (Sp.)

danse hongroise (Fr.)
*czardas
csardas
danza ungharesa (It.)
danza hungara (Sp.)
ungarischer Volktanz (G.)

danza en redondo (Sp.)
round dance
ring dance
girotondo (It.)
danza in tondo (It.)
ronde (Fr.)
Reigen (G.)
ronda (Sp.)

danza tedesca (It.)
waltz
Ländler (G.)
allemande (Fr.)
deutscher Tanz (G.)

Darmsaite (G.)
gut string
catgut string
budello (It.)
boyau (Fr.)
minugia (It.)

Daseian notation
Boethian notation
Greek letter notation (9-10c.)
letter notation
Odoistic notation
Oddonic notation
Guidonian Hand
manus musicalus (Lat.)
manus Guidonis (Lat.)

dasselbe Zeitmass (G.)
*a tempo (It.)
l'istesso tempo (It.)
tempo primo (It.)
premier mouvement (Fr.)
même mouvemrnt (Fr.)
erstes Tempo/Zeitmass (G.)

movimiento anterior (Sp.)
primero tiempo (Sp.)
primero movimiento (Sp.)
first tempo
same tempo
back to the original tempo

dauernd Bewegung (G.)
perpetual motion
perpetuum mobile (Lat.)
moto perpetuo (It.)
mouvement perpétuel (Fr.)
fortwährende Bewegung (G.)
movimiento perpetuo (Sp.)
movimiento continuo (Sp.)

Daumenaufsatz (G.)
thumb position (on 'cello)
capotasto (It.)
démanché, démanchement (Fr.)
position du pouce (Fr.)
posición del pulgar (Sp.)

David's harp
harpe de David (Fr.)
Davidsharfe (G.)
Irish harp
Gaelic harp

vs. pedal harp

dawn song
matin song
mattinata (It.)
aubade (Fr.)
Morgenständchen (G.)
alborada (Sp.)

vs. serenade (evening)

de côté (Fr.)
*aside
in disparte (It.)
à part (Fr.)
beiseite (G.)

a parte (Sp.)

de forme ouverte (Fr.)
through-composed
progressive composition
open form
durchkomponiert (G.)
a forma aperta (It.)
compuesto de principio a fin
(Sp.)

de grado en grado (Sp.)
little by little
gradually
by degrees
poco a poco (It., Sp.)
di grado (It.)
a grado a grado (It.)
per gradi (It.)
poi a poi (It.)
peu à peu (Fr.)
nach und nach (G.)
por grado (Sp.)

vs. subito (It.)

de la pointe (Fr.)
with the point of the bow
*up-bow
a punto d'arco (It.)
mit der Spitze (G.)
a la punta del arco (Sp.)

de memoria (Sp.)
memorized
from memory
by heart
by rote
a memoria (It.)
par coeur (Fr.)
auswendig (G.)

dead march
funeral march
dirge
marcia funebre (It.)

marche funèbre (Fr.)
Trauermarsch (G.)
marcha funebre (Sp.)
epicede
epicedium (Lat.)
epicedio (It., Sp.)

dead room
anechoic chamber
echoless
acoustical ceiling/wall/tiles
soundproof
insosorizzato (It.)
isolato acusticamente (It.)
sourd (Fr.)
insonorisé (Fr.)
Schalltot (G.)
insonoro (Sp.)
antisonoro (Sp.)

vs. live room

début, debut (E., Fr.)
first appearance
premiere performance
première (E., Fr.)
debutto (It.)
esordio (It.)
Debüt (G.)
Erstauffführung (G.)
primer (Sp.)
estreno (Sp.)

decani (Lat.)
(of the Dean)
epistle side of choir
right, or south side
choir, chorus
chancel choir
antiphonal

vs. cantoris (Lat.)

decay
die away
fade out

*decrescendo (It.)
diminuendo (It.)
morendo (It.)

deceptive cadence
false cadence
half-cadence
interrupted cadence
suspended cadence
avoided cadence
irregular cadence
surprise cadence
broken cadence
cadenza evitata (It.)
cadenza d'inganno (It.)
cadence interrompue (Fr.)
cadence évitée (Fr.)
cadence irregulière (Fr.)
Trugkadenz (G.)
Trugschluss (G.)
Halbschluss (G.)
cadencia evitada (Sp.)
cadencia interrumpida (Sp.)

déchant (Fr.)
discant
discantus (Lat.)
Diskant (G.)
treble part
soprano part
superius (Lat.)
lead voice
hymn descant
counter melody
prick song
discanto (It.)
dessus (Fr.)
Oberstimme (G.)
tiple (Sp.)

2. conductus (Lat.)
copula (Lat.)
organum section

decibel
loudness

bel
amplitude
sound level
volume
gain
décibel (Fr.)
Dezibel (G.)
decibelio (Sp.)

decima (Lat., It.)
tenth (interval)
compound third
dixième (Fr.)
Dezime (G.)
décima (Sp.)

decimaquinta (It.)
*fifteenth (interval)
quinzième (Fr.)
quindecima (It.)
Fünfzehntel (G.)
Quindezime (G.)
quincena (Sp.)
double octave
disdiapason (Gr., Lat.)

2. two-foot stop (organ)
super octave
Superoktav(e) (G.)
piccolo (It.)

Decke (G.)
belly (of a violin, etc.)
table (E., Fr.)
soundboard
tavola armonica (It.)
table d'harmonie (Fr.)
Resonanztafel (G.)
tapa, tabla de armonia (Sp.)

declamation
accentuation
text underlay
pronunciation
enunciation
stress, accent

diction
articulation

declamatory (style)
recitative
parlando
declamato (It.)
declamando (It.)
en déclamant (Fr.)
Sprechstimme (G.)
declamado (Sp.)

vs. lyrical

decoration
*ornamentation
florid
embelishment

découpler (Fr.)
cancel (organ stop)
off
auflösen (G.)
ab (G.)

decrescendo (It.)
diminuendo (It.)
get/become softer
decay
fade out
die away
morendo (It.)
calando (It.)
mancando (It.)
diluendo (It.)
estinguendo (It.)
perdendo, perdendosi (It.)
stringuendo (It.)
smortando (It.)
en perdant le son (Fr.)
schwindend (G.)
sterbend (G.)
verhallend (G.)
verlöschend (G.)
verschwindend (G.)
abschwellen (G.)

ersterbend (G.)
expirando (Sp.)

vs. crescendo (It.)

deductio (Lat.)
*hexachord
deduttione (It.)
déduction (Fr.)
deducio (Sp.)
scale
solmization

degree (of a scale)
step
half-step
tone
whole tone
half-tone
semi-tone
hemitone
minor second
major second
apotome (Gr.)
limma (Gr.)
diesis (Gr.)
grado (It., Sp.)
degré (Fr.)
Grad (G.)
Stufe, Tonstufe (G.)
Schritt (G.)

délié (Fr.)
non legato
detatched
détaché (Fr.)
staccato (It.)
spiccato (It.)
abgestossen (G.)
destacado (Sp.)
no ligado (Sp.)

vs. lié (Fr.)

démanché, démanchement (Fr.)
thumb position ('cello)

capotasto (It.)
position du pouce (Fr.)
Daumenaufsatz (G.)
posición del pulgar (.Sp.)

demi-bâton (Fr.)
two-measure rest
pausa di breve (It.)
pause de brève (Fr.)
silence de brève (Fr.)
Zweitaktpause (G.)
Doppeltaktpause (G.)
Zweiganzepause (G.)
silencio de breve (Sp.)
pausa de breve (Sp.)
breve rest

demi-cadence (Fr.)
semi-cadence
half cadence
imperfect cadence
deceptive cadence
Halbschluss (G.)
cadencia suspendida (Sp.)
semicadencia (Sp.)

demi-choeur (Fr.)
semi-chorus
echo choir/chorus
madrigal choir
chamber choir
vocal ensemble
soli (It.)
favoriti (It.)
coro favorito (It.)
concertino (It.)
petit-choeur (Fr.)
Kammerchor (G.)
coro de cámara (Sp.)

demi-pause (Fr.)
half-rest, half-note rest
pausa di minima (It.)
halbe Pause (G.)
silencio de blanca (Sp.)

demi-semiquaver
thirty-second note
demisemiquaver
triple-croche (Fr.)
biscroma (It.)
Zweiunddreissigstel (G.)
fusa (Lat., It., Sp.)
fuse (Fr.)
Fusel (G.)

demi-semitone
quarter-tone
microtone
quarto di tono (It.)
quart de ton (Fr.)
Viertelton (G.)
cuarto di tono (Sp.)

demi-soupir (Fr.)
eighth-rest
eighth-note rest
quaver rest
pausa di croma (It.)
Achtelpause (G.)
silencio de corchea (Sp.)
pausa de corchea (Sp.)

demi-ton (Fr.)
semitone
half-tone
half-step
minor second
degree
demi-ton (Fr.)
semitono (It., Sp.)
Halbton (G.)
limma (Gr.)
diesis (Gr.)
apotome (Gr.)

demi-voix (Fr.)
half-voice
very soft
whispered
stage whisper
under one's breath

*aside
pianissimo (It.)
mezza voce (It.)
sotto voce (It.)
à mi-voix (Fr.)
mit halbe Stimme (G.)
media voz (Sp.)

demiquaver
semiquaver
sixteenth-note
demicroche (Fr.)
double croche (Fr.)
sedicesimo (It.)
semicroma (It.)
Sechzehntel (G.)
semicorchea (Sp.)

demo
audition recording/tape
sample
try-out
screen test

Denkmäler (G.)
collection
historical monuments
edition
corpus (Lat.)
*anthology
collezione (It.)
raccolta (It.)
racueeil (Fr.)
colección (Sp.)

dentist music
light music
*backround music
elevator music
dinner music
salon music
table music
cocktail music
easy listening

déploration (Fr.)

*lament
lamentation
apotheose
elegie
dirge
planh
planctus (Lat.)
requiem (Lat.)
threnody
tombeau (Fr.)
plainte (Fr.)
lamento (It.)
complainte (Fr.)
Klage (G.)
Klagelied (G.)
nenia (E., It., Sp.)
nénia (Fr.)
dompe. dump (17c. E.)
epicede

derechos de ejecución (Sp.)
performing rights
rights
diritti d'esecuzione (It.)
droits d'exécution (Fr.)
Auffürungsrecht (G.)

dernier mouvement (Fr.)
last movement
concluding movement
finale (E., It.)
mouvement final (Fr.)
Finalsatz (G.)
Schlusssatz (G.)
Schlussstück (G.)
movimiento final (Sp.)
conclusión (Sp.)
último movimiento (Sp.)

désacordé (Fr.)
out of tune
*off-key
off pitch
tone-deaf
scordato (It.)
verstimmt (G.)

falsch singen (G.)

descant
superius (Lat.)
soprano
lead voice
melody

2. counter-melody
hymn descant
déchant (Fr.)
discanto (It.)
Diskant (G.)
Oberstimme (G.)

3. prick song

descant clef
soprano clef
violin clef
*C-clef (on first line)

descant flute
flageolet
flautino (It.)
*recorder
fipple flute
fife

descant mass (15-16c.)
cantus firmus in treble
cantus firmus mass
parody mass

descant recorder
soprano recorder

descant viol
treble viol
soprano viol

descort (Prov.)
lai, lay
song
Troubadour song
Leich (G.)

sequence

descriptive music
program music
word painting
program chanson (Fr.)
tone poem
symphonic poem
aria d'imitazione (It.)
storm music
burrasca (It.)

vs. absolute music

desde el principio (Sp.)
*da capo (It.)
D. C.
from the beginning
from the top

desde el signo hasta el fin(Sp.)
dal segno al fine (It.)
D. S. al fine (It.)
from the sign to the end
vom Zeichen bis zum Schluss
(G.)

despacio (Sp.)
slow, slowly
lento (It., Sp.)
adagio (It.)
largo (It.)
lent, lentement (Fr.)
langsam (G.)
lentamente (Sp.)

vs. veloz (Sp.)

dessin (Fr.)
plan (composition)
form
structure
forma (It., Sp.)
fattura (It.)
forme (Fr.)
facture (Fr.)

Faktur (G.)
Aufbau (G.)
Gestalt (G.)

dessus (Fr.)
treble (viol)
violin part
soprano
Diskant (G.)
canto (It., Sp.)

dessus de viole (Fr.)
treble viol
viola da gamba (It.)
Gambe (G.)
viola de gamba (Sp.)

detatched
destacado (Sp.)
non legato (It.)
staccato (It.)
détaché (Fr.)
spiccato (It.)
piccato (It.)
picch(i)ettato (It.)
délié (Fr.)
abgestossen (G.)
no ligado (Sp.)

detuned
voix céleste (organ, Fr.)
*celeste stop
unda maris (organ, Lat.)
vox angelica (Lat.)
vox humana (Lat.)

2. sing off-pitch
*out of tune
off-key
scordato (It.)
détonner (Fr.)
stonare (It.)
detonieren (G.)
desentonar (Sp.)
falsch singen (G.)
unrein singen (G.)

Deutsche Flöte (G.)
transverse flute
orchestral flute
concert flute
cross flute
German flute
flauto traverso (It.)
*flute

vs. recorder

Deutsche Messe (G.)
Lutheran mass
missa brevis (Lat.)
German mass
hymn mass
folk mass

Deutscher Leier (G.)
*hurdy-gurdy
hand piano
street piano/organ
barrel organ/piano
Leier, Drehleier (G.)

Deutscher Tanz (G.)
Ländler (G.)
waltz
danza tedesca (It.)
allemande (Fr.)
Walzer (G.)

development (section)
sonata form
sonata-allegro form
fragmentation of theme
svolgimento (It.)
sviluppo (It.)
développement (Fr.)
Durchführung (G.)
Themenverarbeitung (G.)
desarrollo (Sp.)

devil's box
fiddle
*violin

devil's interval
tritone
Quinta falsa (Lat.)
diabolus in musica (Lat.)
false fifth
diminished fifth
augmented fourth
mi contra fa (Lat)
tritono (It., Sp.)
triton (Fr.)
Tritonus (G., Lat.)

Dezett (G.)
piece for 10 performers
diecetto (It.)
decimino (It.)
decimette (Fr.)
dixtuor (Fr.)
Dixtuor (G.)

Dezibel (G.)
decibel
bel
loudness
sound level
gain
volume
décibel (Fr.)
decibelio (Sp.)

Dezime (G.)
tenth (interval)
compound third
decima (It.)
décima (Sp.)
décime (Fr.)
dixième (Fr.)

di grado (It.)
step-wise
*conjunct motion
melodic
scale passage
par degré (Fr.)
Stufenweise (G.)
por grado (Sp.)

2. litle by little
gradually
step by step
poco a poco (It.)
poi a poi (It.)
per gradi (It.)
a grado a grado (It.)
peu à peu (Fr.)
petit à petit (Fr.)
nach und nach (G.)
de grado en grado (Sp.)
por grado (Sp.)

dialogue (E., Fr.)
*antiphonal
echo
*duet
dialogo (It., Sp.)
Dialog (G.)
jeu-parti (12c. Fr.)
joc-parti (12c.)
partimen (Fr.)
tenso, tenson (Fr.)

dialogue mass
missa dialogata (Lat.)
missa recitata (Lat.)
*mass
missa (Lat.)

diana (It., Sp.)
reveille
wake-up call
bugle call (A.M.)
sveglia (It.)
diane (Fr.)
réveil (Fr.)
sonnerie (Fr.)
Morgensignal (G.)
Wecken (G.)
Weckdienst (G.)
alborada (Sp.)

diapason (organ)
principal (E., Sp.)
foundation stop

principale (It., Fr.)
montre (Fr.)
fond(s) d'orgue
préstant (Fr.)
Prinzipal (G.)
Hauptstimme (G.)
diapasón abierto (Sp.)

diapason (Gr.)
octave
antiphonia (Gr.)
ottava (It.)
Oktav (G.)
octava (Sp.)

2. melody
sound
strain

diapason (E, Fr., It.)
tuning fork
forchetta d'accordo (It.)
fourchette tonique (Fr.)
Stimmgabel (G.)
Gabelton (G.)
diapasón (Sp.)
corista (It., Sp.)
pitchpipe

2. * range
compass
tessitura (It.)
estensione (It.)
Umfang (G.)
extension (Sp.)

3. *pitch
intonation
standard of pitch
concert pitch

diapasón alto (Sp.)
high pitch
concert pitch
philharmonic pitch
diapasón de concierto (Sp.)

diapason normal (Fr.)
international pitch
classical pitch
French pitch
low pitch
Normalton (G.)
Franzton (G.)
diapasón normal (Sp.)
diapasón de bajo (Sp.)

diapente (Gr., Lat.)
fifth (interval)
dioxia (Gr.)
quinta (It., Sp.)
quinte (Fr.)
Quinte (G.)
hemiola (Gr.)
sesquialtera (Lat.)

diaphony, diaphonia (Gr.)
dissonance

vs. symphonia

2. two-part organum
discantus (Lat.)
discant

diaschisma
*comma
didymic comma
cent
microtone

diastema (Gr.)
interval
intervallo (It.)
intervalle (Fr.)
Intervall (G.)
Abstand (G.)
intervalo (Sp.)

diastematic notation
neumes on a staff
definite pitch
square notation

vs. adiastematic
cheironomic

diatesseron (Gr.)
fourth (interval)
Quarta (It.)
quarte (Fr.)
Quart(e) (G.)
cuarta (Sp.)

diatonic
major/ninor scale
white keys
diatonico (It., Sp.)
diatonique (Fr.)
diatonisch (G.)
stufentönig (G.)

vs. chromatic

diaulos (Gr.)
double aulos
*shawm
reed
oboe
calamus (Lat.)
Kalamos (Gr.)

dice music
chance music
*aleatory music
indeterminacy
Wüfelspiel (G.)

dictation (music)
transcribe
ear-training
aural training
write what one hears
dictée musicale (Fr.)
Musikdiktat (G.)

diction
enunciation of text
pronunciation
declamation

articulation

die away
decay
*decrescendo (It.)
diminuendo (It.)
morendo (It.)
ersterbend (G.)
erlöschend (G.)

diecetto (It.)
piece for 10 performers
decimino (It)
decimette (Fr.)
dixtuor (Fr.)
Dezett (G.)
Dixtuor (G.)

diesare (It.)
to sharp a note
alzare (It.)
diéser (Fr.)
hausser (Fr.)
durch Kreuz erhöhen (G.)
erhöhen (G.)
alzar (Sp.)

vs. abbassare (It.)

dièse (Fr.)
sharp sign
dièze (Fr.)
diesis (It.)
Kreuz (G.)
sostenido (Sp.)

vs. bémol (Fr.)

diesis (Gr.)
semitone (Pythagorean)
limma (Gr.)
half-step
half-tone
minor second
demi-ton (Fr.)
semitono (It., Sp.)

Halbton (G.)
diesi (Sp.)
apotome (Gr.)
hemitone

diferencia (16c. Sp.)
variations
divisions
*ornamentation
passaggio (It.)
gorgia (It.)
glosas (Sp.)

differentia (Lat.)
endings in chant psalm tones
cadence
termination
distinctio (Lat.)
euouae, evovae (Lat.)
saeculorum amen (Lat.)
doxology
Gloria Patri (Lat.)
Glory be
Lesser Doxology
oioueae (world without end
amen)

differential tone
resultant tone
difference tone
*combination tone
Tartini's tone
suono differenziale (It.)
son différentiel (Fr.)
Differenzton (G.)
sonido diferencial (Sp.)

digital
key (on piano,etc.)
pedal (on organ)
tasto (It.)
touche
Taste (G.)
tecla (Sp.)

2. binary recording

computerized
sequencer

vs. analogue recording

digital versatile disc
DVD
digital video disc
laserdisc
compact disc
CD
recording

digitazione (It.)
fingering
digitatura (It.)
diteggiatura (It.)
doigté (Fr.)
Fingersatz (G.)
Applikatur (G.)
*applicazione (It.)
digitación (Sp.)

digitazione sulla arpa (It.)
dital harp
harp guitar
harp lute
doigté sur la harpe (Fr.)
Harfenlaute (G.)
digitación sobre la arpa (Sp.)

digitorium
practice keyboard
dumb piano
dumb spinet
dumb organ
Übungsklavier (G.)
stummes Klavier (G.)
Übungsapparat (G.)

diludium (Lat.)
interlude
episode
transition
intermezzo (It.)
intermède (Fr.)

intermedio (It., Sp.)
interludio (It., Sp.)
Zwischenspiel (G.)

diluendo (It.)
*decrescendo (It.)
morendo (It.)
diminuendo (It.)
dying away

Dimanche (Fr.)
Sunday
the Lord's day
Sabbath
dominica (Lat.)
Domenica (It.)
Sonntag (G.)
Domingo (Sp.)

Dimanche de Pâques (Fr.)
Easter Sunday
Resurrection Sunday
Dominica Resurrectionis (Lat.)
Pasqua (It.)
Ostersonntag (G.)
Pascua de Resurrección (Sp.)
Pascua de florida (Sp.)
Domingo de Resurrección (Sp.)
Domingo de Pascua (Sp.)

Dimanche des Rameaux (Fr.)
*Palm Sunday
second Sunday of the Passion
Dominica in Palmis (Lat.)
domenico delle Palme (It.)
Palmsonntag (G.)
Domingo de Ramos (Sp.)

diminished (chord, interval)
diminu(i)to (It.)
diminué (Fr.)
verkleinert (G.)
vermindert (G.)
diminuido (Sp.)

diminished fifth
augmented fourth
tritone
devil's interval
false fifth
mi contra fa (Lat.)
quinta falsa (Lat.)
diabolus in musica (Lat.)
hemidiapente (Gr.)
tritonus (Lat.)
tritono (It., Sp.)
triton (Fr.)
Tritonus (G.)

diminuendo (It.)
*decrescendo (It.)
morendo (It.)
die away
decay
fade out

vs. crescendo (It.)

diminution (E., Fr.)
use of smaller note values
diminutio (Lat.)
diminuzione (It.)
Verkleinerung (G.)
Verkürzung (G.)
di(s)minución (Sp.)

vs. augmentation

2. *ornamentation
divisions
passaggi (It.)

dinamica (It.)
dynamics
dynamique (Fr.)
Dynamik (G.)
dinámica (Sp.)
amplitude
loudness
loud and soft
gain

131

volume

dinner music
light music
light classics
easy listening
elevator music
dentist music
Muzak
cafe music
table music
banquet music
cocktail music
easy listening
salon music
*backround music

diotic
binaural
stereo
stereophonic
hi-fi
two-track, four-track

dioxia (Gr.)
diapente (Gr., Lat.)
fifth (interval)
quinte (Fr., G.)
quinta (It., Sp.)
sesquialtera (Lat.)
hemiola (Gr.)

dip
key fall (keyboard)
vertical key movement

diphona (Gr.)
bicinium (Lat.)
diphonium (Lat.)
duet, duo
duetto (It.)
Duett (G.)
dueto (Sp.)
duplum (Lat.)

direct (vb.)

conduct
lead
dirigere (It.)
diriger (Fr.)
dirigieren (G.)
leiten (G.)
dirigir (Sp.)

direct (n.)
guide
index
cue note
custos (Lat., E.)
tractulus (Lat.)
mostra (It., Sp.)
guidon (Fr.)
guida (It.)
Kustos (G.)

director (E., Sp.)
conductor
leader
batonist, batoneer
bandleader
maestro (It.)
direttore (It.)
directeur (Fr.)
Dirigent (G.)
Leiter (G.)
Kapellmeister (G.)
Capellmeister (G.)
chef d'orchestra (Fr.)

dirge
funeral hymn, song
funeral march
*lament
epicede
epicedium (Lat.)
epicedio (It., Sp.)
requiem (Lat.)
apothéose (Fr.)
Grabgesang (G.)
Klaglied (G.)
Trauergesang (G.)
Trauermarsch (G.)

epiodion (Gr.)

Dirigierpartitur (G.)
full score
complete score
orchestral score
partizione (It.)
grande partition (Fr.)
Partitur (G.)
partición (Sp.)

diritti d'esecuzione (It.)
performing rights
rights
droits d'exécution (Fr.)
Aufführungsrecht (G.)
derechos de ejecución (Sp.)

disc
record(ing)
phonograph record
gramophone record
platter
pressing
shellac record
vinyl record
long-playing record
microgroove record
extended-play (45 rpm)
disco (It., Sp.)
disque (Fr.)
Schallplatte (G.)
album
cylinder
78 (rpm)
LP (33 1/3 rpm)
CD
DVD

disc jockey (DJ)
player of records
host of a record show
Dee-jay
announcer
MC
master of ceremonies

discant (section)
  conductus (Lat.)
  organum section
  *substitute clausula
  clausula (Lat.)
  copula (Lat.)
  discantus (Lat.)
  discanto (It.)
  déchant (Fr.)
  Diskant (G.)

2. treble part
  soprano
  dessus (Fr.)
  Oberstimme (G.)
  vox organalis (Lat.)
  duplum (Lat.)
  motetus (Lat.)

disco
  discothèque (Fr.)
  dance club
  dance hall
  *nightclub
  night spot
  supper club
  cocktail lounge
  cabaret
  à go-go (Fr.)
  discoteca (It., Sp.)
  Diskothek (G.)

2. dance style

3. pop music
  rock
  rock-and-roll
  dance music

discography
  recorded music list
  catalog(ue) of recorded music

disdiapason (Gr., Lat.)
  double octave
  *fifteenth

  quindicesimo (It.)
  pentacordo (It.)
  piccolo (It.)
  quinzième (Fr.)
  Quindezime (G.)
  Doppelocktave (G.)
  decimaquinta (It.)
  quincena (Sp.)

disjunct motion
  skipwise
  chordal
  *arpeggio (It.)

vs. conjunct motion
  stepwise

display pipes (organ)
  dummy pipes
  facade
  canne di facciata (It.)
  montre (Fr.)
  Füllpfeifen (G.)
  Stummepfeifen (G.)
  Prospektpfeifen (G.)

dissonance, dissonant
  clash
  discord
  cacophony
  unstable
  unresolved
  active tone/chord
  jarring sounds
  cross-relation
  falsa (17c.)
  disaccordo (It.)
  désaccord (Fr.)
  Missklang (G.)
  misstönend (G.)
  Kakaphonie (G.)
  diaphony, diaphonia (Gr.)
  dissonanza (It.)
  Dissonanz (G.)
  disonancia (Sp.)

distich
  couplet
  pair of lines/verses
  verse
  strophe
  strofa (It.)
  Strofe (G.)
  copla (Sp.)

distinctio (Lat.)
  *differentia (Lat.)
  endings of chant formulae
  cadence

2. in chant, pauses between
phrases

dital
  a key to change pitch
  a half-step on harp, etc.

dital harp
  harp guitar
  harp lute
  Harfenlaute (G.)
  digitazione sulla arpa (It.)
  doigté sur la harpe (Fr.)
  digitación sobre la arpa (Sp.)

diteggiatura (It.)
  *fingering
  digitazione (It.)
  doigté (Fr.)
  Fingersatz (G.)
  applicazio (It.)
  Applikatur (G.)

diteggiatura cambiata (It.)
  finger substitution
  changer le doigté (Fr.)
  ablösen (G.)
  cambiar la digitación (Sp.)

dithyramb
  hymn to Dionysus

bacchanal
  bacchanalian song
  drinking song
  tavern song
  dithyrambus (Lat.)
  dithyrambos (Gr.)
  ditirambo (It., Sp.)
  dithyrambe (Fr.)
  Dithyrambe (G.)
  Trinklied (G.)

ditone
  major third
  ditonus (Lat.)
  ditonos (Gr.)
  ditono (It., Sp.)
  diton (Fr.)
  terza maggiore (It.)
  tierce majeure (Fr.)
  tierce de Picardie (Fr.)
  Picardy third
  grosse Terz (G.)
  tercera mayor (Sp.)

ditonic comma
  comma
  Pythagorian comma
  ditonisches Komma (G.)
  microtone
  comma maxima (Lat.)
  schisma
  syntonic comma
  diascisma
  didymic comma
  cent
  centitone
  Komma (G.)
  coma (Sp.)

ditty
  *song
  tune
  melody
  jingle
  air

diva
  prima donna (It.)
  opera singer
  cantatrice (It., Fr.)
  divette (Fr.)
  Sängerin (G.)
  cantatriz (Sp.)

divertimento (It.)
  serenade
  cassation
  suite
  divertissement (Fr.)
  divertimiento (Sp.)

divertissement (Fr.)
  serenade
  divertimento (It.)
  suite

2. potpourri
  medley
  entr'acte (Fr.)
  act tune
  curtain tune
  intermezzo (It.)
  interlude

3. episode in a fugue

4. incidental music

5. ballet in an opera

divided choirs
  *antiphonal
  cori spezzati (It.)
  mehrechörig (G.)
  cantoris, decani
  double chorus
  polychoral

divided stop (organ)
  split keyboard
  medio registro (Sp.)

Divine Liturgy
  *Mass (Byzantine)
  Eucharist
  communion service
Divine Service
  St. John Chrisostom
  St. Basil
  *liturgy
  leiturgeia (Gr.)
  ritual

Divine Office
  monastic office
  office (E., Fr.)
  daily office
  officium divinum (Lat.)
  canonical hours
  horae canonicae (Lat.)
  Opus Dei (Lat.)
  ufficio divino (It.)
  uffizio divino (It.)
  office divin (Fr.)
  Stundenoffizium (G.)
  Tagesoffizium (G.)
  oficios (Sp.)
  horas canónicas (Sp.)
  Santo Oficio (Sp.)
  morning/evening prayer
  hours of the day
  rhymed office
  lauds (Lat. laudes)
  prime (Lat. prima)
  terce (Lat. tertia)
  sext (Lat. sexta)
  none (Lat. nona)
  vespers (Lat. vesperae)
  compline (Lat. completa)
  matins (Lat. matutinum)
  night office (Matins)
  Little Hours
  Liturgy of the Hours (1972)
  Night Prayers (1972)
  Liturgia horarum (Lat.1972)

Divine Service
  *mass

missa (Lat.)
Communion service
Lord's Supper
Holy Communion
agape feast
love feast
Eucharist
*liturgy
Abendmahl (G.)
Agende (G.)
Kirchenordnung (G.)
Kirchenamt (G.)

divisi (It.)
  divided (section)
  à 2
  a due (It.)
  à deux (Fr.)
  divisé (Fr.)
  geteilt (G.)
  dividido (Sp.)

divisio (Lat.)
  compound meter (14c. It.)
  battuta composta
  mesure composée (Fr.)
  zusammengesetzte Takt (G.)
  compás compuesto (Sp.)

division
  *manual (organ)
  keyboard
  pedalboard
  partial organ

  2. part (performers)
  section (E., Fr.)
  group
  sezione (It.)
  Gruppe (G.)

  3. excerpt
  movement
  phrase
  period
  part

pars (Lat.)
parte (It., Sp.)
partie (Fr.)
Absatz (G.)
Satz (G.)
Teil (G.)

division viol
  small bass viol
  viola bastarda (It.)
  viola da gamba (It.)
  viola di fagotto (It.)
  Fagottgeige (G.)
  Handbassel (G.)
  bassoon fiddle

divisions
  passage work
  ornamentation
  embellishment
  figuration
  variation
  melismatic
  passaggio (It.)
  coloratura (It.)
  gorgia (It.)
  fioritura (It.)
  fioritures (Fr.)
  Blumen (G.)
  floreos (Sp.)
  glosas (Sp.)
  diferencia (Sp.)

dixieland (jazz)
  New Orleans jazz
  swing
  pop

dixième (Fr.)
  tenth (interval)
  decima (It.)
  Dezime (G.)
  décima (Sp.)
  compound third

do

ut (Lat.)
finalis (Lat.)
C
tonic note
root
keynote

do du milieu du piano (Fr.)
  one-line C
  middle C
  do sotto il rigo (It.)
  eingestrichenes C (G.)
  do medio (Sp.)
  do central (Sp.)

doble (Sp.)
  double (E., Fr.)
  doppio (It.)
  doppel (G.)

doble apoyatura (Sp.)
  double appoggiatura
  non-harmonic tones
  appoggiatura doppia (It.)
  appogiature double (Fr.)
  Anschlag (G.)

doble barra (Sp.)
  double bar
  doppio barro (It.)
  double-barre (Fr.)
  Doppeltakstrich (G.)
  Schlussstriche (G.)

doble bemol (Sp.)
  double-flat
  doppio bemolle (It.)
  Doppel-B (G.)
  double bémol (Fr.)

doble contrapunto (Sp.)
  double counterpoint
  invertible counterpoint
  convertible counterpoint
  contrappunto doppio (It.)
  contrepoint double (Fr.)

doppelter Kontrapunkt (G.)

doble cuerda (Sp.)
double stop
corda doppia (It.)
double corde (Fr.)
Doppelgriff (G.)

doble golpe de lengua (Sp.)
double-tongueing
doppio colpe di lingua (It.)
double coup de langue (Fr.)
Doppelzunge (G.)

doble sostenido (Sp.)
*double sharp
doppio diesis (It.)
double dièse (Fr.)
Doppelkreuz (G.)

dobro
steel guitar
Hawaiian guitar
chitarra Hawayana (It.)
guitare Hawaienne (Fr.)
Hawaii-Gitarre (G.)
guitarra Hawaiana (Sp.)

Docke (G.)
*jack (of a harpsichord)
quill
plectrum
plettro (It.)
plectre (Fr.)
Plektrum (G.)
plectro (Sp.)

Dodecachordon (Gr.)
twelve modes (Glareanus,
1547)
medieval modes

dodecaphonic
twelve-tone music
serial music
tone row

polytonal
atonal (E., Fr., G., Sp.)
atonale (It.)
dodecafonia (It.)
dodécaphonisme (Fr.)
Zwölftontechnik (G.)
Zwölftonmiusik (G.)
dodecafonismo (Sp.)
dodecafónico (Sp.)

dodinette, dodo, dodino (Fr.)
lullaby
cradle song
ninna nanna (It.)
ninnerella (It.)
berceuse (Fr.)
Wiegenlied (G.)
Schlummerlied (G.)
Ständchen (G.)
canción de cuna (Sp.)
nana (Sp.)
arrullo (Sp.)

doghouse bass
string bass
acoustic bass
standup bass
washtub bass
contrabass
bass fiddle
bull fiddle
*bass

doigté (Fr.)
fingering
applicatio (It.)
digituzione (It.)
diteggiatura (It.)
application(Fr.)
Fingersatz (G.)
Applicatur (G.)
aplicación (Sp.)
digitación (Sp.)

dolce (It.)
soft

sweet
piano (It.)
doux (Fr.)
suave (Fr., Sp.)
süss (G.)
sanft (G.)
leise (G.)
lieblich (G.)
dulce (Sp.)

dolcian
fagotto (It.)
bassoon
dolcino (It.)
dulcian
Dulzian (G.)

dolciano (organ)
soft organ stop (wood)
dulciana

dolente (It.)
*sadly
sorrowful
plaintive
doloroso (It., Sp.)
lamentoso (It., Sp.)
douloureux (Fr.)
schmerzvoll (G.)
schmerzlich (G.)

dolzaine (Fr.)
*shawm
dolzaina (It.)
bassoon
*curtal
douçaine (Fr.)
Dulzian (G.)

Dom (G.)
cathedral
duomo (It.)
cattedrale (It.)
cathédrale (Fr.)
catedral (Sp.)
seo (Sp.)

basilica
church

Domchor (G.)
cathedral choir
church choir
coro del duomo (It.)
choeur de cathédrale (Fr.)
Kantorei (G.)
catedralicio (Sp.)
coro de catedral (Sp.)

dominant
fifth tone of the scale
fifth degree
sol (It.)
dominante (Fr., It., G., Sp.)
Oberdominante (G.)

2. recitation note
reciting tone (chant)
psalm-tone
tenor (Lat., E., It., Sp.)
tuba (Lat., E., It.)
recto tono (Lat.)
nota dominans (Lat.)
nota di recitazione (It.)
repercussio (It.)
teneur (Fr.)
Tenor (G.)

dominant of the dominant
five of five (V of V)
secondary dominant
dominante secondaria (It.)
dominante di passaggio (It.)
dominante de passage (Fr.)
Zwischendominante (G.)
Wechseldominante (G.)
dominante secundaria (Sp.)

dominant seventh
five chord plus seventh
settima di dominante (It.)
Dominantseptakkord (G.)
Dominantseptime (G.)

séptima de dominante (Sp.)

dominica (Lat.)
Sunday
the Lord's Day
Sabbath
Domenica (It.)
Dimanche (Fr.)
Sonntag (G.)
Domingo (Sp.)

vs. feria (Lat.)

Domingo de Pascua (Sp.)
Easter Sunday
Resurrection Sunday
Dominica Resurrectionis (Lat.)
Pasqua (It.)
Dimanche de Pâques (Fr.)
Ostersonntag (G.)
Pascua florida (Sp.)
Domingo de Resurrección (Sp.)
Pascua de Resurrección (Sp.)

Dominica in Palmis (Lat.)
Palm Sunday
second Sunday of the Passion
Dominica florum (Lat.)
Dominica capitilavium (Lat.)
Dominica Hosanna (Lat.)
Dominica Ramispalma (Lat.)
Pascha floridum (Lat.)
Pascha competentium (Lat.)
Domenica della palme (It.)
Dimanche des Rameaux (Fr.)
Palmsonntag (G.)
Domingo de Ramos (Sp.)

Dominica Pentecostes (Lat.)
Pentecost
Whit Sunday
Pascha rosarum (Lat.)
Pentecoste (It.)
Pentecôte (Fr.)

Pfingsten (G.)
Pentecostés (Sp.)

domp(e) (keyboard)
dump
elegy
*lament

domra, dombra (Rus.)
balalaika
balalaica (It., Sp.)
lute
guitar

domus organaria (Lat.)
casework
organ case
cassa dell'organo (It.)
buffet (Fr.)
Gehäuse (G.)
Orgelkasten (G.)

Donnermaschine (G.)
thunder machine/sheet
macchina per il tuono (It.)
machine pour le tonnere (Fr.)
maquina por la trueno (Sp.)

doo-wop music
pop music
rock music
rock and roll
rhythm-and-blues

Doppel, doppel- (G.)
double (E., Fr.)
doppio (It.)
doble (Sp.)

Doppelchor (G.)
*double chorus
antiphonal choirs
polychoral
choirwise
cori spezzati (It.)
divided choirs

Doppelfuge (G.)
double fugue
*fugue
double counterpoint
invertible counterpoint
convertible counterpoint

Doppelganze (G.)
breve (E., It., Fr., Sp.)
double whole note
brevis (Lat., G.)
carrée (Fr.)
quarrée (Fr.)
Doppeltaktnote (G.)
cuadrada (Sp.)

Doppelgriff (G.)
double-stop
harmony
doppia corda (It.)
double corde (Fr.)
doble cuerda (Sp.)

Doppelkonzert (G.)
double concerto
two soloists
sinfonie concertante (It.)
symphonie concertante (Fr.)
concerto grosso (It.)

Doppelkreuz (G.)
*double-sharp
Spanisches Kreutz (G.)

Doppelrohrblatt (G.)
*double reed
ancia doppia (It.)
anche double (Fr.)

Doppelschlag (G.)
* turn (ornament)
gruppetto (It.)
groupe (Fr.)
grupo (Sp.)
Gruppe (G.)
noeud (Fr.)

grupeto, grupito (Sp.)

Doppelschlegel (G.)
two-headed drumstick
battente doppio (It.)
mazzuolo a doppia testa (It.)
tampon (Fr.)
mailloche double (Fr.)
mailloche à double tête (Fr.)
zweikopfiger Schlegel (G.)
baqueta de dos cabezas (Sp.)

Doppelstrich (G.)
double bar
Schlussstriche (G.)
doppio barro (It.)
double-barre (Fr.)
doble barra (Sp.)

Doppeltaktpause (G.)
two-measure rest
double whole-note rest
demi-bâton (Fr.)
breve rest
pausa di breve (It.)
pause de breve (Fr.)
Zweitaktpause (G.)
Zweiganzepause (G.)
silencio de breve (Sp.)

doppelte Auslösung (G.)
double escapement
*escapement
doublehopper
doppio scappamento (It.)
double échappement (Fr.)
englische Mechanik (G.)
Repetitionsmechanik (G.)

doppelter Kontrapunkt (G.)
double counterpoint
invertible counterpoint
convertible counterpoint
contrappunto doppio (It.)
double contrepoint (Fr.)
doble contrapunto (Sp.)

Doppelzunge (G.)
double-tongueing
double coup de langue (Fr.
doble golpe de lengua (Sp.)
doppio colpe di lingua (It.)

doppio (It.)
double (E., Fr.)
Doppel (G.)
doble (Sp.)

doppio movimento (It.)
*cut time
twice as fast
double time
march time
alla breve (It.)
double mouvement (Fr.)
doppelte Bewegung (G.)
doble movimiento (Sp.)

vs. tempo ordinario (It.)

Doppler effect
pitch change
effetto Doppler (It.)
effet Doppler (Fr.)
Doppler-Fizeau (Fr.)
Doppler-Effekt (G.)

Dorian mode
first mode
Greek mode
medieval mode
Doric mode
dorico (It., Sp.)
dorisch (G.)
dorien (Fr.)

dosillo (Sp.)
duplet
two notes for three
duina (It.)
duolet (Fr.)
Duole (G.)

dot
punto (It.)
point (Fr.)
Punkt (G.)
puntillo (Sp.)
punctus (Lat.)

dotted (note, rest)
pricked
puntato (It.)
pointé (Fr.)
punktiert (G.)
puntado (Sp.)
double-dotted

dotted rhythm
alla zuppa (It.)
boiteux (Fr.)
hinkend (G.)
cojeando (Sp.)
limping
Scotch snap
reverse dotted

double (E., Fr.)
twice
repeat
additional
substitute
variation (17-18c.)
doppio (It.)
Doppel (G.)
doble (Sp.)

doublé (Fr.)
ornament
*turn
brisé (Fr.)
gruppetto (It.)
Doppelschlag (G.)
noeud (Fr.)
grupeto (Sp.)

double appoggiatura
ornament
non-harmonic tones

*appoggiatura (It.)
appoggiatura doppia (It.)
appogiature double (Fr.)
Anschlag (G.
doble apoyatura (Sp.)

double backfall
slide
*appoggiatura
backfall

double bar
division
doppio barro (It.)
double-barre (Fr.)
Doppel(takt)strich (G.)
Schlussstriche (G.)
doble barra (Sp.)

double bass
contrabass
*bass
string bass
bass viole
bass fiddle
bull fiddle
stand-up bass

double bassoon
contrafagotto (It.)
contrebasson (Fr.)
Kontrafagott (G.)
fagottone (It.)

double cadence
ornamental close
trill cadence

double cadence (Fr.)
*turn
gruppetto (It.)
Doppelschlag (G.)
circolo mezzo (It.)
grupeto (Sp.)

double chant

Anglican chant
single tune for two verses of a
psalm
falso bordone

vs. single chant

double chorus
multiple choirs
divided chorus
antiphonal choirs
polychoral
echo chorus
call and response
choirwise
dialogue, musical
cori spezzati (It.)
cori battente (It.)
double choeur (Fr.)
Doppelchor (G.)
Apsidenchöre (G.)
cantoris, decani
stereophonic
binaural

double concerto
two soloists
Doppelkonzert (G.)
concerto grosso (It.)
sinfonie concertante (It.)
symphonie concertante (Fr.)
konzertanten Sinfonien (G.)

double corde (Fr.)
double stop
corda doppia (It.)
Doppelgriff (G.)
doble cuerda (Sp.)

double counterpoint
invertible counterpoint
inversion
double fugue
convertible counterpoint
contrappunto doppio (It.)
double contrepoint (Fr.)

doppelter Kontrapunkt (G.)
doble contrapunto (Sp.)

double coup de langue (Fr.)
flutter-tonguing
frullato (It.)
articulation double (Fr.)
Flatterzunge (G.)
tripe articulación (Sp.)
raspberry
French kiss

double-croche (Fr.)
sixteenth note
semiquaver
semifusa (Lat.)
semicroma (It.)
sedicesimo (It.)
Sechzehntel (G.)
semicorchea (Sp.)

double cursus (medieval)
repeated melody
sequence
clausulae, motets

double-dièse (Fr.)
double-sharp
doppio diesis (It.)
Doppelkreuz (G.)
Spanischer Kreutz (G.)
doble sostenido (Sp.)

double dotted
*dotted notes
doppelt punktiert (G.)

double drum(s)
kettledrums
*tympani
timpano (It.)
taballo (It.)
timbale (Fr.)
Pauken (G.)
Kesselpauken (G.)
timbal (Sp.)

atabal (Sp.)
atabale (Fr.)

double escapement
*escapement (piano)
doublehopper
doppio scappamento (It.)
double échappement (Fr.)
doppelte Auslösung (G.)
englische Mechanik (G.)
repetitionsmechanik (G.)

double-flat
doppio bemolle (It.)
double bémol (Fr.)
Doppel-B (G.)
doble bemol (Sp.)

double fugue
*fugue
double counterpoint (E., Fr.)
Doppelfuge (G.)

double leading tone cadence
(14-15c.)
Landini cadence
Burgundian cadence
lydian cadence

double mordent
mordent
trill
couble relish
inverted mordent

double note
breve (It., Fr., E., Sp.)
double whole note
brevis (Lat., G.)
carrée (Fr.)
quarrée (Fr.)
Doppelganze (G.)
Doppeltaktnote (G.)
cuadrada (Sp.)

double octave

fifteenth
quinzième (Fr.)
quindicesimo (It.)
piccolo (It.)
Quindezime (G.)
Fünfzehntel (G.)
Doppelocktave (G.)
quincena (Sp.)
disdiapason (Gr., Lat.)

double reed (instrument)
oboe
bassoon
English horn
shawm
ancia doppia (It.)
anche double (Fr.)
Doppelrohrblatt (G.)

double relish
ornament
trill
double mordent

double sharp
doppio diesis (It.)
double dièse (Fr.)
Doppelkreuz(G.)
Spanisches Kreuz (G.)
doble sostenido (Sp.)

double-stop
doppia corda (It.)
double corde (Fr.)
Doppelgriff (G.)
doble cuerda (Sp.)
interval

double-strung
double course
twelve-string guitar
mandolin
*course

double-time
*cut-time

alla breve (It.)
quick time
double-quick time
twice as fast
duple meter
march time
C-barred
a cappella (It.)
à la blanche (Fr.)
doppio movimento (It.)
in halben Noten (G.)
a la breve (Sp.)

vs.common time

double-tongueing
doppio colpe di lingua (It.)
double coup de langue (Fr.)
Doppelzunge (G.)
doble golpe de lengua (Sp.)
trillo (17c. It.)
tremolo

double whole-note
brevis (Lat., G.)
breve (It.,Fr., E.)
quarrée (Fr.)
carrée (Fr.)
Doppelganze (G.)
Doppeltaktnote (G.)
double note

double zither
zither
arpanetta (It., Fr.)
arpa doppia (It.)
arpenette (Fr.)
Spitzharfe (G.)

doublette (Fr.)
*mixture stop (organ)
compound stop
sesquialtera (Lat.)
Hintersatz (G.)
fourniture (Fr.)
cornet (Fr.)

douçaine (Fr.)
*shawm
Dulzian (G.)
dulcina
dulceuse (E.)
dolzaina (It.)
douchaine (Fr.)

2. *dulcian (organ stop)
Dulzian (G.)
dulciana, dolciano
Dulziana (G.)
dulcet (octave)
dulcina
dulceuse
douçaine (Fr.)
douchaine
doussaine (Fr.)
doucine
dolzaina

doucemelle (15c. Fr.)
*clavichord
chekker
doulcemelle (Fr.)

2. *dulcimer

doux (Fr.)
sweet
soft
piano (It.)
dolce (It.)
dulce (Sp.)
Süss (G.)
suave (It., Fr.)
sanft (G.)
leise (G.)
lieblich (G.)

vs. fort (Fr.)

douzième (Fr.)
twelfth (interval)
duodecimo (It.)
Duodezime (G.)

duodécima (Sp.)

down-bow
arco in giù (It.)
arcata in giù (It.)
tiré (Fr.)
à la hausse (Fr.)
tirado (Sp.)
Abstrich (G.)
Herabstrich (G.)
arcada hacia abajo (Sp.)
Herunterstrich (G.)
am Frosch (G.)
al tallone (It.)
au talon (Fr.)
al talón (Sp.)
at the frog

vs. up-bow

downbeat
first beat of a measure
thesis
crusis
masculine
strong beat
abbattimento (It.)
frappé (Fr.)
Abschlag (G.)
Niederschlag (G.)
Herunterschlag (G.)
schwerer Taktteil (G.)

vs. upbeat
last beat of the measure

doxology
hymn to the Trinity
*cherubim song
angelic hymn
hymn to the angels
Gloria Patri (Lat.):
Lesser Doxology
Gloria in excelsis Deo (Lat.):
Greater Doxology

drag
slow down
rallentando (It.)
*ritardando (It.)

2. snare drum stroke
*drumbeat
ruff, ruffle
flam
paradiddle
batterie (Fr.)

3. portamento (It.)
slide
glissando (It.)

4. slow dance (S. Amer.) and its
music

dramatic overture
*overture to an opera
*programmatic
prelude

dramatic tenor/soprano
Heldentenor (G.)
heroic tenor
Wagnerian tenor
tenore robusto (It.)
tenore drammatico (It.)
tenore eroico (It.)
ténor dramatique (Fr.)
fort ténor (Fr.)
tenor dramatico (Sp.)
operatic singer
spinto (It.)

drame lyrique (Fr.)
lyric drama
music drama
dramma per musica (It.)
dramma lirico (It.)
*opera

dramma giocoso (It.)
*comic opera

light opera
operetta
opéra comique (Fr.)
Singspiel (G.)

dramma sacro (It.)
*oratorio
dramatic cantata
*azione sacra (It.)
sacra rappresentazione (It.)
Oratorium (G., Lat.)

draw-knob(s) (org.)
organ stops
draw-stop
stop tabs
bottoni dei registri (It.)
tirante (It., Sp.)
registre (Fr.)
tirant (Fr.)
boutons de registres (Fr.)
Zug, Züge (G.)
Registerzüge (G.)
botones de los registros (Sp.)
botones tiradores (Sp.)
plancas de los registros (Sp.)

drawing-room grand (piano)
*baby grand
semi-grand
boudoir grand
parlor grand
*grand piano
pianoforte a coda (It.)
piano de boudoir (Fr.)
grand piano de concert (Fr.)
Salonflügel (G.)
piano de media cola (Sp.)

drawing-room music
salon music
light music
*backround music
dinner music
easy listening
elevator music

Dreher (G.)
waltz
Ländler (G.)

Drehorgel (G.)
street organ
street piano
*barrel organ
hand organ
*hurdy-gurdy
Drehleier (G.)

Dreiertakt (G.)
triple meter
perfect time
waltz time
three-quarter time
in 3
tempus perfectum (Lat.)
tempus ternarium (Lat.)
tempo ternario (It.)
mesure ternaire (Fr.)
ungerader Takt (G.)
compás ternario (Sp.)
compás de tres tiempo (Sp.)

Dreiklang (G.)
triad
*chord
accordo (It.)
accorde (Fr.)
Akkord (G.)
acorde (Sp.)

Dreitritt (G.)
waltz
three-step
valzer a tre passi (It.)
trois-temps (Fr.)
valse (Fr.)
Walzer (G.)
vals (Sp.)

dress circle
mezzanine
*balcony

142

gallery
prima galleria (It.)
premier balcon (Fr.)
corbeille (Fr.)
erster Rang (G.)

dress rehearsal
open rehearsal
full rehearsal
ultima prova (It.)
Generalprobe (G.)
répétition générale (Fr.)
ensayo general (Sp.)

drill (n.)
exercise
finger exercise
practice piece
study
esercizio (It.)
pezzo per studio (It.)
exercice (Fr.)
*étude (Fr., E.)
study
Übung, Übungstück (G.)
ejercicio (Sp.)
estudio (Sp.)

drill (vb.)
practice
rehearse
go over
run through/over
do over
esercitare (It.)
exercer (Fr.)
üben (G.)
ejercitar (Sp.)

drinking song
tavern song
*bacchanal
dithyramb
brindisi (It.)
carmina burana (Lat.)
air à boire (Fr.)

chanson à boire (Fr.)
Trinklied (G.)
vinata, vinetta (It.)
canción baquica (Sp.)

driving note
*syncopation
off-beat
alla zoppa (It.)
contrattempo (It.)
contre-temps (Fr.)
Gegenzeit (G.)
síncopa (Sp.)

droits d'exécution (Fr.)
rights
performing rights
diritti d'esecuzione (It.)
Aufführungsrecht (G.)
derechos de ejecución (Sp.)

drone
pedal point
pedal note
double pedal point
organ point
drone bass
pedale (It.)
pédale (Fr.)
bajo de organo (Sp.)
point d'orgue (Fr.)
Orgelpunkt (G.)
nota pedal (Sp.)
*bagpipes
cantus firmus (Lat.)
organum

drop
curtain
backdrop
traveler
scrim
cyclorama
telone (It.)
sipario, siparietto (It.)
rideau (Fr.)

Vorhang (G.)
Bühnenvorhang (G.)
telón (Sp.)

Druckknopf (G.)
combination stop (org.)
piston
toe stud/piston
pistoncini (It.)
bouton de combinaison (Fr.)
Kollektivzug (G.)

drum
percussion
tympanum (Lat.)
tabor
cassa (It.)
caisse (Fr.)
tamburo (It.)
Trommel (G.)
tambour (Fr.)
tambor (Sp.)
caja (Sp.)
tabla (Ind.)

drum-beat
flam
ruff, ruffle
paradiddle
drag
roll
rub-a-dub
double-beat
colpo di tamburo (It.)
battement de tambour (Fr.)
batterie (Fr.)
Trommelschlag (G.)
redoble (Sp.)
tantarán, tantarantán (Sp.)

drum-roll
tremolo (It.)
rullo (It.)
roulement (Fr.)
Trommelwirbel (G.)
Paukenwirbel (G.)

redoble (Sp.)

drum set
band percussion set
rhythm drums
traps, trap set
drum kit

drumhead
skin
vellum
membrana (It., Sp.)
peau (Fr.)
Trommelfell (G.)

drumstick
mallet
hammer
bacchetta da tamburo (It.)
mazza, mazzuolo (It.)
battente (It.)
baguette de tambour (Fr.)
mailloche (Fr.)
marteau (Fr.)
Trommelschlegel (G.)
Schlegel (G.)
Hammer (G.)
baqueta (Sp.)
palillo de tambor (Sp.)
macillo, martillo (Sp.)

du signe à la fin (Fr.)
dal segno al fine (It.)
vom Zeidhen bis zum Schluss
(G.)
desde el signo hasta el fin (Sp.)

duct flute
fipple flute
whistle flute
penny whistle
flageolet
recorder
*fife

ductia (Lat.)

instrumental piece
stantipes (Lat.)
estampie (Fr.)

Dudelsack (G.)
*bagpipe
Dudey (G.)
chanter
musette (Fr.)
cornemuse (Fr.)
piva (It.)
zampagna (It.)
gaita (Sp.)

duet, duo
pair
duetto (It.)
duo (Fr.)
Duett (G.)
dueto (Sp.)
bicinium (Lat.)
diphona (Gr.)
dialogue
echo
jeu-parti (Fr.)
joc-partit (Fr.)
partimen (Fr.)
tenso, tenson (Fr.)
four-hand piano/organ
vierhändig (G.)
à quatre mains (Fr.)
a quattro mani (It.)
a cuatro manas (Sp.)

dugazon (Fr.)
soprano
light soprano
soubrette (Fr., It., E., G.)
ingenue (Fr.)
servetta (It.)
*comic role
tiple cómico (Sp.)

dulce (Sp.)
soft
sweet

piano (It.)
dolce (It.)
doux (Fr.)
süss (G.)
sanft (G.)
lieblich (G.)
leise (G.)
suave (It., Fr.)

vs. fuerte (Sp.)
forte (It.)

dulce melos (Lat.)
*dulcimer
hammered dulcimer
clavichord

dulcian (org.)
soft reed stop
Dulzian (G.)
douçaine (Fr.)
doussaine (Fr.)
douchaine
doucine
dolzaina
dulceuse
dulcina
dulcian bass
Dulzianbass (G.)
dulcet (8va)

2. curtal
sordone
dulzian

dulciana (org.)
soft string stop
dolciano

dulcimer
cimbalom
cembalom
dulcimore
psaltery
zither
dulce melos (Lat.)

tympanon (Fr.)
bûche (Fr.)
tamborin à cordes (Fr.)
salterio tedesco (It.)
Hackbrett (G.)
Scheitholt (G.)
Zimbalon (G.)
Hummel, Humle (G.)

2. Appalachian dulcimer
mountain dulcimer
folk zither
mountain zither

dulzian
enclosed reed instrument
curtal
dulcian
sordone (It,)
sourdine (Fr.)
Sordun (G.)
ranket(t) (G.)
*racket
bassoon

dumb piano, organ
practice keyboard
digitorium (Lat.)
dumb spinet
stummes Klavier (G.)
Übungsklavier (G.)
Übungsapparat (G.)

dumka, dumki, dumky
folk ballad (Pol., Rus.)
ballad
song

2. *lament (instr.)
elegy
melancholy romance

dummy pipes (organ)
facade
display pipes
Füllpfeifen (G.)

Stummepfeifen (G.)
Prospektpfeifen (G.)
montre (Fr.)
canne di facciata (It.)

dump, domp, dompe
lament (instr.)
*chaconne
variations (16c. E.)
ground bass

dunce notes
shape(d)-notes
character notes
patent notes
buckwheat notes
fasola
*solmization

duodecimo (It.)
twelfth (interval)
douzième (Fr.)
Duodezime (G.)
duodécima (Sp.)

duomo (It.)
cathedral church
basilica
cattedrale (It.)
cathédrale (Fr.)
Dom (G.)
catedral (Sp.)
seo (Sp.)

duple meter
in 2 or 4
binary measure
imperfect time
tempus imperfectus (Lat.)
*cut time
double time
march time
common time
common measure
ordinary time
tempo ordinario (It.)

ritmo binario (It.)
tempo binario (It.)
mouvement ordinaire (Fr.)
mesure binaire (Fr.)
rythme binaire (Fr.)
Zweiertakt (G.)
Vierertakt (G.)
compás binario (Sp.)
movimiento ordinario (Sp.)

duplet
two notes for three
duina (It.)
duolet
Duole (G.)
dosillo (Sp.)

duplex longa (13c. Lat.)
maxima (Lat.)
nota maxima (Lat.)
large (note)

duplexing (organ)
unified
unit organ
theatre organ
cinema organ
extension organ
organo da teatro (It.)
organo da cinematografo (It.)
orgue de cinéma (Fr.)
Multiplexorgel (G.)
Kinoorgel (G.)
órgano de cine (Sp.)

duplum (Lat., 13c.)
second voice
motetus part (Lat.)
vox organalis (Lat.)
organum

dur (G.)
major
maggiore (It.)
majeur (Fr.)
mayor (Sp.)

Durtonart (G.)

duration (time)
   time value
   length of a note/rest
   valor (Lat., Sp.)
   valore (It.)
   valeur (Fr.)
   Wert (G.)
   Notenwert (G.)

durchbrochene Arbeit (G.)
   motivic treatment
   voice exchange
   *hocket
   hoquetus (Lat.)
   hoquetatio (Lat.)
   truncatio (Lat.)
   ochetus (Lat.)
   ochetti (It.)
   ho(c)quet (Fr.)
   Hoketus (G.)

Durchführung (G.)
   development (section)
   sviluppo (It.)
   svolgimento (It.)
   elaborazione tematica (It.)
   développment (Fr.)
   desarrollo (Sp.)
   elaboración (Sp.)

   *exposition (fugue)

Durchgangsnote (G.)
   passing tone
   Durchgangston (G.)
   nota di passaggio (It.)
   note de passage (Fr.)
   nota de paso (Sp.)
   non-harmonic tone
   pièn-tone
   fill-in tone

durchkomponiert (G.)
   through-composed

progressive composition
open form
oda continua (Lat.)
a forma aperta (It.)
de forme ouverte (Fr.)
compuesto de principio a fin (Sp.)

Durchstreichen (G.)
   strumming
   thrumming
   raking
   twanging
   strappata (It.)
   grattant (Fr.)
   Ausstreifen (G.)
   rasgueado (Sp.)

Dutch concert
   cacaphony
   noise
   charivari (Fr.)
   shivaree
   horning
   mock serenade
   *callithumpian concert
   cat's music
   Katzenmusik (G.)
   scampata (It.)

dux (Lat.)
   subject of a fugue
   antecedent
   proposta (It.)
   guida (It.)
   sujet (Fr.)
   Führer (G.)
   guia (Sp.)

   vs. comes (Lat.)
   consequent

DVD
   digital versatile disc
   digital video disc
   laserdisc

*recording
CD
compact disc

dynamics
   loud and soft
   *amplitude
   loudness
   volume
   gain
   dinamica (It.)
   dynamique (Fr.)
   Dynamik (G.)
   dinámica (Sp.)

.

E

E-string
chanterelle (Fr.)
cantarella (It.)
cantino (It.)
Sangsaite (G.)
Quintsaite (G.)
cantarela (Sp.)
prima (Sp.)
tiple (Sp.)

ear
orecchio (It.)
oreille (Fr.)
Ohr (G.)
oido (Sp.)
oreja (Sp.)

ear (to have an)
hear
listen
appreciate
discriminate

ear (to play by)
extemporize
improvise
fake it
ad -lib

ear-splitting
very loud
too loud
blaring
deafening
fortissimo (It.)
très fort (Fr.)
sehr Laut (G.)
stark (G.)
muy fuerte (Sp.)

ear-training
dictation
listening
sight-singing
Gehörbildung (G.)

early music
pre-Bach
pre-Mozart
pre-classical
renaissance music
medieval music
ancient music
old music
historical music
musica antiqua (Lat.)
musica antico (It.)
musique ancienne (Fr.)
alte Musik (G.)
música antigua (Sp.)

ears (organ)
plates on pipes
Seitenbart (G.)

Easter chant/song
Exultet (Lat.)
praeconium pascale (Lat.)
Easter proclamation

Easter Sunday
Resurrection Sunday
Dominica Resurrectionis (Lat.)
Pasqua (It.)
Dimanche de Pâques (Fr.)
Ostersonntag (G.)
Pascua Florida (Sp.)
Pascua de Resurrección (Sp.)
Domingo de Pascua (Sp.)
Domingo de Resurrección
(Sp.)

Eastern chant
Byzantine chant
Orthodox music

eastern music
oriental music
Asian music

vs. Western music
music of the West

easy listening
light classics
light music
salon music
dinner music
*backround music
furniture music
musica leggiera (It.)
musique légère (Fr.)
musiquette (Fr.)
musichetto (It.)
musiquillo (Sp.)
leichte Musik (G.)
Unterhaltungsmusik (G.)
música ligera (Sp.)

vs. serious music
classical music

eccedente (It.)
augmented
raised
sharped
aumentatio (It.)
augmenté (Fr.)
übermässig (G.)
hochalteriert (G.)
aumentado (Sp.)

vs. diminuito (It.)

ecclesiastical mode
church mode
scale
minor mode
authentic mode
auctoralis (Lat.)
authentischer Modus (G.)
modo ecclesiastico (It.)

mode ecclésiastique (Fr.)
Kirchentonart (G.)
modo eclesiástico (Sp.)

ecclesiastical music
church music
liturgical music
sacred music
religious music
musique d'église (Fr.)
musica da chiesa (It.)
Kirchenmusik (G.)
música de iglesia (Sp.)

vs. secular music

échange de voix (Fr.)
voice exchange
voice-crossing
croisement de voix (Fr.)
Stimmtauch (G.)

échappée (Fr.)
escape note
ornament
*cambiata
changing note
auxiliary note
non-harmonic tone
broderie (Fr.)
Wechselnote (G.)

échappement (Fr.)
escapement (piano)
hopper
grasshopper
release
key release
*double escapement
scappamento (It.)
Auslöser, Auslösung (G.)
escape, escapatoria (Sp.)

échelette (Fr.)
xylophone (E., Fr.)
gigelira (It.)

*claquebois (Fr.)
xilofono (It.)
Xylophon (G.)
xilófono (Sp.)
xilórgano (Sp.)
sticcato (It.)
sticcado pastorale (It.)
marimba
vibraharp
vibraphone
orchestral bells

échelle (Fr.)
scale
gamme (Fr.)
scala (It.)
gamma (It.)
Tonleiter (G.)
Skala (G.)
escala (Sp.)
gama (Sp.)
diatonic scale
pentatonic scale
chromatic scale

echo
reverberation
repeat
resound
resonate
live room
eco (It., Sp.)
écho (Fr.)
Echo (G.)
Nachhall (G.)
retumbo (Sp.)

echo chamber
reverb
ambiance
surround-sound
live room

vs. anechoic chamber
dead room

echo choir
semi-chorus
chamber choir
favoriti (It.)
coro concertato (It.)
semicoro (It., Sp.)
soli (It.)
petit-choeur (Fr.)
demi-choeur (Fr.)
Halbchor (G.)
hemicoro (Sp.)
*antiphonal
double chorus
dialogue
polychoral

echo division (organ)
gallery organ
nave division
antiphonal organ
echo-stop
organo d'eco (It.)
clavier d'écho (Fr.)
Fernwerk (G.)
Echoklavier (G.)
Echowerk (G.)

ecclesiastical mode
Gregorian mode
medieval mode
church mode
scale

echoi, echos (Gr.)
mode
tonoi (Gr.)
oktoechos (Gr.)
enechemata (Gr.)

eclogue
pastoral piece, song
idyl
egloga (It.)
églogue (Fr.)
Hirtengesang (G.)
Schäferstück (G.)

égloga (Sp.)
pastorale (It., Fr.)
pastoral (Sp.)

écossaise (Fr.)
Scottish dance
contradance
polka
Schottische (G.)
Scozzese (It.)
Escocesa (Sp.)
anglaise (Fr.)
française (Fr.)

Edad Media (Sp.)
Middle Ages
medieval period
dark ages
Medio Evo (It.)
Mittelalter (G.)
Moyen Age (Fr.)

edit, edition
transcribe, transcription
*arrange(ment)
adapt(ation)
version
edizione (It.)
edition (Fr.)
tirage (Fr.)
Ausgabe (G.)
Auflage (G.)
edicion (Sp.)

effe (It.)
sound-hole
F-hole
ouïle (Fr.)
F-Loch (G.)
efe (Sp.)
vido (Sp.)

effetti (It.)
*ornaments
grace notes
embellishments

ornamenti (It.)
abbellimenti (It.)
broderies (Fr.)
ornements (Fr.)
Verzierungen (G.)
adornos (Sp.)

eighth (interval)
octave (E., Fr.)
diapason (Lat.)
antiphonia (Gr.)
ottava (It.)
Oktave (G.)
octava (Sp.)

eighth-note
quaver
unca (Lat.)
hooked note
croma (It.)
croche (Fr.)
Achtel (G.)
corchea (Sp.)

eighth-rest
quaver rest
pausa della croma (It.)
demi-soupir (Fr.)
Achtelpause (G.)
silencio de corchea (Sp.)

eighty-eight
piano (E., Fr., Sp.)
keyboard
the ivories
pianoforte (It.)
Klavier (G.)

eilend (G.)
faster
accelerando (It.)
stringendo (It.)
stretto (It.)
plus vite (Fr.)
en pressant (Fr.)
schneller (G.)

vs. langsamer (G.)

eine Saite (G. piano)
soft pedal
una corda (It.)
une corde (Fr.)
una cuerda (Sp.)
soft
muted

Eingang (G.)
ingressa (It., Lat.)
entrance (hymn/song)
introit
introitus (Lat.)
introito (It., Sp.)
entrée (Fr.)
introït (Fr.)
Einleitung (G.)
Introitus (G.)
entrada (Sp.)

eingestrichenes C (G.)
middle C
one-line C
do sotto il rigo (It.)
do du milieu du piano (Fr.)
do medio (Sp.)
do central (Sp.)

einkanalig (G.)
monaural
monophonic
monoaurale (It.)
monofonico (It.)
monophonique (Fr.)
monofónico (Sp.)

vs. stereophonisch (G.)

Einklang (G.)
unison
unisonus (Lat.)
unisson (Fr.)
unisono (It., Sp.)

Einleitung (G.)
  intro, introduction
  introduzione (It.)
  introduction (Fr.)
  Vorspiel (G.)
  Introduktion (G.)
  Auftritt (G.)
  introducción (Sp.)
  intrada (Sp., G.)
  intrata, entrata (It.)
  entrada (Sp.)
  *prelude
  overture
  voluntary

2. introit
  introitus (Lat.)
  ingressa (It.)
  entrée (Fr.)
  *Eingang (G.)

einstimmen (G.)
  tune up
  intonare (It.)
  accordare (It.)
  accorder (Fr.)
  afinar (Sp.)

Einschnitt (G.)
  a cut
  delete
  strike out
  taglio (It.)
  inciso (It., Sp.)
  coupure (Fr.)
  Schnitt (G.)
  corte (Sp.)
  vide, vi - - - de (Lat.)

einstimmig (G.)
  monophonic
  solo
  monody
  unaccompanied
  *unison
  a una voce (It.)

une voix seule (Fr.)
a una voz (Sp.)
für eine Stimme (G.)

vs. vielstimmig (G.)

einthemig (G.)
  single theme
  monothematic
  monotematico (It.)
  monothématique (Fr.)
  monothematisch (G.)
  monotemático (Sp.)
  fugal
  ricercar

Eisenvioline (G.)
  nail violin
  nail fiddle
  nail harmonica
  violino di ferro (It.)
  violon de fer (Fr.)
  Nagelgeige (G.)
  Nagelharmonika (G.)
  Nagelklavier (G.)

ejecución (Sp.)
  execution
  performance
  esecuzione (It.)
  exécution (Fr.)
  Ausführung (G.)

ejercicio (Sp.)
  exercise
  study
  practice
  drill
  *étude (Fr., E.)
  exercice (Fr.)
  esercizio (It.)

ekphonetic notation (Gr.)
  ecphonetic (Gr.)
  cantillation
  cheironomic

oratorical
adiastematic

electronic music
  computer music
  musique concrète (Fr.)
  concrete music
  synthesizer
  Ondes Martenot (Fr.)
  Ondes musicales (Fr.)
  theremin
  electrophone

electronica
  pop music
  hip-hop
  rock
  techno
  rap
  reggae
  ska
  world music

electropneumatic action (organ
  key action

vs. mechanical, tracker action

elegy
  *lament
  plaint
  dirge
  requiem (Lat.)
  planctus (Lat.)
  threnody
  lamento (It., Sp.)
  Klagelied (G.)
  tombeau (Fr.)
  déploration (Fr.)
  elegia (It., Sp.)
  Elegie (G.)
  élégie (Fr.)

élévation (Fr.)
  *upbeat
  weak beat

levé (Fr.)
anacrusis (Lat.)
arsis (Gr.)
arsi (It.)
anacrusi (It., Sp.)
anacrouse (Fr.)
levé (Fr.)
Hebung (G.)
Auftakt (G.)

vs. frappé (Fr.)
downbeat

elevator music
easy listening
light classics
popular music
*backround music
lift music
dinner music
salon music
dentist music

vs. serious music

eleventh (interval)
compound fourth
undicesima/o (It.)
onzième (Fr.)
Undezime (G.)
undecima (It., Sp.)
oncena (Sp.)

embellishment
*ornament
grace note(s)
embroidering
divisions
flos (Lat., 13c.)
coloratura
improvisation
abbellimento (It.)
adornamento (It.)
broderie (Fr.)
ornement (Fr.)
agrément (Fr.)

fioritura (It.)
fregiatura (It.)
Verzierung (G.)
adorno (Sp.)
glosas (Sp.)
melismatic
ornate

embolada (Port.)
Brazilian folk song
patter song
parlando (It.)
comic opera
scat singing
rap

embouchure (E., Fr.)
imboccatura (It.)
Mundloch (G.)
Ansatz (G.)
embocadura (Sp.)
boquilla (Sp.)
lip

2. mouthpiece
bocchino (It.)
Mundstück (G.)
bec (Fr.)
becco (It.)
Schnabel (G.)
cup (brass)
Kessel (G.)

embroider(y)
ornament
embellish
decorate
ornate
florid
melismatic
fioritura (It.)
embellir (Fr.)
verzieren (G.)
abbellire (It.)
adornar (Sp.)

emisión (Sp.)
*broadcast
trasmissione (It.)
émission (Fr.)
Sendung (G.)
radio
television
cable
satellite

emotional
impassioned
passionate
*appassionata (It.)
passionément (Fr.)
avec passion (Fr.)
pasionada (Sp.)
leidenschaftlich (G.)

2. sentimental (E., Fr., Sp.)
sentimentale (It.)
schmaltzy
slushy, mushy
empfindsam (G.)
schmalzig (G.)

emphasized
accented
stressed
*accusé (Fr.)
en déhors (Fr.)
enfatico (It.)
betont (G.)
resaltado (Sp.)

Empore (G.)
choir
choir gallery
choirloft
Chorempore (G.)
cantoria (It.)

empty fifth(s)
open fifth (no third)
naked fifth
offene Quintenparallelen (G.)

empty measure/bar
grand pause
general pause
hold
fermata (It.)
rest
caesura
railroad tracks
cesura (It., Sp.)
césure (Fr.)
Zäsur (G.)
vuoto (It.)
misura vuota (It.)
pausa generale (It.)
pause générale (Fr.)

en allant (Fr.)
going
moderato (It.)
*andante (It.)
gehend (G.)
andando (Sp.)

en aparté (Fr.)
*aside
sotto voce (It.)
very soft
under one's breath
stage whisper

en augmentant (Fr.)
*crescendo (It.)
getting louder

en badinant (Fr.)
playful
sportive
jestingly
scherzo, scherzando (It.)
Scherzhaft (G.)

en chamade (Fr.)
organ pipes lying horizontal
fanfare stop
reed pipes

en coulisse (Fr.)
offstage
*backstage
in the wings
behind the scenes
retroscena (It.)
Hinterbühne (G.)
hinter der Szene (G.)
hinter den Kulissen (G.)
bastidores (Sp.)
entre bastidores (Sp,)

en dehors (Fr.)
emphasized
brought out
prominent
*accusé (Fr.)
con enfasi (It.)
enfatico (It.)
nachdrucklich (G.)

en glissant (Fr.)
*glissando (It.)
portamento (It.)
glissade
sliding
slide
glissé (Fr.)
gleitend (G.)
resbalando (Sp.)

en mesure (Fr.)
*a tempo
in time
in strict time
im Takt (G.)
a compás (Sp.)

en perdant le son (Fr.)
*decrescendo
getting softer
en mourant (Fr.)
morendo (It.)
ersterbend (G.)
expirando (Sp.)

en serrant (Fr.)
*stringendo (It.)
stretto (It.)
accelerando (It.)
en serrant le mouvement (Fr.)
getting faster

vs. en retenant (Fr.)

en sourdain (Fr.)
mutes
dampers
deadened
muffled
piano (It.)
con sordina (It.)
gedämpft (G.)
cubierto (Sp.)
couvert (Fr.)
*coperto (It.)

en su lugar (Sp.)
as written
at (that) pitch
*loco (It.)
ad locum (Lat.)

enchaînement (Fr.)
*voice-leading
part-leading
Stimmführung (G.)
movimento di voci (It.)
conducción de las voces (Sp.)
conduite des voix (Fr.)

enchaînez (Fr.)
segue (It.)
*attacca (It.)
es folg (G.)
sigue (Sp.)

enchiriadis, enchiridion (Gr.)
handbook
manual
collection

*anthology
florigelium (Lat.)
Denkmäler (G.)

enclume (Fr.)
anvil
incudine (It.)
Amboss (G.)
yunque (Sp.)

encore (E., Fr.)
again, more
repeat
ancore (It.)
bis (Fr., G., Lat.)
altra volta (It.)
noch einmal (G.)
Zugabe (G.)
otra vez (Sp.)

end
fine (It.)
fin (Fr., Sp.)
Schluss (G.)

endecha (Sp.)
*funeral song
requiem
*lament
trenodia (It.)
treno (Sp.)

ending
close
*cadence
termination
first, second ending
ouvert, clos (Fr.)
aperto, chiuso (It.)
fine (It.)
finalis (Lat.)
differentiae (Lat.)
distinctio (Lat.)
*coda
clausula (Lat.)

endpin
puntale (It.)
pique, piquet (Fr.)
Stachel (G.)
Knopf (G.)
puntal (Sp.)
peg
spike
tailpin

enechemata (Gr.)
*mode
scale
echos, echoi (Gr.)
tonoi (Gr.)
oktoechos (Gr.)

enfant(s) de choeur (Fr.)
*choirboy(s)
choristers
cantore (It.)
Sängerknabe (G.)
Chorknabe (G.)
Kapelknabe (G.)
putti (It.)
ragazzo-i (It.)
niños de coro (Sp.)

enfatigo (It., Sp.)
*emphasized
accented
stressed
lead voice
en dehors (Fr.)

engagement
concert season
run
tour
gig
club date
booking
stagione (It.)
saison (Fr.)
Spielzeit (G.)
temporada (Sp.)

enganche al pedalero (Sp.)
coupler, pedal coupler (org.)
accoppiamento (It.)
accouplement (Fr.)
tirasse (Fr.)
Koppelpedal (G.)
Pedalkoppel (G.)
acoplamiento (Sp.)

enge Harmonie (G.)
close harmony
barbershop harmony
enge Lage (G.)
equal voices
voci pari (It.)
voix égales (Fr.)
gleiche Stimmen (G.)
Aequalstimmen (G.)
voces iguales (Sp.)

2. close score

Engelstimme (G., organ)
vox angelica (Lat., It.)
voix céleste (Fr.)
céleste (Fr.)
detuned
jeu céleste (Fr.)
jeu d'anges (Fr.)
vox angelica (Lat.)
vox coelestis (Lat.)
unda maris (Lat.)
vox humana (Lat.)

Engführung (G.)
stretto
stringendo (It.)
accelerando (It.)
faster

englische Mechanik (G.)
double escapement
doublehopper (piano)
grasshopper
doppio scappamento (It.)
double échappement (Fr.)

doppelte Auslösung (G.)
Repetitionsmechanik (G.)

English discant (15c.)
fauxbourdon (Fr.)
improvisation
polyphony
homophony
harmonizing

English flute
*recorder
fipple flute
flageolet
vertical flute
whistle flute
flauto a becco (It.)
flûte à bec (Fr.)
flûte à neuf trous (Fr.)
flûte d'Angleterre (Fr.)
Blockflöte (G.)
flauta de pico (Sp.)
flauto diritto (It.)
duct flute
ocarina

vs. German flute

English horn
cor anglais (Fr.)
corno inglese (It.)
Englischhorn (G.)
Enlisch(es) Horn (G.)
corno inglés (Sp.)
oboe da caccia (It.)
oboe d'amore (It.)
alto oboe

English opera
ballad opera
folk opera
Singspiel (G.)
operetta
light opera

enharmonic

equivalent notes
euharmonic
**enharmonische
Entsprechung (G.)
enarmonico (It., Sp.)
enharmonique (Fr.)**
homophone (Fr.)

2. tetrachord (Gr.)
scale

enharmonic modulation
pivotal chord/note
common chord/tone
enharmonische Umdeutung
(G.)

enigmatic canon
riddle canon
puzzle canon
canone enigmatico (It., Sp.)
canon énigmatique (Fr.)
Rätselkanon (G.)

enlever la sourdine (Fr.)
remove mutes
mutes off
take off mutes
levate i sordini (It.)
senza sordino (It.)
sans sourdine (Fr.)
Dämpfer weg/ab/abheben (G.)
*ohne Dämpfer (G.)
sin sordina (Sp.)
levanten la sordina (Sp.)

enregister (Fr.)
to record
to tape, tape-record
registrare (It.)
aufnehmen (G.)
registrar (Sp.)

enregistrement (Fr.)
recording
sound reproduction

pressing
taping
registrazione (It.)
Aufnahme (G.)
registro (Sp.)

ensalada (Sp.)
quodlibet (Lat.)
*medley
pot-pourri (Fr.,E.)
olio
overture
farrago
farragina (It.)
messanza (It.)
mescolanza (It.)
pastiche (Fr.)
salmi(s) (Fr.)
Querschnitt (G.)
olla podrida (Sp.)
program chanson
madrigal

ensayo (Sp.)
rehearsal
practice
run-through
going-over
drill
*dress rehearsal
prova (It.)
repetizione (It.)
répétition (Fr.)
Probe (G.)

ensayo general (Sp.)
dress rehearsal
full rehearsal
ultima prova (It.)
répétition générale (Fr.)
Generalprobe (G.)

ensemble (E., Fr., G.)
consort
broken consort
chamber group

154

combo
band

2. unity
group precision
togetherness
tightness

entertainment
show
spectacle
musical
vaudeville
act
extravaganza
minstrel show
revue
variety show
talent show
floor show
follies
operetta
opera
cork opera
masque
entremet (Fr. 14-15c.)
entremés (Sp.)
zarzuela (Sp.)
Unterhaltung (G.)
Singspiel (G.)
spettacolo (It.)
divertissement (Fr.)

entonación (Sp.)
pitch
*frequency
vibration
oscillation
intonation
tone
intonazione (It.)
diapason (It., Fr.)
hauteur du ton (Fr.)
Tonhöhe (G.)
Kammerton (G.)
Stimmung (G.)

diapasón (Sp.)

entonner (Fr.)
*intone
start off
strike up
begin
introduce
intonare (It.)
anstimmen (G.)
entonar (Sp.)

entr'acte (Fr.)
interlude
intermezzo (It.)
act-tune
*curtain music/tune
divertissement (Fr.)
entreacto (Sp.)
Zwischenspiel (G.)
prelude

2. intermission
*interval
pause

entrada (Sp.)
intrada (It.)
entrata (It.)
entrée (Fr.)
introduction
prélude (Fr.)
*Einleitung (G.)
Vorspiel (G.)
entremés (Sp.)

2. entrance (song/hymn)
processional song
introit
introitus (Lat.)
ingressa (It.)
Eingang (G.)

entrance, entry
statement
theme

dux (Lat.)
comes (Lat.)
subject
answer
Einsatz (G.)

2. introitus (Lat.)
introit
ingressa (Lat., It.)
entrée (Fr.)
introït (Fr.)
Introïtus (G.)
Eingang (G.)
introito (Sp.)
entrada (Sp.)

entre bastidores (Sp.)
in the wings
behind the scenes
*backstage
offstage
retroscena (It.)
en coulisse (Fr.)
hinter der Szene (G.)
hinter den Kulissen (G.)

entresol (Fr.)
mezzanine
*balcony
dress circle
gallery
ammezzato (It.)
Mezzanin (G.)
mezanina (Sp.)
entresuelo (Sp.)

enueg (Fr.)
satiric song (Troubadour)
goliard song

enunciation
diction
declamation
pronunciation
articulation
text

envoi, envoy (Fr.)
  tornada (Prov.)
  concluding section
  *coda
  epilogue
  commiato (It.)

eolifono (It.)
  wind-machine
  éoliphone (Fr.)
  appareil à vent (Fr.)
  machine à vent (Fr.)
  Windmaschine (G.)
  máquina de viento (Sp.)

epicede
  dirge
  *lament
  funeral song
  requiem
  epicedium (Lat.)
  epicedio (It., Sp.)
  epicède (Fr.)
  Trauergesang (G.)
  epiodion (Gr.)

epilogue
  *coda
  envoi (Fr.)
  cauda (Lat.)
  tag

vs. prologue

épinette (Fr.)
  *harpsichord
  spinet
  virginal(s)
  cembalo (It.)
  Kielflügel (G.)
  clavecin (Fr., Sp.)
  chekker

épinette des Vosges (Fr.)
  zither
  bûche (Fr.)

bûche de Flandres (Fr.)
Hummel, Humle (G.)
dulcimer

epinicion (Gr.)
  victory song
  triumphant song
  triumphant hymn
  sanctus (Lat.)
  angelic hymn
  cherubic hymn
  song of the angels
  aius trisagion (Gr.)

episema (Gr.)
  dash over neume
  tenuto (It.)

2. ictus (Lat.)
  vertical episema

episode
  transition
  bridge passage
  soggetto (It.)
  andamento (It.)
  episodio (It., Sp.)
  épisode (Fr.)
  Zwischenspiel (G.)
  Zwischensatz (G.)

epistle side
  decani (Lat.)
  south side
  right side

vs. gospel side

epistrophe (Gr.)
  *refrain
  chorus
  respond
  antistrophe (Gr.)

epithalamium (Lat., E.)
  nuptual song

wedding song
bridal song
epithalamy
epithalamion (Gr.)
epitalamio (It., Sp.)
canto nuziale (It.)
épithalame (Fr.)
chanson de noce (Fr.)
Brautlied (G.)
canto nupcial (Sp.)

epode (Gr.)
  *refrain
  chorus

2. ode
  *coda
  ending

eptacorde (Fr.)
  heptachord
  scale of seven notes
  eptacordo (It.)

2. seventh (interval)
  settima (It.)
  septième (Fr.)
  Septime (G.)
  setima (Sp.)

equal temperament
  equal tuning
  tempered tuning

vs. just intonation
  mean-tone tuning

equal values/rhythm
  free rhythm
  chant rhythm
  ad longum (Lat.)

equal voices
  women's voices
  children's voices
  cherub choir

treble choir
boychoir
men's voices
close harmony
barbershop harmony
voces aequales (Lat.)
voci pari (It.)
voci eguales (It.)
voix égales (Fr.)
gleiche Stimmen (G.)
Aequalstimmen (G.)
voces iguales (Sp.)
enge Harmonie (G.)
enge Lage (G.)

vs. mixed voices

erhöhen (G.)
raise
sharp
hausser (Fr.)
alzare (It.)
alzar (Sp.)

vs, erniedrigen (G.)

Erinnerungsmotiv (G.)
Leitmotiv (G.)
idée fixe (Fr.)
Hauptmotiv (G.)
leitmotif
theme
leading motive
motivo principale (It.)
motif conducteur (Fr.)
motivo principal (Sp.)

erniedrigen (G.)
to flat
lower
abbassare (It.)
baisser (Fr.)
senken (G.)
bajar/rebajar (Sp.)

vs, erhöhen (G.)

ernst (G.)
serioso, serio (It., Sp.)
serious(ly)
ernestly
sérieux (Fr.)

Ersatzklausel (G.)
substitute clausula
clausula (Lat.)
discant section
organum (Lat.)
clausola sostituta (It.)
clausule alternative (Fr.)
clausula sustitutiva (Sp.)

erste Rang (G.)
dress circle
*balcony
gallery
prima galleria (It.)
premier balcon (Fr.)
corbeille (Fr.)

erste Stimme (G.)
top part
highest voice/part
*soprano part
discant
lead voice
superius (Lat.)
cantus (Lat.)
discantus (Lat.)
dessus (Fr.)
melody part

erste Umkehrung (G.)
first inversion chord
sixth chord
chord of the sixth
*six-three chord
primo rivolto (It.)
accordo di sesta (It.)
premier renversement (Fr.)
accord de sixte (Fr.)
Sextakkord (G.)
acorde de sexta y tercera Sp.)

Erzähler (G.)
narrator
evangelist
historicus (Lat.)
evangelium (Lat.)
testo (It.)
récitant (Fr.)
chronista (Lat.)
narratore (It.)
narrateur (Fr.)
Evangelisten (G.)
narrador (Sp.)

Erzlaute (G.)
*archlute
*lute
theorbo
bass lute
chitarrone (It.)
arciliuto (It.)
archiluth (Fr.)
archilaúd (Sp.)

es folg (G.)
segue (It.)
*attacca (It.)
suit, suivez (Fr.)

esacordo (It.)
hexachord
hexachordum (Lat.)
hexacorde (Fr.)
Hexachord (G.)
hexacordo (Sp.)
scale of six notes

2. sixth (interval)
tonus cum diapente (Lat.)
sesta (It.)
sixte, sixième (Fr.)
Sexte (G.)
sexta (Sp.)

escacherium (Lat.)
chekker
*clavichord

clavicordo (It.)
clavicorde (Fr.)
Klavichord (G.)
clavicordio (Sp.)

escala (Sp.)
scale
gamma (It.)
échelle (Fr.)
gamme (Fr.)
Tonleiter (G.)
Skala (G.)
scala (It.)
gama (Sp.)

escape note
*cambiata
passing tone
non-harmonic tone
changing note
échappée (Fr.)
note changée (Fr.)
nota cambiata (It.)
Wechselnote (G.)
note cambiada (Sp.)

escapement (piano)
release, key release
hopper
grasshopper
*double escapement
scappamento (It.)
échappement (Fr.)
Auslöser, Auslösung (G.)
escape, escapatoria (Sp.)

escena, escenario (Sp.)
stage
platform
bandwagon
scena (It.)
scène (Fr.)
Bühne (G.)
tablado (Sp.)

escobillas (Sp.)

brushes
wire/steel brushes
spazzole (It.)
balais de jazz (Fr.)
Rute (G.)
Besen, Jazzbesen (G.)

escocésa (Sp.)
polka
galop
can-can
écossaise (Fr.)
scozzese (It.)
anglaise (Fr.)
française (Fr.)
Schottische (G.)
German polka

escolán (Sp.)
chorister
*choirboy
cantore (It.)
fanciullo del coro (It.)
ragazzi (It.)
putto (It.)
corista (It., Sp.)
enfants de choeur (Fr.)
Chorknaben (G.)
Kapellknaben (G.)
niños de coro (Sp.)

escolanía (Sp.)
*children's choir
boychoir
treble choir
coro di ragazzi (It.)
maîtrise d'enfants (Fr.)
Knabenchor (G.)

escotadura (Sp.)
*mouthpiece
bocca, bocchetta, -ino (It.)
bec (Fr.)
Schnabel (G.)

escuela de música (Sp.)

*choirschool
lyceum
*academy of music
music school
conservatory of music
scuola di música (It.)
conservatoire (Fr.)
Hochschüle für Musik (G.)

esecuzione (It.)
execution
delivery
performance
exécution (Fr.)
Ausführung (G.)
ejecución (Sp.)

esercizio (It.)
exercise
study
practice piece
drill
*étude (Fr., E.)
Etüde (G.)
Übungsstück (G.)
ejercicio (Sp.)

esordio (It.)
première (E., Fr.)
debut, début (E., Fr.)
debutto (It.)
Debüt (G.)
estreno (Sp.)
first performance

espace (Fr.)
space (on the staff)
spazio (It.)
interligne (Fr.)
Zwischenraum (G.)
interlinea (Sp.)

vs. ligne (Fr.)
line

2. interval

esposizione (It.)
    exposition (E., Fr.)
    theme(s)
    Exposition (G.)
    Ausführung (G.)
    exposición (Sp.)

espressivo (It.)
    expressively
    with expression
    with feeling
    expressif (Fr.)
    ausdrucksvoll (G.)
    gefühlvoll (G.)
    expresivo (Sp.)

essential seventh
    leading tone
    subtonic
    note sensible (Fr.)
    sensibile (It.)
    Leitton (G.)
    sensible (Sp.)
    ti, si
    seventh note

esspressione (It.)
    expression (E., Fr.)
    feeling
    emotion
    Ausdruck (G.)
    expresión (Sp.)

estampie (Fr.)
    stantipes (Lat.)
    saltarello (It.)
    istampita (It.)
    estampida (Sp.)
    sequence form
    dance (13-14c.)

estensione (It.)
    range
    compass
    gamut (Lat.)
    tessitura (It.)

ambitus (Lat., Fr., E.)
ambito (It., Sp.)
Umfang (G.)
Raum (G.)
Ausdehnung (G.)
diapason (Fr.)
étendue (Fr.)

estinto (It.)
    very soft
    hushed
    pianissimo (It.)
    éteint (Fr.)

estratto (It.)
    *excerpt
    fragment
    extract
    section
    sample
    example
    movement
    extensión (Sp.)
    tesitura (Sp.)

estreno (Sp.)
    first appearance
    first performance
    *début (Fr.)
    première (Fr.)
    debutto (It.)
    esordio (It.)
    Debüt (G.)

estribillo (Sp.)
    *refrain (E., Fr.)
    chorus
    ripresa (It.)
    rondeau (Fr.)
    ritornello (It.)
    rechant (Fr.)
    burden

ethnic folk music
    folk music
    popular music

Volksmusik (G.)
musica populare (It.)
musique folklorique (Fr.)
musique populaire (Fr.)
música popular (Sp.)
ethnomusicology

ethos (Gr.)
    character of scales
    philosophie (Fr.)
    Gesinnung (G.)

étouffoir (Fr.)
    *mute
    damper
    buff stop (harpsichord)
    lute stop (harpsichord)
    sordino (It.)
    una corda (It.)
    soft pedal (piano)
    Dämpfer (G.)
    sordina (Sp.)

ettacordo (It.)
    eptacordo (It.)
    heptachord
    seven-note scale
    diatonic scale

2. seventh (interval)
    ditonus cum diapente (Lat.)
    settima (It.)
    septième (Fr.)
    Sept, Septime (G.)
    séptima (Sp.)

étude (Fr., E.)
    study
    exercise
    lesson
    invention
    practice piece
    drill

exercitium (Lat.)
    studio (It.)
    esercizio (It.)

159

exercice (Fr.)
Etüde (G.)
Übung (G.)
Handstück (G.)
Übensstück (G.)
Aufgabe (G.)
estudio (Sp.)
ejercicio (Sp.)

etwas (G.)
somewhat
rather
a little
poco (It., Sp.)
peu (Fr.)
wenig (G.)

Eucharist
Holy Communion
Lord's Supper
*mass
missa (Lat.)
agape feast
love feast
communion service
liturgy
Abendmahl (G.)
Kirchenordnung (G.)
Kirchenamt (G.)

euharmonic
*enharmonic
equivalent notes
homophone (Fr.)
enarmonico (It.)
enharmonique (Fr.)
enharmonisch (G.)

eunuch flute
mirliton (Fr.)
flûte eunuque (Fr.)
onion flute
toy flute
toy instrument
kazoo
bazoo

euouae (Lat.)
endings (psalm chants)
differentia (Lat.)
saeculorum amen (Lat.)
Gloria Patri (Lat.)
Lesser Doxology
evovae (Lat.)
aeuia, aevia (Lat.)
oioueae (world without end
amen)

euphonium (E., Fr., G., Sp.)
tuba, tenor tuba
baritone horn
euphone
basse à pistons (Fr.)
flicorno basso (It.)
eufonio (It.)
Baryton (G.)
Barytonhorn (G.)
bombardino (Sp.)
bugle

Evangelist
narrator
historicus (Lat.)
Evangelium (Lat.)
chronista (Lat.)
testo (It.)
narratore (It.)
récitant (Fr.)
narrateur (Fr.)
Erzähler (G.)
Evangelisten (G.)
narrador (Sp.)

evening song/music
nocturne
Nachtmusik (G.)
Abendlied (G.)
*serenade
notturno (It.)
serenata (It.)
serenada (Sp.)
sérénade (Fr.)
Ständchen (G.)

vs. matin song
dawn song

evensong
evening prayer
vespers
vesperae (Lat.)
canonical hour
day hour
monastic office
*Divine office

eversio (Lat.)
inversion (of parts)
reversal
evolutio Lat.)
rivolgimento (It.)
evolution (Fr.)
renversement (Fr.)
Umkehrung (G.)
evolución (Sp.)

evirato (It.)
castrato (It.)
male alto/soprano
eunuch
sopranista (It.)
tenorino (It.)
castrat (Fr.)
Kastrat (G.)
castrado (Sp.)

excerpt
fragment
section
movement
example
extract
estratto (It.)
extrait (Fr.)
Ausschnitt (G.)
Auszug (G.)
extracto (Sp.)

execution
performance

delivery
esecuzione (It.)
exécution (Fr.)
Ausführung (G.)
ejecución (Sp.)

exequiae (Lat.)
*funeral music
requiem (Lat.)
*lament, lamentation
Exequien (G.)
exequies
elegy
planctus (Lat.)
Trauermusik (G.)
tombeau (Fr.)
cantos de velorio (Sp.)

exercise
*étude
study
practice piece
drill
exercitium (Lat.)
esercizio (It.)
exercice (Fr.)
Übung, Übungsstück (G.)
ejercicio (Sp.)
estudio (Sp.)

exitus (Lat.)
*coda
tag
cauda (Lat.)
neupma (Lat.)
envoi, envoy (Fr.)

expirando (Sp.)
decay
dying
fading (away)
decrescendo (It.)
en mourant (Fr.)
morendo (It.)
calando (It.)
ersterbend (G.)

exposition (E., Fr.)
theme(s)
statement
sonata form
sonata-allegro form
esposizione (It.)
Exposition (G.)
Ausführung (G.)
exposición (Sp.)

vs. development section

expression (E., Fr.)
feeling
emotion
esspressione (It.)
Ausdruck (G.)
expresión (Sp.)

expressively
with expression
with feeling
con espressione (It.)
espressivo (It.)
expressif (Fr.)
mit Gefühl (G.)
ausdrucksvoll (G.)
gefühlvoll (G.)
expresivo (Sp.)

Expressivorgel (G.)
*harmonium
reed organ
parlor organ
pump organ
American organ
orgue expressif (Fr.)
Windharmonika (G.)

extempore, extemporize
ad-lib
improvised
impromptu
*freely
played by ear
fake it

ad libitum (It.)
a bene placido (It.)
a piacere (It.)
a capriccio (It.)
libre (Fr.)
au caprice (Fr.)
nach Gefallen (G.)
a placer (Sp.)
a voluntad (Sp.)

extended play
recording
45 rpm record
record
disc
*long-playing record
LP record, 33 1/3 rpm
Langspielplatte (G.)
gramophone record
phonograph record
platter
pressing

extension
shank (brass instr.)
*crook
ritorto (It.)
corpo di ricambio (It.)
corps de rechange (Fr.)
Aufsatzbogen (G.)
Stimmbogen (G.)
cuerpo de recambio (Sp.)

extensión (Sp.)
range
*compass
ambitus (Lat.)
tessitura (It.)
diapason (Fr.)
tessiture (Fr.)
Umfang (G.)
Raum (G.)
Lage (G.)
tesitura (Sp.)
gamut (Lat.)

extension organ
    unified organ
    duplexing
    unit organ
    cinema organ
    theatre organ
    organo da teatro (It.)
    organo da cinematografo (It.)
    orgue de cinéma (Fr.)
    Kinoorgel (G.)
    Multiplexorgel (G.)
    órgano de cine (Sp.)

extra
    bit part
    walk-on
    super
    supernumerary
    minor role
    supporting role
    comprimario/a (It.)
    Statist (G.)

extract
    *excerpt
    fragment
    section
    example
    estratto (It.)
    extrait (Fr.)
    Ausschnitt (G.)
    Auszug (G.)
    extracto (Sp.)

extrasino (Sp.)
    portamento (It.)
    slide
    *glissando (It.)
    gliding

extravaganza
    show
    floor show
    *entertainment
    lavish production
    revue
    spectacular
    variety show
    minstrel show
    follies
    musical
    opera, operetta

exultet (Lat.)
    praeconium pascale (Lat.)
    Easter hymn (vigil)
    Easter proclamation

eye music
    descriptive music
    program music
    tone painting
    tone poem
    word painting
    musica visiva (It.)
    musique oculaire (Fr.)
    Augenmusik (G.)
    música de ojo (Sp.)
    música para la vista (Sp.)

F

F- clef
bass clef
baritone clef
chiave di fa (It.)
chiave di basso (It.)
clef de fa (Fr.)
F-Schlüssel (G.)
Bassschlüssel (G.)
llave de fa (Sp.)
clave de bajo (Sp.)
clave de fa (Sp.)
clave grave (Sp.)

F-hole
sound hole
effe (It.)
ouïle (F.)
efe (Sp.)
vido (Sp.)
F-Loch (G.)

fa (It.)
subdominant
fourth degree

faburden
fauxbourdon (Fr., E.)
harmony
English discant
falsobordone (It.)
fabordón (Sp.)
homophonic
Anglican chant

2. organ voluntary
prelude
postlude

facade, façade
display pipes (organ)

dummy pipes
canne di facciata (It.)
Stummpfeifen (G.)
Prospektpfeifen (G.)
Füllpfeifen (G.)

Fackeltanz (G.)
slow torchlight dance
polonaise (Fr.)
polacca (It.)

fächerförmiges Pedal (G.)
radiating pedalboard (organ)
concave pedals
fan-shaped pedalboard

facture (Fr.)
*form (composition)
structure
plan
fattura (It.)
Faktur (G.)
forma (It., Sp.)
dessin (Fr.)
forme (Fr.)
Aufbau (G.)
Gestalt (G.)

2. scale (organ pipes)
proportion
fattura (It.)
misura (It.)
mesure (Fr.)
diapason (Fr.)
Mensur (G.)
mensura (Sp.)
voicing
regulating

fade out, fading away
decay
morendo (It.)
*decrescendo (It.)
diminuendo (It.)
calando (It.)
perdenosi (It.)

smortando (It.)
spirando (It.)
expirando (Sp.)
en mourant (Fr.)
ersterbend (G.)

fado, fadinho (Port.)
popular song
song of fate

Fagott (G.)
*bassoon
fagotto (It.)
basson (Fr.)
fagote (Sp.)
bajon (Sp.)
curtal
bombard

Fagottgeige (G.)
bassoon fiddle
bass viola
viola bastarda (It.)
viola di fagotto (It.)
Handbassel (G.)
division viol
bass viol (small)

fagottino (It.)
tenor oboe
tenoroon
treble bassoon
high curtal
petit basson (Fr.)
Quintfagott (G.)
Tenorfagott (G.)
fagote quinta (Sp.)

fagottone (It.)
*contrabassoon
double bassoon
contrafagotto (It.)
contrebasson (Fr.)
Kontrafagott (G.)
contrafagot (Sp.)

Fagottzug (G.)
   prepared piano
   piano préparé (Fr.)
   piano preparado (Sp.)

Fahn, Fahne, Fähnchen (G.)
   flag or hook (of a note)
   tail
   codetta (It.)
   crochet (Fr.)
   Notenfahne (G.)
   rabillo (Sp.)
   gancho (Sp.)

fairy bells
   *bell harp
   box zither
   cithare sur caisse (Fr.)
   Kastenzither (G.)

fake book
   score
   lead sheet
   charts
   short score
   condensed score
   improvise
   harmonize
   collection
   anthology
   song collection

fake it
   *improvise
   extemporize
   play by ear
   ad-lib
   *freely
   jam
   read charts
   follow lead sheets

falsa musica (Lat., 13c.)
   musica ficta (Lat., 14c.)
   musica falsa (Lat.)
   false music

   conjuncta, conjunctio (Lat., 14c.)
   synemmenon (Gr.)
   chromatic notes

falsa relazione (It.)
   false relation
   *cross-relation
   fausse relation (Fr.)
   Querstand (G.)
   falsa relación (Sp.)
   *dissonance
   clash
   discord

falsch singen (G.)
   out of tune
   sing off-key, off-pitch
   monotone
   tone-deaf
   scordato (It.)
   stonare (It.)
   désacordé (Fr.)
   verstimmt (G.)

false cadence
   *deceptive cadence
   interrupted cadence
   half-cadence

false fifth, triad
   *diminished fifth
   augmented fourth
   tritone
   devil's interval

false note
   mistake
   wrong note
   sour note
   clinker
   stecca (It.)
   galliparo (It.)
   fausse note (Fr.)
   canard (Fr.)
   Misston (G.)

false relation
   cross-relation
   clash
   dissonance
   falsa relazione (It.)
   fausse relation (Fr.)
   Querstand (G.)
   falsa relación (Sp.)

falsetto (E., It.)
   head voice (male voice)
   mezza voce (It.)
   half-voice
   high tenor
   countertenor
   voix de fausset (Fr.)
   fausset (Fr.)
   Falsett (G.)
   Fistelstimme (G.)
   falsete (Sp.)
   voz de cabeza (Sp.)

falsobordone (It., 16c.)
   harmonized chant
   Anglican chant
   fabordón (Sp.)
   fauxbourdon

fan(s)
   *audience
   listeners
   concertgoers
   groupies
   the public
   congregation

fan-shaped pedals/pedalboard
   concave pedalboard (org.)
   radiating pedalboard
   fächerörmiges Pedal (G.)

fan trumpet/tuba (org.)
   chamade (Fr.)
   horizontal trumpet
   state trumpet

herald's trumpet
*Aïda trumpet

fanciullo del coro (It.)
  *choirboys
  choristers
  cantori (It.)
  ragazzi (It.)
  putti (It.)
  enfants de choeur (Fr.)
  Chorknaben (G.)
  Sängerknaben (G.)
  niños de coro (Sp.)
  escolán (Sp.)

fancy, fancie, fantasy
  fantasia (It., E., Sp.)
  fantaisie (Fr.)
  Fantasie, Phantasie (G.)
  Fantasiestück (G.)
  impromptu
  *arabesque
  rhapsody
  capriccio (It.)
  caprice (Fr.)
  réverie (Fr.)
  sogno (It.)
  stravaganza (It.)
  Träumerei (G.)

2. quodlibet
  potpourri
  *medley

fandango (Sp.)
  Spanish dance, triple meter
  malagueña (Sp.)
  flamenco (Sp.)
  cachucha (Sp.)
  bolero (Sp.)
  chico, chica (Sp.)

fanfare (E., Fr.)
  trumpet call
  bugle call
  flourish

tantara, tarantara
honors
salute
call
tuck, tucket
reveille
taps
Tusch (G.)
chiamata (It.)
fanfara (It.)
squillo di tromba (It.)
sonnerie (Fr.)
chamade (Fr.)
Fanfare (G.)
fanfarria (Sp.)
banda (It., Sp.)
charanga (Sp.)
sonada (Sp.)
toque de trompeta (Sp.)
Blasmusik (G.)
Trompetenstoss (G.)

farandole (Fr.)
  Provencal dance, 6/8 time
  farandola (It.)
  farandula (Sp.)
  branle (Fr.)
  cotillon (Fr.)

faringe (It., Sp.)
  pharynx (E., Fr.)
  voice-box
  larynx
  pipes
  Rachenhöhle (G.)

farsa (Lat.)
  farse
  trope
  tropus (Lat.)

farsa per musica (It.)
  burlesque
  farce
  musical comedy
  minstrel show

follies
comic opera
operetta

fasola
  sol-fa
  tonic solfa
  *solmization
  solfeggio (It.)
  solfège (Fr.)
  character notation
  shape(d) notes
  dunce notes
  buckwheat notes
  music reading

fast
  quick
  lively
  rapid
  brisk
  allegro (It.)
  presto (It.)
  veloce (It.)
  vif (Fr.)
  vite (Fr.)
  rapide (Fr.)
  rasch (G.)
  schnell (G.)
  lebhaft (G.)
  alegre (Sp.)
  pronto (Sp.)
  veloz (Sp.)

vs. slow

faster, getting faster
  accelerando (It.)
  stringendo (It.)
  animando (It.)
  affretando (It.)
  en serrant (Fr.)
  schneller (G.)
  eilend (G.)
  treibend (G.)
  más pronto (Sp.)

vs. slower, getting slower

fattura (It.)
*form
design
plan
structure
forma (It., Sp.)
dessin (Fr.)
forme (Fr.)
facture (Fr.)
Faktur (G.)
Aufbau (G.)
Gestalt (G.)

2. scale (organ pipes)
proportion
misura (It.)
facture (Fr.)
diapason (Fr.)
mesure (Fr.)
Mensur (G.)
mensura (Sp.)

fausse note (Fr.)
false note
mistake
wrong note
stecca (It.)
canard (Fr.)
Misston (G.)
gallipavo (Sp.)

fausse relation (Fr.)
false relation
dissonance
*cross-relation
Querstand (G.)

faux, fausse (Fr.)
off-key, off-pitch
out of tune
flat/sharp
scordato (It.)
stonato (It.)
désacordé (Fr.)

verstimmt (G.)
falsch (G.)
unrein (G.)
falso (It., Sp.)

fauxbourdon (Fr.)
English discant
faburden
harmonized chant

favola per/in musica (It.)
*opera
music drama
opera seria (It.)

favoriti (It.)
semi-chorus
echo chorus
chamber choir
madrigal choir
concertina (It.)
coro concertato (It.)
coro concertino (It.)
coro favorito (It.)
coro recitante (It.)
soli (It.)
solo ensemble
vocal ensemble
petit choeur (Fr.)
demi-choeur (Fr.)
Kammerchor (G.)
Madrigalchor (G.)
coro de càmara (Sp.)

feedback
acoustical feedback
microphone squeal
reazione (It.)
réaction (Fr.)
Ruckkoppelung (G.)
Reaktion (G.)
reacción (Sp.)

feintes (Fr.)
black keys (keyboard)
accidentals

sharps and flats
touches noires (Fr.)
Obertasten (G.)
schwarze Obertasten (G.)

vs. palettes (Fr.)
touches blanches (Fr.)

Feldmusik (G., 17-18 c.)
brass music (outdoors)
field band music
military band music
music for winds

feminine ending
off-beat ending
syncopation
weak beat cadence

vs. masculine ending

feria (Lat.)
weekday
ordinary day

vs. dominica (Lat.)
sunday

ferial tone (chant)
simple tone
ordinary tone
tonus simplex (Lat.)
tonus ferialis (Lat.)
tonus oratorium (Lat.)

vs. solemn tone

fermata (It.)
a hold
a pause
corona (Lat., It.)
punto coronata (It.)
punto d'organo (It.)
couronne (Fr.)
point d'orgue (Fr.)
point d'arrêt (Fr.)

Fermate (G.)
Halt (G.)
Krone (G.)
Orgelpunkt (G.)
calderón (Sp.)
punto de órgano (Sp.)

Fernwerk (G.)
echo organ division
gallery organ
nave organ
antiphonal organ
organo d'eco (It., Sp.)
écho (Fr.)
clavier d'écho (Fr.)
Echoklavier (G.)

festoso (It.)
joyful
gioioso (It.)
festivo (It., Sp.)
gai (Fr.)
joyeux (Fr.)
frölich (G.)
alegre (Sp.)

feuillet d'album (Fr.)
album-leaf
pagina d'album (It.)
foglio d'album (It.)
Albumblatt (G.)
hoja de álbum (Sp.)
short piece

fiati (It.)
wind instruments
aerophones
brass and woodwinds
strumenti a fiato (It.)
instruments à vent (Fr.)
Blasinstrumente (G.)
instrumentos de viento (Sp.)

fiddle
*violin
rebec

viol
devil's box
fidula (Lat., It., Sp.)
viella (Lat.)
violino (It.)
vielle (Fr.)
violon (Fr.)
Fiedel (G.)
Geige (G.)
vihuela de arco (Sp.)

fiddle band
string band
string orchestra
orchestra d'archi (It.)
orchestre à cordes (Fr.)
Streichorchestrer (G.)
orquestra de cuerdas (Sp.)

fiddler
violinist
violinista (It.)
violiniste (Fr.)
Geiger, Geigerin (G.)

fiddlestick
bow
fiddle bow
arco (It., Sp.)
archetto (It.)
archet (Fr.)
Bogen (G.)

fife
flute
piccolo
penny whistle
fipple flute
piffero (It.)
fifre (Fr.)
Pfeife (G.)
pifano, pifaro (Sp.)
Querpfeife (G.)
Schweizeflöte (G.)

fife and drum (corps)

pipe and tabor
whittle and dub
galoubet (Fr.)
Galoubet (G.)
Schwegel und Tamborin (G.)
Querpfeife-Trommel (G.)
fluviol y tambori(l) (Sp.)

fifteenth (interval)
double octave
quindicesimo (It.)
decimaquinta
quizième (Fr.)
quincena (Sp.)
Quindezime (G.)
Fünfzehntel (G.)
Doppeloktave (G.)
disdiapason (Lat., Gr.)

fifteenth (organ)
two-foot stop
double octave
piccolo
super octave

fifth (interval)
diapente (Lat.)
dioxia (Gr.)
sesquialtera (Lat.)
perfect fifth
Quinta (It., Sp.)
quinte (Fr.)
Quinte (G.)
hemiola (medieval Gr.)

figle (Sp.)
tuba
bass trombone
serpent
*ophicleide
Klappenhorn (G.)

figura, figurae (Lat.)
note
neume
ligature

figura muta (Lat.)
　rest sign
　silenzio (It.)
　silence (Fr.)
　silencio (Sp.)
　pausa (It., Sp.)
　Pause (G.)
　pause (Fr.)

Figuralgesang, Figuralmusik (G.)
　figured music
　mensural music
　polyphonic music
　*canto figurato (It.)
　figurata (Lat.)

figuration
　*ornamentation
　decoration
　passage work
　melisma
　passaggio (It.)
　coloratura (It.)
　fioritura (It.)

figure (E., Fr.)
　motif, motive
　theme
　subject
　idea
　strain
　figura (It.)
　Figur (G.)

figured bass
　continuo
　thoroughbass
　basso continuo (It.)
　basso figurato (It.)
　basso generale (It.)
　basso cifrato (It.)
　basso numerato (It.)
　basso seguente (It.)
　basse chiffrée (Fr.)
　basse continue (Fr.)

　basse figurée (Fr.)
　bezifferter Bass (G.)
　Generalbass (G.)
　allgemeiner Bass (G.)
　bajo cifrado (Sp.)
　bajo continuo ,(Sp.)
　bajo numerado (Sp.)

fila (It., organ)
　rank (of pipes)
　set of pipes
　stop
　registro (It., Sp.)
　Register (G.)
　rang (Fr.)
　jeu (Fr.)
　registre (Fr.)
　Stimme (G.)

filar il tuono (It.)
　messa di voce (It.)
　swell the tone
　filar la voce (It.)
　filer la voix (Fr.)
　filer le son (Fr.)
　pose de la voix (Fr.)
　mise de la voix (Fr.)
　Schwellton (G.)
　poner la voz (Sp.)

film music
　underscoring
　incidental music
　*backround music
　musica per film (It.)
　musique de film (Fr.)
　Filmmusik (G.)
　música de película (Sp.)

filum (Lat.)
　stem (of a note)
　plica (Lat.)
　gambo (It.)
　queue (Fr.)
　Hals, Notenhals (G.)
　hampe (Fr.)

final cadence
　full cadence
　perfect cadence
　full close
　*authentic cadence

finale (It., E.)
　concluding movement
　last movement
　final (Fr., Sp.)
　dernier mouvement (Fr.)
　mouvement final (Fr.)
　Schlusssatz (G.)
　Schlussstück (G.)
　Finalsatz (G.)
　movimiento final (Sp.)
　conclusión (Sp.)
　último movimiento (Sp.)

finalis (Lat.)
　tonic note
　do
　ut (Lat.)
　keynote

2. close
　cadence
　affinalis (Lat.)
　confinalis (Lat.)

fine (It.)
　close
　end
　final cadence
　al fine (It.)
　fin (Fr., Sp.)
　Schluss (G.)

finger cymbals
　*crotales
　antique cymbals
　cimbalini (It.)
　cymbales digitales (Fr.)
　Fingercymbeln (G.)
　cymbales antiques (Fr.)
　cimbalillos digitales (Sp.)

finger excercise
  *etude
  drill
  study
  lesson
  practice piece

finger substitution
  ablösen (G.)
  diteggiatura cambiata (It.)
  changer le doigté (Fr.)
  cambiar la digitación (Sp.)

fingerboard
  fretboard
  tastiera (It.)
  touche (Fr.)
  manche (Fr.)
  Griffbrett (G.)
  batidor (Sp.)

fingerhole
  buco (It.)
  foro (It.)
  trou (Fr.)
  Griffloch, Tonloch (G.)
  Fingerloch (G.)
  agujera (Sp.)
  orificio (Sp.)

fingering
  digitazione (It.)
  applicatio (It.)
  diteggiatura (It.)
  doigté (Fr.)
  Fingersatz (G.)
  Applicatur (G.)
  digitación (Sp.)

fioretto (It.)
  grace note
  ornament
  embellishment
  adornamento (It.)
  abbellimento (It.)
  fregiatura (It.)

ornement (Fr.)
agrément (Fr.)
Verzierung (G.)
adorno (Sp.)
glosas (Sp.)

fioritura (It.)
  florid melody
  *ornamentation
  embellishment
  melismatic
  gorgia (It.)
  fioritures (Fr.)
  Blumen (G.)
  fioreos (Sp.)
  glosas (Sp.)

fipple flute
  *recorder
  *fife
  flageolet (Fr.)
  penny whistle
  ocarina
  tin whistle
  whistle flute
  toy flute
  duct flute
  flûte à bec (Fr.)

firing
  ringing all bells at once

vs. chiming
  change-ringing

first (interval)
  unison
  unisonus (Lat.)
  prime
  unisono (It., Sp.)
  unisson (Fr.)
  Prim (G.)
  Einklang (G.)

first (of a part)
  highest

leading
principal
first chair

first appearance
  *début
  première
  first performance
  opening night

first inversion triad
  sixth-chord
  six-three chord
  primo rivolto (It.)
  accordo di sesta (It.)
  premier renversement (Fr.)
  accord de sixte (Fr.)
  erste Umkehrung (G.)
  Sextakkord (G.)
  acorde de sexta (y tercera)
(Sp.)
  Italian sixth
  French sixth
  Gernan sixth
  Neapolitan sixth

first movement form
  sonata form
  sonata-allegro form

first-string player
  top player (instrumental)
  first desk
  principal
  lead player/singer
  lead part

Fistelstimme (G.)
  *falsetto voice
  head voice
  countertenor
  castrato (It.)
  fausset (Fr.)
  Falsett (G.)
  falsete (Sp.)

fistula (Lat.)
   pipe (organ)
   flute

five-part form
   *rondo form

five-three chord
   root position chord
   triad

fixed do
   absolute do

vs. movable do
   relative do

flag
   hook
   tail
   eighth-note
   codetta (It.)
   crochet de la note (Fr.)
   Fahne, Fähnchen (G.)
   Notenfahne (G.)
   rabillo (Sp.)
   gancho (Sp.)

flageolet (Fr.)
   flute
   recorder
   *fife
   fipple-flute
   duct flute
   flagioletto (It.)
   Flageolett (G.)
   flajolé, flajerle (Sp.)

flageolet tones
   *harmonics
   overtones
   partials
   aliquot tones

flam
   drum stroke (snare)

*drumbeat
   paradiddle
   ruff, ruffle
   drag
   rub-a-dub
   roll
   batterie (Fr.)
   redoble (Sp.)
   Trommelschlag (G.)

flamenco
   Spanish dance music
   *cante hondo/jondo (Sp.)
   cante flamenco (Sp.)
   deep song
   fandango (Sp.)
   malagueña (Sp.)
   seguedilla (Sp.)
   soleá (Sp.)
   phrygian mode

flat
   blue note
   half-step lower
   bemolle (It.)
   bémol (Fr.)
   Be, Bemol (G.)
   bemol (Sp.)
   B rotundum (Lat.)

2. below pitch
   off-pitch
   off-key
   detuned
   *out of tune
   sour note

vs. sharp

flat-top guitar
   classical guitar
   folk guitar
   Spanish guitar

vs, arch-top guitar

flatté, flaté (Fr.)
   *balancement (Fr.)
   vibrato
   tremolo
   close shake
   trillo (It.)
   Bebung (G.)

Flatterzunge (G.)
   flutter-tonguing
   frullato, frulando (It.)
   double coup de langue (Fr.)
   articulation double (Fr.)
   triple articulación (Sp.)
   raspberry
   French kiss
   Bronx cheer

flauta alemana (Sp.)
   *flute
   cross flute
   German flute
   concert flute
   flauto traverso (It.)
   flûte traversière (Fr.)
   flûte allemande (Fr.)
   Querflöte (G.)
   flauta travesera (Sp.)

flauta baja (Sp.)
   bass flute
   alto flute
   flautone (It.)
   flûte alto (Fr.)
   Altflöte (G.)

flauta de Pan (Sp.)
   pipes of Pan
   Panpipes
   flauto di Pan (It.)
   siringa (It.)
   syrinx (Gr.),
   syringe (Fr.)
   Panflöte (G.)
   flauta pánica (Sp.)

flauta de pico (Sp.)
  *recorder
  flauto diritto (It.)
  flûte à bec (Fr.)
  Blockflöte (G.)
  flauta sencilla (Sp.)
  flauta silbato (Sp.)

flauta eunuco (Sp.)
  mirliton (Fr.)
  eunuch flute
  onion flute
  toy flute
  flûte à l'oignon (Fr.)
  Zwiebelflöte (G.)
  flauta cebolla (Sp.)
  mirlitón (Sp.)

flauta inglesa (Sp.)
  *recorder
  duct flute
  fipple flute
  English flute

flautando, flautato (It.)
  on the fingerboard
  sul tasto (It.)
  sulla tastiera (It.)
  sur la touche (Fr.)
  am Griffbrett (G.)
  sobre el batidor (Sp.)
  overtones
  harmonics

flautino (It.)
  small flute
  *piccolo
  recorder
  flageolet

flauto (It.)
  recorder
  *flute
  flûte (Fr.)
  Flöte (G.)
  flauta (Sp.)

flauto a becco (It.)
  *recorder
  flauto diritto (It.)
  flauto dolce (It.)
  flûte à bec (Fr.)
  flûte à neuf trous (Fr.)
  Blockflöte (G.)
  Schnabelflöte (G.)
  flauta dulce (Sp.)
  duct flute
  fipple flute

flauto piccolo (It.)
  piccolo (E., It., Fr.)
  piccolo flute
  octave flute
  ottavino (It.)
  flautino (It.)
  petite flûte (Fr.)
  kleine Flöte (G.)
  Pikkelflöte, Pickelflöte (G.)
  Oktavflöte (G.)
  flautin (Sp.)

flauto traverso (It.)
  *flute
  transverse flute
  cross flute
  concert flute
  German flute
  flûte traversière (Fr.)
  flûte à six trous (Fr.)
  flauta travesera (Sp.)

flautone (It.)
  *alto flute
  bass flute

flaviol, flabiol, fluviol (Sp.)
  fife (of fife and drum)
  flaviol y tamboril (Sp.)
  fluviol y tambori (Sp.)
  pipe and tabor
  whittle and dub
  fife and drum
  galoubet (Fr.)

Schwegel (G.)

flexa (Lat.)
  flex (in chant)
  half cadence

Flickwerk, Flickoper (G.)
  cento (Lat.)
  centone (It.)
  centon (Fr.)
  centón (Sp.)
  pasticcio
  quodlibet
  *medley
  olio
  salmagundi, -y

flicorno (It.)
  flugelhorn
  bugle (Fr.)
  flicorne (Fr.)
  Flügelhorn (G.)
  fiscorno (Sp.)

flicorno basso (It.)
  *euphonium
  eufonio (It.)
  baritone horn

flicorno contralto (It.)
  *baritone horn
  *althorn

Flikkanzone (G.)
  quilt canzona
  patch canzona
  ricercare (It.)
  fugue
  carmen (Lat.)

fling
  Scotch dance
  reel
  contredance

floor show

revue
entertainment
musical
vaudeville
follies
night club act
variety show

florid
ornate
ornamented
embellished
melismatic
fioritura (It.)

florigelium (Lat.)
*anthology
collection
corpus (Lat.)
repertoire
raccolta (It.)
recueil (Fr.)
Sammlung (G.)

flos (Lat.)
embellishment
ornament
trill
mordent

Flöte (G.)
*flute
concert flute
transverse flute
cross flute
German flute

flourish
*fanfare
call
salute
honors
trumpet call
tantara
tuck, tucket
fanfara (It.)

squillo di tromba (It.)
sonnerie (Fr.)
Tusch (G.)
fanfarria (Sp.)
sonada (Sp.)
toque de trompeta (Sp.)

flue pipe/stop (organ)
labial
canna d'anima (It.)
canna labiale (It.)
tuyau à bouche (Fr.)
Labialpfeife (G.
tubo de boca (Sp.)

vs. reed pipe

Flügel (G.)
*grand piano
concert grand
pianoforte a coda (It.)
piano à queue (Fr.)
piano de cola (Sp.)

vs. Klavier (G.)

2. harpsichord

flugelhorn
bugle
cornet
flicorno (It.)
flicorne (Fr.)
bugle à pistons (Fr.)
fiscorno (Sp.)
Flügelhorn (G.)
Bügelhorn (G.)
saxhorn
saxtromba

flute
transverse flute
cross flute
concert flute
German flute
flauto (It.)

Flöte (G.)
flûte (Fr.)
flauta (Sp.)
flauto traverso (It.)
flûte traversière (Fr.)
flûte allemande (Fr.)
flûte à six trous (Fr.)
Kreuzflöte (G.)
Querflöte (G.)
Konzertflöte (G.)
flauta travesera (Sp.)
flauta alemana (Sp.)

*piccolo

recorder
English flute
fife
flageolet
duct flute
fipple flute
whistle flute
ocarina
panpipes
pipes of Pan

flûte à cheminée (Fr.)
chimney flute (organ)
Rohrflöte (G.)

flûte à neuf trous (Fr.)
*recorder

flûte à six trous (Fr.)
cross flute
*flute

flûte alto (Fr.)
alto flute
*bass flute
flûte basse (Fr.)

flûte eunuque (Fr.)
eunuch flute
onion flute
toy flute

kazoo
mirliton (Fr.)
flûte à l'oignon (Fr.)

flutophone
recorder (plastic)
tonette
fipple flute
whistle flute
bazooka
slide whistle
ocarina

flutter-tonguing
frullato (It.)
articulation double (Fr.)
double coup de langue (Fr.)
Flatterzunge (G.)
triple articulación (Sp.)
raspberry
French kiss

foglio d'album (It.)
album leaf
short piece
pagina d'album (It.)
feuillet d'album (Fr.)
hoja de album (Sp.)
Albumblatt (G.)

foire d'enfants (Fr.)
toy symphony
symphonie burlesque (Fr.)
Kindersinfonie (G.)

folia, follia (It., 12-18c.)
ground bass
variations
*chaconne
passacaglia
ostinato

2. Spanish dance (15c.)
moresca, morisca (It.)
pantomime dance
morris dance

folio, in folio
full size pages
once-folded sheet
quarto (Lat.)
octavo (Lat.)

folk guitar
acoustic guitar
Spanish guitar
classical guitar
flat-top guitar

vs. electric guitar

folk mass
contemporary mass
*low mass

folk music
ethnic folk music
popular music
old-time music
musica popolare (It.)
musique populaire (Fr.)
Volksmusik (G.)
volkstümliche Musik (G.)
música popular (Sp.)
traditional music
country music
mountain music
hillbilly music
bluegrass music
western music

folk opera
ballad opera
operetta
opéra comique (Fr.)
Singspiel (G.)
Spieloper (G.)
zarzuela (Sp.)
light opera
musical

folk singer
balladeer

*minstrel
troubadour
bard
gleeman
scop
wait

folk song
popular song
ballad
broadside ballad
work song
spinning song
sea shanty
traditional song
Volkslied (G.)

folk zither
dulcimer
Appalachian dulcimer
mountain zither
tamborin à cordes (Fr.)
Scheitholt (G.)
Hummel, Humle (G.)

follies
variety show
revue
musical revue
vaudeville
minstrel show
musical comedy
entertainment
cabaret
floor show

fond(s) d'orgue (Fr.)
foundation stops (organ)
principal (E., Sp.)
principale (It., Fr.)
Prinzipal (G.)
*diapason
montre (Fr.)
préstant (Fr.)
Hauptstimme (G.)
diapasón abierto (Sp.)

vs. mutation stops

fonografo (It.)
   phonograph
   record player
   turntable
   victrola
   record changer
   *gramophone

foot
   piede (It.)
   pied (Fr.)
   Fuss (G.)
   pie (Sp.)
   length of organ pipes
   pitch of pipes

2. unit of poetry

3. bottom of organ pipe
   boot
   staple
   Stiefel (G.)

forchetta d'accordo (It.)
   tuning fork
   diapason
   corista (It., Sp.)
   fourchette tonique (Fr.)
   Gabelton (G.)
   Stimmgabel (G.)
   pitchpipe
   afinador (Sp.)

fore-mass
   ante-communion
   Liturgy of the Word
   Mass of the Catechumens

forefall
   *appoggiatura
   backfall
   ornament

fori, foratura (It.)

bore (of a wind instrument)
   perce (Fr.)
   Bohrung (G.)
   perforación (Sp.)

form
   design
   structure
   plan
   forma (It., Sp.)
   forme (Fr.)
   Form (G.)
   Gestalt (G.)
   Aufbau (G.)
   dessin (Fr.)
   facture (Fr.)
   fattura (It.)
   Faktur (G.)

forme fixe (Fr. 14c.)
   virelai
   ballade
   rondeau
   canso, canzo
   Troubadour song
   Trouvère song

foro (It.)
   fingerhole
   buco (It.)
   trou (Fr.)
   Griffloch (G.)
   Tonloch (G.)
   Fingerloch (G.)
   agujero (Sp.)
   orificio (Sp.)

fort ténor (Fr.)
   *dramatic tenor
   heroic tenor
   Wagnerian tenor
   tenore robusto (It.)
   Heldentenor (G.)
   tenor dramatico (Sp.)

forte, ƒ (It.)

*loud(ly)
   strong
   ear-splitting
   blaring
   fortemente (It.)
   fortissimo (It.)
   fort, fortement (Fr.)
   laut (G.)
   stark (G.)
   fuerte (Sp.)

Forte-Pedal (G.)
   loud pedal
   damper pedal
   sustaining pedal
   sustenuto pedal
   pedale destra (It.)
   pédale droite (Fr.)
   *prolongement (Fr.)
   rechte Pedal (G.)
   pedal fuerte (Sp.)

vs. Dampfer (G.)
   linke Pedal (G.)

forte-piano (It.)
   *accent
   stress
   sforzando, sforzato (It.)

fortepiano (It.)
   pianoforte (It.)
   *piano
   Klavier (G.)

Fortschreitung (G.)
   progression (E., Fr.)
(harmonic, melodic)
   sequence
   progressione (It.)
   progresiön (Sp.)

fortwährende Bewegung (G.)
   perpetual motion
   perpetuum mobile (Lat.)
   moto perpetuo (It.)

mouvement perpétuel (Fr.)
dauernd Bewegung (G.)
movimiento perpetuo (Sp.)
movimiento continuo (Sp.)

forzando, forzato (It.)
accent
stress
sforzando, sforzato (It.)
rinforzando (It.)
fortepiano (It.)
forcé (Fr.)
en forçant (Fr.)
forciert (G.)
verstärkt (G.)
forzado (Sp.)

fossa orchestrale (It.)
orchestra pit
buca dell'orchestra (It.)
fosse d'orchestre (Fr.)
Orchestergraben (G.)
fose de orquestra (Sp.)
fose orquestrale (Sp.)

fouet (Fr.)
whip (percussion)
slapstick
frusta (It.)
Peitsche, Pritsche (G.)
fusta (Sp.)
tralla (Sp.)
zurriaga (Sp.)
látigo (Sp.)

foundation stop (organ)
*diapason
principal (E., Sp.)
principale (Fr., It.)
montre (Fr.)
*fond d'orgue (Fr.)

vs. mutation stop

four hands (keyboard)
piano duet

a quattro mani (It.)
à quatre mains (Fr.)
vierhändig (G.)
a cuatro manas (Sp.)

four-shape notes
fasola
shape-notes
patent notes
character notes
buckwheat notes
*solmization
solfeggio (It.)
sol-fa system

fourchette tonique (Fr.)
tuning fork
forchetta d'accordo (It.)
corista (It., Sp.)
Stimmgabel (G.)
Stimmhammer (G.)
Gabelton (G.)
diapasón (Sp.)
afinador (Sp.)

fourniture (Fr. organ)
*mixture stop
compound stop
furniture
plein jeu (Fr.)
mistura (It.)
Mixtur (G.)
sesquialtera (Lat.)
registro composta (It.)

fourth (interval)
diatessaron (Gr.)
perfect fourth
quarta (It.)
quarte (Fr.)
Quart(e) (G.)
cuarta (Sp.)

fra le quinte (It.)
in the wings
behind the scenes

*backstage
dans les coulisses (Fr.)
hinter den Kulissen (G.)
bastidores (Sp.)

fra se (It.)
*aside
stage whisper
very soft
under one's breath
sotto voce (It.)
à part (Fr.)

fragment (E., Fr.)
*excerpt
extract
selection
frammento (It., Sp.)
Bruchstück (G.)

frammento d'imitazione (It.)
point of imitation
theme of a fugue
dux, comes (Lat.)
motivo d'imitazione (It.)
passage en imitation (Fr.)
motif en imitation (Fr.)
Imitationsabschnitte (G.)
Imitationsmotiv (G.)
punto de imitación (Sp.)
pasaje de imitación (Sp.)
motivo imitado (Sp.)

Française (Fr.)
18c dance
anglaise (Fr.)
écossaise (Fr.)
contredanse (Fr.)
country dance

Franconian notation
mensural notation (13-16c.)
Ars Nova (Lat.)

Franzton (G.)
French pitch

low tuning (435 cps)
low pitch
classical pitch
international pitch
diapason normal (Fr.)
Normalton (G.)

frappé (Fr.)
*downbeat
first beat of a measure
thesis (Lat.)
crusis (Lat.)
masculine
strong beat
abbattimento (It.)
Abschlag (G.)
Niederschlag (G.)
Herunterschlag (G.)
schwerer Taktteil (G.)

vs. élevation, levé (Fr.)

frase (It., Sp.)
phrase (E., Fr.)
period
passage
Satz (G.)
Phrase (G.)

frase musicale completa (Sp.)
period
anticedent/consequent phrases
periodo (It., Sp.)
période (Fr.)
phrase musicale complète (Fr.)
Periode (G.)

fraseggio (It.)
phrasing
bowing
tongueing
shaping
phrasé (Fr.)
fraseo (Sp.)
Phrasierung (G.)

Frauenchor (G.)
women's chorus
female choir/chorus
treble choir
equal voices
close harmony
voci pari (It.)
voix égales (Fr.)
Aequalstimmen (G.)
enge Harmonie (G.)
voces iguales (Sp.)

fredon (Fr.)
trill
tremolo
roulade (Fr.)
run
shake
ornamental passage
florid
embellishment
coloratura

fredonner (Fr.)
to hum
to trill
a bocca chiuso (It.)
canticchiare (It.)
chantonner (Fr.)
avec bouche fermé (Fr.)
trällern (G.)
Brummstimmen (G.)
canturrear (Sp.)
furberia del canto (It.)

free
unrestrained
with abandon
con abbandono (It.)
abandonné (Fr.)
avec abandon (Fr.)
mit Hingabe (G.)
Hingebung (G.)
con abandono (Sp.)

freely

ad libitum (Lat.)
ad placitum (Lat.)
a bene placito (It.)
a piacere (It.)
a capriccio (It.)
libre (Fr.)
au caprice (Fr.)
à plaisir (Fr.)
à votre gré (Fr.)
à volonté (Fr.)
nach Gefallen (G.)
nach Belieben (G.)
a placer (Sp.)
a voluntad (Sp.)
a capricho (Sp.)

free meter
polymetric
irregular barring
uneven barring
vers mesuré (Fr.)
chanson mesurée (Fr.)
musique mesurée (Fr.)

free rhythm (chant)
equal time values
ad longum (Lat.)
Gregorian chant style

vs. metrical

fregiatura (It.)
*ornament
grace note
adornamento (It.)
ornement (Fr.)
agrément (Fr.)
adorno (Sp.)
Verzierung (G.)

French harp
*harmonica
mouth organ
aeoline
armonica (It., Fr.)
armonica a bocca (It.)

Mundharmonika (G.)
armónica (Sp.)

French horn
natural horn
hunting horn
corno (It., Sp.)
cor (Fr.)
Horn (G.)
Waldhorn (G.)
cuerno (Sp.)
trompa (Sp.)

French kiss
*flutter-tonguing
raspberry
Bronx cheer
frullato (It.)
Flatterzunge (G.)

French overture
*overture
prelude
voluntary
Italian overture
sinfonia (It.)
overtura (It.)
introduzione (It.)
ouverture (Fr.)
Vorspiel (G.)
Nachspiel (G.)
Ouvertüre (G.)

French pitch
international pitch
classical pitch
low pitch (435 cps)
diapason normal (Fr.)
Franzton (G.)
Normalton (G.)

French sixth
augmented sixth chord
sixth chord
first inversion triad
German sixth

Italian sixth
Neapolitan sixth
pentatone

frequency
vibration
cycle
sound wave
oscillation
Hertz
pitch
intonation (E., Fr.)
cps
tone
frequenza (It.)
fréquence (Fr.)
Frequenz (G.)
frecuencia (Sp.)
intonazione (It.)
hauteur du ton (Fr.)
Tonhöhe (G.)
entonación (Sp.)
diapason (E., Fr.)
diapasón (Sp.)
Stimmung (G.)
Schwingung (G.)

fret
tasto (It.)
touche, touchette (Fr.)
Bund (G.)
traste (Sp.)

fretboard
fingerboard
tastiera (It.)
manche (Fr.)
Griffbrett (G.)
teclado (Sp.)

fricassée (Fr.)
quodlibet
*medley
olio
pot-pourri (Fr., E.)
pastiche (E., Fr.)

overture
messanza (It.)
mélange (Fr.)
ensalada (Sp.)

2. 18c dance with pantomime

frigio (It., Sp.)
Phrygian mode (mode 3)
Greek mode
ecclesiastical mode
phrygien (Fr.)
phrygisch (G.)

frog
handle of a bow
heel
nut
tacco (It.)
tallone (It.)
talon (Fr.)
hausse (Fr.)
Frosch (G.)
talón (Sp.)

vs. point, tip

frölich (G.)
joyous
happy
festoso (It.)
joyeux (Fr.)
gai (Fr.)
festivo (It., Sp.)
alegre (Sp.)

from memory
by heart
memorized
by rote
a memoria (It.)
par coeur (Fr.)
auswendig (G.)
de memoria (Sp.)

from the top

from the beginning
*da capo (It.)
D.C.
repeat

frons (Fr.)
bar form (AAB)
Aufgesang (G.)
Stolle(n) (G.)
first section of a song
A section
lai
Leich (G.)
pes, pedes (Lat.)
Meistersinger (G.)
Minnesinger (G.)

vs. Abgesang (G.)

frottola (It., E.)
part-song
madrigal
ballet(t)
glee
canzona (It.)
ballata (It.)
capitolo (It.)
barzelletta (It.)
villota (It.)
villancico (Sp.)
motus confectus (Lat.)

Frühlingslied (G.)
spring song
canto di primavera (It.)
canzona della primavera (It.)
reverdie (Fr. Trouvère)
canción de primavera (Sp.)

frullato ((It.)
*flutter-tonguing
French kiss
Flatterzunge (G.)
articulation double (Fr.)
double coup de langue (Fr.)
triple articulación (Sp.)

raspberry
Bronx cheer

frusta (It.)
whip (percussion)
slapstick
fouet (Fr.)
Peitsche, Pritsche (G.)
zurriaga (Sp.)
láligo (Sp.)
tralla (Sp.)
fusta (Sp.)

fuelle (Sp.)
*bellows (organ)
wind chest
wind supply
soffietto (It.)
mantice (It.)
soufflet (Fr.)
Gebläse (G.)

2. *accordion
concertina
squeezebox
Quetche (G.)

fuera (Sp.)
*en dehors (Fr.)
prominent
emphasized
brought out
enfatico (It.)

fuerte (Sp.)
loud
strong
blaring
ear-splitting
deafening
forte, fortissimo (It.)
fort, fortement (Fr.)
laut (G.)
stark (G.)

vs. dulce (Sp.)

fuga (Lat., It., Sp.)
fugue (E., Fr.)
Fuge (G.)
imitation
polyphonic
round
canon
fugato (It.)
in reports
ricercare (It.)
motet (15-16c.)

fuga al contrario (It.)
counterfugue
fugue by inversion
fugue contraire (Fr.)
fuga contraria (Sp.)
Gegenfuge (G.)

fugal
imitation
in reports
fugato (It.)
di fuga (It.)
de fugue (Fr.)
fugué (Fr.)
fugiert (G.)
de fuga (Sp.)

fugue, fuge (E.)
hymn
anthem
round
canon
fuguing tune/piece

Führer (G.)
dux (Lat.)
subject (of a fugue)
antecedent
proposta (It.)
guida (It.)
sujet (Fr.)
guia (Sp.)

vs. Antwort (G.)

comes (Lat.)

full anthem
    choir *anthem
    Tudor church music
    cathedral music

vs. verse anthem

full cadence
    authentic cadence
    *perfect cadence
    full close
    cadenza perfetta (It.)
    cadence parfaite (Fr.)
    cadence authentique (Fr.)
    Ganzschluss (G.)
    vollkommene Kadenz (G.)
    authentische Kadenz (G.)
    cadencia perfecta (Sp.)
    cadencia autentica (Sp.)

vs. half-cadence

full choir/chorus
    tutti (It.)
    coro pieno (It.)
    cappella (It.)
    grand-choeur (Fr.)
    ripieno (It.)
    grosser Chor (G.)

full orchestra
    tutti (It.)
    ripieni (It.)
    concerto (It.)
    piena orchestra (It.)
    tout l'orchestre (Fr.)
    volles Orchester (G.)
    a toda orquesta (Sp.)
    todos (Sp.)

full organ
    great organ
    great chorus
    tutti (It.)

organo pleno/pieno (It.)
grand choeur (Fr.)
grand orgue (Fr.)
grand jeu (Fr.)
volle Orgel (G.)
volles Werk (G.)
Hauptwerk (G.)
Hauptmanual (G.)
Hintersatz (G.)
gran juego (Sp.)
organo lleno (Sp.)

full score
    complete score
    orchestral score
    grande partition (Fr.)
    partizione (It.)
    sparta, -o, spartita, -o (It.)
    spartitura (It.)
    partition (Fr.)
    Sparte (G.)
    Partitur (G.)
    Dirigierpartitur (G.)
    partición (Sp.)

vs. *condensed score
    piano score

full voice
    *chest voice
    belting tone
    voce di petto (It.)
    voix de poitrine (Fr.)
    Bruststimme (G.)
    voz de pecho (Sp.)

vs. half-voice
    sotto voce (It.)

Füllpfeife (G.)
    dummy pipe (organ)
    facade
    display pipes
    Stummepfeifen (G.)
    Prospektpfeifen (G.)
    montre (Fr.)

canne di facciata (It.)

función (Sp.)
    *performance
    show
    concert
    recital
    musicale
    presentation
    spettacolo (It.)
    spectacle (E., Fr.)
    Vorstellung (G.)
    Schauspiel (G.)
    espectáculo (Sp.)

functional music
    utility music
    music for the home
    Hausmusik (G.)
    Gebrauchsmusik (G.)
    musica da consumo (It.)
    musica d'uso (It.)
    musique d'usage (Fr.)
    música de consumo (Sp.)

fundamental tone
1. root of a chord

2. eight-foot stop (organ)

3. first harmonic
    first overtone
    lowest frequency of a tone
    radical bass
    pedal tone
    tuono fondamentale (It.)
    basse fondamentale (Fr.)
    Grundbass (G.)
    Basston, Grundton (G.)
    Fundamentalbass (G.)
    Primärton (G.)
    sonido fundamental (Sp.)

funeral march
    dirge
    *dead march

marcia funebre (It.)
marche funèbre (Fr.)
Trauermarsch (G.)
marcha fúnebre (Sp.)

funeral mass/service
requiem
mass for the dead
memorial mass/service
burial service
missa de profuntis (Lat.)
missa pro defunctis (Lat.)
messa dei/per defunti (It.)
messa da requiem (It.)
messa dei/per morti (It.)
messe funèbre (Fr.)
messe des morts (Fr.)
Totenmesse (G.)
misa de difuntos (Sp.)
misa de réquiem (Sp.)
misa de ánima (Sp.)
misa de muertos (Sp.)
exequies (E.)
exequiae (Lat.)
Exequien (G.)
lament, lamentation

funeral song/music
requiem
*lament
lamentation
elegy
planctus (Lat.)
lamento (It.)
angelito (It.)
déploration (Fr.)
plaint, planh (Fr.)
tombeau (Fr.)
apothéose (Fr.)
Trauermusik (G.)
Grabgesang (G.)
cantos de velorio (Sp.)
musica funebre (It.)
musique funèbre (Fr.)
música fúnebre (Sp.)

Fünfertakt (G.)
5-4 time
Cretic meter
quintuple meter/time
misura a cinque tempos (It.)
quinario (It.)
mesure à cinque temps (Fr.)
compás de cinco tiempos (Sp.)

Fünftonleiter (G.)
*pentatonic scale
whole-tone scale
gamme pentatonique (Fr.)
scala pentatonica (It.)
Ganztonleiter (G.)
pentatonische Skala (G.)
pentacordo (Sp.)

Fünfzehntel (G.)
a fifteenth (interval)
double octave
2-foot stop (org.)
super octave
disdiapason (Lat.)
decimaquinta (It.)
quinzième (Fr.)
doublette (Fr.)
Quin(t)dezime (G.)
Doppeloktave (G.)
quincena (Sp.)

funk(y)
jazz(y)
lowdown
pop music
rock-and-roll
hip-hop music
technomusic
grunge

für eine Stimme (G.)
*solo
monody
monophonic
unaccompanied
a una voce (It.)

à une voix (Fr.)
une voix seule (Fr.)
einstimmig (G.)
a una voz (Sp.)

für sich (G.)
*aside
very soft
stage whisper
whispered
under one's breath
sotto voce (It.)
à part (Fr.)
de côté (Fr.)
a parte (Sp.)

furberia del canto (It.)
to hum
to trill
a bocca chiusa (It.)
canticchiare (It.)
canterellare (It.)
avec bouche fermée (Fr.)
chantonner (Fr.)
fredonner (Fr.)
trällern (G.)
Brummstimmen (G.)
canturrear (Sp.)
canticar (Sp.)

furniture (organ)
fourniture (Fr.)
*mixture
compound stop
plein jeu (Fr.)
mistura (It.)
Mixtur (G.)

furniture music
easy listening
elevator music
lift music
Muzak
*backround music
dentist music
salon music

dinner music
table music
banquet music
cocktail music
light music
musique d'ameublement (Fr.)

fouet (Fr.)
Preitsche, Pritsche (G.)
zurriaga (Sp.)
tralla (Sp.)
látigo (Sp.)

fusa (Lat., It., Sp.)
thirty-second note
demisemiquaver
triple-croche (Fr.)
fuse (Fr.)
Fusel (G.)
Zweiunddreissigstelnote (G.)
biscroma (It.)
biscrome (Fr.)

fusée (Fr.)
a slide (ornament)
rapid passage
coulade (Fr.)
coulé (Fr.)
Schleifer (G.)

fusion
blend of jazz and rock
blend of jazz and classical
classical jazz
jazz
rock
disco
pop music
crossover
third stream

Fussdrücker (G.)
toe piston (org.)
toe stud
pistone (It.)
piston (E., Fr.)
pistòn (Sp.)

fusta (Sp.)
whip (percussion)
slapstick
frusta (It.)

G

G-clef
soprano clef
treble clef
violin clef
chiave di sol (It.)
chiave di violino (It.)
chiave di soprano (It.)
clef de sol (Fr.)
clef de violon (Fr.)
G-Schlüssel (G.)
Sopranschlüssel (G.)
Violinschlüssel (G.)
llave de sol (Sp.)
clave de sol (Sp.)
clave aguda (Sp.)
clave de violin (Sp.)

Gabelton (G.)
*tuning fork
diapason (Fr.)
fourchette tonique (Fr.)
forchetta d'accordo (It.)
Stimmgábel (G.)
afinador (Sp.)
corista (It., Sp,)

gagliarda (It.)
galliard
gaillarde (Fr.)
Gagliarde (G.)
gallarda (Sp.)
saltarello (It.)
tourdion, tordion (Fr.)
tordiglione (It.)
cascarda (It., 16-17c.)

gai (Fr.)
merry
lively
humorously

giocoso (It.)
lustig (G.)
jocoso (Sp.)

gain
volume
loudness
bel
decibel
*amplitude (E., Fr.)
dynamics

gaita (Sp.)
*bagpipe
piva (It.)
musetta (It.)
musette (Fr.)
cornemuse (Fr.)
Dudelsack (G.)
Sackpfeife (G.)

galant style (17-18c.)
rococo
baroque
stile galante (It.)
style galant (Fr.)
galanter Stil (G.)
estilo galante (Sp.)

gallery
*balcony
choir loft
loggione (It.)
galleria (It.)
mezzanine
loge, loggia
box seats
gallerie (Fr.)
Galerie (G.)
galeria (Sp.)

gallery organ
nave organ
*echo organ
antiphonal organ

Gallican chant
*chant
plainsong/plainchant
cantus planus (Lat.)
Gregorian chant
Ambrosian chant
Mozarabic chant

gallipavo (Sp.)
mistake
wrong note
false note
sour note
clinker
stecca (It.)
Misston (G.)
canard (Fr.)
fausse note (Fr.)
galipavo (Sp.)

galop (Fr., E., Sp.))
polka
cancan
quadrille
badinage (Fr.)
badinerie (Fr.)
galoppo (It.)
galopade (Fr.)
Galopp (G.)

galoubet (Fr.)
pipe (of pipe and tabor)
fife (and drum)
whittle and dub
flute
fife
Schwegel (G.)
flaviol y tamboril (Sp.)

gama (Sp.)
scale
gamma (It.)
gamme (Fr.)
scala (It.)
échelle (Fr.)
Tonleiter (G.)

Skala (G.)

gamba (It., Sp.)
  viola da gamba (It.)
  gambe (Fr.)
  Gambe (G.)
  'cello
  violoncello
  bass viol

gamba (organ)
  string stop
  viole d'orchestre (Fr.)
  viola

gambo (It.)
  stem of a note
  filum (Lat.)
  plica (Lat.)
  hampe (Fr.)
  queue (Fr.)
  Hals (G.)

gamelan
  percussion ensemble
  Java, Bali orchestra
  steel band

gamma (Gr.)
  lowest note of the scale
  gamma-ut (Lat.)
  gamut (Lat., entire range)
  gamme (Fr.)

2. tonic note
  do
  ut (Lat.)

3. range
  *compass
  tessitura (It.)
  diapason (Fr.)

gamme pentatonique (Fr.)
  pentatonic scale
  whole-tone scale

anhemitonic
scala pentatonica (It.)
Fünftonleiter (G.)
Ganztonleiter (G.)
pentatonische Skala (G.)
pentacordo (Sp.)

gamut-way (17c. E.)
  notation
  ordinary notation

vs. tablature

gamuza (Sp.)
  chamois horn
  Gemshorn
  goathorn
  recorder
  cor de chamois (Fr.)

ganascione (It.)
  *lute (large)
  archlute
  bass lute
  theorbo

gancho (Sp.)
  tail (of a note)
  flag
  hook
  codetta (It.)
  crochet de la note (Fr.)
  Fahne, Fähnchen (G.)
  Notenfahne (G.)
  rabillo (Sp.)

ganze Note (G.)
  whole note
  punctum inclinatum (Lat.)
  semibrevis (Lat.)
  semibreve (It..E.)
  intera, -o (It.)
  ronde (Fr.)
  Ganzenote (G.)
  redonda (Sp.)

ganze Pause (G.)
  whole-note rest
  semibreve rest
  semipause (Lat.)
  pausa di semibreve (It.)
  pause (Fr.)
  silencio de redonda (Sp.)
  pausa de redonda (Sp.)

Ganzschluss (G.)
  *authentic cadence
  *full cadence
  full close
  perfect cadence
  cadenza perfetta (It.)
  cadence authentique (Fr.)
  authentische Kadenz (G.)
  cadencia autentica (Sp.)

Ganzton (G.)
  whole tone
  whole step
  major second
  seconda maggiore (It.)
  tono (It., Sp.)
  ton (Fr.)
  tonus (Lat.)
  degree
  seconde majeure (Fr.)
  grosse Sekunde (G.)
  tono entero (Sp.)
  segunda mayor (Sp.)

garganta (Sp.)
  throat (of a singer)
  gola (It.)
  gorge (Fr.)
  Hals (G.)
  Kehle (G.)

Gassenhauer (G., 16c.)
  popular song
  street song
  pont-neuf (Fr.)

Gaukler (G.)

goliard
*minstrel
balladeer
folksinger
gleeman
Spielmann (G.)
bard
scop
jo(n)gleur (Fr.)
troubadour
trouvère
Minnesinger
schola mimorum (Lat.)

gavotte, gavot (E., Fr.)
duple dance, 17c.
gavotta (It.)
gavota (Sp.)
Gavotte (G.)
cibell, cebell (E.)
bourée (Fr.)
suite

Gebrauchtmusik (G.)
house music
functional music
practical music
amateur music
Hausmusik (G.)
musica da consumo (It.)
musica d'uso (It.)
musique d'usage (Fr.)
música de consumo (Sp.)

Gebläse (G., organ)
bellows
blower
soffietto (It.)
mantice (It.)
soufflet (Fr.)
Balg (G.)
fuelle (Sp.)
wind chest
wind supply

Gebrauchsmusik (G.)

utility music
functional music
Hausmusik (G.)
musica da consumo (It.)
musica d'uso (It.)
musique d'usage (Fr.)
música de consumo (Sp.)

gebrochene Tasten (G.)
*split keys/keyboard (organ)
divided stop
broken octave
short octave
tasti spezzati (It.)
touches brisées (Fr.)
doppelt Semitonien (G.)
octava corta (Sp.)

gebrochener Akkord (G.)
broken chord
*arpeggio (It.)
rolled chord
Alberti bass
batterie (Fr.)
Brechung (G.)
rasgado (Sp.)

vs. platter Akkord
solid chord

gebunden (G.)
*legato
connected
slurred
lié (Fr.)
louré (Fr.)
ligado (Sp.)

vs. abgestossen (G.)

Gedeckt (organ) (G.)
stopped pipe
stopped diapason
gedackt
bourdon (Fr.)
canna tappata (It.)

tuyau bouché (Fr.)
tubo tapado/tapadillo (Sp.)

vs. offene (G.)

gedämpft (G.)
damped
muted
muffled

Gefährte (G.)
answer
comes (Lat.)
consequent
réponse (Fr.)
consequenza (It.)
Antwort (G.)
consecuente (Sp.)

vs.dux (Lat.)
Führer (G.)

Gefässrassel (G.)
rattle
maraca (E., Fr., It., Sp.)
rainstick
raganella (It.)
crécelle (Fr.)
Knarre (G.)
Ratsche (G.)
Kürbisrassel (G.)
matraca (Sp.)
carraca (Sp.)

geflüstert (G.)
whispered
vary soft
*aside
stage whisper
bisbigliato (It.)
chuchoté (Fr.)
cuchicheado (Sp.)

gefühlvoll (G.)
with feeling
mit Gefühl (G.)

con espressione (It.)
espressivo (It.)
expressif (Fr.)
expresivo (Sp.)

Gegenfuge (G.)
counterfugue
fugue by inversion
fuga al contrario (It.)
fugue contraire (Fr.)
fuga contraria (Sp.)

Gegenbewegung (G.)
contrary motion
opposite motion
oblique motion
inversion (melodic)
a(l) rovescio (It.)
moto contrario (It.)
mouvement contraire (Fr.)
movimiento contrario (Sp.)

Gegenrhythmus (G.)
cross-rhythm
polyrhythm

Gegensatz (G.)
counter-theme
Gegenthema (G.)
counter-subject
second theme
contrasoggetto (It.)
contresujet (Fr.)
Kontrasubjekt (G.)
contrasujeto (Sp.)

gehaucht (G.)
very soft(ly)
whispered
piano, pianissimo (It.)
a fior di labbro (It.)
au bout des lèvres (Fr.)
con la boca chico (Sp.)

Gehäuse (G.)
organ case

casework
cassa dell'organo (It.)
buffet (Fr.)
domus organaria (Lat.)
Orgelkasten (G.)

gehend (G.)
*andante (It.)

Geige (G.)
*violin
fiddle
violino (It.)
violon (Fr.)
vielle (Fr.)
viella (Lat.)
kit
rebec
devil's box
vihuela de arco (Sp.)

Geigenharz (G.)
rosin, resin (for a bow)
colophony
colofonia It., Sp.)
colophane (Fr.)
Kolophon. Kolophonium (G.)
resina (Sp.)

Geigenbauer (G.)
violin maker
luthier (Fr.)
liutaio (It.)
violinaio (It.)
Saiteninstrumentenmacher (G.)
violero (Sp.)

Geisslerlieder (14c. G.)
flagellant songs
laude spirituali (Lat.)
laude (It.)

Geisstriller (G.)
goat's trill
tremolo
vibrato

chevrotement (Fr.)
Bockstriller (G.)
trillo caprino (It.)
trino de cabra (Sp.)

Geisterharfe (G.)
Aeolian harp
wind harp
zither
arpa d'eolo (It.)
harpe éoline (Fr.)
Äolsharfe (G.)
Windharfe (G.)
Wetterharfe (G.)

geistliche (G.)
sacred
religious
holy
spiritual
liturgical
sacra (It.)
religiosa (It., Sp.)
sacrée (Fr.)
religieuse (Fr.)
sagrada (Sp.)

vs. weltliche (G.)

geistliche Spiel (G.)
*liturgical drama
miracle play
mystery play
magi play
religious play
tomb play
sepulcher play
auto (Sp.)
azione sacra (It.)
sacra rappresentazione (It.)

geklimper (G.)
strumming
thrumming
twanging
strimpellio (It.)

tapotage (Fr.)
cencerreo (Sp.)
zangarreo (Sp.)
rasgado, rasgueado (Sp.)

gekröntes Lied (G.)
cantus coronatus (Lat.13c.)
crowned song
prize song
chanson couronée (Fr.)
puy, puit (Fr.)
Trouvère (Fr.)
Preislied (G.)
Meistersinger

gemässigt (G.)
moderato (It.)
modéré (Fr.)
mässig (G.)
moderado (Sp.)
moderate tempo

Gemeindelied (G.)
hymn
church song
shorale
Kirchenlied (G.)
Kirchengesang (G.)
inno (It.)
hymne (Fr.)
himno (Sp.)

gemel, gimel, gymel
parallel thirds
semel
duet
cantus gemellus (Lat.)
Zwillingsgesang (G.)

gemischte Stimmen (G.)
mixed voices
SATB
mixed chorus
voces inaequalis (Lat.)
voci miste (It.)
voix mixtes (Fr.)

voces mezcladas (Sp.)

gemischter Chor (G.)
mixed chorus/choir
SATB choir
coro misto (It.)
choeur mixte (Fr.)
coro mixto (Sp.)

vs. gleiche Stimmen (G.)

Gemshorn (G.)
horn (goat horn)
chamois horn
recorder (15-16 c.)
gamuza (Sp.)

2. organ stop, soft diapason
cor de chamois (Fr.)

general (organ)
piston button
general cancel
*combination button
pre-sets

Generalbass (G.)
thoroughbass
continuo
*figured bass
basso continuo (It.)
basse continue (Fr.)
bajo continuo (Sp.)
allgemeiner Bass (G.)

Generalpause (G.)
G.P
general pause
grand pause
caesura.
empty measure/bar
railroad tracks
vuoto, misura vuota (It.)
pausa generale (It.)
cesura (It., Sp.)
pause/silence générale (Fr.)

césure (Fr.)
Zäsur (G.)

Generalprobe (G.)
*dress rehearsal
open rehearsal
full rehearsal
ultima prova (It.)
répétition générale (Fr.)
ensayo general (Sp.)

German fingering
variant fingering (recorder, piano)

vs. baroque, English fingering

German flute
*flute
transverse flute
cross-flute
concert flute

vs. English flute
recorder

German mass
hymns
chorales
Lutheran liturgy
folk mass
Deutsche Messe (G.)

2. Missa Brevis (Lat.)

German polka
Schottische (G.)
contradance
Scozzese (It.)
écossaise (Fr.)
Escocesa (Sp.)
anglaise (Fr.)
française (Fr.)
Kontertanz (G.)
contredanse (Fr.)

German sixth
 sixth chord
 augmented sixth chord
 French sixth
 Italian sixth
 Neapolitan sixth
 pentatone

German style
 waltz, landler
 alla tedesca (It.)
 à l'allemande (Fr.)
 a la alamana (Sp.)
 nach Deutcher Art (G.)

Gesamtausgabe (G.)
 complete edition
 collected works
 opera omnia (Lat.)
 opere complete (It.)
 oeuvres complètes (Fr.)
 sämtliche Werke (G.)
 gesammelte Werke (G.)
 obres completes (Sp.)
 obras completas (Sp.)

Gesang (G.)
 *song
 melody
 air
 tune
 chant
 cantus (Lat.)
 cantio (Lat.)
 canticum (Lat.)
 canticle
 Lied (G.)
 Weise (G.)
 chanson (Fr.)
 chant (Fr.)
 cantique (Fr.)
 canto, cantico (It.)
 canzona (It.)
 aria (It.)
 cántico (Sp.)
 canción (Sp.)

Gesangbuch (G.)
 hymnal
 songbook
 song collection
 fake book
 *anthology
 cantionale (Lat.)
 canzoniere (It.)
 chansonnier (Fr.)
 Liederbuch (G.)
 cancionero (Sp.)

Gesangverein (G.)
 *choral society
 oratorio society
 chorale
 *choir
 glee club
 schola cantorum (Lat.)
 societá di canto (It.)
 société chorale (Fr.)
 Singakademie (G.)
 Kantorei (G.)
 orfeón (Sp.)

Geschichte der Musik (G.)
 music history
 history of music
 musicology
 storia della musica (It.)
 l'histoire de la musique (Fr.)
 Musikgeschichte (G.)
 historia de la música (Sp.)

Gestalt (G.)
 *form
 design
 structure
 plan
 fattura (It.)
 dessin (Fr.)
 facture (Fr.)
 Aufbau (G.)

Gestaltung (G.)
 interpretation (E., Fr.)

 *arrangement
 version
 rendition
 performance
 interpretazione (It.)
 Interpretation (G.)
 interpretación (Sp.)

gestohlenes Zeitmass (G.)
 altered time
 rubato (It.)
 tempo rubato (It.)
 verrucktes Zeitmass (G.)
 stolen time
 borrowed time

 vs. streng im Takt (G.)

gestopft (G.)
 stopped (horns)
 muted
 chiuso (It.)
 tappato (It.)
 bouché (Fr.)
 étouffé (Fr.)
 gedeckt (G.)
 tapado (Sp.)
 sonido cerrado (Sp.)

 vs. offen (G.)

geteilt (G.)
 divisi (It.)
 divided (parts)
 a due (It.)
 à deux (Fr.)
 divisés (Fr.)
 divisados (Sp.)
 dividido (Sp.)
 diviso (Sp.)

getragen (G.)
 sustained
 sostenuto (It.)
 soutenu (Fr.)
 sostenido (Sp.)s

geworfen (G.)
bouncing the bow
jeté (Fr.)
ricoché (Fr.)
sautillé (Fr.)
saltando (It.)
Springbogen (G.)
saltado (Sp.)

gezupft (G.)
plucked
pizzicato (It.)
pincé (Fr)
zupfend (G.)
punteado (Sp.)

ghironda (It.)
*hurdy-gurdy
street piano
organistrum (Lat.)
ghironda ribeca (It.)
lira organizzata (It.)
lira tedesca (It.)
stampella (It.)
vielle organisée (Fr.)
Leier (G.)
Drehleier (G.)
viela de rueda (Sp.)

gig
engagement
performance
concert season
club date
tour
recital
job playing/singing

gigelira (It.)
xylophone
*claquebois (Fr.)
régale de bois (Fr.)
straw fiddle
Strohfiedel (G.)
xilofono (It.)
Xylophon (G.)

xilófono, xilórgano (Sp.)
sticcado pastorale (It.)
sticcato (It.)
marimba
vibraphone/vibraharp
vibes

gigue (Fr.)
rebec
fiddle (medieval)
giga (It.)
Gige (G.)
viele (Fr.)

2. jig (dance)
canary
canario (It., Sp.)
canarie (Fr.)
giga (It., Sp.)
Gigue (G.)

gimel, gemel
gymel
cantus gemellus (Lat.)
semel
parallel thirds
Zwillingsgesang (G.)

giocoso (It.)
lively
merry
humorously
lustig (G.)
gai (Fr.)
jocosc (Sp.)

gioioso (It.)
joyous(ly)
festoso (It.)
festivo (It., Sp.)
joyeux (Fr.)
frölich (G.)
gai (Fr.)
alegre (Sp.)

giovedi santo (It.)

Holy Thursday
Last Supper
Maundy Thursday
Coena Domini (Lat.)
Jeudi saint (Fr.)
Gründonnerstag (G.)
Jueves santo (Sp.)
Jueves del mandato (Sp.)

giradischi (It.)
phonograph
record player
*gramophone
victrola
fonografo (It.)
grammofono (It.)
tourne-disques (Fr.)
Plattenspieler (G.)
tocadiscos (Sp.)

giraffe (piano)
grand upright
*upright piano
vertical grand
Giraffenklavier (G.)
Giraffenflügel (G.)
piano giraffe (Fr.)
piano jirafa (Sp.)

vs. grand piano

girotondo (It.)
round dance
ring dance
danza in tondo (It.)
ronde (Fr.)
Riegen (G.)
ronda (Sp.)
danza en redondo (Sp.)

Gitarre (G.)
*guitar
Guitarre (G.)

gittern
guitar

ghittern
guiterne (Fr.)
Quinterne (G.)
guitarra (Sp.)

giustiniana (It. 16c.)
*madrigal
part-song
glee
catch
chanson (Fr.)
frottola (It.)
villanella (It.)
trio

giusto (It.)
strict
correct
exact
juste (Fr.)
richtig (G.)
justo (Sp.)

glass harmonica
musical glasses
clavicylinder
*hurdy-gurdy
euphone
armonica (It.)
armonica a vetro (It.)
armonica a calici (It.)
harmonica de Franklin (Fr.)
harmonica de verres (Fr.)
verrillon (Fr.)
Glasharmonika (G.)
Glasspiel (G.)
Glasharfe (G.)
Glasschalenspiel (G.)
glass harp
copólogo (Sp.)

glee
*madrigal
part-song (male voices)
catch
round

caccia (It.)
chanson (Fr.)

glee club
men's chorus
male choir
Apollo club
Liedertafel (G.)
Männergesangverein (G.)
choral society
barbershop choir/chorus

gleeman
*minstrel
bard
balladeer
jongleur (Fr.)
troubadour
Spielmann (G.)
menestrello (It.)
ménétrier, ménestrel (Fr.)
ministril (Sp.)
scop (E.)
goliard

gleiche Stimmen (G.)
equal voices
close harmony
barbershop harmony
men's voices
women's voices
treble choir
voces aequales (Lat.)
voci pari (It.)
voix égales (Fr.)
voces iguales (Sp.)
Aequalstimmen (G.)
enge Harmonie (G.)
enge Lage (G.)

vs. gemischte Stimmen (G.)
mixed voices

glissando (It.)
slur
connect

glide
portamento (It.)
scoop
slide
sdrucciolando (It.)
scivolando (It.)
tirata (It.)
glissé (Fr.)
en glissant (Fr.)
tirade (Fr.)
port-de-voix (Fr.)
gleitend (G.)
glisando (Sp.)
glisado (Sp.)
resbalando (Sp.)

Glocke(n) (G.)
*bell(s)
cloches (Fr.)
cimbalo (Sp.)
campana (It., Sp.)

Glockenklavier (G.)
carillon (E., Fr.)
churchbells
tower bells
steeple bells
cariglione (It.)
carillón (Sp.)

Glockenspiel (G.)
bell lyre
bells
orchestra bells
metal harmonica
campanette (It.)
campanelli (It.)
organo di campane (It.)
carillon (Fr.)
jeu de timbres (Fr.)
sonnante (Fr.)
Lyra (G.)
Stahlspiel (G.)
juego de timbres (Sp.)
campanólogo (Sp.)
celeste

celesta
chimes

Glockenstern (G.)
cimbelstern (organ)
Cymbelstern (G.)
Zimbelstern (G.)

Gloria in excelsis Deo (Lat.)
Greater Doxology
Hymnus angelicus (Lat.)
angelic hymn
hymn of the angels
Cherubim song
Grosse Doxologie (G.)

Gloria Patri (Lat.)
lesser Doxology
Doxology
Glory be
Hymnus glorificationis (Lat.)
kleine Doxologie (G.)
Psalms, etc.
Old Hundredth (tune)

glosa (Sp.)
ornamentation
divisions
passaggio (It.)
coloratura (It.)
diferencia (Sp.)

glottal stop
glottal catch
glottal attack
glottale (It.)
coup de glotte (Fr.)
Kehlschlag (G.)
Kehlverschlusslaut (G.)
Knacklaut (G.)
Glottisschlag (G.)

goathorn
Gemshorn (G.)
chamois horn
recorder

cor de chamois (Fr.)
gamuza (Sp.)

goat's trill
tremolo
vibrato
trill
trillo (It.)
trillo caprino (It.)
chevrotement (Fr.)
trille de chèvre (Fr.)
Bockstriller (G.)
Geisstriller (G.)
trino/trinado de cabra (Sp.)

goliard
*minstrel
gleeman
balladeer
bard
scop
jongleur (Fr.)
Troubadour
Trouvère (Fr.)
Minnesinger (G.)
Spielmann (G.)
carmina burana (Lat.)

golpe de lengua (Sp.)
tonguing
colpo di lingua (It.)
coup de langue (Fr.)
Zungenstoss (G.)
Zungenschlag (G.)
articulation

gondola song/music
barcarole
boat-song
gondoliera (It.)
barcarolle (Fr.)
Gondellied (G.)
barcarola (Sp.)

gong
Chinese gong

tam-tam (It., G., Sp.)
kettle gong
tambour de bronze (Fr.)
Kesselgong (G.)
tantán (Sp.)
batintín (Sp.)
cymbal

Good Friday
Parasceve (E., Lat.)
*Holy Week
Sacred Triduum
Triduum Sacrum (Lat.)
venerdi santo (It.)
Vendredi saint (Fr.)
Karfreitag (G.)
Viernes Santo (Sp.)
reproaches
improperia (Lat.)
veneration of the Cross

Gopak, hopak (R.)
fast duple dance
*polka
can-can
galop

gorge (Fr.)
throat (of a singer)
gola (It.)
Hals (G.)
Kehle (G.)
garganta (Sp.)

gorgia (It.)
*ornamentation
divisions
florid passages
passaggi (It.)
fioritura (It.)
diminutio (Lat.)
fioritures (Fr.)
floreos (Sp.)
glosas (Sp.)
Blumen (G.)

gospel music, song
  soul music
  jazz
  hymns
  spirituals
  pop music
  religious song

gospel side
  cantoris (Lat.)
  north side
  choir
  precentor
  chancel choir

vs. epistle side
  decani (Lat.)

Gothic music
  ars antiqua (Lat.)
  medieval music
  ars vetus (Lat.)
  stile antico (It.)
  ancient style

Gothic notation
  hobnail notation
  Hufnagelschrift (G.)
  chant notation
  neumes

Gottesdienst (G.)
  service
  *liturgy
  religious service
  Mass
  Divine Service
  Agende (G.)

grace notes
  ornaments
  embellishments
  abbellimenti (It.)
  fioretti (It.)
  fregiaturi (It.)
  agréments (Fr.)

  ornements (Fr.)
  Verzierungen (G.)
  adornos (Sp.)

gracioso (Sp.)
  grazioso, gratioso (It.)
  gracieux, gracieuse (Fr.)
  anmutig (G.)
  graceful(ly), gracious

Grad (G.)
  *degree (of a scale)
  step
  tone
  second (interval)
  grado (It., Sp.)
  degré (Fr.)
  Stufe, Tonstufe (G.)
  Schritt (G.)

vs. Sprung (G.)

gradual
  psalm
  song
  chant
  antiphon
  responsory
  graduale (Lat., It.)
  graduel (Fr.)
  Graduale (G.)
  grail (old Anglican)
  responsorium graduale (Lat.)
  Responsorium (Gallican)
  psalmellus (Ambrosian)

2. collection of mass chants
  cantatorium (Lat.)
  antiphonale missarum (Lat.)

gradually
  by degrees
  little by little
  step by step
  poco a poco (It., Sp.)
  di grado (It.)

  per gradi (It.)
  poi a poi (It.)
  a grado a grado (It.)
  peu à peu (Fr.)
  petit à petit (Fr.)
  nach und nach (G.)
  por grado (Sp.)
  de grado en grado (Sp.)

vs. suddenly

Grammy award
  music award

gramophone (E., Fr.)
  phonograph
  record player
  victrola
  talking-machine
  grammofono (It.)
  giradischi (It.)
  fonografo (It.)
  turntable
  tourne-disques (Fr.)
  Grammophon (G.)
  Plattenspieler (G.)
  Sprechmachine (G.)
  gramofono (Sp.)
  tocadiscos (Sp.)
  tape recorder
  wire recorder
  CD player
  DVD player
  sequencer (computer)

gramophone record
  platter
  record
  disc
  album
  phonograph record
  78
  long-playing record (33 1/3rpm)
  extended play (45rpm)
  recording

pressing
cylinder
CD, DVD
disco (It., Sp.)
disque (Fr.)
Schallplatte (G.)

grand-barré (Fr.)
capo (guitar)
*barré (Fr.)
capotasto (It.)
capodastre (Fr.)
Kapodaster (G.)
Saitenfessel (G.)
ceduela (Sp.)
ceja, cejilla, cejita (Sp.)

gran cassa (It.)
bass drum
gran tamburo (It.)
cassa grande (It.)
grosse caisse (Fr.)
gros-tambour (Fr.)
grosse Trommel (G.)
bombo (Sp.)

grand chant (Fr.)
early latin song
grande chanson (Fr.)
chant
plainsong, plainchant

grand choeur (Fr.)
full organ
great organ/division
great chorus
tutti (It.)
organo pleno/pieno (It.)
principale (It.)
gran organo (It.)
grand-jeu (Fr.)
grand-orgue (Fr.)
grosses Spiel (G.)
Hauptwerk (G.)
Hauptorgel (G.)
Hintersatz (G.)

volles Werk (G.)
volles Orgel (G.)
órgano lleno (Sp.)
gran juego (Sp.)
gran'organo (Sp.)
primer manual (Sp.)

2. full chorus/choir
grosser Chor (G.)
Tuttichor (G.)
coro ripieno (It.)
coro pieno (It.)
tutti (It.)
cappella (It.)

grand concerto (Fr.)
*concerto grosso (It.)
grosses Konzert (G.)
gran concierto (Sp.)

grand-messe (Fr.)
high mass
solemn mass
missa cantata (Lat.)
missa solemnis (Lat.)
messa solenne (It.)
Hochamt (G.)
Hauptmesse (G.)
misa solemne (Sp.)
misa mayor (Sp.)

vs. messe basse (Fr.)

grand opera
music drama
opera seria (It.)
dramma per musica (It.)
bel canto (It.)
lyric opera
lyric drama
dramma lirico (It.)
drame lyrique (Fr.)
azione teatrale (It.)
representazione (It.)

vs. operetta

comic opera

grand pause, G.P.
general pause
fermata (It.)
hold
rest
empty measure/bar
railroad tracks
caesura
cesura (It., Sp.)
césure (Fr.)
Zäsur (G.)
pausa generale (It.)
vuoto (It.)
misura vuota (It.)
pause/silence générale (Fr.)
Generalpause (G.)

grand piano
concert grand
full grand
horizontal piano
parlor grand
*baby grand
grand
square piano
pianoforte a coda (It.)
piano à queue (Fr.)
grand piano de concert (Fr.)
Hammerclavier (G.)
Hammerflügel (G.)
Flügel, Salonflügel (G.)
gran cola (Sp.)
piano de cola (Sp.)

vs. upright piano
vertical piano

grande chanson (Fr.)
Troubadour song
Trouvère song
monody
forme fixe (Fr.)
canzo, canso (Fr.)
grande partition (Fr.)

full score
complete score
orchestral score
partizione (It.)
Partitur (G.)
Dirigierpartitur (G.)
partición Sp.)

s. partition réduite (Fr.)
condensed score

ranulato (It.)
non-legato (It.)
not slurred
pas lié (Fr.)
granulé (Fr.)
ungebunden (G.)
granulado (Sp.)
no ligado (Sp.)

s. legato (It.)

rappa (It.)
brace
bracket
graffa (It.)
accolade (E., Fr.)
Akkolade (G.)
Klammer (G.)
corchete (Sp.)

rasshopper (piano)
escapement
*double escapement
hopper
release
key release
scappamento (It.)
échappement (Fr.)
Auslöser (G.)
Auslösung (G.)

ratte (Fr.)
*guitar

ratter (Fr.)

strum
thrum
strimpellare (It.)
tapoter (Fr.)
klimpern (G.)
rasgueado (Sp.)
cencerrear (Sp.)

grave (It.)
solemn
heavy
*slow
grave (E., Sp.)
adagio (It.)
lento (It.)
largo (It.)
lent (Fr.)
pesant (Fr.)
langsam (G.)
schwer (G.)

gravicembalo (It.)
*harpsichord
clavicembalo (It.)
cembalo (It., G., Sp.)
virginal(s)
clavecin (Fr., Sp.)
Kielflügel (G.)
clavier (G.)

grazioso, gratioso (It.)
graceful, gracious
gracieux, gracieuse (Fr.)
anmutig (G.)
gracioso (Sp.)

great (org.)
main division
main manual
great organ
principale (It.)
grand-orgue (Fr.)
Hauptwerk (G.)

Great Antiphons
O Antiphons

Magnificat
antiphon
vespers

great bell
lowest pitched bell
largest bell
tenor
Big Ben
churchbell
steeple bell
bourdon (Fr.)
carillon

great chorus (organ)
full organ
tutti (It.)
organo pleno (It.)
gran organo (It.)
grand choeur (Fr.)
grand-jeu (Fr.)
grand-orgue (Fr.)
Hauptwerk (G.)
gran juego (Sp.)

great mean
third string on bass viol
D-string on violin
Grosssangsaite (G., lute)
gross Mittelsaite (G., lute)

great octave
second C below middle-C

great scale
Guido's scale
solfa
*solmization

Great Service
elaborate setting
morning/evening prayer
canticles
Cathedral music
Tudor church music
verse anthem

full anthem

vs. short service

great staff
combined staves
grand staff
pentagramma (It.)
portée (Fr.)
System, Notensystem (G.)

Greater Doxology
Gloria in excelsis Deo (Lat.)
hymnus angelicus (Lat.)
hymn to the Trinity
hymn of the angels
doxology
*cherubim song

vs. lesser Doxology

greek mode
phrygian mode
ecclesiastical mode
frigio (It., Sp.)
phrygien (Fr.)
phrygisch (G.)

greghesca (It.)
villanella
madrigal
giustiniana (It.)
frottola
canzona, canzonetta (It.)

Gregorian chant
plainsong
plainchant
chant
liturgical song
cantus planus (Lat.)
cantus choralis (Lat.)
cantilena Romana (Lat.)
Choral (G.)
canto plano (It.)
canto liturgico (It.)

canto Gregoriano (It., Sp.)
chant d'eglise (Fr.)
chant Grégorien (Fr.)
Gregorianischer
Gesang/Choral (G.)
canto llano (Sp.)
monody
homophonic song

Gregorian mode
ecclesiastical mode
medieval mode
church mode
modo ecclesiastico (It.)
mode ecclésiastique (Fr.)
Kirchentonart (G.)

Gregorian notation
chant notation
plainsong notation
square notes
quadratic notation
neumes
Aquitanian notation
nota Romana (It.)
nota/notazione quadrata (It.)
note/notation carrée (Fr.)
Quadratnotenschrift (G.)
Quadratnotation (G.)
notación cuadrada (Sp.)
notación Gregoriana (Sp.)

grelots (Fr.)
jingle bells
sleighbells
harness bells
altar bells
Sanctus bells
*bells
pellet bells
sonagliera (It.)
Schellen (G.)
cencerro (Sp.)
cascabel (Sp.)

Griffbrett (G.)

fingerboard (guitar)
fretboard
tastiera (It.)
touche (Fr.)
manche (Fr.)
batidor (Sp.)

Griffbrettsaiten (G.)
stopped string

Griffloch (G.)
fingerhole
buco (It.)
foro (It.)
trou (Fr.)
Tonloch (G.)
Fingerloch (G.)
orificio (Sp.)
agujera (Sp.)

gros-tambour (Fr.)
*bass drum
grosse caisse (Fr.)
gran cassa (It.)
gran tamburo (It.)
cassa grande (It.)
grosse Trommel (G.)
bombo (Sp.)

Gross-Pedal (G.)
loud pedal
sostenuto pedal
damper pedal
sustaining pedal
pedale destra (It.)
pedale forte (It.)
pédale droite (Fr.)
pédale forte (Fr.)
*prolongement (Fr.)
Forte-Pedal (G.)
rechte Pedal (G.)
pedal fuerte (Sp.)

vs. Dämpfer
soft pedal

grosse Messe (G.)
  solemn mass
  *high mass
  hohe Messe (G.)
  Hochamt (G.)
  missa cantata (Lat.)
  missa solemnis (Lat.)
  messe solenne (It.)
  messe cantata (It.)
  messe haute (Fr.)
  grand'messe (Fr.)
  messe solennelle (Fr.)
  misa mayor (Sp.)
  misa solemne (Sp.)

vs. stille Messe (G.)

grosse Oper (G.)
  *grand opera
  music drama
  opera seria (It.)

grosse Sekunde (G.)
  major second
  whole step
  whole tone
  seconda maggiore (It.)
  seconde majeure (Fr.)
  tono entere (Sp.)
  segunda mayor (Sp.)

grosse Terz (G.)
  major third
  ditone
  terza maggiore (It.)
  tierce majeure (Fr.)
  tercera mayor (Sp.)
  Picardy third

grosser Chor (G.)
  full chorus/choir
  coro pieno (It.)
  cappella (It.)
  grand choeur (Fr.)
  ripieno (It.)

ground, ground bass
  basso ostinato (It.)
  ostinato bass
  strophic bass
  strophic variations
  *chaconne (Fr.)
  passacaglia (It.)
  partimento (It.)
  pes
  folia (It.)

group de sons/notes (Fr.)
  tone cluster
  chord
  pitch aggregate
  gruppo di suonori (It.)
  Tonballung (G.)
  Tontraube (G.)

Grundbass (G.)
  root of a chord
  root bass
  radical bass
  basso fondamentale (It.)
  basse fondamentale (Fr.)
  bajo fundamental (Sp.)

Gründonnerstag (G.)
  Holy Thursday
  Last Supper
  Maundy Thursday
  Coena Domini (Lat.)
  giovedi santo (It.)
  Jeudi saint (Fr.)
  Jueves santo (Sp.)
  Jueves del mandato (Sp.)

Grundstellung (G.)
  root position (chord)
  5/3 chord
  posizione fondamentale (It.)
  position fondamentale (Fr.)
  posición fundamental (Sp.)

vs. Umkehrung (G.)

Grundthema (G.)
  Leitmotiv (G.)
  leading motive
  idée fixe (Fr.)
  recurring theme
  theme song/music
  signature music/song

Grundton (G.)
  first partial
  lowest harmonic
  fundamental tone
  suono fondamentale (It.)
  note fondamentale (Fr.)
  nota fundamental

2. key note
  tonic
  do
  ut (Lat.)
  tonica (It.)
  suono fondamentale (It.)
  son fondamentale (Fr.)
  tono fundamental (Sp.)

grunge
  pop music
  rock
  low-squality pop

gruppetto (It.)
  trill
  turn
  ornament
  gruppo, groppo (It.)
  groupe (Fr.)
  grupo, grupeto, grupito (Sp.)
  Doppelschlag (G.)
  Gruppe (G.)
  quiebro (Sp.)

guaracha (Sp.)
  Cuban dance
  Latin music

guías (Sp.)

cue notes
little notes
notine (It.)
petite notes (Fr.)
Stichnoten (G.)

guide
   guida (It.)
   guidon (Fr.)
   guia (Sp.)
   custos (Lat.)
   direct
   Kustos (G.)
   tractulus (Lat.)

2. *subject
   dux (Lat.)
   antecedent

vs. answer
   consequent

Guidonian Hand (12c.)
   manus musicalis (Lat.)
   manus Guidonis (Lat.)
   mano guidoniana (It., Sp.)
   main guidonienne (Fr.)
   Guidonische Hand (G.)
   harmonic hand
   solfeggio (It.)
   solmization
   letter notation
   Oddonic/Odionic notation
   Boethian notation
   Daseian notation

guimbard
   *Jew's-harp
   mouth organ
   crembalum (17-18c.Lat.)
   cymbalum orale (Lat.)
   scacciapensieri (It.)
   spassapensieri (It.)
   ribeba (It.)
   guimbarda (It., Sp.)
   guimbarde (Fr.)

trompe de Béarn (Fr.)
trompe de laquais (Fr.)
rebube (Fr.)
Judenharfe (G.)
Maultrommel (G.)
Mundharmonika (G.)
Brummeisen (G.)
birimbao (Sp.)
trompa de París (Sp.)
trompa gallega (Sp.)
trompa inglesa (Sp.)

guión (Sp.)
   *repeat
   repetition
   ripresa (It.)
   repetizione (It.)
   reprise (E., Fr.)
   répétition (Fr.)
   Wiederholung (G.)
   repetición (Sp.)

güiro (Sp.)
   scraper
   percussion
   rhythm instrument

guitar
   bandore, bandora
   bandura, bandoura
   pandora
   chitarra (It.)
   chitarrino (It.)
   guitarra (It.)
   guitare, guiterne (Fr.)
   gratte (Fr.)
   G(u)itarre (G.)
   Zupfgeige (G.)
   bandola (Sp.)
   chango (Sp.)
   vihuela (Sp.)
   guitarrón (Sp.)
   orpharion
   lute, archlute
   sitar (Ind.)
   koto (Jap.)

bouzouki (Gr.)
Spanish guitar
folk guitar
classical guitar
acoustic guitar
electric guitar

guitare d'amour (Fr.)
   arpeggione (instrument)
   guitar-violoncello
   chitarra d'amore (It.)

guitare en bateau (Fr.)
   chitarra battente (It.)
   chitarra mandola (It.)
   guitar
   guitarra battente (It.)
   guitare capucine (Fr.)
   guitare toscane (Fr.)
   guitare à la capucine (Fr.)
   Kapuzinergitarre (G.)

guitare Hawaïenne (Fr.)
   Hawaiian guitar
   steel guitar
   dobro
   chitarra Hawayana (It.)
   Hawaii-Gitarre (G.)
   guitarra Hawaiana (Sp.)

vs. Spanish guitar

gut string
   catgut
   budello (It.)
   minugia (It.)
   boyau (Fr.)
   Darmsaite (G.)
   cuerda de vihuela (Sp.)
   nylon string

vs. steel string

gymel, gimel, gemell
   cantus gemellus (Lat.)
   duet

divided part
semel
parallel thirds
Zwillingsgesang (G.)

ymnopédie (Fr.)
ancient Greek dance
gymnopaedia (Lat.)
piano piece (Satie)

ypsy scale
minor scale/mode
Hungarian mode/scale
harmonic minor

ypsy song
zingana (It.)
canzone gitana (It.)
zingaresca (It.)
chant tzigane/gitan (Fr.)
Zigeunerlied (G.)
canto gitano (Sp.)
canción gitana/tzigana (Sp.)

ypsy style
alla zingara (It.)
à la tzigane (Fr.)
à la hongroise (Fr.)
nach Art der Zigeuner (G.)
al estilo cingaro (Sp.)

H

habanera (Sp.)
  Cuban slow dance
  Latin dance
  tango
  rumba
  avanera (It.)
  havanaise (Fr.)
  Spanischer Tanz (G.)

hablando (Sp.)
  declamatory
  syllabic
  patter song
  recitando (It.)
  parlando, parlato (It.)
  en parlant (Fr.)
  sprechend (G.)
  Sprechstimme (G.)

Hackbrett (G.)
  dulcimer
  cimbalom, cembalom
  hammered dulcimer
  dulcimore
  *psaltery
  salterio tedesco (It.)
  Zimbalom (G.)
  Cimbalom (G.)

hair(s) (of a bow)
  crini (It.)
  crins (Fr.)
  Bogenhaare (G.)
  cuerdas del arco (Sp.)
  crines (Sp.)

hairpins
  crescendo/decrescendo marks
  messa di voce (It.)
  pose de la voix (Fr.)

Hakenneumen (G.)
  hook neumes
  notation (plainsong)

Halbbass (G.)
  bassetto (It.)
  basso di camera (It.)
  Kammerbass (G.)
  Bassett, Bassettl, Bassl (G.)
  *'cello

Halbchor (G.)
  semi-chorus
  echo chorus
  chamber choir
  soli (It.)
  favoriti (It.)
  coro concertato (It.)
  coro favorito (It.)
  semicoro (It., Sp.)
  petit-choeur (Fr.)
  semi-choeur (Fr.)

Halbe (G.)
  open note
  half-note
  minum
  bianca (It.)
  blanche (Fr.)
  blanca (Sp.)

halbe Pause (G.)
  half-rest
  minum rest
  suspirium (Lat.)
  pausa di minima (It.)
  demi-pause (Fr.)
  silencio de blanca (Sp.)
  pausa de blanca (Sp.)

halbe Stimme, mit (G.)
  soft
  half-voice
  *aside
  stage whisper
  pianissimo (It.)

  mezza voce (It.)
  sotto voce (It.)
  à mi-voix (Fr.)
  demi-voix (Fr.)
  media voz (Sp.)

Halbgeige (G.)
  *kit
  small violin
  rebec
  pocket-violin
  violino piccolo (It.)
  violinette (Fr.)
  petit violon de poche (Fr.)
  Tanzmeistergeige (G.)
  violín de bolsillo (Sp.)

Halbmond (G.)
  Turkish crescent
  Chinese crescent
  Chinese pavilion
  Janissary music
  mezzaluna (It.)
  banda Turca (It.)
  *chapeau Chinois (Fr.)
  pavillon Chinois (Fr.)
  sombrero Chino (Sp.)

half-cadence
  semi-cadence
  half-close
  imperfect cadence
  *deceptive cadence
  cadenza imperfetta (It.)
  cadence imperfaite (Fr.)
  demi-cadence (Fr.)
  Halbschluss (G.)
  Mittelkadenz (G.)
  hängende Kadenz (G.)
  unvollkommene Kadenz (G.)
  gebrochene Kadenz (G.)
  Änderungsabsatz (G.)
  cadencia imperfecta (Sp.)
  semicadencia (Sp.)

half-note

minum
minima (It.)
metá (It.)
bianca (It.)
blanche (Fr.)
halbe Note (G.)
blanca (Sp.)

half-rest
minim rest
pausa di mimima (It.)
demi-pause (Fr.)
halbe Pause (G.)
pausa de blanca (Sp.)
silencio de blanca (Sp.)

half-step
semi-tone
half-tone
minor second
hemitone
apotome (Gr.)
limma (Gr.)
semitono (It., Sp.)
demi-ton (Fr.)
Halbton (G.)
diesis (Gr.)

hallelujah, halleluia (Heb.)
alleluia
praise
refrain
respond
chorus
post Epistolam (Ambrosian)
post evangelium (Ambrosian)
laudes (Gallican, Mozarabic)

Hals (G.)
neck (of violin, etc.)
manico (It.)
manche (Fr.)
mango (Sp.)

2. throat (of a singer)
gola (It.)

gorge (Fr.)
Kehle (G.)
garganta (Sp.)

3. stem (of a note)
Stiel (G.)
gambo (It.)
queue (Fr.)
hampe (Fr.)
Notenhals (G.)
plica (Lat.)
filum (Lat.)

Halt (G.)
hold
*fermata (It.)
pause
corona (It., Sp.)
couronne (Fr.)

Haltepedal (G.)
sustain(ing) pedal (piano)
loud pedal
*damper pedal
sostenuto pedal
right pedal
pedale di resonanza (It.)
pédale grande (Fr.)
rechte Pedal (G.)
Tonhaltungspedal (G.)
pedal fuerte (Sp.)

hammer (piano)
martello, martelletto (It.)
marteau (Fr.)
martillo (Sp.)
Hammer (G.)

hammered dulcimer
dulcimer (Hung.)
cimbalom
cembalom
piano harp
psaltery
salterio tedesco (It.)
Hackbrett (G.)

Zimbalom (G.)

Hammerklavier (G.)
*piano
Klavier (G.)
Hammerflügel (G.)
pianoforte

hand-harmonica
*accordion
concertina
squeezebox
Handharmonika (G.)
bandoneón (Sp.)

hand horn
natural horn
French horn
hunting horn
*horn
cor à main (Fr.)
corno da caccia (It.)
cor de chasse (Fr.)
trompe de chasse (Fr.)
Waldhorn (G.)
Naturhorn (G.)
Jagdhorn (G.)
cuerno de caza (Sp.)
trompa de caza (Sp.)

hand organ
*barrel organ
street organ
*hurdy-gurdy
Drehorgel (G.)

Handbassel (G.)
*division viol
viola bastarda (It.)
viola di fagotto (It.)
Faggotgeige (G.)

handbells
campanelli (It.)
clochettes (Fr.)
sonnettes (Fr.)

Handglocken (G.)
bell choir, handbell choir

Handschrift (G.)
autograph score
manuscript
urtext
hand-written
manoscritto (It.)
manuscrit (Fr.)
manuscrito (Sp.)

Handstück (18c. G.)
study
*étude (E., Fr.)
lesson
exercise
practice piece
studio (It.)
esercizio (It.)
ejercicio (Sp.)
estudio (Sp.)
Übung (G.)

Handtrommel (G.)
tamborine
timbrel
tamburino (It.)
tamburello (It.)
cimbalo (It.)
tamburo Basco (It.)
tamburo di provenza (It.)
tambour de Basque (Fr.)
tambour de Biscaye (Fr.)
Schellentrommel (G.)
Tamburin (G.)
Baskische Trommel (G.)
pandero, pandereta (Sp.)
cimbalo, cimbaletto,
cimbalino (It.)

hard rock
rock-'n'-roll
heavy metal
acid rock
pop music

grunge

hardanger fiddle
fiddle
violin
Norwegian folk fiddle
sympathetic strings
*viola d'amore (It.)
violon de Hardanger (Fr.)
Hardingfele (E., G.)
Hardangerfi(e)del (G.)

Harfe (G.)
*harp
arpa (It., Sp.)
harpe (Fr.)

Harfenlaute (G.)
*dital harp
harp lute
harp guitar

harmoniai (Gr.)
*scale
mode

harmonic(s)
overtone
partial
open note/tone
node
overblow
flageolet tone
aliquot tone
natural tone
chord of Nature
harmonic series
flautato (It.)
suoni armonici (It.)
sons harmoniques (Fr.)
Obertöne (G.)
sónidos armónicos (Sp.)

harmonic close
*cadence (E., Fr.)
Schluss (G.)

Kadenz (G.)
cadentia (Lat.)
cadenza (It.)
cadencia (Sp.)
close
ending

harmonic hand
Guidonian hand
solfege
sol-fa
*solmization

harmonic minor
scale
minor scale
Gypsy scale
Hungarian gypsy scale
natural minor
melodic minor
mode

harmonic progression
chord progression
harmonization
chord changes
harmonic rhythm
**harmonischer Rhythmus
(G.)**

harmonic series
overtones
harmonics
harmoniques (Fr.)
aliquoti (It.)
aliquotes (Fr.)
Aliquottöne (G.)
armonichi (It.)
armónicos (Sp.)
alicuotes (Sp.)
partials
chord of Nature
flageolet tones
aliquot tones

harmonica

mouth organ
French harp
aoline
armonica (It.)
armonica a/di bocca (It.)
verrillon (Fr.)
harmonica à bouche (Fr.)
Mundharmonika (G.)
Harmonika (G.)
armónica (Sp.)

harmonica de bois (Fr.)
xylophone
marimba
sticcato (It.)
xilofono (It.)
organo di legno (It.)
*claquebois (Fr.)
orgue de paille (Fr.)
xilofono (It.)
xilorgano (It.)
Xilophon (G.)
xilófono (Sp.)
xilórgano (Sp.)
armónica de madera (Sp.)

harmonichord
*hurdy-gurdy
sostinente pianoforte (It.)
sympathetic strings

harmonie par quartes (Fr.)
quartal harmony
armonia quartale (It.)
armonia per quarte (It.)
Quartenharmonik (G.)
armonía por cuartes (Sp.)

harmonie par/en tierces (Fr.)
tertian harmony
triadic harmony
harmony in thirds
per terze (It.)
Terzaufbau (G.)
per terceras (Sp.)

Harmoniemusik (G.)
wind ensemble music
band music
music for brass

harmonium (E., Fr., G.)
melodeon
aerophone
aeoline
aeolodicon
American organ
seraphine
reed organ
parlor organ
pump organ
armonio, armonium (It.)
orgue expressif (Fr.)
séraphine (Fr.)
Expressivorgel (G.)
Windharmonika (G.)
armonio (Sp.)

harmonized chant
Anglican chant
falsoborbone (It.)
fauxbourdon (Fr.)

harmony
*chord
triad
tone cluster
vertical aspect
armonia (It.)
harmonie (Fr.)
Harmonie (G.)
armonía (Sp.)
homophonic

harmony of the spheres
music of the spheres
celestial harmony
musica mundana (Lat.)
l'armonia delle sfere/celeste (It.)
musique des spheres célestes (Fr.)

Sphärenmusik (G.)
Sphärenharmonie (G.)
armonía de las esferas celestes (Sp.)
música de las esferes celestes (Sp.)

harness bells
*bells
sleighbells
pellet bells
jingle bells
altar bells
Sanctus bells
sonaglio, sonagliera (It.)
bubboli (It.)
grelots (Fr.)
sonnettes, sonnailles (Fr.)
Rollschellen (G.)
Schellengeläute (G.)
cascabeles (Sp.)
cencerro (Sp.)

harp
lyre
cithara (Lat.)
kithara (Gr.)
arpa (It., Sp.)
harpe (Fr.)
Harfe (G.)
magadis (Gr.)

harp guitar
*dital harp
harp lute
harpe ditale (Fr.)
Harfenlaute (G.)
Guitarrenharfe (G.)

harp stop (harpsichord)
buff stop
lute stop
mute
una corda (It.)
sordina (It., Sp.)
étouffoir (Fr.)

sourdine (Fr.)
Dämpfer (G.)
Harfenzug (G.)

harpe éoline/eolienne (Fr.)
Aeolian harp
arpa eolia (It., Sp.)
Windharfe (G.)
Äolsharfe (G.)

harpe de David (Fr.)
David's harp
Irish harp
Troubadour harp
Gaelic harp
arpa di David (It.)

vs. pedal harp

harpégé, harpégement (Fr.)
broken chord
rolled chord
*arpeggio (It.)
gebrochener Akkord (G.)
batterie (Fr.)
bariolage (Fr.)
arpège (Fr.)

vs. accord plaqué (Fr.)

harpsichord
clavicembalo (It., Sp.)
cembalo (It.)
clavecin (Fr.)
Cembalo (G.)
Kielflügel (G.)
clavecín (Sp.)
virginals
spinet
chekker
clavicimbalum (Lat.)
gravicembalo (17c. It.)
arpicordo (It.)
épinette (Fr.)
Klavizimbel (G.)
clave, clavicordio (Sp.)

pedal harpsichord
clavichord

hasta el fin (Sp.)
al fine (It.)
to the end
à la fin (Fr.)
bis zu Ende (G.)

Hauptmesse (G.)
high mass
solemn mass
missa cantata (Lat.)
missa solemnis (Lat.)
messa solenne (It.)
messa grande (It.)
messe solennelle (Fr.)
grand-messe (Fr.)
Hochamt (G.)
misa solemne (Sp.)
misa mayor (Sp.)

vs. stille Messe (G.)

Hauptmotiv (G.)
Leitmotiv (G.)
idée fixe (Fr.)
leading motive
recurring theme
motivo conduttore (It.)
motif conducteur (Fr.)
motivo conductor (Sp.)
theme song
signature song/music
Erinnerungsmotiv (G.)
rondo
parody mass

Hauptrolle (G.)
principal role/part
leading role/part
prima parte (It.)
parte principale (It.)
ruolo principale (It.)
rôle principal (Fr.)
première partie/rôle (Fr.)

vs. Nebenrolle (G.)

Hauptsatz (G.)
first theme
main theme
principal theme
motivo principale (It.)
motif principal (Fr.)
Hauptthema (G.)

vs. Seitensatz (G.)

Hauptstimme (G.)
foundation stop (organ)
diapason
principal (E., Sp.)
princoipale (It., Fr.)
Prinzipal (G.)
fond(s) d'orgue (Fr.)
préstant (Fr.)
montre (Fr.)
diapasón abierto (Sp.)

Hauptthema (G.)
main theme
principal theme
first theme
tema principale (It.)
thème principal (Fr.)
tema principal (Sp.)

vs. Nebenthema (G.)

Hauptwerk (G.)
great organ/manual
gran organo (It.)
principale (It.)
*grand choeur (Fr.)
grand orgue (Fr.)
Hauptmanual (G.)
Hauptorgel (G.)
primer manual (Sp.)
teclado principal del organo (Sp.)

Hausmusik (G.)

house music
music for the home
functional music
practical music
amateur music
musica de consumo (It.)
musica d'uso (It.)
musica domestica (It.)
musica familiare (It.)
musique domestique (Fr.)
musique d'usage (Fr.)
música de consumo (Sp.)
música en casa (Sp.)
música doméstica (Sp.)
Gebrauchsmusik (G.)

hausse (Fr.)
nut (of a bow)
frog (of a bow)
heel
tallone (It.)
tacco (It.)
talon (Fr.)
Frosch (G.)
talón (Sp.)

vs pointe (Fr.)

hausser (Fr.)
to sharp (a tone)
raise
alzare (It.)
alzar (Sp.)
erhöhen (G.)

vs. baisser (Fr.)

haut-dessus (Fr.)
high soprano
first soprano
*soprano one
treble one

vs. bas-dessus (Fr.)
soprano two

hautbois (Fr.)
oboe
hautboy (E.)
aulos (Gr.)
shawm
diaulos (Gr.)
kalamos (Gr.)
calamus (Lat.)
tibia (Lat.)
reed, double reed
chalumeau (Fr.)
Schalmei (G.)
caramillo (Sp.)
tiple (Sp.)
*English horn
oboe d'amore (It.)
oboe da caccia (It.)
*crumhorn

haute-contre (Fr.)
countertenor
high tenor
alto-tenor
cambiata
Irish tenor
*alto
contralto
falsetto
altus (Lat.)
altista (It.)
alti naturali (Lat., It.)
haute-taille (Fr.)
Alt, Altstimme (G.)
Kontraalt (G.)

hauteur du ton (Fr.)
*pitch
frequency
Hertz
vibration
diapason (Fr., It.)
Tonhöhe (G.)
Kammerton (G.)
entonación (Sp.)
diapasón (Sp.)

hautparleur (Fr.)
loudspeaker
PA system
altoparlante (It.)
Lautsprecher (G.)
altavoz (Sp.)

Hawaiian guitar
steel guitar
dobro
electric guitar with steel bar
chitarra Hawayana (It.)
guitare Hawaïenne (Fr.)
Hawaii-Gitarre (G.)
guitarra Hawaiana (Sp.)

vs. Spanish guitar

hay, haye, heye (16-17c. E.)
*branle (Fr.)
canary
canarie (Fr.)
canario (It., Sp.)
jig
gigue
giga (It.)

hazan (Heb.)
cantor (E., Sp.)
soloist
leader of song
chazzan (H.)
precentor
accentor (E.)
accentus (Lat.)
cantore (It.)
chantre (Fr.)
Vorsänger (G.)

head
main part of a note
testa (It.)
tête (Fr.)
Notenkopf (G.)

2. part of a drum

vellum
membrane
skin
pelle (It.)
peau (Fr.)
Fell (G.)
Schlagfell (G.)

3. point (of a bow)
tip
punta (It., Sp.)
pointe (Fr.)
Spitze (G.)
Kopf (G.)

head arrangement
improvisation
extemporization
ad-lib
swing
jam
jazz

head tone/voice/register
falsetto
high voice
voce di testa (It.)
voix de tête (Fr.)
Kopfstimme (G.)
voz de cabeza (Sp.)

vs. chest tone

heavy metal
rock and roll
hard rock
acid rock
pop music
grunge

Hebdomade Sancte (Lat.)
Holy Week
Passion Week
settimana santa (It.)
semaine sainte (Fr.)
Karwoche (G.)

semana santa (Sp.)

Hebung (G.)
arsis (Gr.)
anacrusis (Lat.)
upbeat
pick-up
feminine
élévation (Fr.)
levé (Fr.)
Auftakt (G.)

vs. Abschlag (G.)
Niederschlag (G.)

heckelphone
bass oboe
baritone oboe
basset oboe
Heckelphon (G.)
basse de musette (Fr.)
Musettenbass (G.)

heel (of a bow)
frog
tallone (It.)
talon (Fr.)
hausse (Fr.)
Frosch (G.)
talón (Sp.)

vs. point, tip

Heerpauke(n) (G., 16c.)
*kettledrum
tympani
timpano (It.)
timbale (Fr.)
Pauke (G.)

heirmos, hirmos (Gr.)
stanza (Byzantine chant)
ode
hymn
strophe

Heldentenor (G.)
Wagnerian tenor
heroic tenor
dramatic tenor
tenore robusto (It.)
tenore drammatico (It.)
tenore eroico (It.)
fort ténor (Fr.)
ténor dramatique (Fr.)
tenor dramatico (Sp.)

helicon
bass tuba
hélicon (Fr.)
Helikon (G.)
elicon(a), helicon (It.)
sousaphone
cavalry horn

hemidemisemiquaver
sixty-fourth note
semidemisemiquaver
semibiscroma (It.)
sessantaquattresimo (It.)
quadruple-croche (Fr.)
Vierundsechzigstel (G.)
semifusa (Sp.)

hemidiapente (Gr.)
diminished fifth
augmented fourth
tritone
tritonus (Lat.)
tritono (It., Sp.)
triton (Fr.)
Tritonus (G.)
devil's interval
diabolus in musica (Lat.)
false fifth
mi contra fa (Lat.)

hemiditone (Gr.)
minor third
terza minore (It.)
tierce mineure (Fr.)
kleine Terz (G.)

tercera menor (Sp.)

hemiola (E., Gr.)
    perfect fifth
    diapente (Gr.)

2. rhythm change in triple meter
    sesquialtera (Lat.)
    emiola (It.)
    hémiole (Fr.)
    Hemiole (G.)

3. proportio hemiola (Lat. 15c.)
    black notes, or red notes to
indicate a 2:3 proportion
    color (Lat.)
    isorhythm
    talea (Lat.)

hemitone
    *half-step
    half-tone
    semitone
    chromatic interval
    minor second
    semitono (It.)
    demi-ton (Fr.)
    Halbton (G.)

hemitonic
    chromatic
    *half-steps
    semitones
    hemitonium (Lat., Gr.)
    Halbton (G.)

vs. anhemitonic (whole steps)

hep-cat
    swing musician
    jazz player
    big band fan

heptachord
    seven-tone scale
    diatonic scale

eptacordo, ettacordo (It.)

Herabstrich (G.)
    *down-bow
    arco in giù (It.)
    arcata in giù (It.)
    tiré (Fr.)
    Abstrich (G.)
Herstrich (G.)
Herunterstrich (G.)
    tirado (Sp.)
    arcada hacia abajo (Sp.)

vs. Heraufstrich (G.)
    up-bow

herald's trumpet
    state trumpet
    natural trumpet
    *Aida trumpet
    chamade (Fr., organ)
    ceremonial trumpet
    long, straight trumpet
    tuba (Lat.ancient Rome)
    trompette thébaine (Fr.)
    buisine (Fr.)
    buccina (Lat., med.)
    Alphorn, Alpenhorn (G.)
    Heroldstrompete (G.)

Hertz
    cycles per second (cps)
    *frequency
    vibration
    sound wave
    pitch
    oscillation
    frequenza (It.)
    fréquence (Fr.)
    Frequenz (G.)
    Schwingung (G.)
    Tonhöhe (G.)
    frecuencia (Sp.)

Herunterschlag (G.)
    *downbeat

thesis (Gr.)
crusis (Lat.)
strong beat
abbattimento (It.)
frappé (Fr.)
Abschlag (G.)

hervorgehoben (G.)
    *emphasized
    lead part
    bring out
    in fuori (It.)
    au dehors (Fr.)
    en dehors (Fr.)
    hervortretend (G.)
    fuera (Sp.)

heterophony
    duplicate melody
    unison (not quite)
    variation
    embroidery
    ornamented melody
    heterofonia (It., Sp.)
    hétérophonie (Fr.)
    Heterophonie (G.)

hexachord
    six-note scale
    solmization
    deductio (Lat.)
    deduttione (It.)
    déduction (Fr.)
    Deductio (G.)
    deducio (Sp.)
    hexachordum (Lat.)
    esacordión (Sp.)
    hexacordo (Sp.)
    hexacorde (Fr.)

2. six-stringed instrument

3. major sixth (interval)

hi-hat, high-hat
    cymbal

choke cymbals
sock cymbals
Charleston (It.)
hi-hat pédal (Fr.)
Charlestonmaschine (G.)
cymbales choquées (Fr.)
pedal del bombo de jazz (Sp.)

hiatus
pause
stop
hold
*fermata
railroad tracks
interrupted melody
Abreissung (G.)
abruptio (Lat.)

hidden fifths, octaves
covered fifths
consecutive fifths
parallel fifths
horn fifths
Ohrenquinten (G.)
verdeckte Quinten (G.)

high-brow music
long-haired music
classical music
serious music
art song, art music
concert music

high curtal
fagottino (It.)
treble bassoon
tenor oboe
tenoroon
petit basson (Fr.)
Tenorfagott (G.)
Quintfagott (G.)
fagote Quinta (Sp.)

high-fi, hi-fi
faithful recording/playback
digital recording

high fidelity
stereo
LP
CD
DVD
audio
sound reproduction

high mass
solemn mass
choral service
missa solemnis (Lat.)
missa cantata (Lat.)
messa solenne (It.)
messa grande (It.)
messa cantata (It.)
messe haute (Fr.)
grand'messe (Fr.)
messe solennelle (Fr.)
messe chantée (Fr.)
hohe Messe (G.)
grosse Messe (G.)
Hochamt (G.)
Choramt (G.)
Chordienst (G.)
Hauptmesse (G.)
Singmesse (G.)
misa solemne (Sp.)
misa mayor (Sp.)
misa cantada (Sp.)

vs. low mass

high pitch
philharmonic pitch
concert pitch
international pitch
diapasón alto (Sp.)
diapasón de concierto (Sp.)

high tenor
Irish tenor
whiskey tenor
countertenor
falsetto

Hilfslinie (G.)
ledger line
righetta, rigo (It.)
riga aggiunta (It.)
ligne supplémentaire (Fr.)
ligne additionelle (Fr.)
ligne ajoutée (Fr.)
linea adicional (Sp.)

Hilfsnote (G.)
non-harmonic tone
auxiliary note
neighbor-note
nota ausiliare (It.)
note auxiliaire (Fr.)
note secondaire (Fr.)
Nebennote (G.)
nota auxiliar (Sp.)

hillbilly music
country music
mountain music
folk music
traditional music
old time music
gospel
bluegrass

himno (Sp.)
hymn
chorale
hymn-tune
sacred song
religious song
anthem
ode
hymnus (Lat.)
hymnos (Gr.)
heirmos, hirmos (Gr.)
inno (It.)
hymne (Fr.)
Lobgesang (G.)
Kirchenlied (G.)
Kirchengesang (G.)
Hymne (G.)
canticle

antiphon
psalm
doxology
exultet
sequence
dithyramb
paean (Gr.)

himno nacional (Sp.)
national hymn
national anthem
inno nazionale (It.)
hymne national (Fr.)
Nationalhymne (G.)

Hinaufstrich (G.)
up-bow
Hinstrich (G.)
arcata in su (It.)
poussé (Fr.)
Aufstrich, Anstrich (G.)
arcada hacia arriba (Sp.)

vs. Herabstrich (G.)

Hingebung (G.)
*free
unrestrained
with abandon
con abbandono (It.)
abandonné (Fr.)
avec abandon (Fr.)
mit Hingabe (G.)
con abandono (Sp.)

hinkend (G.)
*syncopated
off-beat
limping rhythm
alla zoppa (It.)
boiteux, boitement (Fr.)
cojeando (Sp.)

hinter der Szene (G.)
behind the scenes
in the wings

*backstage
offstage
fra le quinte (It.)
dans les coulisses (Fr.)
en coulisse (Fr.)
hinter den Kulissen (G.)
Hinterbühne (G.)
paño, al paño (Sp.)
bastidores (Sp.)
entre bastidores (Sp.)

Hintergrundmusik (G.)
*backround music
light music
easy listening
Muzak
dinner music
cocktail music
cabaret music
café music
dentist music
elevator music
lift music
salon music
incidental music

Hintersatz (G.)
*mixture stop (organ)
compound stop
fourniture (Fr.)
cornet (Fr.)
plein jeu (Fr.)
sesquialtera (Lat.)

2. full organ
organo pieno/pleno (It.)
gran organo (It.)
*grand-choeur (Fr.)
grand-orgue (Fr.)
grand jeu (Fr.)
Werk (G.)
volles Werk (G.)
gran juego (Sp.)
órgano lleno (Sp.)

hinzugefügte Sexte (G.)

added sixth chord
sesta aggiunta (It.)
sixte ajouté (Fr.)
sexta agregada (Sp.)

hip-hop music
pop music
rap
rock
reggae
ska
techno-music
electronica
world music
grunge

hippodrome
arena
stadium
opera house
outdoor theatre
ampitheatre
auditorium

hirmos, heirmos (Gr.)
Byzantine chant
hymn stanza
hymn
strophe

Hirtengesang (G.)
eclogue
pastorale (It., Fr.)
idyl
egloga (It.)
églogue (Fr.)
Schäferstück (G.)
pastoral (Sp.)
égloga (Sp.)

Hirtenpfeife (G.)
tin whistle
tin flute
pipe
chanter (of a bagpipe)
zufolo (It.)

scialumo (It.)
pipeau, pipette (Fr.)
pipa, pipitaña (Sp.)

historicus (Lat.)
narrator
Evangelist
evangelium (Lat.)
chronista (Lat.)
testo (It.)
narratore (It.)
narrateur (Fr.)
récitant (Fr.)
Erzähler (G.)
narrador (Sp.)

historical instrument(s)
period instruments
old instrument
original instrument
authentic instrument
early music
instruments origineaux (Fr.)
Originalinstrumenten (G.)

history of music
music history
musicology
storia della musica (It.)
l'histoire de la musique (Fr.)
Musikgeschichte (G.)
Geschichte der Musik (G.)
historia de la música (Sp.)

hit it!
*attack
attacca (It.)
attaquez (Fr.)
fange an (G.)
falle an (G.)
ataca (Sp.)
*segue (It.)

hit parade (E., Fr.)
best pop songs
charts

top ten, twenty, forty
hits, hit songs
rassegna di successi musicali (It.)
Schlagerparade (G.)

hit song
top of the charts
top-40, top-10
hit record
hit single
canzoni di successo (It.)
chanson à la mode (Fr.)
chanson à succès (Fr.)
Schlager (G.)
canción de moda (Sp.)
canción en boga (Sp.)

hobnail notation
gothic notation (chant)
Hufnagelschrift (G.)
Nagelschrift (G.)

hochalteriert (G.)
augmented
augmentatio (Lat.)
aumentato (It.)
eccedente (It.)
augmenté (Fr.)
übermässig (G.)
aumentado (Sp.)

vs. verkleinert (G.)

Hochamt (G.)
*high mass
solemn mass
sung mass
missa cantata (Lat.)
missa solemnis (Lat.)
messa solenne (It.)
messa grande (It.)
Hauptmesse (G.)
misa mayor (Sp.)
misa solemne (Sp.)

vs. stille Messe (G.)

hochet (Fr.)
*rattle, cog rattle
rainstick
raganella (It.)
crécelle (Fr.)
Rassel, Ratsche (G.)
Knarre (G.)
Schnarre (G.)
maraca (Sp.)
cabaça (Port.)

Hochschule für Musik (G.)
conservatory of music
*academy of music
conservatorio (It., Sp.)
Konservatorium (G.)
music school
music academy
lyceum
schola cantorum (Lat.)
liceo (It.)
scuola di musica (It.)
accademia musicale (It.)
académie de musique (Fr.)
escuela de música (Sp.)

Hochzeitsmarsch (G.)
wedding march
marcia nuziale (It.)
marche nuptiale (Fr.)
marcha nupcial (Sp.)

hocket (13-14c.)
hoquetatio, hoquetus (Lat.)
ochetto (It.)
tactée (Fr.)
ho(c)quet (Fr.)
Hoketus (G.)
hoquet (Sp.)
broken note
interrupted melody
truncatio (Lat.)
occitatio (Lat.)

hoedown
hootnanny
jamboree
square dance
hillbilly music
old-time music
jam session
sing-along
community sing

Hoflied (G.)
courting song
Hofweise (G.)
Minnesinger
Meistersinger
Troubadour (Fr.)
grande chanson (Fr.)

Hoftanz (G.)
*basse danse (Fr.)
court dance
minuet
saltarello (It.)
*branle (Fr.)
pas de Brabant (Fr.)
Nachtanz (G.)

Hohelied (G.)
Song of Songs
Song of Solomon
*Canticle of Canticles
Canticum Canticorum (Lat.)
Cantico dei Cantici (It.)
Cantique des Cantiques (Fr.)
Lied der Lieder (G.)
Cantar de los Cantares (Sp.)

hoja de álbum (Sp.)
*album-leaf
short piece
foglio d'album (It.)
pagina d'album (It.)
feuillet d'album (Fr.)
Albumblatt (G.)

hold

*fermata
pause
*caesura
organ point
corona (It.)
punto d'organo (It.)
couronne (Fr.)
point d'arrêt (Fr.)
point d'orgue (Fr.)
Fermate (G.)
Orgelpunkt (G.)
punto de organo (Sp.)
calderón (Sp.)

Holy Communion
Eucharist
*mass
Lord's Supper
communion service
agape feast
love feast
*liturgy
Divine Service
Abendmahl (G.)
Agende (G.)
Kirchenordnung (G.)
Kirchenamt (G.)

Holy Saturday
Easter Eve
Easter Vigil
Sacred Triduum
Holy Week
Triduum Sacrum (Lat.)
Sabbato Sancto (Lat.)
sabato santo (It.)
Samedi saint (Fr.)
Karsamstag (G.)
Sábado Santo (Sp.)

Holy Thursday
Maundy Thursday
Last Supper
Sacred Triduum
Holy Week
Triduum Sacrum (Lat.)

Coena Domini (Lat.)
giovedi santo (It.)
Jeudi saint (Fr.)
Gründonnerstag (G.)
Jueves Santo (Sp.)
Jueves del mandato (Sp.)

Holy Week
Passion Week
Sacred Triduum
Triduum Sanctum (Lat.)
Hebdomade Sancte (Lat.)
settimana sancta (It.)
semaine sainte (Fr.)
Karwoche (G.)
semana santa (Sp.)

Holzblock (G.)
*Chinese wood-block
temple blocks
Korean temple blocks
clog box
tap box
caisse Chinois (Fr.)
bloc de bois (Fr.)
cassettina (It.)
cassa di legno (It.)
blochetto (It.)
Holzblocktrommel (G.)
caja China (Sp.)

Holzharmonika (G.)
*xylophone
*claquebois (Fr.)
sticcato (It.)
gigelira (It.)
Holzstabspiel (G.)
hölzernes Gelächter (G.)
armonica de madera (Sp.)

homophon (Gr.)
unison (interval)
prime
unisono (It., Sp.)
unisson (Fr.)
Einklang (G.)

homophonic
homogenized melody
omofonico (It.)
homophone (Fr.)
homophon (G.)
homofónico (Sp.)
homorhythmic

vs. polyphonic
homophony
monody
solo
chordal style
familiar style
omofonia (It.)
homophonie (Fr.)
Homophonie (G.)
homofonía (Sp.)

vs. polyphony

homorhythm(ic)
homophony
isorhythm
note-against-note
fauxbourdon
falsobordone (It.)
Anglican chant
Russian chant
frottola (It.)
vers mesuré (Fr.)
musique mesurée (Fr.)
hymns
chorales
conductus style

honky-tonk(y)
pop/jazz style
low-down
funky
cheap
grunge

hook (of a note)
flag
tail

eighth-note, etc.
coda uncinata (It.)
codetta (It.)
crochet de la note (Fr.)
Fahne, Fähnchen (G.)
Notenfahne (G.)
rabillo (Sp.)
gancho (Sp.)

hook neumes
Hakenneumen (G.)
notation
plainsong
chant

hoot(e)nanny
jamboree
sing-along
jam session
community sing
hoedown

hopak
gopak
fast, duple dance
Russian dance
polka
trepak
galop
can-can

Hopp Tancz (G.)
*saltarello (It.)
galliard
gagliarda (It.)
tripla (It.)
rotta (It.)
bassadanza (It.)
quaternaria (It.)
basse danse (Fr.)
sauterelle (Fr.)
to(u)rdion (Fr.)
Sprung (G.)
Nachtanz (G.)
Hupfauf (G.)
segunda danza (Sp.)

hopper (piano)
grasshopper
escapement
key release
scappamento (It.)
Auslöser, Auslösung (G.)
échappement (Fr.)
escape, escapatoria (Sp.)
horae canonicae (Lat.)
canonical hours
*Divine Office
office (E., Fr.)
monastic office
Night Office (Matins)
Little Hours
Morning, Evening Prayer
Night Prayer (1972)
hours of the day
Opus Dei (Lat.)
Stundenoffizium (G.)
Horas Canónicas (Sp.)
Liturgy of the Hours (1972)
Liturgia horarum (Lat. 1972)

horn
French horn
corno (It.)
cor (Fr.)
Horn (G.)
trompa (Sp.)
*valve horn

2. any wind instrument (jazz)

horn fifths
parallel fifths
consecutive fifths
hidden fifths
covered fifths
Hornquinten, Hornsatz (G.)

horning
mock serenade
*shivaree
*callithumpian concert
caterwauling

cacaphony
cat's concert
Dutch concert
charivari (Fr.)
scampata (It.)
musica di gatti (It.)
Katzenmusik (G.)
cencerrada (Sp.)

hornpipe
duple dance
sailor's dance
jig

Hornsignal (G.)
call
signal call
bugle call
chiamata ((It.)
chamade (Fr.)

horse opera
program or film with a
western theme
a western (film)

hot
jazzy
swing
fast and loud

2. very popular
sexy

house of worship
church
synagogue
temple
cathedral
basilica
chapel

Hufnagelschrift (G.)
gothic notation (chant)
hobnail notation
Nagelschrift (G.)

huitième (Fr.)
thirty-second note
demisemiquaver
biscroma (It.)
trentaduesimo (It.)
Zweiunddreissigstel (G.)
fusa (Sp.)

huitième de soupir (Fr.)
thirty-second rest
demisemiquaver rest
pausa di biscroma (It.)
Zweiunddreissigstel Pause
(G.)
silencio de fusa (Sp.)
pausa de fusa (Sp.)

hum, humming
a boc(c)a chiusa (It.)
furberia del canto (It.)
canticchiare (It.)
chantonner (Fr.)
fredonner (Fr.)
avec bouche fermée (Fr.)
Brummstimmen (G.)
trällern (G.)
canticur, canturrear (Sp.)

Hummel, Humle (G.)
zither
dulcimer
bûche (Fr.)
bûche de Flandres (Fr.)
épinette des Vosges (Fr.)
tamborin à cordes (Fr.)
Scheitholt (G.)

Hümmelchen (G.)
*bagpipe
piva (It.)
musette (Fr.)
Dudelsack (G.)
gaita (Sp.)

humoresque (E., Fr.)
umoresca (It.)

Humoreske (G.)
humoresca (Sp.)
caprice (E., Fr.)
fancy
burlesca, burla (It.)
burlesque (E., Fr.)

Hungarian gypsy scale
harmonic minor
gypsy scale

hunting horn
natural horn
French horn
Jagdhorn (G.)
cor de chasse (Fr.)
trompa de caza (Sp.)
trompe (Fr.)

hunting song
caccia (It.)
chace (Fr.)
catch
chase
caça (Sp.)
descriptive music
character piece

hurdy-gurdy
street piano/organ
barrel organ/piano
hand organ
organistrum (Lat.)
lyra rustica (Lat.)
lyra pagano (Lat.)
ghironda (It.)
ghironda ribeca (It.)
sambuca rotata (Lat.)
lira tedesca (It.)
lira organizzata (It.)
organetto (It.)
stampella (It.)
sinfonia (It.)
viola da orbo (It.)
vielle organisée (Fr.)
vielle à roue (Fr.)

vielle d'amour (Fr.)
chifonie (Fr.)
orgue à cilindre (Fr.)
orgue à manivelle (Fr.)
orgue de Barbarie (Fr.)
Drehorgel (G.)
Orgelwalze (G.)
Leier, Drehleier (G.)
Leierkastel (G.)
Bauernleier (G.)
Deutsche Leier (G.)
Radleier (G.)
Bettlorleier (G.)
zanfoña, zanfonía (Sp.)
cifonia (Sp.)
viola de rueda (Sp.)
organillo (Sp.)

hydraulic organ
water organ
hydraulis-os (Gr.)
hydraulus (Lat.)
organum hydraulicum (Lat.)
organo idraulico (It.)
orgue hydraulique (Fr.)
Wasserorgel (G.)
órgano hidráulico (Sp.)

hymn (n.)
church song
chorale
hymn tune
sacred song
religious song
ode
paean
psalm, psalm tune
sequence
dithyramb
doxology
anthem
canticle
heirmos, hirmos (Gr.)
hymnos (Gr.)
hymnus (Lat.)
inno (It.)

hymne (Fr.)
Hymne (G.)
Lobgesang (G.)
Kirchenlied (G.)
Kirchengesang (G.)
himno (Sp.)

2. national hymn
national anthem
inno nazionale (It.)
hymne national (Fr.)
Nationalhymne (G.)
himno nacional

hymn (vb.)
to sing, chant
intone
strike up
cantare (It.)
singen (G.)
chanter (Fr.)
cantar (Sp.)

Hymn of Victory (Byz.)
Triumphant Hymn/Song
Sanctus (Lat.)
Song of the Angels
Cherubic Hymn
Trisagion
epinicion (Gr.)
Kadosh (H.)
Kedusha (H.)

hymnal
hymn book
tune book
song book (religious)
hymnary
psalter
*anthology
repertory
hymn-tune collection
innario (It.)
hymnaire (Fr.)
Hymnar (G.)
Gesangbuch (G.)

Leise (medieval G.)
himnario (Sp.)

Hymnus Ambrosianus (Lat.)
Te Deum (Lat.)
Ambrosian Hymn

Hymnus Angelicus (Lat.)
Angelic Hymn
Hymn of the Angels
Cherubim Song
Greater Doxology
Gloria in excelsis Deo (Lat.)
doxology
trinitarian hymn

Hymnus glorificationis (Lat.)
doxology
Lesser Doxology
Gloria patri (Lat.)

hypoaeolian mode/scale (mode 10)
plagal mode, E-E, final A

hypodorian mode/scale (mode 2)
plagal mode, A-A, final D
natural minor

hypoionian mode/scale (mode 12)
plagal mode, G-G, final C

hypolydian mode/scale (mode 6)
plagal mode, E-E, final F

hypomixolydian mode/scale (mode 8)
plagal mode, D-D, final G

hypophrygian mode/scale (mode 4)
plagal mode, B-B, final E

*pavan
passamezzo (It.)

chiave (It.)
  clef
  clé (Fr.)
  Schlüssel (G.)
  clave (Sp.)
  llave (Sp.)
  staff

2. key on instr.

3. tuning key

chiave di do (It.)
  C-clef
  alto clef
  viola clef
  tenor clef
  chiave di contralto (It.)
  clef d'ut (Fr.)
  clef de do (Fr.)
  C-Schlüssel (G.)
  Altschlüssel (G.)
  llave de do (Sp.)
  clave de do (Sp.)
  clave de contralto (Sp.)

chiave di fa (It.)
  bass clef
  baritone clef
  F-clef
  chiave di basso (It.)
  clef de fa (Fr.)
  F-Schlüssel (G.)
  Bassschlüssel (G.)
  llave de fa (Sp.)
  clave de grave (Sp.)
  clave de bajo (Sp.)

chiave di sol (It.)
  G-clef
  treble clef
  soprano clef
  violin clef

chiave di violino (It.)
chiave di soprano (It.)
chiave di canto (It.)
  clef de sol (Fr.)
  clef de violon (Fr.)
  G-Schlüssel (G.)
  Violinschlüssel (G.)
  Sopranoschlüssel (G.)
  llave de sol (Sp.)
  clave de violin (Sp.)
  clave de sol (Sp.)
  clave aguda (Sp.)

chiavette (It.)
  transposed clefs
  clef system (16c.)
chiavi transportati (It.)

chica, chico (Sp.)
  dance
  fandango
  cachucha (Sp.)
  bolero
  chaconne

chiesa (It.)
  *church
  chapel
  basilica
  cathedral
  house of worship
  église (Fr.)
  Kirche (G.)
  iglesia (Sp.)

chiff (organ, flute)
  *articulation
  attack
  piff

chiffre de mesure (Fr.)
  meter signature
  time signature
  measure signature
  indicazione della misura (It.)
  indicazione del tempo (It.)

segno del tempo (It.)
indication de la mesure (Fr.)
Taktart (G.)
Taktvorzeichnung (G.)
llave de tiempo (Sp.)

chifonie (Fr.)
  *hurdy-gurdy
  barrel organ
  Drehleier (G.)
  cinfonia (Sp.)
  stampella (It.)

chime-bells
  *bells
  glockenspiel

chime (bells)
  peal
  ring
  toll
  sound
  play
  tinkle
  scampanare (It.)
  suonare (It.)
  sonner (Fr.)
  läuten (G.)
  schallen (G.)
  resonar (Sp.)

chimes
  bells
  carillon
  tubular chimes
  orchestra bells
  celesta
  church bells
  tower bells

chimney flute (organ)
  Rohrflöte (G.)
  flûte à cheminée (Fr.)

chin rest
  mentoniera (It.)

mentonnière (Fr.)
Kinnhalter (G.)
mentonera (Sp.)
barbada (Sp.)

Chinese (wood) block
wood blocks
Chinese temple blocks
Korean temple blocks
temple blocks
clog box
tap box
cassettina (It.)
blochetto (It.)
cassa di legno (It.)
bloc de bois (Fr.)
caisse Chinoise (Fr.)
Holzblock (G.)
Holzblocktrommel (G.)
caja China (Sp.)

Chinese crescent
Turkish crescent
Chinese pavilion
Jingling Johnny
Janissary music
padiglione cinese (It.)
mezzaluna (It.)
cappello cinese (It.)
*chapeau Chinois (Fr.)
pavillon Chinois (Fr.)
Schellenbaum (G.)
Halbmond (G.)
chinesco (Sp.)
sombrero chino (Sp.)

Chinese gong
tam-tam
gong
kettle gong
tambour de bronze (Fr.)
Kesselgong (G.)
batintin (Sp.)
tantán (Sp.)

chirimia (Sp.)

*curtal
*bassoon
fagotto (It.)
fagot (Fr.)
Fagott (G.)
fagot(e) (Sp.)

chironomy, cheironomy
staffless notation
neumes
chant notation
in campo aperto (Lat.)
oratorical
adiastematic
nondiastematic

chitarra (It.)
guitar
gittern
guitare (Fr.)
guiterne (Fr.)
Gitarre (G.)
Quinterne (G.)
guitarra (Sp.)
chitarrino (It.)
vihuela
lute
mandora/mandore/mandola

chitarra battente (It.)
mandoline-shaped guitar
guitarra battente (It.)
chitarra mandola (It.)
guitare en bateau (Fr.)
guitare capucine (Fr.)
guitare toscane (Fr.)
guitare à la capucine (Fr.)
Kapuzinergitarre (G.)
*guitar
lute

chitarra Hawayana (It.)
Hawaiian guitar
steel guitar
dobro
guitare Hawaïenne (Fr.)

Hawaii-Gitarre (G.)
guitarra Hawaiana (Sp.)

chitarrone (It.)
* archlute
theorbo
bass lute
archiliuto (It.)
arcichitarra (It.)
Basslaute (G.)

chiuso (It.)
stopped (horn)
closed
muted
bouché (Fr.)

vs. aperto (It.)

2. second ending
seconda volta (It.)
clos (Fr.)

vs. aperto
ouvert (Fr.)
first ending

choeur (Fr.)
choir
chorus
chorale
choral society
coro (It., Sp,)
Chor (G.)

2. *course (strings)

choeur à voix mixtes (Fr.)
mixed chorus
choeur mixte (Fr.)
gemischter Chor (G.)
gemischte Stimmen (G.)
coro misto (It.)

choir
chorus

chorale
coro (It., Sp.)
choeur (Fr.)
glee club
choral society
oratorio society
symphonic chorus
philharmonic choir
chamber choir
schola (Lat.)
schola cantorum (Lat.)
Gesangverein (G.)
Singakademie (G.)
Kantorei (G.)

2. chancel area (church)
decani
cantoris
choir stalls
choir loft
choir gallery
sanctuary

choir director
choirmaster
choral conductor
Kapellmeister (G.)
Chordirigent (G.)
Chorleiter (G.)
Chordirektor (G.)
maestro di coro (It.)
maestro di cappella (It.)
chef de choeur (Fr.)
chef de la maîtrise (Fr.)
maître de chapelle (Fr.)
director de coro (Sp.)
maestro de capilla (Sp.)
regens chori (Lat.)

choir gallery
choir
chancel
cantoria (It.)
choir loft
balcony
Chorempore (G.)

choir organ, manual, division
chair organ
positive organ
organo di coro (It.)
positif (Fr.)
petit orgue (Fr.)
Unterwerk (G.)
Chororgel (G.)
Rückpositiv (G.)
positif de dos (Fr.)
Positiv im Stuhl (G.)
órgano positivo (Sp.)
órgano de coro (Sp.)
órgano de silla (Sp.)

choir pitch
church pitch
organ pitch
tuono chorista (It.)
corista di coro (It.)
ton de choeur (Fr.)
ton de chapelle (Fr.)
Chorton (G.)
Kapellton (G.)

choir school
schola cantorum (Lat.)
*music school
lyceum
conservatory of music
*academy of music
conservatoire (Fr.)
conservatorio (It., Sp.)
Konservatorium
maîtrise (Fr.)

choirbook
collection
*anthology
chorale (It.)
livre de choeur (Fr.)
Chorbuch (G.)
part-books

choirboy(s)
chorister

singer
putti (It.)
ragazzi (It.)
fanciullo del coro (It.)
cantori (It.)
corista (It., Sp.)
enfant de choeur (Fr.)
choriste (Fr.)
Sängerknabe (G.)
Kapellknabe (G.)
Chorknabe (G.)
Chorist, -in (G.)
niños de coro (Sp.)
escolán (Sp.)

choirwise
*antiphonal
polychoral
double chorus

choke cymbals
high-hat
hi-hat
sock cymbals
Charleston (It.)
hi-hat pédal (Fr.)
cymbales choquées (Fr.)
Charlestonmaschine (G.)
pedal de bombo de jazz (Sp.)

Chor (G.)
chorus
choir
chorale
coro (It., Sp.)
choeur (Fr.)

2. *course (strings)

choral
for choir
mixed chorus
choraliter (Lat.)
Choralmässig (G.)
corale (It.)
coral (Sp.)

Choral (G.)
  *chant
  plainsong
  Gregorian chant
  canzone sacra (It.)
  cantique (Fr.)
  cantico (Sp.)

choral bass (organ)
  choralprincipal
  chorus reed
  pedal flute (4 ft.)
  Chorbass (G.)
  Prinzipalbass (G.)

choral music
  choir music
  musica corale (It.)
  musique chorale (Fr.)
  Chormusik (G.)
  música coral (Sp.)

choral service
  *high mass
  sung mass
  service with music
  solemn mass
  missa cantata (Lat.)
  messa cantata (It.)
  messe chantée (Fr.)
  messa solenne (It.)
  messe haute (Fr.)
  grand'messe (Fr.)
  Hochamt (G.)
  Choramt (G.)
  Chordienst (G.)
  misa solemne (Sp.)
  misa mayor (Sp.)
  misa cantada (Sp.)

choral society
  chorale
  community chorus
  oratorio society
  civic chorus
  symphonic choir

philharmonic chorus
associazione corale (It.)
societá di canto (It.)
société chorale (Fr.)
Gesangverein (G.)
Singakademie (G.)
orfeón (Sp.)

chorale
  *hymn (German)
  Chorgesang (G.)
  Kirchenlied (G.)
  Kirchengesang (G.)
  Leise (G. medieval)
  hymnus (Lat.)
  inno (It.)
  hymne (Fr.)
  Hymne (G.)
  himno (Sp.)

2. **choir**
  chorus
  vocal ensemble
  *choral society
  coro (It.. Sp.)
  choeur (Fr.)
  Chor (G.)
  Choral (G.)
  Gesangverein (G.)

chorale-prelude (organ)
  hymn arrangement
  Choralvorspiel (G.)
  organ hymn
  organ mass
  Orgelchoral (G.)

choraleer
  *singer
  vocalist
  songster
  chorister
  cantante (It., Sp.)
  cantore (It.)
  chanteur (Fr.)
  chanteuse (Fr.)

Sänger, Sängerin (G.)

Chorbuch (G.)
  choir book
  part-book
  partitura (It.)
  chorale (It.)
  livre de choeur (Fr.)
  Stimmbuch (G.)
  anthology
  collection

chord
  triad
  harmony
  tone cluster
  homophonic
  accordo (It.)
  accord (Fr.)
  Akkord (G.)
  acorde (Sp.)
  Dreiklang (G.)
  triade (It., Fr.)
  triada (Sp.)

chord change(s)
  chord progression
  harmonic progression
  harmonic sequence
  harmonization

chord of nature
  harmonic series
  *harmonics
  overtones
  partials
  aliquot tones
  open note, tone
  natural tone

chord of the sixth
  sixth chord
  *six-three chord
  first-inversion chord
  French sixth
  German sixth

I

iambus, iamb
rhythmic mode #2

2. metrical foot

Iastian mode
mode eleven, c-c
Ionian mode
hypophrygian
ionico (It.)
ionien (Fr.)
ionisch (G.)
jonico (Sp.)

ictus (chant)
beat
stress
rhythmic sign
episema (vertical)

idea
theme
figure
motive
subject

idée fixe (Fr.)
theme
Leitmotiv(G.)
recurring motive
leading motive
signature theme
motivo conduttore (It.)
motif conducteur (Fr.)
motivo conductor (Sp.)
Erinnerungsmotiv (G.)

idiophone
musical instrument
*instrument

idyl(l)
pastoral
idillio (It.)
idylle (Fr.)
Idyll (G.)
idilio (Sp.)
*eclogue
églogue (Fr.)
pastorale (Fr.)
pastourelle (Fr.)
bergerette (Fr.)
brunette (Fr.)
pastorella (It.)
Hirtengesang (G.)

im Kapellstil (G.)
a cappella (It.)
unacompanied
Palestrina style
stile antico (It.)
stile osservato (It.)
alla Palestrina (It.)
à la Palestrienne (Fr.)
style de chapelle (Fr.)
sans instruments (Fr.)
Palestrina-Stil (G.)
a capilla (Sp.)
música vocal (Sp.)

im Takt (G.)
in time
*a tempo (It.)
en mesure, mesuré (Fr.)
a compás (Sp.)
im Zeitmass (G.)

imboccatura (It.)
lip
embouchure (E., Fr.)
mouthpiece
bocchino (It.)
becco (It.)
bec (Fr.)
Mundstück (G.)
Mundloch (G.)
Mundrohr (G.)

embocadura (Sp.)
boquilla (Sp.)

imbroglio (It.)
scene of confusion (opera)
chaos (dramatic)

imitation (E., Fr.)
fugue
round
canon
motet
madrigal
stretto (It.)
dux, comes (Lat.)
ricercare (It.)
counterpoint
canzona
imitazione (It.)
Nachahmung (G.)
imitación (Sp.)

2. copy
echo
record
reproduce
parody
plagiarize
Ersatz (G.)

Imitationsabschnitte (G.)
points of imitation (fugal)
frammento d'imitazione (It.)
motivo d'imitazione (It.)
passage en imitation (Fr.)
motif en imitation (Fr.)
Imitationsmotiv (G.)
punto de imitación (Sp.)
pasaje de imitación (Sp.)
motivo imitado (Sp.)

imitazione a coppie (It.)
paired imitation
double imitation
double counterpoint
imitation double (Fr.)

paarige Imitation (G.)
paarweise Imitation (G.)

immediately
subito (It.)
suddenly
quickly
subitement (Fr.)
sofort (G.)
sogleich (G.)
inmediato (Sp.)
súbito (Sp.)

imperfect cadence
*half-cadence
semi-cadence
half close
*deceptive cadence
cadenza imperfecta (It.)
cadenza sospesa (It.)
Halbschluss (G.)
demi-cadence (Fr.)
cadence suspendue (Fr.)
semicadencia (Sp.)
cadencia suspendida (Sp.)

vs. authentic cadence

imperfect time
*duple time/meter
tempus imperfectum (Lat.)
common time
ordinary time
binary measure
tempo ordinario (It.)
mouvement ordinaire (Fr.)
movimiento ordinario (Sp.)

impresario
manager
agent
booking agent
producer
sponsor
rep, representative
conductor

impressionism
music of Debussy, Ravel and
others
romanticism of early 20th c.
evocative imagery, and less
formal style

impromptu
ad-lib
extempore
improvisation
play by ear

2. caprice (n.)
*fancy
fantasy
arabesque
rhapsody
romance
romanza (It.)
free form
character piece
invention
bagatelle
free piece

Improperia (Lat.)
reproaches
Holy Week
Good Friday
Veneration of the Cross

improvisation
*ad-lib
extemporization
play by ear
impromptu
ornamentation
divisions
variations
sortisatio (Lat. 16c.)
partimento (It. 18c.)
figured bass
basso continuo (It.)

improvise

play by ear
extemporize
ad-lib
off the cuff
make it up (as you go along)
on the spot
pull it out of the air
fake it
jam
read charts
follow lead sheets
improvvisare (It.)
improviser (Fr.)
improvisieren (G.)
phantasieren (G.)
improvisar (Sp.)

in campo aperto (It.)
notation (chant)
staffless neumes
adiastematic notation
nondiastematic
oratorical
ekphonetic, ecphonetic
cheironomic
cantillation

in der Oktave (G.)
at the octave
all'ottava (It.)
à l'octave (Fr.)
a la octava (Sp.)

in disparte (It.)
*aside
stage whisper
de coté (Fr.)
à part (Fr.)
beiseite (G.)

in four
*binary measure
common time
duple time/meter
in 2
cut-time

march time
tempo binario (It.)
mesure binaire (Fr.)
Vierertakt, Zweiertakt (G.)
movimiento ordinario (Sp.)
compás binario (Sp.)

in halben Noten (G.)
cut time
double time
quick time
march time
in 2
alla breve (it.)
a cappella (It.)
à la blanche (Fr.)
a la breve (Sp.)

in seculum (Lat. 13c.)
cantus firmus (Lat.)
clausula (Lat.)
motet (medieval)

in the wings
*backstage
offstage
retroscena (It.)
dans les coulisses (Fr.)
en coulisse (Fr.)
Hinterbühne (G.)
hinter den Kulissen (G.)
hinter der Szene (G.)
bastidores (Sp.)
entre bastidores (Sp.)

in three
triple meter
perfect time
waltz time
¾ time
three-quarter time
tempus perfectum (Lat.)
tempus ternarium (Lat.)
tempo ternario (It.)
mesure ternaire (Fr.)
ungerader Takt (G.)

Dreiertakt (G.)
compás de tres tiempo (Sp.)
compás ternario (Sp.)

in time
in strict time
keeping the beat
a battuta (It.)
en mesure (Fr.)
au movement (Fr.)
im Takt (G.)
a compás (Sp.)

vs. rubato, tempo rubato (It.)

in tune
in tono (It.)
intonato (It.)
essere intonato (It.)
d'accord (Fr.)
rein singen/spielen (G.)
templado (Sp.)
armoniosamente (Sp.)

vs. out of tune
off-pitch

in two
duple meter
cut time
common time
a 2 (Fr., It.)
in Zwei (G.)

incatenatura (It.)
*quodlibet (G.)
pot-pourri (Fr., E., G., It.)
*medley
overture
cento, centone (It.)
pasticcio (It.)
pastiche (Fr.)
Pastete (G.)

incidental music
play music

film music
*backround music
underscore
musica di scena (It.)
musica scenica (It.)
musique de scène (Fr.)
Bühnenmusik (G.)
música de escena (Sp.)

incipit (Lat.)
intonation (chant)
opening part of a chant
beginning phrase
initium (Lat.)

inciso (It., Sp.)
cut
vide, vi---de (Lat.)
taglio (It.)
incise (Fr.)
Einschnitt (G.)
corte (Sp.)

incomplete stop (organ)
partial stop
short octave
broken octave
split keyboard
divided keyboard
mi re ut (It.)
octave courte (Fr.)
kurze Oktave (G.)
octava corta (Sp.)

incrosciemento (It.)
crossing (of hands, etc.)
croisement (Fr.)
Kreuzung (G.)
cruzamiento (Sp.)

indeterminacy music
chance music
dice music
aleatoric music
pitch aggregate
tone clusters

atonal music
avant-garde
contemporary music

index
guide
direct
cue note
mostra (It., Sp.)
custos (Lat.)
guidon (Fr.)
Kustos (G.)

indicatif musicale (Fr.)
theme song/music
signature song/music
sigla melodica (It.)
idée fixe (Fr.)
Kennmelodie (G.)
Leitmotiv (G.)
caracteristica (Sp.)

indicazione del tempo (It.)
time signature
meter/measure signature
segno del tempo (It.)
indication de la mesure (Fr.)
llave de tiempo (Sp.)
Taktart (G.)
Taktvorzeichnung (G.)

infinite canon
perpetual canon
*circular canon

ingenue (opera)
soubrette
light soprano (role)
comic role
dugazon (Fr.)
servetta (It.)
tiple cómico (Sp.)

ingressa (It., Lat.)
introit
entrance song

opening hymn
introitus (Lat.)
entrée (Fr.)
introït (Fr.)
Introitus (G.)
Eingang (G.)
Einleitung (G.)
entrada (Sp.)
introito (Sp.)

initium (Lat.)
intonation (chant)
incipit (Lat.)

inmediato (Sp.)
immediately
suddenly
quickly
subito (It.)
subitement(Fr.)
sofort (G.)
sogleich (G.)
súbito (Sp.)

vs. poco a poco (It., Sp.)
de grado en grado (Sp.)

inner voice/part
medius (Lat.)
meane, mene
Mittelstimme (G.)
Innenstimme (G.)
voce intermedia (It.)
voix intermédiaire (Fr.)
voz intermediaria (Sp.)

vs. outer voice/part

inno (It.)
*hymn
sacred song
religious song
chorale
anthem
psalm
alma mater (Lat.)

ode
dithyramb
paean (Gr.)
hymnus (Lat.)
hymne (Fr.)
Hymne (G.)
Lobgesang (G.)
Kirchenlied (G.)
Kirchengesang (G.)
himno (Sp.)

inno nazionale (It.)
national hymn
national anthem
hymne national (Fr.)
Nationalhymne (G.)
himno nacional (Sp.)

insonorisé (Fr.)
soundproof
anechoic chamber
dead room
sound-absorbent
isolato acusticamente (It.)
insonorizzato (It.)
Schalltot (G.)
insonoro (Sp.)
antisonoro (Sp.)

institute
*academy of music
conservatory
lyceum
music school
schola cantorum (Lat.)
liceo (It.)
conservatorio (It., Sp.)
conservatoire (Fr.)
Hochschule für Musik (G.)
Musikakademie (G.)

instrument (E., Fr.)
idiophone
membranophone
aerophone
chordophone

electrophone
stromento (It.)
strumento (It.)
istrumento (It.)
Instrument (G.)
instrumento (Sp.)

instrument à anche (Fr.)
reed, reed instrument
strumento ad ancia (It.)
strumento a becco (It.)
Rohrblattinstrument (G.)
Zungeninstrument (G.)
Schnabelinstrument (G.)
instrumento de lengüeta
(Sp.)
instrumento de caña (Sp.)

instrument à l'archet (Fr.)
string instrument
bowed instrument
strumento da arco (It.)
Streichinstrument (G.)
instrumento de arco (Sp.)

instrument à clavier (Fr.)
keyboard instrument
strumento a tastiera (It.)
Klavierinstrument (G.)
Tasteninstrument (G.)
instrumento de teclado (Sp.)

instrument à cordes (Fr.)
string instrument
instrument à l'archet
strumento da corda (It.)
Saiteninstrument (G.)
instrumento de cuerda (Sp.)

instrument à cordes pincées
(Fr.)
plucked (stringed) instrument
strumento a pizzico (It.)
Zupfinstrument (G.)
instrumento punteado (Sp.)

instrument à percution
/percussion (Fr.)
percussion instrument
instrument à batterie (Fr.)
strumento da percossa (It.)
Schlaginstrument (G.)
instrumento de percusión
(Sp.)

instrument à vent (Fr.)
wind instrument
horn (jazz)
strumento da fiato (It.)
strumento a vento (It.)
Blasinstrument (G.)
Windinstrument (G.)
instrumento de viento (Sp.)
instrumento de boca/boquilla
(Sp.)

instrument de bois (Fr.)
woodwind instrument
strumento (a fiato) di legno
(It.)
Holzblasinstrument (G.)
instrumento de madera (Sp.)

instrument de bouche (Fr.)
wind instrument
horn (jazz)
instrument à vent (Fr.)
strumento da fiato (It.)
Blasinstrument (G.)
instrumento de viento (Sp.)
instrumento de boca/boquilla
(Sp.)

instrument de cuivre (Fr.)
brass instrument
strumento di metallo (It.)
strumento d'ottone (It.)
Blechinstrument (G.)
instrumento de metal (Sp.)

instrument transpositeur (Fr.)
transposing instrument

strumento traspositore (It.)
transponierende instrument
(G.)
instrumento de transposición
(Sp.)

instrumentation (E., Fr.)
scoring
orchestration
bandstration
instrumentazione (It.)
Instrumentierung (G.)
instrumentación (Sp.)

intabulation
vocal piece arranged for
instruments (14-16c.)
adaptation
transcription

intavolatura (It.)
tablature (E., Fr.)
letter/number notation
Tabulatur (G.)
tablatura (Sp.)

intera, -o (It.)
whole note
punctum inclinatum (Lat.)
semibrevis (Lat.)
semibreve (E., It.)
ronde (Fr.)
Ganze, Ganzenote (G.)
redonda (Sp.)

interdominant
secondary dominant
pivotal chord
Zwischendominante (G.)

interligne (Fr.)
space on staff
spatium (Lat.)
spazio (It.)
espace (Fr.)
Zwischenraum (G.)

interlinea (Sp.)

vs. ligne (Fr.)
   line

interlude
   entr'acte (Fr.)
   act-tune
   prelude
   verset
   organ piece during a service
   intermezzo (It.)
   intermède (Fr.)
   divertissement (Fr.)
   *curtain music/tune
   Zwischenspiel (G.)
   Zwischenaktmusik (G.)
   entreacto (Sp.)
   intermedio (Sp.)

international pitch
   classical pitch
   philharmonic pitch
   standard pitch
   low pitch
   French pitch
   diapason normal (Fr.)
   Franzton (G.)
   Normalton (G.)
   diapasón normal (Sp.)
   diapasón de bajo (Sp.)

interpretation (E., Fr.)
   rendition
   performance
   reading
   interpretazione (It.)
   Gestaltung (G.)
   interpretación (Sp.)

interrupted cadence
   *deceptive cadence
   false cadence
   suspended cadence
   half-cadence
   imperfect cadence

interrupted melody
   hiatus
   railroad tracks
   *caesura
   abruptio (Lat.)
   pause
   general pause
   *hocket
   Abreissung (G.)

interval
   diastema (Gr.)
   intervallum (Lat.)
   intervallo (It.)
   intervalle (Fr.)
   Abstand (G.)
   intervalo (Sp.)
   espace (Fr.)
   spazio (It.)

2. **intermission**
   break
   pause
   pausa (It.)
   intervallo (It.)
   Pause (G.)
   Intervall (G.)
   pause (Fr., Sp.)
   entr'acte (Fr.)
   entreacto (Sp.)

intonation
   *pitch
   tone
   tuning
   *temperament
   intonazione (It.)
   Stimmung (G.)
   Tongebung (G.)
   entonación (Sp.)
   accorditura (It.)
   corditura (It.)
   accordage (Fr.)
   Tongebung (G.)
   afinación (Sp.)
   diapason (It., Fr., Sp.)

2. incipit
   initium (Lat.)
   accentus ecclesiastici (Lat.)

3. organ prelude
   voluntary
   praeludium (Lat.)
   *prélude (Fr.)
   Vorspiel (G.)
   preludio (Sp.)

intone
   strike up
   begin the song
   start off
   hit it
   sing the incipit
   introduce
   *attacca (It.)
   intonare (It.)
   entonner (Fr.)
   anstimmen (G.)
   entonar (Sp.)

intrada (It. 16c.)
   introduction
   first movement
   entrance piece
   entrata (It.)
   entrée (Fr.)
   Intrada (G.)
   entrada (Sp.)

intro, introduction
   prelude
   overture
   anteludium (Lat.)
   introduzione (It.)
   intrata (It.)
   introduction (Fr.)
   Einleitung (G.)
   Auftritt (G.)
   entrada (Sp.)
   intrada (Sp.)
   introducción (Sp.)
   voluntary

verse of a pop song
preparation to a piece/song
beginning section
vamp, vamp till ready

introit
antiphon & psalm
entrance song
praelegendum (Gallican)
ingressa (Ambrosian)
introitus (Lat.)
introito (It., Sp.)
Introitus (G.)
introït (Fr.)
mass
proper of the mass
hymn
psalm

invention (E., Fr.)
free keyboard piece
*fantasy, fancy
impromptu
bagatelle (Fr.)
prelude
voluntary
étude
inventio (Lat.)
invenzione (It.)
Invention (G.)

inversion (E., Fr.)
reversal
eversio, evolutio (Lat.)
inversione (It.)
rovesciamento (It.)
riversamento (It.)
rivolto, rivoltato (It.)
renversement (Fr.)
évolution (Fr.)
Umkehrung (G.)
invertido (Sp.)
inversión (Sp.)

inverted dotting
Scotch snap

alla zoppa (It.)
stile lombardo (17c.It.)
Lombard style
reversed dotting

2. *syncopated
boiteux (Fr.)

inverted mordent
upper neighbor
ornament
grace note
pincé renversé (Fr.)
Schneller (G.)
Pralltriller (G.)
trill
auxiliary tone
neighbor note/tone
upper neighbor
mordent

invitatory
Matins psalm
Venite antiphon
Ps. 94/95
invititorium (Lat.)
Morning Prayer

Ionian/Ionic mode
mode eleven, c-c
ionico (It.)
ionien (Fr.)
ionisch (G.)
jonico (Sp.)
Iastian
hypophrygian
modus lascivus (Lat.)

Irish harp
celtic harp
clarsach
folk harp
Troubadour harp

vs. pedal harp

Irish organ
union pipes
bagpipes
uilleann pipes

Irish tenor
high tenor
whiskey tenor
countertenor
falsetto

irregular barring
polymetric
uneven barring

irregular cadence
*deceptive cadence
false cadence
half-cadence
avoided cadence
suspended cadence
surprise cadence
broken cadence

isolato acusticamente (It.)
soundproof
*anechoic chamber
dead room
insonorisé (Fr.)
shalltot (G.)
insonoro (Sp.)

isometric (14-15c.)
talea (Lat.)
color (Lat.)
isorhythmic
inversion
cantus firmus (Lat.)

istesso/l'istesso tempo (It.)
same tempo
le même mouvement (Fr.)
dasselbe Zeitmass (G.)
mismo tiempo (Sp.)

istrumento (It.)

*instrument
strumento (It.)
instrumento (It., Sp.)
Instrument (G.)

Italian overture
*overture
French overture
prelude
sinfonia (It.)
overtura (It.)
introduzione (It.)
ouverture (Fr.)
Vorspiel (G.)
Ouvertüre (G.)

Italian sixth
*augmented sixth chord
French sixth
German sixth
Neapolitan sixth

J

jack (on a harpsichord)
plectrum, plectra
quill
plettro (It.)
salterello (It.)
spina (It.)
sautereau (Fr.)
plectre (Fr.)
Kiel (G.)
Plektrum (G.)
Docke (G.)
Springer (G.)
plectro (Sp.)
púa (Sp.)
macillo (Sp.)
martinete (Sp.)

Jagdhorn (G.)
*horn
hunting horn
natural horn
French horn
*corno da caccia (It.)
cor de chasse (Fr.)
trompe de chasse (Fr.)
Waldhorn (G.)
cuerno de caza (Sp.)
trompa de caza (Sp.)

jam session
improvisation
jazz
impromptu
hootnanny
jamboree

Janissary music
Turkish music
jingling Johnny
Turkish crescent
Chinese crescent
Chinese pavilion
banda Turca (It.)
alla Turca (It., Sp.)
*chapeau Chinois (Fr.)
musique à la Turque (Fr.)
musique de Janissaires (Fr.)
Janitscharenmusik (G.)
Schellenbaum (G.)
sombrero Chino (Sp.)

Japanese zither
koto (Jap.)
sitar (Ind.)
lute
*guitar

jazz
improvise on standard tunes
variations
jam session
swing
bounce
blues
soul music
gospel music
Dixieland
barrelhouse
ragtime
boogie-woogie
jive
jitterbug
stride piano
bop, bebop
funk
stomp
pop
rock
reggae
ska
jug band
skiffle band
rhythm and blues
fusion
third stream
progressive
combo

band

jazz band
swing band
big band
stage band
40's band
dance band
Dixieland band
jug band
combo

jazz bass line
walking bass
scale-wise bass line
Laufbass (G.)

jazz choir
show choir
pop choir

jazz chord
blue notes
substitute chord
accordo sostituito (It.)
accord substitué (Fr.)
Substitutklang (G.)
stellvertretender Akkord (G.)
acorde sustitutiva (Sp.)

jazz note
blue note
flatted third
flatted seventh
Bluesterz (G.)

Jazzbesen (G.)
brushes
wire brushes
steel brushes
spazzole (It.)
balais de jazz (Fr.)
Rute (G.)
escobillas (Sp.)

jazzy

syncopated
off-beat
hot
cool
be-bop
sincopato (It.)
syncopé (Fr.)
verschoben (G.)
synkopiert (G.)
sincopado (Sp.)

jeté (Fr.)
bouncing the bow
staccato bowing
spiccato (It.)
saltando (It.)
geworfen (G.)
ricochet (Fr.)
sautillé (Fr.)
Springbogen (G.)
saltado (Sp.)

jeu (Fr.)
rank (organ)
stop
register
registro (It., Sp.)
registre (Fr.)
Register (G.)

2. *course (of strings)
Saitenchor (G.)

jeu céleste (Fr.)
detuned organ stop
céleste stop
jeu d'anges (Fr.)
voce angelica (It.)
vox angelica (Lat.)
voix angélique (Fr.)
voix céleste (Fr.)
vox coelestis (Lat.)
unda maris (Lat.)
Engelstimme (G.)
voz angelica (Sp.)
*vox humana (Lat.)

jeu composé (Fr.)
*mixture stop (organ)
compound stop
sesquialtera (Lat.)
mistura (It.)
Mixtur (G.)

jeu(x) de timbres (Fr.)
glockenspiel
bell lyre
campanetti (It.)
jeu de clochettes (Fr.)
Lyra (G.)
juego de timbres (Sp.)
bells, orchestra bells
carillon

jeu de luth (Fr.)
lute stop
harp stop
buff stop
Lautenzug (G.)
Nasalzug (G.)
jeu de harpe (Fr.)

jeu de mutation (Fr.)
mutation stop (organ)
partials
harmonics
registro di mutazione (It.)
Hilfsstimmen (G.)
Aliquostimmen (G.)
registro de mutación (Sp.)

jeu-parti (Fr.)
dialogue in 12-13c. song
Troubadour
Trouvère
parture (Fr.)
joc-parti (Prov.)
partimen (Prov.)
tenso (Prov.)

Jeudi Saint (Fr.)
Last Supper
Coena Domini (Lat.)

Maunday Thursday
Holy Thursday
giovedi santo (It.)
Gründonnerstag (G.)
Jueves Santo (Sp.)
Jueves del mandato (Sp.)

Jew's harp
crembalum (Lat.)
cymbalum orale (Lat.)
Jew's trump
jaw's harp
mouth-organ
ribeba (It.)
scacciapensieri (It.)
spassapensieri (It.)
guitarraccia (It.)
guimbarde (Fr.)
trompe de Béarn/Berne (Fr.)
trompe de laquais (Fr.)
rebube (Fr.)
Maultrommel (G.)
Mundharmonika (G.)
Brummeisen (G.)
Judenharfe (G.)
birimbao (Sp.)
guitarrón (Sp.)
trompa de París (Sp.)
trompa gallega (Sp.)
trompa inglesa (Sp.)

jig(g) (16-18c.)
ballad opera
entertainment
masque
operetta
light opera
musical
Singspiel (G.)
zarzuela (Sp.)
tonadilla (Sp.)
sainete (Sp.)

2. *gigue (dance)
giga (It., Sp.)
Gigue (G.)

canary
canario (It., Sp.)
canarie (Fr.)

jingle
tune
ditty
melody
*song
air
aria
lay
carol
hymn
ballad
canzona (It.)
chanson (Fr.)
Lied (G.)
cantiga (Sp.)

2. metal disk on tambourine
*crotale (Fr.)
antique cymbal

3. to ring
tinkle
klingen (G.)

jingle bells
pellet bells
sleigh bells
harness bells
*bells
altar bells
Sanctus bells
nolae (Lat.)
campanae (Lat.)
tintinabulum (Lat.)
tintinabolo (It.)
nolettes (Fr.)
Cimbelstern (G.)
cascabeles (Sp.)

jingling Johnny
Turkish crescent
Chinese crescent
Turkish crescent
Chinese pavilion
Janissary music
pavillon Chinois (Fr.)
*chapeau Chinois (Fr.)
Halbmond (G.)
sombrero Chino (Sp.)

jitterbug
swing (dance)
lindy hop
jump
bounce
stomp
jazz
jive

jocoso (Sp.)
*giocoso (It.)
gai (Fr.)
joyeux (Fr.)
lustig (G.)
frölich (G.)
merry
happy

vs. doloroso (It., Sp.)

jodeln (G.)
to **yodel**
alla Tirolese (It.)
fare lo jodel (It.)
à la tyrolienne (Fr.)
jodler (Fr.)
a la tirolesa (Sp.)

jongleur, joglar, jougleur (Fr.)
juggler
joculator (Lat.)
gleeman
minstrel
Gaukler (G.)
balladeer
Troubadour
Trouvère
ménestrier (Fr.)
goliard
Minnesinger

jonico (Sp.)
*Ionian mode
Iastian
mode eleven

jota (Sp.)
dance in triple time
Aragonaise (Fr.)
Aragonesa (Sp.)

jouer (Fr.)
play an instrument
*perform
blow
suonare/sonare (It.)
spielen (G.)
tocar (Sp.)

joueur d'orgue de Barbarie (Fr.)
organ-grinder
sonatore d'organetto (It.)
Leiermann (G.)

joyful
gioioso (It.)
festoso (It.)
joyeux (Fr.)
gai (Fr.)
frölich (G.)
alegre (Sp.)

vs. sad

juba
southern and Haitian dance
breakdown

jubal
shofar
ram's horn
chofar (Fr.)
Schofar (G.)

Jubilate Deo (Lat.)
Psalm 100
morning prayer
Anglican service

jubilus, jubili, jubilatio (Lat.)
pneuma
melisma (on Alleluia chant)
plainsong
proper of the mass

juego de timbres (Sp.)
*glockenspiel
bell lyre
orchestra bells
celesta, celeste
campanette, campanelli (It.)
organo di campane (It.)
carillon (Fr.)
jeu de timbres (Fr.)
Lyra (G.)
Stahlspiel (G.)
campanólogo (Sp.)

Jueves Santo (Sp.)
Holy Thursday
Maunday Thursday
Last Supper
coena Domini (Lat.)
giovedi santo (It.)
Jeudi Saint (Fr.)
Gründonnerstag (G.)
Jueves del Mandato (Sp.)

jug band
folk band
jazz band
country band
skiffle band
washboard band
combo
mountain music
old time music
hillbilly music
hoedown music
bluegrass music

juke-joint
restaurant with a jukebox
diner
tavern
pub
cocktail lounge
disco
night spot/club

jukebox
nickelodeon
music box
automatic phonograph
automatic turntable
juke-box (It., Fr.)
Musikautomat (G.)
Musikbox (G.)
tocadiscos automático (Sp.)
máquina de discos (Sp.)
tragaperras (Sp.)
rocola (Sp.)

jump
dump, domp(e) (E.16-17c.)
slow dance
*lament (keyboard, lute)

2. jazz dance
jive
jitterbug
lindy-hop
stomp
swing
bounce
shake

3. skip (interval)
leap
disjunct motion
broken chord
arpeggio
salto (It., Sp.)
sbalzo (It.)
saut (Fr.)
Sprung (G.)

just intonation
natural tuning
pure tuning
accordatura giusta (It.)
intonation juste (Fr.)
Reine Stimmung (G.)
natürlich Stimmung (G.)
entonación justa (Sp.)
mean-tone temperament

vs. tempered tuning

K

kaddish (Heb,)
doxology
memorial service
*lament

Kadenz (G.)
*cadence(E., Fr.)
close
ending
cadentia (Lat.)
cadenza (It.)
Schluss (G.)
cadencia (Sp.)

2. *clausula (Lat.)
discant
motet (13c.)

3. *cadenza
improvise
concerto
virtuoso
bariolage (Fr.)

Kadosh (Heb.)
trisagion (Gr.)
sanctus (Lat.)
ter sanctus (Lat.)
aius (Lat.)
Kedusha (Heb.)
Cherubic Hymn
Song of the Angels
Angelic Hymn

Kakaphonie (G.)
cacaphony
discord
*dissonance
disaccordo (It.)
désaccord (Fr.)

disonancia (Sp.)

kalamos (Gr.)
calamus (Lat.)
*shawm
aulos (Gr.)
oboe
diaulos (Gr.)
tibia (Lat.)
reed, double reed
syrinx
panpipe
chalumeau (Fr.)

k kalinda
calypso
calenda
carnival

Kalkant (G.)
blower (organ)
bellows
wind supply
mantice (It.)
soffietto (It.)
souflet (Fr.)
Gebläse (G.)
Balg (G.)
fuelle (Sp.)

Kammerbass (G.)
*bassetto (It.)
basso di camera (It.)
Halbbass (G.)
cello

Kammerchor (G.)
*chamber choir
semi-chorus
petit-choeur (Fr.)
madrigal choir
echo-chorus/choir
vocal ensemble

Kammermusik (G.)
chamber music

musica da camera (It.)
musique de chambre (Fr.)
música de cámara (Sp.)

Kammerton (G.)
*pitch
*intonation
frequency
diapason (Fr., It.)
intonazione (It.)
hauteur du ton (Fr.)
Tonhöhe (G.)

2. chamber pitch
ton de chambre (Fr.)
diapason normale (Fr.)
corista di camera (It.)
tonalidad de camera (Sp.)

Kanon (G.)
*canon
fugue
catch
imitation
round
rota

2. canon (of the mass)
eucharist
communion
Mass of the Faithful

Kanon (Gr.)
hymns (Byzantine)
odes (Gr.)
troparion (Gr.)
heirmos (Gr.)

2. monochord
tromba marina (It.)
*trumpet marine

Kantate (G.)
*cantata (It., E., Sp.)
oratorio
ode

rappresentazione (It.)
pasticcio (It.)
cantate (Fr.)
cantada (Sp.)

Kantilene (G.)
*cantilena (Lat, It., Sp.)
song
chant
ditty
lullaby
cantilène (Fr.)
chanson (polyphonic)
lyrical melody (19c.)

Kantor (G.)
*cantor (E., Sp.)
cantore (It.)
lead singer
choir director
chantre (Fr.)

Kantorei (G.)
chorus, choir
*choral society
oratorio society
community chorus
schola cantorum (Lat.)
associazione corale (It.)
société chorale (Fr.)
Singakademie (G.)
orfeón (Sp.)

Kanzone, Kanzonette (G.)
*canzona, canzonette (It.)
song
part-song
madrigal
villanella (It.)
chanson (Fr.)

2. *canso, canzo (Fr.)
bar form
AAB form
formes fixes (Fr.)

Kapelle (G.)
*chapel
church
cappella (It.)
chapelle (Fr.)
capilla (Sp.)

2. music ensemble employed by a
court or a church/chapel
performing group unattached
*band
orchestra

Kapellknabe (G.)
*choirboy
chorister
Chorknabe (G.)
Sängerknabe (G.)
enfant de choeur (Fr.)
putto (It.)
ragazzo (It.)
cantore (It.)
niños de coro (Sp.)

Kapellmeister (G.)
*choir director
choirmaster
regens chori (Lat.)
maestro di cappella (It.)
maître de chapelle (Fr.)
chef d'orchestre (Fr.)
Dirigent (G.)
Leiter (G.)
Capellmeister (G.)
maestro de capilla (Sp.)

Kapellton (G.)
choir pitch
church pitch
organ pitch
corista di coro (It.)
tuono corista (It.)
ton de choeur (Fr.)
ton de chapelle (Fr.)
Chorton (G.)

Kapodaster (G.)
capo (guitar)
bar
transposer
capotasto (It.)
barré (Fr.)
capodastre (Fr.)
Saitenfessel (G.)
ceduela (Sp.)
ceja, sejilla (Sp.)

Karaoke music
music minus one
split track
canned music
recorded accompaniments

Karsamstag (G.)
Holy Saturday
Easter vigil
Sabbato Sancto (Lat.)
Sabato Santo (It.)
Samedi Saint (Fr.)
Sábado Santo (Sp.)

Karwoche (G.)
Holy Week
Passion Week
Hebdomade Sancte (Lat.)
settimada santa (It.)
semaine sainte (Fr.)
semana santa (Sp.)

Kassation (G.)
*cassation
serenade
divertimento (It.)
cassatio (It.)
cassazione (It.)
sérénade (Fr.)
suite

Kastagnetten (G.)
*castanets
clappers
claves

bones
spoons
nacchere (It.)
castagnettes (Fr.)
castañetas (Sp.)

Kastenzither (G.)
zither
box zither
*bell harp
fairy bells
cithare sur caisse (Fr.)
salterio (It., Sp.)

Kastrat (G.)
castrato (E., It.)
male singer
countertenor
male soprano
castrated male singer
eunuch
evirato (It.)
sopranista (It.)
tenorino (It.)
castrat (Fr.)
castrado (Sp.)

Katzenmusik (G.)
shivaree
cat's music
cacaphony
noise
Dutch concert
*callithumpian concert
scampanata (It.)
chiasso (It.)
charivari (Fr.)
Lärm (G.)

kazoo
mirliton (Fr.)
eunuch flute
onion flute
toy instrument
bazoo

keep time
count beats/measures
stay with the beat
in strict time
a battuta (It.)
en mesure (Fr.)
au mouvement (Fr.)
im Takt (G.)
a compás (Sp.)

Kehle (G.)
throat (of a singer)
gola (It.)
gorge (Fr.)
Hals (G.)
garganta (Sp.)

Kehlkopf (G.)
larynx (E., Fr.)
voice box
vocal cords/folds
pipes
laringe (It., Sp.)
pharynx
syrinx

Kehlschlag (G.)
glottal stop/catch
glottal attack
glottale (It.)
occlusiva glottale (It.)
coup de glotte (Fr.)
Glottisschlag (G.)
Kehlverschlusslaut (G.)
Knacklaut (G.)
Stimmritzenverschlusslaut (G.)

Kennmelodie (G.)
theme song/music
signature song/music
sigla melodica (It.)
indicatif musicale (Fr.)
idée fixe (Fr.)
Leitmotiv (G.)
caracteristica (Sp.)

Kern (organ)
languid
languette
tongue for tuning
anima (It.)
biseau (Fr.)
alma (Sp.)
bisel (Sp.)

Kernspaltflöte (G.)
duct flute
fipple flute
whistle flute
tonette
flutophone
toy flute
flageolet
*recorder
ocarina

Kessel (G.)
cup (of a brass mouthpiece)
tazza (It.)
bassin (Fr.)
taza (Sp.)

Kesselgong (G.)
gong
Chinese gong
tam-tam
kettle gong
tambour de bronze (Fr.)
batintín (Sp.)
tantán (Sp.)

Kettledrum
timpani
double-drum
timpano (It.)
timbalo (It.)
timbale (Fr.)
atabale (Fr.)
Pauke (G.)
Kesseltrommel (G.)
Kesselpauke (G.)
timbal (Sp.)

atabal (Sp.)

key (an instrument)
digital
chiave (It.)
clef (Fr.)
Klappe (G.)
llave (Sp.)

(of a keyboard)
tasto (It.)
touche (Fr.)
Taste (G.)
tecla (Sp.)

(of tonality)
scale
mode
modality
tonal center
tono (It.)
modo (It.)
tonalita (It.)
Tonart (G.)
Tonalität (G.)
tonalité (Fr.)
tonalidad (Sp.)

key change
change of key
transposition (E., Fr.)
transporto (It.)
Transposition (G.)
transportición (Sp.)
modulation (E., Fr.)
modulazione (It.)
Modulation (G.)
modulación (Sp.)

key chord
tonic chord
I (one) chord

key signature
armatura di chiave (It.)
armure, armature (Fr.)

signes accidentals (Fr.)
Tonartvorzeichnung (G.)
Vorzeichnung (G.)
armadura (Sp.)
sharps and flats
key indicator

keyboard
manual (E., Sp.)
pedalboard
tastatura (It.)
clavier (E.,Fr., G.))
Klaviatur, claviatur (G.)
teclado (Sp.)
Manual (G.)
manuel (Fr.)

Keyed bugle
Royal Kent bugle
Kent bugle/horn
Key bugle
Regent's bugle
clairon à clefs (Fr.)
Klappelhorn (G.)
ophicleide
cimbasso (It.)
bombardon (Fr.)
bugle à clés (Fr.)
serpent
cornet
trumpet

keyfall (keyboard)
dip

keynote
tonic
do
ut
finalis (Lat.)
root

kiddush (Heb.)
sabbath
festival
Shabbat (Heb.)

Lord's Day
Sunday
vigil

Kiel (g.)
jack
plectrum
pick
quill
plettro (It.)
petaccha (It.)
saltarello (It.)
sautereau (Fr.)
plectre (Fr.)
médiator (Fr.)
Plektrum (G.)
Mediator (G.)
Docke (G.)
Springer (G.)
plectro (Sp.)
púa (Sp.)

Kielflügel (G.)
*harpsichord
clavicembalum (Lat.)
clavicembalo (It., Sp.)
cembalo (It.)
gravicembalo (It.)
arpicordo (It.)
épinette (Fr.)
clavecin (Fr., Sp.)
Klavizimbel (G.)
clave, clavicordio (Sp.)
virginals
spinet
chekker
clavichord
pedal harpsichord

Kinderflöte (G.)
tin whistle
penny whistle
fife
flutophone
fipple flute
tonette

ocarina
recorder
duct flute
toy flute
piffero (It.)
fifre (Fr.)
pifano (Sp.)

Kindersinfonie (G.)
toy symphony
foire des enfants (Fr.)
symphonie burlesque (Fr.)

King of instruments
organ
organum (Lat.)
organo (It., Sp.)
orgue (Fr.)
Orgel (G.)
re degli strumenti (It.)
roi des instruments (Fr.)
Königin der Instrumente (G.)
rey de los instrumentos (Sp.)
positive
portative
organetto
calliope
barrel organ
pipe organ
chamber organ
electric/electronic organ
theatre organ

Kinnhalter (G.)
chin rest (violins)
mentoniera (It.)
mentonnière (Fr.)
mentonera (Sp.)
barbada (Sp.)

Kinoorgel (G.)
cinema organ
theatre organ
unit organ
unified organ
duplexing

extension organ
organo da teatro (It.)
organo da cinematografo (It.)
orgue de cinéma (Fr.)
Multiplexorgel (G.)
órgano de cine (Sp.)

kiosque à musique (Fr.)
bandstand
bandshell
bandwagon
stage
platform
carro della banda musicale (It.)
palco della banda (It.)
palco dell'orchestra (It.)
Musikpavillon (G.)
Konzertpavillon (G.)
quiosco de música (Sp.)
plataforma con concha
acústica (Sp.)

Kirchenlied (G.)
*hymn
chorale
sequence
canticle
Kirchengesang (G.)
inno (It.)
hymne (Fr.)
hymnos (Gr.)
hymnus (Lat.)
Hymne (G.)
himno (Sp.)

Kirchenmusik (G.)
church music
sacred music
religious music
liturgical music
ecclesiastical music
Cathedral music
Anglican music
musica da chiesa (It.)
musique d'église (Fr.)
música de iglesia (Sp.)

Kirchenordnung (G.)
*liturgy
service
Eucharist
Lord's Supper
Holy Communion
rite, ritual
Agende (G.)
Kirchenamt (G.)
Abendmahl (G.)
*Mass

Kirchenschluss (G.)
plagal cadence
church cadence
amen cadence
cadenza plagale (It.)
cadence plagale (Fr.)
plagale Kadenz (G.)
cadencia plagal (Sp.)

Kirchentonart (G.)
church mode
authentic mode
ecclesiastical mode
modo ecclesiastico (It.)
mode ecclesiasrique (Fr.)
modo eclesiástico (Sp.)
scale
diatonic scale
minor mode

kit
small violin
rebec
pocket-fiddle
linterculus (Lat.)
sordino (It.)
poccetta (It.)
violino di pochetto (It.)
violino piccolo (It.)
pochette (Fr.)
petit violon de poche (Fr.)
Taschengeige (G.)
Sackgeige (G.)
Halbgeige (G.)

Quartgeige (G.)
Terzgeige (G.)
Tanzmeistergeige (G.)
violinette (Fr.)
violin de bolsillo (Sp.)
violin pequeño (Sp.)

kithara (Gr.)
cithara, cythara (Lat.)
harp
lyre

Klagenlied (G.)
*lament, lamentation
elegy
Klage (G.)
lamento (It., Sp.)
plainte (Fr.)
tombeau (Fr.)
dirge
requiem
threnody
planctus (Lat.)
dump, dompe
taps

klagend (G.)
plaintive
*sadly
addolorito (It.)
lagnoso (It.)
plaintif (Fr.)
douloureux (Fr.)
schmerzlich (G.)
lamentoso (Sp.)
doloroso (It., Sp.)

Klammer (G.)
brace
bracket
grappa (It.)
accolade (Fr.)
Akkolade (G.)
corchete (Sp.)
staves
grand staff

Klang (G.)
sound
sonority
tone
note
suono (It.)
son (Fr.)
Ton (G.)
Schall
sonido (Sp.)

Klangstäbe (G.)
rhythm sticks
claves (Sp., E., Fr., It.)
clappers
bones
spoons

Klappenhorn (G.)
tuba
trombone
serpent
*ophicleide
bombardon (Fr.)
*keyed bugle

Klarinette (G.)
*clarinet
licorice stick
basset horn
clarinetto (It.)
clarinette (Fr.)
chalumeau (Fr.)
clarinete (Sp.)

Klausel (G.)
*cadence (16c.)

2. *clausula

Klaviatur (G.)
*keyboard
manual
tastiera (It.)
touche (Fr.)
Tastatur (G.)

teclado (Sp.)

Klavichord (G.)
*clavichord
clavicordo (It.)
clavicorde (Fr.)
clavicordio (Sp.)
chekker
escacherium (Lat.)

Klavier (G.)
piano
pianoforte (It.)
grand piano
upright piano
studio piano
spinet

2. manual (of an organ)
*keyboard
division

Klavierquartett (G.)
piano quartet
quartetto con pianoforte (It.)
quatuor avec piano (Fr.)
cuarteto con piano (Sp.)

Klavizimbel (G.)
*harpsichord
cembalo (It.)
clavecin (Fr., Sp.)
Kielflügel (G.)
chekker

Klavizitherium (G.)
upright harpsichord
clavicytherium

kleine Flöte (G.)
*piccolo
octave flute
flauto piccolo (It.)
ottavino (It.)
flautino (It.)
petite flûte (Fr.)

kleine Messe (G.)
  missa brevis (Lat.)
  messa brevi (It.)
  petite messe (Fr.)
  kurze Messe (G.)
  misa breve (Sp.)

kleine Trommel (G.)
  side drum
  military drum
  snare drum
  cassa, cassa rulante (It.)
  caisse roulante (Fr.)
  caisse militaire (Fr.)
  caisse clair (Fr.)
  tambour (Fr.)
  Militärtrommel (G.)
  casa viva (Sp.)
  tambor (Sp.)

Kleinintervalle (G.)
  microtone
  quarter tone
  *comma
  cent, centitone
  schisma (Lat.)
  Mikrointervalle (G.)

klingen (G.)
  sound, resound
  reverberate
  echo
  ring out
  rimbombare (It.)
  riverberare (It.)
  réverbérer (Fr.)
  nachhallen (G.)
  reverberar (Sp.)

Knabenchor (G.)
  boychoir
  maîtrise d'enfants (Fr.)
  coro di raggazzi (It.)
  putti (It.)

Knacklaut (G.)

glottal stop/catch
glottal attack
glottale (It.)
occlusiva glottale (It.)
coup de glotte (Fr.)
Glottisschlag (G.)
Kehlschlag (G.)
Kehlverschlusslaut (G.)
Stimmritzenverschlusslaut (G.)

Knarre (G.)
  *rattle
  maraca
  rainstick
  cog rattle
  crécelle (Fr.)
  raganella (It.)
  Rassel (G.)
  Ratsche (G.)
  Schnarre (G.)
  matraca (Sp.)
  carraca (Sp.)

Kniegeige (G.)
  viol
  viola da gamba (It.)
  gamba (It.)
  Gambe (G.)
  viole (Fr.)
  viola de gamba (Sp.)
  'cello
  bass viol

Knopf (G.)
  endpin
  tailpin
  peg
  spike
  puntale (It.)
  pique, piquet (Fr.)
  Stachel (G.)
  puntal (Sp.)

Knote (G.)
  node (on a string)
  nodal point

harmonics
nodo (It.)
noeud (Fr.)
Knotenpunkt (G.)
nudo (Sp.)

Koda (G.)
  *coda (It., E.)
  tag
  epilogue
  cauda (Lat.)
  Anhang (G.)
  codetta (It.)
  partie finale (Fr.)
  cola (Sp.)

Kodaly system
  hand signals
  *solmization
  fasola
  solfa
  solfeggio

kolenda, koleda (Pol.)
  carol
  Christmas carol
  canzona di natale (It.)
  chant/cantique de noël (Fr.)
  Weinachtslied (G.)
  Quempas (G.)
  villancico (Sp.)
  cántico de Navidad (Sp.)
  zéjel (Sp.)

Kollektivschweller (G.)
  crescendo pedal
  crescendo rotativo (It.)
  rouleau crescendo (Fr.)
  Crescendowalze, -zug (G.)
  Registerrad, -walze (G.)
  Rollschweller (G.)
  rodillo del crescendo (Sp.)

Kollektivzug (G. organ)
  combination stop/button
  piston

toe stud
pre-sets
pédale de combinaison (Fr.)
pédale d'accouplement (Fr.)
Kombinationspedal (G.)
Druckknopf (G.)
pistoni, pistoncini (It.)
thumb piston
bouton de combinaison (Fr.)

Kolophon, Kolophonium (G.)
rosin, resin (for a bow)
colophony
colofonia (It., Sp.)
colophane (Fr.)
Geigenharz (G.)
resina (Sp.)

Koloratursopran (G.)
high and light soprano
coloratura soprano
soprano di coloratura (It.)
soprano legg(i)era (It.)
soprano sfogato (It.)
soprano léger (Fr.)
tiple ligera (Sp.)
soprano ligera (Sp.)

Kombinationston (G.)
*combination tone
resultant tone
differential/difference tone
summation tone
suono di combinazione (It.)
son combiné (Fr.)
sonido de combinación (Sp.)
acoustic bass (organ)

Komma (G.)
*comma
breath mark
breathing sign
comma
virgla (It.)
virgule (Fr.)
Atempause (G.)

coma (Sp.)

Komplet (G.)
compline (office)
night song/prayer
completorium (Lat.)
compieta (It.)
complies (Fr.)
completas (Sp.)
office
caonical hours

Komponieren (G.)
to compose
write music
set to music
score, underscore
comporre (It.)
composer (Fr.)
componer (Sp.)

Königin der Instrumente (G.)
King of Instruments
*organ
re degli instrumenti (It.)
roi des instruments (Fr.)
rey de los instrumentos (Sp.)

Komponist (G.)
composer
writer of music
compositore (It.)
compositeur (Fr.)
Tonkünstler (G.)
compositor (Sp.)

konkrete Musik (G.)
electronic music
concrete music
musique concrète (Fr.)
musica concreta (It.)
música concreta

Konservatorium (G.)
lyceum
academy of music

*conservatory of music
music school
conservatorio (It.)
conservatoire (Fr.)
Hochschule für Musik (G.)
escuela de música (Sp.)
schola cantorum (Lat.)

Konsonant (G.)
*consonant
stable
at rest
consonante (It., Sp.)
accordant (Fr.)

vs. dissonant (G., E.)

Konsonanz (G.)
*consonance (E., Fr.)
consonanza (It.)
accord (Fr.)
consonna (Fr.)
consonancia (Sp.)

vs. Dissonanz (G.)

Kontertanz (G.)
contradance
Schottisches
German polka
anglaise (Fr.)
française (Fr.)
contredanse (Fr.)
Kontratanz (G.)
Contretanz (G.)

Kontra-tempo (G.)
*syncopation
contrattempo (It.)
contre-temps (Fr.)
alla zoppa (It.)
boiteux (Fr.)
Synkope (G.)
syncopé (Fr.)

Kontraalt (G.)

contralto
alto voice
mezzo-soprano
counter-tenor
altista (It.)
haute-contre (Fr.)
altus (Lat.)
Alt, Altistin (G.)
Altstimme (G.)

Kontrabass (G.)
doublebass
*bass
contrabass
standup bass
string bass
bass fiddle
bull fiddle
octobasse (Fr.)
contrabajo (Sp.)
violone (It., Fr.)
basse-contre de violon (Fr.)

Kontrafagott (G.)
contrabassoon
double bassoon
contrafagotto (It.)
contrebasson (Fr.)
contrafagot (Sp.)
fagottone (It.)

Kontrapunkt (G.)
counterpoint
polyphony
imitation
round
canon
motet
contrapunctus (Lat.)
contrappunto (It.)
contrepoint (Fr.)
contrapunto (Sp.)

Kontrasubjekt (G.)
counter-subject
counter-melody

contrasoggetto (It.)
contre-sujet (Fr.)
Gegensatz (G.)
Gegenthema (G.)
contresujeto (Sp.)

Konzert (G.)
concerto
solo and orchestra
concierto (Sp.)

2. concert (E., Fr.)
performance
rendition
execution
recital
musicale
concerto (It.)
concierto (Sp.)

konzertanten Sinfonien (G.)
symphonie concertante (Fr.)
sinfonie concertante (It.)
double concerto
concerto grosso (It.)

konzertierende Sinfonie (G.)
*concerto grosso (It.)
grand concerto (Fr.)
grosses Konzert (G.)
gran concierto (Sp.)

Konzertina (G.)
concertina
*accordion
squeezebox
bandoneon
Schifferklavier (G.)

Konzertmeister (G.)
concertmaster
conductor
leader
assistant conductor
first chair violin
violino primo (It.)

chef d'attaque (Fr.)
Primgeiger (G.)
Vorgeiger (G.)
concertino (Sp.)

Konzertpavillon (G.)
band shell
bandstand
bandwagon
stage
platform
carro della banda musicale (It.)
palco della banda (It.)
palco dell'orchestra (It.)
kiosque à musique (Fr.)
quiosco de música (Sp.)
platforma con concha acústica (Sp.)

Konzertsaal (G.)
*concert hall
recital hall
music hall
opera house
symphonic hall
philharmonic hall
hippodrome
academy of music
auditorium
fellowship hall
social hall
sala da concerto (It.)
salle de concert (Fr.)
salón de concierto (Sp.)

Konzertstück (G.)
concertino (It.)
concerto (small)
concert piece
concertante (It.)
concerto grosso
pezzo da concerto (It.)
pièce de concert (Fr.)
pieza de concierto (Sp.)

Kopfstimme (G.)

head voice/tone
falsetto voice
yodeling
voce di testa (It.)
vois de tête (Fr.)
voz de cabeza (Sp.)

vs. Bruststimme (G.)
chest voice

Koppel, Koppelung (G.)
coupler (organ)
piston, thumb piston
accoppiamento (It.)
accouplement (Fr.)
copula (Lat.)
acoplamiento (Sp.)

2. *pedal coupler
tirasse (Fr.)

Korean temple blocks
Chinese temple blocks
*Chinese (wood) blocks
clog box
tap box
wood block
cassa di legno (It.)
caisse Chinoise (Fr.)
Holzblock (G.)
caja China (Sp.)

Kornett (G.)
*mixture stop (organ)
cornet (Fr.)
compound stop
sesquialtera (Lat.)
mistura (It.)
plein jeu (Fr.)
Mixtur (G.)

Korpus, Körper (G.)
*body (of instrument)
corpo (It.)
corps (Fr.)
coffre (Fr.)

cuerpo (Sp.)

Korrepetitor (G.)
coach
teacher
ripetitore (It.)
maestro sostituto (It.)
répétiteur (Fr.)
repetidor (Sp.)

Kortholt (G.)
*curtal
bassoon
Kurzholz (G.)
courtaut (E.)
sordone (It.)
sourdine (Fr.)
Sordun (G.)
chirimia (Sp.)

Kotillon (G.)
cotillion
square dance
quadrille (Fr.)
cotillon (Fr.)

koto (Jap.)
*zither
Japanese zither
guitar
sitar (Ind.)
lute

Krakowiak (E., It., G.)
fast duple dance
polka
cracoviana (It., Sp.)
Cracoviak (Fr.)
Cracovienne (Fr.)
Krakauer Tanz (G.)

Krebskanon (G.)
crab canon
*canon
canon cancrizans (Lat.)
recte et recto (Lat.)

retrograde canon
al rovescio (It.)
Krebsgang (G.)

Kreuz (G.)
a sharp
accidental sign
diesis (It.)
dièse (Fr.)
sostenido (Sp.)

vs. Bemol (G.)

Kreuzflöte (G.)
*flute
cross flute
transverse flute
concert flute
German flute
flauto (It.)
flûte (Fr.)
flûte traversière (Fr.)
Flöte (G.)
Querflöte (G.)
flauta (Sp.)
flauta travesera (Sp.)

vs. Blockflöte (G.)

Kreuzung (G.)
crossing (of parts, voices)
incrosciemento (It.)
croisement (Fr.)
cruzamiento (Sp.)

Krippenspiel (G.)
Nativity play
Christmas play
Christmas pageant
*liturgical drama
Magi play
Mystery play

Krone (G.)
fermata (It., Sp.)
hold

caesura
organ point
corona (It.)
punto d'organo (It.)
point d'orgue (Fr.)
point d'arrêt
couronne (Fr.)
Fermate (G.)
Orgelpunkt (G.)
punto de organo (Sp.)

Krummhorn (G.)
crumhorn
oboe
cromorno (It., Sp.)
cromorne (Fr.)
tournabout (Fr.)
storto (It.)
piva torto (It.)
orlo (Sp.)

Kuhglocken (G.)
cowbells
Kuhschelle (G.)
Alpenglocken (G.)
campanaccio (It.)
cloches de vaches (Fr.)
sonnaille (Fr.)
cencerros (Sp.)

Kunstlied (G.)
art song
classical song
Lied, Lieder (G.)
mélodie (Fr.)
chanson (Fr.)
concert song/aria
aria, air, ayre

Kürbisrassel (G.)
*rattle
ratchet
*crécelle (Fr.)
raganella (It.)
hochet (Fr.)
Knarre (G.)

Schnarre (G.)
Gefässrassel (G.)s
maraca
carraca (Sp.)

kurze Messe (G.)
missa brevis (Lat.)
messa brevi (It.)
petite messe (Fr.)
kleine Messe (G.)
misa breve (Sp.)

vs. grosse Messe (G.)

kurze Oktave (G.)
short octave (organ)
broken octave
mi re ut (It.)
octave courte (Fr.)
octava corta (Sp.)

2. partial stop
incomplete stop
split keys

kurzer Vorschlag (G.)
*acciaccatura (It.)
*mordent
ornament
grace note
trill
neighbor note
shake
mordente (It., Sp.)
mordant (Fr.)
mordiente (Sp.)

Kustos (G.)
guide (to the next note)
direct
custos (Lat.)
tractulus (Lat.)
cue note
index
mostra (It., Sp.)
guida (It.)

guidon (Fr.)

Kyriale (Gr., Lat.)
collection of chants
ordinary of the Mass
*anthology

Kyrie Eleison (Gr.)
Mass chant
ordinary of the Mass
lesser litany

kyrielle (Fr.)
litany
letany
litany of the Saints
litany of Loreto
greater litany
litaniae Lauretaniae (Lat.)
suffrages
prayers
orations
call-and-response
Kyrie (Gr.)
lesser litany
preces (Lat.)
litania (It.)
litanie (Fr.)
Litanei (G.)

L

la
sixth degree of the scale
letter A
submediant
superdominant
sopraddominante (It.)
sus-dominante (Fr.)
sous-médiante (Fr.)
Untermediante (G.)
superdominante (Sp.)

la-la music
zydeco music
cajun music

labbro (It.)
lip
labium (Lat.)
lèvre (Fr.)
Lippe (G.)
labio (Sp.)

labial pipe (organ)
flue pipe
canna labiale (It.)
canna d'anima (It.)
tuyau à bouche (Fr.)
Labialpfeife (G.)
tubo de boca (Sp.)

vs. reed pipe

Lage (G.)
range
*compass
ambitus (Lat., Fr., E.)
gamut (Lat.)
tessitura (It.)
tessiture (Fr.)
Raum (G.)

tesitura (Sp.)

lagnoso (It.)
plaintive
sad(ly)
addolorato (It.)
plaintif (Fr.)
klagend (G.)
schmerzlich (G.)
lamentoso (It., Sp.)
doloroso (It., Sp.)

lai, lay (13-14c.)
*song
Troubadour song
Trouvère song
Leich (G.)
Stollen (G.)
canzo (Fr.)
ballade (Fr.)
bar form
AAB form
Minnesinger
formes fixes (Fr.)
sequence
descort (Prov.)

laisse (Fr.)
strophe
stanza
chanson de geste (Fr.)
Troubadour song
Trouvère song

Lamb of God
Agnus Dei (Lat.)
Mass
ordinary of the Mass
common of the Mass
Mass movement

lame musicale (Fr.)
musical saw
sega (It.)
scie musicale (Fr.)
singende Säge (G.)

serrucho (Sp.)

lament
threnody
apotheosis
lamentation (E., Fr.)
dirge
elegy
plaint
funeral song
requiem (Lat.)
planctus (Lat.)
trenodia (It.)
lamento (It., Sp.)
plainte (Fr.)
planh (Prov.)
complainte (Fr.)
tombeau (Fr.)
élégie (Fr.)
elegia (It., Sp.)
Elegie (G.)
nenia (E., It., Sp.)
nénie (Fr.)
déploration (Fr.)
apothéose (Fr.)
Trauergesang (G.)
Klage, Klagelied (G.)
Grabgesang (G.)
dump, dompe
epicede
epicedium (Lat.)
epicedio (It., Sp.)
epiodion (Gr.)
kaddish (Heb.)
taps
sonnerie aux morts (Fr.)
Zapfenstreich (G.)
treno (Sp.)
endecha (Sp.)
canto fúnebre (Sp.)
toque de silencio (Sp.)

Landini cadence
Burgundian cadence
double leading-tone cadence
cadence

lydian cadence

Ländler (G.)
waltz
Dreher (G.)
danza tedesca (It.)
allemanda (It.)
allemande (Fr.)
alemana, alemanda (Sp.)

Langspielplatte (G.)
long-playing record
LP record, 33 1/3 rpm
microgroove record
platter
a 45
CD, DVD
microsolco (It.)
microsillon (Fr.)
microsurco (Sp.)

languid (organ)
tongue of pipe
tuning device
languette (E., Fr.)
anima (It.)
biseau (Fr.)
Kern (G.)
alma (Sp.)
bisel (Sp.)

larga (Lat.)
maxima (Lat.)
a large
duplex longa (Lat.)
early notation (13c.)

largo (It.)
slow
broad
lento (It., Sp.)
adagio (It.)
grave (E., It.)
large (Fr.)
lent, lentement (Fr.)
langsam (G.)

breit (G.)
amplio (Sp.)
ancho (Sp.)
despacio (Sp.)
lentamente (Sp.)

larigot (organ)
nineteenth (1 1/3 ft.)
mutation stop
mixture rank

l'armonia delle sfere/celeste (It.)
harmony of the spheres
music of the spheres
celestial music
musica mundana (Lat.)
musique des spheres célestes
(Fr.)
Sphärenmusik (G.)
Sphärenharmonie (G.)
armonía de las esferas celestes
(Sp.)
música de las esferas celestes
(Sp.)

larynx (E., Fr.)
vocal cords/folds
voice box
laringe (It., Sp.)
Kehlkopf (G.)
syrinx
pharynx

last movement
finale (E., It.)
concluding movement
dernier mouvement (Fr.)
mouvement final (Fr.)
Finalsatz (G.)
Schlusssatz (G.)
Schlussstück (G.)
final (Sp.)
movimiento final (Sp.)
conclusión (Sp.)
último movimiento (Sp.)

Last Supper
Coena Domini (Lat.)
Maunday Thursday
Holy Thursday
giovedi santo (It.)
Jeudi Saint (Fr.)
Gründonnerstag (G.)
Jueves Santo (Sp.)
Jueves del mandato (Sp.)

látigo (Sp.)
whip
slapstick
frusta (It.)
fouet (Fr.)
Peitsche, Pritsche (G.)
tralla (Sp.)
fusta (Sp.)
zurriaga (Sp.)

latin dance music
South-American
Latin-American music
latin disco
afro-cuban
salsa music
musica sudamericana (It.)
musique d'Amérique latine
(Fr.)
musique latino-Américaine
(Fr.)
**lateinamerikanische Musik
(G.)**
música tropical (Sp.)
música latinoamericana (Sp.)

latin song (medieval)
monody
goliard
lauda (It.)
laudi spirituali (It. plur.)
plainsong
Gregorian chant
grand chant (Fr.)
grande chanson (Fr.)
Geisslerlieder (G.)

laúd (Sp.)
  *lute
  cittern
  bandurria (Sp.)
  bandore
  pandore
  bandola, bandolin (Sp.)

laud(s)
  hymn of praise
  Alleluia (Gallican, Mozarabic)
  laudes (Lat.)
  response
  proper of the mass

2. *Divine Office
  hours of the day
  monastic office
  morning prayer
  Laudes (Lat.)
  laudi (It.)
  Laudes (Fr.)
  Lauden (G.)
  laudes (Sp.)
  matins and lauds

3. trope (on the Gloria)
  tropus (Lat.)
  sequence
  prosa (Lat.)

lauda, laude (It.)
  spiritual songs (13-16c.)
  religious songs
  *hymns
  laude spirituale (It.)
  laudi spirituali (Lat.)

Lauf (G.)
  a run (rapid scale notes)
  veloce passaggio di note (It.)
  passage rapide de notes (Fr.)
  pasaje rápida (Sp.)
  escale rápida (Sp.)
  passaggio (It.)
  coloratura (It.)

glosas (Sp.)
glissando (It.)
divisions
diminutions

laut (G.)
  loud
  strong
  blaring
  ear-splitting
  deafening
  forte, fortissimo (It.)
  fort (Fr.)
  stark (G.)
  fuerte (Sp.)

vs. leise (G.)
  sanft (G.)

Laute (G.)
  *lute
  lauto (It.)
  liuto, leuto (It.)
  luth (Fr.)
  theorbo
  archlute
  laúd (Sp.)

läuten (G.)
  peal (bells)
  ring
  toll
  chime
  tinkle
  sound
  play
  scampanare (It.)
  suonare (It.)
  sonner (Fr.)
  klinge(l)n (G.)
  resonar (Sp.)

Lautenist (G.)
  lute player
  lutanist, lutenist
  liutista (It.)

Lautenspieler (G.)
  luthiste (Fr.)

Lautenwerk (G.)
  lute harpsichord
  clavecin-luth (Fr.)
Lautenklavier (G.)

Lautenzug (G.)
  lute stop
  buff stop
  *mute
  jeu de luth (Fr.)
  jeu de harpe (Fr.)
  Nasalzug (G.)

Lautsprecher (G.)
  loudspeaker
  PA system
  altoparlante (It.)
  hautparleur (Fr.)
  altavoz (Sp.)

lavish production
  extravaganza
  spectacle
  show
  entertainment
  musical
  opera
  masque

lay, lai (13c.)
  *song
  Troubadour song
  descort (Fr.)
  Leich (G.)
  Stollen (G.)
  Minnesinger
  bar form
  canzo
  ballade
  formes fixes (Fr.)

lay
  *song

melody
air
strain
tune
ditty

le même mouvement (Fr.)
same tempo
l'istesso tempo (It.)
medesimo tempo/moto (It.)
tempo primo (It.)
même temps (Fr.)
à la même (Fr.)
dasselbe Zeitmass (G.)
el mismo tiempo (Sp.)
mismo movimiento (Sp.)

lead, lead part
principal part
prima parte (It.)
prima voce (It.)
parte principale (It.)
première partie (Fr.)
erste Stimme (G.)
primera parte (Sp.)

2. main theme
en dehors (Fr.)
accusê (Fr.)
con enfasi (It.)
enfatico (It.)
nachdrucklich (G.)
betont (G.)
fuera (Sp.)

lead-in
cue
intro, introduction
vamp
pick-up

lead sheet
chart
fake book
short score
condensed score

improvise
harmonize
*basso continuo (It.)
figured bass

lead voice
melody
tune
cantus (Lat.)
superius (Lat.)
soprano

leader
director
*conductor
maestro (It.)
directeur de musique (Fr.)
Dirigent (G.)
Leiter (G.)

leading motive
idée fixe (Fr.)
Leitmotiv (G.)
Grundthema (G.)
recurring theme
theme song

leading role/part
principal role
lead, lead part
ruolo principale (It.)
rôle principal (Fr.)
Hauptrolle (G.)
papel principal (Sp.)

vs. secondary role

leading tone
ti, si
7th note of the scale
subtonic
essential 7th
sensibile (It.)
nota sensibile (It.)
note sensible (Fr.)
Leitton (G.)

sensible nota (Sp.)

leaning note
*appoggiatura
ornament
grace note
backfall
forefall
suspension
non-harmonic tone
coulé (Fr.)
Nachschlag (G.)
Steigend (G.)
Vorschlag (G.)
appogiature (Fr.)
apoyatura (Sp.)

leap (interval)
skip
jump
disjunct motion
salto (It., Sp.)
sbalzo (It.)
saut (Fr.)
Sprung (G.)

vs. step

lebhaft (G.)
*animato, animando (It.)
animated
lively
spirited
con moto (It.)
vivace (It.)
con spirito (It.)
spirit(u)oso (It.)
mosso (It.)
animé (Fr.)
belebt (G.)
munter (G.)
animado (Sp.)

lectionary
*proper of the mass
Proprium missae (Lat.)

proper of the time
proper of the saints

lectern
   podium (E., Fr.)
   stand
   rostrum
   stage
   pulpit
   podio (It.)
   Podium (G.)
   tablado (Sp.)

le(d)ger line(s)
   extra lines and spaces
   ligne d'aiuto (It.)
   rigo, righetta (It.)
   rigo aggiunto (It.)
   lignes postiches (Fr.)
   lignes supplémentaires (Fr.)
   ligne ajoutée (Fr.)
   Hilfslinien (G.)
   Nebenlinien (G.)
   linea adicional (Sp.)

leere Dreiklang (G.)
   empty chord/triad (no third)
   incomplete chord/triad
   open/empty fifth
   naked fifth
   leere Quinte (G.)

leere Saite (G.)
   open string
   open note
   unstopped string
   corda vuota (It.)
   corde à vide (Fr.)
   corde à jour (Fr.)
   offene Saite (G.)
   cuerda al aire (Sp.)

vs. abgegriffene Saiten (G.)
   Griffbrettsaiten (G.)

legato (It.)

slurred
connected
smooth
lié (Fr.)
louré (Fr.)
gebunden (G.)
geschleift (G.)
ligado (Sp.)

vs. staccato (It.)

legato-staccato (It.)
   hooked
   portato (It.)
   mezzo-staccato (It.)
   louré (Fr.)
   piqué (Fr.)
   picchiettato (It.)

legatura (It.)
   slur
   legato sign
   liaison (Fr.)
   Bindung (G.)
   Bindebogen (G.)
   ligadura (Sp.)

2. tie
   legatura di valore (It.)
   signe de tenue (Fr.)
   Haltebogen (G.)
   ligadura de valor (Sp.)

3. ligature (chant notation, etc.)
   ligatura (Lat, It.)
   ligature (Fr.)
   Ligatur (G.)
   ligadura (Sp.)

leggio (It.)
   music stand
   music desk
   podium
   lectern
   Notenständer (G.)
   Notenpult (G.)

pupitre (Fr.)
podio (Sp.)
atril (Sp.)

Leich (G.)
   lai
   bar form
   AAB form
   Abgesang
   Stollen (G.)
   canzo (12c. Fr.)
   Minnesinger
   Troubadour
   ballade (Fr.)
   formes fixes (Fr.)

leichte Musik (G.)
   light music
   easy listening
   *backround music
   elevator music
   lift music
   dinner music
   salon music
   café music
   cocktail music
   Musak
   muaica leggiera (It.)
   musique légère (Fr.)
   Unterhaltungsmusik (G.)
   música ligera (Sp.)

leichter (G.)
   easier version
   ossia (It.)
   ou bien (Fr.)
   plus facile (Fr.)
   oder (G.)
   o bien (Sp.)

Leier (G.)
   lyre (E., Fr.)
   lyra (Gr.)
   chelys (Gr.)
   lira (Lat., It., Sp.)
   Lyra (G.)

kithara (Gr.)
cithara
rotta
harp
crotta (It.)
rota (Sp.)
crwth
barbiton, barbitos
phorminx

2. *hurdy-gurdy
organistrum (Lat.)
street piano/organ
barrel organ/piano
lira rustica (It.)
lira tedesca (It.)
vielle (Fr.)
vièle à roue (Fr.)
Leierkasten (G.)
Drehorgel (G.)
Drehleier (G.)
organillo (Sp.)
viela de rueda (Sp.)

3. *glockenspiel (E., G.)
bell lyre
orchestra bells
campanette, campanelli (It.)
jeu de timbres (Fr.)
juego de timbre (Sp.)

Leiermann (G.)
organ-grinder
sonatore d'organetto (It.)
joueur d'orgue de Barbarie
(Fr.)

Leise (G.)
*hymn (medieval)
chorale
sacred song

leise (G.)
soft
piano (It.)
dolce (It.)

doux (Fr.)
dulce (Sp.)
sanft (G.)

vs. laut (G.)

leiten (G.)
lead
direct
conduct
dirigere (It.)
diriger (Fr.)
dirigieren (G.)
dirigir (Sp.)

Leiter (G.)
scale
Skala (G.)
Tonleiter (G.)
scala (It.)
gamma (It.)
gamme (Fr.)
échelle (Fr.)
escala (Sp.)
gama (Sp.)

2. director
conductor
bandleader
maestro (It.)
Dirigent (G.)
Kapellmeister (G.)

Leitmotiv (G.)
leading motive
recurring theme
theme song
signature song
motivo conduttore (It.)
motif conducteur (Fr.)
motivo conductor (Sp.)
idée fixe (Fr.)

Leitton (G.)
*leading-tone
ti, si

subtonic
seventh note of the scale

leiturgeia (Gr.)
*liturgy
mass
worship service
ritual
liturgia (Lat., It., Sp.)
liturgie (Fr.)
Liturgie (G.)

lengüeta (Sp.)
reed
ancia (It.)
anche (Fr.)
Rohr, Rohrblatt (G.)
*reed instrument
woodwind instrument
organ pipes

lento (It.)
slow
adagio (It.)
largo (It.)
grave (It.)
lent, lentement (Fr.)
langsam (G.)
lentamente (Sp.)
despacio (Sp.)

vs. allegro (It.)
presto (It.)

lesser
minor
minore (It.)
mineur (Fr.)
kleiner (G.)
moll (G.)
menor (Sp.)

vs. greater
major

lesser doxology

gloria patri (Lat.)
hymnus glorificationis (Lat.)
kleine Doxologie (G.)
psalm ending
Old Hundreth (tune)

vs. greater doxology
Gloria in excelsis Deo (Lat.)

lesser hours
*Divine Office
little hours
little office
minor hours
terce sext, none
oficio parvo (Sp.)

lesser litany
Kyrie (Gr.)

lesson
keyboard piece
study
exercise
practice piece
invention
esercizi (It.)
lezione (It.)
leçon (Fr.)
*étude (Fr.)
Übungsstück (G.)
ejercicio (Sp.)

letania (Sp.)
litany
letany
prayers
suffrages
lesser litany
Kyrie (Gr.)
greater litany
litany of the Saints
litany of Loreto
litaniae Lauretanae (Lat.)
preces (Lat.)
litania, letania (Lat., It.)

litanie (Fr.)
Litanei (G.)

letter notation
Boethian notation
Odoistic/Oddonic notation
Daseian notation
Guidonian letters

leuto (It.)
*lute
liuto (It.)
lauto (It.)
luth (Fr.)
Laute (G.)
laúd (Sp.)
theorbo
archlute

levate i sordini (It.)
remove mutes
take off mutes
mutes off
senza sordino (It.)
sans sourdine (Fr.)
enlever les sourdines (Fr.)
Dämpfer abheben (G.)
*ohne Dämpfer (G.)
levanten la sordina (Sp.)
sin sordina (Sp.)

vs. con sordina (It., Sp.)

levé (Fr.)
*up-beat
arsis (Gr.)
anacrusis (Lat,)
pick-up
élévation (Fr.)
Auftakt (G.)
Hebung (G.)

vs. frappé (Fr.)
downbeat

liaison (Fr.)

tie
slur
phrase mark
bind
ligature
portato (It.)
fascia (It.)
legatura (It.)
légature (Fr.)
chapeau (Fr.)
coulé (Fr.)
Bind(e)bogen (G.)
Haltebogen (G.)
ligadura (Sp.)

Liber Usualis (Lat.)
chant collection
plainsong collection
*anthology
Graduale Romanum (Lat.)
Antiphonale (Lat.)

libre, librement (Fr.)
free, *freely
ad libitum (Lat.)

vs. juste (Fr.)
giusto (It.)

libretto (It., E.)
script
book
play
plot
screenplay
lyrics
livret (Fr.)
Libretto (G.)
Textbuch (G.)
libreto, -a, -e (Sp.)

libro da messa (It.)
missal
mass book
missale (Lat.)
Graduale (Lat.)

Gradual
missel (Fr.)
Messbuch (G.)
misal (Sp.)
libro de misa (Sp.)

liceo (It.)
music academy
*academy of music
lyceum
conservatory of music
music school
institute
schola cantorum (Lat.)
Hochschule für Musik (G.)
escuela de música (Sp.)

lick
riff
hot lick
break
solo passage (jazz)
cadenza (It.)
virtuoso (It., E.)

licorice stick
*clarinet

lidio (It., Sp.)
lydian mode
mode #5, F-F
lydien (Fr.)
lydisch (G.)

lié (Fr.)
*legato (It.)
connected
slurred
louré (Fr.)
gebunden (G.)
geschleift (G.)
ligado (Sp.)

Lied, Lieder (G.)
*song
art song

air
aria
melody
cantus (Lat.)
canto (It., Sp.)
canzona (It.)
chanson (Fr.)
Gesang (G.)
Weise (G.)
canzón (Sp.)
canción (Sp.)

Lied der Lieder (G.)
Song of Songs
Canticle of Canticles
Song of Solomon
Canticum Canticorum (Lat.)
Cantico dei Cantici (It.)
Cantique des Cantiques (Fr.)
Hohelied (G.)
Lied der Lieder (G.)
Cantar de los Cantares (Sp.)

Lied ohne Worte (G.)
song without words
romanza senza parole (It.)
romance sans paroles (Fr.)
romanza sin palabras (Sp.)

Liederkranz (G.)
*choral society
chorale
civic chorus
symphonic choir
community chorus
societá di canto (It.)
société chorale (Fr.)
Gesangverein (G.)
orfeón (Sp.)

Liederkreis (G.)
song cycle
set, series
suite of songs
cycle de lieder (Fr.)
cycle de mélodies (Fr.)

Liederzyklus (G.)
ciclo di canzoni (It.)
ciclo de canciones (Sp.)

Liederspiel (G.)
ballad opera
operetta
musical
masque
Singspiel (G.)
zarzuela (Sp.)
vaudeville

2. vocal concerto
cantata
choral suite

3. liturgical drama
mystery play
miracle play
magi play
azione sacra (It.)
sacra rappresentazione (It.)
drame lyrique (Fr.)
geistliche Spiel (G.)
auto sacramental (Sp.)

Liedertafel (G.)
male chorus
men's choir
Apollo club
glee club (men's)
Orphéon (Fr.)
Liederkranz (G.)
Männergesangverein (G.)
barbershop chorus

lift music
elevator music
*backround music
light music
easy listening
dinner music
salon music
dentist music
Muzak

ligado (Sp.)
  slurred
  connected
  legato (It.)
  lié (Fr.)
  louré (Fr.)
  gebunden (G.)
  geschleift (G.)

vs. destacado (Sp.)

ligature
  *slur
  tie
  bind
  ligatura (Lat.)
  legatura (It.)
  liaison (Fr.)
  Bindung (G.)
  Bindebogen (G)
  ligadura (Sp.)
  neume

light classics
  semiclassical music
  popular classics
  easy listening
  *backround music
  dinner music
  salon music

light music
  popular music
  easy listening
  dinner music
  salon music
  *backround music
  musica leggera (It.)
  musique légère (Fr.)
  leichte Musik (G.)
  Tafelmusik (G.)
  Unterhaltungsmusik (G.)
  música ligera (Sp.)

light opera
  operetta

masque
musical
opérette (Fr.)
Singspiel (G.)
Spieloper (G.)
Operette (G.)
opereta (Sp.)
zarzuela (Sp.)
tonadilla (Sp.)

vs. grand opera

ligne ajoutée (Fr.)
  le(d)ger line
  rigo, righetta (It.)
  rigo aggiunto (It.)
  ligne d'aiuto (It.)
  ligne postiche (Fr.)
  ligne supplémentaire (Fr.)
  Nebenlinie (G.)
  linea adicional (Sp.)

lilt, lilting
  light rhythm
  swing
  dance-like
  lyrical
  melodic
  song-like

limma (Gr.)
  half-step
  half-tone
  semitone
  apotome

lindy
  jitterbug
  swing
  stomp
  jump
  jive
  jazz dance
  lindy-hop
  two-step
  Charleston

line
  staff-line
  linea (It., Sp.)
  ligne (Fr.)
  Linie (G.)
  Zeile (G.)

2. line of music
  score
  system

3. vocal line/part
  instrumental line/part
  part
  parte (It., Sp.)
  part, partie (Fr.)
  Stimme (G.)

linea divisoria (Sp.)
  bar-line
  sbarra (It.)
  stranghetta (It.)
  barra (It., Sp.)
  barra de compás (Sp.)
  Taktstrich (G.)
  Mensurstrich (G.)
  *double-bar

linear (E., G.)
  melodic line
  horizontal
  voice-leading
  contrapuntal
  lineare (It.)
  linéaire (Fr.)

vs. vertical
  harmony

linear analysis
  analysis (tonal)
  Schenker system

liner notes
  program notes
  analytical notes

Liniensystem (G.)
staff, stave
great staff
grand staff
system
five-line staff
pentagramma (It.)
rigo musicale (It.)
sistema (It.)
portée musicale (Fr.)
Notensystem (G.)
System (G.)
pentagrama (Sp.)
pauta (Sp.)

liniertes Papier (G.)
music paper
manuscript paper
*staff paper
carta da musica (It.)
carta rigata (It.)
carta pentagrammato (It.)
Notenpapier (G.)
papier à musique (Fr.)
pautada (Sp.)
papel de música (Sp.)

linke Pedal (G.)
left pedal
*soft pedal
damper pedal
una corda (It.)
pédal gauche (Fr.)
pedal soave/sordina (Sp.)

vs. rechte Pedal (G.)

linterculus (Lat.)
*kit
rebec
pocket-fiddle
violino di pochetto (It.)
poche, pochette (Fr.)
Sackgeige (G.)
violín de bolsillo (Sp.)

lip
imboccatura (It.)
embouchure (Fr.)
Mundloch (G.)
Ansatz (G.)
boquilla (Sp.)
embocadura (Sp.)

lira (It.)
*lyre
Leier (G.)

2. viol (16-18c.)
   lirone (It.)
   lirone perfetto (It.)
   bass lyre
   accordo (It.)
   archiviola di lira (It.)
   lira da gamba (It.)
   lira da braccio (It.)
   lira tedesca (It.)

lira organizzata (It.)
*hurdy-gurdy
vielle organisée (Fr.)
lira rustica (It.)
lira tedesca (It.)

listener(s)
*audience
fans
spectators
concert-goers
the public
congregation

l'istesso tempo (It.)
same tempo
original tempo
a tempo (It.)
tempo primo (It.)
medesimo tempo (It.)
à la même (Fr.)
le même mouvement (Fr.)
die gleiche Geschwindigkeit (G.)

el mismo tiempo (Sp.)

litany
prayers
supplications
suffrages
letany
greater and lesser litanies
litany of the Saints
litany of Loreto
litania Lauretana (Lat.)
litaniae Lauretanae (Lat.)
preces (Lat.)
litania (Lat., It.)
litanie (Fr.)
Litanei (G.)
letania (Lat., Sp.)
Kyrielle (Fr.)

little by little
gradually
by degrees
step by step
poco a poco (It., Sp.)
poi a poi (It.)
a grado a grado (It.)
per gradi (It.)
di grado (It.)
peu à peu (Fr.)
petit à petit (Fr.)
nach und nach (G.)
por grado (Sp.)
de grado en grado (Sp.)

vs. subito (It.)
suddenly

Little Hours
minor hours (prime, terce, sext, none)
day hours
office
monastic office
Little Office
*Divine Office
oficio parvo (Sp.)

liturgical chant/song
  *chant
  Gregorian chant
  plainsong
  plainchant
  cantus planus (Lat.)
  cantus choralis (Lat.)
  canto Gregoriano (It.)
  corale (It.)
  chant Romain (Fr.)
  chant Grégorien (Fr.)
  chant d'église (Fr.)
  plain-chant (Fr.)
  chant (E., Fr.)
  Choral (G.)
  Gregorianischer Gesang (G.)
  cantico (It., Sp.)

liturgical drama
  miracle play
  mystery play
  morality play
  magi play
  passion play
  nativity play
  Christmas pageant
  sepulcrum play
  liturgical play
  sacra rappresentazione (It.)
  rappresentazione sacra (It.)
  azione sacra (It.)
  sepolcro (It.)
  mystère (Fr.)
  moralité (Fr.)
  miracle (Fr.)
  geistliche Spiel (G.)
  Mysterien (G.)
  misterio (Sp.)
  auto sacramental (Sp.)
  milagro (Sp.)
  cantata
  oratorio (staged)

liturgical music
  sacred music
  church music

religious music
ecclesiastical music
  *chant
  plainsong
  motet
  mass
  anthem
  musica liturgica (It., Sp.)
  musique liturgique (Fr.)
  liturgische Musik (G.)

vs. secular music

liturgical season
  Proper of the Season/Time
  Proprium de Tempore (Lat.)
  Proper of the Mass
  Proprium Missae (Lat.)
  Proper of the Saints
  Proprium Sanctorum (Lat.)

liturgy
  *mass
  service
  Divine Service
  Holy Communion
  Lord's Supper
  Eucharist
  *Divine Office
  rite, ritual
  rubrics
  ceremony
  devotion
  worship
  use
  ordo (Lat.)
  Ordo Romanus (Lat.)
  Morning/Evening Prayer
  canonical hours
  hours of the day
  leiturgeia (Gr.)
  liturgia (Lat., It., Sp.)
  liturgie (Fr.)
  Liturgie (G.)
  Agende (G.)
  Kirchenordnung (G.)

Kirchenamt (G.)

Liturgy of the Word
  fore-mass
  ante-communion
  Mass of the Catechumens

liutaio (It.)
  violin maker
  violinaio (It.)
  luthier (Fr.)
  Geigenbauer (G.)
  Saiteninstrumentenmacher (G
  violero (Sp.)

liuto (It.)
  *lute
  lauto (It.)
  luth (Fr.)
  Laute (G.)
  laúd (Sp.)
  theorbo
  archlute

lituus (Lat.)
  trumpet (ancient Roman)
  straight trumpet
  state trumpet
  herald's trumpet
  *Aïda trumpet
  cornett
  crumhorn
  salpinx (Gr.)
  buccina (Lat.)
  buisine (Fr.)
  tuba (Lat.)
  cromorne (Fr.)
  Zink (G.)
  cornetto (It.)

liutaio (It.)
  luthier (Fr., E., Sp.)
  violin maker
  Saiteninstrumentenmacher (G
  violero (Sp.)

live music/performance
  in person
  in the flesh
  live recording
  dal vivo (It.)
  sur le vif (Fr.)
  en chair et en os (Fr.)
  direkt (G.)

vs. recorded
  canned

live room
  echo
  reverberation
  ambiance

vs.dead room

lively
  animated
  spirited
  animato, animando (It.)
  vivace (It.)
  spirituoso (It.)
  mosso (It.)
  animé (Fr.)
  lebhaft (G.)
  belebt (G.)
  munter (G.)
  animado (Sp.)

livre de cantiques/choeur (Fr.)
  songbook
  *anthology
  repertoire
  part-book
  voice part
  chorale (It.)
  Chorbuch (G.)
  Stimmbuch (G.)

livret (Fr.)
  libretto
  book
  script

screenplay
  Textbuch (G.)
  libreto (Sp.)

llave (Sp.)
  clef (E., Fr.)
  chiave (It.)
  Schlüssel (G.)
  clave (Sp.)

llave de do (Sp.)
  *C-clef
  alto clef
  viola clef
  tenor clef
  chiave de do (It.)
  clef d'ut (Fr.)
  C-Schlüssel (G.)
  clave de do (Sp.)

llave de fa (Sp.)
  *F-clef
  bass clef
  baritone clef
  chiave di fa (It.)
  clef de fa (Fr.)
  F-Schlüssel (G.)
  clave de bajo (Sp.)

llave de sol (Sp.)
  *G-clef
  soprano clef
  treble clef
  violin clef
  chiave de sol (It.)
  clef de sol (Fr.)
  G-Schlüssel (G.)
  clave aguda (Sp.)

llave de tiempo (Sp.)
  time signature
  meter/measure signature
  segno del tempo (It.)
  indicazione del tempo (It.)
  indication de la mesure (Fr.)
  Taktart (G.)

Taktvorzeichnung (G.)

Lobgesang (G.)
  *hymn of praise
  theody
  paean
  lauda (It.)
  doxology
  canticle

locale notturno (It.)
  *night club
  night spot
  supper club
  cabaret
  cocktail lounge
  ritrovo notturno (It.)
  discothèque (Fr., E.)
  boîte de nuit (Fr.)
  Nachtlokal (G.)
  Nachtklub (G.)
  café-cantante (Sp.)

loco (It.)
  as written
  at pitch
  ad locum (Lat.)
  al luogo (It.)
  come stà (It.)
  à sa place (Fr.)
  comme il écrit (Fr.)
  an seinem Platz (G.)
  am Orte (G.)
  wie es dasteht (G.)
  wie geschrieben steht (G.)
  en su lugar (Sp.)
  a su puesto (Sp.)
  como está (Sp.)

locrian mode
  authentic mode #11, B-B
  hypophrygian mode #4, B-B

loges
  *balcony
  mezzanine

gallery
dress circle
loggia (It.)
loggione (It.)
box seats

Lombardic style
reversed dotting
inverted dotting
stile Lombardo (It.)
Lombard rhythm

2. organum in parallel fourths
simple organum

London street cries
street cries
country cries
madrigal
cries of London
cris de Paris (Fr.)
cris de la rue (Fr.)
musique de la rue (Fr.)

longa (Lat.)
notula caudata (Lat.)
a long (note)
maxima (Lat.)

vs. brevis (Lat.)

long-haired music
classical music
serious music
high-brow music
art music
concert music
great music
the classics

vs. pop music
vs. folk music

long-playing record
LP record
33 1/3 rpm

vinyl record
microgroove record
pressing
platter
disk
microsolco (It.)
microsillon (Fr.)
Langspielplatte (G.)
microsurco (Sp.)

lontano (It.)
distant
from a distance
far off
da lontano (It.)
entfernt (G.)
lointain (Fr.)
lejano (Sp.)
fern (G.)
weit entfernt(G.)

Lord's Day
Sunday
Sabbath
Dominica (Lat.)
Domenica (It.)
Dimanche (Fr.)
Sonntag (G.)
Domingo (Sp.)

Lord's Prayer
Our Father
Paternoster
Pater Noster (Lat.)
Notre Père (Fr.)
Vaterunser (G.)
Padre Nuestro (Sp.)

Lord's Supper
Holy Communion
Eucharist
communion service
Divine Service
agape feast
love feast
Agende (G.)

Abendmahl (G.)
Kirchenamt (G.)
Kirchenordnung (G.)

loud
strong
forceful
blaring
ear-splitting
deafening
forte, fortissimo (It.)
fort, fortement (Fr.)
laut (G.)
stark (G.)
fuerte (Sp.)

vs. soft

loud pedal
sustaining pedal
damper pedal
sostenuto pedal
pedale forte (It.)
pedale destra (It.)
*prolongement (Fr.)
pédale droite (Fr.)
rechte Pedale (G.)
pedal fuerte (Sp.)

vs, soft pedal

louder
crescendo (It.)
en augmentant (Fr.)
anschwellen(d) (G.)
zunehmen(d) (G.)
Wachsend (G.)
cresciendo (S.)

vs. softer
decrescendo (It.)

loudness
amplitude (E., Fr.)
volume
gain

dynamics
bel, decibel
ampiezza (It.)
Amplitude (G.)
amplitud (Sp.)

loudspeaker
PA system
altoparlante (It.)
hautparleur (Fr.)
Lautsprecher (G.)
altavoz (Sp.)

loure (Fr.)
dance in slow triple time

2. *bagpipe (16-17c.)

louré (Fr.)
slurred
*legato (It.)
legato-staccato (It.)
mezzo-staccato (It.)
hooked
portato (It.)
piqué (Fr.)
porté (Fr.)
getragen (G.)

vs. staccato (It.)
détaché (Fr.)

lourer (Fr.)
slur
play legato
portato (It.)

2. notes inégales (Fr.)
couler (Fr.)
pointer (Fr.)

low mass
said mass
missa lecta (Lat.)
messa letta (It.)
messa bassa (It.)

messe basse (Fr.)
stille Messe (G.)
misa lezada (Sp.)

vs. high mass
missa cantata (Lat.)

low pitch
French pitch
international pitch
classical pitch
diapason normal (Fr.)
Franzton (G.)
Normalton (G.)
diapasón normal (Sp.)
diapasón de bajo (Sp.)

low voice
chest voice
full voice
voce di petto (It.)
registro di petto (It.)
voix de poitrine (Fr.)
Bruststimme (G.)
Brustregister (G.)
voz de pecho (Sp.)

vs. head voice

lower (the pitch)
flat a note
abbassare (It.)
baisser/abaisser (Fr.)
senken (G.)
erniedrigen (G.)
bejar/rebejar (Sp.)

vs. raise the pitch

lucernarium (Lat.)
Ambrosian chant
responsory
Vespers
Divine Office
hours of the day

Luftpause (G.)
breath
pause
rest
caesura
respiro (It.)
respiration (Fr.)
pausa de respiración (Sp.)

lullaby
cradle song
slumber song
serenade
by by
nenia song, naenia
lullatio (Lat.)
nanna, ninna nanna (It.)
ninnerella (It.)
fascinina, falcinine (It.)
berceuse (Fr.)
dodinette, dodo, dodino (Fr.)
Schlummerlied (G.)
Ständchen (G.)
Wiegenlied (G.)
canción de cuna (Sp.)
nana (Sp.)
arrullo (Sp.)

lutanist, lutenist
lute player
liutista (It.)
luthiste (Fr.)
Lautenspieler (G.)

lute
liuto, lauto. leuto (It.)
luth (Fr.)
Laute (G.)
laúd (Sp.)
citole
theorbo
oud
almérie (Fr.)
archlute
chitarrone (It.)
angelica

angelique (Fr.)
orpharion
testudo (Lat.)
chelys (Lat.)
domra, dombra
mandola, mandore (It.)
colascione (It.)
colachon (Fr.)
archlute
Erzlaute (G.)
arciliuto (It.)
archilaúd (Sp.)
bandora
ganascione (It.)
guitar
vihuela (Sp.)
sitar
koto
zither
bouzouki

lute harpsichord
clavecin-luth (Fr.)
Lautenwerk (G.)
Lautenklavier (G.)

lute stop (harpsichord)
buff stop
*mute
harp stop
jeu de luth (Fr.)
jeu de harpe (Fr.)
Lautenzug (G.)

Lutheran Mass
missa brevis (Lat.)
hymn mass
Deutsche Messe (G.)
German mass

luthier (Fr., E., Sp.)
violin maker
liutaio (It.)
violinaio (It.)
Geigenbauer (G.)
Saiteninstrumentenmacher (G.)

violero (Sp.)

lutrin (Fr.)
music desk
*music stand
music rack
podium
lectern
leggio (It.)
pupitre (Fr.)
Notenhalter (G.)
Notenpult (G.)
Notenständer (G.)
podio (Sp.)
atril (Sp.)

lyceum
*academy of music
music school
conservatory
institute
schola cantorum (Lat.)
liceo (It.)
conservatoire (Fr.)
Musikakkademie (G.)
Hochschule für Musik (G.)
escuela de música (Sp.)

lydian mode
mode #5, F-F
lidio (It., Sp.)
lydien (Fr.)
lydisch (G.)

lydian cadence
doudle leading-tone cadence
Landini cadence
Burgundian cadence

lyra viol
viola bastarda
viola da gamba (It.)
division viol
barytone, baritone

lyre (E., Fr.)

rotta
cithara
kithara (Gr.)
harp
phorminx
crotta (It.)
crwth
rota (Sp.)
lyra (It., Sp.)
Lyra (G.)
chelys (Gr.)

2. *glockenspiel
Stahlspiel (G.)

lyric
song-like
melodious
tuneful
lyrical
bel canto (It.)
cantabile, cantando (It.)

2. text
words
poem
verses
lyric(s)
libretto
versi (It.)
paroles (Fr.)
Schlagertext (G.)

lyric bass
*baritone (singer)
bass-baritone
high bass
first bass
baritono (It., Sp.)
basso cantante (It.)
basse chantante (Fr.)
basse noble (Fr.)

lyric drama
*opera
music drama

grand opera
    dramma per musica (It.)
    opera seria (It.)
    Musikdrama (G.)
    grosse Oper (G.)

vs. light opera
    operetta

lyric theatre
    opera house
    the opera
    lyric stage
    lyceum
    auditorium
    concert hall
    *academy of music
    teatro lirico (It.)
    teatro dell'opera (It.)
    liceo (It.)
    opéra (Fr.)
    Opernhaus (G.)
    teatro de la ópera (Sp.)

lyrichord
    sostinente pianoforte
    piano-violin
    harmonichord
    melopiano
    Geigenwerk (G.)
    Gambenwerk (G.)
    *hurdy-gurdy

lyzarden
    cornett
    crumhorn
    lituus (Lat.)
    trumpet (Roman)
    cornetto (It.)
    cromorne (Fr.)
    Zink (G.)

M

ma non troppo (It.)
but not too much
mais pas trop (Fr.)
aber nicht zu viel (G.)
pero no demasiado (Sp.)

macaronic carol, motet, or madrigal
multiple/mixed languages
bitextual
zweitextig (G.)

machicotage (Fr. 14-18c.)
*ornamentation of chants
embellishment
melismatic
coloratura (It.)

machine à vent (Fr.)
wind machine
eolifono (It.)
éoliphone (Fr.)
appareil à vent (Fr.)
Windmaschine (G.)
máquina de viento (Sp.)

machine pour le tonnere (Fr.)
thunder machine/sheet
macchina per il tuono (It.)
Donnermaschine (G.)
máquina por la trueno (Sp.)
máquina de truenos (Sp.)

macillo (Sp.)
*drumstick
hammer (piano)
mallet (percussion)
martillo (Sp.)
martello (It.)
marteau (Fr.)
Hammer (G.)

jack (harpsichord)

madrigal (E., Fr., G., Sp.)
part-song
glee
catch
chanson (polyphonic)
frottola (It.)
villancico (Sp.)
canzona, -e (It.)
ballata (It.)
capitolo (It.)
caccia (It.)
greghesca (It.)
giustiniana (It.)
villanella (It.)
barzellatta (It.)
motus confectus (Lat.)
mandrialis (Lat.)
madrigale, madriale (It.)

madrigal choir
chamber choir
vocal/choral ensemble
semi-chorus
echo choir
concertina (It.)
favoriti (It.)
coro favorito (It.)
coro recitante (It.)
coro concertato (It.)
coro concertino (It.)
petit-choeur (Fr.)
demi-choeur (Fr.)
Kammerchor (G.)
Halbchor (G.)
Madrigalchor (G.)
coro de cámera (Sp.)

madrigal comedy/opera
madrigals telling a story
part-song comedy
Madrigalkomödie (G.)
madrigal cycle

maestoso (It.)

majestic
pomposo (It.)
majestueux (Fr.)
majestätisch (G.)
majestuoso (Sp.)

maestro (It., Sp.)
director
*conductor
leader
maestro di cappella (It.)
maître (de chapelle) (Fr.)
Meister (G.)
Kapellmeister (G.)
maestro de capilla (Sp.)

maestro sostituto (It.)
coach
teacher
tutor
ripetitore (It.)
répétiteur (Fr.)
Korrepetitor (G.)
repetidor (Sp.)
maestro concertador (Sp.)

maggiolata (It.)
spring song
May song
villanella (It.)
Mailied (G.)
chanson de mai (Fr.)
canción de mayo (Sp.)

maggiore (It.)
major
dur, durtonart (G.)
majeure (Fr.)
mayor (Sp.)
modus lascivus (Lat.)
Ionian mode

vs. minore (It.)

magi play
mystery play

morality play
miracle play
tomb play
sepulcrum play
*liturgical drama

Magnificat (Lat.)
Canticle of the Virgin
Canticle of Mary
Song of Mary
vespers
evensong

main droite (Fr.)
right hand
mano destra (It.)
mano dritta (It.)
manritta (It.)
rechte Hand (G.)
mano derecha (Sp.)

vs. main gauche (Fr.)

mailloche double (Fr.)
padded, two-headed drumstick
tampon (Fr.)
battente doppio (It.)
mazzuolo a doppia testa (It.)
mailloche à double tête (Fr.)
zweikopfiger Schlegel (G.)
Doppelschlegel (G.)
baqueta de dos cabezas (Sp.)

main gauche (Fr.)
left hand
mano sinistra (It.)
mano manca (It.)
linke Hand (G.)
mano izquierda (Sp.)

main guidonienne (Fr.)
Guidonian hand
harmonic hand
manus guidonis (Lat.)
manus musicalis (Lat.)
mano guidoniana (It., Sp.)

mano harmonica (It.)
main harmonique (Fr.)
Guidonische Hand (G.)
solmization

main theme
principal theme
first theme
tema principale (It.)
thème principal (Fr.)
Hauptthema (G.)
tema principal (Sp.)

vs. secondary theme

maîtrise (Fr.)
choir school
choir
conservatory
institute
*academy of music

maîtrise d'enfants (Fr.)
boychoir
coro di raggazzi (It.)
putti (It.)
Knabenchor (G.)

major (mode, interval)
maggiore (It.)
majeur (Fr.)
Dur, Durtonart (G.)
mayor (Sp.)

major bass (organ)
32 ft. bourdon
16 ft. pedal diapason

major second
whole step/tone
tone
seconda maggiore (It,)
seconde majeure (Fr.)
grosse Sekunde (G.)
segunda mayor (Sp.)

vs. minor second

major seventh (interval)
heptachord
ditonus cum diapente (Lat.)
*seventh
settima maggiore (It.)
sptième majeure (Fr.)
grosse Sept, Septime (G.)
septima mayor (Sp.)
eptacordo (It., Sp.))
eptacorde (Fr.)

major sixth (interval)
hexachord
tonus cum diapente (Lat.)
*sixth
sesta maggiore (It.)
sixte majeur (Fr.)
grosse Sexte (G.)
sexta mayor (Sp.)
esacordo (Sp.)

major third
*ditone
Picardy third
tierce de Picardy (Fr.)
*third
terza maggiore (It.)
tierce majeure (Fr.)
grosse Terz (G.)
tercera mayor (Sp.)

make music
perform
concertize
conduct
play, sing
ring out
sonare (It.)
fare musica (It.)
faire de la musique (Fr.)
musiquer (Fr.)
jouer (Fr.)
sonner (Fr.)
spielen (G.)

klingen (G.)
musizieren (G.)
sonar (Sp.)
tocar (Sp.)
hacer música (Sp.)
tickle the ivories (piano)
blow the trumpet
beat the drums

malagueña (Sp.)
fandango (Sp.)
folk music
flamenco (Sp.)
seguidilla (Sp.)

male alto
countertenor
falsetto
head tone
contratenor (Lat.)
tenorino (It.)
alti naturali (It.)
tenore leggero (It.)
haute-contre (Fr.)
Männeraltist (G.)
Kontraalt (G.)
Alt'stimme (G.)

mallet
hammer
*drumstick
martello, martelletto (It.)
marteau (Fr.)
mailloche (Fr.)
Hammer (G.)
Schlegel (G.)
martillo (Sp.)
macillo (Sp.)
palillo (Sp.)

mambo
afro-Cuban
Latin music
merengue (Sp.)

manager

agent
impresario
booking agent
representative

mancando (It.)
*decrescendo (It.)
morendo (It.)
diminuendo (It.)
decay
fade out

manche (Fr.)
neck (violin, etc.)
manico (It.)
Hals (G.)
mango (Sp.)
mástil (Sp.)

mandola, mandora, -e (It.)
lute (small)
gittern
pandora, pandorina
quinterna (Lat.)
tenor mandolin
mandore (Fr.)
Mandorlauten (G.)
Mandora (G.)
Pandurzither (G.)
mandola (Sp.)
bandola (Sp.)

mandolin(e)
mandolino (It.)
mandoline (Fr.)
Mandoline (G.)
mandolina (Sp.)
bandolín, bandore (Sp.)
bandurria (Sp.)
mandola (E., It.)

manicorde (E., Fr.)
*clavichord
manicordion (Fr.)
manichord

Manier (G.)
grace note
*ornament
agrément (Fr.)

Männergesangverein (G.)
male chorus
glee club
Männerchor (G.)
Apollo club
barbershop chorus

mano destra (It.)
right hand
mano dritta (It.)
main droite (Fr.)
rechts Hand (G.)
mano derecha (Sp.)

mano guidoniana (It., Sp.)
Guidonian hand
harmonic hand
manus guidonis (Lat.)
manus musicalis (Lat.)
main guidonienne (Fr.)
Guidonische Hand (G.)
*solmization

mano sinistra (It.)
left hand
mano manca (It.)
main gauche (Fr.)
linke Hand (G.)
mano izquiera (Sp.)

mantice (It.)
*bellows
soffietto (It.)
soufflet (Fr.)
Balg (G.)
Gebläse (G.)
fuelle (Sp.)
wind chest
wind supply

manual (org., harpsichord)

keyboard
clavier (Fr.)
division
partial organ
manualis (Lat.)
manuale (It.)
tastatura, tastiera (It.)
Klaviatur (G.)
Tastatur (G.)
Manual (G.)
manuel (Fr.)
manual (Sp.)
teclado (Sp.)
pedalboard

manualiter (Lat.)
manuals only
manualmente (It.)
per manuale solo (It.)
ohne Pedal (G.)
manuel solo (Fr.)
manual solo (Sp.)

manubrio (It.)
organ stop knobs
drawpulls/drawknobs
manubrium (Lat.)
Manubrien (G.)
bottoni dei registri (It.)
registre (Fr.)
boutons de registres (Fr.)
Züge (G.)
Registerzüge (G.)
botones de los registros (Sp.)

manuscript
autograph score
hand-written music
codex (Lat.)
manoscritto (It.)
manuscrit (Fr.)
Handschrift (G.)
Urtext (G.)
manuscrito (Sp.)

manuscript paper

music paper
*staff paper
carta da musica (It.)
papier à musique (Fr.)
Notenpapier (G.)
pautada (Sp.)
papel de música (Sp.)

máquina de discos (Sp.)
jukebox
nickelodeon
automatic turntable
automatic phonograph
juke-box (It., Fr.)
Musikbox (G.)
Musikautomat (G.)
rocola (Sp.)
tocadiscos automático (Sp.)

máquina de truenos (Sp.)
thunder machine/sheet
macchina per il tuono (It.)
machine pour le tonnere (Fr.)
Donnermaschine (G.)
máquina por la trueno (Sp.)

máquina de viento (Sp.)
wind machine
eolifono (It.)
machine à vent (Fr.)
appareil à vent (Fr.)
éoliphone (Fr.)
Windmaschine (G.)

maraca (E., Fr., It., Sp.)
rattle
gourd
raganella (It.)
*crécelle (Fr.)
hochet (Fr.)
Ratsche (G.)
Knarre (G.)
Gefässrassel (G.)
Kürbisrassel (G.)
carraca (Sp.)
matraca (Sp.)

marcato (It.)
accented
stressed
marcando (It.)
marqué (Fr.)
markiert (G.)
marcado (Sp.)

march
quick-step
marcia (It.)
marche (Fr.)
Marsch (G.)
marcha (Sp.)
duple

march time
*cut time
duple
double time
quick time
C-barred
alla breve (It.)
à la blanche (Fr.)
in halben Noten (G.)
a la breve (Sp.)

marcha funebre (Sp.)
funeral march
*dead march
dirge
funeral processional
marcia funebre (It.)
marche funèbre (Fr.)
Trauermarsch (G.)

marche nuptiale (Fr.)
wedding march
nuptual march
marcia nuziale (It.)
marcha nupcial (Sp.)

marching band
*band
brass band
military band

banda (It.)
musica militar (It.)
bande (Fr.)
musique militaire (Fr.)
Militär Musikcorps (G.)
música militar (Sp.)

mariachi (Sp.)
Mexican folk band
*band
ensemble
cobla (Sp.)

Marian hymn
akathistos (Gr.)
alabado, alabanza (Sp.)
cantiga de Santa Maria (Sp.)

marimba
*xylophone
vibraharp
vibraphone
vibes
Marimbaphon (G.)

marine trumpet
trumpet-marine
sea-trumpet
tromba marina (It.)
trompette marine (Fr.)
Trumscheit (G.)
Trompetegeige (G.)
Seetrompete (G.)
trompeta marina (Sp.)

marteau (Fr.)
hammer (piano)
mallet
martello, martelletto (It.)
Hammer (G.)
martillo (Sp.)

martelé (Fr.)
detatched
non-legato
hammered

staccato (It.)
gehämmert (G.)

vs. legato (It.)
lié (Fr.)

martellement (Fr., 17-18c.)
mordent
trill
grace note
ornament

masculine ending
cadence on strong beat

vs. feminine ending

masque (E., Fr.)
pastoral opera
operetta
musical
mask
mascherata (It.)
mascarade, masquerade (E., Fr.)
Maskenspiel (G.)
mascarada, máscara (Sp.)
Singspiel (G.)
ballet
opéra-ballet (Fr.)
ballet de cour (Fr.)

Mass
*liturgy
service
Divine Service
Holy Communion
Lord's Supper
ritual, rite
eucharist
communion service
agape feast
love feast
worship service
leiturgeia (Gr.)
liturgia (Lat., It., Sp.)

liturgie (Fr.)
Mass of the Faithful
missa (Lat.)
messa (It.)
messe (Fr.)
misa (Sp.)
Messe (G.)
Agende (G.)
Abendmahl (G.)
Kirchenordnung (G.)
Kirchenamt (G.)

Mass (G.)
measure
bar
misura (It.)
mesure (Fr.)
Mensur (G.)
meter
time
tempo (It.)

mass book
missal
missale (Lat.)
messal (It.)
missel (Fr.)
Missale (G.)
Messbuch (G.)
misal (Sp.)
gradual
graduale (Lat.)
Liber Usualis (Lat.)

mass movement
ordinary of the mass
common of the mass
proper of the mass

Mass of the Catechumens
fore-mass
ante-communion
Liturgy of the Word

mässig (G.)
moderato (It.)

modéré (Fr.)
gemässigt (G.)
moderately
moderado (Sp.)

massima (It.)
double long (note)
maxima Lat.)
longa (Lat.)
duplex longa (Lat.)

masterpiece, masterwork
chef d'oeuvre (Fr.)
opus magnus (Lat.)
major work
capolavoro (It.)
Meisterwerk (G.)
Meisterstück (G.)
obra maestra (Sp.)

mastersinger
Meistersinger (G.)
Minnersinger (G.)
Troubadour (Fr.)
Trouvère (Fr.)
*minstrel
bard
balladeer
gleeman
goliard
wandering minstrel
singer

matasin(e), matassin (Fr.)
sword dance(r)
dance of death
buffoon
moresca (It.)
mattacino (It.)
danse macabre (Fr.)
Totentanz (G.)
matachín (Sp.)
morris dance(r)

matelot(t)e (Fr.)
sailor's dance

hornpipe
Matrosentanz (G.)

matin song
serenade
mattinata (It.)
aubade (Fr.)
*alba (Prov.)
Morgenständchen (G.)
alborada (Sp.)

matinee
afternoon performance
mattinata (It.)
Vormittagsveranstaltung (G.)
Nachmittagsvorstellung (G.)
matinée (Fr.)
Matinee (G.)

matins (and lauds)
morning prayer
day hours
*Divine Office
nocturns
night office
Night Prayer (1972)
first hour
officium matutinum (Lat.)
matutinae (Lat.)
Mette (G.)

matizado (Sp.)
shading
inflection
nuance (E., Fr.)
sfumatura (It.)
graduare (It.)
Abstufung (G.)

matraca (Sp.)
rattle
cog rattle
ratchet
raganella (It.)
hochet (Fr.)
crécelle (Fr.)

Rassel (G.)
Ratsche (G.)
Knarre (G.)
Schnarre (G.)
carraca (Sp.)
maraca (Sp.)
sonajero (Sp.)
Gefässrassel (G.)
Kürbisrassel (G.)
rainstick

Maultrommel (G.)
*Jew's-harp
Jew's trump
mouth organ
Mundharmonika (G.)
crembalum (Lat.)

Maunday Thursday
Last Supper
Holy Thursday
coena Domini (Lat.)
giovedi santo (It.)
Jeudi Saint (Fr.)
Gründonnerstag (G.)
Jueves Santo (Sp.)
Jeuves del Mandato (Sp.)

maxixe (Port.)
Brazilian dance music
polka
samba
bossa-nova
carioca
batuque
jazz (cool)

mayor (Sp.)
major
maggiore (It.)
majeur (Fr.)
Dur, Durtonart (G.)

vs. menor (Sp.)

mazurka (E., Fr.)

Polish dance
waltz
redowa
mazurca (It., Sp.)
masurka (Fr.)
Mazurka (G.)

mazzuolo a doppia testa (It.)
two-headed padded drumstick
tampon (Fr.)
mailloche double (Fr.)
mailloche à double tête (Fr.)
battente doppio (It.)
Doppelschlegel (G.)
zweikopfiger Schlegel (G.)
baqueta de dos cabezas (Sp.)

mean, meane, mene
inner voice, part
medius (Lat.)
parte/voce intermedia (It.)
voix intermédiaire (Fr.)
voix intérieure (Fr.)
Innenstimme (G.)
Mittelstimme (G.)
voz/parte intermediaria (Sp.)

mean-tone tuning
just intonation
equal temperament
tempered tuning
mean-tone temperament

measure
bar
meter
mensural
misura (It.)
mesure (Fr.)
Takt (G.)
medida (Sp.)
compás (Sp.)

measure signature
time signature
meter signature

prolation sign
segno del tempo (It.)
indicazione del tempo (It.)
indicazione della misura (It.)
indication de la mesure (Fr.)
chiffre de mesure (Fr.)
Taktart (G.)
Taktvorzeichnung (G.)
llave de tiempo (Sp.)

measured music
mensural music
metrical psalms
mensural notation

mécanique (Fr.)
*action (of a piano)
mechanism
meccanica (It.)
Mechanik (G.)
mecanismo (Sp.)

mechanical action (organ)
tracker action
mecanismo dell'organo (It.)
mécanisme de l'orgue (Fr.)
Abstraktur (G.)
mecanismo de los grandes
organos (Sp.)

mechanical piano
player piano
pianola (It.)
piano mécanique (Fr.)
planchette (Fr.)
automatisches Klavier (G.)
autopiano (Sp.)
piano mecánico (Sp.)
piano automático (Sp.)
piano rolls

medesimo tempo/moto (It.)
same tempo
l'istesso tempo (It.)
a tempo (It.)
tempo primo (It.)

même mouvement (Fr.)
dasselbe Zeitmass (G.)
mismo tiempo (Sp.)

media voz (Sp.)
*aside
sotto voce (It.)
stage whisper
very soft
half-voice
under one's breath
mezza voce (It.)
fra se (It.)
à part (Fr.)
à mi-voix (Fr.)
für sich (G.)
a parte (Sp.)

mediant
third degree of the scale
mi
mediante (It., Sp.)
médiante (Fr.)
Mediante (G.)

medida (Sp.)
meter
time
measure
metrical
mensural
mensura (Lat.)
misura (It.)
tempo (It.)
mesure (Fr.)
Takt, Taktart (G.)
Mass (G.)
compás (Sp.)
tiempo (Sp.)

medieval mode
authentic mode
ecclesiastical mode
liturgical mode
church mode
auctoralis (Lat.)

plagal mode
scale
tonos (Gr.)
octave-species
greater perfect system
lesser perfect system

Medio Evo (It.)
middle ages
dark ages
medieval
Mittelalter (G.)
Moyen Age (Fr.)
Edad Media (Sp.)

medio registro (Sp.)
divided stop (organ)
split keyboard
partial stop
incomplete stop

Mediolanensis (Lat.)
Ambrosian chant
plainsong
chant
cantus planus (Lat.)

medisimo tempo (It.)
same tempo
tempo one
*a tempo (It.)
l'istesso tempo (It.)
tempo primo (It.)
à la même (Fr.)
le même mouvement (Fr.)
dasselbe Zeitmass (G.)
die gleiche Geschwindigkeit
(G.)
mismo tiempo (Sp.)
el mismo movimiento (Sp.)

medley
potpourri
quodlibet
olio
olla podrida (Sp.)

pastiche (Fr.)
fricassée (Fr.)
salmi(s) (Fr.)
salmigondis (Fr.)
overture
suite
musical miscellany
salmagundi, -y
program chanson/madrigal
pasticcio (It.)
mescolanza (It.)
mistichanza (It.)
messanza (It.)
zibaldone (It.)
ensalada (Sp.)
centone (It.)
mélange (Fr.)
Querschnitt (G.)
Flickwerk (G.)
Flickoper (G.)
centón (Sp.)
mezcla (Sp.)

mehrstimmiges Lied (G.)
part-song
madrigal
glee
choral piece/composition
polyphonic
homophonic
canto polifonico (It.)
chanson à parties (Fr.)

vs. einstimmiges Lied (G.)

Mehrstimmigkeit (G.)
polyphonic
contrapuntal
fugal
imitative
polifonico (It.)
polyphonique (Fr.)
polyphon (G.)
polifónico (Sp.)

Meistergesang (G.)

song
Meistersinger's song
prize song

Meistersinger (G. 15-16c.)
minstrel
bard
gleeman
scop
Troubadour, Trouvère (Fr.)
Minnesinger (G.12-14c.)
Spielmann (G.)
*bar form

melisma, melismatic (chant)
embellishment
ornamented melody
slurring
jubilus, jubilatio (Lat.)
pneuma (Lat., Gr.)
neuma, neupma (Lat.)
neume
*ligature

vs. note-for-note

melismatic (chant)
ornamented
florid
embellished
slurred

vs. syllabic

mellophone
ballad horn
alto horn
tenor cor
concert horn
Althorn (G.)
ficorno contralto (It.)
saxhorn ténor (Fr.)
bugle contralto (Sp.)

melodeon
reed organ

*harmonium
American organ
melodium
parlor organ
pump organ

melodia (organ)
soft flute stop
labial stop (8-foot)

melodic
lyrical
tuneful
melodious
cantabile (It.)
cantando (It.)
bel canto (It.)

2. stepwise motion
conjunct motion
scale patterns

vs. chordal
skipwise

melodic minor
minor mode
harmonic minor
natural minor
modal scale

melodrama
drama with music
monodrama
duodrama
mélodrame (Fr.)
Melodram (G.)
Singspiel (G.)
Sprechstimme (G.)

melodramma (It.)
*libretto
book
text for an opera

melody

*song
air, ayre
aria
strain
lay
ballad
ditty
tune
chant
art song
folk song
melos (Gr.)
melodia (Lat., It., Sp.)
round
plainsong
jingle
theme
idée fixe (Fr.)
Leitmotiv (G.)
subject
motive
monody
carmen, carmina (Lat.)
canto (It., Sp.)
canzona, canzonetta (It.)
cavatina (It.)
cabaletta (It.)
lauda (It.)
chant, chanson (Fr.)
cantique (Fr.)
mélodie (Fr.)
Lied (G.)
Gesang (G.)
Weise (G.)
canción (Sp.)
cantar (Sp.)
cantiga (Sp.)
hymn
anthem
roundel, roundelay
carol
arioso
monody

lai, laisse (Fr.)
virelai (Fr.)

rotrouenge (Fr.)
canso/canzo (Fr.)
alba (Fr.)
plahn (Prov.)
rota, rotula (Lat.)
planctus (Lat.)
vers (Fr.)
rondeau (Fr.)
ballade (Fr,)
brunette (Fr.)
bergerette (Fr.)
pastourelle (Fr.)
Meistergesang, Meistersang (G.)
Minnegesang (G.)

melody part
lead voice
superius (Lat.)
cantus (Lat.)
soprano
tenor
cantus firmus (Lat.)

melomane (It.)
music lover
concert-goer
fan
mélomane (Fr.)
Musikliebhaber (G.)
melómano (Sp.)

membranophone
drums
kazoo
tambourine

memorized
by heart
from memory
by ear
by rote
a memoria (It.)
par coeur (Fr.)
auswendig (G.)
de memoria (Sp.)

ménestrel, méné(s)trier (Fr.)
  *minstrel
  jongleur
  songster
  goliard
  gleeman
  singer
  bard
  scop
  troubadour
  menestrello (It.)
  Spielmann (G.)

meno mosso (It.)
  slower
  più lento (It.)
  moins animé (Fr.)
  weniger bewegt (G.)
  menos agitado (Sp.)

vs. mosso (It.)

menor (Sp.)
  minor
  minore (It.)
  mineur (Fr.)
  moll, molltonart (G.)

vs. mayor

Mensur (G.)
  time
  measure
  mensura (Lat.)
  misura (It.)
  tempo (It.)
  mesure (Fr.)
  Takt (G.)
  Mass (G.)
  medida (Sp.)
  compás (Sp.)
  tiempo (Sp.)

2. scale (organ pipes)
  voicing
  regulating

misura (It.)
  fattura (It.)
  mesure (Fr.)
  taille (Fr.)
  facture (Fr.)
  mensura (Sp.)

mensural music
  measured music
  figured music
  cantus mensurabilis (Lat.)
  musica mensurata (It.)
  canto figurato (It.)
  musique mesurée (Fr.)
  Mensuralgesang (G.)
  Mensuralmusik (G.)
  Figuralmusik (G.)
  música mensural (Sp.)

mensural notation (13-16c.)
  Franconian notation
  Ars nova (Lat.)

menuet (Fr.)
  minuet
  minuetto (It.)
  Menuett (G.)
  minuete (Sp.)
  waltz
  Ländler (G.)

mentoniera (It.)
  chin rest (violin)
  mentonnière (Fr.)
  Kinnhalter (G.)
  barbada (Sp.)
  mentonera (Sp.)

merengue (Sp.)
  latin dance in duple meter
  mambo (Sp.)
  tango (Sp.)
  rumba (Sp.)
  bolero (Sp.)
  béguine (Fr.)

mescolanza (It.)
  *medley
  potpourri
  musical miscellany
  olio
  salmagondi, -y
  quodlibet (Lat., G.)
  pastiche (Fr.)
  salmis (Fr.)
  pasticcio (It.)
  ensalada (It.)
  *messanza (It.)
  zibaldone (It.)
  centone (It.)
  olla podrida (Sp.)
  mezcla (Sp.)
  centón (Sp.)

messa (It.)
  mass
  eucharist
  worship service
  Divine Service
  communion service
  *liturgy
  rite, ritual
  missa (Lat.)
  messe (Fr.)
  misa (Sp.)
  Messe (G.)
  Agende (G.)
  Kirchenamt (G.)

messa bassa (It.)
  low mass
  missa lecta (Lat.)
  said mass
  messa letta (It.)
  messe basse (Fr.)
  messe petite (Fr.)
  stille Messe (G.)
  misa rezada (Sp.)
  misa leída (Sp.)

vs. messa solenne (It.)

messa da requiem (It.)
  requiem mass
  *funeral mass
  memorial service
  mass for the dead
  missa pro defunctis (Lat.)
  messa funebre (It.)
  messa dei/per morti (It.)
  messe des morts (Fr.)
  Totenmesse (G.)
  Exequien (G.)
  misa de difuntos (Sp.)
  misa de réquiem (Sp.)

messa di voce (It.)
  crescendo and decrescendo
  ornament
  swell the tone
  hairpins
  filar il tuono (It.)
  filar la voce (It.)
  mise de la voix (Fr.)
  pose de la voix (Fr.)
  filer la voix (Fr.)
  filer le son (Fr.)
  Schwellton (G.)
  poner le voz (Sp.)

messa nuziale (It.)
  nuptual mass
  wedding mass
  messe de mariage (Fr.)
  messe nuptuale (Fr.)
  Hochzeitsmesse (G.)
  misa de relaciones (Sp.)
  misa de esponsales (Sp.)

messa parodia (It.)
  parody mass
  missa parodia (Lat.)
  parodie-messe (Fr.)
  Parodiemesse (G.)
  misa parodia (Sp.)
  contrafactum (Lat.)

messa solenne (It.)

high mass
solemn mass
missa cantata (Lat.)
missa solemnis (Lat.)
messa grande (It.)
messe solennelle (Fr.)
grand-messe (Fr.)
messe haute (Fr.)
Hochamt (G.)
Hauptmesse (G.)
misa solemne (Sp.)
misa mayor (Sp.)

vs. messa letta (It.)

messanza (It.)
  *medley
  quodlibet (Lat.)
  potpourri
  salmagundi. -y
  olio
  olla podrida (Sp.)
  pastiche (Fr.)
  mélange (Fr.)
  salmi(s) (Fr.)
  salmigondis (Fr.)
  overture
  suite
  musical miscellany
  pasticcio (It.)
  enssalada (It.)
  centone (It.)
  mescolanza (It.)
  mezcla (Sp.)
  ensalada (It.)
  Querschnitt (G.)
  centón (Sp.)

messe basse (Fr.)
  low mass
  missa lecta (Lat.)
  messe petite (Fr.)

messe chantée (Fr.)
  sung mass
  high mass

choral service
missa cantata (Lat.)
messa cantata (It.)
misa cantada (Sp.)
Choramt (G.)
Singmesse (G.)

vs. messe basse (Fr.)

messe de minuit (Fr.)
  midnight mass (for Christmas
  ad primum missam in nocte
(Lat.)
  first mass at Christmas
  messa di mezzanotte (It.)
  Mitternachtsmesse (G.)
  misa del gallo (Sp.)

Messebuch (G.)
  missal
  mass book
  missel (Fr.)
  missale (Lat.)
  messale (It.)
  Missale (G.)
  libro da messa (It.)
  libro de misa (Sp.)
  misal (Sp.)
  Gradual
  Graduale (Lat.)

Messglöckchen (G.)
  altar bells
  sanctus bells
  pellet bells
  *bells
  jingle bells
  sleighbells
  harness bells
  campanelli della messa (It.)
  clochettes pour la messe (Fr.)
  Messklingeln (G.)

mesto, mestamente (It.)
  pensive
  melancholy

sad
plaintive
triste (Fr., Sp.)
traurig (G.)
betrübt (G.)

vs. giocoso (It.)

mesure (Fr. organ)
scale, scaling
proportion
voicing
regulating
fattura (It.)
misura (It.)
taille (Fr.)
diapason (Fr.)
Mensur (G.)
mensura (Sp.)

mesuré (Fr.)
in (strict) time
in tempo
a tempo (It.)
a battuta (It.)
im Takt (G.)
im Zeitmass (G.)
a compás (Sp.)

vs. libre (Fr.)

mesure á cinque temps (Fr.)
5-4 time
Cretic meter
quintuple meter/time
misura a cinque tempi (It.)
quinario (It.)
Fünfertakt (G.)
compás de cinco tiempos (Sp.)

mesure binaire (Fr.)
rythme binaire (Fr.)
binary measure
duple meter
ordinary time
common measure

2/4, 2/2, 4/4 time
ritmo binario (It.)
tempo binario (It.)
Zweiertakt (G.)
Vierertakt (G.)
compás binario (Sp.)

mesure composée (Fr.)
compound meter
battuta composta (It.)
divisio (14c. It.)
zusammengesetzte Takt (G.)
compás compuesto (Sp.)

mesure ternaire (Fr.)
triple time
triple meter
in 3
waltz time
perfect time
tempus perfectus (Lat.)
tempo ternario (It.)
ungerader Takt (G.)

metá (It.)
half-note
minum
minima (It., Sp.)
bianca (It.)
blanche (Fr.)
halbe Note (G.)
blanca (Sp.)

metal harmonica
*glockenspiel
bell lyre

metallophone
percussion instrument
orchestra bells
glockenspiel
celesta
tuned metal bars

meter
measures

pattern of beats
bars
metrical
mensural
mensura (Lat.)
misura (It.)
tempo (It.)
mesure (Fr.)
Takt, Taktart (G.)
Mass (G.)
Mensur (G.)
compás (Sp.)
tiempo (Sp.)
medida (Sp.)

meter signature
time signature
measure signature
prolation sign
segno del tempo (It.)
indicazione del tempo (It.)
indicazione della misura (It.)
chiffre de mesure (Fr.)
indication de la mesure (Fr.)
Taktart (G.)
Taktvorzeichnung (G.)
llave de tiempo (Sp.)

metrical accent
beat (strong)
time
tactus (Lat.)
pulse
meter

vs. tonic, agogic accent

metrical psalm
psalter
hymn
psalm tune
Anglican chant

metronome
mechanical beat
meter

chronometer
metronomo (It., Sp.)
métronome (Fr.)
Metronom (G.)
Taktmesser (G.)

Mette (G.)
matins
morning prayer
day hours
*Divine Office
nocturns
night office
Night Prayer (1972)
first hour
officium matutinum (Lat.)
matutinae (Lat.)

mezza voce (It.)
half-voice
piano (It.)
soft
falsetto voice
head voice
mi-voix (Fr.)
mit halber Stimmkraft/Stimme (G.)
media voz (Sp.)

vs. voce di petto (It.)
full voice

mezzaluna (It.)
Chinese crescent
Turkish crescent
Chinese pavilion
Janissary music
jingling Johnny
*chapeau Chinois (Fr.)
Schellenbaum (G.)
Halbmond (G.)
sombrero chino (Sp.)

mezzanine
*balcony
dress circle

loges
galleria (It.)
corbeille (Fr.)
galería (Sp.)

mezzo, mezzo-soprano
second soprano
alto voice
bas-dessus (Fr.)
second-dessus (Fr.)
Mittelsopran (G.)
Mezzosopran (G.)

mezzo staccato (It.)
portato (It.)
slurred-detatched
legato-staccato (It.)
hooked
louré (Fr.)
piqué (Fr.)
porté (Fr.)
picchiettato (It.)

mi (It.)
third note of the scale
mediant
third degree

mi contra fa (Lat.)
tritone
false fifth
devil's interval
diabolus in musica (Lat.)
mi-fa (Lat.)
augmented fourth
diminished fifth
tritonus (Lat.)
tritono (It., Sp.)
triton (Fr.)
Tritonus (G.)

mi re ut (It.)
short octave (org.)
broken octave
incomplete stop
partial stop

octave courte (Fr.)
kurze Oktave (G.)
octava corta (Sp.)

microgroove record
long-playing record
LP
45
platter
disc
CD, DVD
microsolco (It.)
microsillon (Fr.)
Mikrorille (G.)
Mikrorillenschallplatte (G.)
Langspielplatte (G.)
microsurco (Sp.)

microphone squeal
feedback
acoustical feedback
reazione (It.)
réaction (Fr.)
Rückkoppelung (G.)
Reaktion (G.)
reacción (Sp.)

microtone
quarter-tone
demi-semitone
*comma
cent, centitone
schisma (Lat.)
diacisma, diaschisma
Mikrointervalle (G.)
Kleinintervalle (G.)

Middle Ages
medieval period
dark ages
Medio Evo (It.)
Moyen Age (Fr.)
Mittelalter (G.)
Edad Media (Sp.)

middle C

one-line C
do sotto il rigo (It.)
do du milieu du piano (Fr.)
eingestrichenes C (G.)
do medio (Sp.)

middle pedal (piano)
sostenuto pedal
bass-sustain pedal
pedale centrale (It.)
pédale centrale (Fr.)
Mittelpedal (G.)
pedal del medio (Sp.)
pedal central (Sp.)
pedal sostenuto (Sp.)

middle section
B section
contrasting section
break
bridge
channel
trio (of a minuet)
alternativo (It.)
alternativement (Fr.)
Überleitung (G.)

milagro (Sp.)
mystery play
*miracle play
magi play
morality play
*liturgical drama

Milanese chant
Ambrosian chant
plainsong
plainchant
chant

military band/music
band
wind band
marching band
brass band
banda militare (It.)

musique militaire (Fr.)
Militärkapelle (G.)
banda (militar) (Sp.)

military call
call
signal call
*bugle call
caccia (It.)
chiamata (It 17c.)
chasse (Fr.)
chamade (Fr.)
Hornsignal (G.)
toque de corneta (Sp.)

military drum
snare drum
side drum
cassa, cassa chiara (It.)
tamburo militare (It.)
tamburo piccolo (It.)
caisse clair (Fr.)
petit tambour (Fr.)
tambour militaire (Fr.)
kleine Trommel (G,)
Militärtrommel (G.)
tambor, tambor militar (Sp.)
caja, caja militar (Sp.)

miniature score
pocket score
partitura tascabile (It.)
partition du poche (Fr.)
Taschenpartitur (G.)
partitura de bolsillo (Sp.)
partitura miniatura (Sp.)

vs. full score

minim (E.)
half note/rest
minima (Lat., It., Sp.)
bianca (It.)
méta (It.)
blanche (Fr.)
minime (Fr.)

Halbe (G.)
blanca (Sp.)

minimalism, minimalist
systematic music
motivic repetition

Minnelied (G. 12-13c.)
love song
courtly music
monophonic
carmina burana (Lat.)
canzo, canso (Prov.)
Minnesang (G.)
Frauenlied (G.)
Wechsel (G.)
Tagelied (G.)
Tanzlied (G.)
Kreuzlied (G.)
Spruch, Sangspruch (G.)
Troubadour (Fr.)
Minnesinger (G.)
minstrel

minor (mode, interval)
smaller
lesser
lower
modal
natural minor
melodic minor
harmonic minor
minore (It.)
mineur (Fr.)
menor (Sp.)
moll, Molltonart (G.)

vs. major

minor hours
Little office
day hours (prime. terce, sext, none)
little hours
monastic office
*Divine Office

oficio parvo (Sp.)

minor role
    supporting role
    secondary part
    comprimario/a (It.)
    ruolo secondario (It.)
    rôle secondaire (Fr.)
    Nebenrolle (G.)
    papel secundario (Sp.)

vs. lead part
    leading role

ninor second
    half-step
    half-tone
    semitone
    hemitone
    apotome (Gr.)
    semitonium (Lat.)
    seconda minore (It.)
    semit(u)ono (It.)
    seconde mineure (Fr.)
    semi-ton (Fr.)
    kleine Sekunde (G.)
    Halbton (G.)
    segunda menor (Sp.)
    semitono (Sp.)

minor semitone
    *quarter-tone
    demi-semitone
    *comma
    microtone
    limma (Gr.)
    diesis (Gr.)
    schisma (Lat.)

minor seventh
    settima minore (It.)
    septième mineure (Fr.)
    kleine Septime (G.)
    septima menor (Sp.)

minor sixth

sesta minore (It.)
sixte mineure (Fr.)
kleine Sexte (G.)
sexta menor (Sp.)

minor third
    terza minore (It.)
    tierce mineure (Fr.)
    kleine Terz (G.)
    tercera menor (Sp.)

minstrel
    singer
    bard
    balladeer
    gleeman
    goliard
    scop
    wait
    folk singer
    Troubadour (Fr.)
    Trouvère (Fr.)
    jongleur (Fr.)
    menestrello (It.)
    ménéstrier (Fr.)
    ménestrel (Fr.)
    Spielmann (G.)
    Gaukler (G.)
    Minnesinger
    Meistersinger
ministril (Sp.)
ministerialis (Lat.)

minstrel show
    vaudeville
    revue
    entertainment
    follies
    floor show
    musical
minstrelsy

minuet (and trio)
    waltz
    minuetto (It.)
    menuet (Fr.)

Menuett (G.)
minué, minuete (Sp.)
paspy
passepied (Fr.)

minugia (It.)
    gut string
    budello (It.)
    boyou (Fr.)
    Darmsaite (G.)
    cuerda de vihuela (Sp.)
    nylon string

minuti (It.)
    ornamentation
    divisions
    diminutions
    passage work
    figuration
    coloratura
    passagi (It.)
    roulade (Fr.)
    Roulade (G.)
    Diminution (G.)
    división (Sp.)

miracle play
    mystery play
    magi play
    morality play
    *liturgical drama
    tomb play
    sepulcrum play
    sacra rappresentazione (It.)
    azione sacra (It.)
    miracolo (It.)
    miracle (Fr.)
    moralité (Fr.)
    geistliche Spiel (G.)
    Mirakelspiel (G.)
    auto sacramental (Sp.)
    drama litúrgico (Sp.)
    milagro (Sp.)

mirliton (Fr.)
    eunuch flute

onion flute
toy flute
kazoo
bazoo

mirror canon
inverted canon
retrograde canon
crab canon
*canon
canon al rovescio (It.)
canon rétrograde (Fr.)
Krebskanon (G.)
Spiegelkanon (G.)

misa (Sp.)
*mass
missa (Lat.)
messa (It.)
messe (Fr.)
Messe (G.)
eucharest
Lord's Supper

misa corta (Sp.)
*missa brevis (Lat.)
misa breve (Sp.)

misa de ánima (Sp.)
requiem mass
mass for the dead
*funeral mass
missa pro defunctis (Lat.)
misa de difuntos (Sp.)
misa de muertos (Sp.)
misa de réquiem (Sp.)
messa da requiem (It.)
messe des morts (Fr.)
Totenmesse (G.)
Exequien (G.)

misa de relaciones (Sp.)
nuptual mass
wedding mass
missa nuptualis (Lat.)
messa nuziale (It.)

messe de mariage (Fr.)
messe nuptuale (Fr.)
Hochzeitsmesse (G.)
misa de esposales (Sp.)

misa del gallo (Sp.)
midnight mass (Christmas)
first mass at Christmas
ad primum in nocte (Lat.)
messa di mezzanotte (It.)
messe de minuit (Fr.)
Mitternachtsmesse (G.)

misa mayor (Sp.)
*high mass
missa cantata (Lat.)
solemn mass
choral service
missa solemnis (Lat.)
messa solenne (It.)
messe haute (Fr.)
grand'messe (Fr.)
hohe Messe (G.)
Hochamt (G.)
misa solemne (Sp.)
misa cantada (Sp.)

misa parodia (Sp.)
parody mass
missa parodia (Lat.)
messa parodia (It.)
parodie-messe (Fr.)
Parodiemesse (G.)
contrafactum (Lat.)

misa rezada (Sp.)
low mass
said mass
missa lecta (Lat.)
messa bassa (It.)
messa letta (It.)
messe basse (Fr.)
messe petite (Fr.)
stille Messe (G.)
misa leída (Sp.)

miscella (Lat.)
*mixture stop (organ)
sesquialtera (Lat.)
fourniture (Fr.)
registro composta (It.)
mistura (It.)
plein jeu (Fr.)
jeu composé (Fr.)
cornet (Fr.)
Mixtur (G.)
Kornett (G.)
Scharf(f) (G.)
Cimbale (G.)

mise de la voix (Fr.)
messa di voce (It.)
swell the tone
filar la voce (It.)
filar il tuono (It.)
filer la voix (Fr.)
filer le son (Fr.)
pose de la voix (Fr.)
Schwellton (G.)
poner le voz (Sp.)

mismo movimiento (Sp.)
same tempo
tempo one
l'istesso tempo (It.)
*a tempo (It.)
tempo primo (It.)
medesimo tempo (It.)
à la même (Fr.)
le même mouvement (Fr.)
die gleiche Geschwindigkeit (G.)
dasselbe Zeitmass (G.)

missa (Lat.)
*mass
eucharist
communion service
Divine Service
messa (It.)
messe (Fr.)
Messe (G.)

misa (Sp.)
agape feast
love feast

missa brevis (Lat.)
short mass setting
quick/brief mass
messa brevi (It.)
messe brevi (Fr.)
petite messe (Fr.)
kurze Messe (G.)
kleine Messe (G.)
misa breve (Sp.)
misa corta (Sp.)

2. shortened mass (Kyrie and Gloria only)
incomplete Mass
Lutheran Mass

missa cantata (Lat.)
sung mass
*high mass
solemn mass
missa solemnis (Lat.)
messa solenne (It.)
messa cantata (It.)
messe haute (Fr.)
messe chantée (Fr.)
hohe Messe (G.)
Choramt (G.)
Singmesse (G.)
misa mayor (Sp.)
misa cantada (Sp.)

missa de profuntis (Lat.)
requiem mass
*funeral mass
burial service
mass for the dead
missa pro defunctis (Lat.)
messa da requiem (It.)
messe funèbre (Fr.)
messe des morts (Fr.)
Totenmesse (G.)
misa de difuntos (Sp.)

misa de muertos (Sp.)
misa de ánima (Sp.)

missa lecta (Lat.)
low mass
said mass
messa letta (It.)
messa bassa (It.)
messe basse (Fr.)
messe petite (Fr.)
stille Messe (G.)
misa rezada (Sp.)
misa leída (Sp.)

missal
mass book
missalette
missale (Lat.)
missel (Fr.)
liber missalis (Lat.)
libro da messa (It.)
messale (It.)
Messbuch (G.)
misal (Sp.)
libro de misa (Sp.)
Graduale (Lat.)
gradual (mass book with music)

Missklang (G.)
discord
*dissonance
cacaphony

Misston (G.)
wrong note(s)
mistake
false note
sour note
clinker
stecca (It.)
falsa nota (It.)
fausse note (Fr.)
canard (Fr.)
falsche Note (G.)
gallipavo (Sp.)

misterio (Sp.)
mystery play
*liturgical drama
morality play
miracle play
magi play
tomb play
sepulrum play
azione sacra (It.)
sacra rappresentazione (It.)
sepolcro (It.)
miracle (Fr.)
moralité (Fr.)
mystère (Fr.)
geistliche Spiel (G.)
Mysterien (G.)
drama litúrgico (Sp.)
auto sacramental (Sp.)
milagro (Sp.)

mistichanza (It.)
quodlibet
*medley
potpourri
pastiche
olio
musical miscellany
overture
salmagundi, -y
mélange (Fr.)
salmi(s) (Fr.)
salmigondis (Fr.)
pasticcio (It.)
mescolanza (It.)
messanza (It.)
ensalada (It.)
Querschnitt (G.)
mezcla (Sp.)
olla podrida (Sp.)
centón (Sp.)
centone (It.)

misura (It.)
time
bar
measure

mensura (Lat.)
mesure (Fr.)
Mensur (G.)
Takt (G.)
Mass (G.)
medida (Sp.)
compás (Sp.)
tiempo (Sp.)

2. scale (organ pipes)
proportion
voicing
fattura (It.)
diapason (Fr.
facture (Fr.)
taille (Fr.)
mesure (Fr.)
Mensur (G.)
mensura (Sp.)

misura a cinque tempi (It.)
5-4 time
quintuple meter/time
Cretic meter
quinario (It.)
mesure à cinq temps (Fr.)
Fünfertakt (G.)
compás de cinco tiempos (Sp.)

misura vuota (It.)
grand pause
general pause
hold
rest
empty measure/bar
caesura
railroad tracks
cesura (It., Sp.)
césure (Fr.)
Zäsur (G.)
pausa generale (It.)
vuoto (It.)
pause générale (Fr.)
Generalpause (G.)

mit Dämpfer (G.)

with mute(s)
con sordina/i (It., Sp.))
una corda (It.)
avec sourdine (Fr.)
sotto voce (It.)

vs. ohne Dämpfer (G.)

mit der Bogenstange (G.)
with the wood of the bow
col legno (del arco) (It.)
avec le bois (Fr.)
avec le dos (Fr.)
mit dem Holze des Bogen (G.)
mit der Stange (G.)
mit dem Bogen schlagen (G.)
con la varilla (Sp.)
con la madera (Sp.)

mit der Oktav (G.)
with the octave
coll'ottava (It.)
à l'octave (Fr.)
con ottava (Sp.)

mit der Spitze (G.)
with the point of the bow
*up-bow
a punta d'arco/dell'arco (It.)
à/de la pointe (Fr.)
a la punta del arco (Sp.)

vs. am Frosch (G.)
down-bow

mit Emphase (G.)
emphasized
*accusé (Fr.)
con enfasi (It.)
avec emphase (Fr.)
en déhors (Fr.)
con énfasis (Sp.)
resaltado (Sp.)

mit Feuer (G.)

with fire
con fuoco (It.)
con brio (It.)
avec brio (Fr.)
avec feu (Fr.)
con fuego (Sp.)

mit Gefühl (G.)
with feeling
with expression
con anima (It.)
expressif (Fr.)
avec âme (Fr.)
con alma (Sp.)

mit halbe Stimme (G.)
*aside
sotto voce (It.)
mezza voce (It.)
à part (Fr.)
à mi-voix (Fr.)
a parte (Sp.)
media voz (Sp.)

mit Hingabe (G.)
*free
unrestrained
with abandon
con abbandono (It.)
avec abandon (Fr.)
con abandono (Sp.)
Hingebung (G.)

vs. streng (G.)

mit Kraft (G.)
with force
con forza (It.)
avec force (Fr.)
con fuerza (Sp.)

Mitklang (G.)
resonance
risonanza (It.)
résonance (Fr.)
Resonanz (G.)

269

Nachklang (G.)
resonancia (Sp.)

Mittelkadenz (G.)
semi-cadence
half-cadence
*imperfect cadence
half close
cadenza imperfetta (It.)
cadence imparfaite (Fr.)
Halbschluss (G.)
cadencia imperfecta (Sp.)

Mittelpedal (G.)
middle pedal
sostenuto pedal
bass-sustain pedal
pedale centrale (It.)
pédale centrale (Fr.)
pedal central (Sp.)
pedal del medio (Sp.)
pedal sostenuto (Sp.)

Mittelsopran (G.)
mezzo, mezzo-soprano
second soprano
alto voice
second-dessus (Fr.)
bas-dessus (Fr.)
Mezzosopran (G.)

Mittelstimme(n) (G.)
middle voice(s)
inner voices/parts
mean, mene
medius (Lat.)
voce intermedia (It.)
voix intermédiaire (Fr.)
voz intermediaria (Sp.)

mixed chorus
mixed voices
coro misto (It.)
choeur mixte (Fr.)
gemischter Chor (G.)
coro mixto (Sp.)

vs. men's chorus
treble choir

mixed consort
broken consort
mixed ensemble
company of musicians
*band

vs. whole consort

mixed voices
SATB ensemble
unequal voices
voces inaequalis (Lat.)
voci miste (It.)
voix mixtes (Fr.)
gemischte Stimmen (G.)
voces mixto (Sp.)

vs. equal voices

Mixolydian mode
seventh mode
septimus tonus (Lat.)
tetratus (Lat.)
mixolidio (It.)
mixolydisch (G.)
mixolydien (Fr.)
mixolidio (Sp.)

mixture (organ)
compound stop
furniture
partials
overtones
harmonics
sesquialtera (Lat.)
miscella (Lat.)
acuta (Lat.)
ripieno (It.)
pieno (It.)
accordo (It.)
mistura (It.)
jeu composé (Fr.)
plein jeu (Fr.)

grand jeu (Fr.)
mixture composée (Fr.)
cornet (Fr.)
fourniture (Fr.)
Mixtur (G.)
Scharf(f) (G.)
Cimbale (G.)
Hintersatz (G.)
cimbala (Sp.)
lleno (Sp.)

mock serenade
*shivaree
charivari (Fr.)
*callithumpian concert
Dutch concert
horning
catawauling
cat's music
scampata (It.)
Katzenmusik (G.)
cencerrada (Sp.)

mock trumpet
trumpet marine
marine trumpet
monochord
nun's fiddle
tromba marina (It.)
trompette marine (Fr.)
Nonnengeige (G.)
Trompetengeige (G.)
Trumscheit (G.)
trompa marina (Sp.)

2. *chalumeau (Fr.)
clarinet
shawm

modal music, modality
minor mode
medieval music
ancient music
church modes
ecclesiastical modes

vs. tonal music

mode (E., Fr.)
  scale
  octave species
  harmoniai (Gr.)
  echos (Gr.)
  tonoi (Gr.)
  oktoechos (Gr.)
  enechemata (Gr.)
  modus (Lat.)
  modo (It., Sp.)
  Tongeschlecht (G.)
  Modus (G.)
  raga (Ind.)

mode ecclésiastique (Fr.)
  church mode
  authentic mode
  plagal mode
  ecclesiastical mode
  auctoralis (Lat.)
  modo ecclesiastico (It.)
  Kirchentonart (G.)
  modo eclesiástico (Sp.)

mode hellénistique (Fr.)
  Dorian/Doric mode (mode 1)
  Greek mode
  dorico (It., Sp.)
  dorien (Fr.)
  dorisch (G.)

mode majeur (Fr.)
  major mode
  modo maggiore (It.)
  Durtonart (G.)
  modo mayor (Sp.)

mode mineur (Fr.)
  minor mode
  modo minore (It.)
  Molltonart (G.)
  modo menor (Sp.)

mode relatif (Fr.)

relative key/mode
  tono relativo (It., Sp.)
  Paralleltonart (G.)
  clave paralela (Sp.)

moderato (It.)
  moderately
  modéré (Fr.)
  mässig (G.)
  gemässigt (G.)
  moderado (Sp.)
  moderademente (Sp.)

modern music
  contemporary music
  avant-garde music
  20th-century music
  electronic music
  serial music
  new music
  new wave
  new age
  musicum novum (Lat.)
  ars nova (Lat. 14c.)
  nuove musiche (It.)

modulate
  to change key
  modulare (It.)
  moduler (Fr.)
  modulieren (G.)
  modular (Sp.)

modulation (E., Fr.)
  key change
  change of key
  modulatio (Lat.)
  modulazione (It.)
  Modulation (G.)
  modulación (Sp.)

modus lascivus (Lat.)
  Ionian mode
  C-major
  major mode

moll (G.)
  minor
  minore (It.)
  mineur (Fr.)
  menor (Sp.)
  Molltonart (G.)

vs. dur (G.)

momentulum (Lat.)
  16th rest
  semiquaver rest
  pause di semicroma (It.)
  quart de soupir (Fr.)
  sechzehntel Pause (G.)
  silencio de semicorchea (Sp)
  pausa de semicorchea (Sp.)

momentum (Lat.)
  eighth-rest
  quaver rest
  pausa di croma (It.)
  demi-soupir (Fr.)
  Achtelpause (G.)
  silencio de corchea (Sp.)

monacordo (It. 16c.)
  clavichord
  sonometer
  monochord
  monacorde
  monocordo (It.)
  monocorde (Fr.)
  Monochord (G.)
  Einsaiter (G.)
  trumpet marine
  marine trumpet

monastic office
  *Divine Office
  daily office
  canonical hours
  hours of the day
  morning/evening prayer
  officium divinum (Lat.)
  horae canonicae (Lat.)

Liturgy of the Hours (1972)
Liturgia horarum (1972)
Opus Dei (Lat.)

monaural
monophonic
single channel
monoaurale (It.)
monofonico (It.)
monophonique (Fr.)
einkanalig (G.)
monofónico (Sp.)

vs. binaural
stereophonic

monody
solo song
chant
homophony
cantio (Lat.)
melody

monophonic
solo
unaccompanied
a cappella (It.)
a una voce (It.)
monodico (It.)
une voix seule (Fr.)
für ein Stimme (G.)
einstimmig (G.)
a una voz (Sp.)
monódico (Sp.)

2. *monaural
single channel

monothematic
one theme
fugal
monotematico (It.)
monothématique (Fr.)
monothematisch (G.)
einthemig (G.)
monotemático (Sp.)

monotone
recitation tone
recto tono (Lat.)
tenor
*dominant

2. out-of-tune singer
*tone-deaf
amusia
off-pitch, off-key
can't carry a tune
have a tin ear

montre (Fr.)
foundation stop (organ)
diapason
principal (E., Sp.)
principale (Fr., It.)
fond(s) d'orgue (Fr.)
préstant (Fr.)
Prinzipal (G.)
Hauptstimme (G.)
principal (Sp.)
diapasón abierto (Sp.)

2. display pipes (organ)
dummy pipes
facade, façade
canne di facciata (It.)
Stummepfeifen (G.)
Prospektpfeifen (G.)
Füllpfeifen (G.)

mood music
dinner music
light music
table music
easy listening
Muzak
café music
cocktail music
*backround music
musica d'ambiente (It.)
musique d'ambiance (Fr.)
Stimmungsmusik (G.)
música de ambiente (Sp.)s

morality play
miracle play
*liturgical drama
mystery play
passion play
magi play
tomb play
sepulcrum play

morceau (Fr.)
piece (of music)
*composition
selection
number
excerpt
work
opus (Lat.)
pezzo (It.)
brano musicale (It.)
pièce (Fr.)
oeuvre (Fr.)
Werk (G.)
Stück (G.)
obra (Sp.)
pieza (Sp.)
trozo (Sp.)

mordent
grace note
ornament
neighbor-note
lower neighbor
acciaccatura (It.)
tremulus (Lat.)
trill
shake
flos (Lat. 13c.)
tiret (Fr.)
mordente (It., Sp.)
pincé (Fr.)
battement (Fr.)
mordant (Fr.)
pincement (Fr.)
Pralltriller (G.)
Praller (G.)
Mordent (G.)

Brisser (G.)
quiebro (Sp.)

morendo (It.)
die away
fade out
decay
diminuendo (It.)
*decrescendo (It.)
calando (It.)
perdendosi (It.)
smortando (It.)
smorendo (It.)
en perdant le son (Fr.)
en mourant (Fr.)
sterbend, ersterbend (G.)
expirando (Sp.)

moresca, morisca (It.)
pantomime dance
folia, follia (It.)
morris dance
moresque (Fr.)
Moriskentanz (G.)

Morgensignal (G.)
reveille
wake-up call
sveglia (It.)
diana (It., Sp.)
réveil (Fr.)
Reveille (G.)
toque de alborada (Sp.)

mormorando (It.)
*soft
murmuring
pianissimo (It.)
en murmurant (Fr.)
murmelnd (G.)
murmurando (Sp.)

Morning Prayer
Matins and Lauds
day hours
*Divine Office

canonical hours
monastic office
Opus Dei (Lat.)

vs. Evening Prayer
Vespers

morning song
dawn song
matin song
mattinata (It.)
*alba (Prov.)
aubade (Fr.)
Tagelied (G.)
Morgenständchen (G.)
alborada (Sp.)

mosso (It.)
*fast
rapid
lively
animated
moving along
animé (Fr.)
bewegt (G.)
munter (G.)
movido (Sp.)
animado (Sp.)

vs. meno mosso (It.)

mostra (It., Sp.)
guide
direct
cue note
index
custos (Lat.)
tractulus (Lat.)
guida (It.)
guidon (Fr.)
Kustos (G.)

motet (E., Fr.)
anthem
polyphonic sacred latin song
latin hymn

canticle
antiphon
cantio sacra (Lat.)
canzona spirituale (It.)
motetus (Lat.)
motectum (Lat. 16c.)
motellus (Lat. 13-14c.)
motetto (It.)
Motette, Moteta (G.)
motete (Sp.)

motetus (Lat.)
second voice part
duplum (Lat.)
vox organalis (Lat.)
organum

motive
theme
subject
figure
idea
motivo (It., Sp.)
motif (Fr.)
Motiv (G.)
motto (It.)
Spielfigur (G.)
Komplementärfigur (G.)

motivo conduttore (It.)
leading motive
theme song
signature song
Leitmotiv (G.)
Hauptmotiv (G.)
Hauptsatz (G.)
idée fixe (Fr.)
motif conducteur (Fr.)
motivo conductor (Sp.)
motivo principale (It.)
motif principal (Fr.)
motivo principal (Sp.)

motivo d'imitazione (It.)
point of imitation (fugal)
subject

theme
dux (Lat.)
frammento d'imitazione (It.)
passage en imitation (Fr.)
motif en imitation (Fr.)
Imitationsabschnitte (G.)
Imitationsmotiv (G.)
motivo imitado (Sp.)
punto de imitación (Sp.)
pasaje de imitación (Sp.)

moto contrario (It.)
contrary motion
motus contrarius (Lat.)
mouvement contraire (Fr.)
Gegenbewegnung (G.)
movimiento contrario (Sp.)

moto obliquo (It.)
oblique motion
motus obliquus (Lat.)
mouvement oblique (Fr.)
Seitenbewegung (G.)
movimiento oblicuo (Sp.)

moto perpetuo (It.)
perpetual motion
perpetuum mobile (Lat.)
mouvement perpetuel (Fr.)
fortwährende Bewegung (G.)
dauernd Bewegung (G.)
movimiento continuo (Sp.)
movimiento perpetuo (Sp.)

motus confectus (Lat.)
madrigal
part-song
polyphonic chanson
frottola (It.)

mountain zither
dulcimer
Appalachian dulcimer
folk zither
tamborin à cordes (Fr.)
Hummel, Humle (G.)

Scheitholt (G.)

mouth organ
harmonica
mouth harp
mouth harmonica
French harp
aoline
armonica (It.)
armonica a/di bocca (It.)
harmonica à bouche (Fr.)
Harmonika (G.)
Mundharmonika (G.)
armónica (Sp.)

2. panpipes
syrinx
pipes of Pan

mouthpiece
bocchino (It.)
imboccatura (It.)
cicogna (It.)
becco (It.)
embouchure (Fr.)
bec (Fr.)
Mundstück (G.)
Schnabel (G.)
boquilla (Sp.)
embocadura (Sp.)
pico (Sp.)
escotadura (Sp.)

mouvement (Fr.)
part (of a larger work)
division
movement
pars (Lat.)
parte (It.)
part (Fr.)
Teil (G.)
Satz (G.)

2. tempo
motion
rhythm

movement
movimento (It.)
Bewegung (G.)
movimiento (Sp.)
tiempo (Sp.)

mouvement ordinaire (Fr.)
*common time/measure
ordinary time
4/4 meter
binary meter
duple meter
tempo ordinario (It.)
Viervierteltakt (G.)
movimiento ordinario (Sp.)

movable do system
*solmization
solfa
fasola
tonic sol-fa
relative do system
solfeggio (It.)
solfège (Fr.)
Solfeggio (G.)
solfeo (Sp.)

vs. fixed-do system
absolute do

movimento di voci (It.)
voice-leading
part-leading
condotta delle voces (It.)
conduite des voix (Fr.)
enchaînement (Fr.)
Stimmführung (G.)
conducción de las voces (Sp.)

movimiento final (Sp.)
finale (E., It.)
last movement
concluding movement
mouvement final (Fr.)
dernier mouvement (Fr.)
Finalsatz (G.)

Schlusssatz (G.)
Schlussstück (G.)
conclusión (Sp.)
último movimiento (Sp.)

Mozarabic chant
Spanish chant
Visigothic chant
Romano-Seraphicum (Lat.)

mue de la voix (Fr.)
voice-change
register-change
*mutation
mutazione della voce (It.)
Stimmbruch (G.)
Stimmwechsel (G.)
mudanza de la voz (Sp.)

muffled
muted
damped
veiled
covered (tone)
velato (It.)
coperto (It.)
sourd (Fr.)
couvert (Fr.)
bedeckt (G.)
cubierto (Sp.)

multiple choirs
polychoral
double chorus
*antiphonal choirs
divided choirs
cori spezzati (It.)
cori battente (It. 16c.)
double choeur (Fr.)
Doppelchor (G.)
Apsidenchöre (G.)
policoral (Sp.)
coro dividido (Sp.)
coro separado (Sp.)

Multiplexorgel (G.)

theater organ
cinema organ
unit, unified organ
extension organ
duplexing
organo da teatro (It.)
organo da cinematografo (It.)
orgue de cinéma (Fr.)
órgano de cine (Sp.)
Kinoorgel (G.)

Mundharmonika (G.)
harmonica
mouth organ
French harp
armonica (It., Fr.)
armonica a bocca (It.)
harmonica à bouche (Fr.)
armónica (Sp.)
Harmonika (G.)

Mundloch (G.)
lip
imboccatura (It.)
embouchure (Fr.)
Ansatz (G.)
embocadura (Sp.)
boquilla (Sp.)

Mundstück (G.)
*mouthpiece
becco (It.)
embouchure (Fr.)
bec (Fr.)
boquilla (Sp.)

munter (G.)
lively
animated
spirited
animato (It.)
*mosso (It.)
animé (Fr.)
bewegt (G.)
animado (Sp.)

murky
18c. piece with broken octaves
in the bass
murky bass
walking bass
boogie-woogie
jazz
Laufbass (G.)

muse (E., Fr.)
Greek goddess (of arts and
learning)
musa (Lat., It., Sp.)
Muse (G.)

2. *bagpipe
pipes
piva (It.)
zampagna (It.)
musetta (It.)
musette (Fr.)
cornemuse (Fr.)
Sackpfeife (G.)
Dudelsack (G.)

musette (Fr.)
pastoral piece
musetta (It.)
use of drones

2. *bagpipe
musetta (It.)
piva (It.)
cornemuse (Fr.)
gaita (Sp.)

Musettenbass (G.)
bass oboe
baritone oboe
Heckelphone
basse de musette (Fr.)

music
tones
notes
harmony

rhythm
musica (Lat. It.)
musique (Fr.)
Musik (G.)
música (Sp.)

2. score, full score
notation
parts written out

3. performance
recital
concert
muicale
rendition

4. CDs, tapes (of music)

music box
Swiss music box
scatola musicale (It.)
scatola armonica (It.)
tabatière à musique (Fr.)
boîte à musique (Fr.)
carillon à musique (Fr.)
Spieldose (G.)
caja de música (Sp.)

2. *jukebox
nickelodeon
phonograph
gramophone
record player
record changer
victrola
Musikbox (G.)
Musikautomat (G.)
rocola (Sp.)
tragaperras (Sp.)
máquina de discos (Sp.)
tocadiscos automático (Sp.)

music desk
music stand
podium
lectern

leggio (It.)
pupitre ä musique (Fr.)
lutrin (Fr.)
Notenständer (G.)
Notenpult (G.)
atril (Sp.)
podio (Sp.)

music dictionary
lexicon
encyclopedia
glossary
terms in music
musical terms
dizionario di musica (It.)
Wörterbuch der Musik (G.)
musikalisches Lexicon (G.)
dictionnaire de la musique
(Fr.)
diccionario de la música (Sp.)

music director
conductor
band leader
choral/orchestral director
choirmaster
regens chori (Lat.)
maestro (It.)
maestro di cappella (It.)
capo d'orchestra (It.)
direttore d'orchestra (It.)
chef d'orchestre (Fr.)
maître de chapelle (Fr.)
Kapellmeister (G.)
Capellmeister (G.)
Dirigent (G.)
Leiter (G.)
director de orquestre (Sp.)

music drama
*opera
grand opera
liturgical drama
opera seria (It.)
dramma per musica (It.)
melodramma (It. 17c.)

drame lyrique (Fr.)
azione teatrale (It.)
Musikdrama (G.)
auto (Sp.)

music hall
concert hall
theater
auditorium
recital hall
academy of music
philharmonic hall
symphonic hall
opera house
sala da concerto (It.)
salle de concert (Fr.)
Konzertsaal (G.)
salón de concierto (Sp.)

music history
history of music
musicology
musica historica (Lat.)
storia della musica (It.)
l'histoire de la musique (Fr.)
Musikgeschichte (G.)
Geschichte der Musik (G.)
historia de la música (Sp.)

music lover
concert-goer
fan
melomane (It.)
mélomane (Fr.)
Musikliebhaber (G.)
melómano (Sp.)

music-minus-one
recorded accompaniment
split track
karaoke music
canned music

music of the spheres
harmony of the spheres

musica mundana/mondana (Lat.)
  celestial harmony
  l'armonia delle sfere/celeste (It.)
  musique des spheres célestes (Fr.)
  Sphärenmusik (G.)
  Sphärenharmonie (G.)
  armonía de las esferas celestes (Sp.)
  música de las esferas celestes (Sp.)

music paper
  *staff paper
  carta da musica (It.)
  papier à musique (Fr.)
  Notenpapier (G.)
  papel de música (Sp.)
  papel pautado (Sp.)

music school
  academy of music
  conservatory of music
  lyceum
  music institute
  schola cantorum (Lat.)
  conservatorio (It., Sp.)
  scuola di musica (It.)
  accademia di musica (It.)
  liceo (It.)
  conservatoire (Fr.)
  akadémie de musique (Fr.)
  maître (Fr.)
  Konservatorium (G.)
  Musikakademie (G.)

music stand
  music desk
  music rack
  podium
  leggio (It.)
  pupitre (Fr.)
  lutrin (Fr.)
  Notenpult (G.)

Notenständer (G.)
  atril (Sp.)
  podio (Sp.)

music store
  music seller/dealer
  music shop
  magasin de musique (Fr.)
  Musikalienhandlung (G.)
  Musikalienhändler (G.)

music theory
  musica theoretica (Lat.)
  teoria musicale (It.)
  théorie musicale (Fr.)
  Musiktheorie (G.)
  teoría musical (Sp.)

music therapy
  terapia (It.)
  thérapie (Fr.)
  Musiktherapie (G.)
  terapia musical (Sp.)

musica a programma (It.)
  program music
  descriptive music
  tone poem
  word painting
  musique à programme (Fr.)
  Programm-Musik (G.)
  música de programa (Sp.)

musica antiqua (Lat.)
  ancient music
  early music
  historical music
  pre-Bach
  musica antico (It.)
  musique ancienne (Fr.)
  alte Musik (G.)
  música antigua (Sp.)

musica assoluta (It.)
  absolute music
  pure music

abstract music
  musica pura (It.)
  musique pure (Fr.)
  absolute Musik (G.)
  música absoluta (Sp.)
  música pura (Sp.)

música catedralícia (Sp.)
  *cathedral music
  Tudor church music
  Anglican music
  Episcopal music
  musique cathédrale (Fr.)

musica concreta (It.)
  concrete music
  electronic music
  computer music
  musique concrète (Fr.)
  konkrete Musik (G.)
  mùsica concreta (Sp.)

musica contemporanea (It.)
  contemporary music
  modern music
  new music
  avant-garde music
  new wave
  new age
  musique contemporaine (Fr.)
  zeitgenössische Musik (G.)
  neue Musik (G.)
  música contemporánea (Sp.)

musica corale (It.)
  choral/choir music
  musique de choeur (Fr.)
  musique chorale (Fr.)
  Chormusik (G.)
  música coral (Sp.)

musica da camera (It.)
  chamber music
  salon music
  musique de chambre (Fr.)
  Kammermusik (G.)

música de cámara (Sp.)

musica da chiesa (It.)
church music
musique d'église (Fr.)
Kirchenmusik (G.)
música de iglesia (Sp.)

musica da consumo (It.)
functional music
practical music
utility music
music for the home
school music
musica d'uso (It.)
musique d'usage (Fr.)
Gebrauchsmusik (G.)
Hausmusik (G.)
mùsica de consumo (Sp.)

musica da salotto (It.)
salon music
dinner music
table music
light music
*backround music
musique de salon (Fr.)
Salonmusik (G.)
mùsica de salón (Sp.)

musica da tavola (It.)
table music
dinner music
*backround music
musique de table (Fr.)
Tafelmusik (G.)
música de mesa (Sp.)

musica d'ambiente (It.)
mood music
*backround music
musique d'ambiance (Fr.)
Stimmungsmusik (G.)
música de ambiente (Sp.)

música de las catedrales (Sp.)

cathedral music
Tudor church music
Anglican music
Episcopal music
musique de cathédrale (Fr.)

música de ojo (Sp.)
eye music
descriptive music
program music
word painting
tone painting
musica visiva (It.)
musique oculaire (Fr.)
Augenmusik (G.)
música para la vista (Sp.)

musica descrittiva (It.)
descriptive music
*program music
tone painting
tone poem
symphonic poem
musique descriptive (Fr.)
Programm-Musik (G.)
música descriptiva (Sp.)

musica di fondo (It.)
*backround music
musique de fond (Fr.)
Hintergrundmusik (G.)
música de fondo (Sp.)

musica di giannizeri (It.)
Janissary music
jingling Johnny
Turkish music
banda Turca (It.)
*chapeau Chinois (Fr.)
musique de Janissaires (Fr.)
Janitscharenmusik (G.)
sombrero chino (Sp.)
chinesco (Sp.)

musica di gatti (It.)
shivaree

cat's concert
caterwauling
*callithumpian concert
horning
charivari (Fr.)
Katzenmusik (G.)
cencerrada (Sp.)

musica di scena (It.)
incidental music
music for a play
underscore (film)
film music
*backround music
musica scenica (It.)
musique de scène (Fr.)
Bühnenmusik (G.)
música de escena (Sp.)

musica divina (Lat., It.)
sacred music
religious music
church music
musica sacra (It.)
musia religiosa (It.)
musica ecclesiastica (It.)
musique sacrée (Fr.)
musique religieuse (Fr.)
geistliche Musik (G.)
música sagrada (Sp.)
música religiosa (Sp.)

musica elettronica (It.)
electronic music
musique élétronique (Fr.)
elektronische Musik (G.)
música electrónica (Sp.)

música en hojas (Sp.)
sheet music
partitions (Fr.)
Notenblätter (G.)

musica familiare (It.)
music for the home/school
musica domestica (It.)

Hausmusik (G.)
música doméstica (Sp.)
música en casa (Sp.)

musica ficta (Lat., It.)
   chromatic alteration (in early
music)
   musica falsa (Lat.)

musica figurata (Lat.)
   figured/figural music
   florid music
   polyphony
   mensural music

vs. musica plana (Lat.)

música folklórico (Sp.)
   folk music
   ethnic folkmusic
   musica popolare (It.)
   musique folklorique (Fr.)
   musique populaire (Fr.)
   Volksmusik (G.)
   música popular (Sp.)

musica istrumentale (It.)
   instrumental music
   band music
   orchestral music
   musique instrumentale (Fr.)
   Instrumentalmusik (G.)
   música instrumental (Sp.)

musica legg(i)era (It.)
   light music
   *backround music
   musique légère (Fr.)
   Unterhaltungsmusik (G.)
   leichte Musik (G.)
   música ligera (Sp.)

musica liturgica (It.)
   liturgical music
   religious music
   musique liturgique (Fr.)

liurgische Musik (G.)
música litúrgica (Sp.)

musica mensurabilis (Lat.)
   mensural music
   measured music
   metrical music
   metrical psalms
   musica mensurata (It.)
   canto figurato (It.)
   musique mesurée (Fr.)
   vers mesuré (Fr.)
   musique mesurée (Fr.)
   Mensuralgesang (G.)
   Mensuralmusik (G.)
   Figuralmusik (G.)
   música mensural (Sp.)

musica mundana (Lat.)
   harmony of the spheres
   *music of the spheres
   celestial harmony
   mundane music
   musica mondana (It.)
   **música de las esferas celestes
(Sp.)**

musica nova (It.)
   new music
   modern music
   contemporary music
   new age
   new wave
   musicum novum (Lat.)
   ars nova (Lat. 13-14 c.)
   nuove musiche (It.17c.)
   avant-garde (E., Fr.)
   neue Musik (G.)
   nueva música (Sp.)

vs. musica antico (It.)

musica plana (Lat.)
   plainsong
   *chant
   plainchant

Gregorian chant
   cantus planus (Lat.)
   cantus choralis (Lat.)
   cantus Romanus (Lat.).
   cantico (It., Sp.)
   musica piana (It.)
   chant d'église (Fr.)
   Choral (G.)

vs. musica figurata (Lat.)

musica popolare (It.)
   folk music
   popular music
   musique folklorique (Fr.)
   musique populaire (Fr.)
   Volksmusik (G.)
   volkstümliche Musik (G.)
   música popular (Sp.)

musica profana (Lat., It.)
   secular music
   musica vulgaris (Lat.)
   musique profane (Fr.)
   weltliche Musik (G.)
   música profana (Sp.)

musica pura (It.)
   absolute music
   pure music
   abstract music
   musica assoluta (It.)
   musique pure (Fr.)
   absolute Musik (G.)
   música absoluta (Sp.)

musica reservata (Lat.)
   16c. polyphony
   chromaticism
   expressiveness

musica sacra (Lat., It.)
   sacred music
   church music
   liturgical music
   religious music

Kirchenmusik (G.)
musique sacrée (Fr.)
música sacra (Sp.)

musica sudamericana (It.)
Latin-American music
Latin disco
Afro-Cuban music
musique d'Amérique latine
(Fr.)
musique latino-Américaine
(Fr.)
lateinamerikanische Musik
(G.)
música tropical (Sp.)
**música latinoamericano
(Sp.)**

musica visiva (It.)
eye music
tone poem
tone painting
word painting
*program music
descriptive music
musique oculaire (Fr.)
Augenmusik (G.)
música para la vista (Sp.)
música de ojo (Sp.)

musical, musical comedy
Broadway musical
musical play
musical revue
revue
operetta
masque
burlesque
vaudeville
revue
minstrel show
variety show
follies
olio
caberet
extravaganza

burletta (It.)
Singspiel (G.)
comedia musical (Sp.)
revista (Sp.)

musical artist
performer
recitalist
entertainer
singer
soloist
diva
instrumentalist
artiste

musical glasses
*glass harmonica
armonica (It.)
verrillon (Fr.)
Glasspiel (G.)
Glasharfe (G.)
copólogo (Sp.)

musical joke
*burlesca (It.)
humoresque (E., Fr.)
scherzo (It.)
capriccio (It.)
caprice (E., Fr.)
musikalischer Spass (G.)

musical miscellany
potpourri
quodlibet
*medley
olio
overture
revue
musical revue
pastiche (Fr.)
salmi(s) (Fr.)
salmigondis (Fr.)
pasticcio (It.)
messanza (It.)
mescolanza (It.)
Querschnitt (G.)

mezcla (Sp.)
olla podrido (Sp.)

musical saw
sega (It.)
lame musicale (Fr.)
seie musicale (Fr.)
singende Säge (G.)
serrucho (Sp.)

musicale
concert
recital
performance
rendition
musical offering

musichetto (It.)
easy listening
light music
salon music
dinner music
*backround music
musiquette (Fr.)
leichte Musik (G.)
musiquillo (Sp.)

musician
performer
singer
player
musical artist
artiste
conductor
concert artist
bard
scop
troubadour
musico, musicista (It.)
musicien (Fr.)
Musiker (G.)
Spielmann (G.)
músico (Sp.)

musicology
music history

musicologia (It.)
musicologie (Fr.)
Musikologie (G.)
Musikwissenschaft (G.)
musicología (Sp.)

musicum novum (Lat.)
new music
new wave
new age
contemporary music
*avant-garde (E., Fr.)
Ars Nova (Lat. 14c.)
Nuove Musiche (It.17c.)
musica nova (It.)
neue Musik (G.)
nueva música (Sp.)

Musik (G.)
music
musica (It.)
musicum (Lat.)
musique (Fr.)
música (Sp.)

musikalischer Spass (G.)
musical joke
burlesca (It.)
humoresque (Fr.)
scherzo
caprice (E., Fr.)

Musikant (G.)
minstrel
strolling minstrel
wandering minstrel
goliard
scop
bard
jongleur (Fr.)
troubadour, troubador
Troubadour (Fr.)
Trouvère (Fr.)
Minnesinger (G.)
Meistersinger (G.)

Musikautomat (G.)
jukebox
nickelodeon
music box
automaic turntable
automatic phonograph
juke-box (It., Fr.)
Musikbox (G.)
rocola (Sp.)
tocadiscos automático (Sp.)
máquina de discos (Sp.)

Musikgeschichte (G.)
music history
history of music
musicology
musica historica (Lat.)
storia della musica (It.)
l'histoire de la musique (Fr.)
Geschichte der Musik (G.)
historia de la música (Sp.)

Musikpavillon (G.)
bandstand
band shell
bandwagon
stage
platform
carro della banda musicale
(It.)
palco della banda (It.)
palco dell'orchestra (It.)
kiosque à musique (Fr.)
Konzertpavillon (G.)
quiosco de música (Sp.)
platforma con concha acústica
(Sp.)

musique à la Turque (Fr.)
jingling Johnny
Turkish crescent
Chinese crescent
Chinese pavilion
Janissary music
banda Turca (It.)
*chapeau Chinois (Fr.)

musique Janissaires (Fr.)
Schellenbaum (G.)
sombrero Chino (Sp.)

musique à programme (Fr.)
program music
*musica programmatica (It.)

musique absolute (Fr.)
absolute music
abstract music
pure music
*musica assoluta (It.)
musique pure (Fr.)
absolute Musik (G.)
música pura (Sp.)

musique ancienne (Fr.)
early music
ancient music
historical music
pre-Bach music
old music
*musica antiqua (Lat.)
stile antico (It.)
alte Musik (G.)
música antigua (Sp.)

musique chorale (Fr.)
choral/choir music
*musica corale (It.)
Chormusik (G.)
música coral (Sp.)
música para coro (Sp.)

musique concrète (Fr.)
concrete music
tape music
electronic music
musica concreta (It.)
konkrete Musik (G.)
música concreta (Sp.)

musique d'ameublement (Fr.)
furniture music
easy listening

*backround music
Muzak
elevator music
salon music
musique d'ascenseur (Fr.)
musique de supermarché (Fr.)

musique de cathédrale (Fr.)
*cathedral music
Tudor church music
Anglican music
Episcopal music
Kirchenmusik (G.)
música de las catedrales (Sp.)

musique de chambre (Fr.)
chamber music
*musica da camera (It.)
música de camara (Sp.)

musique de la rue (Fr.)
street cries
London cries
hollers, field hollers
cries de la rue (Fr.)
cris de Paris (Fr.)

musique de scène (Fr.)
incidental music
underscore
film music
*musica di scena (It.)
Schauspielmusik (G.)
Bühnenmusik (G.)
música de escena (Sp.)

musique d'église (Fr.)
church music
religious music
sacred music
liturgical music
cathedral music
*musica da chiesa (It.)
musique liturgique (Fr.)
musique sacrée (Fr.)

Kirchenmusik (G.)
música sacra (Sp.)

musique de salon (Fr.)
salon music
light music
dinner music
*backround music
*musica da salotto (It.)
Salonmusik (G.)
música de salón (Sp.)

musique des spheres célestes (Fr.)
music of the spheres
harmony of the spheres
celestial music
l'armonia delle sfere/celeste (It.)
Sphärenmusik (G.)
música de las esferas celestes (Sp.)
armonía de las esferas celestes (Sp.)

musique domestique (Fr.)
music for the home/school
musica domestica (It.)
musica familiare (It.)
Hausmusik (G.)
música en casa (Sp.)
música doméstica (Sp.)

musique d'usage (Fr.)
practical music
music for the home/school
*musica da consumo (It.)
Hausmusik (G.)
música de consumo (Sp.)

musique instrumentale (Fr.)
instrumental music
orchestral music
band music
chamber music
*musica (i)strumentale (It.)

Instrumentalmusik (G.)
música instrumental (Sp.)

musique latino-Américaine (Fr.)
Latin-American music
Afro-Cuban music
salsa music
Latin dance music
musica sudamericana (It.)
musique d'Amérique latine (Fr.)
lateinamerikanische Musik (G.)
música tropical (Sp.)
música latinoamericana (Sp.)

musique mesurée (Fr.)
metrical music
vers mesuré (Fr.)

musique nouvelle (Fr.)
new music
modern music
contemporary music
musicum novum (Lat.)
Ars Nova (Lat.)
nuove musiche (It.)
seconda prattica (It.)
musica nova (It.)
avant-garde (Fr.)
neue Musik (G.)
nueva música (Sp.)

musique oculaire (Fr.)
eye music
word painting
tone painting
*program music
musica visiva (It.)
Augenmusik (G.)
música para la vista (Sp.)
música de ojo (Sp.)

musique populaire (Fr.)
folk music

popular music
*musica popolare (It.)
musique folklorique (Fr.)
Volksmusik (G.)
música popular (Sp.)
música folklórico (Sp.)

musique profane (Fr.)
secular music
musica vulgaris (Lat.)
*musica profana (Lat., It.)
weltliche Musik
música profana (Sp.)

musique pure (Fr.)
absolute music
pure music
*musica pura (It.)
música absoluta (Sp.)

musiquette (Fr.)
easy listening
light music
salon music
dinner music
*backround music
musichetto (It.)
leichte Musik (G.)
musiquillo (Sp.)

mutation (E., Fr.)
voice-change
breaking of the voice
register-change
mutazione della voce (It.)
mue de la voix (Fr.)
Stimmbrach (G.)
Mutierung (G.)
Mutation (G.)
mudanza de la voz (Sp.)

mutation stop (organ)
harmonics
partials
overtones
registro di mutazione (It.)

jeu de mutation (Fr.)
mixture simple (Fr.)
Aloquostimmen (G.)
Mutazionsregister (G.)
Hilfsstimmen (G.)
registro de mutación (Sp.)
mutación (Sp.)
quint
tierce (1 2/3)
larigot (1 1/3)
nazard (2 2/3)

mute
damper
sordino (It.)
étouffoir (Fr.)
Dämpfer (G.)
sordina (Sp.)
una corde (It.)
soft pedal
buff stop
lute stop
wa-wa mute
Harmon mute
plunger mute

muted
muffled
damped
covered (tone)
veiled
velato (It.)
coperto (It.)
sorda (It., Sp.)
couvert (Fr.)
sourd (Fr.)
bedeckt (G.)
cubierto (Sp.)

mutes off
remove mutes
take off mutes
tutte corde (It.)
toutes les cordes (Fr.)
alle Saiten (G.)
*ohne Dämpfer (G.)

Dämpfer weg/ab (G.)
todas las cuerdas (Sp.)

mutes on
muted
con sordina (It., Sp.)
aves sourdine (Fr.)
mit Dämpfer (G.)
Dämpfer aufsetzen (G.)

muy fuerte (Sp.)
very loud
ear-splitting
deafening
*forte, fortissimo (It.)
fort (Fr.)
sehr laut (G.)

vs. pianissimo (It.)

mystery play
miracle play
*liturgical drama
morality play
magi play
passion play
sepulcrum play
tomb play

N

nacaire (Fr.)
  kettledrum
  timpani
naccara, naccherone (It.)
nacara (Sp.)

nacchera (It.)
  castanets
  clappers
  bones
  castagnettes (Fr.)
  Kastagnetten (G.)
  postizas (Sp.)
  castañetas (Sp.)
  castañuelas (Sp.)
  spoons
  maracas
  rattle

2. *kettledrums
  tympani
  double-drum
  timpano, timbalo (It.)
  timbale (Fr.)
  Pauken (G.)
  atabal (Sp.)

nach Art der Zigeuner (G.)
  gypsy style
  alla zingara (It.)
  à la tzigane (Fr.)
  al estilo cingaro (Sp.)
  all'ongarese (It.)
  à la hongroise (Fr.)

nach Belieben (G.)
  ad lib
  *freely
  ad libitum (Lat.)
  ad placitum (Lat.)

a piacere (It.)
a bene placito (It.)
au caprice (Fr.)
à volonté (Fr.)
nach Gefallen (G.)
a placer (Sp.)
a voluntad (Sp.)

nach Deutscher Art (G.)
  German style
  alla tedesca (It.)
  à l'allemande (Fr.)
  a la alemana (Sp.)

2. in the style of a waltz, landler,
or allemande

nach Türkischer Art (G.)
  Turkish style
  alla Turca (It.)
  à la Turque (Fr.)
  a la Turca (Sp.)

nach und nach (G.)
  gradually
  little by little
  step by step
  by degrees
  poco a poco (It., Sp.)
  poi a poi (It.)
  di grado (It.)
  per gradi (It.)
  a grado a grado (It.)
  peu à peu (Fr.)
  petit à petit (Fr.)
  por grado (Sp.)
  de grado en grado (Sp.)

Nachhall (G.)
  echo
  reverb, reverberation
  live room
  eco (It., Sp.)
  écho (Fr.)
  Echo (G.)
  retumbo (Sp.)

Nachschlag (G.)
  ornament
  grace note
  passing tone
  *anticipation tone
  non-harmonic tone
  trill ending

Nachspiel (G.)
  postlude
  voluntary
  postludium (Lat.)
  postludio (It., Sp.)
  clôture (Fr.)

vs. Vorspiel (G.)

Nachtanz (G.)
  after-dance
  second dance of a pair
  court dance
  galliard
  proporzione (It.)
  tripla (It.)
  rotta (It.)
  bassadanza (It.)
  basse-danse (Fr.)
  branle (Fr.)
  sauterelle (Fr.)
  Proportz, Proportio (C
  Hupfauf, Hoftanz (G.)
  segunda danza (Sp.)

Nachthorn (G.)
  soft 8-ft organ stop
  cor-de-nuit (Fr.)
  pastorita (It.)
  Quintatön (G.)

Nachtklub (G.)
  night club
  night spot
  cabaret
  cocktail lounge
  supper club
  disco

Nachtlokal (G.)
locale notturno (It.)
ritrovo notturno (It.)
boîte de nuit (Fr.)
discothèque (Fr.)
café-cantante (Sp.)

Nachtmusik (G.)
serenade
nocturne (E., Fr.)
evening music
Abendmusik (G.)
Nachtstück (G.)
serenata (It., Sp.)
sérénade (Fr.)

Nagelschrift (G.)
gothic neumes
hobnail notation
chant notation
Hufnagelschrift (G.)

Nagelgeige (G.)
nail violin
nail fiddle
nail harmonica
Nagelklavier (G.)
Nagelharmonika (G.)
Eisenvioline (G.)
violon de fer (Fr.)
violino di ferro (It.)

naked fifths
open fifths (no third)
empty fifths
pure fifths
offene Quintenparallelen (G.)

naker
kettledrum
tympani
nacchera, naccherone (It.)
nacaire (Fr.)
timbales (Fr.)
Pauken (G.)
nácara (Sp.)

nana (Sp.)
lullaby
cradle song
ninnananna (It.)
ninnerella (It.)
berceuse (Fr.)
dodinette, dodo, dodino (Fr.)
Schlummerlied (G.)
Ständchen (G.)
Wiegenlied (G.)
arrullo (Sp.)
canción de cuna (Sp.)
nana (Sp.)

napolitana, napoletana (It.)
part-song (16-17c.)
madrigal
glee
catch
villanella (It.)
canzonetta (It.)
villanelle (Fr.)

narrator
Evangelist
Evangelium (Lat.)
historicus (Lat.)
chronista (Lat.)
testo (It.)
narratore (It.)
récitant (Fr.)
narrateur (Fr.)
Erzähler (G.)
narrador (Sp.)

nasard, nazard, nassart (Fr.)
twelth (organ stop – 2 2/3)
Nasat (G.)
nasardo (It., Sp.)

nasetto (It.)
point of the bow
tip
peak
punta d'arco (It.)
pointe (Fr.)

Spitze (G.)
punta del arco (Sp.)

vs. tallone (It.)

natalizio (It.)
Christmas carol/song
canzona di natale (It.)
chant de noël (Fr.)
cantique de noël (Fr.)
Quempas (G.)
Weinachtslied (G.)
villancico (Sp.)
cántico de Navidad (Sp.)
zéjel (Sp.)

national anthem
*hymn
patriotic hymn
national hymn
national air
inno nazionale (It.)
hymne national (Fr.)
Nationalhymne (G.)
himno nacional (Sp.)

nativity play
*liturgical drama
Christmas play
Christmas pageant
magi play
miracle play
mystery play
Krippenspiel (G.)

natural
accidental
cancel sign
B cancellatum (Lat.)
B quadrum (Lat.)
B quadratum (Lat.)
quadro (It.)
bequadro (It.)
bécarre (Fr.)
naturel (Fr.)
Quadrat, B-Quadrat (G.)

Auflöser (G.)
Auflösungszeichen (G.)
becuadro (Sp.)

natural harmonic
*harmonic
partial
overtone

natural horn
French horn
Waldhorn (G.)
Jagdhorn (G.)
Naturhorn (G.)
hunting horn
hand horn
corno naturale (It.)
corno da caccia (It.)
cor de chasse (Fr.)

natural minor (scale)
minor mode
aeolian mode
hypodorian mode
melodic minor
harmonic minor

natürlich (G.)
bell down (horn)
posizione normale (It.)
position naturelle (Fr.)
normalmente (Sp.)

vs. Stürze hoch (G.)
Schalltrichter hoch (G.)

Natur(lich)töne (G.)
unstopped horn tone
open notes
suoni naturali (It.)
sons naturels/ouverts (Fr.)
notas naturales (Sp.)

vs. Stopftöne (G.)

nave organ (division)

echo organ
gallery organ
antiphonal organ
organo d'eco (It.)
clavier d'echo (Fr.)
Fernwerk (G.)
Echoklavier (G.)
Echowerk (G.)

Neapolitan sixth
augmented sixth-chord
sixth chord
accordo di sesta Napoletana
(It.)
sesta Napoletana (It.)
accord de sixte Napolitaine
(Fr.)
**Neapolitanischer Sextakkord
(G.)**
acorde de sexta Napoletana
(Sp.)
Italian sixth
German sixth
French sixth

Nebenlinie (G.)
ledger line
ligne d'aiuto (It.)
rigo, righetta (It.)
rigo aggiunto (It.)
lignes postiches (Fr.)
lignes supplémentaires (Fr.)
ligne ajoutée (Fr.)
Hilfslinien (G.)
linea adicional (Sp.)

Nebennote (G.)
auxiliary note
non-harmonic tone
neighbor-note
ornament
nota ausiliare (It.)
note secondaire (Fr.)
note auxiliaire (Fr.)
Hilfsnote (G.)
nota auxiliar (Sp.)

Nebenrolle (G.)
minor role
secondary role
supporting role
comprimario/a (It.)
ruolo secondario (It.)
rôle secondaire (Fr.)
papel secundario (Sp.)

vs. Hauptrolle (G.)

Nebenthema (G.)
second theme
secondary theme
subordinate theme
thème secondaire (Fr.)

vs. Hauptthema (G.)

neck (of an instrument)
manico (It.)
manche (Fr.)
Hals (G.)
mango (Sp.)

negra (Sp.)
quarter note
crotchet
nera (It.)
semiminima (It.)
quarto (It.)
noire (Fr.)
Viertel (G.)
schwarze Note (G.)
semínima (Sp.)

neighbor-note
auxiliary note
non-harmonic tone
*mordent
trill
grace note
*ornament
acciaccatura (It.)
appoggiatura (It.)

nenia (E., It., Sp.)
*lament
nénie (Fr.)
Klagelied (G.)

neoclassicism
16c. humanism
20c. modernism
contemporary music

neue Musik (G.)
new music
contemporary music
modern music
new age
new wave
Ars Nova (Lat. 14c.)
musicum novum (Lat.)
musica nova (It.)
nuove musiche (It.)
musique nouvelle (Fr.)
avant-garde (Fr.)
nueva música (Sp.)

vs. alte Musik (G.)
Ars Antiqua (Lat.)
musica antiqua (Lat.)

neumatic chant
slightly ornamented

vs. syllabic chant
melismatic chant

neume (chant)
note
square note
group of notes
ligature
figure
neuma (Lat.)
figura (Lat.)
punctum (Lat.)

neupma (Lat.)
cauda (Lat. 13c.)

coda
tag
epilogue
exitus (Lat.)
codetta (It.)
partie finale (Fr.)
envoi, envoy (Fr.)
Koda (G.)
Anhang (G.)
Schlussgruppe (G.)
cola (Sp.)

neuvième (Fr.)
ninth
compound second
nona, -o (It.)
None (G.)
novena (Sp.)

New Orleans jazz
Dixieland jazz
jazz combo
street band

Nicene creed
creed
credo (Lat.)
credo in unum Deo (Lat.)
mass section/movement
ordinary of the mass

nicht zu viel (G.)
not too much
non troppo/tanto (It.)
pas trop/tant (Fr.)
no demasiado (Sp.)

nickelodeon
*jukebox
music box
automatic record player
automatic turntable
juke-box (It., Fr.)
Musikbox (G.)
Musikautomat (G.)
tocadiscos automático (Sp.)

máquina de discos (Sp.)
tragaperras (Sp.)
rocola (Sp.)

2. automatic piano
player piano
mechanical piano
piano rolls
pianola (It.)
planchette (Fr.)
piano mécanique (Fr.)
automatisches Klavier (G.)
autopiano (Sp.)
piano automático (Sp.)
piano mecánico (Sp.)

3. movie theater
movies
cinema

nicolo (It.)
bombardon (17c.)
bombard
bombarde (Fr.)
bombarda (It., Sp.)
Bombard (G.)
bassoon
shawm
tenor shawm
Basspommer (G.)
basset Pommer (G.)
tenor Pommer (G.)

Niederschlag (G.)
*downbeat
first beat of a measure
thesis (Gr.)
crusis (Lat.)
abbattimento (It.)
frappé (Fr.)
Abschlag (G.)

vs. Aufschlag (G.)

Nietenbecken (G.)
sizzle cymbals

rivet cymbals
  piatti chiodati (It.)
  cymbales sur tiges (Fr.)
  Sizzle-Becken (G.)
  Zischbecken (G.)
  cimbales sobre palillos (Sp.)

night club
  cabaret
  night spot
  cocktail lounge
  discothèque (Fr.)
  disco
  dance club
  supper club
  boîte de nuit (Fr.)
  locale notturno (It.)
  ritrovo notturno (It.)
  Nachtklub (G.)
  Nachtlokal (G.)
  café-cantante (Sp.)

Night Song
  compline
  office
  night office
  canonical hours
  *Divine office
  completorium (Lat.)
  compieta (It.)
  complies (Fr.)
  Komplet (G.)
  completas (Sp.)

nineteenth (interval)
  larigot (Fr.)
  1 1/3 foot stop (organ)
  mutation stop
  overtone

ninnananna (It.)
  lullaby
  cradle song
  ninnerella (It.)
  berceuse (Fr.)
  dodinette, dodo, dodino (Fr.)

Wiegenlied (G.)
Schlummerlied (G.)
nana (Sp.)
arrullo (Sp.)
canción de cuna (Sp.)

niños de coro (Sp.)
  choristers
  *choirboys
  cantori (It.)
  putti (It.)
  ragazzi (It.)
  choriste (Fr.)
  enfants de choeur (Fr.)
  Chorknaben (G.)
  Kapellknaben (G.)
  escolán (Sp.)

ninth (interval, chord)
  compound second
  nona, -o (It.)
  neuvième (Fr.)
  None (G.)
  novena (Sp.)

nocturn
  Matins section
  *Divine office
  Night Hours
  horae nocturnae (Lat.)
  nocturnae orationes (Lat.)

nocturne (Fr., E.)
  evening song/music
  serenade
  notturno (It.)
  serenata (It.)
  Nachtmusik (G.)
  Abendlied, Abendmusik (G.)
  Nachtstück (G.)
  Ständchen (G.)
  nocturno (Sp.)
  instrumental piece

node (on a string)
  harmonics touch point

partials
overtones
nodule
nodus, nodulus (Lat.)
nodo (It.)
noeud (Fr.)
Knote, Knotenpunkt (G.)
nudo (Sp.)

node (on the vocal chords)
  injury
  strain
  swelling
  enlargement
  growth

noeud (Fr.)
  turn
  ornament
  grace notes
  gruppetto, groppo, gruppo (It
  groupe (Fr.)
  tour de Gosier (Fr.)
  doublé (Fr.)
  brisé (Fr.)
  double cadence (Fr.)
  Doppelschlag (G.)
  Halbzirkel (G.)
  grupeto, grupito (Sp.)

2. *node
  *harmonics

noel, nowell
  Christmas carol
  canzona di Natale (It.)
  natalizio (It.)
  chant de noël (Fr.)
  cantique de noël (Fr.)
  noël, noé, nouel (Fr.)
  Weinachtslied (G.)
  Quempas (G.)
  cántico de Navidad (Sp.)
  villancico (Sp.)
  zéjel (Sp.)

noire (Fr.)
  quarter note
  crotchet
  nera (It.)
  quarto (It.)
  semiminima (It.)
  Viertel, Virtelnote (G.)
  schwarze Note (G.)
  negra (Sp.)
  semínima (Sp.)

nolae (Lat.)
  small *bells
  pellet bells
  jingle bells
  harness bellss
  sanctus bells
  altar bells
  tintinnabulae (Lat.)
  campanae (Lat.)
  campanelli (It.)
  nolettes (Fr.)
  grelots (Fr.)
  Cimbelstern (G.)
  Zimbelstern (G.)
  Schelle (G.)
  cascabels (Sp.)

non-harmonic tone
  altered tones
  chromatic notes
  half-steps
  accidentals

2. passing tone
  neighbor note
  auxiliary tone
  appoggiatura (It.)
  mordent
  cambiata (It.)
  échappée (Fr.)

non-legato (It.)
  *detatched
  staccato (It.)
  spiccato (It.)

délié (Fr.)
détaché (Fr.)
abgestossen (G.)
no ligado (Sp.)
destacado (Sp.)

non troppo (It.)
not too much
non tanto (It.)
pas trop (Fr.)
pas tant (Fr.)
nicht zuviel (G.)
no demasiado (Sp.)
no mucho (Sp.)
no tanto (Sp.)

nona, -o (It.)
  ninth (interval, chord)
  compound second
  neuvième (Fr.)
  None (G.)
  novena (Sp.)

nondiastematic notation
  staffless neumes (chant)
  in campo aperto (It.)
  cheironomic
  ekphonetic, ecphonetic
  oratorical
  adiastematic

none
  hours of the day
  fifth of the canonical hours
  ninth hour
  *Divine Office
  monastic office
  nona (Lat., It., Sp.)
  None (G.)

nonet
  work for nine musicians
  nonetto (It.)
  nonette (Fr.)
  Nonett (G.)
  noneto (Sp.)

Nonnengeige (G.)
  trumpet marine
  marine trumpet
  nun's-fiddle
  tromba marina (It.)
  trompette marine (Fr.)
  Trumscheit (G.)

normalmente (Sp.)
  bell down (horn)
  posizione normale (It.)
  position naturelle (Fr.)
  natürlich (G.)

vs. pabellón al aire (Sp.)

Normalton (G.)
  international pitch
  classical pitch
  low pitch
  French pitch
  diapason normal (Fr.)
  Franzton (G.)
  diapasón normal (Sp.)
  diapasón de bajo (Sp.)

nota cambiata (It.)
  *cambiata
  ornament
  escape note
  changing note
  non-harmonic tone
  échapée (Fr.)
  note de rechange (Fr.)
  Wechselnote (G.)
  nota cambiada (Sp.)

nota di passaggio (It.)
  passing tone/note
  auxiliary tone
  non-harmonic unaccented tone
  note de passage (Fr.)
  Durchgangsnote (G.)
  Durchgangston (G.)
  nota de paso (Sp.)
  pièn-tone

nota di recitazione (It.)
reciting note/tone
dominant
tenor
tuba (Lat., It., E.)
nota dominans (Lat.)
recto tono (Lat.)
repercussio (Lat.)
teneur (Fr.)
Tenor (G.)

nota fundamentale (It., Sp.)
pedal tone
fundamental tone
first harmonic
pedaltono (It.)
ton de pédale (Fr.)
note fondamentale (Fr.)
Pedalton (G.)

nota pedal (Sp.)
drone
pedal note
pedal point
organ point
pedale (It., Sp.)
pédale (Fr.)
point d'orgue (Fr.)
Orgelpunkt (G.)
bajo de órgano (Sp.)
organum
bagpipe

nota puntata (It.)
dotted note
pricked note
note pointé (Fr.)
punktierte Note (G.)
nota con puntillo (Sp.)

nota sensibile (It.)
leading tone
7th note of the scale
ti, si
subtonic
sensibile (It.)

note sensible (Fr.)
Leitton (G.)
sensible nota (Sp.)

notación cuadrada (Sp.)
square notation
quadratic notation
chant notation
plainsong notation
Gregorian notation
Aquitanian notation
neumes
nota Romana (It.)
nota quadrata (It.)
notazione quadrata (It.)
note/notation carrée (Fr.)
Quadratnotenschrift (G.)
Quadratnotation (G.)
notación Gregoriana (Sp.)

notation (E., Fr.)
written music
notes and rests
tablature
notatio (Lat.)
notazione (It.)
semeiografia (It.)
séméographie (Fr.)
Tonschrift (G.)
Notenschrift (G.)
notación (Sp.)

note (E., Fr.)
musical sign/sound
neume
ligature
*tone
pitch
figura (Lat., It.)
nota (It., Sp.)
tono, tuono (It.)
sono, suono (It.)
ton (Fr.)
son (Fr.)
Note (G.)
Tonzeichen (G.)

Klang (G.)

note-against-note
simple counterpoint
first species counterpoint
homophonic
homorhythmic
note-for-note
punctus contra punctum (Lat.)
Note-gegen-Note (G.)
nota contre nota (It., Sp.)
suono contro suono (It.)
point-contre-point (Fr.)
note-contre-note (Fr.)

note de pédale (Fr.)
pedal point
pedal note
organ point
drone bass
organum
bagpipes
pedal d'armonia (It.)
pédale (Fr.)
point d'orgue (Fr.)
Orgelpunkt (G.)
nota de pedal (Sp.)
bajo de organo (Sp.)

note head
capocchia (It.)
testina (It.)
tête de la note (Fr.)
Notenkopf (G.)
cabeza de las notas (Sp.)
punto de las notas (Sp.)

Notenbalken (G.)
beam
cross-bar
tratto d'unione (It.)
stanghetta (It.)
barre transversale (Fr.)
barre de liaison (Fr.)
barre horizontale (Fr.)
Balken (G.)

Querbalken (G.)
Balkenverbindung (G.)
barra de compás (Sp.)

Notenblätter (G.)
sheet music
folio
partitions (Fr.)
música en hojas (Sp.)

Notenpapier (G.)
music paper
*staff paper
carta da musica (It.)
carta rigata (It.)
carta pentagrammato (It.)
papier à musique (Fr.)
liniertes Papier (G.)
pautada (Sp.)
papel de música (Sp.)

Notensystem (G.)
staff, stave
five-line staff
four-line staff (chant)
pentagramma (It.)
rigo musicale (It.)
portée musicale (Fr.)
Liniensystem (G.)
pentagrama (Sp.)

Notenwert (G.)
time value
duration
length of a note/rest
valor (Lat., Sp.)
valore (It.)
valeur (Fr.)
Wert (G.)

notes inégales (Fr.)
unequal notes
ungleiche Noten (G.)

Notre Dame school (10-12c.)
organum

tropes
sequences
St. Martial school

Notre Père (Fr.)
Lord's Prayer
Our Father
Pater Noster (Lat.)
Paternoster (It.)
Vaterunser (G.)
Padre Nuestro (Sp.)

notturno (It.)
nocturne
evening serenade

2. serenade
serenata (It.)
divertimento (It.)
cassation
suite

novena (Sp.)
ninth (interval)
nona (It.)
neuvième (Fr.)
None (G.)

nowell
Christmas carol
noel
natalizio (It.)
canzona di natale (It.)
chant de noël (Fr.)
cantique de noël (Fr.)
Quempas (G.)
Weinachtslied (G.)
villancico (Sp.)
cántico de navidad (Sp.)
zéjel (Sp.)

nuance (E., Fr.)
shading
inflection
ombra (It.)
sfumatura (It.)

graduare (It.)
abstufen (G.)
matizar (Sp.)

nueva música (Sp.)
new music
contemporary music
modern music
avant-garde
new age
new wave
Ars Nova (Lat.)
musicum novum (Lat.)
musica nova (It.)
nuova musiche (It.)
musique nouvelle (Fr.)
neue Musik (G.)

vs. música antigua (Sp.)

number opera
operetta
light opera
opéra comique (Fr.)
Singspiel (G.)
Nummeroper (G.)

Nunc Dimittis (Lat.)
Song of Simeon
Canticle of Simeon
Evensong
Vespers
Canticum Simeonis (Lat.)

nuptual mass
wedding ceremony/mass
missa nuptualis (Lat.)
messa nuziale (It.)
messe de mariage (Fr.)
messe nuptuale (Fr.)
Hochzeitsmesse (G.)
misa de relaciones (Sp.)
misa de esposales (Sp.)

nuptual song
wedding song

bridal song
epithalamy
epithalamion (Gr.)
epithalamium (Lat., E.)
epitalamio (It., Sp.)
canto nuziale (It.)
chanson de noce (Fr.)
épithalame (Fr.)
Brautlied (G.)
canto nupcial (Sp.)

nut
    frog (of a bow)
    hausse (Fr.)
    talon (IFr.)
    Frosch (G.)

vs. point
    tip

2. (on the fingerboard)
    saddle
    capotasto (It.)
    sella (It.)
    sillet (Fr.)
    Sattel (G.)
    ceja, cejilla (Sp.)

nylon string
    *gut string
    catgut

vs. steel string

nymphale (Fr.)
    *portative organ (16c.)

O

O antiphons
Great Antiphons
*Magnificat
vespers

o bien (Sp.)
alternate
another way
ossia (It.)
ov(v)ero (It.)
ou bien (Fr.)
oder (G.)

obbligato (It.)
neccessary part
required
obligé (Fr.)
Obligat (G.)
obligado (Sp.)

vs. ad libitum (Lat.)
a piacere (It.)

Oberdominante (G.)
dominant
sol
fifth note of the scale
dominante (Fr., It., Sp.)
Dominante (G.)

Oberstimme (G.)
*descant
counter melody
hymn
discanto (It.)
déchant (Fr.)
Diskant (G.)

Obertasten (G.)
*black keys of the piano
sharps and flats
tasto nero (It.)
touche noir (Fr.)
feintes (Fr.)
Halbtotaste (G.)
schwarze Obertasten (G.)
tecla negra (Sp.)

v vs. Untertasten (G.)
white keys.

Oberwerk (G. organ)
clavier de récit (Fr.)
swell division, choir organ, or
solo division
récit (Fr.)
Schwellwerk (G.)
Brustwerk (G.)

oblique motion
contrary motion
motus obliquus (Lat.)
moto obliquo (It.)
mouvement oblique (Fr.)
Seitenbewegung (G.)
movimiento oblicuo (Sp.)

oboe (E., It.)
double-reed
hautboy, hoboy
shawm
Schalmei (G.)
aulos (Gr.)
diaulos (Gr.)
kalamos (Gr.)
calamus (Lat.)
tibia (Lat.)
crumhorn
English horn
haubois (Fr.)
chalumeau (Fr.)
Oboe (G.)
óboe (Sp.)
caramillo (Sp.)
tiple (Sp.)
chirimía (Sp.)

oboe d'amore (It.)
oboe da caccia (It.)

obra (Sp.)
opus (Lat.)
work, numbered work
*composition
piece
number
movement
excerpt
pezzo (It.)
opera (It.)
oeuvre (Fr.)
pièce (Fr.)
Werk (G.)
Stück (G.)
pieza (Sp.)
trozo (Sp.)

ocarina (E., It., Fr., Sp.)
oval whistle-flute
sweet potato
duct flute
fipple flute
Okarina (G.)
recorder
flageolet
flutophone
tonette

occhiali (It.)
Alberti bass
Brillenbässe (G.)
broken chords
*arpeggio (It.)
batterie (Fr.)
bariolage (Fr.)
Albertischer Bass (G.)
rasgado, rasgueado (Sp.)

vs. accordo incollato (It.)
concento (It.)

occitatio (Lat.)
hocket

broken note
interrupted melody
truncatio (Lat.)
hoquetus, hoquetatio (Lat.)
ochetus (Lat.)
ochetto (It.)
ho(c)quet (Fr.)
Hoketus (G.)
hoquet (Sp.)

occlusiva glottale (It.)
glottal stop
glottal catch
glottale (It.)
coup de glotte (Fr.)
Kehlschlag (G.)
Kehlverschlusslaut (G.)
Knacklaut (G.)
Stimmritzenverschlusslaut (G.)
Glottisschlag (G.)

occursus (Lat.)
organum at the 4 th (9-10c.)
converging organum
parallel organum

octave (E., Fr.)
eighth (interval)
diapason (Lat.)
antiphonia (Gr.)
ottava (It.)
Oktav(e) (G.)
octava (Sp.)

2. 4-foot stop (organ)

octave courte (Fr.)
short octave (org.)
broken octave
incomplete stop
partial stop
mi re ut (It.)
kurze Oktave (G.)
octava corta (Sp.)

octave flute

piccolo (E., It., Fr.)
piccolo flute
fife
ottavino (It.)
flautino (It.)
flauto piccolo (It.)
petite flûte (Fr.)
kleine Flöte (G.)
Pickelflöte, Pikkoloflöte (G.)
Oktavflöte (G.)
flautin (Sp.)

octave species
diatonic scale
mode

octave-string (on a banjo)
drone
*chanterelle (Fr.)
organ point
pedal point

octavier (Fr.)
overblow (on wind instr.)
overtones
partials
harmobics
ottavizzare (It.)
überblasen (G.)
octavar (Sp.)

octavo music
choral music (printed)
music for choirs
sheet music
vocal music
folio size
quarto (Lat.)

octet
ensemble of eight
ottetto (It.)
octette (Fr.)
octuor (Fr.)
Oktett (G.)
octeto (Sp.)

octobasse (Fr.)
contrabass
doublebass
*bass
octo-bass
basse gigantique (Fr.)

oda continua (Lat.)
through-composed
open form
a forma aperta (It.)
de forme ouverte (Fr.)
durchkomponiert (G.)
compuesto de principio a fin
(Sp.)

Oddonic notation (10th c.)
letter notation
solmization
Odoistic notation
Boethian notation
Daseian notation
Guidonian letters/hand

ode (Lat., E., It., Fr.)
lyric poem
hymn
paean
anthem
canticle
cantata
oratorio
Ode (G.)
oda (Lat., Sp.)

oder (G.)
alternatively
otherwise
or
ossia (It.)
ovvero (It.)
ou bien (Fr.)
o bien (Sp.)

oeuvre (Fr.)
work

composition
opus (Lat.)
opera (It.)
Werk (G.)
obra (Sp.)

off-beat
syncopated
jazzy
contrattempo (It.)
alla zoppa (It.)
contretemps (Fr.)
syncopé(e) (Fr.)
Gegenzeit (G.)
synkopiert (G.)

off-key
out of tune
flat/sharp
off-pitch
scordato (It.)
stonato (It.)
faux, fausse (Fr.)
désacordé (Fr.)
unrein (G.)
falsch (G.)
verstimmt (G.)
unrichtig (G.)
falso (Sp., It.)

vs. in tune

offene Quintenparallelen (G.)
open fifth/triad
naked fifth
empty fifths
leere Quinten (G.)

offene Saite (G.)
open string
unstopped string
corda vuota (It.)
corde à vide (Fr.)
corde à jour (Fr.)
leere Saite (G.)
cuerda al aire (Sp.)

vs. Griffbrettsaiten (G.)
stopped strings

offertory
Mass Proper
Mass movement
psalm for presentation of gifts
during Mass
offertorium (Lat.)
offerenda (Lat. Ambrosian)
sonus (Gallican)
sacrificium (Lat. Mozarabic)
offertorio (It.)
offertoire (Fr.)
ofertorio (Sp.)

Office
monastic office
*Divine Office
daily office
canonical hours
hours of the day
morning/evening prayer
Opus Dei (Lat.)
horae canonicae (Lat.)

offstage
*backstage
behind the scenes
in the wings
retroscena (It.)
en coulisse (Fr.)
hinter den Kulissen (G.)
entre bastidores (Sp.)

oficio parvo (Sp.)
Little Office
Little Hours
minor hours
prime, terce, sext, none
day hours
monastic office
*Divine Office
Opus Dei (Lat.)
oficio (Sp.)
Santo Oficio (Sp.)

oficio rimado (Sp.)
rhymed office
*Divine Office
Reimoffizium (G.)

ohne Dämpfer (G.)
mutes off
remove mutes
take off mutes
levate i sordini (It.)
togliere la sordina (It.)
senza sordina (It.)
tutte (le) corde (It.)
senza sordini (It.)
toutes les cordes (Fr.)
ôter la sourdine (Fr.)
sans sourdine (Fr.)
alle Saiten (G.)
Dämpfer weg/ab/absetzen (G.)
Dämpfer abheben/abnehmen (G.)
todas las cuerdas (Sp.)
retirar la sordina (Sp.)
levanten la sordina (Sp.)
sin sordina (Sp.)

vs. mit Dämpfer (G.)

ohne Instrumente (G.)
a cappella (It.)
unaccompanied
sans instruments (Fr.)
style de chapelle (Fr.)
im Kapellstil (G.)
a capilla (Sp.)
música vocal (Sp.)

vs. mit Begleitung (G.)

Ohrenquinten (G.)
parallel fifths
hidden fifths
covered fifths
horn fifths
Hornquinten (G.)
verdeckte Quinten (G.)

oído (Sp.)
ear
orecchio (It.)
oreille (Fr.)
Ohr (G.)
oreja (Sp.)

oído absoluto (Sp.)
absolute pitch
perfect pitch
true pitch
orecchio assoluto (It.)
oreille absolue (Fr.)
absolutes Gehör (G.)

vs. oído relativo (Sp.)

oído relativo (Sp.)
relative pitch
orecchio relativo (It.)
oreille relative (Fr.)
relatives Gehör (G.)

vs. oído absoluto (Sp.)

oioueae
world without end amen
Glory be
Lesser Doxology
Gloria Patri (Lat.)
Euouae (Lat.)
evovae (Lat.)
aeuia, aevia (Lat.)
endings (psalm chants)
terminations
distinctio (Lat.)
differentia (Lat.)
saeculorum amen (Lat.)

Oktave (G.)
*octave
8va

old-time music
traditional music
folk music

mountain music
hillbilly music
bluegrass music
country music

olio
*medley
musical miscellany
revue
musicale
vaudeville
minstrel show
follies
potpourri
quodlibet
salmagundi, -y
overture
suite

oliphant, olifant (Fr.)
cor d'olifant (Fr.)
horn of ivory
bugle
elephant horn/tusk
Signalhorn (G.)
olifante (It., Sp.)
Olifant (G.)
ram's horn
Gemshorn (G.)
Shofar (Heb.)

ombra (It.)
nuance(E., Fr.)
shading
inflection
sfumatura (It.)
graduare (It.)
abstufen (G.)
matizado (Sp.)

omnes, omnia (Lat.)
all everyone
tutti (It.)
tous (Fr.)
Alle(s) (G.)
todos (Sp.)

omofonia (It.)
homophony
harmonized melody
homophonie (Fr.)
Homophonie (G.)
homofonia (Sp.)

vs. polyphonia (It.)

on the air
broadcasting
radio
over the airways
television
cable
satellite
wireless
trasmissione (It.)
radiodiffusione (It.)
émission (Fr.)
radiodiffusion (Fr.)
Rundfunk (G.)
Sendung (G.)
emisión (Sp.)
radiodifusión (Sp.)

vs. off the air

on the bridge (strings)
near the bridge
sul ponticello (It.)
au chevalet (Fr.)
près du chevalet (Fr.)
am Steg (G.)
sobre el puentecillo (Sp.)

oncena (Sp.)
eleventh (interval, chord)
undicesima -o (It.)
undecimo (It., Sp.)
onzième (Fr.)
Undezime (G.)

ondeggiando (It.)
tremolo (strings)
undulating effect

*bariolage (Fr.)
ondulé (Fr.)
bariolage (Fr.)
tremblant (Fr.)
Bebung (G.)

Ondes Martenot (Fr.)
electronic music
electrophone
Ondes Musicales (Fr.)
Ondium Martenot
theremin
synthesizer
*musique concrète (Fr.)

one-foot stop (organ)
sifflöte (G.)
sifflet (Fr.)

one-line C
middle C
do sotto di rigo (It.)
do du milieu du piano (Fr.)
eingestrichenes C (G.)
do medio (Sp.)
do central (Sp.)

onion flute
mirliton (Fr.)
flûte à l'oignon (Fr.)
flûte eunuque (Fr.)
Zwiebelflöte (G.)
flauta eunuco (Sp.)
flauta cebolla (Sp.)
mirlitón (Sp.)
eunuch flute
toy flute
kazoo, bazoo

onzième (Fr.)
eleventh (interval, chord)
undicesimo –a (It.)
undecimo (It., Sp.)
Undezime (G.)

open (cadence, ending)

first ending
half- cadence
semi-cadence
apertum (Lat.)
aperto (It.)
prima volta (It.)
ouvert (Fr.)
offen (G.)
Halbschluss (G.)

vs. clos (Fr.)
clausum (Lat.)
closed

open diapason
foundation stop (organ)
principal
montre (Fr.)
prestante (It.)
prestant (Fr.)
Prinzipal (G.)
Hauptstimme (G.)

open fifth (interval, triad)
incomplete triad
empty fifth
naked fifth
offene Quintenparallelen (G.)
leere Quinte (G.)

open form
through-composed
progressive composition
a forma aperta (It.)
de forme ouverte (Fr.)
durchkomponiert (G.)
compuesto de principio a fin
(Sp.)

open harmony
open position
open chord
open triad
wide spacing
offene Dreiklang (G.)
leere Dreiklang (G.)

vs. close position/spacing
close harmony
barbershop harmony

open note
white note
half/whole note

2. harmonic
overtone
partial
open tone

3. open string
unstopped string
leere Saite (G.)

4. unstopped horn tone
*Naturtöne (G.)

open pipe (organ)
canna aperto (It.)
offene Pfeife (G.)
tuyau ouvert (Fr.)
tubo abierto (Sp.)

vs. stopped pipe

open score
conducting score
full score
partitura, partizione (It.)
sparta, spartito –a, spartitura
(It.)
partition (Fr.)
grande partition (Fr.)
Partitur (G.)

vs. close score
condensed score
reduction

open string
unstopped string
open note
corda vuota (It.)

corde à jour (Fr.)
corde à vide (Fr.)
leere Saite (G.)
offene Saite (G.)
cuerda al aire (Sp.)

vs. stopped string

opera
grand opera
lyric opera
music drama
concert opera
dramma per musica (It.)
opera seria (It.)
opera per drammatico (It.)
dramma lirico (It.)
azione teatrale (It.)
melodramma (It., 17c.)
drame lyrique (Fr.)
tragédie en musique (Fr.)
tragédie lyrique (Fr.)
opéra (Fr.)
Oper (G.)
Musikdrama (G.)
grosse Oper (G.)
ópera (Sp.)
ópera cómico (Sp.)
zarzuela (Sp.)
verismo (It.)
bel canto (It.)
operetta
masque
ballad opera
folk opera
light opera
opérette (Fr.)
Operette (G.)
Singspiel (G.)
Spieldose (G.)
komische Oper (G.)
opéra comique (Fr.)
opera buffo (It.)
opéra bouffe (Fr.)
Oper (G.)
obra (Sp.)

opéra-ballet (Fr.)
ballet
ballet de cour (Fr.)
ballo (It.)
Ballett-Oper (G.)

opera house
lyric theatre
auditorium
academy of music
*concert hall
teatro lirico (It.)
opéra (Fr.)
Opernhaus (G.)
teatro de la ópera (Sp.)

opera singer
diva (It.)
prima donna (It.)
volal artist
soloist
cantatrice (It., Fr.)
divette (Fr.)
Sängerin (G.)
cantatriz (Sp.)

ophicléide (Fr., E.)
tuba
keyed bugle/horn
Kent bugle
officleide (It.)
cimbasso (It.)
basse d'harmonie (Fr.)
bombardon (Fr.)
bugle à clés (Fr.)
Ophikleide (G.)
Klappenhorn (G.)
figle (Sp.)

opposite motion
contrary motion
inversion
motus contrarius (Lat.)
moto contrario (It.)
a rovescio (It.)
mouvement contraire (Fr.)

Gegenbewegung (G.)
movimiento contrario (Sp.)

vs. parallel motion

opus (Lat.)
piece
*composition
work
number
selection
pezzo (It.)
opera (It.)
oeuvre (Fr.)
morceau (Fr.)
Werk (G.)
Stück (G.)
obra (Sp.)
pieza (Sp.)

Opus Dei (Lat.)
*Divine Office
monastic office
daily office
canonical hours
morning/evening prayers
hours of the day
rhymed office

or, or else
alternatively
otherwise
ossia (It.)
ovvero (It.)
ou bien (Fr.)
oder (G.)
o bien (Sp.)

oratio (Lat.)
prayer
collect
oration
preces (Lat.)
*litany
suffrages
oremus (Lat.)

colletta (It.)
orazione (It.)
collecte (Fr.)
Tagesgebet (G.)
colecta (Sp.)
oración (Sp.)

oratorical neumes
staffless neumes
in campo aperto (It.)
cheironomic notation
nondiastematic notation
adiastematic notation
ekphonetic, ecphonetic

oratorio (E., Fr., Sp.)
cantata
opera
Passion
Crucifixion
azione sacra (It.)
oratorium (Lat.)
sacra rappresentazione (It.)
sacro per musica It.)
Oratorium (G.)

oratorio society
choral society
community chorus/chorale
civic chorale
symphonic choir
philharmonic chorus
societá corale (It.)
société chorale (Fr.)
Gesangverein (G.)
Singakademie (G.)
orfeón (Sp.)

orchestra (E., It.)
instrumental ensemble
band
symphony orchestra
philharmonic orchestra
concert orchestra
community orchestra
orchestre (Fr.)

Orchester (G.)
orquesta (Sp.)

2. main seating section
floor seats
orchestra circle
parterre (E., Fr., It., Sp.)
parquet

orchestra bells
*bells
chimes
glockenspiel

orchestra leader
*conductor
maestro
director
maestro di cappella (It.)
capo d'orchestra (It.)
chef d'orchestre (Fr.)
Kappelmeister (G.)
Dirigent (G.)
Leiter (G.)
director de orquesta (Sp.)

orchestra pit
buca dell'orchestra (It.)
fossa orchestrale (It.)
fosse d'orchestre (Fr.)
Orchestergraben (G.)
foso de orquesta (Sp.)
foso orquestrale (Sp.)

orchestral chimes
tubular bells
chimes
clock chimes
campane tubolari (It.)
cloches tubulaires (Fr.)
Röhrenglocken (G.)
campanólogo (Sp.)

orchestration (E., Fr.)
scoring
bandstration

instrumentation
orchestrazione (It.)
Orchestrierung (G.)
orquestración (Sp.)
instrumentación (Sp.)

orden (Sp.)
*course of strings (lute, etc.)
double course
coro (It., Sp.)
choeur (Fr.)
cours (Fr.)
ordre (Fr.)
jeu (Fr.)
Chor (G.)
Saiten (G.)
Saitenchor (G.)

ordinarium missae (Lat.)
common of the mass
ordinary of the mass

vs. proprium missae (Lat.)
proper of the mass

ordinary time
common time (4/4)
common measure
duple meter
*binary measure
tempo ordinario (It.)
passo ordinario (It.)
mouvement ordinaire (Fr.)
movimiento ordinario (Sp.)
Zweiertakt (G.)
Viervieltakt (G.)

vs. cut time

2. liturgically less important part
of the church year
Sundays after Pentecost until
Advent
Sundays after Epiphany until
Lent

ordo (Lat.)
  liturgy (7-9c.)
  Ordo Romanus (Lat.)
  ordo missae (Lat.)
  rite, ritual
  rubrics
  ceremony
  calendar

ordre (Fr.)
  suite
  partita
  serenade
  cassation
  divertimento (It.)
  divertissement (Fr.)
  divertimiento (Sp.)

2. *course (strings)
  coro (It., Sp.)
  choeur (Fr.)
  Saitenchor (G.)
  *orden (Sp.)

orecchio (It.)
  ear
  oreille (Fr.)
  Ohr (G.)
  oído (Sp.)
  oreja (Sp.)

orecchio assoluto (It.)
  absolute pitch
  perfect pitch
  true pitch
  oreille absolue (Fr.)
  absolutes Gehör (G.)
  oído absoluto (Sp.)

vs. orecchio relativo (It.)

orecchio relativo (It.)
  relative pitch
  oreille relative (Fr.)
  relatives Gehör (G.)
  oído relativo (Sp.)

vs. orecchio assoluto (It.)

oremus (Lat.)
  prayer
  collect
  oration
  litany
  suffrages
  *oratio (Lat.)
  orationes (Lat.)

orfeón (Sp.)
  choral society
  oratorio society
  chorale
  chorus
  community chorus
  philharmonic choir
  symphonic choir
  associazione corale (It.)
  societá di canto (It.)
  société chorale (Fr.)
  Kantorei (G.)
  Gesangverein (G.)
  Singakademie (G.)

organ
  pipe organ
  King of instruments
  re degli instrumenti (It.)
  roi des instruments (Fr.)
  Königin der Instrumente (G.)
  rey de los instrumentos (Sp.)
  organum (Lat.)
  organo (It.)
  orgue (Fr.)
  Orgel (G.)
  órgano (Sp.)
  calliope
  electric/electronic organ
  theatre organ
  positive organ
  portative organ
  chamber organ
  organetto (It.)
  reed organ

regal
hydraulos (Gr.)
barrel organ
street organ

2. division of the organ
  manual, pedal
  great organ/division
  swell organ
  choir organ
  solo organ
  pedal organ
  chair organ
  nave organ
  echo organ

organ case
  casework
  cassa dell'organo (It.)
  buffet (Fr.)
  Gehäuse (G.)
  Orgelkasten (G.)

organ chorale
  organ prelude
  voluntary
  organ hymn/ mass
  Choralvorspiel (G.)
  Orgelchoral (G.)

organ crawl
  visits of several organs
  organ demonstrations

organ-grinder
  street-organ player
  sonatore d'organetto (It.)
  joueur d'orgue de Barbarie
(Fr.)
  Leiermann (G.)

organ mass
  alternatim mass
  antiphonal (choir vs. organ)
  organ hymn
  Orgelmesse (G.)

organ metal
    pipe metal (lead and tin)
    tin metal
    common metal
    plain metal
    spotted metal

organ pipe
    canna d'organo (It.)
    tuyau d'orgue (Fr.)
    Pfeife (G.)
    Orgelpfeife (G.)
    tubo (Sp.)
    caño (Sp.)

organ pitch
    choir pitch
    church pitch
    tuono corista (It.)
    corista di coro (It.)
    Chorton (G.)
    Kapellton (G.)
    ton de chapelle (Fr.)
    ton de choeur (Fr.)

organ point
    pedal point
    pedal note
    drone bass
    organum
    bagpipes
    pedal d'armonia (It.)
    punto d'organo (It.)
    pédale (Fr.)
    point d'orgue (Fr.)
    note de pédale (Fr.)
    Orgelpunkt (G.)
    nota de pedal (Sp.)
    baja de organo (Sp.)

organetto (It.)
    portative organ
    regal
    chamber organ

2. barrel organ

    street organ
    hand organ
    *hurdy-gurdy
organistrum (Lat.)
    bird organ
organillo (Sp.)

organo da teatro (It.)
    theater organ
    cinema organ
    unified, unit organ
    extension organ
    duplexing
organo da cinematografo (It.)
    orgue de cinéma (Fr.)
    Kinoorgel (G.)
    Multiplexorgel (G.)
    órgano de cine (Sp.)

organo d'eco (It.)
    echo organ/division/manual
    gallery organ
    antiphonal organ
    nave organ
    clavier d'écho (Fr.)
    Fernwerk (G.)
    Echowerk, Echoklavier (G.)

organo di Barberia (It.)
    *barrel organ
    street organ
    *hurdy-gurdy
organo a manovella (It.)
    organetto (It.)
orgue de Barbarie (Fr.)
    Drehorgel (G.)
organillo (Sp.)

organo di campane (It.)
    *glockenspiel (G.)
    bell lyre
    orchestra bells
    campanette, campanelli (It.)
    carillon (Fr.)
    jeu de timbres (Fr.)

    Lyra (G.)
    juego de timbres (Sp.)

organo di coro (It.)
    choir organ/division/manual
    chair organ
    positive organ
    positif (Fr.)
    petit orgue (Fr.)
    positif de dos (Fr.)
    Unterwerk (G.)
    Chororgel (G.)
    Positiv im Stuhl (G.)
    Rückpositiv (G.)
    órgano de coro (Sp.)
    órgano positivo (Sp.)
    órgano de silla (Sp.)

organo di legno (It.)
    cabinet organ
    positive organ
    portative organ
    bible organ
    orgue positif/portatif (Fr.)
    Flötenwerk (G.)
    Positiv (G.)

2. xylophone
    gigelira (It.)
    sticcado pastorale (It.)
    sticcato (It.)
    harmonica de bois (Fr.)
    *claquebois (Fr.)
    armonoica de madera (Sp.)

organo espressivo (It.)
    swell organ/division/manual
    under expression
    clavier de récit (Fr.)
    récit expressif (Fr.)
    Schwellwerk (G.)

organo pieno/pleno (It.)
    full organ
    plein jeu (Fr.)
    grand choeur (Fr.)

volle Orgel (G.)
órgano lleno (Sp.)

organum (E., Lat.)
polyphony
drone
cantus firmus (Lat.)
discant
clausula (Lat.)
diaphony (Gr.)
Notre-Dame school

Orgel (G.)
*organ
King of Instruments
organum (Lat.)
organo (It.)
orgue (Fr.)
órgano (Sp.)

Orgelkasten (G.)
organ case
casework
cassa dell'organo (It.)
buffet (Fr.)
Gehäuse (G.)

Orgelpunkt (G.)
fermata
*corona

2. *organ point
pedal point

Orgelwalze (G.)
*barrel organ
street piano/organ
hurdy-gurdy
orgue à cilindre (Fr.)
orgue à manivelle (Fr.)
orgue de Barbarie (Fr.)
Drehorgel (G.)

orgue à vapeur (Fr.)
calliope
steam organ/piano

street organ
Dampforgel (G.)
órgano de vapor (Sp.)

orgue de paille (Fr.)
xylophone
straw fiddle
marimba
vibraharp
sticcato (It.)
gigelira (It.)
*claquebois (Fr.)
harmonica de bois (Fr.)
Strohfiedel (G.)
armonica de madera (Sp.)

orgue expressif (Fr.)
reed organ
*harmonium
organo d'espressione (It.)
Expressivorgel (G.)

orificio (Sp.)
fingerhole
buco (It.)
foro (It.)
trou (Fr.)
Griffloch (G.)
Tonloch (G.)
Fingerloch (G.)
agujera (Sp.)

original instruments
historical instruments
early instruments
period instruments
authentic instruments
old instruments
instruments origineaux (Fr.)
Originalinstrumenten (G.)

original version/edition
versione originale (It.)
version originale (Fr.)
Urtext (G.)
Originalausgabe (G.)

version primitiva (Sp.)

orlo (Sp.)
*crumhorn
cromorno (It., Sp.)
cormorne (Fr.)
Krummhorn (G.)

orlo (It.)
rim (of a drum)
bord (Fr.)
Rand (G.)
borde (Sp.)

ornament(s)
grace note
embellishment
decoration
effetti (It.)
abbellimento (It.)
fregiatura (It.)
ornamento (It., Sp.)
adornamento (It.)
agrément(s) (Fr.)
broderie (Fr.)
ornement (Fr.)
Verzierung (G.)
Zierraten, Ziernoten (G.)
adorno (Sp.)
decoración (Sp.)

ornamentation
decoration
embellishment
passage work
melismatic
rococo
elaboration
diminution
breaking (17c.)
diminutio (Lat.)
minuritio (Lat.)
coloratura (It.)
gorgia (It.)
passaggio (It.)
fioritura (It.)

fioretti (It.)
abbellimenti (It.)
broderie (Fr.)
roulade (Fr.)
battement (Fr.)
machicotage (Fr.)
Koloratur (G.)
glosa (Sp.)
differencia (Sp.)

orpharion
cittern
lyre
lute
cruit
rotta
*cithara (Lat.)

orphéon (Fr.)
glee club (men's)
men's choir/chorus
Apollo club
choral society
Liedertafel (G.)
Männergesangverein (G.)
barbershop chorus

orquestración (Sp.)
scoring
instrumentation
*orchestration
bandstration

oscillation
vibration
beating
cps's
Herz (G.)
frequency
pitch
sound

ossia (It.)
alternate version
or, otherwise
ov(v)ero (It.)

ou bien (Fr.)
oder (G.)
o bien (Sp.)

Ostersonntag (G.)
Easter Sunday
Resurrection Sunday
Dominica Resurrectionis (Lat.)
Pasqua (It.)
Dimanche de Pâques (Fr.)
Pascua florida (Sp.)
Pascua de Resurrección (Sp.)
Domingo de Resurrección (Sp.)
Domingo de Pasqua (Sp.)

ostinato (bass)
ground bass
strophic bass
strophic variations
chaconne
passacaglia
basso ostinato (It.)
folia (It.)
basse obstinée (Fr.)
basse constrainte (Fr.)
pes
variations
bajo obstinado (Sp.)

ôter la sourdine (Fr.)
remove mute
take off mute
mutes off
togliere la sordina (It.)
sans sourdine (Fr.)
*ohne Dämpfer (G.)
leventen la sordina (Sp.)

vs. avec sourdine (Fr.)

otra vez (Sp.)
*encore (E., Fr.)
repeat
once again
ancore (It.)

altra volta (It.)
bis (G., Lat., Fr.)
noch einmal (G.)

ottava (It.)
octave higher/lower
ottava alta/bassa (It.)
ottava sopra/sotto (It.)
octave supérieure/inférieure (Fr.)
octave du haut/du bas (Fr.)
obere/untere Oktav (G.)
hohe/tiefe Oktav (G.)

ottavina (It.)
spinet (at four ft.)
virginals
harpsichord
spinetta ottavina (It.)
spinettino (It.)
Oktavspenett (G.)

ottavino (It.)
octave flute
*piccolo (flute)
petite flûte (Fr.)
piccolo clarinet
Pikkolo (G.)
Oktavflöte (G.)

ottavizzare (It.)
overblow (on wind instr.)
overtones
partials
harmonics
octavier (Fr.)
überblasen (G.)
octavar (Sp.)

ottetto (It.)
octet
double quartet
octuor (Fr.)
octette (Fr.)
Oktet (G.)
octeto (Sp.)

303

ottoni, d'ottone (It.)
  brass instruments
  horns (jazz)
  cuivres (Fr.)
  Blechinstrumente (G.)
  metales (Sp.)

oud, ud
  lute
  theorbo
  guitar
  cittern
  archlute

ouïe (Fr.)
  sound-hole (on an instrument)
  F-hole
  effe (It.)
  F-Loch (G.)
  efe (Sp.)
  vido (Sp.)

Our Father
  Lord's Prayer
  Pater Noster (Lat.)
  Paternoster (It.)
  Notre Père (Fr.)
  Vaterunser (G.)
  Padre Nuestro (Sp.)

out of tune
  off-key
  off-pitch
  sharp/flat
  detuned
  stonare (It.)
  scordato (It.)
  détonner (Fr.)
  désaccordé (Fr.)
  falsch singen (G.)
  detonieren (G.)
  verstimmt (G.)
  desafinar (Sp.)

vs. in tune

outer voice/parts
  parte estrema (It.)
  partie extrême (Fr.)
  Aussenstimmen (G.)
  voz extrema (Sp.)
  parte extrema (Sp.)

vs. inner voices/parts

ouvert (Fr. 14c.)
  first ending
  apertum (Lat.)
  aperto (It.)
  prima volta (It.)
  offen (G.)
  abierto (Sp.)

vs. clos (Fr.)

ouvert (Fr.)
  unstopped (horn)
  open
  suoni aperti (It.)
  Naturtöne (G.)
  offene Töne (G.)
  abierto (Sp.)

vs. bouché (Fr.)

ovation
  applause
  accolades
  clapping
  standing ovation
  bravo (It.)
  applauso (It.)
  applaudissement (Fr.)
  Beifall (G.)
  aplauso (Sp.)

over the airways
  on the air
  *broadcasting
  telecasting
  radio, TV
  cable, satellite

  wireless
  trasmissione (It.)
  radiodiffusione (It.)
  radio diffusion (Fr.)
  émission (Fr.)
  Sendung (G.)
  Rundfunk (G.)
  emisión (Sp.)
  radiodifusión (Sp.)

vs. off the air

overblow (on wind instr.)
  harmonics
  partials
  nodes
  chord of nature
  overtones
  flageolet tones
  aliquot tones
  ottavizzare (It.)
  octavier (Fr.)
  octavar (Sp.)
  umschlagen (G.)
  überblasen (G.)

overtone(s)
  partials
  harmonics
  open note/tone
  chord of nature
  natural tones
  aliquot tones
  flageolet tones
  suoni armonici (It.)
  sons harmoniques (Fr.)
  Obertöne (G.)
  armónico (Sp.)
  tono parcial (Sp.)

overture
  prelude
  act-tune
  curtain tune/music
  intermezzo (It.)
  entr'acte (Fr.)

salmis (Fr.)
sinfonia (It.)
ovatura (It.)
ouverture (Fr.)
Ouvertüre (G.)
*medley
potpourri
salmagundi, -y
pastiche (Fr.)
olio
suite
French overture
Italian overture
olla podrida (Sp.)

ovvero (It.)
ossia (It.)
alternate passage
or
ou bien (Fr.)
oder (G.)
o bien (Sp.)

P

Päan (G.)
hymn of praise
paean
canticle
anthem
ode
lauda (It.)
peana (It.)
péan (Fr.)
Lobgesang (G.)
peán (Sp.)

pabellón al aire (Sp.)
bell in the air (horns)
campana in alto (It.)
padiglioni in alto (It.)
pavillon en l'air (Fr.)
Stürze hoch (G.)
Schalltrichter hoch (G.)

vs. **normalmente (Sp.)**
bell down

padiglione cinese (It.)
Chinese crescent
Turkish crescent
Chinese pavilion
jingling Johnny
Janissary music
cappello cinese (It.)
*chapeau Chinois (Fr.)
Schellenbaum (G.)
sombrero chino (Sp.)

padovana, padoana (It.)
pavane, pavenne (Fr.)
pavana (It., Sp.)
pavan, paven, pavin (E.)
passamezzo (It.)
padouenne (Fr.)

piva (It.)

Padre Nuestro (Sp.)
Our Father
Lord's Prayer
Pater Noster (Lat.)
Paternoster (It.)
Notre Père (Fr.)
Vaterunser (G.)

pageant
*liturgical drama
magi play
miracle play
mystery play
tomb play

pagina d'album (It.)
album-leaf
foglio d'album (It.)
feuillet d'album (Fr.)
Albumblatt (G.)
hoja de album (Sp.)

paired imitation
double imitation
imitation by pairs
imitazione a coppie (It.)
imitation double (Fr.)
paarweise Imitation (G.)
paarige Imitation (G.)
polyphony
counterpoint
*double counterpoint

palco della banda (It.)
bandstand
bandwagon
stage
platform
carro della banda musicale (It.)
kiosque à musique (Fr.)
Konzertpavillon (G.)
Musikpavillon (G.)
quiosco de música (Sp.)

plataforma con concha
acústica (Sp.)

Palestrina style
a cappella style
without accompaniment
unaccompanied
stile antico (It.)
stile osservato (It.)
style de chapelle (Fr.)
à la Palestrienne (Fr.)
im Kapellstil (G.)
Palestrina-Stil (G.)
música vocal (Sp.)
a capilla (Sp.)

vs. accompanied
with accompaniment

palette (Fr.)
white key (keyboard)
tasto bianco (It.)
touche blanche (Fr.)
weisse Taste (G.)
Untertaste (G.)
tecla blanca (Sp.)

vs. **feintes (Fr.)**
black keys

palillo (Sp.)
*drumstick
mallet
hammer
bacchetta (It.)
battente (It.)
baguette (Fr.)
mailloche (Fr.)
Schlegel (G.)
baqueta (Sp.)
macillo (Sp.)

Palm Sunday
Pascha competentium (Lat.)
Pascha floridum (Lat.)
Dominica in Palmis (Lat.)

Dominica capitilavium (Lat.)
Dominica florum (Lat.)
Dominica olivarum (Lat.)
Dominica Hosanna (Lat.)
Dominica Ramispalma (Lat.)
second Sunday of the Passion
*Holy Week
Domenica della palme (It.)
Dimanche des Rameaux (Fr.)
Palmsonntag (G.)
Domingo de Ramos (Sp.)

panderete (Sp.)
  *tambourine
  timbrel
  cimbalo, cimbaletto, -ino (It.)
  tamburino (It.)
  tamburo basco (It.)
  tambour de Basque (Fr.)
  Baskische Trommel (G.)
  Schellentrommel (G.)

pandora (16c.)
  guitar
  lute
  bandora, bandore

pandoura, pandura (Gr.)
  lute
  *archlute
  theorbo
  trichordon (Gr.)
  colascione (It.)
  chitarrone (It.)

panpipes
  pipes of Pan
  Pandean pipes
  mouth organ
  syrinx
  cicuta (Lat.)
  flauto di Pan (It.)
  siringa (It., Sp.)
  fistola (It.)
  flûte de Pan (Fr.)
  fretel, fretèle (Fr.)

sifflet de Pan (Fr.)
sifflet des chaudronniers (Fr.)
Panflöte (G.)
Papagenoflöte (G.)
flauta de Pan (Sp.)
flauta pánica (Sp.)

papel secundario (Sp.)
  supporting role
  minor role
  secondary part
  comprimario (It.)
  ruolo secondario (It.)
  rôle secondaire (Fr.)
  Nebenrolle (G.)

vs. parte principale (Sp.)

papier à musique (Fr.)
  music paper
  staff paper
  carta da musica (It.)
  portée musicale (Fr.)
  Notenpapier (G.)
  papel de música (Sp.)
  pautada (Sp.)
  papel pautado (Sp.)

par degré (Fr.)
  step-wise
  melodic
  di grado (It.)
  Stufenweise (G.)
  per grado (Sp.)

paradiddle
  drum stroke (snare drum)
  flam
  roll
  ruff, ruffle
  batterie (Fr.)
  Trommelschlag (G.)
  redoble (Sp.)

paraiso (Sp.)
  *balcony

gallery
peanut gallery
choir loft
il paradiso (It.)
galleria (It.)
gallerie (Fr.)
Galerie (G.)
galeria (Sp.)

parallel motion
  moto retto (It.)
  mouvement parallèle (Fr.)
  Parallelbewegung (G.)
  movimiento paralelo (Sp.)
  consecutive fifths, octaves

vs. contrary motion
  oblique motion

Paralleltonart (G.)
  relative key/mode
  tono relativo (It., Sp.)
  tono somigliante (It.)
  mode relatif (Fr.)
  verwandte Tonart (G.)
  clave paralela (Sp.)

vs. tonic major/minor
  parallel key

paraphrase
  parody (mass, motet)
  quote
  *arrangement
  variation

pardessus de viole (Fr.)
  descant (viol)
  viola da gamba (It.)
  quinton (Fr.)

parlando, parlante (It.)
  speaking style
  declamatory
  recitative
  patter song

parlato (It.)
en parlant (Fr.)
sprechend (G.)
redend (G.)
Sprechstimme (G.)
hablando (Sp.)

parlor grand
*grand piano
*baby grand
drawing-room grand
boudoir grand
pianoforte a coda intera (It.)
piano de boudoir (Fr.)
Salonflügel (G.)
piano de media cola (Sp.)

vs. upright piano

parlor organ
harmonium
reed organ
cabinet organ
pump organ
American organ
armonio (It., Sp.)

parody
paraphrase
trope
clausula (Lat.)
adaptation
*arrangement
use of borrowed material
parodia (It., Sp.)
Parodie (G.)
parodie (Fr.)

2. satire
caricature
take-off
spoof

parody mass
imitation mass
*arrangement

adaptation
modeled on
paraphrase
borrowed material
quote
contrafactum (Lat.)
missa parodia (Lat.)
messa parodia (It.)
parodie-messe (Fr.)
misa parodia (Sp.)
Parodiemesse (G.)

parole (Fr.)
text
words
libretto
script
parola (It.)
palabra (Sp.)
Wort (G.)

pars (Lat.)
part
section of a longer work
movement
division
phrase
excerpt
parte (It., Sp.)
partie (Fr.)
Teil (G.)
Satz, Absatz (G.)

2. voice
vox (Lat.)
voce (It.)
voix (Fr.)
Stimme (G.)
voz (Sp.)

part-leading
*voice-leading
condotta delle voci (It.)
conduite des voix/parties (Fr.)
Stimmführung (G.)
dirigiendo la voz (Sp.)

conducción de las voces/parte
(Sp.)

part-music
polyphony
harmony
part-song
concentus (Lat.)
madrigal
glee
chanson
chanson à parties (Fr.)
mehrstimmiges Lied (G.)
villancico (Sp.)
motet
anthem

partbook
voice-part
chorale (It.)
livre de choeur (Fr.)
Chorbuch (G.)
Stimmbuch (G.)

parterre (E., Fr., It.)
orchestra seats (theater)
orchestra circle
parquet circle
platea (It., Sp.)
Parquett (G.)
Parterre (G.)

Partie, Partia, Parthie (G.)
suite (17-18c.)
partita (It.)
variations

partie extrême (Fr.)
outer voice/part
parte estrema (It.)
Aussenstimme (G.)
parte extrema (Sp.)
voz extrema (Sp.)

vs. voix intermédiaire (Fr.)

partial
  overtone
  harmonic
  aliquot tone
  open note/tone
  flageolet tone
  natural tone
  flautato (It.)
  suoni armonici (It.)
  sons harmoniques (Fr.)
  Obertöne (G.)
  Teilton (G.)
  sónidos armónicos (Sp.)
  tono armónico (Sp.)

partial organ
  division
  manual

partial signature
  key signature
  conflicting signatures
  musica ficta (Lat.)

partial stop (organ)
  incomplete stop
  short octave
  broken octave
  mi re ut (It.)
  octave courte (Fr.)
  kurze Oktave (G.)
  octava corta (Sp.)

partie finale (Fr.)
  *coda
  tag
  Anhang (G.)

vs. introduction (Fr., E.)

partimen (Fr.)
  jeu-partie
  parture (Fr.)
  joc-partit (Fr.)
  tenso (Fr.)
  Troubadour song

partimento (It.)
  division on a ground
  divisions
  improvisation
  ground bass

partita (It.)
  suite
  serenade
  cassation
  divertimento (It.)

2. variations
  variations on a theme
  theme and variations

partitions (Fr.)
  sheet music
  folio size
  Notenblätter (G.)
  música en hojas (Sp.)

partitur(a) (It., Sp.)
  score
  full score
  partizione (It.)
  partition (Fr.)
  Partitur (G.)

partitura ridotta (It.)
  condensed score
  piano reduction
  piano-vocal score
  short score
  charts
  lead sheet
  fake book
  partition réduite (Fr.)
  Partiturauszug (G.)

partitura tascabile (It.)
  pocket score
  miniature score
  partition de poche (Fr.)
  Taschenpartitur (G.)
  partitura de bolsillo (Sp.)

pas de Brabant (Fr.)
  *saltarello (It.)
  passo brabante (It.)
  duet dance
  pas de deux (Fr.)

Pascha competentium (Lat.)
  *Palm Sunday
  second Sunday of the Passion
  Dominica in Palmis (Lat.)
  Pascha floridum (Lat.)
  dominica florum (Lat.)
  dominica capitilavium (Lat.)
  dominica Hosanna (Lat.)
  dominica Ramispalma (Lat.)
  Domenica della palma (It.)
  Dimanche des Rameaux (Fr.)
  Palmsonntag (G.)
  Domingo de Ramos (Sp.)

Pascha rosarum (Lat.)
  Pentecost
  Whit Sunday
  Dominica Pentecostes (Lat.)
  Pentecoste (It.)
  Pentecôte (Fr.)
  Pfingsten (G.)
  Pentecosté (Sp.)

paso doble (Sp.)
  fast two-step dance
  march
  galop
  polka
  passo doppio (It.)
  pas double (Fr.)

Pasqua (It.)
  Easter Sunday
  Resurrection Sunday
  Dominica Resurrectionis (Lat.)
  Dimanche de Pâques (Fr.)
  Ostersonntag (G.)
  Pascua Florida (Sp.)
  Pascua de Resurrección (Sp.)
  Domingo de Pascua (Sp.)

Domingo de Resurrección (Sp.)

passacaglia (It.)
   ground bass
   ostinato bass
   strophic bass
   strophic variations
   chaconne (Fr.)
   ciaconna (It.)
   chacona (Sp.)
   variations
   basso ostinato (It.)
   bergamasca (It.)
   folia (It.)
   romanesca (It.)
   passamezzo (It.)
   passacaille (Fr.)
   passacalle (Sp.)

passage (E., Fr.)
   section
   excerpt
   fragment
   example

2. break in the voice
   register change
   cavaletto (It.)

3. passaggio (It.)
   ornamentation
   divisions

passage en imitation (Fr.)
   point of imitation (fugal)
   frammento d'imitazione (It.)
   motivo d'imitazione (It.)
   motif en imitation (Fr.)
   Imitationsabschnitte (G.)
   Imitationsmotiv (G.)
   pasaje de imitación (Sp.)
   punto de imitación (Sp.)
   motivo imitado (Sp.)

passaggio (It.)

embellishment
ornament
flourish
florid
divisions
diminutions
passage-work
passo (It.)
passage (Fr.)
Passagenwerk (G.)
paso, pasaje (Sp.)

2. break in the voice
   register change
   cavaletto (It.)

3. *modulation
   key change
   transition

passamezzo (It.)
   pavan, paven, pavin
   slow, duple dance
   passymeasure
   cinque-pace
   pavane (Fr.)
   pavana (It., Sp.)
   pas'e mez(z)o (It.)
   quadran pavan

passepied (Fr.)
   lively dance in triple
   minuet
   paspy
   sarabande
   paspié (Sp.)

passing chord
   secondary, unaccented chord
   accordo di passaggio (It.)
   accord de passage (Fr.)
   durchgehender Akkord (G.)
   acorde de paso (Sp.)

passing tone/note
   non-harmonic unaccented tone

pièn-tone
nota di passaggio (It.)
note de passage (Fr.)
Durchgangston (G.)
Durchgangsnote (G.)
nota de paso (Sp.)

Passion (E., Fr.)
   cantata
   oratorio
   Seven last words of Christ
   passione (It.)
   Passion (G.)
   Passionsoratorium (G.)
   Choralpassion (G.)

Passion play
   *liturgical drama
   mystery play
   miracle play
   morality play
   tomb play
   sepulcrum play

Passion week
   Holy week
   Hebdomade Sancte (Lat.)
   settimada sancta (It.)
   semaine sainte (Fr.)
   Karwoche (G.)
   semana santa (Sp.)

passo (It.)
   step
   pas (Fr.)
   Schritt (G.)
   paso (Sp.)

2. time
   measure
   meter

passo Brabante (It.)
   saltarello (It.)
   pas de Brabant (Fr.)
   duet dance

passo doppio (It.)
   paso doble (Sp.)
   pas double (Fr.)
   two-step dance
   galop
   march
   polka

passo ordinario (It.)
   4/4 time
   ordinary time
   common time/measure

pasticcio (It.)
   *medley
   potpourri
   pastiche (Fr.)
   quodlibet (Lat.)
   musical miscellany
   salmi(s) (Fr.)
   salmigondis (Fr.)
   salmagundi, -y
   olio
   overture
   suite
   masque

pastorale (E., It., Fr.)
   idyl
   bucolic song
   eglogue (Fr.)
   pastourelle (Fr.)
   sicilienne (Fr.)
   Hirtenstück (G.)
   pastoral (Sp.)
   siciliano, -a (It.)
   pifa (It.)
   bergerette (Fr.)
   brunette (Fr.)

Pater Noster (Lat.)
   Lord's Prayer
   Our Father
   Paternoster (It.)
   Notre Père (Fr.)
   Vaterunser (G.)

Padre Nuestro (Sp.)

patent notes
   shape notes
   character notes
   buckwheat notes
   dunce notes
   *solmization
   solfeggio (It.)
   fasola

patouille (Fr.)
   xylophone
   gigelira (It.)
   organo di legno (It.)
   *claquebois (Fr.)
   harmonica de bois (Fr.)
   Xylophon (G.)
   armonica de madera (Sp.)
   marimba

patriotic song
   national anthem/hymn/air
   inno nazionale (It.)
   hymne national (Fr.)
   Nationalhymne (G.)
   himno nacional (Sp.)

patter song
   parlando style
   syllabic
   Wortwiederholung (G.)

patapatapan (Fr.)
   *drumbeat
   paradiddle
   flam
   ruff, ruffle
   patapan
   tantarán, tantarantán (Sp.)

Pauken (G.)
   *kettledrums
   timpani
   double-drum
   timbales (Fr.)

timbals (Sp.)
atabals (Sp.)

Paukenwirbel (G.)
   drum-roll
   tremolo (It.)
   rullo (It.)
   gruppo (It.)
   roulement (Fr.)
   Trommelwirbel (G.)
   redoble (Sp.)

pausa (It., Sp.)
   rest
   silence (E., Fr.)
   silenzio (It.)
   pause (Fr.)
   Pause (G.)
   figura muta (Lat., It.)

pausa di biscroma (It.)
   32nd rest
   demisemiquaver rest
   huitième de soupir (Fr.)
   zweiunddreissigstel Pause (G.)
   silencio de fusa (Sp.)
   pausa de fusa (Sp.)

pausa di breve (It.)
   two-measure rest
   pause de breve (Fr.)
   demi-bâton (Fr.)
   Zweiganzepause (G.)
   Zweitaktpause (G.)
   Doppeltaktpause (G.)
   silencio de breve (Sp.)
   breve rest

pausa di croma (It.)
   eighth-note rest
   quaver rest
   demi-soupir (Fr.)
   Achtelpause (G.)
   silencio de corchea (Sp.)
   pausa de corchea (Sp.)

pausa di minima (It.)
half-rest
minim rest
demi-pause (Fr.)
halbe Pause (G.)
silencio de blanca (Sp.)
pausa de blanca (Sp.)

pausa di semibreve (It.)
whole rest
semibreve rest
semipausa (Lat.)
pause (Fr.)
ganze Pause (G.)
silencio de redonda (Sp.)
pausa de redonda (Sp.)

pausa di semicroma (It.)
16th rest
semiquaver rest
quart de soupir (Fr.)
sechzehntel Pause (G.)
silencio de semicorchea (Sp.)
pausa de semicorchea (Sp.)

pausa di semiminima (It.)
quarter rest
crotchet rest
soupir (Fr.)
viertel Pause (G.)
silencio de negra (Sp.)
pausa de negra (Sp.)

pausa generale (It.)
general pause
break
caesura
pausa generalis (Lat.)
pause générale (Fr.)
Generalpause (G.)
pausa general (Sp.)

pause
rest
caesura
hold

railroad tracks
corona (It.)
*fermata (It.)
punto coronata (It.)
point d'orgue (Fr.)
Fermate (G.)

pause (Fr.)
whole rest
semibreve rest
*pausa di semibreve (It.)

pauta (Sp.)
staff, stave
pentagramma (It.)
rigo musicale (It.)
portée musicale (Fr.)
Notensystem (G.)
Liniensystem (G.)
pentagrama (Sp.)

pautada (Sp.)
*music paper
staff paper
carta da musica (It.)
papier à musique (Fr.)
Notenpapier (G.)
papel de música (Sp.)

pavane (Fr.)
slow duple dance
paduana (16-17c.)
pavan, paven, pavin
pavana (It., Sp.)
passamezzo (It.)
pass'e mezzo (It.)
chiarenzana (It.)
Paduana, Padoana (G.)

pavillon (Fr.)
bell (of wind instrument)
flair of a horn
campana (Lat., It., Sp.)
padiglione (It.)
Schallbecher (G.)
Schallstück (G.)

Schalltrichter (G.)
Stürtze (G.)
pabellón (Sp.)

pavillon Chinois (Fr.)
Chinerse crescent
Chinese pavilion
Chinese hat
Janissary music
Turkish pavilion/crescent
jingling Johnny
cappello Cinese (It.)
*chapeau Chinois (Fr.)
Schellenbaum (G.)
Halbmond (G.)
sombrero Chino (Sp.)

pavillon en l'air (Fr.)
bell in the air
padiglione in alto (It.)
campana in alto (It.)
Stürze hoch (G.)
Schalltrichter hoch (G.)
pabellón al aire (Sp.)

vs. position naturelle (Fr.)
bell down

peak (of a bow)
tip
point
punta (It., Sp.)
pointe (Fr.)
Spitze (G.)

vs. frog, heel

peal (bells)
ring
toll
chime
sound
play
strike
läuten (G.)
schallen (G.)

klingen, klingeln (G.)
sonner (Fr.)
scampanare (It.)
suonare (It.)
resonar (Sp.)
campanear (Sp.)

peal-ringing
change-ringing
carillon-ringing
sonnerie (Fr.)

peanut gallery
gallery
*balcony
bleachers
choir loft
paradiso (It.)
galleria (It.)
gallerie (Fr.)
Galerie (G.)
galeria (Sp.)
paraiso (Sp.)

pear-shaped tone
full tone (voice)
rounded ton
bel canto (It.)

pedal (organ, piano, harp)
foot-key
pedal-key
pedale (It.)
pédale (Fr.)
Pedal (G.)
pedal (Sp.)

pedal-board (organ)
pedal organ/division
pedal keyboard
pedaliera (It.)
pédalier (Fr.)
clavier de pédales (Fr.)
Pedalklaviatur (G.)
Orgelpedal (G.)
pedalero (Sp.)

pedal clarinet
contrabass clarinet
doublebass clarinet
Kontrabassklarinette (G.)

pedal flute (organ)
choral bass
chorus reed
Chorbass (G.)
Prinzipalbass (G.)

pedal harp
concert harp
chromatic harp
double-action harp
Trittharfe (G.)
Pedalharfe (G.)

vs. Irish harp

pedal coupler (org.)
accoppiamento (It.)
accouplement (Fr)
tirasse (Fr.)
Koppelpedal (G.)
Pedalkoppel (G.)
acoplamiento (Sp.)
enganche al pedalero (Sp.)

pedal note
drone
pedal point
organ point
point d'orgue (Fr.)
pedale (It., Sp.)
pédale (Fr.)
Orgelpunkt (G.)
nota pedal (Sp.)
bajo de órgano (Sp.)
burden
bourdon (Fr.)
organum
*bagpipe

pedal tone (brass instrument)
fundamental note (lowest note)

first harmonic/partial
pedaltono (It.)
nota fundamentale (It., Sp.)
ton de pédale (Fr.)
note fondamentale (Fr.)
Pedalton (G.)
tono de pedal (Sp.)

pédale douce (Fr.)
soft pedal
una corda (It.)
pedale sordina (It.)
pedale sinistra (It.)
pedale piano (It.)
pédale gauche (Fr.)
pédale sourde (Fr.)
petite pédale (Fr.)
eine Saite (G.)
linke Pedal (G.)
Dämpfer (G.)
pedal sordina/suave (Sp.)
*mute

pédale droite (Fr.)
loud pedal
sustaining pedal
damper pedal
pedale forte (It.)
pedale destra (It.)
rechte Pedal (G.)
pedal fuerte (Sp.)
pedal de sostén (Sp.)

pedal sostenuto (Sp.)
middle pedal
sostenuto pedal
pedale centrale (It.)
pédale centrale (Fr.)
Mittelpedal (G.)
pedal del medio (Sp.)
pedal central (Sp.)

pédale de la boîte expressive (Fr.)
swell pedal
swell shoe

staffa crescendo (It.)
Schwelltritt (G.)
pedal de crescendo (Sp.)

pédales de combination (Fr.)
toe studs (organ)
pistons
couplers
pédales d'accouplement (Fr.)
pédale de combinaison (Fr.)
Kombinationspedal (G.)

Pedalpauke (G.)
timpani
pedal timps
pedal drum
timpano pedale (It.)
timbale chromatique (Fr.)
timbale méchanique (Fr.)
Maschinenpauken (G.)
timbal de pedal (Sp.)
tambor de pedal (Sp.)

pedes (Lat.)
lai
Stollen (G.)
Leich (G.)

vs. cauda (Lat.)
Abgesang (G.)

peg
tuning peg
bischero (It.)
pirolo, pirone (It.)
voluta (It.)
cheville (Fr.)
Wirbel (G.)
clavija (Sp.)

2. 'cello/bass peg
endpin
tailpin
spike
puntale (It.)
pique, piquet (Fr.)

pied (Fr.)
Stachel (G.)
Knopf (G.)
puntal (Sp.)

Peitsche (G.)
whip (percussion)
slapstick
horsewhip
frusta (It.)
fouet (Fr.)
Pritsche (G.)
zurriaga (Sp.)
látigo (Sp.)
tralla (Sp.)

pellet bells
jingle bells
*bells
sanctus bells
*altar bells
sleighbells
harness bells
sonaglio (It.)
grelots (Fr.)
Schelle (G.)
cascabel (Sp.)

penna (It.)
plectrum
pick
jack
quill
plettro (It.)
plectre (Fr.)
plectro(Sp.)
púa (Sp.)
Plektrum (G.)
Kiel (G.)

pen(n)illion, pennill
Welsh harp and song
bard
scop
minstrel
troubadour

improvised song

penny whistle
tin whistle
fife
fipple flute
whistle flute
toy flute
piffero (It.)
fifre (Fr.)
flageolet (Fr.)
Kinderflöte (G.)
pifano (Sp.)

pentachord
five-note scale
diatonic scale
pentacordo (It.)
pentacorde (Fr.)
Pentachord (G.)
pentacordio (Sp.)
tetrachord
hexachord

pentagramma (It.)
staff, stave
five-line staff
four-line staff (chant)
rigo musicale (It.)
portée musicale (Fr.)
Notensystem (G.)
Liniensystem (G.)
pentagrama (Sp.)
pauta, pautada (Sp.)

pentatone
interval of five whole-steps
pentanonon (Gr.)
augmented sixth (interval)
minor seventh
Italian sixth
French sixth
German sixth
Neapolitan sixth

pentatonic scale

whole-tone scale
anhemitonic
scala pentatonica (It.)
gamme pentatonique (Fr.)
Ganztonleiter (G.)
Fünftonleiter (G.)
pentatonische Skala (G.)
pentacordo (Sp.)

Pentecost
Whit Sunday
Dominica Pentecostes (Lat.)
Pascha rosarum (Lat.)
Pentecoste (It.)
Pentecôte (Fr.)
Pfingsten (G.)
Pentecostés (Sp.)

per gradi (It.)
by degree (of the scale)
step-wise
scalewise
melodic
*conjunct motion
di grado (It.)
par degré (Fr.)
Stufenweise (G.)

2. little by little
step by step
gradually
a grado a grado (It.)
poco a poco (It., Sp.)
poi a poi (It.)
di grado (It.)
peu à peu (Fr.)
petit à petit (Fr.)
nach und nach (G.)
de grado per grado (Sp.)
por grado (Sp.)

perce (Fr.)
bore (of a wind instr.)
fori, foratura (It.)
Bohrung (G.)
perforación (Sp.)

perceptible (E., Fr., Sp.)
audible (E., Sp.)
percettibile (It.)
hörbar (G.)

percussion instrument
idiophone
rhythm instruments
pulsatile instrument
strumento a percussione (It.)
instrument à percussion (Fr.)
instrumento de percusion (Sp.)
Schlaginstrument (G.)

perdendosi (It.)
dying away
fading out
decay
morendo (It.)
*decrescendo (It.)
diminuendo (It.)
en perdand le son (Fr.)
Sterbend (G.)
expirando (Sp.)

perfect cadence
full cadence
authentic cadence
full close
final cadence
cadenza perfetta (It.)
cadence parfaite (Fr.)
cadence authentique (Fr.)
Ganzschluss (G.)
authentische Kadenz (G.)
vollkommene Kadenz (G.)
cadencia perfecta (Sp.)
cadencia autentica (Sp.)

perfect fifth (interval)
pure fifth
quinta giusta (It.)
quinte juste (Fr.)
reine Quinte (G.)
quinta perfecta (Sp.)

perfect fourth
pure fourth
Quarta giusta (It.)
quarte juste (Fr.)
reine Quart (G.)
cuarta perfecta (Sp.)

perfect pitch
absolute pitch
true pitch
orecchio assoluto (It.)
oreille absolue (Fr.)
absolutes Gehör (G.)
oïdo absoluto (Sp.)

vs. relative pitch

perfect time
*triple meter
tempus perfectum (Lat.)
tempus ternarium (Lat.)
three-quarter time
waltz time
tempo ternario (It.)
mesure ternaire (Fr.)
Dreiertakt (G.)
compás ternario (Sp.)

vs. imperfect time
duple meter

perform
sing
play
concertize
execute
render
interpret
give a reading
give a recital
eseguire (It.)
exécuter (Fr.)
ausführen (G.)
vortragen (G.)
ejecutar (Sp.)

performance
concert
recital
presentation
program
production
rendition
reading
interpretation
show
spettacolo (It.)
rappresentazione (It.)
représentation (Fr.)
spectacle (E., Fr.)
Schauspiel (G.)
Vorstellung (G.)
Aufführung (G.)
Vortrag (G.)
espectáculo (Sp.)
representación (Sp.)
función (Sp.)

performance center
*concert hall
auditorium
recital hall
academy of music

performance practices
practical music
applied music
pratico d'esecuzione (It.)
prassi d'esecuzione (It.)
pratique de l'exécution (Fr.)
Auffürungspraxis (G.)
práctica de ejecución (Sp.)

performer
singer
player
musical artist
musician
concert artist
virtuoso
soloist
concertista (It., Sp.)

concertiste (Fr.)
Konzertist (G.)
Konxertgeber (G.)
ejecutante (Sp.)

performing rights
rights
diritti d'esecuzione (It.)
droits d'exécution (Fr.)
Aufführungsrecht (G.)
derechos de ejecución (Sp.)

perifrasi (It.)
paraphrase (E., Fr.)
quote
*parody
Paraphrase (G.)
parafrasis (Sp.)

Perinetventil (G.)
valve (brass instr.)
piston (E., Fr.)
pistone (It.)
valvola (It.)
Ventil (G.)
Pumpventil (G.)
pistón (Sp.)

period
phrases (pair of)
antecedent/consequent phrases
periodo (It., Sp.)
période (Fr.)
phrase musicale complète (Fr.)
Periode (G.)
frase musicale completa (Sp.)

period instruments
original instruments
historical instruments
authentic instruments
old instruments
early music
instruments originaux (Fr.)
Originalstrumenten (G.)

perpetual canon
circular canon
infinite canon
perpetual motion
canone perpetuo (It., Sp.)
canon perpétuel (Fr.)
unendlicher Kanon (G.)

perpetual motion
perpetuum mobile (Lat.)
moto perpetuo (It.)
mouvement perpétuel (Fr.)
dauernd Bewegung (G.)
fortwährende Bewegung (G.)
movimiento continuo (Sp.)
movimiento perpetuo (Sp.)

pes (Lat.)
ostinato tenor/bass
ground bass
basso ostinato (It.)
chaconne (Fr.)
passacaglia (It.)

2. pedes (Lat.)
frons
Stolle (G.)
Aufgesang (G.)

pesante (It.)
heavy
pesant (Fr.)
schwerfällig (G.)
pesado (Sp.)

petaccha (It.)
pick
plectrum
jack
quill
plettro (It.)
plectre (Fr.)
médiator (Fr.)
Mediator (G.)
Plektrum (G.)
Kiel (G.)

plectro (Sp.)
púa (Sp.)

petit basson (Fr.)
treble bassoon
tenor oboe
tenoroon
fagottino (It.)
Quintfagott (G.)
Tenorfagott (G.)
fagote Quinta (Sp.)

petit choeur (Fr.)
chamber choir/chorus
semi-chorus
echo choir
soli (It.)
semicoro (It., Sp.)
demi-choeur (Fr.)
Halbchor (G.)
hemicoro (Sp.)

2. concertino (It.)
solo instrumental group
favoriti (It.)
soli (It.)
coro concertino (It.)
coro principali (It.)
coro concertato (It.)
coro favorito (It.)

petit violon de poche (Fr.)
*kit
small violin
rebec
pocket-fiddle
violino di pochetto (It.)
poche, pochette (Fr.)
Sackgeige (G.)
Taschengeige (G.)
violín de bolsillo (Sp.)
violín pequeño (Sp.)

petite flûte (Fr.)
piccolo
octave flute

ottavino (It.)
Oktavflöte (G.)
kleine Flöte (G.)
Pikkoloflöte (G.)

petite pédal (Fr.)
soft pedal (piano)
una corda (It.)
damper pedal
pedale piano (It.)
pedale sinistra (It.)
pédale douce (Fr.)
pédale gauche (Fr.)
Dämpfer (G.)
linke Pedal (G.)
pedal sordina (Sp.)
pedal suave (Sp.)

petites notes (Fr.)
cue notes
little notes
lead-in
notine (It.)
Stichnoten (G.)
guías (Sp.)

peu (Fr.)
somewhat
rather
a little
poco (It., Sp.)
wenig (G.)

peu à peu (Fr.)
by degrees
gradually
little by little
step by step
poco a poco (It., Sp.)
di grado (It.)
per gradi (It.)
a grado a grado (It.)
poi a poi (It.)
petit à petit (Fr.)
nach und nach (G.)
por grado (Sp.)

de grado en grado (Sp.)

vs. subito (It.)

pezzo (It.)
piece (of music)
*composition
selection
number
work
opus
brano (It.)
pièce (Fr.)
oeuvre (Fr.)
morceau (Fr.)
Stück (G.)
Werk (G.)
pieza (Sp.)
trozo (Sp.)

pezzo di reserva (It.)
shank (brass instr.)
*crook
extension
ritorto (It.)
corpo di ricambio (It.)
corps de rechange (Fr.)
Aufsatzbogen (G.)
cuerpo de recambio (Sp.)

Pfeife (G.)
*fife
piccolo
penny whistle
tin whistle
fipple flute
piffero (It.)
fifre (Fr.)
Querpfeife (G.)
pifano, pifaro (Sp.)

2. organ pipe
canna d'organo (It.)
tuyau (Fr.)
tubo (Sp.)
cañón (Sp.)

Orgelpfeife (G.)

Pfingsten (G.)
Whit Sunday
*Pentecost
Dominica Pentecostes (Lat.)

Phantasie (G.)
fancy, fantasy
impromptu
arabesque
rhapsody
fantasia (It., E., Sp.)
capriccio (It.)
stravaganza (It.)
caprice (Fr.)
fantasie (Fr.)
Fantasie, Fantasiestück (G.)
Phantasiebilder (G.)

Phantasieren (G.)
improvise
extemporize
play by ear
ad-lib
impromptu

pharynx (E., Fr.)
vocal organs
throat
larynx
voice-box
syrinx
faringe (It., Sp.)
Rachenhöhle (G.)

philharmonic
symphonic
concert
classical

philharmonic hall
symphonic hall
*concert hall
recital hall
auditorium

academy of music

philharmonic pitch
concert pitch
high pitch
diapasón alto (Sp.)
diapasón de concierto (Sp.)

philharmonic society
music society
symphonic society
accademia (It.)

2. *orchestra (It., E.)
symphony orchestra
orchestre (Fr.)
Orchester (G.)
orquesta (Sp.)

philosophical pitch
scientific pitch
Stuttgart pitch

phonograph
record player
*gramophone
turntable
victrola
CD, DVD player
giradischi (It.)
grammofono (It.)
piatto portadischi (It.)
tourne-disques (Fr.)
plateau (Fr.)
Grammophon (G.)
Plattenteller (G.)
Plattenspieler (G.)
Sprechmachine (G.)
tocadiscos (Sp.)
gramófono (Sp.)
fonógrafo (Sp.)
plato (Sp.)

phonograph record
record, recording
platter

gramophone record
LP record
long-playing record
extended play record
disc
pressing
disco (It., Sp.)
disque (Fr.)
Schallplatte (G.)
CD, DVD
audio tape recording
cassette recording

phorminx (Gr.)
*lyre
harp
cithara (Lat.)
kithara (Gr.)

phrase (E., Fr.)
melodic unit
musical sentence
period
passage
fragment
sequence
motive
figure
frase (It., Sp.)
Satz (G.)

phrasing
bowing
tongueing
shaping
expression
articulation
fraseggio (It.)
phrasé (Fr.)
Phrasierung (G.)
fraseo (Sp.)

Phrygian mode
mode 3
Greek mode
ecclesiastical mode

minor mode
Phrygian cadence
frigio (It., Sp.)
phrygisch (G.)
phrygien (Fr.)

pianette
small upright piano
pianino (It.)
pianet (Fr.)
piano droite (Fr.)
Kleinklavier (G.)

piano (instrument)
fortepiano
grand piano
concert grand
parlor grand
baby grand
piano de boudoir (Fr.)
grand piano de concert (Fr.)
upright piano
console piano
studio piano
spinet
cottage piano
cabinet piano
vertical piano
pianoforte (It.)
pianoforte a coda(intera) (It.)
pianoforte verticale (It.)
piano à queue (Fr.)
piano droit (Fr.)
piano à tavolins (Fr.)
piano vertical (Fr., Sp.)
Flügel (G.)
Klavier (G.)
Hammerflügel (G.)
Hammerklavier (G.)
piano de (media) cola (Sp.)

piano, pianissimo (It.)
soft, very soft
quiet
dolce (It.)
doux (Fr.)

leise (G.)
dulce (Sp.)

vs. forte, fortissimo (It.)

piano accordion
*accordion
concertina
squeezebox

piano armonico (It.)
soundboard
table
belly
tavola armonico (It.)
table d'harmonie (Fr.)
Resonanzboden (G.)
caja armónica (Sp.)

piano giraffe (Fr.)
giraffe piano
grand upright
vertical grand
Giraffenklavier (G.)
Giraffenflügel (G.)
piano jirafa (Sp.)

piano harp
hammered dulcimer
cimbalom, cembalom
Hackbrett (G.)

piano préparé (Fr.)
prepared piano
altered sounds
Fagottzug (G.)
piano preparado (Sp.)

piano-organ
street piano
street organ

2. piano organisé (Fr.)
piano-orgue (Fr.)
Orgelklavier (G.)

piano quartet
quartetto con pianoforte (It.)
quatuor avec piano (Fr.)
Klavierquartett (G.)
cuarteto con piano (Sp.)

piano-roll
mechanical piano
player-piano roll
cilindro (It., Sp.)
rouleau (Fr.)
cylindre (Fr.)
Walze (G.)

piano score
condensed score
piano-vocal score
piano reduction
conductor's score
short score
close score
lead sheet
partitura ridotta (It.)
partition réduite (Fr.)
Partiturauszug (G.)

vs. full score

piano-violin
sostinente pianoforte
hurdy-gurdy
Streichklavier (G.)

pianola (E., It.)
player piano
mechanical piano
nickelodeon
piano méchanique (Fr.)
planchette (Fr.)
automatisches Klavier (G.)
autopiano (Sp.)
piano mecánico (Sp.)
piano automático (Sp.)

piatto portadischi (It.)
*phonograph

gramophone
record player
record changer
talking machine
victrola
turntable
grammofono (It.)
giradischi (It.)
tourne-disques (Fr.)
Plattenteller (G.)
tocadiscos (Sp.)

piatti (It.)
cymbals
crash cymbals
choke cymbals
ride cymbals
high-hat
acetabula (Lat.)
cinelli (It.)
cembali (It.)
cymbales (Fr.)
Becken (G.)
Schallbecken (G.)
cimbalos (Sp.)
platillos (Sp.)

piatti chiodati (It.)
sizzle cymbales
rivet cymbales
cymbales sur tiges (Fr.)
Sizzle-Becken (G.)
Nietenbecken (G.)
Zischbecken (G.)
cimbales sobre palillos (Sp.)

Picardy third
major third
ditone
raised third
tierce de Picardie (Fr.)
tierce majeur (Fr.)
terza maggiore (It.)
Pikardische Terz (G.)
grosse Terz (G.)
tercera mayor (Sp.)

picchettato, picchiettato (It.)
*detatched
piccato (It.)
staccato (It.)
spiccato (It.)
détaché (Fr.)
pikiert (G.)
abgestossen (G.)
destacado (Sp.)

vs. legato (It.)

piccolo (E., It., Fr.)
flute
fife
octave flute
ottavino (It.)
flautino (It.)
flauto piccolo (It.)
petite flûte (Fr.)
Pikkoloflöte (G.)
kleine Flöte (G.)
Oktavflöte (G.)
Pickelflöte (G.)
flautin (Sp.)

piccolo trumpet
Bach trumpet
trumpet in D
baroque trumpet
clarion
clarino (It.)
clairon (Fr.)

pick (vb.)
play a guitar, banjo, etc.
strum
pluck
finger-pick
pizzicato (It.)
pizzicare (It.)
pincer (Fr.)
zupfen (G.)
puntear (Sp.)

vs. to bow

pick (n.)
plectrum
quill
jack
plettro (It.)
penna (It.)
petaccha (It.)
plectre (Fr.)
médiator (Fr.)
bec (Fr.)
Plektrum (G.)
Kiel (G.)
plectro (Sp.)
pua (Sp.)

pick-up
*upbeat
lead-in
cue
vamp
arsis (Gr.)
anacrusis (E.)
anacrusi (It., Sp.)
arsi (It.)
anacrouse (Fr.)
levé (Fr.)
élévation (Fr.)
Anakrusis (G.)
Auftakt (G.)
Hebung (G.)

vs. downbeat

picker
plucker
strummer
player of plucked string instr.

pico (Sp.)
*mouthpiece
imboccatura (It.)
becco (It.)
embouchure (Fr.)
bec (Fr.)
Schnabel (G.)
Mundstück (G.)

embocadura (Sp.)
boquilla (Sp.)

piece
composition
selection
set piece
number
work
opus (Lat.)
pezzo (It.)
brano musicale (It.)
pièce (Fr.)
morceau (Fr.)
oeuvre (Fr.)
Werk (G.)
Stück (G.)
obra (Sp.)
pieza (Sp.)
trozo (Sp.)

pied (Fr.)
endpin
tailpin
spike
peg
puntale (It.)
pique(t) (Fr.)
Stachel (G.)
puntal Sp.)

pièn-tone
ornamental tone
passing tone
fill-in tone
non-harmonic,unaccented tone
nota di passaggio (It.)
note de passage (Fr.)
Durchgangston (G.)
Durchgangsnote (G.)
nota de paso (Sp.)

pieno (It.)
mixture stop (organ)
compound stop
overtones

harmonics
partials
sesquialtera (Lat.)
miscella (Lat.)
ripieno (It.)
accordo (It.)
plein jeu (Fr.)
Hintersatz (G.)
Mixtur (G.)
lleno (Sp.)

2. full
plein (Fr.)
rempli (Fr.)
voll (G.)
lleno (Sp.)

pifa (It.)
pastorale
idyl
bucolic piece
siciliano, -a (It.)
sicilienne (Fr.)
pastourelle (Fr.)
Hirtenstück (G.)
pastoral (Sp.)

pifano (Sp.)
penny whistle
fife
tin whistle
duct flute
whistle flute
toy flute
piffero (It.)
fifre (Fr.)
mirleton (Fr.)
Kinderflöte (G.)

piff
chiff (organ)
buzz
articulation
attack

piffaro, piffero (It.)

*shawm
oboe
cialamello (It.)
chalumeau (Fr.)
Schalmei (G.)
chirimia (Sp.)
caramillo (Sp.)

pin
tuning pin/peg (on piano and strings)
bischero (It.)
pirolo (It.)
voluta (It.)
cheville (Fr.)
Wirbel (G.)
Stimmnagel (G.)
clavija (Sp.)

2. endpin
tailpin
peg
puntale (It.)
pied (Fr.)
pique (Fr.)
Stachel (G.)
Knopf (G.)
puntal (Sp.)

pin-block (piano)
tuning pin holder
wood block
sommier de chevilles (Fr.)
Stimmstock (G.)
clavijero (Sp.)

pincé (Fr.)
plucked
strummed
picked
pizzicato (It.)
zupfen (G.)
punteado (Sp.)

vs. arco (It.)
à l'archet (Fr.)

2. *mordent
ornament
grace note
mordente (It., Sp.)
mordant (Fr.)
battement (Fr.)
Pralltriller (G.)

pincé étouffé (Fr.)
*acciaccatura
crushed note
mordent
appoggiatura brève (Fr.)
pincement (Fr.)
Quetschung (G.)
apoyatura breve (Sp.)

pincé renversé (Fr.)
inverted mordent
trill
upper neighbor
ornament
grace note
Schneller (G.)
Pralltriller (G.)

pipe (organ)
canna d'organo (It.)
tuyau d'orgue (Fr.)
Pfeife (G.)
tubo (Sp.)
caño (Sp.)

pipe and tabor
whittle and dub (old E.)
fife and drum
galoubet (Fr.)
Schwegel und Tamburin (G.)
Querpfeife-Trommel (G.)
fluviol y tambori(l) (Sp.)

pipe metal (organ)
organ metal
alloy: tin and lead (and zinc)
tin metal

common metal
plain metal
spotted metal

pipe organ
*organ
King of the Instruments
organo (It., Sp.)
orgue (Fr.)
Orgel (G.)

vs. electronic organ

pipeau (Fr.)
tin whistle
tin flute
pipe
zufolo (It.)
pipette (Fr.)
Hirtenpfeife (G.)
pipa, pipitaña (Sp.)
chalumeau (Fr.)
scialumo (It.)
chanter (of bagpipe)

pipes of Pan
panpipes
mouth organ
syrinx
Pandean pipes
cicuta (Lat.)
flauto di Pan (It.)
siringa (It., Sp.)
fistola (It.)
flte de Pan (Fr.)
fretel, fretèle (Fr.)
sifflet des chaudronniers (Fr.)
Panflöte (G.)
Papagenoflöte (G.)
flauta de Pan (Sp.)
flauta pánica (Sp.)

pique, piquet (Fr.)
endpin (of a cello, etc.)
spike
*pin, peg

piqué (Fr.)
semi-detatched
mezzo staccato (It.)
picchiettato (It.)
portato (It.)

pirolo (It.)
tuning peg/pin
bischero (It.)
caviglia (It.)
cheville (Fr.)
Wirbel (G.)
Stimmnagel (G.)

pista (It., Sp.)
band on a disk
track
traccia (It.)
piste (Fr.)
Spur, Tonspur (G.)

pista sonora (Sp.)
sound track
sound stripe
film recording
collona sonora (It.)
colonne sonore (Fr.)
bande sonore (Fr.)
Tonspur (G.)
banda de sonido (Sp.)

piston (organ)
combination
coupler
copula (Lat.)
unione (It.)
accopiamento (It.)
accouplement (Fr.)
Koppel, Koppelung (G.)
acopiamiento (Sp.)

piston (wind instruments)
valve
pistone (It.)
cylindre (Fr.)
Ventil (G.)

Pumpventil (G.)
Perinetventil (G.)
pistón (Sp.)
valvula de pistón (Sp.)

pit band/orchestra
theater orchestra
buca dell'orchestra (It.)
fauteuils d'orchestre (Fr.)

pitch
frequency
intonation
vibration
cps
Hertz
oscillation
intonazione (It.)
hauteur du ton (Fr.)
diapason (It., Fr.)
Tonhöhe (G.)
entonación (Sp.)
diapasón (Sp.)

pitch aggregate
tone cluster
aleatory
gruppo di suonori (It.)
groupe de son/notes (Fr.)
Tonballung (G.)
Tontraube (G.)

pitchpipe
tuning pipe
corista (It.)
diapason (It.)
diapason de bouche (Fr.)
Stimmflöte (G.)
Stimmpfeife (G.)

più (It.)
more
plus (Fr.)
mehr (G.)
mas (Sp.)

vs. meno (It.)

piva (It.)
*bagpipe
zampogna, sampogna (It.)
cornamusa (It., Sp.)
musetta (It.)
musette (Fr.)
cornrmuse (Fr.)
Dudelsack (G.)
Sackpfeife (G.)
gaita (Sp.)

2. bass dance
*basse danse (Fr.)
bassa danza (It.)
Hoftanz (G.)
baxa (Sp.)

piva torto/storto (It.)
*crummhorn
oboe
cromorno (It., Sp.)
cromorne (Fr.)
Krummhorn (G.)
orlo (Sp.)

pivotal chord
modulating chord
common chord
interdominant
secondary dominant
Zwischendominanten (G.)
acorde pivote (Sp.)

pizzicato (It.)
plucked
staccato (It.)
pincé (Fr.)
arraché (Fr.)
gezupft, gezwickt (G.)
anreissen (G.)
punteado (Sp.)

vs. bowed
arco (It.)

plagal cadence
amen cadence
church cadence
*imperfect cadence
cadenza plagale (It.)
cadence plagale (Fr.)
Kirchenschluss (G.)
plagale Kadenz (G.)
unvollkommene Kadenz (G.)
cadencia plagal (Sp.)

plagal mode
modus plagius (Lat.)
modo plagale (It.)
mode plagale (Fr.)
plagale Tonart (G.)

vs. authentic mode

plagiarize
copy
steal
imitate
quote
parody
plagiare (It.)
plagier (Fr.)
abschreiben (G.)
plagiar (Sp.)

plainsong
*chant
plainchant
Gregorian chant
liturgical song
monophonic
cantus planus (Lat.)
cantus choralis (Lat.)
cantus Romanus (Lat.)
cantilena Romana (Lat., Sp.)
cantico (It., Sp.)
canto Gregoriano (It., Sp.)
chant d'église (Fr.)
chant Romain (Fr.)
chant Grégorien (Fr.)
Choral (G.)

Gregorianische Gesang (G.)

plainte (Fr.)
 *lament
 dirge
 elegy
 plaint
 funeral song
 taps
 planctus (Lat.)
 requiem (Lat.)
 lamento (It., Sp.)
 tombeau (Fr.)
 déploration (Fr.)
 Klage, Klagelied (G.)
 Grabgesang (G.)

2. ornament (17c.)
 neighbor-note
 afterbeat
 portamento (It.)
 glissando (It.)
 Nachschlag (G.)

plaintive
 sad, sadly
 addolorato (It.)
 plaintif (Fr.)
 douloureux (Fr.)
 klagend (G.)
 schmerzlich (G.)
 lamentoso (Sp.)
 dolorido (Sp.)

plan
 form
 structure
 forma (It., Sp.)
 fattura (It.)
 dessin (Fr.)
 forme (Fr.)
 facture (Fr.)
 Faktur (G.)
 Gestalt (G.)
 Aufbau (G.)

plancas de los registros (Sp.)
 draw-knobs (organ)
 draw-stops
 bottoni dei registri (It.)
 boutons de registres (Fr.)
 Registerzüge (G.)
 Registerknöpfe (G.)
 Züge (G.)
 botones tiradores (Sp.)
 botones de los registros (Sp.)

planchette (Fr.)
 mechanical piano
 player piano
 nickelodeon
 pianola (It.)
 piano mécanique (Fr.)
 automatisches Klavier (G.)
 autopiano (Sp.)
 piano mecánico (Sp.)
 piano automático (Sp.)

plantation song
 song of the south
 Steven Foster song
 Plantagengesang (G.)

plaqué (Fr.)
 non-arpeggio
 solid chord
 unbroken chord
 accordo incollato (It.)
 accord plaqué (Fr.)
 platter Akkord (G.)
 Akkord anschlagen (G.)
 acorde apoyado (Sp.)

vs. brisé
 broken chord

plataforma con concha acústica (Sp.)
 band shell
 bandstand
 bandwagon
 stage

platform
 palco della banda (It.)
 palco dell'orchestra (It.)
 carro della banda musicale (It
 kiosque à musique (Fr.)
 Musikpavillon (G.)
 Konzertpavillon (G.)
 quiosco de música (Sp.)

platillos (Sp.)
 *cymbals
 acetabulum (Lat.)
 crotalum (Lat.)
 crash cymbals
 finger cymbals
 choke cymbals
 piatti (It.)
 cinelli (It.)
 cymbales (Fr.)
 Becken (G.)
 Schallbecken (G.)
 cimbalos (Sp.)

Plattenspieler (G.)
 phonograph
 *gramophone
 record player
 turntable
 victrola
 talking machine
 grammofono (It.)
 giradischi (It.)
 fonografo (It.)
 tourne-disques (Fr.)
 plateau (Fr.)
 Grammophon (G.)
 Sprechmachine (G.)
 Plattenteller (G.)
 plato (Sp.)
 tocadiscos (Sp.)
 gramofono (Sp.)

platter
 record
 phonograph record
 grammophone record

long-playing record
extended play
disk
CD, DVD
pressing
disco (It., Sp.
disco da grammofono (It.)
disque (Fr.)
disque de phonographé (Fr.)
Platte (G.)
Schallplatte (G.)

platter Akkord (G.)
unbroken chord
solid chord
simultaneous
non-arpeggio (It.)
accordo incollato (It.)
concento (It.)
accord plaqué (Fr.)
Akkord anschlagen (G.)
acorde apoyado (Sp.)

vs. gebrochener Akkord (G.)

play
perform
concertize
execute
give a recital
suonare (It.)
jouer (Fr.)
spielen (G.)
tocar (Sp.)

play by ear
improvise
ad-lib
extemporize
impromptu
off the cuff
make it up (as you go along)
on the spot
pull it out of the air
fake it
jam

read charts
follow lead sheets
improvvisare (It.)
improviser (Fr.)
improvisieren (G.)
phantasieren (G.)
improvisar (Sp.)

player piano
mechanical piano
automatic piano
pianola (It.)
nickelodeon
piano mécanique (Fr.)
planchette (Fr.)
automatisches Klavier (G.)
autopiano (Sp.)
piano mecánico (Sp.)
piano automático (Sp.)

playhouse
theater
ampitheater
auditorium
colosseum
lyceum
hippodrome
Greek theater
music hall
concert hall
recital hall
opera house
teatro (It., Sp.)
théatre (Fr.)
Theater (G.)

plectrum
pick
jack
quill
saltarello (It.)
petaccha (It.)
plettro (It.)
plectre (Fr.)
plectro (Sp.)
púa (Sp.)

plein-jeu (Fr.)
full organ
organo pieno/pleno (It.)
tutti (It.)
grand orgue (Fr.)
grand choeur (Fr.)
grand jeu (Fr.)
volle Orgel (G.)
volles Werk (G.)
Hauptwerk (G.)
gran juego (Sp.)
organo lleno (Sp.)

2. *mixture
compound stop
sesquialtera (Lat.)
mistura (It.)
registro composta (It.)
fourniture (Fr.)
Mixtur (G.)
lleno (Sp.)

plenary mass
full mass
complete mass
ordinary and proper combined
Plenarmesse (G.)

pluck
pick
strumm
pizzicare (It.)
pincer (Fr.)
zupfen (G.)
puntear (Sp.)

vs. bow
arco (It.)

plus facile (Fr.)
easier version
alternate way
ossia (It.)
ovvero (It.)
ou bien (Fr.)
oder (G.)

leichter (G.)
o bien (Sp.)

pneuma (Gr.)
melisma (chant)
vocalise
jubilation
jubilus (Lat.)
coloratura (It.)

pneumatic action (organ)
tubular-pneumatic action
pneumatic lever
sistema pneumatico tubulare
(It.)
**pneumatische
Spieleinrichtung(G.)**
Röhrenpneumatik (G.)

poche, pochette (Fr.)
kit
small violin
pocket-fiddle
rebec
linterculus (Lat.)
sordino (It.)
violino di pochetto (It.)
violino piccolo (It.)
violinette (Fr.)
petit violon de poche (Fr.)
Taschengeige (G.)
Sackgeige (G.)
Halbgeige (G.)
Terzgeige (G.)
Tanzmeistergeige (G.)
violín de bolsillo (Sp.)
violín pequeño (Sp.)

pocket score
miniature score
partitura tascabile (It.)
partition de poche (Fr.)
Taschenpartitur (G.)
partitura de bolsillo (Sp.)

vs. full score

poco (It., Sp.)
a little
somewhat
rather
peu (Fr.)
wenig (G.)
etwas (G.)

poco a poco (It., Sp.)
little by little
gradually
step by step
poi a poi (It.)
a grado a grado (It.)
di grado (It.)
per gradi (It.)
peu à peu (Fr.)
petit à petit (Fr.)
nach und nach (G.)
de grado en grado (Sp.)
por grado (Sp.)

vs. subito (It.)

podium (E., Fr.)
rostrum
stand
stage
lectern
pulpit
podio (It., Sp.)
Podium (G.)
tablado (Sp.)
tarima (Sp.)

poème symphonique (Fr.)
symphonic poem
tone poem
program music
descriptive music
word painting
tone painting
poema sinfonico (It.)
poema sinfónico (Sp.)
symphonische Dichtung (G.)

point (n.)
tip of bow
peak
head
punta (It., Sp.)
punta d'arco (It.)
nasetto (It.)
pointe (Fr.)
Spitze (G.)
punto del arco (Sp.)

vs. frog
heel

2. mensural notation
punctus, punctum (Lat.13c.)
punctum perfectionis (Lat.)
point of division
dot of perfection
dot of addition
punctus additionis (Lat.)
divisio modi (Lat.)

point, pointing (vb.)
mark chants for performance
chanting the psalms
psalm singing
Anglican chanting

point d'arrêt (Fr.)
hold
pause
*fermata (It.)
corona (Lat., It.)
punto coronata (It.)
punto d'organo (It.)
couronne (Fr.)
point d'orgue (Fr.)
point de repos (Fr.)
Halt (G.)
Pause (G.)
Krone (G.)
Orgelpunkt (G.)
punto de órgano (Sp.)
calderón (Sp.)
pausa (Sp.)

point d'augmentation (Fr.)
  dot after a note
  punto di valore (It.)
  Verlängerungspunkt (G.)
  puntillo (Sp.)

point d'orgue (Fr.)
  point d'arrêt (Fr.)
  hold
  *fermata (It.)

2. pedal point
  pedal note
  organ point
  drone bass
  organum
  bagpipes
  pedal d'armonia (It.)
  punto d'organo (It.)
  pédale (Fr.)
  note de pédale (Fr.)
  pédale harmonique (Fr.)
  Orgelpunkt (G.)
  nota de pedal (Sp.)
  baja de órgano (Sp.)

3. *cadenza (of concerto)

point de repos (Fr.)
  rest
  pause (E., Fr.)
  caesura
  cadence
  silence (E., Fr.)
  figura muta (Lat., It.)
  pausa (It.,Sp.)
  silenzio (It.)
  Pause (G.)
  Schweigezeichen (G.)
  silencio (Sp.)

point neumes (chant)
  neumes
  punctum (Lat.)
  Aquitanian neume/dot
  Punktneumen (G.)

pointe (Fr.)
  tip of the bow
  peak
  punta (It., Sp.)
  Spitze (G.)

vs. talon (Fr.)

2. toe (in organ playing)

pointé (Fr.)
  dotted
  pricked
  puntato (It.)
pointillé (Fr.)
  punktiert (G.)
  puntado (Sp.)
  con puntillo (Sp.)

pointer (Fr.)
  make notes unequal in length
  notes inégales (Fr.)
  inégaliser (Fr.)
  lourer (Fr.)
  couler (Fr.)

points de reprise (Fr.)
  repeat marks
  repeat sign
  segno di ripetizione (It.)
  signe de répétition (Fr.)
  Wiederholungszeichen (G.)
  signo de repetición (Sp.)

points of imitation (fugal)
  subject
  answer
  theme
  dux (Lat.)
  comes (Lat.)
  motivo d'imitazione (It.)
  frammento d'imitazione (It.)
  passage en imitation (Fr.)
  motif en imitation (Fr.)
  Imitationsabschnitte (G.)
  Imitationsmotiv (G.)

  punto de imitación (Sp.)
  pasaje en imitación (Sp.)
  motivo imitado (Sp.)

polka
  duple fast dance
  galop
  can-can
  trepak
  scozzese (It.)
  polca (It., Sp.)
  Écossaise (Fr.)
  anglaise (Fr.)
  française (Fr.)
  Schottische (G.)
  Kwacowiak (G.)

polonaise (E., Fr.)
  dance in triple time
  mazurka
  polacca (It.)
  Polonaise, Polonäse (G.)
  polonesa (Sp.)

polso (It.)
  beat
  rhythm
  pulse
  tactus (Lat.)
  meter
  pouls (Fr.)
  Puls (G.)
  pulso (Sp.)

polychoral
  multiple choirs
  double chorus
  *antiphonal
  divided choirs
  cori spezzati (It.)
  cori battente (It.)
  double choeur (Fr.)
  Doppelchor (G.)
  coro separado (Sp.)
  coro dividido (Sp.)

polymetric, polymeter
  irregular barring
  uneven barring
  free meter
  vers mesuré (Fr.)
  musique mesurée (Fr.)

polyphony
  counterpoint
  fugue
  imitation
  multi-voiced
  heterophony
  polifonia (It., Sp.)
  polyphonie (Fr.)
  Mehrstimmigkeit (G.)
  Polyphonie (G.)

vs. monophony
  homophony

polyrhythm
  cross-rhythm
  poliritmica (It.)
  polyrythmie (Fr.)
  Polyrhythmik (G.)
  Gegenrhythmus (G.)
  poliritmia (Sp.)

polythematic
  multi-thematic
  politematico (It.)
  polythématique (Fr.)
  vielthemig (G.)
  politemático (Sp.)

vs. monothematic

polytonal
  bitonal
  atonal
  multi-tonal
  politonale (It.)
  polytonale (Fr.)
  polytonal (G.)
  politonal (Sp.)

Pommer, Pomhart (G.)
  bass shawm
  tenor shawm
  helicon
  bombardon
  bass tuba
  bombardo (It.)
  bombarde (Fr.)
  Bombard (G.)

pomposo (It., Sp.)
  majestic
  pompous
  pompeux, -euse (Fr.)
  feierlich (G.)
  prächtig (G.)

poner le voz (Sp.)
  messa di voce (It.)
  swell the tone
  filar il tuono (It.)
  filar la voce (It.)
  filer le son (Fr.)
  filer la voix (Fr.)
  mise de la voix (Fr.)
  pose de la voix (Fr.)
  Schwellton (G.)

pont (Fr.)
  *bridge section
  transition
  episode
  release
  channel
  alternative
  B-section
  alternativo (It.)

pont-neuf (Fr.)
  street song
  vulgar song
  popular song
  canzonaccia (It.)
  Gassenhauer (G.)

ponticello (It.)

bridge (of a violin, etc.)
  cavalletto (It.)
  scagnello (It.)
  chevalet (Fr.)
  Steg (G.)
  puente (Sp.)

pop/popular music
  Broadway music
  hit songs
  top-40, top-20, top-10
  light music
  commercial songs
  light and easy
  light classics
  semiclassical
  easy listening
  rock and roll
  heavy metal
  acid rock
  world music
  doo-wop music
  bubblegum music
  bobby-sox music
  jazz
  blues
  rhythm-and-blues
  reggae
  ska
  hip-hop
  rap
  electronica
  techno

vs. classical music
  folk music

pops concert
  light classics
  popular music
  revue
  *medley

por grado (Sp.)
  little by little
  by degrees

gradually
step by step
di grado (It.)
per gradi (It.)
poi a poi (It.)
poco a poco (It., Sp.)
a grado a grado (It.)
peu à peu (Fr.)
petit à petit (Fr.)
nach und nach (G.)
de grado en grado (Sp.)

vs. subito (It.)

port-de-voix (Fr.)
ornament
grace note
backfall
appoggiatura (It.)
coulé (Fr.)
Nachschlag (G.)
apoyatura (Sp.)

2. slide
scoop
bend (electronic keyboards)
portamento (It.)
portar la voce (It.)
glissando (It.)
glissade (Fr.)
coulade (Fr.)
porter la voix (Fr.)
tragend (G.)
Schleifer (G.)
llever la voz (Sp.)
extrasino (Sp.)

portative organ
regal
bible/book regal
positive organ
chamber organ
cabinet organ
portable organ
organetto (It.)
organo picciolo (It.)

organo portativo (It.)
orgue positif (Fr.)
orgue portatif (Fr.)
Portativ, Positiv (G.)
órgano positivo (Sp.)
órgano portátil (Sp.)

portato (It.)
legato-staccato (It.)
mezzo-staccato (It.)
hooked
louré (Fr.)
porté (Fr.)

Posaune (G.)
trombone (E., It., Fr.)
bass trumpet
slide,valve trombone
Busaune (G.)
trombón (Sp.)
sackbut

2. organ reed stop

pose de la voix (Fr.)
messa di voce (It.)
swell the tone
filar la voce (It.)
filar il tuono (It.)
filer la voix (Fr.)
mise de la voix (Fr.)
Schwellton (G.)
poner le voz (Sp.)

position (E., Fr.)
chord spacing
chord inversions
posizione (It.)
Lage (G.)
Position (G.)
posición (Sp.)

2. string shifts
hand positions

position naturelle (Fr.)

bell down (horns)
posizione normale (It.)
natürlich (G.)
normalmente (Sp.)

vs. pavillon en l'aire (Fr.)

position du pouce (Fr.)
thumb position ('cello)
capotasto (It.)
démanché, démanchement
(Fr.)
Daumenaufsatz (G.)
posición del pulgar (Sp.)

posizione fondamentale (It.)
root position (chord)
5/3 chord
position fondamentale (Fr.)
Grundstellung (G.)
posición fundamental (Sp.)

positive organ
*portative organ
organetto (It.)
regal
reed organ
bible regal

2. choir organ/division
organo di coro (It.)
positif (Fr.)
positif de dos (Fr.)
Positiv (G.)
Positiv im Stuhl (G.)
Unterwerk (G.)
Rückpositiv (G.)

post Epistolum (Lat.)
Alleluia mass section
(Ambrosian)
Hallelujah
post Evangelium (Lat.)

posthorn
coach-horn

straight horn
corno da posta (It.)
cornetta da postiglione (It.)
cor, cornet de poste (Fr.)
cornet (Fr.)
corneta de posta/postillón (Sp.)
trumpet
cornet
bugle

postizas (Sp.)
  *castanets
  clappers
  bones
  naccheres (It.)
  castagnettes (Fr.)
  Kastagnetten (G.)
  castañetas (Sp.)

postlude
  voluntary
  postludium (Lat.)
  postludio (It., Sp.)
  clôture (Fr.)
  Nachspiel (G.)
  Postludium (G.)

vs. prelude

potpourri
  *medley
  olio
  overture
  suite
  salmagundi, -y
  centone (It.)
  pastiche (E., Fr.)
  divertissement (Fr.)
  salmis, salmigondis (Fr.)
  pot-pourri (Fr.)
  quodlibet (Lat.)
  olla potrida (Sp.)
  centón (Sp.)

poulailler (Fr.)
  gallery

*balcony
peanut gallery
galleria (It.)
gallerie (Fr.)
Galerie (G.)
galería (Sp.)
paraíso (Sp.)

pouls (Fr.)
  beat
  rhythm
  pulse
  polso (It.)
  Puls (G.)
  pulso (Sp.)

poussé, poussez (Fr.)
  *up-bow
  arcata in su (It.)
  Aufstrich (G.)
  Hinaufstrich (G.)
  Anstrich (G.)
  arco por arriba (Sp.)
  arco hacia arriba (Sp.)

vs. tiré (Fr.)

practical music
  applied music
  performance practice
  *Aufführungspraxis (G.)

practice (vb)
  rehearse
  run through
  go over
  drill
  esercitare (It.)
  provare (It.)
  répéter (Fr.)
  exercer (Fr.)
  üben (G.)
  proben (G.)
  ejercitar (Sp.)
  ensayar (Sp.)

practice (n)
  rehearsal
  run-through
  drill
  dress rehearsal
  prova (It.)
  répétition (Fr.)
  Probe (G.)
  ensayo (Sp.)

praeambulum (Lat.)
  prelude
  voluntary
  prologue (opera)
  pro(h)emium (Lat.)
  intonazione (It.)
  prélude (Fr.)
  préambule (Fr.)
  Vorspiel (G.)
  Präludium (G.)
  preludio (Sp.)

vs. postludium (Lat.)

praecentor (Lat.)
  *cantor
  choir leader
  precentor
  accentor
  cantore (It.)
  chantre (Fr.)
  préchantre (Fr.)
  Kantor (G.)

praeconium paschale (Lat.)
  ex(s)ultet (Lat.)
  Easter proclamation

praelegendum (Lat.)
  introit (Gallican, Mozarabic)
  entrance song
  ingressa (Lat., Ambrosian)
  mass
  proper of the mass

praise song

song of praise
*hymn
anthem
doxology
theody
paean
canticle
Lobgesang (G.)

Pralltriller (G.)
upper neighbor note
auxiliary tone
ornament
grace note
inverted mordent
half-shake
mordente superiore (It.)
mezzo trillo (It.)
tremblement (Fr.)
pincé (Fr.)
Praller (G.)
Schneller (G.)
mordente invertido (Sp.)

prayer(s)
collect
litany
sufferages
orations
preces (Lat.)
oratio (Lat.)
oremus (Lat.)
oración (Sp.)

pre-sets (organ)
combination pistons
thumb pistons
toe studs/pistons
generals
pistoni (It.)
bouton-pistons (Fr.)
boutons de combinaison (Fr.)
Druckknopf (G.)

Preislied (G.)
*prize song

crowned song
cantus coronatus (Lat.)
chanson couronnée (Fr.)
Meistersinger (G.)

prelude
introduction
overture
voluntary
verset
verse (of a popular song)
anabole (Gr.)
praeludium (Lat.)
anteludium (Lat.)
praeambulum (Lat.)
sinfonia (It.)
intonazione (It.)
preludio (It., Sp.)
prélude (Fr.)
Präludium (G.)
Vorspiel (G.)

vs. postlude

premier (Fr.)
lead part
upper part (piano duet)
primo (It.)
erste (G.)
primero (Sp.)

premier balcon (Fr.)
first *balcony
dress circle
mezzanine
loges
gallery

premier dessus (Fr.)
soprano (E., It., Fr., Sp.)
high voice
lead voice/part
melody (voice)
dessus, haut-dessus (Fr.)
cantus (Lat.)
superius (Lat.)

erste Stimme (G.)
erste Sopran (G.)
tiple (Sp.)

premier mouvement (Fr.)
*a tempo (It.)
primo tempo (It.)
first tempo
erstes Tempo/Zeitmass (G.)
primero tiempo (Sp.)

premier pupitre (Fr.)
first stand/desk
principal
primo leggio (It.)
erstes Pult (G.)
premer atril (Sp.)

première E., Fr.)
first performance
*début (E., Fr.)
debutto (It.)
Erstaufführung (G.)
estreno (Sp.)

preparation (tone/note)
anticipation tone
ornament
non-harmonic tone
prepared dissonance
suspension

preparation hymn
sermon hymn

prepared piano
altered sounds
piano préparé (Fr.)
Fagottzug (G.)
piano preparado (Sp.)

presentation
*performance
concert
recital
reading

interpretation
engagement
gig

pressante (It.)
accelerando (It.)
accelerato (It.)
stringendo (It.)
accéléré (Fr.)
pressez (Fr.)
eiland (G.)
acelerado (Sp.)

pressing
a *record
platter
disk
LP
CD, DVD
microgroove record
long-playing record
extended-play (45 rpm)
disco (It., Sp.)
disque (Fr.)
Schallplatte (G.)

préstant (Fr., org.)
principal
octave
diapason
montre (Fr.)
Hauptstimme (G.)
diapasón abierto (Sp.)

presto, prestissimo (It.)
fast, very fast
rapid
quick
vite (Fr.)
rapide (Fr.)
schnell (G.)
presto (Sp.)

vs. lento, largo (It.)

prick song (16c.)

contrapuntal music
figural music
mensural music
polyphonic music

pricked note
dotted note
nota puntata (It.)
note pointé (Fr.)
punktierte Note (G.)
nota con puntillo (Sp.)

prima (Sp.)
E-string (violin)
cantino (It.)
soprana corda (It.)
chanterelle (Fr.)
Sangsaite (G.)
E-Saite (G.)
tiple (Sp.)

prima donna (It.)
opera singer
leading singer (soprano)
diva
principal singer
cantatrice (It., Fr.)
première dame (Fr.)
primo uomo (It.)
Primadonna (G.)
primera dama (Sp.)

prima galleria (It.)
dress circle
first balcony
mezzanine
*balcony
premier balcon (Fr.)
corbeille (Fr.)
erster Rang (G.)
galería principal (Sp.)

prima prattica (It. 17c.)
polyphonic music
16c. style
Palestrina style

old style
ars antiqua (Lat.)
stile antico (It.)

vs. seconda prattica (It.)

prima vista (It.)
at (first) sight
sight-read
à vue (Fr.)
vom Blatt (G.)
a primera vista (Sp.)

prima volta (It.)
first ending
apertum (Lat.)
première fois (Fr.)
ouvert (Fr. 14c.)
erste Mal (G.)
primera vez (Sp.)

vs. seconda volta (It.)
second ending

2. *at (first) sight
sight read

Primärton (G.)
*fundamental tone
root
first harmonic/partial
overtone series
Grundton (G.)

prime (pitch)
unison
unisonus (Lat.)
unisono (It.)
unisson (Fr.)
Einklang (G.)
Prim (G.)

2. tonic note
first note of the scale
do
ut (Lat.)

Prime (E., Fr. religious)
Divine office
first day hour
hora prima (Lat.)
prima (It., Sp.)
Prime (G.)

primer manual (Sp.)
great organ/division
grand'organo (It.)
principale (It.)
grand-orgue (Fr.)
Hauptwerk (G.)
Hauptorgel (G.)
gran'órgano (Sp.)

Primgeiger (G.)
principal violin
first violin
concertmaster
primo violino (It.)
premier violon (Fr.)
Konzertmeister (G.)
erste Geige (G.)
primer violín (Sp.)

primicerius (Lat.)
precentor
*cantor
succentor
primicerio (It., Sp.)
Kantor (G.)

primo (It.)
lead part
upper part (piano duet)
premier (Fr.)
erste (G.)
primero (Sp.)

vs. secondo (It.)

primo uomo (It.)
leading male singer
principal singer
prima donna (It.)

erste Tenorist (G.)
primer hombre (Sp.)

primo rivolto (It.)
first inversion (chord)
chord of the sixth
six-three chord
sixth chord
accordo di sesta (It.)
premier renversement (Fr.)
accord de sixte (Fr.)
Sextakkord (G.)
erste Umkehrung (G.)
acorde de sexta (y tercera)
(Sp.)

primo tempo (It.)
a tempo (It.)
first tempo
premier mouvement (Fr.)
erstes Zeitmass (G.)
primero tiempo (Sp.)
primero movimiento (Sp.)

principal
section leader
first desk/chair
*premier pupitre (Fr.)

principal (organ)
diapason
principale (It.)
principal(e) (Fr.)
montre (Fr.)
Prinzipal (G.)
principal (Sp.)

principal theme
main theme
first theme
tema principale (It.)
thème principal (Fr.)
Hauptsatz (G.)
Hauptthema (G.)
tema principal (Sp.)

vs. second(ary) theme

principale (It. org.)
great organ/division/manual
grand'organo (It.)
grand-orgue (Fr.)
Hauptwerk (G.)
Hauptorgel (G.)
primer manual (Sp.)
gran órgano (Sp.)

Prinzipalbass (G. org.))
Choral bass
chorus reed
pedal flute (4 ft.)
choralbass (Fr.)
Chorbass (G.)
contras en octava (Sp.)

Pritsche (G.)
whip (percussion)
slapstick
horsewhip
frusta (It.)
fouet (Fr.)
Peitsche (G.)
zurriaga (Sp.)
látigo (Sp.)
tralla (Sp.)

prize song
crowned song
cantus coronatus (Lat. 13c.)
chanson couronnée (Fr.)
gekröntes Lied (G.)
Preislied (G.)
puy, puit (Fr.)
Trouvère song (Fr.)
Meistersinger (G.)

Probe (G.)
rehearsal
practice
run-through
drill
prova (It.)

répétition (Fr.)
ensayo (Sp.)

processional
chant book
music for processions
processionale (Lat., Fr.)

2. music for processing
processional hymn

proemium (Lat.)
*prelude
anabole (Gr.)

profane music
secular music
musica profana (It.)
musique profane Fr.)
weltliche Musik (G.)
música profano (Sp.)

vs. sacred music

program
concert
recital
presentation
musicale
musical event
rendering
gig
programma (It.)
programme (E., Fr.)
Programm (G.)
programa (Sp.)

2. menu
listing
order
playbill
bulletin (church)

3. a story, poem or picture
symphonic poem
word-painting

*program music

program music
tone poem
symphonic poem
program symphony
descriptive music
word painting
tone painting
character piece
characteristic piece
program chanson
caprice (Fr.)
pastorale
musica a programma (It.)
musica descritiva (It.)
musique à programme (Fr.)
programm Musik (G.)
música programatica (Sp.)
música programa (Sp.)
música descriptiva (Sp.)

vs. absolute music

program notes
liner notes (record jackets)
analytical notes

progression (E., Fr.)
sequence
movement
progressione (It.)
Fortschreitung (G.)
progresión (Sp.)

progressive composition
through-composed
open form
a forma aperta (It.)
de forme ouverte (Fr.)
Durchkomponieren (G.)
compuesto de principio a fin
(Sp.)

progressive jazz
experimental jazz

avant-garde
fusion
way-out jazz

prolation (14c.)
prolatio (Lat.)
mensuration
proportional rhythm
meter
time changes

prolation sign
meter signature
measure signature
*time signature

prolongement (Fr.)
sostenuto pedal
sustaining pedal
loud pedal
damper pedal
pedale (dell) forte (It.)
pedale destra (It.)
pédale droite (Fr.)
pédale forte (Fr.)
pédale de prolongation (Fr.)
pédale grande (fr.)
Gross-Pedal (G.)
Forte-Pedal (G.)
rechte Pedale (G.)
Tonhaltepedal (G.)
pedal fuerte (Sp.)
pedal de prolongación (Sp.)

prolongation
extention (of tones or tonality)
tonal structure
Schenker analysis

prominent
emphasized
brought out
en dehors (Fr.)
con anfasi (It.)
enfatico (It.)
accusé (Fr.)

nachdrucklich (G.)

prompt(er)
cue
cue card
teleprompter
prompt-box
prompter's box
suggeritore (It.)
buca del suugeritore (It.)
trou de souffleur (Fr.)
souffleur, -euse (Fr.)
Souffleurkasten (G.)
Souffleur, -euse (G.)
apuntador, -ora (Sp.)
concha del apuntador (Sp.)

pronto (Sp.)
allegro (It.)
fast
vite (Fr.)
Schnell (G.)

vs. lentamente (Sp.)
despacio (Sp.)

proper (of the mass)
lectionary
proper of the time
proprium missae (Lat.)
proprium de tempore (Lat.)
proper of the saints
proprium sanctorum (Lat.)
proprio della messa (It.)
propre de la messe (Fr.)
Proprium Missae (G.)
proprio de la misa (Sp.)

proportion (of organ pipes)
scale
voicing
regulating
misura (It.)
taille (Fr.)
facture (Fr.)
diapason (Fr.)

mesure (Fr.)
Mensur (G.)
mensura (Sp.)

Proportz (G.)
after-dance
galliard
gagliarda (It.)
proporzione, proporzio (It.)
tripla (It.)
rotta (It.)
saltarello (It.)
gagliarda (It.)
bassadanza (It.)
quaternaria (It.)
basse-danse (Fr.)
sauterelle (Fr.)
to(u)rdion (Fr.)
Nachtanz (G.)
Hupfauf (G.)
Hopp Tancz (G.)
Sprung (G.)
segunda danza (Sp.)

proposta (It.)
dux (Lat.)
antecedent
subject
theme
antecedente (It., Sp.)
guida (It.)
antécédent (Fr.)
proposition (Fr.)
Proposta (G.)
Leitmelodie (G.)
propuesta (Sp.)

prosa, prosula (Lat.)
sequence (in the mass)
hymn
trope
sequentia (Lat.)
prose (Fr.)

prova (It.)
rehearsal

practice
run-through
drill
dress rehearsal
répétition (Fr.)
Probe (G.)
ensayo (Sp.)

psallenda (Lat.)
*antiphon (Ambrosian)
processional psalm
psalm antiphon
gradual psalm
psalmellus (Lat. Ambrosian)

psalm
sacred song
hymn
Songs of Sion/Zion
metrical psalm
introit
gradual
offertory
psalmus (Lat.)
salmo (It., Sp.)
psaume (Fr.)
Psalm (G.)

psalm book
*hymnal
tune book
hymn book
psalter
*anthology

psalm tone
modes
formula
tono salmodico (It.)
ton psalmodique (Fr.)
Psalmton (G.)
tono salmódico (Sp.)
tono de recitación (Sp.)

psalm tune
hymn-tune

song
metrical psalm

psalmus idioticus (Lat.)
psalm-like chant
gloria, exultet, Te Deum (Lat.)

psalter
psalm book
collection of psalms
hymnal
hymn book
*anthology
salterio (It., Sp.)
psaultier (Fr.)
Psalter (G.)

psaltery
lyre
dulcimer
harp
bell harp
fairy bells
psalterium (Lat.)
salterio (It., Sp.)
psaltérion (Fr.)
Psalterium (G.)

puente (Sp.)
*bridge (strings)
ponticello (It.)
chevalet (Fr.)
Steg (G.)

pulse
beat
rhythm
accent
meter
tactus (Lat.)
polso (It.)
pouls (Fr.)
Puls (G.)
pulso (Sp.)

Pult (G.)

chair
desk
stand
leggio (It.)
pupitre (Fr.)
atril (Sp.)

pump organ
harmonium
reed organ
cabinet organ
parlor organ
American organ
armonio (It., Sp.)

vs. pipe organ

Pumpventil (G.)
valve (brass instr.)
piston (E., Fr.)
pistone (It.)
valvola (It.)
Ventil (G.)
Perinetventil (G.)
pistón (Sp.)

punctum (Lat.)
note
neume
square note
short note
*brevis (Lat.)

punctum inclinatum (Lat.)
semibrevis (Lat.)
semibreve (E., It.)
whole note
intera, -o (It.)
ronde (Fr.)
Ganze, Ganzenote (G.)
redonda (Sp.)

punctus Lat.)
dot
punctus additionis (Lat.)

punctus augmentationis (Lat.)
punctus divisionis (Lat.)
punto (It., Sp.)
point (Fr.)
Punkt (G.)
puntillo (Sp.)

Punktneume (G.)
punctus (Lat., Fr., Sp.)
square note(Gregorian chant)
neume
Aquitanian notation
punto (It., Sp.)
point (Fr.)

punta, punto (It., Sp.)
point (of a bow)
tip
peak
pointe (Fr.)
Spitze (G.)

vs. talón (Sp.)
tallone (It.)

puntale (It.)
endpin (cello, bass)
tailpin
peg
spike
pied (Fr.)
Stachel (G.)
puntal (Sp.)

puntato (It.)
dotted
pointé (Fr.)
coulée (Fr.)
punktiert (G.)
puntado (Sp.)
con puntillo (Sp.)

2. notes inégales (Fr.)

punteado (Sp.)

plucked
strummed
thrummed
pizzicato (It.)
staccato (It.)
pincé (Fr.)
arraché (Fr.)
gezupft, gezwickt (G.)

vs. arco, arcata (It.)

punto coronato (It.)
corona
pause
*fermata (It.)
hold
point d'orgue (Fr.)
calderón (Sp.)
punto de organo (Sp.)
punto d'organo (It.)

punto de imitación (Sp.)
point(s) of imitation
theme
dux (Lat.)
subject
frammento d'imitazione (It.)
motivo d'imitazione (It.)
passage en imitation (Fr.)
motif en imitation (Fr.)
Imitationsabschnitte (G.)
Imitationsmotiv (G.)
motivo imitado (Sp.)
pasaje de imitación (Sp.)

punto de las notas (Sp.)
note head
capocchia (It.)
testina (It.)
tête de la note (Fr.)
Notenkopf (G.)
cabeza de las notas (Sp.)

pupitre (Fr.)
desk
stand

music stand
chair
rostrum
leggio (It.)
Pult (G.)
atril (Sp.)

pure music
abstract music
absolute music
musica assoluta (It.)
musique pure (Fr.)
absolute Musik (G.)
música absoluta (Sp.)
música pura (Sp., It.)

vs. program music

putti (It.)
choirboys
cantori (It.)
ragazzi (It.)
fanciullo del coro (It.)
enfants de choeur (Fr.)
Sängerknaben (G.)
Chorknaben (G.)
niños de coro (Sp.)
escolán (Sp.)

puy, pui (Fr. 13c.)
festival (Troubadour)
competition
song contest
prize song
crowned song
cantus coronatus (Lat.)
chanson couronnée (Fr.)
Preislied (G.)
puy d'amour (Fr.)
Sängerkriege (G.,
Minnesinger)

puzzle canon
riddle canon
enigma/enigmatic canon
canone enigmatico (It.)

canon énigmatique (Fr.)
Rätselkanon (G.)
canon enigmatico (Sp.)

Pythagorean comma
ditonic comma
comma
syntonic comma
schisma
centitone
comma maxima (Lat.)
pythagoreisches Komma (G.)

Pythagorean scale
diatonic scale
major, minor scale
fifths, pure fifths

Q

quadran pavan
  pass'e mez(z)o moderno (It.)
  *passamezzo (It.)
  pavan
  pavana (It.)
  pavane (Fr.)

quadraphonic sound
  four-way, four-track
  surround-sound
  stereophonic sound

vs. monophonic sound

Quadrat (G.)
  natural sign
  cancel sign
  quadro (It.)
  bequadro (It.)
  bécarre (Fr.)
  naturel (Fr.)
  Auflösungszeichen (G.)
  B-Quadrat (G.)
  becuadro (Sp.)

quadrat
  *breve
  square note
  neume
  brevis (Lat.)
  quadratum (Lat.)

Quadratnotation (G.)
  square notation
  chant notation
  neumes
  Aquitanian notation
  quadratic notation
  notazione quadrata (It.)

  notation carrée (Fr.)
  notación cuadrada (Sp.)

quadracinium (Lat.)
  *quartet
  bicinium (Lat.)
  tricinium (Lat.)

quadrille (E., Fr.)
  square dance
  galop
  polka
  cancan
  vaudeville
  quadriglia (It.)
  cuadrilla (Sp.)
  Quadrille (G.)

quadruple counterpoint
  four-part
  invertable counterpoint
  convertible counterpoint
  *paired imitation

quadruple-croche (Fr.)
  64th-note
  hemi-demisemiquaver
  semibiscroma (It.)
  Vierundsechzigstel-Note (G.)
  semifusa (Sp.)

quadruplet
  four notes in place of three
  triplet
  duplet
  quartina (It.)
  quartolet (Fr.)
  Quartole (G.)
  cuatrillo (Sp.)

quadruplum (Lat.)
  four-part organum
  fourth voice

quarré (Fr.)
  *breve (E., It., Fr., Sp.)

  brevis (Lat.)
  double whole-note
  carrée (Fr.)
  Doppelganze (G.)
  Doppeltaktnote (G.)

quart de soupir (Fr.)
  16th-note rest
  semiquaver rest
  pausa di semicroma (It.)
  Sechzehntelpause (G.)
  silencio de semicorchea (Sp.)
  pausa de semicorchea (Sp.)

quart de ton (Fr.)
  quarter-tone
  micro-tone
  demi-semitone
  minor semitone
  limma (Gr.)
  diesis (Gr.)
  quarto di tono (It.)
  cuarto de tono (Sp.)
  *comma
  schisma (Lat.)
  cent, centitone
  Viertelton (G.)
  Kleinintervalle (G.)
  Mikrointervalle (G.)

quartal harmony
  based on fourths
  armonia quartale (It.)
  armonia per quarte (It.)
  harmonie par quartes (Fr.)
  Quartenharmonik (G.)
  armonía por cuartes (Sp.)

vs. triadic harmony
  tertian harmony

quarte (Fr.)
  fourth (interval)
  quarta (Lat., It.)
  Quart(e) (G.)
  cuarta (Sp.)

338

*quarter note

quarter note
crotchet
nera (It.)
semiminima (It.)
quarto (It.)
noire (Fr.)
Viertel(note) (G.)
schwarze Note (G.)
negra (Sp.)
semínima (Sp.)

quarter rest
crotchet rest
pausa di semiminima (It.)
quarto d'aspetto (It.)
soupir (Fr.)
Viertelpause (G.)
silencio de negra (Sp.)
pausa de negra (Sp.)
pausa de semimina (Sp.)

quartet
four performers
a work for four performers
quatricinium (Lat.)
quatuor (Fr.)
quartetto (It.)
Quartett (G.)
cuarteto (Sp.)

quartetto con pianoforte (It.)
piano quartet
quatuor avec piano (Fr.)
Klavierquartett (G.)
cuarteto con piano (Sp.)

quartetto d'archi (It.)
string quartet
quatuor à cordes (Fr.)
Streichquartett (G.)
cuarteto de cuerdas (Sp.)

Quartgeige (G.)
small violin (quarter-size)

*kit
pocket fiddle/violin
poccetta (It.)
pochette (Fr.)
violino piccolo (It.)
violon piccolo (Fr.)
Terzgeige (G.)
Taschengeige (G.)
Sackgeige (G.)
violin pequeño (Sp.)

quarto, in quarto (Lat.)
sheet folded in four
sheet music
smaller than folio size
octavo (choral music)
folio

quarto di tono/tuono (It.)
quarter-tone
***quart de ton (Fr.)**
Viertelton (G.)
cuarto de tono (Sp.)

quaternaria (Lat., It.)
*basse danse (Fr.)
minuet
bassadanza (It.)
saltarello todescho (It.)
branle (Fr.)
Hoftanz (G.)
Nachtanz (G.)

2. ligature of four notes

quatrible
descant a 4th above
organum
quartal harmony

Quartsextakkord (G.)
six-four chord
2nd inversion of a triad
accordo di quarta e sesta (It.)
accord de sixte et quart (Fr.)
acorde de sexta-cuarta (Sp.)

quatricinium (Lat.)
music in four parts (voices)
tricinium (Lat.)
bicinium (Lat.)
*quartet

quattricroma (It.)
64th-note
hemidemisemiquaver
semibiscroma (It.)
sessantaquattresimo (It.)
quadruple croche (Fr.)
vierundsechzigstel Note (G.)
semifusa (Sp.)

quatuor (Fr.)
*quartet
quartetto (It.)

quatuor à cordes (Fr.)
string quartet
chamber music
quartetto di corde (It.)
quartetto d'archi (It.)
Streichquartett (G.)
cuartete de cuerdas (Sp.)

quaver
eighth-note
croma (It.)
ottavo (It.)
croche (Fr.)
Achtel (G.)
corchea (Sp.)

quedo (Sp.)
in a low voice
quietly
softly
whispered
*aside
sotto voce (It.)
à part (Fr.)
beiseite (G.)
a parte (Sp.)

Quempas (G.)
Christmas carol/song
collection of carols
canzona di natale (It.)
natalizio (It.)
chant de noël (Fr.)
cantique de noël (Fr.)
Weinachtslied (G.)
villancico (Sp.)
cántico de Navidad (Sp.)
zéjel (Sp.)

Querbalken (G.)
beam
cross-bar
tratto d'unione (It.)
stanghetta (It.)
barre tranversale (Fr.)
Notenbalken (G.)
Balkenverbindung (G.)
travesaño (Sp.)

Querflöte (G.)
*flute
concert flute
transverse flute
cross flute
German flute
flauto (It.)
flûte (Fr.)
flauta (Sp.)
flauto traverso (It.)
flûte traversière (Fr.)
flauto travesera (Sp.)

vs. Blockflöte (G.)
recorder

Querflügel (G.)
spinet
cottage piano
cabinet piano
upright piano
studio upright
couched harp
spinetta (It.)

épinette (Fr.)
Spinett (G.)
espineta (Sp.)

vs. Hammerflügel (G.)
Flügel (G.)

Querpfeife (G.)
fife
piccolo (It.)
penny whistle
tin whistle
fipple flute
piffero (It.)
fifre (Fr.)
Pfeife (G.)
Schweizeflöte (G.)
pifano, pifaro (Sp.)

Querpfeife-Trommel (G.)
pipe and tabor
whittle and dub (old E.)
galoubet (Fr.)
Schwegel (G.)
flaviol y tambori(l) (Sp.)

Querschnitt (G.)
*medley
potpourri
overture
pasticcio (It.)
pastiche (Fr.)
quodlibet
mezcla (Sp.)

Querstand (G.)
cross relation
false relation
clash
dissonance
discord
falsa relazione (It.)
falsa relación (Sp.)
fausse relation (Fr.)

question

antecedent
subject
theme
motive
statement
phrase
period
dux (Lat.)
antecedente (It.)
proposta (It.)
guida (It.)
thème (Fr.)
Führer (G.)

vs. answer
consequent

Quetsche (G.)
*accordion
concertina
squeezebox
hand-harmonica
fisarmonica (It.)
organetto (It.)
soufflet (Fr.)
accordéon (Fr.)

Quetschkommode (G.)
fuelle (Sp.)
bandoneón (Sp.)

Quetschung (G.)
mordent
*acciaccatura (It.)
grace note
ornament
crushed note
appoggiatura (It.)
apoyatura breve (Sp.)

queue (Fr.)
tail (of a note)
stem
gambo della nota (It.)
hampe (Fr.)
Hals (G.)
Notenhals (G.)

Stiel, Notenstiel (G.)
plica (Sp.)

quick step
march
quick time
*cut time
double time
fast duple time
marcia (It.)
marche (Fr.)
Marsch (G.)
marcha (Sp.)

2. foxtrot
two-step

quickly
immediately
suddenly
subito (It.)
subitement (Fr.)
sofort (G.)
sogleich (G.)
inmediato (Sp.)
súbito (Sp.)

quiebro (Sp.)
trill
ornament
roll
mordent
gruppo (It.)
redoble (Sp.)

quill
jack (harpsichord)
plectrum
spina (It., Sp.)
sautereau (Fr.)
Kiel (G.)
púa (Sp.)

quilt canzona
patch canzona

canzona
ricercar
carmen (Lat.)
fugue
Flikkanzone (G.)

Quin(t)dezime (G. org.)
fifteenth
double octave
doublette (E., Fr.)
superoctave
two-ft. stop
quindecima (It.)
quintadecima (It.)
decimaquinta (It.)
quinzième (Fr.)
Fünfzehntel (G.)
Doppeloktave (G.)
quincena (Sp.)

quint
fifth interval
quinta (It., Sp.)
quinte (Fr.)
Quinte (G.)

2. viola, viola part
fifth voice in four-part piece
Quinta, Quinta vox (Lat.)

3. *E-string on violin
chanterelle (Fr.)
Quintsaite (G.)

4. organ stop
twelfth
mutation stop (2 2/3)

quinta falsa (Lat.)
tritone
false fifth
augmented fourth
mi contra fa (Lat.)
diabolus in musica (Lat.)
devil's interval

*diminished fifth

quintadena (It. organ)
twelfth is prominent
quintaton (Fr.)
Quintatön (G.)
quintatón (Sp.)

Quinte parallele (It.)
parallel fifths
hidden fifths
consecutive fifths
covered fifths
quinte seguito (It.)
quintes parallèles (Fr.)
succession de quintes (Fr.)
verdekte Quinten (G.)
quintas paraleles (Sp.)

Quintenzirkel (G.)
circle of fifths
circolo/ciclo della quinte (It.)
cycle des quintes (Fr.)
ciclo de quintas (Sp.)
escala de quintas (Sp.)

quintet
five performers
quintetto (It.)
quintette (Fr.)
quintuor (Fr.)
Quintett (G.)
quinteto (Sp.)

Quintfagott (G.)
tenor oboe
small bassoon
treble bassoon
English horn
tenoroon
fagottino (It.)
oboe da caccia (It.)
cor Anglais (Fr.)
petit basson (Fr.)
Tenorfagott (G.)

fagote quinta (Sp.)

quinton (Fr.)
  5-string violin
  violin
  pardessus de viole (Fr.)

Quintsaite (G.)
  E-string (violin)
  cantarella (It.)
  soprana corda (It.)
  cantino (It.)
  chanterelle (Fr.)
  Sangsaite (G.)
  cantarela (Sp.)

quintuple meter/time
  5/4 time
  Cretic meter (Gr.)
  misura a cinque tempi (It.)
  quinario (It.)
  mesure à cinq temps (Fr.)
  Fünfertakt (G.)
  compás de cinco tiempos (Sp.)

quiosco de música (Sp.)
  *bandstand
  stage
  band shell
  platform
  palco (It.)
  kiosque à musique (Fr.)
  Musikpavillon (G.)

quire (old E.)
  *choir
  chorus

quirister (old E.)
  *chorister
  choir singer

quiterne (Fr., old E.)
  gittern
  *guitar
  ghiterna (It.)

guiterne (Fr.)
Quinterne (G.)

quodlibet (Lat.)
  *medley
  potpourri
  olio
  overture
  salmagundi, -y
  ensalada (It.)
  fricassée (Fr.)
  salmi(s) (Fr.)
  salmigondis (Fr.)
  pastiche (Fr.)
  messanza (It.)
  Querschnitt (G.)
  ensalada (Sp.)
  mezcla (Sp.)

quote
  borrow
  plagiarize
  steal
  copy
  prendere a prestito (It.)
  faire un emprunt (Fr.)
  entlehnen (G.)
  hacer un préstamo (Sp.)

R

rabec(a)
rebec (E., Fr.)
rebeck(e)
small violin
kit
rebeca (Lat.)
ribeca (It.)
rebebe (Fr.)
rebelle
ribibe
rubeba
rabel (Sp.)

rabillo (Sp.)
tail, flag (on a note)
hook
codetta (It.)
crochet de la note (Fr.)
Fahne, Fähnchen (G.)
Notenfahne (G.)
gancho (Sp.)

raccolta (It.)
*anthology
collection
sampling
repertoire
corpus (Lat.)
anthologium (Lat.)
recueil (Fr.)
Sammlung (G.)
Denkmäler (G.)
colección (Sp.)

racket(t) (E., Fr., Sp.)
sausage bassoon
racket bassoon
cervellato (It.)
rocchetta (It.)
cervelas, cervelat (Fr.)

Rackett, Rankett (G.)
Rankett-Fagott (G.)
Stockfagott (G.)
Wurstfagott (G.)
cervelas (Sp.)

Radel (G. 14c.)
round
*canon
rota
catch
caccia (It.)

radiating pedals (organ)
concave pedalboard
fan-shaped pedalboard
Clutsam keyboard
fächerförmiger Pedal (G.)

radical bass
fundamental bass
root bass
basso fondamentale (It.)
basse fondamentale (Fr.)
Grundbass (G.)
bajo fundamental (Sp.)

radio
*broadcast
on the air
television
satellite
cable

Radleier, Radleyer (G.)
*hurdy-gurdy
street organ
hand organ
organistrum (Lat.)
ghironda (It.)
organetto (It.)
vielle organisée (Fr.)
orgue de Barbarie (Fr.)
Dreorgel (G.)
Dreleier (G.)
organillo (Sp.)

viela de rueda (Sp.)

raga (Ind.)
melody
theme
motive
mode

raganella (It.)
*rattle
cog rattle
crécelle (Fr.)

ragazzi (It.)
chorister
*choirboys
putti (It.)
fanciullo del coro (It.)
enfants de choeur (Fr.)
kapelknaben (G.)
Chorknaben (G.)
niños de coro (Sp.)
escolán (Sp.)

ragtime
jazz
jive
blues
swing
cakewalk
stomp
stride piano
syncopation

railroad tracks
pause
break
*breath mark
hiatus
*caesura
abruptio (Lat.)
Abreissung (G.)

rainstick
*rattle
maracas

raise (pitch)
  sharp(en)
  alzare (It.)
  hausser (Fr.)
  erhöhen (G.)
  alzar (Sp.)

vs. lower
  flat

raise the bell
  bell in the air
  campana in alto (It.)
  padiglioni in alto (It.)
  pavillon en l'air (Fr.)
  Schalltrichter hoch (G.)
  Stürze hoch (G.)
  pabellón al aire (Sp.)

vs. bell down

raised (fifth)
  *augmented (fifth)
  sharped (fifth)
  aumentato (It.)
  augmenté (Fr.)
  übermässig (G.)
  aumentado (Sp.)

raised third
  major third
  Picardy third
  ditone
  terza maggiore (It.)
  tierce de Picardie (Fr.)
  tierce majeur (Fr.)
  grosse Terz (G.)
  Pikardische Terz (G.)
  tercera mayor (Sp.)

raking (on lute, etc.)
  broken chords
  strumming
  thrumming
  plucking
  twanging

  arpeggiating
  strappata (It.)
  Ausstreifen (G.)
  Durchstreichen (G.)
  rasgado, rasgueado (Sp.)
  toque rasgueado (Sp.)

rallentando (It.)
  slowing down
  broadening
  ritardando (It.)
  raffrenando (It.)
  ralentir (Fr.)
  en retardant (Fr.)
  nachgebend (G.)
  nachgiegig (G.)
  langsamer werdend (G.)

vs. accelerando (It.)
  stringendo (It.)

Rand (G.)
  rim (of a drum)
  orlo (It.)
  bord (Fr.)
  borde (Sp.)

rang (Fr.)
  course (strings)
  set of strings
  muta (It.)
  Chor (G.)
  orden (Sp.)

Rang (G.)
  *balcony
  gallery
  circle
  mezzanine
  dress circle
  loges
  galleria (It.)
  balconata (It.)
  balcon (Fr.)
  gallerie (Fr.)
  balcón (Sp.)

  galería (Sp.)

range
  tessitura (E., It.)
  ambitus (E., Fr.)
  compass
  ambito (It., Sp.)
  estensione (It.)
  étendue (Fr.)
  diapason (Fr.)
  Raum (G.)
  Umfang (G.)
  Lage (G.)
  Ausdehnung (G.)
  extensión (Sp.)
  tesitura (Sp.)

rank (organ)
  set of pipes
  stop
  register
  tier
  fila (It., Sp.)
  registro (It., Sp.)
  rang (Fr.)
  jeu (Fr.)
  Stimm (G.)

rant (17c.)
  jig
  dance movement
  courante (E., Fr., Sp.)
  corant(o) (E.)
  corrente (It.)

ranz des vaches (Fr.)
  Swiss mountain air
  Kuhreigen, Kuhreihen (G.)
  Lobetanz (G.)
  yodel

rap music
  pop
  parlando
  hip-hop
  reggae

ska
patter song
talking blues
Sprechstimme (G.)
techno-music
electronica
world music

rapidamente (It.)
fast
allegro (It.)
animato (It.)
presto (It.)
vite (Fr.)
Schnell (G.)
rasch (G.)
quick
pronto (E., Sp.)
affrettato (It.)
rapido (It., Sp.)
rapide (Fr.)
eilig (G.)
apresurado (Sp.)
veloz (Sp.)

vs. lentamente (It.)

rappresentazione sacra (It.)
oratorio
*liturgical drama
mystery play
miracle play
tomb play
sepulcrum play
passion play
geistliches Schauspiel (G.)

rapsodie (Fr.)
rhapsody
fantasy
through-composed
rhapsodie (Fr.)
rapsodia (It., Sp.)
Rhapsodie (G.)

raspberry

*flutter-tonguing
French kiss
Bronx cheer
frullato (It.)
double coup de langue (Fr.)
Flatterzunge (G.)
triple articulación (Sp.)

Rätselkanon (G.)
riddle canon
puzzle canon
enigmatic canon
canone enigmatico (It.)
canon énigmatique (Fr.)
Rätselkanon (G.)

rattenendo, rattenuto (It.)
ritenuto (It.)
rallentando (It.)
ritardando (It.)
slowing down
retenu (Fr.)
zurückgehalten (G.)
retrasado (Sp.)

vs. accelerando (It.)

rattle
ratchet
cog rattle
maraca
rainstick
raganella (It.)
crécelle (Fr.)
hochet (Fr.)
Ratsche (G.)
Rassel (G.)
Klapper (G.)
Knarre (G.)
Schnarre (G.)
sonajero (Sp.)
matraca (Sp.)
carraca (Sp.)

Raum (G.)
range

compass
tessitura
ambitus
ambito (It.)
estensione (It.)
étendue (Fr.)
extensión (Sp.)
ámbito (Sp.)

Rauscher (G.)
repeated notes (fast)
batteria (It.)
trillo (It.)
batterie (Fr.)

Rauschpfeife (G. organ)
mixture stop
compound stop
Rauschflöte (G.)
Rauschquinte (G.)
Rauschwerk (G.)

re
second degree of the scale
supertonic
sopratonica (It.)
sus-tonique (Fr.)
Subdominantparallele (G.)
Wechseldominante (G.)
supertónica (Sp.)

Re degli Strumenti (It.)
organ
King of Instruments
Roi des Instruments (Fr.)
Königin der Instrumente (G.)
Re de los Instrumentos (Sp.)

réaction (Fr.)
feedback (microphone)
microphone squeal
acoustical feedback
reazione (It.)
Reaktion (G.)
Ruckkoppelung (G.)
reacción (Sp.)

reading
  interpretation (E., Fr.)
  performance
  concert
  recital
  rendition
  interpretazione (It.)
  Gestaltung (G.)
  interpretación (Sp.)

realization
  filling in (continuo harmony)
  transcription
  arrangement
  figured bass
  continuo
  read charts
  lead sheet
  realizzazione (It.)
  réalisation (Fr.)
  Aussetzung (G.)
  realización (Sp.)

rebajar (Sp.)
  lower (a pitch)
  flat(ten) a note
  abbassare (It.)
  bemolisar (It.)
  baisser, abaisser (Fr.)
  bémoliser (Fr.)
  senken (G.)
  erniedrigen (G.)
  abemolar (Sp.)
  bajar (Sp.)

vs. alzar (Sp.)

rebec
  small violin
  fiddle
  kit
  rabec(a)
  rubebe (Lat., It.)
  ribeba, ribeca (It.)
  rébec (Fr.)
  Rubebe (G.)

rabe, rabel (Sp.)

rebube (Fr.)
  *Jew's harp
  jaw's harp
  mouth-organ
  ribeba (It.)
  guitarraccia (It.)
  guimbarde (Fr.)
  Maultrommel (G.)
  Judenharfe (G.)
  birimbao (Sp.)
  guitarrón (Sp.)

recapitulation/recap
  reprise (E., Fr.)
  repeat
  restatement
  sonata form
  da capo (It.)
  themes
  subject
  ripresa (It.)
  riesposizione (It.)
  réexposition (Fr.)
  Reprise (G.)
  Wiederkehr (G.)
  Wiederholung (G.)
  retorno (Sp.)
  reaparición (Sp.)
  reexposición (Sp.)

recercada, recercario (Sp.)
  fugal, fugue
  imitative instrumental piece
  *ricercare (E., It.)
  ricercar (Fr.)
  recherché (Fr.)
  Ricercar (G.)
  tiento (Sp.)

recessional
  exit hymn/chant
  closing hymn
  postlude
  voluntary

  postludium (Lat.)
  postludio (It., Sp.)
  clôture (Fr.)
  Nachspiel (G.)

vs. processional

rechant (Fr.)
  *refrain
  chorus
  burden
  respond

rechte Pedal (G.)
  loud pedal (piano)
  right pedal
  sustaining pedal
  sostenuto pedal
  pedale forte (It.)
  pedale destra (It.)
  pédale droite (Fr.)
  prolongement (Fr.)
  pedal fuerte (Sp.)

vs. linke Pedal (G.)
  soft pedal

récit (Fr. organ)
  solo organ manual
  swell division
  clavier de récit (Fr.)
  Soloklavier (G.)
  Oberwerk (G.)
  Schwellwerk (G.)

recital (E., Sp.)
  concert (E., Fr.)
  performance
  rendition
  chamber music concert
  concerto (It.)
  récital (Fr.)
  Konzert (G.)
  concierto (Sp.)

recital hall

*concert hall
auditorium
music hall
academy of music
sala da concerto (It.)
salle de concert (Fr.)
Konzertsaal (G.)
salón de conciertos (Sp.)

reciting note/tone (chant)
tenor
dominant
psalm-tone
tuba (Lat., It., E.)
repercussio (Lat.)
recto tono (Lat.)
nota dominans (Lat.)
nota di recitazione (It.)
teneur (Fr.)
Tenor (G.)

recitalist
performer
musician
artiste
soloist
concert artist

recitando (It.)
declamatory
syllabic
patter song
parlando, parlato (It.)
en parlant (Fr.)
sprechend (G.)
Sprechstimme (G.)
hablando (Sp.)

recitative
parlando (It.)
declamatory
*narrator, narration
evangelist
testo (Lat.)
historicus (Lat.)
Sprechstimme (G.)

stile recitativo (It.)
recitativo (It., Sp.)
récitatif (Fr.)
Rezitativ (G.)
recitado (Sp.)

reclamo (Sp.)
bird-call (organ)
richiamo per ucelli (It.)
cri d'oiseau (Fr.)
appeau (Fr.)
Vogelsang, Vogelgesang (G.)
Vogelpfeife (G.)

record (vb.)
registrare (It.)
enregister (Fr.)
aufnehmen (G.)
registrar (Sp.)
tape (record)

record (n.)
*recording
platter
pressing
disc
long-playing record
microgroove record
shellac record
vinyl record
cylinder
extended play (a 45)
an LP
a 78
CD, DVD
disco (It., Sp.)
disque (Fr.)
Schallplatte (G.)

record player
*phonograph
gramophone
victrola
turntable
CD player
record changer

giradischi (It.)
grammofono (It.)
tourne-disques (Fr.)
Grammophon (G.)
Plattenspieler (G.)
Plattenwechsler (G.)
tocadiscos (Sp.)
gramófono (Sp.)
fonógrafo (Sp.)

recorder (instr.)
English flute
vertical flute
beak flute
whistle flute
duct flute
fipple flute
flageolet
ocarina
tonette
song flute
slide whistle
Swanee whistle
bazooka
flutophone
flauto (up to 18th c.)
flauto a becco (It.)
flauto diritto (It.)
flauto dolce (It.)
flûte à bec (Fr.)
flûte douce (Fr.)
flûte droite (Fr.)
flûte d'Angleterre (Fr.)
flûte à neuf trous (Fr.16-17c.)
Blockflöte (G.)
Sifflöte (G., and org.)
Schnabelflöte (G.)
flauta de pico (Sp.)
flauta dulce (Sp.)
flauta recta (Sp.)

recording
*record
sound reproduction
tape
cassette

cylinder
a 78, 45, 33 1/3
LP
CD
DVD
player piano
sequencer
cartridge (tape)
reel-to-reel tape
registrazione (It.)
enregistrement (Fr.)
Aufnahme (G.)
registro (Sp.)

recte et retro (Lat.)
crab canon
retrograde canon
mirror canon
*canon cancrizans (Lat.)

recto tono (Lat.)
reciting tone (chant)
dominant
nota dominans (Lat.)
repercussio (Lat., It.)
tenor (Lat., It., E., Sp.)
tuba (Lat., It.)
teneur (Fr.)
Tenor (G.)
*recitative

recueil (Fr.)
*anthology
collection
repertory
corpus (Lat.)
raccolta (It.)
repertorio (It., Sp.)
Sammlung (G.)
Denkmäler (G.)

red(d)ita (It.)
repeat, return
recap, recapitulation
rondo theme
ripetizione (It.)

ritornello (It.)
ripresa (It.)
ritorno (It.)
reprise (Fr.)
redite, retour (Fr.)
Wiederholung (G.)
Rückkehr (G.)
retorno (Sp.)
repetición (Sp.)

redoblante (Sp.)
tenor drum
side/snare drum
cassa rullante (It.)
caisse roulante (Fr.)
tambour roulant (Fr.)
caisse sourde (Fr.)
Wirbeltrommel (G.)
Rührtrommel (G.)

redoble (Sp.)
trill
gruppo (It.)

2. drum-roll
tremolo (It.)
rullo (It.)
roulement (Fr.)
Trommelwirbel (G.)
Paukenwirbel (G.)

redonda (Sp.)
whole note
punctum inclinatum (Lat.)
semibrevis (Lat.)
semibreve (E., It.)
intera, -o (It.)
ronde (Fr.)
Ganze, ganze Note (G.)

redowa
Bohemian dance in ¾
waltz
mazurka
rédowa (Fr.)

reed(s)
mouthpiece of cane, etc.
woodwind instrument
reed instrument
aulos (Gr.)
tibia (Lat.)
ancia (It.)
anche (Fr.)
Rohr, Rohrblatt (G.)
lengüeta (Sp.)
caña (Sp.)
strumento ad ancia (It.)
instrument à anche (Fr.)
Rohrblattinstrument (G.)
instrumento de lengüeta (Sp.)

2. organ reed pipe(s)

reed organ
cabinet organ
positive organ
portative organ
*regal
bible/book regal
American organ
parlor organ
pump organ
melodeon
harmonium (E., It., Fr.)
armonio (It., Sp.)
orgue expressif (Fr.)
Harmonium (G.)
Expressivorgel (G.)

reel
Virginia reel
*contradance
line dance
Schottisch

2. recording tape holder
take-up reel
reel-to-reel tape recorder

réexposition (Fr.)
*recapitulation, recap

restatement of themes
repeat
return
da capo (It.)
ripresa (It.)
reprise (Fr.)
Wiederholung (G.)
reexposición (Sp.)

reforzado (Sp.)
accented
stressed
forte-piano (It.)
rinforzando, -ato (It.)
forzato, -ando, sforzato (It.)
renforcé (Fr.)
verstärkt (G.)

refrain (E., Fr.)
chorus
antiphon
respond
burden
rondo theme
epode, epistrophe (Gr.)
ritornello (It.)
ripresa (It.)
rondeau (Fr.)
rechant (Fr.)Widerkehr (G.)
Kehrreim (G.)
estribillo (Sp.)

regal, regall
portative organ
reed organ
positive organ
bible/book organ
pair of regalls
chamber organ
organetto (It.)
regale (It.)
positif (Fr.)
régale (Fr.)
Positiv (G.)
Regal (G.)
realejo (Sp.)

regalía (Sp.)

régale de bois (Fr.)
xylophone
gigelira (It.)
sticcato (It.)
harmonica de bois (Fr.)
patouille (Fr.)
*claquebois (Fr.)
régale de percussion (Fr.)
Xylophon (G.)
Strohfiedel (G.)
armonia de madera (Sp.)

regens chori (Lat.)
choirmaster
*choir director
maestro di cappella (It.)
maestro di coro (It.)
chef de choeur (Fr.)
Kapellmeister (G.)
maestro de capilla (Sp.)
director de coro (Sp.)

regent's bugle
bugle
*key(ed) bugle
Royal Kent bugle
cimbasso (It.)
bugle à clés (Fr.)
Klappenhorn (G.)
cornet
ophicleide

reggae
Jamaican pop/rock music
rap
ska
hip-hop

register
*range
ambitus
tessitura
compass
gamut

ambito (It., Sp.)
diapason (Fr.)
Raum (G.)

2. stop (organ)
rank
registro (It., Sp.)
registre (Fr.)
Stimmlage (G.)

Registerrad (G.)
crescendo pedal (org.)
crescendo rolativo (It.)
rouleau crescendo (Fr.)
Crescendowalze, -zug (G.)
Registerwalze (G.)
Kollektivschweller (G.)
Rollschweller (G.)
rodillo del crescendo (Sp.)

Registerzüge (G.)
draw-knobs (organ)
draw-stops
stop tabs
bottoni dei registri (It.)
boutons de registres (Fr.)
Registerknöpfe (G.)
Züge (G.)
botones tiradores (Sp.)
plancas de los registros (Sp.)

regulation, regulating
voicing
adjusting
regulazione (It.)
réglage (Fr.)
Regulierung (G.)
regulación (Sp.)

rehearsal
practice
run-through
going over
drill
full rehearsal
dress rehearsal

prova (It.)
repetizione (It.)
répétition (Fr.)
Probe (G.)
ensayo (Sp.)

rehearse
practice
go over
run through
drill
ripetere (It.)
répéter (Fr.)
Wiederholen (G.)
repetir (Sp.)

Reigen (G.)
round dance
ring dance
girotondo (It.)
danza in tondo (It.)
ronde (Fr.)
ronda (Sp.)
danza en redondo (Sp.)

Reihe (G.)
row
series
tone row
serial music
twelve-tone music
dodecaphonic music
atonal music

Reimoffizium (G.)
rhymed office
monastic office
hours of the day
Breviary
Opus Dei (Lat.)
*Divine Office
oficio rimado (Sp.)

relative key/mode
  relative minor/major
  tono relativo (It., Sp.)

mode relatif (Fr.)
Paralleltonart (G.)
verwandte Tonart (G.)
clave paralela (Sp.)

vs. tonic major/minor
  parallel key

relative pitch
orecchio relativo (It.)
oreille relative (Fr.)
relatives Gehör (G.)
oído relativo (Sp.)

vs. absolute pitch

release
bridge
channel
B-section
middle section
trio (of minuet)
alternative
alternativo (It.)
alternativement (Fr.)
Überleitung (G.)
Übergang (G.)
Rückgang (G.)
Rückführung (G.)

religious music
sacred music
liturgical music
church music
musica divina (Lat., It.)
musica religiosa (It.)
musica sacra (It.)
musica da chiesa (It.)
musica ecclesiastica (It.)
musique religieuse (Fr.)
musique sacrée (Fr.)
musique d'église (Fr.)
geistliche Musik (G.)
Kirchenmusik (G.)
música sagrada (Sp.)
música religiosa (Sp.)

música de iglesia (Sp.)

vs. secular music

relish
ornament
grace note
trill
double trill
mordent
beat
backfall
shake
appoggiatura (It.)

remove mutes
levate i sordini (It.)
senza sordino (It.)
sans sourdine (Fr.)
enlever la sourdine (Fr.)
Dämpfer abheben (G.)
Dämpfer weg (G.)
ohne Dämpfer (G.)
levanten la sordina (Sp.)
sin sordina (Sp.)

vs. with mutes

Renaissance (E., Fr., G.)
  rebirth
rinascimento (It.)
renacimiento (Sp.)

rendition
performance
concert
recital
interprétation (E., Fr.)
presentation
reading
interpretazione (It.)
Gestaltung (G.)
Vortrag (G.)
interpretación (Sp.)

renforcé (Fr.)

*accented
stressed
rinforzando, -ato (It.)
forte-piano (It.)
forzato, -ando (It.)
sforzando, -ato (It.)
verstärkt (G.)
reforzado (Sp.)

renversement (Fr.)
inversion (E., Fr.)
rivolto (It.)
rovescio, rovesciamento (It.)
Umkehrung (G.)
inversión (Sp.)

renvoi (Fr.)
return sign
repeat (sign)
recapitulation
reprise (E., Fr.)
dal segno (It.)
da capo (It.)
Wiederholungszeichen (G.)

repeat (n.)
repetition
reprise (E., Fr.)
ripresa (It.)
ripetizione (It.)
répétition (Fr.)
Wiederholung (G.)
repetición (Sp.)

repeat (vb.)
bis
once more/again
encore
from the beginning
from the top
D.C.
da capo (It.)
ancora una volta (It.)
encore une fois (Fr.)
noch einmal (G.)
repetieren (G.)

otra vez (Sp.)

repeat sign
segno di ripetizione (It.)
replica (It.)
signe de répétition (Fr.)
bâton de reprise (Fr.)
points de reprise (Fr.)
wiederholungszeichen (G.)
Rückweiser (G.)
signo de repetición (Sp.)

repeating action (piano)
double escapement
doublehopper
grasshopper
doppio scappamento (It.)
double échappement (Fr.)
Repetitionsmechanik (G.)
doppelte Auslösung (G.)
Englische Mechanik (G.)
doble escape (Sp.)
escapatoria (Sp.)

**repercussio, repercussus, -a
(Lat.)**
reciting note (chant)
tenor (Lat., E., Sp.)
dominant
psalm tone
recto tono (Lat.)
tuba (Lat., It., E.)
nota dominans (Lat.)
nota di recitazione (It.)
repercussione (It.)
teneur (Fr.)
répercussion (Fr.)
Tenor (G.)
Reperkussion (G.)
repercusion (Sp.)

repertoire (E., Fr.)
performance material
repertory
repertorio (It., Sp.)
Repertoire (G.)

Spielplan (G.)

2. *anthology
corpus (Lat.)
body of music
collection
compendium

répétiteur (Fr.)
coach
tutor
teacher
ripetitore (It.)
maestro sostituto (It.)
Korrepetitor (G.)
maestro concertador (Sp.)
repetidor (Sp.)

repetitio (Lat.)
repetition
*repeat
reprise
encore
once again, once more

2. concluding section
bar form
lai (Fr.)
cauda (Lat.)
Abgesang (G.)

répétition (Fr.)
rehearsal
prova (It.)
repetizione (It.)
ripetizione (It.)
Probe (G.)
ensayo (Sp.)
repetición (Sp.)

répétition générale (Fr.)
dress rehearsal
full rehearsal
prova generale (It.)
Generalprobe (G.)
ensayo general (Sp.)

repicar (Sp.)
  ring (bells)
  peal
  toll
  chime
  play
  sound
  scampanare (It.)
  carillonner (Fr.)
  Glöcke läuten (G.)
  klinge(l)n (G.)
  tocar las campanas (Sp.)

replica (It.)
  answer
  reply
  comes (Lat.)
  consequent
  fugue
  riposta (It.)
  réplique (Fr.)
  réponse (Fr.)
  Antwort (G.)
  respuesta (Sp.)

2. *repeat

3. cue
  chiamata (It.)
  Stichwort (G.)
  entrada (Sp.)

répons (Fr.)
  respond, responsory
  responsorium (Lat.)
  responsorio (It., Sp.)
  Responsorium (G.)

reports, in reports
  imitation
  fugal, fugue
  motet
  fugato (It.)
  di fuga (It.)
  fugué (Fr.)
  de fugue (Fr.)

fugiert (G.)
de fuga (Sp.)

representative
  agent
  booking agent
  manager
  impresario

reproaches
  improperia (Lat.)
  Good Friday
  Holy Week
  Veneration of the Cross

requiebro (Sp.)
  fast trill
  flutter
  shake
  trillo rapido (It.)
  trille rapide (Fr.)
  schneller Triller (G.)
  quiebro (Sp.)

requiem (Lat., E.)
  mass for the dead
  *funeral mass
  funeral song
  *lament
  missa pro defunctis (Lat.)
  messa da requiem (It.)
  messe des morts (Fr.)
  Totenmesse (G.)
  misa de difuntos (Sp.)

res facta (Lat.)
  written music (15-16c.)
  unadorned chant
  cantus compositus (Lat.)
  chose faite (Fr.)

resaltado (Sp.)
  emphasized
  stressed
  accented
  enfatico (It.)

*accusé (Fr.)
en déhors (Fr.)
betont (G.)

resbalando (Sp.)
  *glissando (It.)
  sliding
  gliding
  scooping
  portamento (It.)
  en glissant (Fr.)
  gleitend (G.)

resin (for a bow)
  rosin
  colophony
  colofonia (It., Sp.)
  colophane (Fr.)
  Kolophon, Kolophonium (G.)
  Geigenharz (G.)
  resina (Sp.)

resolution
  progression
  cadence
  consonant
  resolutio (Lat.)
  risoluzione (It.)
  sauvement (Fr.)
  résolution (Fr.)
  Auflösung (G.)
  resolución (Sp.)

resonance
  echo
  reverberation
  resounding
  risonanza (It.)
  résonance (Fr.)
  Resonanz (G.)
  Nachklang (G.)
  resonancia (Sp.)

Resonanzboden (G.)
  sound box/chest
  resonance chamber

cassa di resonanza (It.)
caisse de résonance (Fr.)
caja de resonancia (Sp.)

2. soundboard
table
belly
tavola armonico (It.)
piano armonico (It.)
table d'harmonie (Fr.)
caja armónica (Sp.)

Resonanzsaite (G.)
sympathetic string
aliquot string
corda simpatica (It.)
corda di risonanza (It.)
corde sympathique (Fr.)
corde de résonance (Fr.)
cuerda simpática (Sp.)
cuerda de resonancia (Sp.)

Resonanztafel (G.)
belly (of a vionin, etc.)
table (E., Fr.)
soundboard
tavola armonica (It.)
table d'harmonie (Fr.)
Decke (G.)
tapa, tabla de armonia (Sp.)

resound
reverberate
echo
ring, ring out
sound
resonate
rimbombare (It.)
riverberare (It.)
réverbérer (Fr.)
nachhallen (G.)
klingen (G.)
reverberar (Sp.)

respiro (It.)
breath pause

comma
suspension de respiration (Fr.)
Atempause (G.)
respiración (Sp.)

respond
responsory
responsorium (Lat.)
refrain
antiphon

response
reply
answer
consequent
comes (Lat.)
riposta (It.)
réponse (Fr.)
Antwort (G.)
respuesta (Sp.)

responsorial
antiphonal
call and response
refrain

respond
responsorium (Lat.)

2. book of responses
responsoriale (Lat.)

responsorium (Lat.)
Gradual psalm (Gallican)
proper of the mass
gradual
graduale (Lat.)
psalmellus (Lat. Ambrosian)
psallenda (Lat. Ambrosian)

ressortir (Fr.)
emphasize
bring out
accent
stress
marcare (It.)

mettere in rilievo (It.)
souligner (Fr.)
mettre en relief (Fr.)
en déhors (Fr.)
hervorheben (G.)
subrayar (Sp.)
hacer resaltar (Sp.)
poner en de relieve (Sp.)

rest
silence (E., Fr.)
silenzio (It.)
figura muta (Lat., It.)
caesura
cadence
pausa (It., Sp.)
pause (E., Fr.)
point de repos (Fr.)
Pause (G.)
silencio (Sp.)

restatement
*recapitulation
recap
reprise
return

restrictio (Lat.)
stretto (It.)
fugue, fugal
strette (Fr.)
Engführung (G.)
Stretta (G.)
estrecho (Sp.)
stretta (Sp.)
getting faster
stringendo (It.)
accelerando (It., Sp.)
en serrant (Fr.)
eilend (G.)
beschleunigend (G.)

resultant bass (organ)
acoustic bass
resultant tone
*combination tone

summation tone
differential/difference tone

retard (vb.)
  slow down
  ritardando (It., Sp.)
  rallentando (It.)
  en retardant (Fr.)
  langsamer werdend (G.)
  retardando (Sp.)

vs. accelerate
  speed up

retornelo (Sp.)
  refrain
  *ritornello (It.)

retroscena (It.)
  behind the scenes
  *backstage
  offstage
  in the wings
  dans les coulisses (Fr.)
  Hinterbühne (G.)
  hinter den Kulissen (G.)
  bastidores (Sp.)

retrograde
  cancrizans (Lat.)
  recte et retro (Lat.)
  crab-wise
  crab canon
  retrograde inversion
  al rovescio (It.)
  à l'écrevisse (Fr.)
  Krebsgang (G.)

reveille
  wake-up call
  bugle call
  sveglia (It.)
  diana (It., Sp.)
  réveil (Fr.)
  sonnerie (Fr.)
  diane (Fr.)

Reveille (G.)
Wecksignal (G.)
Morgensignal (G.)
Weckdienst (G.)
alborada (Sp.)
toque de alborada (Sp.)

vs. lullaby
  taps

reverberation
  echo
  live hall, etc.
  resonance
  riverberazione (It.)
  réverbération (Fr.)
  Nachhall (G.)
  reverberación (Sp.)
  retumbo (Sp.)

reverdie (Fr.)
  spring song
  may song
  Trouvère song
  canto di primavera (It.)
  canzona della primavera (It.)
  Frühlingslied (G.)
  canción de primavera (Sp.)

rêverie (Fr.)
  fantasy
  prelude
  sogno (It.)
  Träumerei (G.)
  soño (Sp.)

revue, musical (E., Fr.)
  musical
  entertainment
  extravaganza
  vaudeville
  burlesque (Fr., E.)
  variety show
  floor show
  follies
  minstrel show

cabaret
masque
operetta
burletta, burlesca (It.)
rivista (It.)
Ausstattungsstück (G.)
Burleske (G.)
Singspiel (G.)
revista (Sp.)

Rezitativ (G.)
  recitative
  narration
  declamatory
  sung dialogue
  rap
  recitativo (It., Sp.)
  stile recitativo (It.)
  récitatif (Fr.)
  Sprechstimme (G.)
  recitado (Sp.)
  opera, oratorio, cantata

rhapsody
  fantasy
  fantasia
  free form
  through-composed
  capriccio (It.)
  r(h)apsodie (Fr.)
  caprice (Fr.)
  rapsodia (It., Sp.)
  Rhapsodie (G.)

rhythm
  time
  movement
  motion
  rhythmus (Lat.)
  ritmo (It., Sp.)
  rythme (Fr.)
  rhythme (Fr.)
  Rhythmus (G.)
  Takt (G.)

rhythm and blues

jazz
pop
rock
blues
torch songs

rhythm band
percussion section (pop)
rhythm section
rhythm back-up/backround

2. children's band
toy instruments
Kindersinfonie (G.)
Musikalische Schlittenfahrt
(G.)

rhythm sticks
claves (Sp.,E., Fr., It.)
clappers
bones
spoons
Klangstäbe (G.)

rhythmed office
Office
*Divine Office
night office
ufficio rimato (It.)
office rimé (Fr.)
Reimoffizium (G.)
oficio rimado (Sp.)

rhythmic modes (13c.)
meter
rhythm
metrical time
mensural music
musica mensurabilis (Lat.)
*organum

ribattuto (It.)
*trill
shake
relish
double mordent

ornament
tremolo
gruppo (It.)
trillo (It.)
trille (Fr.)
Triller (G.)
trino (Sp.)

ribeba, ribebe, ribeca (It.)
*rebec
small violin
kit
rabeca, rebelle, ribibe (It.)
rubèbe (Fr.)

**ricercare, ricercata, ricercada
(It.)**
imitative instrumental piece
fugal
ricercar (E., Fr.)
recherché (Fr.)
Ricercar (G.)
rececada, recercario (Sp.)
tiento (Sp.)

ricochet (Fr.)
staccato bowing
bounced
spiccato (It.)
saltando (It.)
sautillé (Fr.)
jeté (Fr.)
Springbogen (G.)
saltado (Sp.)

vs. lié (Fr.)
legato (It.)

riddle canon
enigma, enigmatic canon
puzzle canon
canone enigmatico (It.)
canon énigmatique (Fr.)
Rätselkanon (G.)
canon enigmatico (Sp.)

rideau (Fr.)
curtain
drop
backdrop
traveler
scrim
cyclorama
sipario, siparietto (It.)
telone (It.)
Vorhang (G.)
telón (Sp.)

ridotto (It.)
masque
masqued entertainment
spectacle
show

2. arrangement
abridgement
reduced score
piano score
vocal score
riduzione (It.)

vs. full score

riff (jazz)
lick
hot lick
solo passage
break
virtuoso passage
cadenza (It.)

rigaudon (Fr.)
duple dance
rigadoon
gavotte
bourrée (Fr.)
suite

riga (It.)
staff line(s)
rigo musicale (It.)
pentagramma (It.)

portée musicale (Fr.)
Liniensystem (G.)
Notenlinie (G.)
pentagrama (Sp.)

righetta (It.)
ledger/leger line
ligne d'aiuto (It.)
rigo aggiunto (It.)
ligne postiche (Fr.)
ligne supplémentaire (Fr.)
ligne ajoutée (Fr.)
Hilfslinie (G.)
Nebenlinie (G.)
linea adicional (Sp.)

rim (of a drum)
drum hoop
orlo (It.)
bord (Fr.)
Rand (G.)
borde (Sp.)

rim shot
sul bordo (It.)
sur le bord (Fr.)
am Rand (G.)
sobre el borde (Sp.)

rinforzando, -ato (It.)
*accent(ed)
stress
forte piano (It.)
sforzando (It.)
forzato, -ando (It.)
renforcé (Fr.)
verstärkt (G.)
reforzado (Sp.)

ring
resound
sound
echo
resonate

2. strike

sound
play handbells
chime
peal
toll
suonare (It.)
scampanare (It.)
sonner (Fr.)
carillonner (Fr.)
läuten (G.)
klinge(l)n (G.)
tocar las campanas (Sp.)
repicar (Sp.)

ringer
bell ringer
campanist
campanista (It.)
carilloneur (Fr.)
Glockenspieler (G.)
campanero (Sp.)

2. professional musician assisting
an amateur group

ripetitore (It.)
coach
tutor
maestro sostituto (It.)
répétiteur (Fr.)
Korrepetitur (G.)
repetidor (Sp.)
maestro concertador (Sp.)

ripieno (It.)
full complement
everybody
tutti (It.)
cappella (It.)
concerto grosso (It.)

vs. concertino (It.)
favorito (It.)

ripresa (It.)
repeat

varied repeat
once more/again
from the top
from the beginning
da capo (It.)
repetition
reprise
recapitulation
refrain (14c.)
ballata (It.)
piedi (It.)
volta (It.)

risposta (It.)
answer (fugal)
consequent
comes (Lat.)
réponse (Fr.)
conséquent (Fr.)
Risposta (G.)
respuesta (Sp.)
consecuente (Sp.)

vs. proposta (It.)

risaltato (It.)
emphasized
stressed
con enfasi (It.)
enfatico (It.)
avec emphase (Fr.)
emphatique (Fr.)
en dehors (Fr.)
accusé (Fr.)
betont (G.)
hervorgehoben (G.)
nachdrucklich (G.)
resaltado (Sp.)
enfático (Sp.)
con énfasis (Sp.)

ritardando (It.)
slowing down
broadening
ritard
ritenuto (It.)

ritenente, ritenendo (It.)
rallentando (It.)
allargando (It.)
raffrenando (It.)
slargando (It.)
ralentir (Fr.)
en retardant (Fr.)
en ralentissant (Fr.)
nachgebend (G.)
nachgiegig (G.)
langsamer werdend (G.)
zurückhaltend (G.)
retardando (Sp.)

vs. accelerando (It.)

rite, ritual
liturgy
ceremony (religious)
service
use (Sarum)
rubrics
order of service
ordo (Lat.)
Mass
Eucharist
Agende (G.)
Kirchenamt (G.)
Kirchenordnung (G.)
rito, rituale (It.)
rite, rituel (Fr.)
Ritus, Ritual (G.)
Zeremoniell (G.)
rito (Sp.)

ritmo (It., Sp.)
*rhythm
time
movement
motion

ritornello (It.)
*refrain
returning theme/section
burden
rondo theme

ritournelle (Fr.)
Ritornell (G.)
ritornelo, retornelo (Sp.)

ritorto (It.)
shank (brass instr.)
*crook
extension
corpo di ricambio (It.)
corps de rechange (Fr.)
Aufsatzbogen (G.)
cuerpo de recambio (Sp.)

Rituale (Lat.)
book of rites
ordo (Lat.)
Sacramentary
Sacramentarium (Lat.)
book of worship
Book of Common Prayer

ritrovo notturno (It.)
nightclub
night spot
cabaret
cocktail lounge
locale notturno (It.)
discothèque (Fr.)
Nachtklub (G.)
Nachtlokal (G.)
café-cantante (Sp.)

riverso, rivolto (It.)
inversion
retrograde

rivet cymbals
sizzle cymbals
piatti chiodati (It.)
cymbales sur tiges (Fr.)
Sizzle-Becken (G.)
Nietenbecken (G.)
Zischbecken (G.)
cimbales sobre palillos (Sp.)

rivista musicale (It.)

periodical
review
journal
revue musicale (Fr.)
Musikzeitschrift (G.)
revista musical (Sp.)

rivista (It.)
revue (musical)(E., Fr.)
floor show
vaudeville
minstrel show
variety show
follies
musical
*medley
potpourri
olio
Ausstatungsstück (G.)
revista (Sp.)

road company
touring company
road show
touring show
traveling show
showboat
showmobile

rocchetta (It.)
*racket(t) (E., Fr., Sp.)
sausage bassoon
racket bassoon
Rankett (G.)

rock, rock and roll
pop music
hard rock
acid rock
heavy metal
reggae
ska
rap
hip-hop
electronica
techno-music

world music
rock'n'roll
rockabilly
jazz
blues
disco music

rococo
baroque (late)
classical (early)
gallant style
style gallant (Fr.)
galante Stil (G.)
Rokoko (G.)

rocola (Sp.)
*jukebox
record player
nickelodeon
Musikbox (G.)
tocadiscos automático (Sp.)

rodillo del crescendo (Sp.)
crescendo pedal (organ)
crescendo rolativo (It.)
rouleau crescendo (Fr.)
Crescendowalze, -zug (G.)
Registerrad, -walze (G.)
Kollektivrad, -walze (G.)
Rollschweller (G.)

Rohr, Rohrblatt (G.)
reed, reed instrument
woodwind instrument
mouthpiece of cane, etc.
aulos (Gr.)
tibia (Lat.)
ancia (It.)
canna (It.)
strumento ad ancia (It.)
instrument à anche (Fr.)
anche (Fr.)
Zunge (G.)
Rohrblattinstrument (G.)
caña (Sp.)
lengüeta (Sp.)

instrumento de lengüeta (Sp.)

2. organ pipe

Röhrenglocken (G.)
tubular bells
*bells
chimes, cathedral chimes
campane tubolari (It.)
cloches tubulaires (Fr.)
campanólogo (Sp.)

Rohrflöte (G. organ)
flute stop
chimney flute
rohr flute
flauto a camino (It.)
flûte à cheminée (Fr.)
flauta de chimenea (Sp.)

Roi des Instruments (Fr.)
organ
King of Instruments
Re degli Strumenti (It.)
Königin der Instrumente (G.)
Re de los Instrumentos (Sp.)

rolata (It.)
roulade (Fr.)
melisma
ornamenation
figurations
florid passage
diminutions
passage-work
runs
cadenzas
passaggio (It.)
fioritura (It.)
gorgia (It.)
Blumen (G.)
Lauf

role (opera)
a part
ruolo (It.)

parte (It.)
rôle (Fr.)
Rolle (G.)
Part (G.)
papel (Sp.)
parte (Sp.)

rôle secondaire (Fr.)
secondary role
minor role
supporting role
comprimario (It.)
ruolo secondario (It.)
Nebenrolle (G.)
papel secundario (Sp.)

vs. première partie (Fr.)

roll
drum roll
tambourine roll
tremolo
trill
rollo (It.)
gruppo (It.)
roulement (Fr.)
Wirbel (G.)
Trommelwirbel (G.)
Paukenwirbel (G.)
redoble (Sp.)

Rolle (G. 18c.)
ornament
turn
gruppetto (It., Fr.)
tour de gosier (Fr.)
grupeto (Sp.)

rolled chord
broken chord
arpeggio (It.)
Alberti bass
strumming
battery
crackle
battimento (It.)

arpège, arpègement (Fr.)
arpégé (Fr.)
Akkordpassage (G.)
Rauscher (G.)
Brechung (G.)
gebrochener Akkord (G.)
rasgado, rasgueado (Sp.)
arpegio (Sp.)

vs. solid chord

Rollschellen (G.)
  *bells
  pellet bells
  sleighbells
  jingle bells
  harness bells
  altar bells

Rollschweller (G. organ)
  crescendo pedal
  crescendo rotativo (It.)
  rouleau crescendo (Fr.)
  Crescendowalze (G.)
  Crescendozug (G.)
  Registerrad, -walze (G.)
  Kollektivschweller (G.)
  rodillo del crescendo (Sp.)

Rolltrommel (G.)
  tenor drum
  side/snare drum
  cassa rulante (It.)
  tamburino, -ello (It.)
  tamburo rullante (It.)
  caisse roulante (Fr.)
  tambour roulant (Fr.)
  caisse sourde (Fr.)
  Wirbeltrommel (G.)
  Rührtrommel (G.)
  Tenortrommel (G.)
  redoblante (Sp.)

Roman chant
  plainchant, plainsong
  Gregorian chant

liturgical song
cantus planus (Lat.)
cantus choralis (Lat.)
cantus Romanus (Lat.)
cantilena Romana (Lat., Sp.)
cantico (It., Sp.)
canto Gregoriano (It., Sp.)
chant d'église (Fr.)
chant Romain (Fr.)
chant Grégorien (Fr.)
Choral (G.)
Gregorianische Gesang (G.)

romance (E., Fr.)
  lyrical song/piece
  ballad
  fantasy
  tone poem
  rhapsody
  romanza (It.)
  Romanze (G.)

romanesca (It.)
  ground bass melody
  chaconne
  passacaglia
  bergamesca (It.)
  folia (It.)

Romano-Seraphicum (Lat.)
  Mozarabic chant
  Spanish chant
  Visigothic chant

Romanian letters (chant)
  litterae significativae (Lat.)
  neumes
  Romanus letters
  lettere di Romanus (It.)
  lettere Romaniane (It.)
  lettres romaines (Fr.)
  caractères romains (Fr.)
  Romanos-Buchstaben (G.)
  letras romanas (Sp.)

Romanticism

19c. style
subjective
emotional
dramatic
romanticismo (It., Sp.)
romantisme (Fr.)
Romantik (G.)

romanza senza parole (It.)
  song(s) without words
  lyrical piano pieces
  romance sans paroles (Fr.)
  Lieder ohne Worte (G.)
  romanza sin palabras (Sp.)

ronde (Fr.)
  whole note
  punctum inclinatum (Lat.)
  semibrevis (Lat.)
  semibreve (E., It.)
  intera, -o (It.)
  Ganze, ganze Note (G.)
  redonda (Sp.)

2. round dance
  circle dance
  carole (Fr.)
  carola (It.)
  Rundtanz (G.)

3. round (vocal)
  catch
  canon
  roundelay
  ronde de table (Fr.)
  Rundgesang (G.)
  rota (Lat.)

rondeau (Fr.)
  monophonic song (med.)
  forme fixe (Fr.)
  refrain
  rondo
  rondellus (Lat.)
  rondel, roundel
  rondelet

rondó (Sp.)
Rondo (G.)

rondo
  five-part form
  ABACA
  refrain
  ritornello (It.)
  rondino (It.)

root (of a chord)
  base/bass note of a chord
  fundamental note
  nota fondamentale (It.)
  suono fondamentale (It.)
  son fondamental d'un accord
(Fr.)
  Grundton (G.)
  Akkordgrundton (G.)
  sonido fundamental del acorde
(Sp.)
  nota fundamental (Sp.)

root position (chord)
  5/3 chord
  posizione fondamentale (It.)
  position fondamentale (Fr.)
  Grundstellung (G.)
  positión fundamental (Sp.)

vs. inversion

rosalia (It.)
  sequence
  repetition
  rosalie (Fr.)
  Rosalie (G.)
  Schusterfleck (G.)
  rosalía (Sp.)

rose, rose hole (guitar, etc)
  sound-hole (ornamental)
  knot (E. 17c.)
  rosa (It., Sp.)
  rose, rosette, rosace (Fr.)
  Rose (G.)

Stern (G. 16c.)
roseta (Sp.)

rosin, resin (for bows)
  colophony
  colofonia (It., Sp.)
  colophane (Fr.)
  Geigenharz (G.)
  Kolophon, Kolophonium (G.)
  resina (Sp.)

rostrum
  *podium

rota (Lat.)
  round
  canon
  catch
  *ronde (Fr.)

2. crowd, crowth, crwth
  cruit
  lyre
  psaltery
  harp
  rote (med.)
  rotta (Lat.)
  chrotta (Lat., Fr.)
  crotta (It.)
  rote, rota (Fr.)
  Rotte (G.)
  Chrotta (G.)
  rota (Sp.)

rote, by rote
  by memory
  memorized
  by heart
  by ear
  a mamoria (It.)
  par coeur (Fr.)
  auswendig (G.)
  de memoria (Sp.)

rotta (It. 14c.)
  dance variation

after-dance
proporzione (It.)
tripla (It.)
Proporz (G.)
Nachtanz (G.)
segunda danza (Sp.)

roulade (Fr.)
  ornamentation
  divisions
  diminutions
  passage-work
  fioritura (It.)
  coloratura (It.)

rouleau (Fr.)
  piano roll
  player-piano roll
  cilindro (It., Sp.)
  cylindre (Fr.)
  Walze (G.)
  rollo (Sp.)

rouleau crescendo (Fr.)
  crescendo pedal (organ)
  crescendo rolativo (It.)
  Crescendowalze, -zug (G.)
  Registerrad, -walze (G.)
  Kollektivschweller (G.)
  Rollschweller (G.)
  rodillo del crescendo (Sp.)

roulement (Fr.)
  drum roll
  *roll
  rullo (It.)
  Trommelwirbel (G.)
  redoble (Sp.)

round
  canon
  perpetual canon
  catch
  fugue
  roundelay
  troll

rota (Lat.)
caccia (It.)
chasse (Fr.)
*ronde (Fr.)
Radel (G.)
Rotula (G.)
Zirkelkanon (G.)

round dance
circle dance
girotondo (It.)
ronde (Fr.)
Reigen (G.)
ronda (Sp.)
rueda (Sp.)

roundelay
song
tune
round
refrain song
rondeau (Fr.)

rovescio, rovesciamento (It.)
retrograde
inversion
crabwise
fugue, fugal

row, tone row
series
serial music
dodecaphonic
twelve-tone music
serie (It., Sp.)
série (Fr.)
Reihe (G.)

royalties
performance fees
license fees
copyright
author's fees
diritti d'autore (It.)
droits d'auteur (Fr.)
Tantiemen (G.)

derechos de autor (Sp.)

rubato (It.)
tempo rubato (It.)
altered time
borrowed time
stolen time
free rhythm

vs. tempo giusto (It.)
strict tempos

rubebe (Lat., It.)
rebec
small violin
kit
ribebe, ribeca (It.)
rébec (Fr.)
Rubebe (G.)
rabe, rabel (Sp.)

Rückfall (G.)
backfall
ornament
forefall
relish
mordent
appoggiatura (It.)

Rückführung (G.)
transition (E., Fr.)
bridge
release
channel
ponte (It.)
pont (Fr.)
Überleitung (G.)
Übergang (G.)
Rückgang (G.)
puente (Sp.)
pasaje (Sp.)

Rückpositiv (G.)
organ division/manual
chair organ
choir organ

organo di coro (It.)
petit orgue (Fr.)
positif (Fr.)
positif de dos (Fr.)
Positiv im Stuhl G.)
Unterwerk (G.)
Chororgel (G.)
órgano de coro (Sp.)
órgano positivo (Sp.)

Rückweise (G.)
dal segno sign
segno (It.)

rueda (Sp.)
round dance
circle dance
girotondo (It.)
*ronde (Fr.)
Reigen (G.)
ronda (Sp.)

ruff, ruffle
snare drum stroke
*drum beat
paradiddle
flam
roll
rullo (It.)
dreifacher Vorschlag (G.)
triple golpe (Sp.)

ruggiero (It.)
repeating bass
ground bass
ostinato bass
*chaconne (Fr.)
passacaglia (It.)
folia (It.)

Ruhepunkt (G.)
*fermata
hold
pause
corona (It.)
couronne (Fr.)

Krone (G.)
Ruhezeichen (G.)
calderón (Sp.)

ruhig (G.)
calm
calmo, calmato (It.)
calme (Fr.)
calmo (Sp.)

Rührtrommel (G.)
tenor drum
cassa rullante (It.)
caisse roulante (Fr.)
tambour roulant (Fr.)
caisse sourde (Fr.)
Wirbeltrommel (G.)
Rolltrommel (G.)
redoblante (Sp.)

rumba (Sp.)
Latin dance
bolero (Sp.)
béguine (Fr.)

run (n.)
a number of performances
tour
engagement
season
concert season
stagione (It.)
saison (Fr.)
Spielzeit (G.)
temporada (Sp.)

2. rapid scale passage
divisions
diminutions
passage work
glissando
gorgia, gorgheggio (It.)
volate (It.)
roulade (Fr.)
volatine (Fr.)
Volate (G.)

glosas (Sp.)

Rundgesang (G.)
round, roundelay
canon
catch
fugal
refrain song
rondo (It.)
caccia (It.)
chasse (Fr.)
rondeau (Fr.)
ronde de table (Fr.)
canción coreada (Sp.)

ruolo secondario (It.)
secondary role
minor role
supporting role
comprimario (It.)
rôle secondaire (Fr.)
Nebenrolle (G.)
papel secundario (Sp.)

vs. ruolo principale (It.)

Russian bassoon
serpent
*bass horn
keyed horn
corno basso (It.)
cor basse (Fr.)
basson Russe (Fr.)
serpent droit (Fr.)
Basshorn (G.)

Rute (G.)
brushes
wire/steel brushes
spazzole (It.)
balais de jazz (Fr.)
Besen, Jazzbesen (G.)
escobillas (Sp.)

Rutscher (G.)
*galop

can-can
polka
quadrille

rythme (Fr.)
rhythm
time
movement
meter
ritmo (It., Sp.)
Rhythmus (G.)

S

Sabbath
Sunday
Saturday
Shabbat (Heb.)
the Lord's Day
Sabbatum (Lat.)
Dominica (Lat.)
Domenica (It.)
Dimanche (Fr.)
Sonntag (G.)
Domingo (Sp.)

Sabbato Sancto (Lat.)
Holy Saturday
Sabato Santo (It.)
Samedi Saint (Fr.)
Karsamstag (G.)
Sábado Santo (Sp.)

sackbut, sagbut
trombone
slide trombone
valve trombone
bass trumpet
saqueboute (Fr.)
Posaune (G.)
Busaune (G.)
trombón (Sp.)
sacabuche (Sp.)

Sackgeige (G.)
kit
small violin
pocket-fiddle
rebec
poccetta (It.)
sordino (It.)
pochette (Fr.)
Taschengeige (G.)

violin pequeño (Sp.)
violin de bolsillo (Sp.)

Sackpfeife (G.)
*bagpipe
zampogna (It.)
piva (It.)
musette (Fr.)
cornemuse (Fr.)
gaita (Sp.)
Dudelsack (G.)

sacra rappresentazione (It.)
music-drama
oratorio
opera
*azione sacra (It.)
rappresentazione sacra (It.)
miracle (Fr.)
geistliche Spiel (G.)
auto sacramental (Sp.)

sacred music
religious music
church music
liturgical music
ecclesiastical music
sacred song
musica sacra (Lat., It.)
musica religiosa (Lat., It.)
musica ecclesiastica (Lat.)
musique sacrée (Fr.)
musique religieuse (Fr.)
musique d'église (Fr.)
Kirchenmusik (G.)
música sagrada (Sp.)
música religiosa (Sp.)

vs secular music

sacred triduum
*Holy Week
Passion Week
Hebdomade Sancte (Lat.)
settimada sancta (It.)
semaine sainte (Fr.)

Karwoche (G.)
semana santa (Sp.)

sacrificium (Lat.)
offertory chant (Mozarabic)
proper of the mass
offertorium (Lat.)
offerenda (Lat. Ambrosian)
sonus (Lat. Gallican)
offertorio (It.)
offertoire (Fr.)
Offertorium (G.)
ofertorio (Sp.)

sad, sadly
plaintive
doleful
addolorato (It.)
lagnoso (It.)
lamentoso (It., Sp.)
doloroso (It., Sp.)
plaintif (Fr.)
klagend (G.)
schmerzlich (G.)

vs. joyful, joyfully

saddle
nut (at the end of the
fingerboard)
sella (It.)
sillet (Fr.)
Sattel (G.)
ceja, cejilla (Sp.)

saeta (Sp.)
sacred song for *Holy Week
Good Friday processional
song

said mass
*low mass
missa lecta (Lat.)
messa letta (It.)
messa bassa (It.)
messe basse (Fr.)

363

stille Messe (G.)
misa lezada (Sp.)

vs. High Mass

sainete (Sp.)
one-act comic opera
intermedium (Lat.)
intermedio (It.)
intermède (Fr.)
opera buffa (It.)
saynète (Fr.)
Singspiel (G.)
Zwischenspiel (G.)
tonadilla (Sp.)
zarzuela (Sp.)

St. Martial school (10-12c.)
organum
tropes
sequences
motets (medieval)
Notre Dame school

saison théâtrale (Fr.)
season
run
tour
engagement
stagione teatrale (It.)
Spielzeit (G.)
temporada teatral (Sp.)

Saite (G.)
string
string instrument
corda (It.)
corde (Fr.)
Saiteninstrument (G.)
cuerda (Sp.)

Saitenchor (G.)
*course (multiple strings on a
lute, guitar, etc.)
coro (It., Sp.)
choeur (Fr.)

jeu (Fr.)
Chor (G.)
orden (Sp.)

Saitenfessel (G.)
capo (guitar)
bar
transposer
capotasto (It.)
capo di tasto (It.)
barré (Fr.)
grand-barré (Fr.)
capodastre (Fr.)
Kapodaster (G.)
ceduela (Sp.)
ceja, cejilla (Sp.)

Saiteninstrumentenmacher (G.)
violin maker
luthier (E., Fr., Sp.)
violinaio (It.)
liutaio (It.)
Geigenbauer (G.)
violero (Sp.)

sala da concerto (It.)
*concert hall
recital hall
auditorium
symphony hall
philharmonic hall
salle de concert (Fr.)
Konzertsaal (G.)
salón/sala de concierto (Sp.)

salicional (organ)
soft string stop
salicet (4-ft.)
dulciana
gamba

salmi(s) (Fr.)
quodlibet
*medley
potpourri

olio
salmagundi, -y
overture
pasticcio (It.)
mescolanza (It.)
pastiche (Fr.)
salmigondis (Fr.)
Querschnitt (G.)
mezcla (Sp.)
ensalada (Sp.)

salmo (It., Sp.)
*psalm
hymn
metrical psalm
anthem
psalter
psalmus (Lat.)
psaume (Fr.)
Psalm (G.)

saloma (Sp.)
shanty, chanty
sea shanty
sailor's work song
sea song
boat song

salon music
chamber music
ensemble music
musica da camera (It.)
musique de chambre (Fr.)
Kammermusik (G.)
música de camara (Sp.)

2. light music
dinner music
table music
café music
cocktail music
*backround music
musica da salotto (It.)
musique de salon (Fr.)
Salonmusik (G.)
música de salón (Sp.)

Salonflügel (G.)
  parlor grand
  baby grand
  boudoir grand
  drawing-room grand
  *grand piano
  pianoforte a coda (intera) (It.)
  piano de boudoir (Fr.)
  grand piano de concert (Fr.)
  Stutzflügel (G.)
  gran cola (Sp.)
  piano de media cola (Sp.)

vs. Klavier (G.)
  upright piano

salpinx (Gr.)
  straight trumpet
  lituus (Lat.)
  tuba (Lat.)
  buccina (Lat.)
  trombetta (It.)

salsa music
  Latin dance/pop music
  Latin disco
  Afro-Cuban music
  Latin-American music
  musica sudamericana (It.)
  musique d'Amérique latine (Fr.)
  musique latino-Américaine (Fr.)
  lateinamerikanische Musik (G.)
  música tropical (Sp.)
  música latinoamericana (Sp.)

saltando, saltato (It.)
  bouncing bow
  detatched
  spiccato (It.)
  détaché (Fr.)
  sautillé (Fr.)
  Springbogen (G.)
  saltillo, saltado (Sp.)

vs. legato (It.)

saltarello (It.)
  lively Italian dance
  estampie (14c.)

2. slow dance
  altadanza (It.15c.)
  pas de Brabant (Fr.)
  basse danse (Fr.)
  bassadanza (It.)
  quaternaria (It.)
  piva ((It.)

3. galliard
  gagliarda (It. 16c.)
  tripla (It.)
  rotta (It.)
  pavana (It.)
  sauterelle (Fr.16c.)
  to(u)rdion (Fr.)
  Sprung (G.)
  Hoftanz (G.)
  Hopp Tancz (G.)
  Hupfauf (G.)
  Proportz (G.)
  Nachtanz (G.)
  segunda danza (Sp.)

salterello (It.)
  *jack (harpsichord)
  sautereau (Fr.)
  Springer (G.)
  macillo (Sp.)
  martinete (Sp.)

salterio (It., Sp.)
  psaltery
  dulcimer
  psalterium (Lat.)
  psaltérion (Fr.)
  Psalterium (G.)

salto (It., Sp.)
  skip
  leap

  jump
  taglio (It.)
  sbalzo (It.)
  saut (Fr.)
  Sprung (G.)

vs. grado (It.)

salute
  honors
  *fanfare (E., Fr.)
  flourish
  call, trumpet call
  fanfara (It.)
  squillo di tromba (It.)
  sonnerie (Fr.)
  Tusch (G.)
  fanfarria (Sp.)
  sonada (Sp.)
  toque de trompeta (Sp.)

samba (Port.)
  Brazilian dance
  carioca (Port.)
  bossa-nova (Port.)
  batuque (Port.)
  maxixe (Port.)
  tango (Sp.)

sambuca (Lat., It.)
  psaltery
  harp
  cruit
  crwth
  hackbrett
  hurdy-gurdy
  sambuca rotata (Lat.)
  sackbut
  pipe

same tempo
  *a tempo (It.)
  l'istesso tempo (It.)
  tempo primo (It.)
  medesimo tempo (It.)
  à la même (Fr.)

le même mouvement (Fr.)
die gleiche Geschwindigkeit
(G.)
el mismo tiempo (Sp.)

Sammlung, Sammelwerk (G.)
*anthology
collection
repertoire
assortment
examples
album
sampling
corpus (Lat.)
raccolta (It.)
recueil (Fr.)
Sammeldruck (G.)
colección (Sp.)

sampogna, zampogna (It.)
*bagpipe
piva (It.)
musette (Fr.)
cornemuse (Fr.)
Sackpfeife (G.)
gaita (Sp.)

sampled sound(s)
recorded live
pre-recorded
faithful reproduction
midi
sequencer
synthesizer
digitalized

sanctorale (Lat.)
music for saints days (chant)
proper/common of the saints
proprium sanctorum (Lat.)
commune sanctorum (Lat.)

sanctus (Lat.)
Holy, holy, holy
ordinary of the Mass
cherubic hymn

Song of the Angels
aius Tris(h)agion (Gr.)
epinicion (Gr.)
ter sanctus (Lat.)
Triumphant Hymn
Hymn of Victory

Sanctus bells
altar bells
mass bells
pellet bells
*bells
sleighbells
harness bells
jingle bells
nolae (Lat.)
campanelli della messa (It.)
clochettes pour la messe (Fr.)
Schelle (G.)
Messglöckchen (G.)
Messklingeln (G.)

sanft (G.)
soft
sweet
dolce (It.)
soave (It.)
piano (It.)
doux (Fr.)
süss (G.)
lieblich (G.)
dolce, dulce (Sp.)

Sänger, Sängerin (G.)
singer
vocalist
songster
cantante (It.)
chanteur, chanteuse (Fr.)
cantatrice (Fr.)
cantante, cantatrice (Sp.)

Sängerknabe(n) (G.)
*choirboy(s)
chorister
putti (It.)

ragazzi (It.)
enfant de choeur (Fr.)
Chorknabe (G.)
Kapellknabe (G.)
niños de coro (Sp.)

sanglot (Fr.)
appoggiatura (It.)
sobbing effect
anticipation note
singhiozzare, -ando (It.)
chûte (Fr.)
schluchzend (G.)
sollozo (Sp.)

Sangsaite (G.)
highest string (violin)
E-string
cantino (It.)
chanterelle (Fr.)
tiple (Sp.)
prima (Sp.)

sans instruments (Fr.)
*a cappella (It.)
unaccompanied
stile antico (It.)
style de chapelle (Fr.)
im Kapellstil (G.)
a capilla (Sp.)

vs. avec instruments (Fr.)

sans sourdine(s) (Fr.)
mutes off
senza sordini (It.)
alle Saiten (G.)
ohne Dämpfer (G.)
todas las cuerdas (Sp.)

vs. avec sourdine(s) (Fr.)

Santo Oficio (Sp.)
*Divine Office
monastic office
ufficio (It.)

oficio (Sp.)

saqueboute (Fr.)
*sackbut
trombone
bass trumpet
Posaune (G.)
Busaune (G.)
trombón (Sp.)
sacabuche (Sp.)

sarabande (Fr.)
slow triple dance
minuet
saraband
sarabanda (It., Sp.)
Sarabande (G.)
zarabanda (Sp., It.)

sardana (Sp.)
fast 6/8 dance (Catalonia)
tarantella (It.)
jig

sarrusophone (E., Fr.)
double-reed brass instrument
saxophone
bassoon
contra-bassoon
sarrusofono (It.)
Sarrusophon (G.)
sarrusofón(o) (Sp.)

Sarum rite/use (chant)
plainsong
plainchant
Gregorian chant
*liturgy
Salisbury Cathedral

Satz(G.)
movement
part
section

2. theme

subject
motive

3. phrase
period
antecedent
question

4. style
texture
Satzart (G.)

Sattel (G.)
nut (at the end of the
fingerboard)
saddle
sella (It.)
sillet (Fr.)
ceja, cejilla (Sp.)

sausage bassoon
racket(t) (E., Fr., Sp.)
racket bassoon
cervellato (It.)
rocchetta (It.)
cervelas, cervelat (Fr.)
Stockfagott (G.)
Wurstfagott (G.)
cervelas (Sp.)

saut (Fr.)
skip
jump
leap
disjunct motion
taglio (It.)
salto (It., Sp.)
sbalzo (It.)
Sprung (G.)

vs. degré (Fr.)
step

sautereau (Fr.)
a jack (harpsichord)
plecktrum

quill
pick
plettro (It.)
salterello (It.)
plectre (Fr.)
Kiel (G.)
Docke (G.)
Springer (G.)
púa (Sp.)
plectro (Sp.)
macillo (Sp.)
martinete (Sp.)

sauvement (Fr.)
resolution (of a dissonance)
rizoluzione (It.)
résolution (Fr.)
Auflösung (G.)
resolución (Sp.)

saxhorn
tuba
baritone horn
bass saxhorn
saxotromba
saxtuba
saxhorn tenor

saxophone (E., Fr.)
brass reed instrument
clarinet
horn (jazz)
sassofono (It.)
Saxophon (G.)
saxofóno, saxófono (Sp.)

saynète (Fr.)
short comic opera
opera buffa (It.)
intermedio (It.)
Singspiel (G.)
Zwischenspiel (G.)
sainete (Sp.)
tonadilla (Sp.)
zarzuela (Sp.)

sbalzato (It.)
bouncing bow
detatched
spiccato (It.)
staccato (It.)
saltando (It.)
sautillé (Fr.)
jeté (Fr.)
ricochet (Fr.)
Springbogen (G.)
saltado, saltillo (Sp.)

sbarra (It.)
*bar, bar-line
stranghetta (It.)
barre de mesure (Fr.)
Taktstrich (G.)
barra de compás (Sp.)

scacciapensieri (It.)
*Jew's-harp
trump
mouth-organ
guimbarde (Fr.)
trompe laquais (Fr.)
Trümpe (G.)
Maultrommel (G.)
birimbao (Sp.)
guimbarda (Sp.)

scagnello (It.)
bridge (on a violin, etc.)
ponticello (It.)
chevalet (Fr.)
Steg (G.)
puente (Sp.)
cavalletto (It.)
caballete (Sp.)

scala pentatonica (It.)
pentatonic scale
whole-tone scale
anhemitonic
gamme pentatonique (Fr.)
Ganztonleiter (G.)
Fünftonleiter (G.)

pentatonische Skala (G.)
pentacordo (Sp.)

scale
octave species
diatonic scale
mode
gamut
Greater Perfect System
disdiapason (Gr.)
diapason (Gr.)
tetrachord (Gr.)
harmoniai (Gr.)
diagramma (Lat.)
scala (Lat., It.)
gamma (It.)
gamme (Fr.)
échelle (Fr.)
Tonleiter (G.)
Skala (G.)
escala (Sp.)
gama (Sp.)

2. ratio (organ pipes)
proportion
fattura (It.)
misura (It.)
facture (Fr.)
diapason (Fr.)
Mensur (G.)
mensura (Sp.)

scampanare (It.)
ring bells
peal
chime
toll
play
strike
carillonner (Fr.)
Glocke läuten (G.)
repicar (Sp.)
tocar las campanas (Sp.)

scampata, scampanata (It.)
mock serenade

shivaree
cat's concert
Dutch concert
*callithumpian concert
musica di gatti (It.)
charivari (Fr.)
Katzenmusik (G.)
cencerrada (Sp.)

scappamento (It.)
escapement (piano)
double escapement
key release
hopper
grasshopper
échappement (Fr.)
Auslösung (G.)
escape (Sp.)
escapatoria (Sp.)

scat singing
jazz vocals
bebop
swing
improvisation

scatola musicale (It.)
music box
scatola armonica (It.)
boîte à musique (Fr.)
carillon à musique (Fr.)
Spieldose (G.)
caja de música (Sp.)

scelta (It.)
selection
piece
movement
excerpt
extract
selezione (It.)
sélection (Fr.)
Auswahl (G.)
selección (Sp.)

Schachtbrett (G.)

*clavichord
chekker
scacarum (Lat.)
escacherium (Lat.)

Schäferpfeife (G.)
*bagpipe
piva (It.)
sampogna, zampogna (It.)
musetta (It.)
musette (Fr.)
cornemuse (Fr.)
Dudelsack (G.)
gaita (Sp.)

Schalenglöckchen (G.)
small bells
pellet bells
jingle bells
sleighbells
harness bells
altar bells
Sanctus bells
*bells
campanelle (It.)
piccole campane (It.)
clochettes (Fr.)
campanillas (Sp.)

Schall (G.)
sound
sonority
tone
resonance
suono (It.)
son (Fr.)
Klang (G.)
sonido (Sp.)

Schallbecher (G.)
bell (of a horn)
campana (It., Sp.)
padiglione (It.)
pavillon (Fr.)
bonnet (Fr.)
Becher (G.)

Schalltrichter (G.)
Stürze (G.)
pabellón (Sp.)

Schallbecken (G.)
cymbals
crash cymbals
acetabulum (Lat.)
crotalum (Lat.)
piatti (It.)
cinelli (It.)
cymbales (Fr.)
Becken (G.)
platillos (Sp.)
cimbalos (Sp.)

Schalloch (G.)
soundhole
F-hole
foro di risonanza (It.)
ouïe (Fr.)
oído (Sp.)
abertura acustica (Sp.)

Schallplatte (G.)
*record
phonograph record
gramophone record
disk
CD, DVD
platter
pressing
dico (It., Sp.)
disque (Fr.)

Schallplattenspieler (G.)
record player
phonograph
turntable
gramophone
victrola
giradischi (It.)
grammofono (It.)
tourne-disques (Fr.)
Grammophon (G.)
Plattenspieler (G.)

tocadiscos (Sp.)
gramófono (Sp.)
fonógrafo (Sp.)

schalltot (G.)
soundproof
dead room
anechoic chamber
lack of resonance
insonorizzato (It.)
isolato acusticamente (It.)
sourd (Fr.)
insonorisé (Fr.)
insonoro (Sp.)
antisonoro (Sp.)

vs. live room

Schalltrichter hoch (G.)
bell in the air (horn)
raise the bell
campana in alto (It.)
padiglioni in alto (It.)
pavillon en l'air (Fr.)
Stürtze hoch (G.)
pabellón al aire (Sp.)

vs. natürlich (G.)

Schalmei, Schalmey (G.)
*shawm, shalme
oboe
calamus (Lat.)
ciaramello, -a (It.)
chalumeau, chalemelle (Fr.)
caramillo (Sp.)
chirimía, xirimía (Sp.)

2. reed organ stop
clarinet stop

Scharf(f) (G.)
sharp mixture (organ)
acute mixture
acuta (Lat.)
compound stop

harmonics
*mixture

Scheitholt (G.)
dulcimer
zither
tamborin à cordes (Fr.)
Hummel, Humle (G.)

Schauspielmusik (G.)
incidental music
backround music
musica di scena (It.)
musique de scène (Fr.)
música incidental (Sp.)
música de escena (Sp.)

Schellen (G.)
*bells
jingle bells
pellet bells
harness bells
sleighbells
nolae (Lat.)
sonaglio (It.)
grelots (Fr.)
Rollschellen (G.)
Schellengeläute (G.)
cascabeles (Sp.)

Schellenbaum (G.)
Turkish crescent
Chinese crescent
Jingling Johnny
mezzaluna (It.)
cappello cinese (It.)
pavillon chinois (Fr.)
*chapeau chinois (Fr.)
Halbmond (G.)
sombrero chino (Sp.)

Schellentrommel (G.)
tambourine
timbrel
tamburo basco (It.)
tambour de Basque (Fr.)

Baskische Trommel (G.)
Tamborin (G.)
pandero, pandereta (Sp.)

Schenker system
analysis (tonal)
linear analysis

scherzo (It.)
playful
sportive
jesting
scherzando, scherzoso (It.)
en badinent (Fr.)
Scherzhaft (G.)

2. fast minuet
symphony movement

3. 17c light vocal works

Schifferklavier (G.)
concertina
*accordion
bandoneon
squeezebox
Konzertina (G.)

schisma
microtone
*comma
quarter-tone
microinterval

Schlag (G.)
beat (of a drum)
stroke
strike
colpo (It.)
coup (Fr.)
batido (Sp.)
golpe (Sp.)

2. *beat (of time)
conductor's beat
metrical accent

pulse
count
tactus (Lat.)
battuta (It.)
temps (Fr.)
Takt (G.)
tiempo (Sp.)

schlagen (G.)
to beat
strike
hit
play
battere (It.)
bussare (It.)
battre (Fr.)
frapper (Fr.)
tocar (Sp.)
golpear (Sp.)
pegar (Sp.)

Schlager (G.)
hit song
a hit
top ten/twenty/forty
chanson à la mode (Fr.)
chanson à succès (Fr.)
canción de moda (Sp.)
canción en boga (Sp.)

Schlaginstrument (G.)
percussion instrument
strumento a percussione (It.)
strumento de percossa (It.)
instrument à percussion (Fr.)
instrument à batterie (Fr.)
instrumento de percusión
(Sp.)

Schlagzither (G.)
zither (plucked)
cembalom
hammered dulcimer
cetra da tavolo (It.)
cetra a percussione (It.)
cithare (Fr.)

tympanon (Fr.)
Hackbrett (G.)
citara punteada (Sp.)
timpanón (Sp.)

Schlegel (G.)
drumstick
mallet
bacchetta (It.)
mazza, mazzuolo (It.)
battente (It.)
baguette (Fr.)
mailloche (Fr.)
palillo (Sp.)
baqueta (Sp.)

2. baton (conducting)
bâton de mesure (Fr.)
Taktstock, Taktstab (G.)

Schleifbogen (G.)
slur
bind
tie
ligature
melismatic
neume
legato (It.)
legatura (It.)
légature (Fr.)
liaison (Fr.)
Schleifzeichen (G.)
Legatobogen (G.)
Bindebogen (G.)
ligadura (Sp.)

Schleifer (G.)
slide
ornament
whole fall
double appoggiatura
double backfall
acciaccatura doppia/tripla
(It.)
coulé (Fr.)
apoyatura breve (Sp.)

Schlummerlied (G.)
lullaby
slumber song
cradle song
ninnananna (It.)
ninnerella (It.)
berceuse (Fr.)
dodinette, dodo, dodino (Fr.)
Wiegenlied (G.)
nana (Sp.)
arrullo (Sp.)
canción de cuna (Sp.)

Schluss (G.)
*cadence (E., Fr.)
close (E., Fr.)
ending
clausula (Lat.)
cadenza (It.)
chiusa (It.)
fine (It.)
fin (Fr.)
Kadenz (G.)
cadencia (Sp.)
final (Sp.)

Schlüssel (G.)
clef (E., Fr.)
chiave (It.)
clé (Fr.)
Notenschlüssel (G.)
clave (Sp.)
llave (Sp.)

Schlusssatz (G.)
last movement
concluding movement
finale (It., E.)
mouvement final (Fr.)
dernier mouvement (Fr.)
Finalsatz (G.)
Schlussstück (G.)
final (Sp.)
movimiento final (Sp.)
conclusión (Sp.)
último movimiento (Sp.)

schmalzig (G.)
sentimental (E., Fr., Sp.)
emotional
schmaltzy
slushy, mushy
sentimentale (It.)
empfindsam (G.)

Schnabel (G.)
mouthpiece
lip
becco (It.)
bocchino (It.)
imboccatura (It.)
embouchure (Fr.)
bec (Fr.)
pico (Sp.)
embocadura (Sp.)
boquilla (Sp.)

Schnabelflöte (G.)
*recorder
English flute
vertical flute
duct flute
whistle flute
beak flute
fipple flute
flageolet
flauto a becco (It.)
flauto dritto (It.)
flûte à bec (Fr.)
flûte droite (Fr.)
Blockflöte (G.)
flauta de pico (Sp.)

vs. Querflöte (G.)

Schnarre (G.)
*rattle, cog rattle
maraca
rainstick
raganella (It.)
crécelle (Fr.)
Ratche (G.)
carraca (Sp.)

matraca (Sp.)

Schnarrsaite (G.)
snare (of a drum)
bordoniera (It.)
timbre (Fr.)
Trommelsaite (G.)
bordón (Sp.)

schnell (G.)
*fast
quick
lively
rapid
allegro (It.)
presto (It.)
veloce (It.)
vite (Fr.)
rapide (Fr.)
lebhaft (G.)
pronto (Sp.)
alegre (Sp.)
alegro (Sp.)

vs. langsam (G.)

Schneller (G.)
inverted mordent
*mordent
ornament
mordente superiore (It.)
pincé (Fr.)
mordente invertido (Sp.)

Schnitt (G.)
*cut
delete, deletion
omit
strike-out
omission
abridgement
taglio (It.)
coupure (Fr.)
Einschnitt (G.)
corte (Sp.)
vide, vi----de (Lat.)

schola, schola cantorum (Lat.)
*choir
chorus
chorale
choir school
music school
lyceum
*academy of music

schola mimorum (Lat.)
school for Gaukler,
Spielmann in the middle ages

Schottische (G.)
duple dance
polka
round dance
Scozzese (It.)
ecossaise (Fr.)
anglaise (Fr.)
française (Fr.)
escocesa (Sp.)

Schritt (G.)
step (of a scale)
tone
degree
grado (It., Sp.)
degré (Fr.)
Stufe, Tonstufe (G.)

vs. Sprung (G.)

Schusterfleck (G.)
sequence
repetition
rosalia (It.)
rosalie (Fr.)
Rosalie (G.)
rosalía (Sp.)

Schwärmer (G.)
rapidly repeated notes
battery
crackle
tremolo (It.)

trillo (It.)
trémolo (Fr., Sp.)
batterie (Fr.)
Rauscher (G.)
Brechung (G.)

schwarze Note (G.)
quarter note
crotchet
quarto (It.)
nera (It.)
semiminima (Lat., It.)
noire (Fr.)
Viertelnote (G.)
negra (Sp.)
semínima (Sp.)

Schwebung (G.)
a beat (acoustical)
battimento (It.)
battement (Fr.)
batimiento (Sp.)

2. vibrato (organ)
tremulant
langueur (Fr.)
Bebung (G.)

Schwellkasten (G.)
swell-box (organ)
under expression
cassa espressiva (It.)
cassa d'organo (It.)
boîte expressive (Fr.)
caja expresiva (Sp.)
caja de expresión (Sp.)

Schwellton (G.)
*messa di voce (It.)
swell (the) tone
mise de la voix (Fr.)
poner le voz (Sp.)

Schwelltritt (G.)
swell pedal
swell shoe

staffa crescendo (It.)
pédale de la boîte expressive (Fr.)
pedal de crescendo (Sp.)

Schwellwerk (G.)
swell organ/division
in cassa espressiva (It.)
récit, clavier de récit (Fr.)
Oberwerk (G.)
expresivo (Sp.)

schwindend (G.)
dying away
fade out
decay
morendo (It.)
*decrescendo (It.)
diminuendo (It.)
en perdant le son (Fr.)
sterbend (G.)
expirando (Sp.)

Schwingung (G.)
vibration (E., Fr.)
cycle
oscillation
frequency
Hertz
sound wave
pitch
vibrazione (It.)
vibración (Sp.)

scivolando (It.)
*glissando (It.)
sliding
gliding
scoop, scooping
portamento (It.)
glissé (Fr.)
englissant (Fr.)
gleitend (G.)
glisado (Sp.)
resbalando (Sp.)

scop
epic poet/singer
bard
minstrel
jo(n)gleur (Fr.)
gleeman
goliard
troubadour
minnesinger (G.)
Gaukler (G.)
Spielmann (G.)

scordato (It.)
out of tune
off-pitch
off-key
detuned
tone-deaf
monotone
stonare (It.)
désaccordé (Fr.)
detonieren (G.)
desafinar (Sp.)

vs. intonato (It.)

2. scordatura (It., Fr., E., Sp.)
varied tuning
different tuning
re-tuned
Umstimmung (G.)
Skordatur (G.)

score (n.)
musical score
notation of all parts
full score
pocket score
condensed score
piano-vocal score
partitur(a), partizione (It.)
sparta, -o, spartita, -o (It.)
spartitura (It.)
partition (Fr.)
Partitur (G.)

Sparte (G.)
partitura (Sp.)

2. a line of music
staff (combined staves)
system

3. musical setting of a symphony, opera, film, musical, etc.

score (vb.)
orchestrate
set/put to music
arrange
transcribe
strumentare (It.)
instrumenter (Fr.)
bezetzen (G.)
instrumentar (Sp.)
orquestar (Sp.)

scoring
orchestration
instrumentation (E., Fr.)
bandstration
vocalstration
organico strumentale (It.)
instrumentazione (It.)
strumentazione (It.)
distribution (Fr.)
Instrumentierung (G.)
Besetzung (G.)
instrumentación (Sp.)

Scotch snap
reverse-dotted eighth
inverted dotting
Lombardy rhythm
syncopated
alla zoppa (It.)
ritmo Lombardo (It, Sp.)
manière Lombarde (Fr.)
rythmeLombard (Fr.)
Lombardischer Rhythmus (G.)

Scozzese (It.)
contredance
polka
can-can
Schottisch
Écossaise (Fr.)
Anglaise (Fr.)
Française (Fr.)
Schottische (G.)
escocesa (Sp.)
chotis (Sp.)

screen test
*audition
tryout
demo

scucito (It.)
detatched
non-legato (It.)
staccato (It.)
spiccato (It.)
piccato (It.)
détaché (Fr.)
délié (Fr.)
sec (Fr.)
abgestossen (G.)
destacado (Sp.)
no ligado (Sp.)

vs. legato (It.)

scuola di musica (It.)
music school
lyceum
conservatory
music institute
*academy of music
schola cantorum (Lat.)
conservatorio (It., Sp.)
liceo (It.)
conservatoire (Fr.)
Musikakademie (G.)
escuela de música (Sp.)

sea chanty/shanty

sea song
sailor's song
boat song
barcarole
work song
folk song

sea trumpet
marine trumpet
trumpet-marine
tromba marina (It.)
trompette marine (Fr.)
Trumscheit (G.)
Trompetengeige (G.)
Seetrompete (G.)
trompeta marina (Sp.)

season
run
tour
engagement
stagione teatrale (It.)
saison théâtrale (Fr.)
Spielzeit (G.)
temporada teatral (Sp.)

secco (It.)
dry
crisp
staccato (It.)
sec (Fr.)
trocken (G.)
sekko (G.)
seco (Sp.)

2. simple
plain
unembellished
accompaniment by continuo
only, not orchestra
secco recitative
recitativo secco (It.)
récitatif secco (Fr.)
Sekko-Rezitativ (G.)
recitativo seco (Sp.)

Sechzehntel(note) (G.)
sixteenth note
semiquaver
semicroma (It.)
sedicesimo (It.)
double-croche (Fr.)
semicorchea (Sp.)

Sechzehntelpause (G.)
sixteenth-note rest
semiquaver rest
pausa di semicroma (It.)
quart de soupir (Fr.)
silencio de semicorchea (Sp.)
pausa de semicorchea (Sp.)

second (interval)
tone
whole step/tone
half-step/tone
tonus (Lat.)
seconda (It.)
seconde (Fr.)
Sekunde (G.)
segunda (Sp.)

2. lower part/voice
subordinate part/player
secondo, -a (It.)
second(e) (Fr.)
zweiter, -e, -es (G.)
segundo (Sp.)

second dessus (Fr.)
mezzo, mezzo-soprano
second soprano
alto voice
bas-dessus (Fr.)
Mittelsopran (G.)
Mezzosopran (G.)

second ending
seconda volta (It.)
chiuso (It.)
clos (Fr.)
zweite Schluss (G.)

374

vs. first ending

second fiddle
assistant
second violin

second inversion (chord)
six-four chord
fifth in the bass
secondo rivolto (It.)
accordo di quarto e sesta (It.)
deuxième renversement (Fr.)
accord de sixte et quarte (Fr.)
Quartsextakkord (G.)
zweite Umkehrung (G.)
acorde de sexta y cuarta (Sp.)

second theme
subordinate theme
secondary theme
exposition
secondo tema (It.)
seconda idea (It.)
idea secondaria (It.)
idée secondaire (Fr.)
second thème (Fr.)
Seitensatz, -thema (G.)
segundo tema (Sp.)
tema secundario (Sp.)

vs first/principal theme

seconda maggiore (It.)
major second (interval)
whole step/tone
seconde majeure (Fr.)
grosse Sekunde (G.)
segunda mayor (Sp.)
tono entere (Sp.)

seconda prattica (It.)
new music
contemporary music
modern muaic
musicum novum (Lat.)
Ars Nova (Lat.)

Nuove Musiche (It.)
monody (17c.)
stile moderno (It.)
musica nova (It.)
musique nouvelle (Fr.)
neue Musik (G.)
nueva música (Sp.)

vs. prima prattica (It.)

seconda volta (It.)
*second ending
clos (Fr.)

secondary dominant
dominant of the dominant
five of five
Wechseldominante (G.)
Zwischendominante (G.)

secondo (It.)
lower part (piano duet)
second (E., Fr.)
zweite (G.)
segundo (Sp.)

vs. primo (It.)

section (E., Fr.)
group (performers)
division
part
sezione (It.)
Gruppe (G.)

2. part (of a piece)
pars (Lat.)
movement
excerpt
phrase
selection
fragment
parte (It., Sp.)
partie (Fr.)
Teil (G.)
Satz, Absatz (G.)

secular music
profane music
musica profana (It.)
musique profane (Fr.)
weltliche Musik (G.)
música profane (Sp.)

vs. sacred music

sedicesimo (It.)
16th note
semiquaver
semicroma (It.)
double-croche (Fr.)
Sechzehntelnote (G.)
semicorchea (Sp.)

Seele (G.)
soundpost (string instr.)
anima (It.)
âme (Fr.)
Stimmstock (G.)
alma (Sp.)

Seelenamt (G.)
Requiem mass
*funeral mass
mass for the dead
burial service
missa pro defunctis (Lat.)
messa da requiem (It.)
messe des morts (Fr.)
Totenmesse (G.)
Seelenmesse (G.)
misa de difuntos (Sp.)

segno (It.)
sign from which to repeat
*dal segno (It.)
segno di ripetizione (It.)
signe de répétition (Fr.)
Wiederholungszeichen (G.)
signo de repetición (Sp.)

segue
continue without pause

go right on
attaca (It.)
enchaînez (Fr.)
suit, suivez (Fr.)
es folg (G.)
sigue (Sp.)

2. continue the same
in similar fashion
simile (It.)

seguidilla (Sp.)
fast dance in triple
flamenco
fandango (Sp.)
malagueña (Sp.)

sehr (G.)
very
rather
*assai (It.)
molto (It.)
très (Fr.)
beaucoup (Fr.)
ziemlich (G.)
viel (G.)
mucho, muy (Sp.)

sehr laut (G.)
very loud
ear-splitting
blaring
deafening
fortissimo (It.)
très fort (Fr.)
muy fuerte (Sp.)

seisillo (Sp.)
sextuplet
sestina (It.)
sextolet (E., Fr.)
Sextole (G.)

Seitenbewegung (G.)
oblique motion
motus obliquus (Lat.)

moto obliquo (It.)
mouvement oblique (Fr.)
movimiento oblicuo (Sp.)

Seitensatz, -thema (G.)
*second theme (sonata form)
subordinate theme

vs. Hauptsatz (G.)

Sekunde (G.)
second (interval)
whole-tone
whole-step
major/minor second
half-step/tone
tonus (Lat.)
seconda (It.)
seconde (Fr.)
segunda (Sp.)

selection
piece
excerpt
extract
selezione (It.)
scelta (It.)
sélection (Fr.)
choix (Fr.)
morceau (Fr.)
selección (Sp.)

sella (It.)
nut (at the end of the
fingerboard)
saddle
sillet (Fr.)
Sattel (G.)
ceja, cejilla (Sp.)

Semaine Sainte (Fr.)
Holy Week
Passion Week
Hebdomade Sancte (Lat.)
Settimana Santa (It.)
Karwoche (G.)

Semana Santa (Sp.)

semel
gymel, gimel, gemel
cantus gemellus (Lat.)
parallel thirds
duet
Zwillingsgesang (G.)

semi-cadence
*half-cadence
half-close
imperfect cadence
deceptive cadence
cadenza imperfetta (It.)
cadence imperfaite (Fr.)
Halbschluss (G.)
hängende Kadenz (G.)
cadencia imperfecta (Sp.)
semicadencia (Sp.)

vs. full cadence

semi-chorus
chamber chorus/choir
solo ensemble
madrigal choir
concertino (It.)
*favoriti (It.)
coro concertato (It.)
coro favorito (It.)
petit-choeur (Fr.)
demi-choeur (Fr.)
Kammerchor (G.)
coro de cámara (Sp.)

semi-grand (piano)
*baby grand
parlor grand
boudoir grand
drawingroom-grand
pianoforte a mezza coda (It.)
piano de boudoir (Fr.)
piano à queue mignon (Fr.)
grand piano de concert (Fr.)
Stutzflügel (G.)

gran cola (Sp.)
piano de media cola (Sp.)

vs. upright piano

semi-opera
operetta
masque
musical
light opera
opérette (Fr.)
Singspiel (G.)
Spieloper (G.)
opereta (Sp.)
zarzuela (Sp.)

semibiscroma (It.)
64th-note
hemidemisemiquaver
semidemisemiquaver
sessantaquattresimo (It.)
quadruple-croche (Fr.)
Vierundsechzigstelnote (G.)
semifusa (Sp.)

semibreve (E., It.)
whole note
punctum inclinatum (Lat.)
semibrevis (Lat.)
ronde (Fr.)
semi-brève (Fr.)
Semibrevis (G.)
Ganze, ganze Note (G.)
redonda (Sp.)

semibreve rest
semipausa (Lat.)
whole note rest
pausa di semibreve (It.)
pause (Fr.)
ganze Pause (G.)
silencio de redonda (Sp.)
pausa de redonda (Sp.)

semicadencia (Sp.)
*half-cadence

half-close
imperfect cadence
deceptive cadence
cadenza imperfetta (It.)
cadence imperfaite (Fr.)
Halbschluss (G.)
cadencia imperfecta (Sp.)

vs. cadencia perfecta (Sp.)

semiclassical music
light classics
popular classics
easy listening
Muzak
salon music
dinner music
table music
*backround music

semidiapente (Lat., It.)
diminished fifth
augmented fourth
imperfect fifth
tritone
false fifth
devil's interval
hemidiapente (Gr.)
diabolus in musica (Lat.)
quinta falsa (Lat.)
quinta deficiens (Lat.)
mi contra fa (Lat.)
tritonus (Lat.)
tritono (It., Sp.)
triton (Fr.)
Tritonus (G.)

semiditonus (Lat.)
minor third
semiditone
semiditono (It.)
semi-diton (Fr.)
kleine Terz (G.)
terza minore (It.)
tierce mineure (Fr.)
tercera menor (Sp.)

· **semifusa (Sp.)**
64th note
hemidemisemiquaver
semibiscroma (It.)
sessantaquattresimo (It.)
quadruple-croche (Fr.)
Vierundsechzigstelnote (G.)

semiminima (Lat., It.)
quarter-note
semiminum
crotchet
nera (It.)
quarto (It.)
noire (Fr.)
Viertelnote (G.)
schwarze Note (G.)
semínima (Sp.)
negra (Sp.)

semiquaver
16th-note
bis unca (Lat.)
semifusa (Lat.)
semicroma (It.)
sedicesimo (It.)
double-croche (Fr.)
Sechzehntel (G.)
semicorchea (Sp.)

semiquaver rest
16th-rest
pausa di semicroma (It.)
quart de soupir (Fr.)
Sechzehntelpause (G.)
pausa de semicorchea (Sp.)
silencio de semicorchea (Sp.)

semitone
half-step
half-tone
minor second
hemitone
semitonium (Lat.)
apotome (Lat.)
semitono (It., Sp.)

demi-ton (Fr.)
Halbton (G.)

vs whole tone

sempre (It.)
always
all the time
continually
throughout
toujours (Fr.)
immer (G.)
siempre (Sp.)

Sendung (G.)
*broadcast
telecast
transmissione radiofonica
(It.)
transmission (Fr.)
émission (Fr.)
emisión (Sp.)
transmisión (Sp.)

senken (G.)
to lower
flat, flatten
abbassare (It.)
bemolisar (It.)
bémoliser (Fr.)
abaisser (Fr.
baisser (Fr.)
erniedrigen (G.)
abemolar (Sp.)
bajar, rebajar (Sp.)

vs. erhöhen (G.)

Senkung (G.)
*downbeat
strong beat
first beat of a measure
thesis (Gr.)
crusus (Lat.)
tesis (It.)
thésis (Fr.)

Thesis (G.)
tesis (Sp.)

vs. Auftakt (G.)

sensible (Fr.)
leading-tone
seventh degree
si, ti
subtonic
essential seventh
nota sensibile (It.)
sensibile (It.)
note sensible (Fr.)
Leitton (G.)
sensible nota (Sp.)

sentence
period
double period
phrase
periodo (It., Sp.)
période (Fr.)
Periode (G.)
frase (Sp.)

senza battuta (It.)
in free time
altered time
borrowed time
stolen time
rubato, tempo rubato (It.)
senza misura (It.)
sans mesure (Fr.)
ohne bestimmtes Mass (G.)
sin compas (Sp.)

vs. tempo giusto (It.)

senza sordini (It.)
mutes off
take off mutes
remove mutes
levati i sordini (It.)
alle Saiten (G.)
*ohne Dämpfer (G.)

toutes les cordes (Fr.)
sans sourdine (Fr.)
sin sordina (Sp.)

vs. sordini, con sordini (It.)

seo (Sp.)
cathedral church
basilica
duomo (It.)
cattedrale (It.)
cathédrale (Fr.)
Dom (G.)
catedral (Sp.)

Septakkord (G.)
seventh chord
chord of the seventh
major/minor/dominant 7th
accordo di settima (It.)
accord de septième (Fr.)
acorde de séptima (Sp.)

septet
chamber ensemble
septetto, settimino (It.)
septuor (Fr.)
Septett (G.)
septeto, septimino (Sp.)

septième (Fr.)
seventh (interval)
settima (It.)
Septime (G.)
séptima (Sp.)

2. mutation stop: 1 1/7 (organ)

septième de dominante (Fr.)
dominant seventh (chord)
acordo di settima di
dominante (It.)
accord de septième de
dominante (Fr.)
Dominantsept(imen)akkord
(G.)

acorde de séptima de dominante (Sp.)

sepulcrum play
Easter play
mystery play
miracle play
Passion play
tomb play
passion play
*liturgical drama
sepolcro (It.)
cantata
oratorio

sequence (E.)
prosa
trope
hymn
song
motet
anthem
sequentia (Lat.)
prosa, prosula (Lat.)
sequenza (It.)
séquence (Fr.)
prose (E., Fr.)
Sequenz (G.)
secuencia (Sp.)

2. repeated phrase, higher or lower

3. progression (E., Fr.)
progressione (It.)
Fortschreitung (G.)
progresión (Sp.)

sequencer
recording device
midi
synthesizer
keyboard
computer music
digital music
séquenceur (Fr.)

Sequenzer (G.)

seraphine
reed organ
*harmonium
parlor organ
American organ
séraphine (Fr.)

serenade (n.)
suite
cassation
divertissement (E., Fr.)
divertimento (It.)
potpourri
nocturne
masque
serenata (It.)
notturno (It.)
sérénade (Fr.)
Ständchen (G.)
Nachtmusik (G.)
Nachtständchen (G.)
Kassation (G.)
serenada (Sp.)

serenade (vb.)
perform (for someone)
sing, play
entertain

serial music
twelve-tone music
dodecaphonic music
atonal
tone row
musica seriale (It.)
musique sérielle (Fr.)
serielle Musik (G.)
música serial (Sp.)
Reihe (G.)
Zwölftonreihe (G.)
Grundgestalt (G.)

serinette (Fr.)
bird organ

*barrel organ
organetto (It.)
Vogelorgel (G.)

serioso, serio (It., Sp.)
ernest(ly)
serious
sérieux (Fr.)
ernst (G.)

sermon hymn
preparation hymn

serpent (E., Fr.)
bass horn
ophicleide
bass cornett
bass trumpet
tuba
Russian bassoon
serpent-bassoon
serpente, serpentone (It.)
serpent droit (Fr.)
Schlangenbass (G.)
Schlangenrohr (G.)
serpentón (Sp.)

servetta (It.)
ingenue
comic soprano role
soubrette (Fr.)
dougazon (Fr.)
tiple cómico (Sp.)

service (E., Fr.)
liturgy
Mass
prayer service
religious service
servizio (It.)
Gottesdienst (G.)
Agende (G.)
servicio (Sp.)

musical setting of Morning or Evening Prayer canticles, etc

Anglican service music
Short Service
Great Service
Full Service

sesquialtera (Lat.)
mixture stop (org.)
compound stop

2. proportion of 3:2
hemiola

3. perfect fifth interval

sessantaquattresimo (It.)
64th-note
hemidemisemiquaver
semibiscroma (It.)
quadruple-croche (Fr.)
Vierundsechzigstelnote (G.)
semifusa (Sp.)

sesta (It.)
sixth (interval)
sixième (Fr.)
sixte (Fr.)
Sexte (G.)
sexta (Sp.)

2. *Sext (canonical hour)
Divine Office

sesta aggiunta (It.)
added sixth chord
sixte ajouté (Fr.)
hinzugefügte Sexte (G.)
sexta agregada (Sp.)

sesta eccedente (It.)
*augmented sixth chord
sesta aumentata (It.)
accord de sixte augmentée
(Fr.)
übermässige Sexte (G.)
sexta aumentada (Sp.).

sestetto (It.)
sextet
sestet
group of six performers
piece for six musicians
sextuor, sextette (Fr.)
Sextett (G.)
sexteto (Sp.)

sestina (It.)
sextuplet, sextolet
sextolet (Fr.)
Sextole (G.)
seisillo (Sp.)

2. six-line stanza
madrigal (16-17c.)

set, sett (n.)
*suite
cassation
divertimento (It.)

2. group of songs
*medley
song cycle

3. stage scenery
scena, scenario (It.)
décor (Fr.)
Szenenbild (G.)
Bühnenbild (G.)
decorado (Sp.)
escenografia (Sp.)

set (vb.)
put words to music
write music to a text
compose

set piece
composition
formal composition
piece
number
concert aria

settima di dominante (It.)
dominant seventh (chord)
*septième de dominante (Fr.

Settimana Santa (It.)
Holy Week
Passion Week
Hebdomade Sancte (Lat.)
Semaine Sainte (Fr.)
Karwoche (G.)
Semana Santa (Sp.)

settimino (It.)
septet
group of seven musicians
settetto (It.)
septetto (It.)
septuor (Fr.)
Septett (G.)
septeto, septimino (Sp.)

setting
composition
arrangement
scoring
version
mise en musique (Fr.)
Vertonung (G.)

seule (Fr.)
solo
allein (G.)

seventh (interval)
ditonus cum diapente (Lat.)
settima (It.)
septième (Fr.)
Sept, Septime (G.)
séptima (Sp.)

seventh chord
dominant seventh chord
diminished seventh chord
major seventh chord
accordo di settima (It.)
accord de septième (Fr.)

Septakkord (G.)
Septimenakkord (G.)
acorde de séptima (Sp.)

Sext (Office)
canonical hour
sixth hour
lesser hour
*Divine Office
Sexta (Lat., Sp.)
sesta (It.)
sexte (Fr.)
Sext (G.)

sextet
group of six performers
piece for six performers
sestetto (It.)
sextuor (Fr.)
sextette (Fr.)
Sextett (G.)
sexteto (Sp.)

sextolet (Fr.)
sextuplet
sestina (It.)
sextole (Fr.)
Sextole (G.)
seisillo (Sp.)

sextus (Lat.)
sixth voice part (16-17c.)
pars sexta (Lat.)
sextuplum (Lat.)

sforzando, sforzato (It.)
stress
accent (strong)
fortepiano (It.)
rinforzando (It.)

shading
nuance (E., Fr.)
inflection
expression
graduare (It.)

sfumatura (It.)
Abstufung (G.)
matizado (Sp.)

shake
ornament
grace note
anticipation note
trill
close shake
trillo (It.)
bebung
beat, shaked beat
cadent
backfall

shalm
shawm
oboe
calamus (Lat.)
ciaramello (It.)
chalumeau, chalemelle (Fr.)
Schalmei (G.)
caramillo (Sp.)
chirimía, xirimía (Sp.)

shank
crook (brass instrument)
ritorto (It.)
corps de rechange (Fr.)
Stimmbogen (G.)
Aufsatzbogen (G.)
tonillo (Sp.)
cuerpo de recambio (Sp.)

shanty, chanty, chantey
sea shanty
sea song
boat song
barcarole
sailor's song
work song
folk song
canto di lavoro (It.)
chant de travail (Fr.)
Arbeitslied (G.)

saloma (Sp.)

shape(d)-notes
character notes
buckwheat notes
patent notes
dunce notes
fasola
*solmization
sol-fa system

sharp (n.)
accidental
half-step higher
diesis (It.)
dièse (Fr.)
Kreuz (G.)
sostenido (Sp.)

2. out of tune
off-pitch
off-key
too high

3. *black key
sharp keys
tasto nero (It.)
touche noire (Fr.)
feinte (Fr.)
Obertaste (G.)
tecla negra (Sp.)

sharp, sharpen (vb.)
raise (the pitch)
alzare (It.)
hausser (Fr.)
erhöhen (G.)
alzar (Sp.)

vs. flat, flatten
lower

sharp mixture (org.)
acuta (Lat.)
acute mixture
compound stop

fourniture (Fr.)
Scharf(f) (G.)

shawm
oboe
shalme
hoboy
aulos (Gr.)
kalamos (Gr.)
tibia (Lat.)
calamus (Lat.)
cialamello (It.)
ciaramella (It.)cennamella
(It.)
zampogna (It.)
piffaro (It.)
chalumeau (Fr.)
pipeau (Fr.)
chalemelle (Fr.)
chalemie (Fr.)
haulxbois (Fr.)
Shalmei, -y (G.)
caramillo (Sp.)
chirimía (Sp.)

sheet music
songs printed in large size
folio size
popular music
partitions (Fr.)
Notenblätter (G.)

shivaree
horning
Dutch concert
cat's concert
cacaphony
catawauling
mock serenade
*callithumpian concert
charivari (Fr.)
scampata (It.)
chiasso (It.)
Katzenmusik (G.)
cencerrada (Sp.)

shofar, shophar (Heb.)
ram's horn
natural horn
horn
signal horn
posthorn

short octave (org.)
partial stop
incomplete stop
broken octave
mi re ut (It.)
octave courte (Fr.)
kurze Oktave (G.)
octava corta (Sp.)

short score
condensed score
piano score
piano-vocal score
reduction
conductor's score/part
lead sheet
fake book
charts
partitura ridotta (It.)
partition réduite (Fr.)
Partiturauszug (G.)

vs. full score

short service
syllabic style
homophonic style
modest style

vs. great service
full service

show choir
jazz choir
pop choir/chorus

show girl
chorus girl (on Broadway)

show tune
pop song
song from a musical
musical comedy song

showboat
road company
road show
traveling show
touring show
showmobile
touring company

shrill
loud
acuto (It.)
squillante (It.)
aigu (Fr.)
durchdringend (G.)
hoch (G.)
agudo (Sp.)

si (It.)
ti (in a scale)
seventh step of the scale
leading tone
subtonic
essential seventh
sensibile (It.)
note sensible (Fr.)
Leitton (G.)
sensible nota (Sp.)

sicigia (Sp.)
chord
triad
syzygy
syzygia (Lat.)
sizigia (It.)

siciliano (It.)
dance movement in 6/8
pastorale
pifa (It.)
sicilienne (Fr.)

Siziliano (G.)
siciliana (Sp.)

side drum
snare drum
military drum
cassa (It.)
cassa chiara (It.)
tamburo militare (It.)
tamburo piccolo (It.)
caisse clair (Fr.)
petit tambour (Fr.)
tambour militaire (Fr.)
kleine Trommel (G.)
Militärtrommel (G.)
tambor, tambor militar (Sp.)
caja, caja militar (Sp.)

sifflet de Pan(Fr.)
*panpipes
pipes of Pan
Pandean pipes
mouth organ
syrinx
flauto di Pan (It.)
flûte de Pan (Fr.)
Panflöte (G.)
flauta de Pan (Sp.)

Sifflöt(e) (G.)
whistle flute
*recorder
duct flute

2. organ stop
ottavino (It.)
sifflet (Fr.)
chiflete (Sp.)
nazardo (Sp.)

sight-singing
at sight
at first sight
sight-reading
a prima vista (It.)
à livre ouvert (Fr.)

à (premier) vue (Fr.)
vom Blatt-Spiel (G.)
a primera vista (Sp.)

sigla melodica (It.)
theme song
signature song/music
idée fixe (Fr.)
indicatif musicale (Fr.)
Leitmotiv (G.)
Kennmelodie (G.)
caracteristica (Sp.)

signal
*fanfare (E., Fr.)
call
reveille
flourish
salute

Signalhorn (G.)
*bugle
keyed bugle
biucolo (It.)
clairon (Fr.)
cor bugler (Fr.)
Jagdhorn (G.)

signature song
theme song
sigla melodica/musicale (It.)
indicatif musical (Fr.)
idée fixe (Fr.)
Leitmotiv (G.)
Kennmelodie (G.)
característica (Sp.)

sign
mark
symbol
siglum
signum (Lat.)
segno (It.)
signe (Fr.)
Zeichen (G.)
signo (Sp.)

signe accidentel (Fr.)
*accidental
sharps and flats
Vorzeichen (G.)
accidente (Sp.)

signum modi (Lat.)
*time signature
meter signature
measure signature

sigue (Sp.)
continue without pause
segue (It.)
*attacca (It.)
suivez (Fr.)
es folg (G.)

silence (E., Fr.)
rest
pause (E., Fr.)
silenzio (It.)
pausa (It., Sp.)
Pause (G.)
silencio (Sp.)

silence générale (Fr.)
*grand pause
general pause
caesura
empty measure/bar
pausa generale (It.)
pause générale (Fr.)
Generalpause (G.)

silencio de blanca (Sp.)
half-rest
minum rest
pausa di minima (It.)
demi-pause (Fr.)
halbe Pause (G.)
pausa de blanca (Sp.)

silencio de breve (Sp.)
breve rest
two-measure rest

383

pausa di breve (It.)
pause de breve (Fr.)
demi-bâton (Fr.)
Zweitaktpause (G.)
Zweiganzepause (G.)
Doppeltaktpause (G.)
pausa de breve (Sp.)

silencio de corchea (Sp.)
eighth-rest
quaver rest
pausa di croma (It.)
demi-soupir (Fr.)
achtel Pause (G.)
pausa de corchea (Sp.)

silencio de fusa (Sp.)
32nd rest
demisemiquaver rest
pausa di biscroma (It.)
huitième de soupir (Fr.)
zweiunddreissigstel Pause
(G.)
pausa de fusa (Sp.)

silencio de negra (Sp.)
quarter-rest
crotchet rest
pausa di semiminima (It.)
soupir (Fr.)
viertel Pause (G.)
pausa de negra (Sp.)

silencio de redonda (Sp.)
whole rest
semibreve rest
semipausa (Lat.)
pausa di semibreve (It.)
pause (Fr.)
ganze Pause (G.)
Ganzepause (G.)
pausa de redonda (Sp.)

silencio de semicorchea (Sp.)
16th-rest
semiquaver rest

pausa di semicroma (It.)
quart de soupir (Fr.)
sechzentel Pause (G.)
Sechzentelpause (G.)
pausa de semicorchea (Sp.)

silencio de semifusa (Sp.)
64th rest
hemidemisemiquaver rest
pausa di semibiscroma (It.)
seizième de soupir (Fr.)
vierundsechzigstel Pause (G.)
Vierundsechzigstelpause (G.)
pausa de semifusa (Sp.)

silent, silence, be silent
tacet (Lat.)
rest for a movement
do not play
tace, taci (It.)
se taire (Fr.)
ne pas jouer (Fr.)
schweigen (G.)
pausieren (G.)
callarse (Sp.)
silencio (Sp.)
cállate (Sp.)

sillet (Fr.)
nut (at the end of the
fingerboard)
saddle
sella (It.)
Sattel (G.)
ceja, cejilla (Sp.)

simile, simili (It.)
continue as before
in the same manner
in like manner
semblable (Fr.)
gleich (G.)
símil (Sp.)

simple meter
regular meter

2/4, 3/4, 4/4 time

vs. compound meter

sincopato (It.)
syncopated
off-beat
jazzy
syncopé (Fr.)
synkopiert (G.)
verschoben (G.)
sincopado (Sp.)

sinfonia (It.)
early composition
overture
prelude
introduction

2. suite
cassation
divertimento (It.)
sonata

3. symphony

sinfonia concertante (It.)
double *concerto
symphony with soloists

sinfonietta (It.)
chamber orchestra
string orchestra
small orchestra
ensemble
orchestra da camera (It.)
orchestre de chambre (Fr.)
Kammerorchester (G.)
orquestra de camara (Sp.)

2. short symphony
chamber symphony

sinfonische Dichtung (G.)
symphonic poem
tone poem

tone painting
program music
descriptive music
poema sinfonico (It.)
poème symphonique (Fr.)
Tondichtung (G.)
poema sinfónico (Sp.)

vs. absolute Musik (G.)

sing
vocalise
chant
make melody
break out in song
intone
warble
lilt
croon
trill
cantare (It.)
chanter (Fr.)
singen (G.)
cantar (Sp.)

sing-along
songfest
sing-in
community sing
hootnanny
jamboree
jam session
hymn-sing
hymn-fest

Singakademie (G.)
choral society
oratorio society
chorale
chorus
community choir
symphonic choir/chorus
philharmonic choir
associazione corale (It.)
societá di canto (It.)
société chorale (Fr.)

Gesangverein (G.)
orfeón (Sp.)

singen (G.)
to sing
to chant
intone
croon
warble
cantare (It.)
chanter (Fr.)
cantar (Sp.)

singende Säge (G.)
musical saw
singing saw
sega (It.)
lame musicale (Fr.)
serrucho (Sp.)

singer
vocalist
artiste
diva
crooner
chantuese
song stylist
songster, songstress
choraleer
minstrel
bard
Troubadour
Trouvère
jongleur
goliard
scop
minnesinger
Meistersinger
crooner
chanteuse
cantor

single chant
Anglican chant
falsobordone

vs. double chant

Singmesse (G.)
*high Mass
missa cantata (Lat.)
messa cantata (It.)
messe chantée (Fr.)
misa cantada (Sp.)

Singspiel (G.)
operetta
*opera
ballad opera
folk opera
masque
musical
dramma per musica (It.)
opéra comique (Fr.)
saynète (Fr.)
Zwischenspiel (G.)
zarzuela (Sp.)
tonadilla (Sp.)
sainete (Sp.)

sink-a-pace
cinque-pace (E.)
cinque passi (It.)
cinq pas (Fr.)
galliard
saltarello

siparo, siparietto (It.)
curtain (stage)
drop
traveler
rideau (Fr.)
Vorhang (G.)
telón (Sp.)

siringa (It.)
Panpipes
pipes of Pan
flauto di Pan (It.)
syrinx, syringe (Fr.)
Panflöte (G.)
flauta de Pan (Sp.)

sirventes (Prov.)
Troubadour satirical song
satire
goliard song
political song
parody
sirventois (Fr.)
Spruch (G.)

sistema (It.)
staff, stave
great staff
pentagramma (It.)
rigo musicale (It.)
portée musicale (Fr.)
Notensystem (G.)
Liniensystem (G.)
pentagrama (Sp.)
pauta, pautada (Sp.)

sistre (Fr.)
cittern
citole
cither
zither
guitar
cetera, cetra (It.)
Cister (G.)

sitar (Ind.)
lute
guitar
koto (Jap.)

six-four chord
second inversion triad
fifth in the bass
accordo di quarto e sesta (It.)
secondo rivolto (It.)
accord de sixte et quarte (Fr.)
deuxième renversement (Fr.)
Quartsextakkord (G.)
zweite Umkehrung (G.)
acorde de sexta-cuerta (Sp.)
acorde de sexta y cuerta (Sp.)

six-three chord
first inversion triad
chord of the sixth
sixth chord
third in the bass
primo rivolto (It.)
accordo di sesta (It.)
premier renversement (Fr.)
accord de sixte (Fr.)
Sextakkord (G.)
erste Umkehrung (G.)
acorde de sexta (y tercera)
(Sp.)

sixte, sixième (Fr.)
sixth (interval)
tonus cum diapente (Lat.)
sesta (It.)
esacordo (It.)
Sexte (G.)
sexta (Sp.)

sixte ajouté (Fr.)
added sixth (chord)
sesta aggiunta (It.)
hinzugefügte Sexte (G.)
sexta agregada (Sp.)

sixteenth note
semiquaver
semifusa (Lat.)
bis unca (Lat.)
semicroma (It.)
sedicesimo (It.)
double-croche (Fr.)
Sechzehntel (G.)
semicorchea (Sp.)

sixteenth rest
semiquaver rest
pausa di semicroma (It.)
quart de soupir (Fr.)
Sechzehntelpause (G.)
pausa de semicorchea (Sp.)
silencio de semicorchea (Sp.)

sixty-fourth note
hemidemisemiquaver
semibiscroma (It.)
sessantaquatresimo (It.)
quadruple-croche (Fr.)
Vierundsechzigstelnote (G.)
semifusa (Sp.)

sixty-fourth rest
pausa di semibiscroma (It.)
seizième de soupir (Fr.)
Vierundsechzigstelpause (G
silencio de semifusa (Sp.)
pausa de semifusa (Sp.)

sizigia (It.)
chord
triad
syzygy
syzygia (Lat.)
syzygie (Fr.)
sicigia (Sp.)

sizzle cymbals
rivet cymbals
piatti chiodati (It.)
cymbales sur tiges (Fr.)
Zischbecken (G.)
Nietenbecken (G.)
Sizzle-Becken (G.)
cimbalos sobre palillos (Sp.)

ska
reggae
pop music
rap
rock and roll

Skala (G.)
*scale
octave species
gamut
diagramma (Lat.)
scala (Lat., It.)
gamma (It.)

gamme (Fr.)
échelle (Fr.)
Tonleiter (G.)
escala (Sp.)
gama (Sp.)

sketch
short composition
character piece
descriptive piece
*program music
outline
schizzo (It.)
esquisse (Fr.)
Skizze (G.)
bosquejo (Sp.)
boceto (Sp.)

skiffle band
jug band
washboard band
folk band
mountain music
jazz band
combo

skiffleboard
washboard
scraper
jug band
skiffle band
tavola da lavare (It.)
planche à laver (Fr.)
Waschbrett (G.)
tabla a lavar (Sp.)
güiro (Sp.)

skip
jump
leap
disjunct interval
salto (It., Sp.)
saut (Fr.)
Sprung (G.)

vs. step

skipwise
disjunct motion
skipping
chordal
broken chords
arpeggiated
arpeggiando (It.)

vs. stepwise

Skolie (G.)
*drinking song
bacchanalian song
tavern song
brindisi (It.)
chanson à boire (Fr.)
Trinklied (G.)
canción de taberna (Sp.)

slapstick
whip (percussion instr.)
horsewhip
frusta (It.)
fouet (Fr.)
Peitsche (G.)
zurriaga, -o (Sp.)
látigo (Sp.)

slargando (It.)
slowing down
rallentando (It.)
allargando (It.)
largando (It.)
lentando (It.)
slentando (It.)
en ralentissant (Fr.)
en retardant (Fr.)
langsamer werden (G.)
retardando (Sp.)

vs. stringendo (It.)

slave song
spiritual
folk hymn
shout

ring shout

sleighbells
jingle bells
harness bells
pellet bells
altar bells
*bell(s)
nolae (Lat.)
sonaglio, sonagliera (It.)
nolettes (Fr.)
grelots (Fr.)
Schellen (G.)
Schellengeläute (G.)
cascabeles (Sp.)

slide
portamento (It.)
*glissando (It.)
slissando (It.)
scoop
glide
glissade (Fr.)
coulade (Fr.)
*port-de-voix (Fr.)
Schleifer (G.)
extrasino (Sp.)
glisado (Sp.)

2. coulisse (of a trombone) (Fr.)
tiro (It.)
pompa (a tiro) (It.)
Stimmzug, Zug (G.)
Scheide (G.)
Kulisse (G.)
bomba (Sp.)
corredera (Sp.)
vara (Sp.)

3. ornament
backfall
double backfall
sliding relish
appoggiatura (It.)
flatté (Fr.)
Schleifer (G.)

slide flute/whistle
 piston flute
 song whistle
 Swanee whistle
 piston flute/pipe
 bazooka
 toy instrument/flute
 flauto a tiro (It.)
 flauto da jazz (It.)
 zufolo a pistone (It.)
 flûte à coulisse (Fr.)
 flûte lotine (Fr.)
 Lotosflöte (G.)
 Stempelflöte (G.)

slow
 lento (It.)
 adagio (It.)
 largo (It.)
 tardo (It.)
 grave (It., E.)
 broad
 lent, lentement (Fr.)
 langsam (G.)
 despacio (Sp.)
 lentamente (Sp.)

vs. fast
 allegro (It.)

slumber song
 *lullaby
 cradle song
 ninna nanna (It.)
 ninnerella (It.)
 berceuse (Fr.)
 Schlummerlied (G.)
 Wiegenlied (G.)
 canción de cuna (Sp.)

vs. reveille

slur
 ligature
 legato sign
 bind

tie
 neume
 melismatic
 legatura (It.)
 portato (It.)
 liaison (Fr.)
 légature (Fr.)
 Bindung (G.)
 Schleifbogen (G.)
 Legatobogen (G.)
 Bindebogen (G.)
 Bindungszeichen (G.)
 ligadura (Sp.)

smorzando (It.)
 fading away
 dying
 slower and softer
 morendo (It.)
 calando (It.)
 decrescendo (It.)
 diminuendo (It.)
 en mourant (Fr.)
 sterbend (G.)
 expirando (Sp.)

snare (of a drum)
 bordoniera (It.)
 timbre (Fr.)
 Schnarrsaite (G.)
 Trommelsaite (G.)
 bordón (Sp.)

snare drum
 side drum
 military drum
 tamburo militare (It.)
 tamburo piccolo (It.)
 cassa militare (It.)
 cassa chiara (It.)
 petit tambour (Fr.)
 caisse claire (Fr.)
 kleine Trommel (G.)
 Militärtrommel (G.)
 tambor, tambor militar (Sp.)
 caja, caja militar (Sp.)

sobre el batidor (Sp.)
 bow on the fingerboard
 harmonics
 overtones
 sul tasto (It.)
 sulla tastiera (It.)
 flautando (It.)
 sur la touche (Fr.)
 am Griffbrett (G.)

sobre el puentecillo (Sp.)
 play near the bridge
 on the bridge
 sul ponticello (It.)
 au chevelet (Fr.)
 près du chevelet (Fr.)
 am Steg (G.)

sock cymbals
 choke cymbals
 hi-hat, high-hat cymbals
 Charleston (It.)
 cymbales choquées (Fr.)
 hi-hat pédal (Fr.)
 Charleston-Maschine (G.)
 pedal del bombo de jazz (Sp.

soffiare (It.)
 blow (a wind instr.)
 play
 sound
 souffler (Fr.)
 blasen (G.)
 soplar (Sp.)

soffietto (It.)
 bellows (org.)
 blower
 wind supply
 wind chest
 mantice (It.)
 soufflet (Fr.)
 Balg (G.)
 Gebläse (G.)
 fuelle (Sp.)

sofort (G.)
   subito (It.)
   suddenly
   quickly
   immediately
   subitement (Fr.)
   sogleich (G.)
   inmediato (Sp.)
   súbito (Sp.)

vs. nach und nach (G.)

soft, softly
   quiet(ly)
   piano (It.)
   dolce (It.)
   doux (Fr.)
   doucement (Fr.)
   leise (G.)
   sanft (G.)
   suave (Sp.)
   dulce (Sp.)

vs. loud,loudly

soft pedal
   una corda pedal
   damper pedal
   una corda (It.)
   pedale sordina (It.)
   pedale sinistra (It.)
   pedale piano (It.)
   pédale douce (Fr.)
   pédale gauche (Fr.)
   pédale sourde (Fr.)
   petite pédale (Fr.)
   linke Pedal (G.)
   eine Saite (G.)
   Dämpfer (G.)
   Verschiebung (G.)
   pedal sordina/suave (Sp.)
   mute

vs. loud/sustaining pedal

soggetto (It.)

subject (of a fugue)
   theme
   antecedent
   dux (Lat.)
   episode
   andamento (It.)
   proposta (It.)
   guida (It.)
   sujet (Fr.)
   Thema (G.)
   Führer (G.)
   guia (Sp.)
   sujeto (Sp.)

vs. riposta (It.)
   *answer

sol
   dominant note
   fifth degree of the scale
   dominante (It., Fr., Sp.)
   Dominante (G.)
   Oberdominante (G.)

soleá (Sp.)
   *flamenco song

solemn (high) Mass
   high Mass
   missa solemnis (Lat.)
   missa cantata (Lat.)
   messa grande (It.)
   messa solenne (It.)
   grand-messe (Fr.)
   messe haute (Fr.)
   messe solennelle (Fr.)
   Hochamt (G.)
   Hauptmesse (G.)
   misa solemne (Sp.)
   misa mayor (Sp.)

vs. low Mass

solemn tone (chant)
   ornate tone
   festal tone

tonus solemnis (Lat.)
tonus festivus (Lat.)

vs. ferial tone
   simple tone

solid chord
   unbroken chord
   accordo incollato (It.)
   accordo sovrapposto (It.)
   concento (It.)
   accord plaqué (Fr.)
   platter Akkord (G.)
   Akkord anschlagen (G.)
   acorde apoyado (Sp.)

vs. broken chord

solmization
   sol-fa
   do-re-mi
   solfa system
   sol-fa-ing
   music reading
   sight-singing
   scale
   letter notation
   vocal excercise
   tonic solfa
   solfeggio (It.)
   solfège (Fr.)
   Solfeggio (G.)
   Abc-diren (G.)
   solfeo (Sp.)
   character notation
   shape-notes
   patent notes
   buckwheat notes
   dunce notes
   bebization
   damenization
   bocedization
   chevé system
   jamization
   Aretinian syllables
   Guidonian hand

solo
music for a single performer
art song
aria
sonata
cantata
concerto
lead part
monody

solo ensemble
chamber group
madrigal singers
soli (It.)
favorito (It.)
concertino (It.)

solo manual/organ
orchestral manual
organo d'assolo (It.)
clavier des bombardes (Fr.)
Soloklavier (G.)

soloist
lead performer
solo singer/player
prima donna (It.)
virtuoso
artiste
diva
first chair
concert artist
section leader
cantor
solista (It., Sp.)
cantatrice (It.)
soliste (Fr.)
Solist (G.)

sombrero Chino (Sp.)
Turkish crescent
Chinese crescent
Chinese pavilion
jingling Johnny
Janissary music
banda Turca (It.)

mezzaluna (It.)
*chapeau Chinois (Fr.)
Halbmond (G.)
chinesco (Sp.)

son (Fr., Sp.)
sound
sonority
tone
sonus (Lat.)
suono (It.)
tono (It., Sp.)
tuono (It.)
Klang (G.)
Ton (G.)
sonido (Sp)

son additionell (Fr.)
summation tone
resultant tone
combination tone
suono/tono addizionale (It.)
suono d'addizione (It.)
tono combinato (It.)
son combiné (Fr.)
Summationston (G.)
Kombinationston (G.)
Zusatzton (G.)
sonido adicional (Sp.)
sonido de combinación
(Sp.)

son bouché (Fr.)
stopped note (horn)
suono chiuso (It.)
son étouffé (Fr.)
Stopfton (G.)
sonido tapado (Sp.)
sonido cerrado (Sp.)

vs. son ouvert (Fr.)

son différentiel (Fr.)
difference tone
differential tone
resultant tone

Tartini tone
suono diferenziale (It.)
Differenzton (G.)
sonido diferencial (Sp.)

son ouvert (Fr.)
open tone (on a horn)
natural tone/note
tono aperto (It.)
tono naturale (It.)
ton ouvert (Fr.)
ton naturel (Fr.)
offener Ton (G.)
Naturton (G.)

sonada (Sp.)
*fanfare
flourish
call
bugle call
tuck, tucket
squillo di tromba (It.)
sonnerie (Fr.)
Tusch (G.)
fanfarria (Sp.)
charanga (Sp.)

sonaglio, sonagliera (It.)
jingle bells
pellet bells
*bell(s)
altar bells
harness bells
sleighbells
jingle bells
bubboli (It.)
grelots (Fr.)
nolettes (Fr.)
sonnettes (Fr.)
Schellen (G.)
Rollschellen (G.)
cascabeles (Sp.)
sonaja (Sp.)

sonajero (Sp.)
*rattle

ratchet
cog rattle
maraca
rainstick
raganella (It.)
crécelle (Fr.)
hochet (Fr.)
Rassel (G.)
Ratsche (G.)
matraca (Sp.)

sonare (It.)
to sound
vibrate
resound
resonate
ring
toll
play
suonare, risonare (It.)
sonner, résonner (Fr.)
jouer (Fr.)
klingen (G.)
spielen (G.)
sonar, resonar (Sp.)

sonata (It., E., Sp.)
solo work
trio sonata
chamber sonata
church sonata
sonatina (It.)
sonatine (Fr.)
sonate (Fr.)
Sonate, Sonatine (G.)

sonata da camera (It.)
chamber sonata
sonate de chambre (Fr.)
Kammersonate (G.)
sonata de camara (Sp.)

sonata da chiesa (It.)
church sonata
sonate d'église (Fr.)
Kirchensonate (G.)

sonata de iglesia (Sp.)

sonata (allegro)form
first movement form
ternary form
forma sonata (It., Sp.)
forme sonate (Fr.)
Sonatenform (G.)

song
melody
tune
air, ayre
lay
ditty
strain
jingle
ballad
carol
hymn
chant
canticle
art song
folk song
cantio (Lat.)
cantus (Lat.)
canticum, canticulum (Lat.)
carmen, carmina (Lat.)
aria, arioso (It.)
canzona (It.)
canto, cantino (It.)
cavatina (It.)
cabaletta (It.)
ballata (It.)
canso (Prov.)
lai (Fr.)
chant (Fr.)
mélodie (Fr.)
chanson, chansonette (Fr.)
rondeau (Fr.)
Gesang (G.)
Lied (G.)
Weise (G.)
canción (Sp.)
cantiga (Sp.)

song collection
*anthology
song book
fake book
repertory, repertoire
cantionale (Lat.)
canzoniere (It.)
chansonnier (Fr.)
Gesangbuch (G.)
Liederbuch (G.)
cancionero (Sp.)

song cycle
suite of songs
song series/set
ciclo di canzoni (It.)
cycle de mélodies (Fr.)
cycle de lieder (Fr.)
Liederkreis (G.)
Liederzyklus (G.)
ciclo de canciones (Sp.)

song form
ABA form
ternary form
three-part form
tripartite form
arch form
bow form
da-capo form
Liedform (G.)
Bogenform (G.)

Song of Hannah
Canticle of Anna
Exultavit cor meum (Lat.)

Song of Mary
Canticle of Mary
Canticle of the (Blessed)
Virgin
Magnificat (Lat.)
Office
Evening Prayer
Vespers

Song of Moses
Canticle of Moses (I, II)
Song of the Sea
Moses' and Miriam's Song
Cantemus Domino (Lat.)
Audite Coeli (Lat.)

Song of Simeon
Nunc Dimittis (Lat.)
Canticle of Simeon
Canticum Simeonis (Lat.)
Evening Prayer
Vespers
Compline
Office

Song of Songs
Canticle of Canticles
Song of Solomon
Canticum Canticorum (Lat.)
Cantico dei Cantici (It.)
Cantique de Cantiques (Fr.)
Lied der Lieder (G.)
Hohelied (G.)
Cantar de los Cantares (Sp.)

Song of the Angels
Sanctus (Lat.)
Ter Sanctus (Lat.)
Hymn of the Angels
angelic hymn
cherubic hymn
Aius Trisagion (Lat.)

Song of the Three (Holy) Children
Canticle of the Three Children
Canticle of the Three Young Men
Benedicite (Lat.)
Office
Lauds

Song of Zechariah
Canticle of Zachary

Canticum Zachariae (Lat.)
Benedictus Dominus Deus Israel (Lat.)
Office
Lauds

Song(s) of Zion/Sion
the Psalms
sacred song
psalmus (Lat.)
salmo (It., Sp.)
psaume (Fr.)
Psalm (G.)

song stylist
singer (pop music)
songster, songstress
songbird
vocalist
artiste
crooner
chanteur, chanteuse (Fr.)
Sänger(in) (G.)

song whistle
Shawnee whistle
piston flute/pipe
slide whistle/flute
bazooka
toy flute
flauto a tiro (It.)
flauto da jazz (It.)
zufolo a pistone (It.)
flûte à coulisse (Fr.)
flûte lotine (Fr.)
Lotosflöte (G.)
Stempelflöte (G.)

songfest
sing-along
hymnfest
community sing
hootnanny
jamboree
jam session

songs without words
piano pieces
descriptive pieces
romanza senza paroles (It.)
romances sans paroles (Fr.)
Lieder ohne Worte (G.)
romanza sin palabras (Sp.)

songsmith
composer of songs
songwriter
tunesmith
melody-maker

sonido (Sp.)
*sound
tone
*sono (It.)
son (Fr.)
Klang (G.)

sonido de combinación (Sp.)
resultant tone
combination tone
summation tone
*son additionell (Fr.)

sonnaille (Fr.)
cowbell
campanaccio (It.)
cloche de vache (Fr.)
Kuhschelle (G.)
Kuhglocke (G.)
Alpenglocke (G.)
cencerro (Sp.)

sonnante (Fr.)
*glockenspiel
bell lyre

sonnerie (Fr.)
signal call
bugle call
*fanfare
flourish
honors

salute
chiamata (It.)
fanfara (It.)
squillo di tromba (It.)
Fanfare (G.)
Blasmusik (G.)
charanga (Sp.)
toque de trompeta (Sp.)

2. chimes
carillon
churchbells
campanelli (It.)
carillon (Fr.)
Geläute (G.)
campanólogo (Sp.)

3. the peal of bells
chime
tolling
ringing

sonnerie aux morts (Fr.)
taps
*lament
silenzio (It.)
Zapfenstreich (G.)
toque de silencio (Sp.)

sonnette (Fr.)
handbell
*bell

Sonntag (G.)
Sunday
Sabbath
Lord's Day
Dominica (Lat.)
Domenica (It.)
Dimanche (Fr.)
Domingo (Sp.)

sono (It.)
*sound
tone
sonority

sonus (Lat.)
suono (It.)
tono (It., Sp.)
son (Fr., Sp.)
Klang (G.)
Ton (G.)
sonido (Sp.)

Sonus (Lat.)
Offertory (Gallican rite)
Offertorium (Lat.)
Offerenda (Lat. Ambrosian)
sacrificium (Lat. Mozarabic)
offertorio (It.)
offertoire (Fr.)
ofertorio (Sp.)

sopraddominante (It.)
sixth degree
la
submediant
superdominant
sus-dominante (Fr.)
sous-médiante (Fr.)
Untermediante (G.)
superdominante (Sp.)

soprana corda (It.)
E-string (violin)
cantarella (It.)
cantino (It.)
chanterelle (Fr.)
Sangsaite (G.)
Quintsaite (G.)
cantarela (Sp.)

sopranino (It.)
higher range than soprano
piccolo (It.)

soprano
high voice
treble voice
top part/voice
male soprano
cantus (Lat.)

superius (Lat.)
sopranista (It.)
sopraniste (Fr.)
dessus, haut-dessus (Fr.)
Sopran, Sopranist, -in (G.)
erste Stimme (G.)
tiple (Sp.)

soprano clef
C-clef on first line
Sopran-Schlussel (G.)
*G-clef
treble clef
chiave di soprano (It.)
clef de violon (Fr.)
clave aguda (Sp.)

soprano recorder
descant recorder
recorder
Sopranblockflöte (G.)

soprano legg(i)ero (It.)
coloratura soprano
soprano di coloratura (It.)
soprano sfogato (It.)
soprano léger (Fr.)
Koloratursopran (G.)
tiple ligera (Sp.)
soprano ligera (Sp.)

sopratonica (It.)
second degree
re
supertonic
sus-tonique (Fr.)
Wechseldominante (G.)
supertónico (Sp.)

sordellina (It.)
*bagpipe
musetta (It.)
piva (It.)
ceramella (It.)
musette (Fr.)
cornemuse (Fr.)

biniou (Fr.)
sourdeline (Fr.)
Dudelsack (G.)
Sackpfeife (G.)
gaita (Sp.)

sordino (It.)
mute
damper
étouffoir (Fr.)
sourdine (Fr.)
Dämpfer (G.)
sordina (Sp.)

2. *kit
pocket fiddle
poccetta (It.)
pochette (Fr.)
Quartgeige (G.)
Taschengeige (G.)
violin de bolsillo (Sp.)

3. *clavichord
chekker
clavicordo (It.)
doucemelle (Fr.)
Klavichord (G.)
clavicordio (Sp.)

sordone (It.)
soft double-reed instr.
curtal
courtaut
bassoon
sourdine (Fr.)
dolzaine, dolçaina (Fr.)
Sordun (G.)
dulzaina (Sp.)

sortisatio (Lat. 16c.)
improvised counterpoint

sortita (It. 18c.)
entry aria (opera)

2. *postlude

closing voluntary

sostenido (Sp.)
sharp sign
diesis (It.)
dièse (Fr.)
Kreuz (G.)

sostenente piano
bowed keyboard instrument
piano-violin
harmonichord
lyrichord
melopiano
*hurdy-gurdy
Geigenwerk (G.)
Gambenwerk (G.)

sostenuto, sostenendo (It.)
sustaining, sustained
soutenu (Fr.)
aus(ge)halten (G.)
sostenido (Sp.)

sostenuto pedal (piano)
middle pedal
bass-sustain pedal
pedale centrale (It.)
pédale centrale (Fr.)
Mittelpedal (G.)
pedal del medio (Sp.)
pedal central (Sp.)
pedal sostenuto (Sp.)

sotto voce (It.)
*aside
under one's breath
stage whisper
whispered
undertone
very soft(ly)
pianissimo (It.)
fra se (It.)
mezza voce (It.)
à part (Fr.)
de coté (Fr.)

à mi-voix (Fr.)
beiseite (G.)
mit halbe Stimme (G.)
für sich (G.)
geflüstet (G.)
chuchoté (Sp.)
a parte (Sp.)
a sovoz (Sp.)

sottodominante (It.)
fourth degree of the scale
fa
subdominant
sous-dominante (Fr.)
Unterdominante (G.)
Subdominante (G.)
subdominante (Sp.)

soubasse, sous-basse (Fr.)
sub-bass (org.)
subbasso (It.)
Subbass (G.)
Untersatz (G.)
sub-bajo (Sp.)

soubrette (It., Fr. E.)
comic role (female)
ingenue (Fr.)
servetta (It.)
dugazon (Fr.)
tiple cómico (Sp.)

souffler (Fr.)
to blow (a wind instr.)
sound
play
soffiare (It.)
blasen (G.)
soplar (Sp.)

soufflet (Fr.)
bellows (org.)
wind supply
blower
soffietto (It.)
tiramantici (It.)

souffleur (Fr.)
Kalkant (G.)
Balgentreter (G.)
Gebläse (G.)
fuelle (Sp.)

souffleur, -euse (Fr.)
prompter
teleprompter
cue cards
suggeritore (It.)
Souffleur (G.)
apuntador (Sp.)
prompt box

soul music
gospel music
jazz
black pop music

sound (n.)
acoustic waves
vibration
sound waves
oscillation
sonority
tone
cycles per second (cps)
audio
stereo
suono (It.)
tuono (It.)
son (Fr.)
Klang (G.)
Schall (G.)
sonido (Sp.)

sound (vb.)
vibrate
echo
resound
reverberate
*s(u)onare (It.)
sonner (Fr.)
klingen (G.)
sonar, resonar (Sp.)

sound box/chest
resonance chamber
hollow body of a string instr.
cassa armonica (It.)
caisse de résonance (Fr.)
Resonanzboden (G.)
caja de resonancia (Sp.)

sound hole
F-hole
effe (It.)
occhi (It.)
ouïe (Fr.)
F-Loch (G.)
Schalloch (G.)
abertura acustica (Sp.)
efe (Sp.)
oído (Sp.)

sound post
anima (It.)
âme (Fr.)
Stimmstock (G.)
Seele (G.)
alma (Sp.)

sound reproduction
recording
canned music
taped music
riproduzione sonora (It.)
reproduction sonore (Fr.)
Schallwiedergabe (G.)
reproducción sonora (Sp.)

sound track
sound stripe (film)
film recording
colonna sonora (It.)
bande sonore (Fr.)
colonne sonore (Fr.)
Tonspur (G.)
banda de sonido (Sp.)
pista sonora (Sp.)

2. band on a disk

track
cut
channel
pista (It., Sp.)
traccia (It.)
piste (Fr.)
Spur, Tonspur (G.)

sound wave
vibration
cycle
pressure wave
onda sonora (It., Sp.)
onde sonore (Fr.)
Schallwelle (G.)

soundboard
belly
table
tavola armonico (It.)
piano armonico (It.)
table d'harmonie (Fr.)
Resonanzboden (G.)
caja armónica (Sp.)

soupir (Fr.)
quarter rest
crotchet rest
pausa di semiminima (It.)
quarto d'aspetto (It.)
Viertelpause (G.)
silencio de negra (Sp.)
pausa de negra (Sp.)
pausa de semínima (Sp.)

sour note
wrong note
false note
mistake
clinker
stecca (It.)
falsa nota (It.)
canard (Fr.)
fausse note (Fr.)
Misston (G.)
falsche Note (G.)

gallipavo (Sp.)

sourd (Fr.)
muted
muffled
damped
covered (tone)
sorda (It., Sp.)
coperto (It.)
velato (It.)
couvert (Fr.)
bedeckt (G.)
cubierto (Sp.)

sourdine (Fr.)
*mute
damper

2. *kit
pochette (Fr.)
pocket violin

3. sordone (It.)
*courtaut
curtal
Sordun (G.)
bassoon

4. clavichord (soft)
spinet

sous-dominante (Fr.)
fourth degree of the scale
fa
subdominant
sottodominante (It.)
Subdominante (G.)
Unterdominante (G.)
subdominante (Sp.)

sous-médiante (Fr.)
sixth degree
la
superdominant
submediant
sopraddominante (It.)

sus-dominante (Fr.)
Untermediante (G.)
superdominante (Sp.)

sous-tonique (Fr.)
seventh degree
ti, si
leading tone
subtonic
essential seventh
sensibile (It.)
nota sensibile (It.)
note sensible (Fr.)
Leitton (G.)
sensible nota (Sp.)

sousaphone
tuba
helicon
bass tuba
bombard, bombardon

soutenu (Fr.)
*sostenuto (It.)
sustained
ausgehalten (G.)

space (on the staff)
spatium (Lat.)
spazio (It.)
interligne (Fr.)
espace (Fr.)
Zwischenraum (G.)
Zwischenzeile (G.)
espacio (Sp.)
interlinea (Sp.)

Spanisches Kreuz (G.)
double sharp sign
doppio diesis (It.)
double dièse (Fr.)
Doppelkreuz (G.)
doble sostenido (Sp.)

Spanish guitar
classical guitar

folk guitar
flat-top guitar

vs. electric guitar

sparta, -o, spartita, -o (It.)
score, full score
spartitura (It.)
partition (Fr.)
Sparte (G.)
partitura (Sp., It.)

vs. partitura tascabile (It.)

spassapensiero (It.)
*Jew's harp
Jew's trump
jaw's harp
mouth-organ
ribeba (It.)
guitarraccia (It.)
guimbarde (Fr.)
trompe de Berne/Béarn (Fr.)
birimbao (Sp.)
guitarrón (Sp.)
trompa gallega (Sp.)
Judenharfe (G.)
Maultrommel (G.)

spazzole (It.)
brushes
wire/steel brushes
balais de jazz (Fr.)
Rute (G.)
Besen, Jazzbesen (G.)
escobillas (Sp.)

species counterpoint
strict counterpoint
practice of counterpoint
contrapuntal writing
specie di contrappunto (It.)
espèces de contrepoint (Fr.)
Kontrapunktgattungen (G.)
especies de contrapunto (Sp.

spectator(s)
    *audience
    fans
    concert-goer
    congregation

speed
    tempo
    pace
    velocity
    velocitá (It.)
    vélocité (Fr.)
    vitesse (Fr.)
    Geschwindigkeit (G.)
    velocidad (Sp.)

spettacolo (It.)
    show
    spectacle
    extravaganza
    *entertainment
    musical
    opera
    follies
    burlesque
    divertissement (Fr.)
    Unterhaltung (G.)
    entremés (Sp.)

Spärenmusik (G.)
    Music of the Spheres
    Harmony of the Spheres
    Celestial Harmony
    l'armonia delle sfere/celeste (It.)
    musique des spheres célestes (Fr.)
    armonía/música de las esferas celestes (Sp.)

spiccato (It.)
    detatched (bowing)
    staccato (It.)
    saltato, saltellato (It.)
    sauté, sautillé (Fr.)
    détaché (Fr.)

gehopst (G.)
gesprungen (G.)
losgetrennt (G.)
saltado (Sp.)
desatado (Sp.)

vs. legato (It.)

Spiegelkanon (G.)
    *crab canon
    retrograde canon
    mirror canon
    *canon
    canon cancrizans (Lat.)
    recte et retro (Lat.)
    al rovescio (It.)
    canone retrogrado (It.)
    à l'écrevisse (Fr.)
    Krebskanon (G.)
    Krebsgang (G.)
    canon cancrizante (Sp.)
    canon retrógrado (Sp.)

Spieldose (G.)
    music box
    scatola musicale (It.)
    scatola armonica (It.)
    carillon à musique (Fr.)
    boite à musique (Fr.)
    caja de música (Sp.)

spielen (G.)
    to play (an instrument)
    perform on
    to play upon
    make music
    suonare (It.)
    jouer (Fr.)
    tocar (Sp.)

Spieler (G.)
    player
    instrumentalist
    suonatore, suonatrice (It.)
    instrumentiste (Fr.)
    instrumentista (Sp.)

Spielmann (G.)
    goliard
    minstrel
    Troubadour
    Trouvère
    Minnesinger
    Meistersinger
    jongleur
    bard
    scop
    performer
    entertainer

Spieloper (G.)
    comic opera
    *opera
    operetta
    light opera
    ballad opera
    masque
    musical comedy
    opera buffa (It.)
    opérette (Fr.)
    Operette (G.)
    Singspiel (G.)
    zarzuela (Sp.)
    tonadilla (Sp.)
    sainete (Sp.)

vs. Oper (G.)

Spieltisch (G.)
    console (org. E., Fr.)
    consolle (It.)
    consola (Sp.)
    caja del órgano (Sp.)

Spielzeit (G.)
    season, concert season
    engagement
    run
    tour
    stagione (It.)
    saison (Fr.)
    temporada (Sp.)

spike
pin
tailpin
*endpin
peg
puntale (It.)
spina (It.)
pique, piquet (Fr.)
Stachel (G.)
Knopf (G.)
puntal (Sp.)

spina (It., Sp.)
*jack (harpsichord)
quill
plectrum
salterello (It.)
sautereau (Fr.)
Kiel (G.)
Docke (G.)
Springer (G.)
púa (Sp.)

2. *spike
peg
endpin

spinet
harpsichord (small)
virginal(s)
spiked harp
cembalo traverso (It.)
spinetta (It.)
épinette (Fr.)
Spinett (G.)
Querflügel (g.)
espineta (Sp.)

2. upright piano
cabinet piano
cottage piano
console piano
studio piano

vs. grand piano

spinning song
ballad
work song
canzona della tela (It.)
chanson de toile (Fr.)
Spinn(er)lied (G.)
canciön de tela (Sp.)

spinto (It.)
soprano, dramatic soprano
tenor, dramatic tenor

spiritoso (It.)
spirited, with spirit
energetic
con spirito (It.)
*animato (It.)
avec esprit (Fr.)
geistreich (G.)
feurig (G.)

spiritual
hymn
gospel song
praise song
Negro spiritual
slave song
white spiritual
religious song

Spitze (G.)
tip of the bow
point
peak
head
nasetto (It.)
punta (It., Sp.)
punta d'arco (It.)
pointe (Fr.)
punto del arco (Sp.)

vs. Frosch (G.)

Spitzflöte (G.)
open flute stop (org.)
tibia cuspida (Lat.)

Spillflöte (G.)

Spitzharfe (G.)
psaltery
small harp
double zither
arpa doppia (It.)
arpanetta (It.)
arpanette (Fr.)
Zwischerharfe (G.)
Harfenett (G.)
Flügelharfe (G.)

split keys/keyboard
divided stop (org.)
short octave
broken octave
partial stop
incomplete stop
medio registro (It.)
mi re ut (It.)
tasti spezzati (It.)
ottava corta (It.)
octave courte (Fr.)
touches brisêe (Fr.)
kurze Oktave (G.)
gebrochene Tasten (G.)
octava corta (Sp.)

split track
sound track
recorded music
music minus one
karaoke music
canned music

spoons
bones
castanets
clappers
rhythm sticks
Klangstäbe (G.)
claves (Sp.)

Sprechmaschine (G.)
phonograph

*gramophone
talking machine
turntable
victrola
giradischi (It.)
tourne-disques (Fr.)
tocadiscos (Sp.)

Sprechstimme (G.)
recitative
declamation
parlando (It.)
recitando (It.)
recitativo parlante (It.)
récitatif parlant (Fr.)
rezitierend (G.)
Sprechgesang (G.)
recitado (Sp.)

spring song
may song
canto di primavera (It.)
canzona della primavera (It.)
reverdie (Fr.)
Frülingslied (G.)
canción de primavera (Sp.)

Springer (G.)
*jack (harpsichord)
quill
plectrum
spina (It.)
salterello (It.)
sautereau (Fr.)
Kiel (G.)
Docke (G.)
macillo (Sp.)
martinete (Sp.)
púa (Sp.)

springer
ornament
grace
anticipation note (E., Fr.)
anticipazione (It.)
Antizipation (G.)

Nachschlag (G.)
anticipación (Sp.)

Spruch (G.)
proverb song
Minnesinger song
Minnesang (G.)
Sangspruch (G.)
Meistersinger song

Sprung (G.)
skip
leap
jump
disjunct motion
salto (It., Sp.)
sbalzo (It.)
saut (Fr.)

vs. Stufe (G.)

2. Nachtanz (G.)
after-dance
second dance of a pair
tripla (It.)
rotta (It.)
proporzione (It.)
Proportz, Proporzio (G.)
segunda danza (Sp.)

square neumes/notation
quadratic notation (chant)
Aquitanian notation
notazione quadrata (It.)
nottation carrée (Fr.)
Quadratnotation (G.)
notación cuadrada (Sp.)

squeezebox
*accordion
concertina
hand harmonica
piano accordion
fisarmonica (It.)
accordéon (Fr.)
Handharmonika (G.)

Quetsche (G.)
Quetschkommode (G.)
bandoneón (Sp.)
fuelle (Sp.)

squilla (It.)
little bell
cowbell
*bell

squillare (It.)
*ring
peal
toll
strike

squillo di tromba (It.)
*fanfare
trumpet call
flourish
bugle call

staccato (It.)
detatched and short
non-legato (It.)
spiccato (It.)
piccato (It.)
picch(i)ettato (It.)
détaché (Fr.)
délié (Fr.)
brisé (Fr.)
abgestossen ((G.)
no ligado (Sp.)
destacado (Sp.)

vs. legato (It.)

Stachel (G.)
endpin
*spike
tailpin
peg

staff
notation
pentagramma (It.)

rigo musicale (It.)
sistemi (It.)
portée (Fr.)
System (G.)
Notensystem (G.)
Liniensystem (G.)
pentagrama (Sp.)
pauta (Sp.)

staff paper
music paper
manuscript paper
carta da musica (It.)
carta rigata (It.)
carta pentagrammato (It.)
papier à musique (Fr.)
Notenpapier (G.)
liniertes Papier (G.)
pautada (Sp.)
papel de música (Sp.)
papel pautado (Sp.)

staffa crescendo (It.)
swell pedal
swell shoe
crescendo pedal
pédale de la boîte expressive (Fr.)
Schwelltritt (G.)
pedal de crescendo (Sp.)

staffless neumes/notation
adiastematic
cheironomic
oratorical
nondiastematic
in campo aperto (It.)

stage
platform
bandwagon
scena (It.)
palcoscenico (It.)
scène (Fr.)
Bühne (G.)
escena, escenario (Sp.)

tablado (Sp.)

stage band
swing band
big band
dance band
jazz band
combo
40's band
Dixiland band

stage whisper
*aside
very soft
whispered
under one's breath
sotto voce (It.)
fra se (It.)
mezza voce (It.)
à part (Fr.)
en aparté (Fr.)
mit halbe Stimme (G.)
a parte (Sp.)
cuchicheado (Sp.)

stagione (It.)
season
engagement
run
tour
saison (Fr.)
Spielzeit (G.)
temporada (Sp.)

Stahlspiel (G.)
lyra
bell lyra
*glockenspiel
orchestra bells
metal harmonica
campanette (It.)
organo di campane (It.)
jeu de timbres (Fr.)
Lyra (G.)
juego de timbres (Sp.)

Stahltrommel (G.)
*steel drum

stampita (It.)
estampie (Fr.)
stantipes (Lat.)
*saltarello (It.)
istampita, stampita (It.)
estampida (Sp.)

stand-up bass
*bass
bass fiddle
bull fiddle
double bass
string bass
upright bass
bass viol
contrabasso (It.)
contrebasse (Fr.)
Kontrabass (G.)
contrabajo (Sp.)

Ständchen (G.)
*serenade
*lullaby
suite
cassation
divertimento (It.)
serenata (It.)
sérénade (Fr.)
Nachtmusik
serenada (Sp.)

stanghetta (It.)
bar line
*bar
sbarra (It.)
barra (It., Sp.)
barre (Fr.)
Taktstrich (G.)
Mensurstrich (G.)
linea divisoria (Sp.)

2. beam
cross-bar

tratto d'unione (It.)
barre tranversale (Fr.)
Notenbalken (G.)
Querbalken (G.)
Balkenverbindung (G.)
travesaño (Sp.)

stanza (E., It.)
verse
strophe
couplet
stance (Fr.)
Stanze (G.)
copla (Sp.)

stark (G.)
forte (It.)
loud
strong
blaring
fort, fortement (Fr.)
laut (G.)
fuerte (Sp.)

vs. leise, sanft (G.)

state trumpet
herald's trumpet
straight trumpet
*Aida trumpet
ceremonial trumpet
salpinx (Gr.)
tuba (Lat.)
lituus (Lat.)
buccina (Lat.)
buisine (Fr.)
trompette thébaine (Fr.)
chamade (Fr. org.)
Fanfarentrompete (G.)
Heroldstrompete (G.)
Alp(en)horn (G.)

steam organ/piano
calliope
organo a vapore (It.)
orgue à vapeur (Fr.)

Dampforgel (G.)
órgano de vapor (Sp.)

stecca (It.)
bad note
wrong note
false note
canard (Fr.)
fausse note (Fr.)
Misston (G.)
galipavo (Sp.)

steel band
oil drums played
percussion orchestra
calypso band

steel brushes
brushes
wire brushes
spazzole (It.)
balais de jazz (Fr.)
Rute (G.)
Besen, Jazzbesen (G.)
escobillas (Sp.)

steel drum (tuned)
tamburo di latta (It.)
tamburo d'acciaio (It.)
tambour d'acier (Fr.)
Calypsotrommel (G.)
Stahltrommel (G.)
Benzinfass (G.)
tambor metálico (Sp.)
steel drum band
gamelan orchestra
percussion ensemble

steel guitar
Hawaiian guitar
dobro
chitarra Hawayana (It.)
guitare Hawaïenne (Fr.)
Hawaii-Gitarre (G.)
guitarra Hawaiana (Sp.)

vs. Spanish guitar

steel string(s)
metal strings
corda d'acciaio (It.)
corde d'acier (Fr.)
corde métallique (Fr.)
Stahlsaite (G.)
cuerda metálica (Sp.)
cuerda de alambre (Sp.)

vs. gut/nylon strings

Steg (G.)
bridge (of a violin)
ponticello (It.)
scagnello, scannello (It.)
cavalletto (It.)
chevalet (Fr.)
puente (Sp.)

stellvertretender Akkord (G.)
substitute chord
jazz chord
accordo sostituito (It.)
accord substitué (Fr.)
Substitutklang (G.)
acorde sustituido (Sp.)

stem (of a note)
vertical line
tail
filum (Lat.)
gambo (It.)
queue (Fr.)
hampe (Fr.)
Hals, Notenhals (G.)
plica (Sp.)

step (interval)
tone (half, whole)
degree of the scale
second (major, minor)
grado (It., Sp.)
degré (Fr.)
Schritt (G.)

Stufe, Tonstufe (G.)

vs. skip

sterbend (G.)
dying away
fading out
decay
*decrescendo (It.)
morendo (It.)
en perdant le son (Fr.)
expirando (Sp.)

stereo(phonic)
bi-naural
dual channel
hi-fi, high fidelity
antiphonal
quadraphonic

vs. mono(phonic)

sticcato, sticcado (It.)
xylophone
straw fiddle
gigelira (It.)
organo di legno (It.)
*claquebois (Fr.)
harmonica de bois (Fr.)
orgue de paille (Fr.)
Strohfiedel (G.)
armonica de madera (Sp.)

Stichnoten (G.)
cue notes
little notes
lead-in
notine (It.)
petites notes (Fr.)
guías (Sp.)

stick (conducting)
baton
bacchetta (It.)
baguette (Fr.)
Taktstock (G.)

batuta (Sp.)

2. *drumstick
bacchetta da tamburo (It.)
battente (It.)
baguette de tambour (Fr.)
Schlegel (G.)
Trommelschlegel (G.)
baqueta (Sp.)
palillo de tambor (Sp.)

stile antico (It.)
ars antiqua (Lat.)
ars vetus (Lat.)
renaissance style
older style
outdated
*Palestrina style
16c. polyphony
stile osservato (It.)
a cappella (It.)
alla Palestrina (It.)
style de chapelle (Fr.)
Palestrina-Slit (G.)

vs. stile moderno

stile concertato (It.)
concerto (grosso) style
baroque style

stile concitato (It.)
expressive style
Monteverdi style
baroque style

stile moderno (It.)
modern style
17c. baroque style
concerto style

stile rappresentativo (It.)
dramatic style
early baroque style
operatic style
recitative style

stille Messe (G.)
said Mass
low Mass
missa lecta (Lat.)
messa letta (It.)
messa bassa (It.)
messe basse (Fr.)
messe petite (Fr.)
misa rezada (Sp.)
misa leida (Sp.)

vs. grosse Messe (G.)
high Mass

Stimmbänder (G.)
vocal cords
vocal folds
vocal organs
voice-box
pipes
corde vocali (It.)
cordes vocales (Fr.)
cuerdas vocales (Sp.)

Stimmbogen (G.)
crook (brass instr.)
shank
extension
tuning slide
ritorto (It.)
corpo di ricambio (It.)
corps de rechange (Fr.)
Tonbogen (G.)
Aufsatzbogen (G.)
tonillo (Sp.)
cuerpo de recambio (Sp.)

Stimmbruch (G.)
change of voice
breaking of a voice
voice-change
cambiata
mutazione (It.)
mue (Fr.)
Stimmwechsel (G.)
cambio de voz (Sp.)

mudanza de la voz (Sp.)

Stimme (G.)
  voice
  part
  line of music
  voce (It.)
  parte (It., Sp.)
  voix (Fr.)
  partie (Fr.)
  Part (G.)
  voz (Sp.)

2. sound post
  anima (It.)
  âme (Fr.)
  Stimmstock (G.)
  alma (Sp.)

Stimmführung (G.)
  *voice-leading
  part-leading
  condotta delle voci (It.)
  conduite des voix (Fr.)
  dirigiendo la voz (Sp.)
  conducción (Sp.)

Stimmgabel (G.)
  tuning fork
  diapason (E., Fr., It.)
  corista (It., Sp.)
  forchetta d'accordo (It.)
  fourchette tonique (Fr.)
  Gabelton (G.)
  diapasón (Sp.)
  afinador (Sp.)

Stimmtausch (G.)
  voice exchange
  scambio di parti (It.)
  êchange des parties (Fr.)
  intercambio de voces (Sp.)

Stimmung (G.)
  tuning
  accordatura (It.)

accord (Fr.)
afinación (Sp.)

Stimmwerk (G.)
  consort (of instruments)
  chest
  set of similar instruments
  choir of instruments
  Akkord (G.)

stinguendo (It.)
  morendo (It.)
  fading away
  *decrescendo (It.)

Stockfagott (G.)
  racket
  sausage bassoon

stolen time
  borrowed time
  flexible tempo
  rubato (It.)

vs. strict time

Stollen (G.)
  pedes (Lat.)
  lai (Fr.)
  song section
  bar form

vs. Abgesang (G.)

stomp
  swing
  jive
  *jazz
  ragtime

stonare (It.)
  sing/play out of tune
  détonner (Fr.)
  detonieren (G.)
  desenttonar (Sp.)

stonato (It.)
  out of tune
  off-pitch
  off-key
  flt/, sharp
  dissonant
  scordato (It.)
  falso (It., Sp.)
  désaccordé (Fr.)
  faux, fausse (Fr.)
  unrein (G.)
  falsch (G.)
  verstimmt (G.)
  unrichtig (G.)

stop (n. organ)
  register
  voice
  rank
  sound
  registro (It.)
  registre (Fr.)
  jeu d'orgue (Fr.)
  Register (G.)

stop (vb. strings)
  change pitch
  hold down a string

stop tabs (org.)
  draw-knobs
  bottoni dei registri (It.)
  pomelli dei registri (It.)
  boutons de registres (Fr.)
  pommettes (Fr.)
  Registerknöpfe (G.)
  registros (Sp.)
  botones (Sp.)
  botones (Sp.)

Stopftöne (G.)
  stopped notes (horn)
  suoni chiusi (It.)
  sons bouchés (Fr.)
  sons étouffés (Fr.)
  sonidos tapados (Sp.)

vs. Naturtöne (G.)

storia della musica (It.)
music history
history of music
musicology
l'histoire de la musique (Fr.)
Geschichte der Musik (G.)
Musikgeschichte (G.)
historia de la música (Sp.)

storm and stress
Sturm und Drang (G.)

storto (It.)
*crumhorn
oboe
lituus (Lat.)
cromoro (It., Sp.)
cromorne (Fr.)
Krummhorn (G.)
orlo (Sp.)

straight trumpet
state trumpet
herald's trumpet
long trumpet
tuba (Lat.)
buccina (Lat.)
trompette thébaine (Fr.)
chamade (Fr.)
*Aida trumpet
Alphorn (G.)

strain
melody
*song
air
tune
ditty

strambotto (It.)
frottola (It.)
part-song
*madrigal
glee

canzona (It.)

straw fiddle
xylophone
marimba
xilofono (It.)
organo di legno (It.)
harmonica de bois (Fr.)
orgue de paille (Fr.)
*claquebois (Fr.)
Strohfiedel (G.)
armonica de madera (Sp.)

street cries
hollers, field-hollers
cries of London
grida dei venditori ambulanti (It.)
musique de la rue (Fr.)
cris de la rue (Fr.)
cris de Paris (Fr.)

street organ/piano
hurdy-gurdy
*barrel organ
organetto (It.)
orgue de Barbarie (Fr.)
Drehorgel (G.)
Leierkasten (G.)
organillo (Sp.)

Streichinstrumente (G.)
stringed instruments (bowed)
the strings
strumenti ad arco (It.)
strumenti a corde (It.)
instruments à cordes (Fr.)
cordes (Fr.)
Saiteninstrumte (G.)
instrumentos de cuerda (Sp.)
cuerdas (Sp.)

Streichorchester (G.)
string orchestra/ensemble
orchestra d'archi (It.)

orchestre à cordes (Fr.)
orquesta de cuerdas (Sp.)

Streichquartett (G.)
string quartet
quartetto d'archi (It.)
quatuor à cordes (Fr.)
cuarteto de cuerdas (Sp.)

stress
*accent
fortepiano (It.)
forzato, forzando (It.)
rinforzato (It.)
szorzato, sforzando (It.)
Betonung (G.)

stretto (It.)
faster
stringendo, stringere (It.)
accelerando (It.)
stretta (It.)
strette (Fr.)
en serrant (Fr.)
Engführung (G.)
estrecho (Sp.)

2. overlapping imitation of a fugal subject

strict time
in strict time
non rubato (It.)
a tempo (It.)
a tempo giusto (It.)
en mesure (Fr.)
mesuré (Fr.)
im Takt (G.)
im Zeitmass (G.)
a compás (Sp.)
tiempo justo (Sp.)

vs. rubato (It.)

stride piano
jazzy style

stomping
boogie-woogie
ragtime

strike up
begin/start to play
intone
attacca (It.)
segue(It.)
intonare (It.)
entonner (Fr.)
anstimmen (G.)
entonar (Sp.)

string
corda (It.)
corde (Fr.)
Saite (G.)
cuerda (Sp.)

string band
folk ensemble
bluegrass band
country band
fiddle band

string bass
double bass
*bass
bass fiddle
bull fiddle
contrabass
upright bass
stand-up bass
contrabasso (It.)
contrebasse (Fr.)
Kontrabass (G.)
contrabajo (Sp.)

stromento (It.)
*strumento (It.)
istrumento (It.)
instrument

strong beat
first beat of a measure

downbeat
accent
stress
thesis (Gr.)
crusis (Lat.)
abbatimento (It.)
frappé (Fr.)
Abschlag (G.)

vs. weak beat
last beat of a measure

strophe (E., Fr.)
stanza
couplet
verse
strofa (It.)
Strophe (G.)
estrofa (Sp.)
copla (Sp.)

strophic
having several stanzas
same music, different verses
strofico (It.)
strophique (Fr.)
strophisch (G.)
estrófico (Sp.)

strophic bass
ostinato bass
ground bass
strophic variations
basso ostinato (It.)
ciac(c)ona (It.)
chaconne (Fr.)
passacaglia (It.)

strum, strumming
pluck
pick
twang
thrum
arpeggio
pizzicato (It.)
strimpellare (It.)

tapoter (Fr.)
gratter (Fr.)
racler (Fr.)
klimpern (G.)
cencerrear (Sp.)
rasguear (Sp.)
rasgado, rasgueado (Sp.)

vs. bowing

strumento (It.)
instrument (E., Fr.)
Instrument (G.)
instrumento (Sp.)

strumento a corda (It.)
stringed instrument
instrument à cordes (Fr.)
instrument à l'archet (Fr.)
Saiteninstrument (G.)
Streichinstrumente (G.)
instrumento de cuerda (Sp.)

strumento a fiato (It.)
wind instrument
horn (jazz)
strumento a vento (It.)
instrument à vent (Fr.)
instrument à bouche (Fr.)
Blasinstrument (G.)
Windinstrument (G.)
instrumento de viento (Sp.)
instrument de boca/boquilla
(Sp.)

**strumento (a fiato) di legno
(It.)**
woodwind instrument
instrument à vent en bois
(Fr.)
instrument à bouche (Fr.)
instrument de bois (Fr.)
Holzblasinstrument (G.)
instrumento de madera (Sp.)

strumento a/di percussione (It.)
   percussion instrument
   strumento da percussa (It.)
   instrument à batterie (Fr.)
   instrument à percution/ percussion (Fr.)
   Schlaginstrument (G.)
   instrumento de percussión (Sp.)

strumento a tastiera (It.)
   keyboard instrument
   instrument à clavier (Fr.)
   Klavierinstrument (G.)
   instrumento de teclado (Sp.)

strumento ad ancia (It.)
   reed instrument
   horn (jazz)
   strumento a becco (It.)
   instrument à anche (Fr.)
   Rohrblattinstrument (G.)
   Zungeninstrument (G.)
   Schnabelinstrument (G.)
   iinstrumento de caña (Sp.)
   instrumento de lengüeta (Sp.)

strumento ad arco (It.)
   stringed instrument
   instrument à cordes (Fr.)
   Saiteninstrument (G.)
   instrumento de cuerda (Sp.)

strumento da pizzico (It.)
   plucked (stringed) instrument
   instrument à cordes pincées (Fr.)
   Zupfinstrument (G.)
   instrument punteado (Sp.)

strumento d'acciaio (It.)
   bell lyre
   celesta
   orchestra bells
   *glockenspiel (G.)

Stahlspiel (G.)
Lyra (G.)

strumento d'ottone (It.)
   brass instrument
   horn
   instrument de cuivre (Fr.)
   Blechinstrument (G.)
   instrumento de metal (Sp.)

strumento traspositore (It.)
   transposing instrument
   instrument transpositeur (Fr.)
   transponierende Instrument (G.)
   instrumento de transposición (Sp.)

vs. C-instrument

Stück (G.)
   piece
   *composition
   selection
   work
   opus (Lat.)
   pezzo (It.)
   brano (It.)
   morceau (Fr.)
   pièce (Fr.)
   Werk (G.)
   pieza (Sp.)
   obra (Sp.)
   trozo (Sp.)

studio (It.)
   *étude (E., Fr.)
   lesson
   practice piece
   study
   exercise
   drill
   Übung (G.)
   Aufgabe (G.)
   estudio (Sp.)

studio (E.)
   practice room
   recording room

   2. teaching business

studio upright (piano)
   console piano
   spinet
   cottage piano
   cabinet piano
   vertical piano
   *piano

vs. grand piano

study
   *étude (E., Fr.)
   exercise
   lesson
   practice piece
   invention
   drill
   studio (It.)
   exercice (Fr.)
   Übung (G.)
   Aufgabe (G.)
   estudio (Sp.)

study score
   miniature score
   pocket score
   partitura tascabile (It.)
   partiturina (It.)
   partition du poche (Fr.)
   Taschenpartitur (G.)
   Studienpartitur (G.)
   partitura de bolsillo (Sp.)
   partitura miniatura (Sp.)

vs. full score

Stufe (G.)
   *degree of a scale
   step
   tone (whole, half)

grado (It., Sp.)
degrê (Fr.)
Grad (g.)
Schritt (G.)

vs. Sprung (G.)

Stufenweise (G.)
stepwise
step by step
conjunct motion
di grado (It.)
par degrés (Fr.)
Schrittweise (G.)
por grados (Sp.)

vs. Sprungweise (G.)

stummes Klavier (G.)
practice piano/keyboard
digitorium (Lat.)
dumb piano
dumb organ
dumb spinet
Übungsklavier (G.)

Stundenoffizium (G.)
*Divine Office
Office
monastic office
hours of the day
canonical hours
Opus Dei (Lat.)
offizio divino (It.)
office des heures (Fr.)
oficios (Sp.)

Sturm und Drang (G.)
storm and stress
melodramatic music
turbulence
imbroglio (It.)

Stürze (G.)
*bell of a horn
flair

campana (Lat., It., Sp.)
padiglione (It.)
pavillon (Fr.)
Schalltrichter (G.)
pabellón (Sp.)

Stürze hoch (G.)
*bell in the air
bell up
raise the bell
campana in alto (It.)
padiglione in alto (It.)
pavillon en l'air (Fr.)
Schalltrichter hoch (G.)
pabellón al aire (Sp.)

vs. natürlich (G.)

Stutzflügel (G.)
*baby grand (piano)
semi-grand
parlor grand
boudoir grand
pianoforte a mezza coda (It.)
piano à queue mignon (Fr.)
piano de media cola (Sp.)

style de chapelle (Fr.)
unaccompanied
*a cappella (It.)
stile antico (It.)
stile osservato (It.)
sans instruments (Fr.)
im Kapellstil (G.)
a capilla (Sp.)

vs. avec instruments (Fr.)

style galant (Fr.)
galant style
roroco style
stile galante (It.)
galanter Stil (G.)
estilo galante (Sp.)

sub-bass (organ)

subbasso (It.)
soubasse, sous-basse (Fr.)
Subbass (G.)
Untersatz (G.)
sub-bajo (Sp.)

subdominant
fourth degree of the scale
fa
sottodominante (It.)
sous-dominante (Fr.)
Subdominante (G.)
Unterdominante (G.)
subdominante (Sp.)

subito (It., Sp.)
suddenly
quickly
immediately
subitement (Fr.)
aussitôt (Fr.)
plötzlich (G.)
sofort (G.)
sogleich (G.)
inmediato (Sp.)
súbito (Sp.)

vs. poco a poco (It., Sp.)

subject
theme
question
answer
melody
fragment
motive
soggetto (It.)
andamento (It.)
tema (It., Sp.)
sujet (Fr.)
thème (Fr.)
demande (Fr.)
Thema (G.)
Subjekt (G.)
Führer (G.)
dux (Lat.)

sujeto (Sp.)

submediant
  sixth degree of the scale
  la
  superdominant
  sopraddominante (It.)
  sus-dominante (Fr.)
  sous-médiante (Fr.)
  Untermediante (G.)
  superdominante (Sp.)

subordinate theme
  second/secondary theme
  subsidiary theme
  secondo tema (It.)
  tema secondario (It.)
  thème secondaire (Fr.)
  Nebenthema (G.)
  Seitenthema (G.)
  segundo tema (Sp.)
  tema secundario (Sp.)

vs. primary theme

substitute chord
  jazz chord
  substitution chord
  accordo sostituito (It.)
  accord substitué (Fr.)
  Substitutklang (G.)
  stellvertretender Akkord (G.)
  acorde sustituido (Sp.)

substitute clausula (organum)
  discant section
  organum
  clausola sostituta (It.)
  clausule alternative (Fr.)
  Ersatzklausel (G.)
  clausula sustitutiva (Sp.)

subtonic
  seventh degree
  leading tone
  essential seventh

ti, si
subsemitonium (Lat.)
  sensibile (It., Fr.)
  nota sensibile (It.)
  note sensible (Fr.)
  Leitton (G.)
  sensible nota (Sp.)

succentor (Lat.)
  subcantor
  deputy precentor
  cantor

succession de quintes (Fr.)
  *parallel fifths
  hidden fifths
  consecutive fifths
  quinte parallele (It.)
  verdekte Quinten (G.)
  quintas paraleles (Sp.)

suffrages
  prayers
  collect
  litany
  orations
  preces (Lat.)
  oremus (Lat.)
  oración (Sp.)

suggeritore (It.)
  prompter
  teleprompter
  cue cards
  prompt box
  souffleur, -euse (Fr.)
  Souffleuse (G.)
  apuntador (Sp.)

suite
  serenade
  cassation
  partita
  *medley
  set, sett
  divertimento (It.)

diverissement (Fr.)
ordre (Fr.)
Kammersuite (G.)
Parthie, Partie (G.)

sul ponticello (It.)
  near (on) the bridge
  au chevelet (Fr.)
  près du chevelet (Fr.)
  am Steg (G.)
  sobre el puente (Sp.)

sul tasto (It., Sp.)
  on the fingerboard
  sulla tastiera (It.)
  flautando, flautato (It.)
  sur la touche (Fr.)
  am Griffbrett (G.)
  sobre el batidor (Sp.)

summation tone
  resultant tone
  *combination tone
  difference tone
  differential tone
  Tartini's tone
  tono combinato (It.)
  suono addizionale (It.)
  suono di combinazione (It.
  son combiné (Fr.)
  Summationston (G.)
  Kombinationston (G.)
  sonido adicional (Sp.)

Summstimme (G.)
  *hum, humming
  a bocca chiusa (It.)
  furberia del canto (It.)
  avec bouche fermée (Fr.)
  Brummstimme (G.)
  canturear (Sp.)

sung mass
  high Mass
  solemn Mass
  missa cantata (Lat.)

messa cantata (It.)
messa solenne (It.)
messe haute (Fr.)
messe chantée (Fr.)
Choramt (G.)
misa cantada (Sp.)

vs. low mass
said Mass

suoni armonici (It.)
*harmonics
overtones
partials
flageolet tones

suono chiuso (It.)
stopped notes (on a horn)
muted notes
sons bouchés (Fr.)
sons étouffés (Fr.)
Stopftöne (G.)
sonidos tapados (Sp.)

vs. tono aperto/naturale (It.)

super (theater)
extra
supernumerary
walk-on part
bit part
comparsa (It., Sp.)
comprimario, -a (It.)
figurante (It., Sp.)
figurant(e) (Fr.)
Komparse, -in (G.)
Statist, -in (G.)

superdominant
sixth degree
la
submediant
sopraddominante (It.)
sus-dominante (Fr.)
sous-médiante (Fr.)
Untermediante (G.)

superdominante (Sp.)

superius (Lat.)
highest part
soprano
cantus (Lat.)
treble part/voice
lead voice
melody part

supertonic
second degree
re
sopratonica (It.)
sus-tonique (Fr.)
Wechseldominante (G.)
supertónico (Sp.)

supper club
*night club
night spot
cocktail lounge
cabaret
locale notturno (It.)
ritrovo notturno (It.)
boîte de nuit (Fr.)
Nachtlokal (G.)
Nachtklub (G.)
café-cantante (Sp.)

supporting role (theater)
minor role
secondary role
ruolo secondario (It.)
rôle secondaire (Fr.)
Nebenrolle (G.)
papel secundario (Sp.)

vs. principal role
major role

suspended cadence
*deceptive cadence
semi-cadence
interrupted cadence
half-cadence

avoided cadence
cadenza evitata (It.)
cadence évitée (Fr.)
Trugschluss (G.)
Halbschluss (G.)
cadencia evitada (Sp.)

suspension
delayed cadential note
syncopation
appoggiatura (It.)
sospensione (It.)
retard (Fr.)
Vorhalt (G.)
Verzögerung (G.)
retardo (Sp.)

suspirium (Lat.)
minim rest
half rest
pausa di minima (It.)
demi-pause (Fr.)
halbe Pause (G.)
silencio de blanca (Sp.)

süss (G.)
soft
sweet
dolce (It.)
doux (Fr.)
sanft (G.)
lieblich (G.)
dulce (Sp.)

sustained
held
long
sostenuto (It.)
soutenu (Fr.)
gestützt (G.)
gehalten (G.)
getragen (G.)
aushalten (G.)
sostenido (Sp.)

sustain(ing) pedal (piano)

loud pedal
*damper pedal
sostenuto pedal
right pedal
pedale destra (It.)
pedale di risonanza (It.)
pédale droite (Fr.)
pédale grande (Fr.)
rechte Pedal (G.)
Sustain-Pedal (G.)
Haltepedal (G.)
Tonhaltepedal (G.)
pedal fuerte (Sp.)

vs. soft pedal

sveglia (It.)
*reveille
wake-up call
bugle call (A.M.)
diana (It.. Sp.)
diane (Fr.)
réveil (Fr.)
Wecken (G.)
alborada (Sp.)

sviluppo (It.)
development (sonata form)
fragmentation of theme(s)
svolgimento (It.)
développement (Fr.)
Durchführung (G.)
Themenverbearbeitung (G.)
desarrollo (Sp.)
elaboración (Sp.)

Swanee whistle
song whistle/flute
piston flute
toy flute
bazooka
flauto a tiro (It.)
flauto da jazz (It.)
zufolo a pistone (It.)
flûte lotine (Fr.)
flûte à coulisse (Fr.)

Lotosflöte (G.)
Stempelflöte (G.)
flauta de pistón (Sp.)
flauta de émbolo (Sp.)

sweet potato
ocarina
oval whistle-flute
duct flute
recorder
fipple flute
toy flute
Okarina (G.)
flutophone
song flute
tonette

swell
under expression (org.)
swell organ/division
swell manual/keyboard
recitativo (It.)
organo espressivo (It.)
organo d'espressione (It.)
clavier de récit (Fr.)
récit (Fr.)
Oberwerk (G.)
Schwellwerk, Schweller (G.)
expresivo (Sp.)

2. crescendo and decrescendo
*messa di voce (It.)
mise de la voix (Fr.)
pose de la voix (Fr.)
Schwellton (G.)
poner le voz (Sp.)

swell box
expression box
cassa espressiva (It.)
boîte expressive (Fr.)
Schwellkasten (G.)
caja expresiva (Sp.)

swell pedal
swell shoe

crescendo pedal
staffa crescendo (It.)
pédale de la boîte expressive
(Fr.)
Schwelltritt (G.)
pedal de crescendo (Sp.)

swing
*jazz
jive
bounce
stomp
hot
barrelhouse
blues
popular music

swing band
big band
jazz band
dance band
stage band
combo
40's band

Swiss music box
*music box
scatola musicale (It.)
boîte à musique (Fr.)
Spieldose (g.)
caja de música (Sp.)

syllabic chant
simple chant
neumatic style
chant syllabique (Fr.)
sillabischer Gesang (G.)

vs. melismatic chant

symbolum (Lat.)
credo (Lat. Ambrosian)
creed
confession of faith
**symbolum apostolicum
(Lat. Mozarabic)**

sympathetic strings
aliquot strings
viola d'amore (It.)
trumpet marine
hurdy-gurdy
baryton
bourdon (Fr.)
viole d'amour (Fr.)
corda simpatica (It.)
coeda di risonanza (It.)
corde sympathique (Fr.)
corde harmonique (Fr.)
corde de résonance (Fr.)
Resonanzsaite (G.)
Aliquot-Saite (G.)
cuerda simpatica (Sp.)
cuerda de resonancia
(Sp.)

symphonette, -a
chamber orchestra
string orchestra
sinfonietta (It.)
orchestra da camera (It.)
orchestre de chambre (Fr.)
Kammerorchester (G.)
orquestra de camara (Sp.)

symphonia (Gr.)
unison

2. consonance

3. hurdy-gurdy
bagpipe
clavichord

4. symphony
sinfonia (It.)

5. polyphony
organum

symphonic
philharmonic
classical

concert
full
sinfonia (It.)
symphonique (Fr.)
symphonisch (G.)
sinfónico (Sp.)

symphonic band
concert band
brass band
military band
*band

symphonic poem
tone poem
*program music
program symphony
tone painting
descriptive music
poema sinfonico (It.)
poème symphonique (Fr.)
symphonische Dichtung (G.)
poema sinfónico (Sp.)

vs. absolute music

symphonia concertante (It.)
double concerto
triple concerto
concerto for orchestra
concerto grosso (It.)
concerto-sinfonia (It.)
sinfonie concertante (Fr.)
Konzertanten Sinfonien (G.)
Konzertsinfonie (G.)
sinfonía concertante (Sp.)

symphony
sonata for orchestra
orchestral piece in several
movements
sinfonia (It.)
symphonie (Fr.)
Symphonie (G.)
sinfonía (Sp.)

symphony form
sonata form
sonata-allegro form
first movement form

symphony hall
*concert hall
symphonic hall
philharmonic hall
orchestra hall
*academy of music
auditorium

symphony orchestra
classical orchestra
philharmonic orchestra
orchestra sinfonica (It.)
orchestre syphonique (Fr.)
Symphonieorchester (G.)
orquesta sinfónica (Sp.)

synagoga (Lat.)
crowd in a Passion play,
oratorio
turba (Lat.)
the multitude

syncopated, syncopation
off-beat
driving note
hemiola
jazzy
*contrattempo (It.)
alla zuppa (It.)
sincope (It.)
contre-temps (Fr.)
syncope (Fr.)
Gegenzeit (G.)
Synkope (G.)
contratiempo (Sp.)
síncopa (Sp.)
sincopación (Sp.)

synthesizer
electronic keyboard
digital music

sintetizzatore (It.)
synthétiseur (Fr.)
Sybthesizer (G.)
sintetizador (Sp.)

syntonic comma
  *comma
  ditonic comma
  comma sintonico (It.)
  comma syntonique (Fr.)
  syntonisches Komma (G.)
  coma sintónica (Sp.)

syrinx
  panpipes
  pipes of Pan
  Pandean pipes
  mouth organ
  siringa (It., Sp.)
  flauto di Pan (It.)
  flûte de Pan (Fr.)
  Panflöte (G.)
  flauta de Pan (Sp.)

2. larynx (esp. of birds)

3. calamus (Lat.)
  tibia (Lat.)
  *shawm

system
  score
  line of music
  staves, grand staff
  systema (Lat.)
  Liniensystem (G.)

systema (Gr., Lat.)
  filling-in of large intervals
with smaller ones

2. the staff
  great staff
  rigo musicale (It.)
  sistemi (It.)
  portée (Fr.)

System (G.)
Notensystem (G.)
pauta (Sp.)
pentagrama (Sp.)

3. tones of a hexachord

syzygia, sysygia (Lat.)
  syzygy
  chord
  triad
  sizigia (It.)
  syzygie (Fr.)
  sicigia (Sp.)

T

taballo (It.)
kettledrum
timpani
timbale (Fr.)
atabale (Fr.)
Kesselpauke (G.)
Pauke (G.)
timbal (Sp.)
atabal (Sp.)

tabatière de musique (Fr.)
music box
Swiss music box
scatola musicale (It.)
scatola armonica (It.)
boîte à musique (Fr.)
carillon à musique (Fr.)
Spieldose (G.)
caja de música (Sp.)

tablature (E., Fr.)
notation for plucked stringed
instruments and organ
letter notation
finger notation
intavolatura (It.)
Tabulatur (G.)
Griffnotation (G.)
Intabulierung (G.)
tablatura (Sp.)
cifra (Sp.)

table (E., Fr.)
belly (of a stringed instr.)
soundboard
tavola armonica (It.)
table d'harmonie (Fr.)
Resonanztafel (G.)
Resonanzboden (G.)

Decke (G.)
tapa (Sp.)
tabla de armonia (Sp.)

**tabor, tabour, taborel, tabourin,
tabret, taboret (E., Fr.)**
small drum
timbrel
hand drum
tamburin, tamburello (It.)
tamborin de Provence (Fr.)
Tabor (G.)
tamboril, tamborino, tamborín
(Sp.)
pipe and tabor

tacco (It.)
frog (of a bow)
heel
tallone (It.)
talon (Fr.)
hausse (Fr.)
Frosch (G.)
talón (Sp.)

vs. punta (It., Sp.)

tace, tacet (It., Lat.)
do not play
silent for a movement or so
rest (long)
ne pas jouer (Fr.)
tais-toi (Fr.)
Schweigt (G.)
cállate (Sp.)

tactée (Fr.)
curtailed note
broken note
interrupted melody
truncatio (Lat.)
occitatio (Lat.)
*hocket

tacto (Sp.)
touch (n.)

tocco (It.)
toucher (Fr.)
Anschlag (G.)

tactus (Lat.)
a *beat
time
metrical accent
pulse
tempus (Lat.)
battuta (It.)
temps (Fr.)
Schlag, **Taktschlag (G.)**
Takt (G.)
Taktteil (G.)
tiempo (Sp.)

Tafelmusik (G.)
table music
banquet music
dinner music
café music
cocktail music
*backround music
musica da tavola (It.)
musique de table (Fr.)
música de mesa (Sp.)

2. part-book for singing part-
music around a table

tag
*coda
cauda (Lat.)
codetta (It.)
envoi (Fr.)
Anhang (G.)
cola (Sp.)

Tagelied (G.)
morning song
serenade
matin song
Minnesinger
mattinata (It.)
aubade (Fr.)

*alba (Prov.)
Wächterlied (G.)

Tagesoffizium (G.)
daily office
day hours
*Divine Office
monastic office
canonical hours
officium divinum (Lat.)
ufficio divino (It.)
office divin (Fr.)
oficios (Sp.)

tagliato (It.)
*alla breve sign
cut time
C-barred
C-barré (Fr.)

taglio (It.)
a *cut
deletion
coupure (Fr.)
Schnitt, Einschnitt (G.)
corte (Sp.)
vide, vi---de (Lat.)

2. cut-off sign (conducting)
coupé (Fr.)
Abschlag (G.)

tail
flag (on a note)
hook
codetta (It.)
crochet (Fr.)
Fahn(e), Fähnchen (G.)
Notenfahne (G.)
rabillo (Sp.)
gancho (Sp.)

2. stem (of a note)
filum (Lat.)
gambo (It.)
hampe (Fr.)

queue (Fr.)
Hals, Notenhals (G.)
plica (Sp.)

taille (Fr.)
viola (part)
*alto (It., Fr.)
taille de violon (Fr.)
Altgeige (G.)
Bratsche (G.)

2. middle voice
tenor
alto-tenor
countertenor
haute-taille (Fr.)
*haute-contre (Fr.)
voz intermedia (Sp.)

3. tenor oboe
*oboe da caccia (It.)
taille de basson (Fr.)

tailpin
endpin
spike
peg
puntale (It.)
spina (It.)
pique, piquet (Fr.)
Knopf (G.)
Stachel (G.)
puntal (Sp.)

take-off
parody
satire
spoof
caricature
copy

Takt (G.)
*beat
pulse
count
metrical accent

time
*tactus (Lat.)

2. measure
bar
meter
misura (It.)
battuta (It.)
Taktart (G.)
barra (Sp.)
medida (Sp.
compás (Sp.)

Taktmesser (G.)
metronome
mechanical/electronic beats
chronometer
metronomo (It., Sp.)
métronome (Fr.)
Metronom (G.)

Taktnote (G.)
whole note
intero (It.)
semibreve (It., E.)
ronde (Fr.)
Ganze, ganze Note (G.)
redonda (Sp.)

Taktpause (G.)
whole-measure rest
whole-note rest
semibreve rest
pause di semibreve (It.)
pause (Fr.)
ganze Pause (G.)
silencio de redonda (Sp.)
pausa de redonda (Sp.)

Taktstock (G.)
baton (for conducting)
stick
bacchetta di direttore (It.)
baguette (Fr.)
bâton de mesure (Fr.)
Taktstab (G.)

baqueta (Sp.)
batuta (Sp.)
Schlegel (G.)

Taktstrich (G.)
bar line
measure line
barra (It., Sp.)
sbarra (It.)
stranghetta (It.)
barre (Fr.)
Mensurstrich (G.)
linea divisoria (Sp.)
barra de compás (Sp.)

Taktvorzeichnung (G.)
time-signature
meter signature
prolation sign
segno del tempo (It.)
indicazione del tempo (It.)
indicazione della misura (It.)
chiffre de mesure (Fr.)
indication de la mesure (Fr.)
Taktart (G.)
llave de tiempo (Sp.)

talea (Lat.)
isorhythm (14-15c.)
tenor part
repetition
polyphony
color (Lat.)

talking machine
phonograph
gramophone
victrola
record player
turntable
giradischi (It.)
grammofono (It.)
tourne-disques (Fr.)
Plattenspieler (G.)
Grammophon (G.)
Sprechmaschine (G.)

tocadiscos (Sp.)
gramófono (Sp.)
fonógrafo (Sp.)

tallone (It.)
heel of a bow
nut
frog
talon (Fr.)
hausse (Fr.)
Frosch (G.)
talón (Sp.)

vs. punta (It.)

2. heel (in org. playing)

tam-tam
gong, kettle gong
tambour de bronze (Fr.)
Kesselgong (G.)
batintin (Sp.)
tantán (Sp.)
Chinese gong

tambour (Fr.)
drum
tabor
tympanum (Lat.)
cassa (It.)
caisse (Fr.)
tambourin (Fr.)
Trommel (G.)
tambor, tambora (Sp.)
tamboril (Sp.)

tambour militaire (Fr.)
*snare drum
*side drum
military drum
cassa militare
tambourin de Suisse (Fr.)
Militärtrommel (G.)
tambor militar (Sp.)
caja militar (Sp.)

tambourine
hand drum with jingles
timbrel
tamburino, tamburello (It.)
tamburo Basco (It.)
cimbalo, cimbalino, cimbaletto
(It.)
tambour de Basque (Fr.)
Tamburin (G.)
Baskische Trommel (G.)
Schellentrommel (G.)
Handtrommel (G.)
pandera, pandero, pandereta/e
(Sp.)

tamburo (It.)
drum
*kettledrum
timpano/i
tambura (Lat.)

tamburo d'aciaio (It.)
steel drum
tamburo di latta (It.)
tambour d'acier (Fr.)
Calypsotrommel (G.)
Stahltrommel (G.)
Benzinfass (G.)
tambor metálico (Sp.)

tamburo grande/grosso (It.)
bass drum
cassa grande/grosso (It.)
gran cassa (It.)
gran tamburo (It.)
grosse caisse (Fr.)
gros-tambour (Fr.)
grosse Trommel (G.)
bombo (Sp.)

tamburo rullante (It.)
tenor drum
cassa rullante (It.)
caisse roulante (Fr.)
Rolltrommel (G.)
Rührtrommel (G.)

redoblante (Sp.)

tampon (Fr.)
padded drumstick
double-headed drumstick
mallet
mazza (It.)
battente doppio (It.)
mazzuolo a doppia testa (It.)
mailloche à double tête (Fr.)
mailloche double (Fr.)
Doppelschlegel (G.)
zweikopfiger Schlegel (G.)
baqueta de dos cabezas (Sp.)
maza, -o (Sp.)

tañer (Sp. n.)
toccata
prelude
tastar (It.)

(Sp. vb.)
2. to play an instr
perform.
sonare, suonare (It.)
jouer (Fr.)
spielen (G.)
tocar (Sp.)

tangent
hammer of a clavichord
key
tangente (It., Fr., Sp.)
Tangente (G.)

tango (Sp.)
Spanish (Argentine) dance
latin dance
habanera

tantara
fanfare
trumpet call
tarantara
*flourish
salute

tuck, tucket
fanfara (It.)
sonnerie (Fr.)
Tusch (G.)
fanfarria (Sp.)

Tanz (G.)
*dance
ball
ballet
ballo (It.)
danza (It., Sp.)
bal (Fr.)
Ball (G.)
baile (Sp.)

tanzen (G.)
dance
cut a rug
trip the light fantastic
danzare (It.)
ballare (It.)
danser (Fr.)
danzar (Sp.)
bailar (Sp.)

tap box (percussion)
clog box
wood block
*Chinese wood-block
temple blocks
Korean temple blocks
cassettina (It.)
cassa di legno (It.)
bloc de bois (Fr.)
caisse Chinois (Fr.)
Holzblocktrommel (G.)
caja China (Sp.)

tapa (Sp.)
*table
belly
soundboard

tapado (Sp.)
stopped (horn)

muted
muffled
tappato (It.)
chiuso (It.)
bouché (Fr.)
gedekt (G.)
gestopft (G.)

vs. open note
no tapados (Sp.)

tape recorder
reel-to-reel recorder
magnetic tape recorder
casette recorder
tape machine
cartridge player
wire recorder
registratore a nastro magnetic
(It.)
magnétophone (Fr.)
Tonbandgerät (G.)
Magnettonbandgerät (G.)
magnetofón (Sp.)

taps
bugle call
elegy
*lament
silenzio (It.)
sonnerie aux morts (Fr.)
Zaptenstreich (G.)
toque de silencio (Sp.)

tarantella (It.)
fast dance in 6/8 or12/8
tarantelle (Fr.)
tarantela (Sp.)

tardo (It.)
slow
lento (It., Sp.)
adagio (It.)
tardamente (It.)
lent, lentement (Fr.)
langsam (G.)

vs. presto (It.)

Tartini's tone
  *combination tone
  summation tone
  resultant tone
  difference tone
  differential tone
  suono di combinazione (It.)
  son combiné (Fr.)
  Kombinationston (G.)
  sonido de combinación (Sp.)

Taschengeige (G.)
  *kit
  small violin
  pocket violin/fiddle
  rebec
  violino di pochetto (It.)
  pochette (Fr.)
  petit violon de poche (Fr.)
  Sackgeige (G.)
  Quartgeige (G.)
  violin de bolsillo (Sp.)
  violin pequeño (Sp.)

Taschenpartitur (G.)
  pocket score
  miniature score
  study score
  partitura tascabile (It.)
  partition de poche (Fr.)
  Studienpartitur)G.)
  partitura de bolsillo (Sp.)
  partitura miniatura (Sp.)

vs. Partitur, Dirigierpartitur (G.)

tastar (It.)
  *prelude
  voluntary
  overture
  introduction
  intonazione (It.)
  sinfonia (It.)
  toccata (It.)

Vorspiel (G.)
tañer (Sp.)

tastiera (It.)
  keyboard
  fingerboard
  fretboard
  manual
  manuale (It.)
tastatura (It.)
  clavier (Fr.)
  Klaviatur (G.)
teclado (Sp.)

tastiera muta (It.)
  dumb piano/organ
  practice keyboard
  dumb spinet
  digitorium (Lat.)
  pianoforte per studio (It.)
  piano d'étude (Fr.)
  stummes Klavier (G.)
  Übungsklavier (G.)
  Übungsapparat (G.)
  teclado de estudio (Sp.)
  piano de estudio (Sp.)

tastiera per luce (It.)
  color organ
  tastiera a colori (It.)
  clavecin oculaire (Fr.)
  orgue de couleur (Fr.)
  Farbenklavier (G.)
  órgano de colores (Sp.)
  clavecin ocular (Sp.)

tasto (It.)
  key (of a keyboard)
  digital
  foot-pedal key
  touche (Fr.)
  Taste (G.)
  tecla (Sp.)

2. fret
  touchette (Fr.)

Bund (G.)
traste (Sp.)

3. fingerboard
  fretboard
  touche (Fr.)
  manche (Fr.)
  Griffbrett (G.)
  batidor (Sp.)

4. touch
  feel
  weight of arm, hand, etc.
  tocco (It.)
  toucher (Fr.)
  Anschlag (G.)
  tasto (Sp.)

tasto solo (It.)
  solo bass (instr.)
  no harmony/chords
  thoroughbass
  figured bass

tavern song
  drinking song
  bacchanal
  carmina burana (Lat.)
  brindisi (It.)
  canto bacchico (It.)
  chanson à boire (Fr.)
  chanson bacchique (Fr.)
  Trinklied (G.)
  canción báquica (Sp.)
  canción de taberna (Sp.)

techno
  pop music
  electronica
  hip-hop
  rock
  rap
  reggae
  ska
  world music

tedesca/o (It.)
German dance
alman(d), almain, almayne
allemanda (It.)
allemande (Fr.)
Teutschertanz (G.)
Ländler (G.)
aleman(d)a (Sp.)

teeny-bop music
pop music
bubblegum music
rock-n-roll

Teil (G.)
part
section (E., Fr.)
parte (It., Sp.)
sezione (It.)
partie (Fr.)
sección (Sp.)

Teilton (G.)
*harmonic
overtone
partial
aliquot tone
flageolet tone
suono parziale (It.)
son harmonique (Fr.)
son partiel (Fr.)
Partialton (G.)
sonido parcial (Sp.)

tel quel (Fr.)
as written
come stà (It.)
comme c'est écrit (Fr.)
nach Vorschrift (G.)
wie es dasteht (G.)
como está (Sp.)

teleprompter
prompter
cue cards
prompt-box

prompt side
stage right
suggeritore (It.)
souffleur, -euse (Fr.)
Souffleur (G.)
apuntador (Sp.)

telón (Sp.)
curtain (stage)
drop
backdrop
traveler
scrim
sipario, siparietto (It.)
telone (It.)
rideau (Fr.)
Vorhang (G.)
Bühnenvorhang (G.)

tema (It., Sp.)
theme
*subject
idea
fragment
motive
thème (Fr.)
Thema (G.)
dux (Lat.)

temperament (E., Fr.)
tuning
tempered tuning
tuning compromise
equal temperament
temperamento (It.)
Temperatur (G.)

temple block(s)
*Chinese temple blocks
Korean temple block
wood block
clog box
tap box
cassa di legno (It.)
cassettina (It.)
blochetto (It.)

caisse Chinoise (Fr.)
bloc de bois (Fr.)
Holtzblocktrommel (G.)
caja China (Sp.)

tempo (It.)
time
speed
pace
tempus (Lat.)
temps (Fr.)
mouvement (Fr.)
Zeitmass (G.)
tiempo (Sp.)

tempo giusto (It.)
strict time/tempo
non rubato (It.)
a tempo (It.)
en mesure (Fr.)
mesuré (Fr.)
im Takt (G.)
im Zeitmass (G.)
a compásw (Sp.)
tiempo justo (Sp.)

tempo ordinario (It.)
duple meter
4/4 time
common time
common measure
*binary measure
passo ordinario (It.)
mouvement ordinaire (Fr.)
Viervierteltakt (G.)
Zweiertakt (G.)
movimiento ordinario (Sp.)

2. moderate tempo
moderato (It.)

tempo primo (It.)
back to the original tempo
a tempo (It.)
l'istesso tempo (It.)
tornando al tempo (It.)

en revenant au mouvement (Fr.)
  temps primaire (Fr.)
  im ersten Zeitmass (G.)
  zum Zeitmass zurückkehrend (G.)
  movimiento anterios (Sp.)
  volviendo al movimiento (Sp.)

tempo rubato (It.)
  rubato (It.)
  free/flexible tempo

vs. tempo giusto (It.)

tempo ternario (It.)
  triple meter
  three-quarter time
  waltz time
  in 3
  perfect time
  tempus perfectum (Lat.)
  tempus ternarium (Lat.)
  mesure ternaire (Fr.)
  Dreiertakt (G.)
  compás ternario (Sp.)
  compás de tres tiempo (Sp.)

tempus (Lat. 13-17c.)
  meter
  time
  prolatio (Lat.)
  tactus (Lat.)
  proportion
  mensuration
  tempus perfectum (Lat.)
  tempus imperfectum (Lat.)

tenebrae (Lat.)
  Matins and Lauds during Holy Week
  nocturnes

tenor (E., Sp.)
  high male voice
  tenore (It.)

ténor (Fr.)
Tenor (G.)

2. reciting note (chant)
  dominant
  psalm-tone
  tuba (Lat., It.)
  recto tono (Lat.)
  nota dominans (Lat.)
  nota di recitazione (It.)
  repercussio (It.)
  teneur (Fr.)

3. cantus firmus (Lat.)
  canto fermo (It.)
  taille (Fr.)
  melody part
  tenor Mass/motet

4. low instrument
  tenor or alto instr./part

tenor clef
  C-clef on the fourth line (trombone, bassoon, 'cello)

tenor drum
  cassa rullante (It.)
  tamburo rullante (It.)
  tambour roulant (Fr.)
  caisse sourde (Fr.)
  caisse roulante (Fr.)
  Rührtrommel (G.)
  Rolltrommel (G.)
  Wirbeltrommel (G.)
  redoblante (Sp.)

vs. bass drum

tenor hautboy
  tenor oboe
  English horn
  *tenoroon
  fagottino (It.)
  oboe da caccia (It.)
  cor Anglais (Fr.)

taille des hautbois (Fr.)
taille (Fr.)

tenor tuba
  baritone horn
  euphonium
  saxhorn

tenor violin
  *viola
  violotta (It.)
  alto (It., Fr.)
  basse de violon (Fr.)
  taille (Fr.)
  cinquième (Fr.)
  Bratsche (G.)
  Altgeige (G.)
  Altviole (G.)
  Tenorgeige (G.)

tenore buffo (It.)
  comic tenor
  *comic role
  buffo tenor
  comic opera
  trial (Fr.)

tenore robusto (It.)
  dramatic tenor
  Wagnerian tenor
  heroic tenor
  tenore eroico (It.)
  tenore drammatico (It.)
  ténor drammatique (Fr.)
  Heldentenor (G.)
  tenor dramatico (Sp.)

tenorino (It.)
  falsetto tenor
  high tenor
  whiskey tenor
  Irish tenor
  countertenor
  castrato (It.)
  sopranista (It.)
  castrat (Fr.)

Kastrat (G.)
castrado (Sp.)

tenoroon
small bassoon
treble bassoon
tenor oboe
fagottino (It.)
oboe da caccia (It.)
petit basson (Fr.)
Tenorfagott (G.)
Quintfagott (G.)
fagote quinta (Sp.)

tenso, tenson (Fr.)
Troubadour dialogue song
debate song
jeu-parti, joc-partit (Fr.)
partimen (Fr.)
tenzone (It.)

tenth (interval)
compound third
decima (It.)
dixième (Fr.)
décime (Fr.)
Dezime (G.)
décime (Sp.)

tenue (Fr.)
sustained
sostenuto (It.)
tenuto (It.)
legato (It.)
fermata
organ-point
Bindung (G.)
gehalten, ausgehalten (G.)

vs. staccato (It.)

ter Sanctus (Lat.)
Holy, holy, holy
Tersanctus (Lat.)
trisag(h)ion (Gr.)
epinicion (Gr.)

Sanctus (Lat.)
cherubic hymn
Song of the Angels
Triumphant Hymn
Hymn of Victory
Kadush (Heb.)

terapia (It.)
music therapy
thérapie (Fr.)
Musiktherapie (G.)
terapia musical (Sp.)

Terce
canonical hour (third)
*Divine Office
monastic office
hora tertia (Lat.)
little hours

tercera, tercia (Sp.)
third (interval)
terza (It.)
tierce (Fr.)
Terz (G.)

tercera mayor (Sp.)
major third
Picardy third
ditone
terza maggiore (It.)
tierce majeur (Fr.)
tierce de Picardy (Fr.)
grosse Terz (G.)

tercera menor (Sp.)
minor third
terza minore (It.)
tierce mineur (Fr.)
kleine Terz (G.)

tercet (Fr.)
triplet
terzina (It.)
triolet (Fr.)
Triole (G.)

tresillo (Sp.)

terceto (Sp.)
trio
terzetto (It.)
Terzett (G.)

ternary form
ABA form
three-part form
song form
tri-partite form
arch form
bow form
da capo (aria) form
ternario (It.)
ternaire (Fr.)
Bogenform (G.)

tertian harmony
triadic harmony
triads
per terza (It.)
en/par tierce (Fr.)
Terzaufbau (G.)
per tercera (Sp.)

vs. quartal harmony

terzo suono (It.)
resultant tone
difference tone
differential tone
*combination tone
Tartini's tone
tono combinato (It.)
son combiné (Fr.)
Kombinationston (G.)
sonido adicional (Sp.)

tesi (It.)
thesis (Gr.)
*downbeat
crusis (Lat.)
thésis (Fr.)
Thesis (G.)

Senkung (G.)
tesis (Sp.)

vs. arsis (Gr.)
arsi (It.)

tessitura (It.)
range
compass
ambitus (E., Lat., Fr.)
gamut (Lat.)
estensione (It.)
tessiture (Fr.)
diapason (Fr.)
Raum (G.)
Umfang (G.)
tesitura (Sp.)

testina (It.)
note head
capocchia (It.)
tête de la note (Fr.)
Notenkopf (G.)
cabeza de las notas (Sp.)
punto de las notas (Sp.)

testo (It.)
narrator
Evangelist
historicus (Lat.)
evangelium (Lat.)
chronista (Lat.)
narratore (It.)
narrateur (Fr.)
récitant (Fr.)
Erzähler (G.)
Evangelisten (G.)
narrador (Sp.)
recitante (Sp.)

text
libretto
words
lyrics
script
book

texte (Fr.)
Text (G.)
texto (Sp.)

tetrachord
4-note scale section
scale
mode
tetracordo (It., Sp.)
tétracorde (Fr.)
Tetrachord (G.)

2. instr.of 4 strings

3. perfect fourth interval

tetratone
interval of three whole tones
*augmented fourth
tritone
devil's interval
diabolus in musica (Lat.)

text underlay
fitting words to rhythm
placement of the text
accentuation
declamation
accents

texture
richness of scoring
voicing
instrumentation

theater, theatre
playhouse
the stage
music hall
opera house
concert hall
auditorium
academy of music
teatro (It., Sp.)
théâtre (Fr.)
Theater (G.)

theater organ
cinema organ
unit organ
unified organ
extension organ
organo da teatro (It.)
organo da cinematografo (It.)
orgue de cinéma (Fr.)
Kinoorgel (G.)
Multiplexorgel (G.)
órgano de cine (Sp.)

theme
subject
melody
motive
idea
dux (Lat.)
comes (Lat.)
Leitmotiv (G.)
leading motive
soggetto (It.)
andamento (It.)
idée fixe (Fr.)
tema (It., Sp.)
thème (Fr.)
Thema (G.)

theme and variations
variations on a theme
partita

theme song
signature song
sigla melodica/musicale (It.)
indicatif musical (Fr.)
idée fixe (Fr.)
Leitmotiv (g.)
Kennmelodie (G.)
caracteristica (Sp.)
cortina musical (Sp.)

Themenverarbeitung (G.)
development (section)
sonata (allegro) form
fragmentation of themes

sviluppo (It.)
svolgimento (It.)
elaborazione tematica (It.)
développment (Fr.)
Durchführung (G.)
thematische Arbeit (G.)
desarrollo (Sp.)

Themenaufstellung (G.)
exposition (E., Fr.)
sonata form
esposizione (It.)
Exposition (G.)
Ausführung (G.)
exposición (Sp.)
elaboración (Sp.)

theody
hymn of praise
lauda (It.)
canticle
paean
praise song

theorbo
large lute
*archlute
chitarrone
bass lute
ganascione (It.)
tiorba (It., Sp.)
théorbe (Fr.)
Theorbe (G.)

theory, music theory
harmony
counterpoint
form
fundamentals
ear-training
analysis
teoria musicale (It.)
théorie musicale (Fr.)
Musiktheorie (G.)
teoria musical (Sp.)

thérapie (Fr.)
music therapy
terapia (It.)
Musiktherapie (G.)
terapia musical (Sp.)

theremin
electrophone
Ondes Martinot (Fr.)
Ondes Musicales (Fr.)
electronic music
synthesizer
hellertion
Aetherophone

thesis (Gr.)
*downbeat
first beat of a measure
strong beat
crusis (Lat.)
tesi (It.)
thésis (Fr.)
Thesis (G.)
Senkung (G.)
tesis (Sp.)

third (interval)
small interval
ditonus (Lat.)
terza (It.)
tierce (Fr.)
Terz(e) (G.)
tercera (Sp.)

third stream
fusion (jazz)
classical jazz
jive

thirty-second note
demisemiquaver
biscroma (It.)
trentaduesimo (It.)
triple croche (Fr.)
Zweiunddreissigstel (G.)
fusa (Sp.)

thirty-second rest
demisemiquaver rest
pausa di biscroma (It.)
huitième de soupir (Fr.)
Zweiunddreissigstelpause (G.
silencio de fusa (Sp.)
pausa de fusa (Sp.)

thorough-bass
*figured bass
through bass
continuo, basso continuo (It.)
basso generale (It.)
basso figurato (It.)
basse continue (Fr.)
Generalbass (G.)
allgemeiner Bass (G.)
bajo continuo (Sp.)

three-part form
ABA form
song form
arch form
bow form
tripartite form
ternary form
da capo form
Bogenform (G.)
Liedform (G.)

threnody
dirge
*lament
elegy
requiem (Lat.)
funeral song
planctus (Lat.)
lamento (It., Sp.)
plainte (Fr.)
déploration (Fr.)
Trauergesang (G.)
Klage, Klagelied (G.)
taps

throat (of a singer)
gola (It.)

gorge (Fr.)
Kehle (G.)
Hals (G.)
garganta (G.)

through-composed
progressive composition
free form
rhapsodic
fantasy
a forma aperta (It.)
de forme ouverte (Fr.)
Durchkomponiert (G.)
de melodîa no estrófica (Sp.)

thrumming, thrum
*strum, strumming
plucking
twang
strimpellare (It.)
tapoter (Fr.)
klimpern (G.)
rasgado (Sp.)

vs. bowing

thumb position ('cello, bass)
capotasto (It.)
position du pouce (Fr.)
démanché, démanchement (Fr.)
Daumenaufsatz (G.)
posición del pulgar (Sp.)

thunder machine/sheet
macchina per il tuono (It.)
machine pour le tonnere (Fr.)
Donnermaschine (G.)
máquina de truenos (Sp.)
máquina por le trueno (Sp.)

ti, si
seventh degree of the scale
leading tone
subtonic
essential seventh

sensibile, nota sensibile (It.)
note sensible (Fr.)
Leitton (G.)
sensible nota (Sp.)

tibia (Lat.)
*oboe
reed instrument
shawm
syrinx
aulos (Gr.)
calamus (Lat.)
tibialis)Lat.)

2. organ stop
flute stop
*diapason

tickle the ivories
play the piano
perform on the piano
concertize

tie
bind
ligature
slur
portato (It.)
legatura di valore (It.)
liaison (Fr.)
signe de tenue (Fr.)
chapeau (Fr.)
Bindbogen (G.)
Haltebogen (G.)
ligadura de valor (Sp.)

tiempo (Sp.)
*beat
pulse
count
time
tempus (Lat.)
tactus (Lat.)
battuta (It.)
temps (Fr.)
Takt (G.)

Taktschlag (G.)

tiento (Sp.)
ricercar
toccata
prelude
fantasia

tierce (Fr.)
*third (interval)
terza (It.)
Terz (G.)
tercera (Sp.)

2. organ stop (1 3/5, 1 1/3)
seventeenth
mutation stop

3. canonical hour
*terce

tierce de Picardie (Fr.)
major third
ditone
Picardy third
terza maggiore (It.)
tierce majeure (Fr.)
grosse Terz (G.)
tercera mayor (Sp.)

timbale(s) (Fr.)
*kettledrum
timpano, timpani, timballo (It.)
atabale (Fr.)
Pauken (G.)
timbal (Sp.)

timbre (E., Fr., Sp.)
tone quality
tone color
character
timbro (It.)
colorito (It.)
Tonfarbe (G.)
Klangfarbe (G.)

timbrel
    small hand-drum
    tabor
    *tambourine

time
    meter
    beat
    pulse
    count
    tempus (Lat.)
    tempo (It.)
    mesure (Fr.)
    Takt, Taktart (G.)
    tiempo (Sp.)

time signature
    measure signature
    meter signature
    prolation sign
    signum modi (Lat.)
    segno del tempo (It.)
    indicazione del tempo (It.)
    indicazione della misura (It.)
    chiffre de mesure (Fr.)
    indication de la mesure (Fr.)
    Taktart (G.)
    Takt(vor)zeichnung (G.)
    llave de tiempo (Sp.)

time value
    duration
    rhythmic value
    length of a note/rest
    valor (Lat., Sp.)
    valore (It.)
    valeur (Fr.)
    Wert (G.)
    Notenwert (G.)

timpan, timpanum (Lat.)
    psaltery
    timpe (old E.)

2. *kettledrum
    timpani

timpani (It.), timpano (sing.)
    *kettledrum(s)
    timbales (Fr.)
    Pauken (G.)
    timbal (Sp.)
    atabal (Sp.)

tin ear
    poor pitch discrimination
    off-key
    off pitch
    out of tune
    monotone
    bad ear
    tone deaf
    have no ear
    can't carry a tune
    amusia
    scordato (It.)
    stonato (It.)
    faux, fausse (Fr.)
    désacordé (Fr.)
    unrein (G.)
    verstimmt (G.)
    unrichtig (G.)
    falso (Sp.)

Tin Pan Alley
    popular music
    hit songs
    top 40
    Broadway show music

tin whistle
    penny whistle
    fife
    pipe
    fipple flute
    toy flute
    tonette
    flutophone
    piffero (It.)
    fifre (Fr.)
    flageolet (Fr.)
    Kinderflöte (G.)
    pifano (Sp.)

tinkle
    to ring (small bells)
    chime
    tintinnare (It.)
    tinter (Fr.)
    klingeln (G.)
    läuten (G.)
    tintinar (Sp.)

tintinabula, -um (Lat.)
    small bells
    *bells
    pellet bells
    jingle bells
    harness bells
    Sanctus bells
    altar bells
    nolae (Lat.)
    campanae (Lat.)
    tintinnabolo (It.)
    campanella (It.)
    clochette (Fr.)
    Schelle (G.)
    Glöckchen (G.)
    campanilla (Sp.)

tiorba (It., Sp.)
    *theorbo
    archlute
    lute
    chitarrone (It.

tip (of a bow)
    point
    peak
    end
    punta (It., Sp.)
    pointe (Fr.)
    Spitze (G.)

vs. frog

tiple (Sp.)
    treble part
    soprano
    superius (Lat.)

2. E-string
   cantino (It.)
   chanterelle (Fr.)
   Sangsaite (G.)

3. shawm
   xirimia (Sp.)
   chirimía (Sp.)

tiple cómica (Sp.)
   comic soprano (role)
   servetta (It.)
   dugazon (Fr.)
   soubrette (Fr.)
   ingenue (Fr.)

tirade (Fr.)
   ornament
   fill-in scale notes
   tirata (It.)
   *glissando (It.)
   glissade (Fr.)

tirage (Fr.)
   edition (E., Fr.)
   transcription
   arrangement
   adaptation
   version
   edizione (It.)
   Ausgabe (G.)
   Auflage (G.)
   edición (Sp.)

tirant (Fr.)
   draw-stop
   *drawknobs
   stops
   stop tabs
   tirante (It., Sp.)
   registre (Fr.)
   Zug (G.)
   registro (Sp.)

tirasse (Fr.)
   coupler (org.)

pedal coupler
   accoppiamento (It.)
   accouplement (Fr.)
   Pedalkoppel (G.)
   Koppelpedal (G.)
   acoplamiento (Sp.)
   enganche al pedalero (Sp.)

tiré, tirer, tirez (Fr.)
   *down bow
   tirato (It.)
   arco in giù (It.)
   Abstrich (G.)
   arco por bajo (Sp.)

vs. poussé (Fr.)

2. draw stops (org.)

3. slow down, slower
   retard
   rallentando (It.)
   ritardando (It.)

vs. en serrant (Fr.)

tiret (Fr.)
   ornament
   *mordent
   neighbor-note
   shake
   trill
   trillo (It.)
   mordente (It., Sp.)
   battement (Fr.)
   Pralltriller (G.)
   quiebro (Sp.)
   trino (Sp.)

tiro (It.)
   *slide (trombone)
   coulisse (Fr.)
   Zug (G.)
   Kulisse (G.)
   Scheide (G.)
   bomba (Sp.)

corredera (Sp.)
   vara (Sp.)

Tischharfe (G.)
   autoharp
   zither
   dulcimer
   cetra ad accordi (It.)
   autoarpa (It.)
   cithare d'amateur (Fr.)
   Akkordzither (G.)

tocadiscos (Sp.)
   *phonograph
   record player
   gramophone
   victrola
   turntable
   talking machine
   giradischi (It.)
   tourne-disques (Fr.)
   Plattenspieler (G.)
   gramofono (Sp.)

tocadiscos automático (Sp.)
   jukebox
   Musikbox (G.)
   Musikautomat (G.)
   máquina de discos (Sp.)
   tragaperras (Sp.)
   rocola (Sp.)

toccata (It., E.)
   prelude
   fantasia
   toquet (Fr.)
   toccate (Fr.)
   Tokkate (G.)
   tocada (Sp.)

tocco (It.)
   touch
   manner of playing
   toucher (Fr.)
   Anschlag (G.)
   tacto (Sp.)

tocsin (Fr., E.)
  alarm bell
  warning bell
  toxin
  beffroi (Fr.)
  Glocke (G.)

todos (Sp.)
  everyone, everybody
  full orchestra, etc.
  tutti (It.)
  tous (Fr.)
  Alles (G.)

toe stud (org.)
  toe piston
  combination stop
  coupler
  pistone (It.)
  piston (E., Fr.)
  Fussdrücker (G.)

togliere le sordine (It.)
  mutes off
  remove mutes
  senza sordini (It.)
  tutte corde (It.)
  toutes les cordes (Fr.)
  sans sourdines (Fr.)
  *ohne Dämpfer (G.)
  alle Saiten (G.)
  todas las cuerdas (Sp.)
  sin sordina (Sp.)

vs. con sordini (It.)

toll
  ring (bells)
  peal
  chime
  strike
  play
  sound
  scampanare (It.)
  carillonner (Fr.)
  Glocke läuten (G.)

tocar las campanas (Sp.)
  repicar (Sp.)

tom-tom(s)
  pair of drums
  bongo drums
  conga drums

2. tam-tam
  *gong

tombeau (Fr.)
  *lament
  elegy
  dirge
  plaint
  funeral song
  requiem (Lat.)
  lamento (It., Sp.)
  plainte (Fr.)
  déploration (Fr.)
  Grabgesang (G.)
  Trauergesang (G.)

ton (Fr.)
  a pitch
  musical sound
  tone
  note
  tono (It., Sp.)
  suono (It.)
  nota (It., Sp.)
  Ton, Tonhöhe (G.)
  Tonart (G.)

2. key
  mode
  scale

3. step of the scale
  whole tone
  whole-step
  major second
  tonos (Gr.)
  tonus (Lat.)
  tono intero (It.)

ton entier (Fr.)
  Ganzton (G.)
  tono entero (Sp.)

ton de chambre (Fr.)
  chamber pitch
  corista di camera (It.)
  diapason normale (Fr.)
  Kammerton (G.)
  tonalidad de camara (Sp.)

ton de chapelle (Fr.)
  church pitch
  choir pitch
  tuono chorista (It.)
  corista di coro (It.)
  ton de choeur (Fr.)
  Kapellton (G.)
  Chorton (G.)

Tonabstand (G.)
  *interval
  diastema (Gr.)
  intervallum (Lat.)
  intervallo (It.)
  intervalle (Fr.)
  Intervall (G.)
  Abstand (G.)
  intervalo (Sp.)

tonada (Sp.)
  folk song
  lyrical song

tonadilla escénica (Sp.)
  intermezzo
  short comic opera
  opera buffa (It.)
  intermedio (It.)
  seynète (Fr.)
  intermède (Fr.)
  sainete (Sp.)
  zarzuela (Sp.)
  operetta
  Singspiel (G.)
  Zwischenspiel (G.)

musical comedy

tonal answer (fugue)
altered subject
imitation

vs.real answer

tonality
key
modality
tonal center
tonalita (It.)
tonalité (Fr.)
Tonalität (G.)
Tonart (G.)
tonalidad (Sp.)

vs. atonality, polytonality

Tonballung (G.)
tone cluster
cluster
pitch aggregate
aleatory
chance music
gruppo di suonori (It.)
groupe de son/notes (Fr.)
Tontraube (G.)

Tonbandgerät (G.)
*tape recorder
tape machine
registratore a nastro magnetico
(It.)
magnétophone (Fr.)
magnetafón (Sp.)

Tonbogen (G.)
*crook (of a horn)
shank
extension
corpo di ricambio (It.)
corps de rechange (Fr.)
Stimmbogen (G.)
tonillo (Sp.)

cuerpo de recambio (Sp.)

Tondichtung (G.)
tone poem
symphonic poem
*program music
tone painting
descriptive music
word painting
poema sinfonico (It.)
poème symphonique (Fr.)
symphonische Dichtung (G.)
Tonmalerei (G.)
poema sinfónico (Sp.)

tone
musical sound
pitch
note
character
type of sound
tono (It., Sp.)
*ton (Fr.)
Ton (G.)

tone color
tone
tone quality
timbre (E., Fr., Sp.)
character
timbro (It.)
Tonfarbe (G.)
Klangfarbe (G.)

tone-deaf
off-key
off pitch
out of tune
monotone
have a bad ear
have no ear
have a tin ear
can't carry a tune
amusia
che non ha orecchio musicale
(It.)

ne pas avoir d'oreille
manque d'oreille (Fr.)
tonhöhentaub (G.)
que tiene mal oído (Sp.)
falto de oído musical (Sp.)

tone row
serial music
twelve-tone music
dodecaphonic
atonal, atonality
serie di suoni (It.)
série (Fr.)
Reihe, Tonreihe (G.)
serie (Sp.)

tonette
flutophone
fipple flute
recorder
whistle flute
toy flute
ocarina
penny whistle
duct flute
fife
slide whistle/flute
bazooka

tonguing
phrasing
articulation
bowing
colpo di lingua (It.)
coup de langue (Fr.)
Zungenschlag (G.)
Zungenstoss (G.)
golpe de lengua (Sp.)

Tonhaltungpedal (G.)
*loud pedal
sustaining pedal
damper pedal
sostenuto pedal

vs. Dämpfer (G.)

tonic
first degree of the scale
do
ut (Lat.)
home key
key note
gamut
finalis (Lat.)
tonica (It.)
fonique (Fr.)
Tonika (G.)
Grundton (G.)
tónica (Sp.)

tonic accent
high or low peak note

vs. agogic accent
metrical accent

tonic chord
I-chord
key chord
chord of the first degree

tonic major/minor
parallel key (same tonic)

vs. relative key

tonic sol-fa
*solmization
sol-fa
movable do
music-reading

Tonkunst (G.)
*music
the art of music
arte dei suoni (It.)
art des sons (Fr.)
arte de los sonidos (Sp.)

Tonkünstler (G.)
musician
composer

writer of music
music maker
compositore (It.)
compositeur (Fr.)
Komponist (G.)
Tonsetzer (G.)
componer (Sp.)

Tonleiter (G.)
*scale
octave species
gamut
scala (Lat., It.)
gamma (It.)
gamme (Fr.)
échelle (Fr.)
Skala (G.)
escala (Sp.)
gama (Sp.)

Tonloch (G.)
fingerhole
buci (It.)
foro (It.)
trou (Fr.)
Griffloch (G.)
Fingerloch (G.)
agujero (Sp.)
orificio (Sp.)

Tonmalerei (G.)
tone painting
tone poem
program music
symphonic poem

tono (It., Sp.)
tone
*ton (Fr.)
Ton (G.)

tono aperto (It.)
open notes (horn)
suoni naturali (It.)
sons naturels (Fr.)
sons ouverts (Fr.)

Naturtöne (G.)
notas naturales (Sp.)

vs. suoni chiusi (It.)

tonos, tonoi (Gr.)
whole tone
whole step
tonus (Lat.)
major second

2. scale
mode
echos, echoi (Gr.)

Tonsatz (G.)
piece
*composition
work
opus
pezzo (It.)
pièce (Fr.)
morceau (Fr.)
Stück (G.)
pieza (Sp.)

Tonspur (G.)
sound track(film music)
sound stripe
colonna sonora (It.)
bande sonore (Fr.)
colonne sonore (Fr.)
banda de sonido (Sp.)
pista sonora (Sp.)

Tonstärke (G.)
volume (E., Fr.)
loudness
amplitude
gain
dynamics
ampiezza (It.)
Amplitude (G.)
amplitud (Sp.)

Tonstufe (G.)

degree
step of the scale
tone
grado (It., Sp.)
degré (Fr.)
Grad (G.)

tonus oratorium (Lat.)
simple tone (chant)
ordinary tone
ferial tone
tonus simplex (Lat.)
tonus ferialis (Lat.)
tonus communis (Lat.)

vs. tonus solemnis (Lat.)

tonus peregrinus (Lat.)
chant psalm tone having two
reciting tones
wandering tone

tonus solemnis (Lat.)
solemn tone
tonus festivus (Lat.)

vs. tonus ferialis (Lat.)

top-40, -20, -10
pop songs
hit songs
top of the charts
hit parade
rassenga di successi musicali
(It.)
canzoni di successi (It.)
chansons à la mode (Fr.)
chanson à succès (Fr.)
Schlager(parade (G.)
canción de moda (Sp.)
canción en boga (Sp.)
Tin Pan Alley
standard tunes/songs

top voice/part
highest voice/part

soprano
treble
lead voice/part
discant
discantus (Lat.)
superius (Lat.)
cantus (Lat.)
dessus (Fr.)
erste Stimme (G.)

vs. low voice/part
bottom voice

toque (Sp.)
call (military)
signal call
taps
toll
bugle call
caccia (It.)
squillo di tromba (It.)
chasse (Fr.)
Hornsignal (G.)
toque de corneta (Sp.)
toque de silencio (Sp.)
toque de trompeta (Sp.)

toque de alborada (Sp.)
*reveille
wake-up call
bugle call
diana (It., Sp.)
diane (Fr.)
Wecksignal (G.)
alborada (Sp.)

toquet (Fr.)
toccata (It.)
fantasy
prelude

torch song
sad love song
blues
jazz
popular song

torch singer

tordion (Fr.)
bass dance movement
*basse danse (Fr.)
bassadanza (It.)
saltarello (It.)
tordiglione (It.)
cascarda (It.)
piva (It.)
tourdion (Fr.)
galliard (Fr.)
pas de Brabant (Fr.)
Hoftanz (G.)
baxa (Sp.)

tornada (Fr.)
envoy, envoi (Fr.)
*coda
tag
commiato (It.)

tornada (Sp.)
old folk ballad
estribillo (Sp.)
refrain

Totenmesse (G.)
requiem Mass
Mass for the dead
*funeral Mass
missa pro defunctis (Lat.)
messa da requiem (It.)
messe des morts (Fr.)
Esequien (G.)
misa de difuntos (Sp.)

touch (n.)
way of playing
expression
the feel
weight of hand, arm
technique
tocco (It.)
tasto (It., Sp.)
toucher (Fr.)

Anschlag (G.)

touch (vb.)
play
sound
sonare (It.)
toucher (Fr.)
sonner (Fr.)
jouer (Fr.)
spielen (G.)
klingen (G.)
tönen (G.)
sonar (Sp.)
tocar (Sp.)
tañer (Sp.)

touche (Fr.)
key (of a piano)
digital
tasto (It.)
touchette (Fr.)
Taste (G.)
tecla (Sp.

2. fret
tasto (It.)
sillet (Fr.)
touchette (Fr.)
Bund (G.)
traste (Sp.)

3. key (of a wind instr.)
digital
chiave (It.)
clef (Fr.)
Klappe (G.)
llave (Sp.)

4. fingerboard (violin)
tastiera (It.)
manche (Fr.)
Griffbrett (G.)
batidor (Sp.)

5. orchestral *toccata

touches blanches (Fr.)
white keys
tasto bianco (It.)
Untertaste (G.)
weisse Taste (G.)
tecla blanca (Sp.)

touches noires (Fr.)
*black keys
sharp/flat keys
accidentals
tasto nero (It.)
feintes (Fr.)
schwarze Obertasten (G.)
tecla negra (Sp.)

tour de gosier (Fr.)
ornament
turn
trill ending (vocal)
gruppetto, groppo (It.)
doublé (Fr.)
Doppelschlag (G.)

touring company
road company
concert/opera tour
on the road
traveling company
showboat
showmobile
a tour

tourne-disques (Fr.)
*phonograph
record player
gramophone
victrola
turntable
talking machine
giradischi (It.)
fonografo (It.)
piatto portadischi (It.)
plateau (Fr.)
Plattenteller (G.)
Plattenspieler (G.)

plato (Sp.)
tocadiscos (Sp.)

tournebout (Fr.)
double reed instr.
oboe
crumhorn
lituus (Lat.)
cromorno (It., Sp.)
piva torto (It.)
storto (It.)
cromorne (Fr.)
Krummhorn (G.)
orlo (Sp.)

toutes les cordes (Fr.)
mutes off
remove mutes
tutte corde (It.)
tre corde (It.)
*ohne Dämpfer (G.)
Dämpfer weg (G.)
alle Saiten (G.)
todas las cuerdas (Sp.)

vs. une corde (Fr.)

tower bells
church bells
steeple bells
carillon music
tower music
cariglione (It.)
carillon (E., Fr.)
Glockenklavier (G.)

tower music
brass ensemble
brass quartet, etc.
Turmmusik (G.)

toy instruments
children's instruments
rhythm instruments
rhythm band

toy symphony
foire des enfants (Fr.)
symphonie burlesque (Fr.)
Kindersymphonie (G.)

toye (old E.)
keyboard piece
jigg
bagatelle (Fr.)

tracción (Sp.)
*action (keyboard)
trasmissione (It.)
traction (Fr.)
Traktur (G.)

tracker action (org.)
mechanical action
trasmissione meccanica (It.)
traction mécanique (Fr.)
transmission mécanique (Fr.)
mechanische Speiltraktur (G.)
transmisión mecánica (Sp.)

vs. electromagnetic action

tract
song after the gradual at Mass
during lent, etc.
Proper of the Mass
tractus (Lat.)
cantus tractus (Lat.)
cantus (Lat. Ambrosian)
tratto (It.)
trait (Fr.)
Trakt (G.)
tracto (Sp.)

tractulus (Lat.)
guide
direct
custos (E., Lat.)
cue sign
index
mostra (It., Sp.)
guida (It.)

guidon (Fr.)
Kustos (G.)

traditional music
folk music
ethnic folk music
mountain music
hillbilly music
bluegrass music
old-time music
country music

traduzione (It.)
translation
traduction (Fr.)
Übersetzung (G.)
traducción (Sp.)

tragédie lyrique (Fr. 17-18c.)
opera
tragic opera
opera seria (It., Sp.)
grand opera
tragédie en musique (Fr.)
grosse Oper (G.)
Musikdramma (G.)

vs. opéra bouffe (Fr.)

trait (Fr.)
*tract
tractus (Lat.)

2. a *run
rapid scale passage
slide
glissando (It.)

tralla (Sp.)
whip
slapstick
frusta (It.)
fouet (Fr.)
Peitsche, Pritsche (G.)
zurriaga (Sp.)
fusta (Sp.)

látigo (Sp.)

trällern (G.)
to hum
trill
a bocca chiusa (It.)
canticchiare (It.)
furberia del canto (It.)
avec bouche fermée (Fr.)
fredonner (Fr.)
Brummstimmen (G.)
canturrear (Sp.)
canticar (Sp.)

transcribe
edit
arrange
adapt
put into modern notation
trascrivere (It.)
transcrire (Fr.)
übertragen (G.)
transcribir (Sp.)

transcription (E., Fr.)
copy
arrangement
adaptation
trascrizione (It.)
Übertragung (G.)
transcripción (Sp.)

transition (E., Fr.)
bridge passage
episode
transizione (It.)
Übergang (G.)
Durchgang (G.)
transición (Sp.)

2. *modulation
key change

transitorium (Lat. Ambrosian)
communion song/antiphon
confractorium (Lat.)

trecanum (Lat. Gallican)

transpose
    change key
    modulate
    shift key
    transmutatio (Lat.)
    trasportare (It.)
    variare il tuono (It.)
    transposer (Fr.)
    transponieren (G.)
    transportar (Sp.)
    modulare (It.)
    moduler (Fr.)
    modulieren (G.)
    modular (Sp.)

transposing instrument
    sounds in another key than
written (clarinet, trumpet, horn,
saxophones, etc.)

vs. C-instrument (strings, flute,
trombone, etc.)

transverse flute
    *flute
    concert flute
    cross flute
    German flute
    flauto traverso (It.)
    flûte allemande (Fr.)
    flûte traversière (Fr.)
    flûte à six trous (Fr.)
    Querflöte (G.)
    Kreuzflöte (G.)
    Konzertflöte (G.)
    flauta travesera (Sp.)
    flauta alemana (Sp.)

vs. recorder

traps (percussion)
    drum set/kit
    trap set
    rhythm section

trasmissione (It.)
    action (organ.)
    traction (Fr.)
    Traktur (G.)
    tracción (Sp.)

traste (Sp.)
    fret
    tasto (It.)
    touche, touchette (Fr.)
    Bund (G.)

tratto d'unione (It.)
    *beam (on notes)
    cross-bar
    barre transversale (Fr.)
    Balken, Notenbalken (G.)
    barra de compás (Sp.)

traveler (curtain)
    curtain
    drop, backdrop
    scrim
    cyclorama
    telone (It.)
    siparia, siparietto (It.)
    rideau (Fr.)
    Vorhang (G.)
    Bühnenvorhang (G.)
    telón (Sp.)

Trauermarsch (G.)
    funeral march
    dead march
    dirge
    marcia funebre (It.)
    marche funèbre (Fr.)
    marcha fúnebre (Sp.)

Trauermusik (G.)
    *lament
    lamentation
    elegy
    requiem (Lat.)
    funeral music
    planctus (Lat.)

lamento (It.)
    musica funebre (It.)
    musique funèbre (Fr.)
    déploration (Fr.)
    tombeau (Fr.)
    Grabgesang (G.)
    cantos de velorio (Sp.)
    música funeral/fúnebre (Sp.)

tre corde (It.)
    release soft pedal
    tutte le corde (It.)
    toutes les cordes (Fr.)
    alle Saiten (G.)
    *ohne Dämpfer (G.)
    todas las cuerdas (Sp.)

vs. una corda (It.)

treble
    soprano
    cantus (Lat.)
    superius (Lat.)
    discantus (Lat.)
    high voice/part
    child's voice
    discant
    canto (It,)
    dessus (Fr.)
    Diskant (G.)

2. high tones (audio)
    tone control
    high frequency control

treble choir
    children's chorus
    cherub choir
    equal voices (high)
    women's voices
    high voices
    close harmony

treble clef
    *G-clef
    violin clef

soprano clef
chiave di sol (It.)
clef de sol (Fr.)
G-Schlüssel (G.)
llave de sol (Sp.)
clave aguda (Sp.)

treble viol
descant viol
Diskantviole (G.)

trecanum (Lat.)
communion antiphon
(Gallican)
confractorium (Lat.
Ambrosian)
transitorium (Lat. Ambrosian)

treibend (G.)
*faster, getting faster
accelerando (It.)
stringendo (It.)
stretto (It.)
en serrant (Fr.)
schneller (G.)
más pronto (Sp.)

vs. nachgebend (G.)
rallentando (It.)

treizième (Fr.)
13th (interval)
tredicesima (It.)
Tredezime (G.)
Terzdezime (G.)
dreizehnte (G.)
decimotercio (Sp.)

tremando, tremanto (It.)
tremolando, -oso (It.)
tremolo, tremulant
vibrato
trillo (It.)
gruppo (It.)
balancement (Fr.)
zitternd (G.)

Schwebung (G.)
Bebung (G.)

tremblement (Fr.)
trill
shake
mordent
ornament
trillo (It.)
groppo (It.)
gruppo, gruppetto (It.)
cadence (Fr.)
trille (Fr.)
Triller (G.)
trino (Sp.)
redoble (Sp.)
quiebro (Sp.)

trenchmore
a lively country dance
English country dance
contredance

treno (Sp.)
*funeral song
dirge
*lament
endecha (Sp.)
canto fúnebre (Sp.)
trenodia (It.)

trentaduesimo (It.)
32nd-note
demisemiquaver
biscroma (It.)
triple-croche (Fr.)
Zweiunddreissigstel (G.)
fusa (Sp.)

trepak
Cossack dance in fast duple
polka
can-can
galop

très (Fr.)

very
rather
much
molto (It.)
assai (It.)
beaucoup (Fr.)
assez (Fr.)
viel (G.)
sehr (G.)
mucho, muy (Sp.)

très fort (Fr.)
very loud
blaring
ear-splitting
deafening
fortissimo (It.)
laut (G.)
stark (G.)
fuerte (Sp.)

tresillo (Sp.)
triplet (3 eighths in the time of
2 eighths)
terzina (It.)
triolet, tercet (Fr.)
Triole (G.)

tresque (Fr.)
13c.dance song
carole
estampie
tresca (It.)
Tresca (G.)

Trezza (G. 17c.)
dance movement of a suite
courante
galliard

triad
chord made up of thirds
harmony
trias (Lat.)
trias harmonica (Lat.)
triade (It., Fr.)

accordo (It.)
accord (Fr.)
Deiklang (G.)
Akkord (G.)
acorde (Sp.)
triada (Sp.)

triadic harmony
   based on thirds
   tertian harmony
   per terza (It.)
   par/en tierce (Fr.)
   Terzaufbau (G.)
   per tercera (Sp.)

vs. quartal harmony

trial (Fr.)
   comic tenor
   buffo tenor
   *comic role
   comic opera
   tenore buffo (It.)

triangle (percussion)
   triangle beater
   triangulum (Lat.)
   triangolo (It.)
   triangel (Fr.)
   treple (Fr.)
   Triangel (G.)
   triángulo (Sp.)

trichordon (Gr.)
   pandora
   lyre
   lute

tricinium (Lat.)
   vocal *trio, unaccompanied
   a cappella trio
   bicinium (Lat.)

Triduum Sacrum (Lat.)
   last three days of Holy Week
   *Holy Week services

Sacred Triduum

trill
   shake
   relish
   tremolo
   vibrato
   double mordent
   flos (Lat. 13c.)
   trillo (It.)
   Gruppo, groppo, grupetto (It.)
   trille (Fr.)
   cadence (Fr.)
   tremblement (Fr.)
   Triller (G.)
   trino (Sp.)

trillo (It.)
   rapid repetition of one note
   tremolo

2. *trill (two-note rapid
repetition)
   gruppo (It.)
   ribattuta (It.)

trillo caprino (It.)
   goat's trill
   wide tremolo
   chèvrotement (Fr.)
   Bockstriller (G.)
   trino de cabra (Sp.)

Trinitarian Hymn
   *Doxology
   Gloria Patri (Lat.)
   Gloria in excelsis Deo (Lat.)
   Cherubim Song

Trinklied (G.)
   drinking song
   tavern song
   bacchanal
   bacchanalian song/dance
   dithyramb
   carmina burana (Lat.)

brindisi (It.)
canto bacchico (It.)
chanson à boire (Fr.)
chanson bacchique (Fr.)
canción báquica (Sp.)
canción de taberna (Sp.)

trio (E., It., Fr., Sp.)
   group of three performers
   piece for three performers
   chamber music
   terzetto (It.)
   tricinium (Lat.)

2. middle section of a minuet a⸱
scherzo
   B-section
   alternativo (It.)
   alternativement (Fr.)

trio sonata
   chamber sonata
   sonata da camera (It.)
   sonata da chiesa (It.)
   sonata a tre (It.)
   sonate en trio (Fr.)
   Triosonate (G.)
   sonata de trío (Sp.)

Triole (G.)
   triplet
   terzina (It.)
   tripla (It.)
   triolet (Fr.)
   tercet (Fr.)
   tresillo (Sp.)

tripartite form
   ternary form
   *three-part form
   ABA form
   song form
   arch form
   bow form

triple articulación (Sp.)

flutter-tonguing
raspberry
French kiss
Bronx cheer
frullato (It.)
articulation double (Fr.)
double coup de lange (Fr.)
Flatterzunge (G.)

triple concerto (E., Fr., Sp.)
for three solo instr. and
orchestra
concerto triplo (It.)
Tripelkonzert (G.)

triple-croche (Fr.)
32nd-note
demisemiquaver
biscroma (It.)
trentaduesimo (It.)
Zweiunddreissigstel (G.)
fusa (Sp.)

triple meter
perfect time
tempus perfectus (Lat.)
triple time
in 3
three-quarter time
waltz time
tempo ternario (It.)
mesure ternaire (Fr.)
ungerader Takt (G.)

triplum (Lat.)
third voice in an organum
treble
top voice/part
superius (Lat.)
discantus (Lat.)
triplex (Lat.)
soprano

tris(h)agion (Gr.)
Reproaches
Good Friday

Holy Week
Sanctus (Lat.)
ter Sanctus (Lat.)
Aius (Mozarabic, Gallican)
Holy, holy, holy
Song of the Angels
Cherubim Song
Hymn of Victory
Triumphant Hymn/Song
Kadosh, Kedusha (Heb.)

triste, tristement (Fr.)
sad, sadly
plaintive
lamentoso (It.)
addolorato (It.)
mesto, mestamente (It.)
betrübt (G.)
tristemente (Sp.)

tritone
diminished fifth
augmented fourth
false fifth
devil's interval
mi contra fa (Lat.)
diabolus in musica (Lat.)
tritonium (Lat.)
tritono (It., Sp.)
triton (Fr.)
Tritonus (G.)

Trittharfe (G.)
pedal harp
concert harp
chromatic harp
double-action harp
arpa a pedali (It.)
harpe à pédales (Fr.)
Pedalharfe (G.)
arpa de pedal (Sp.)

vs. Irish harp

triumphant march
marcia trionfale (It.)

marche triomphale (Fr.)
Triumphmarsch (G.)
marcha triunfal (Sp.)

trobairitz (Prov.)
female *troubadour
minstrel
bard

trois-temps (Fr.)
waltz
three-step
valzer a tre passi (It.)
valse (Fr.)
Walzer (G.)
Dreitritt (G.)
vals (Sp.)

troll
a *round
canon
catch

tromba (It., E., Fr.)
trumpet
trumpet stop (org.)
cornet
bugle
tromba spezzata (It.)
clairon (Fr.)
trompette (Fr.)
Trompete (G.)
Zugtrompete (G.)
trompeta (Sp.)

tromba da tirarsi (It.)
slide trumpet
trombone
tromba a tiro (It.)
trompette à coulisse (Fr.)
Zugtrompete (G.)
trompeta de varas (Sp.)

tromba marina (It.)
monochord
marine trumpet

trumpet marine
sea-trumpet
mock-trumpet
unichord
kanon (Gr.)
unichordum (Lat.)
trompette marine (Fr.)
Trumscheit (G.)
Nonnengeige (G.)
Seetrompete (G.)
trompeta/trompa marina (Sp.)

trombone (E., Fr., It.)
slide trombone
bass trumpet
valve trombone
*sackbut
Posaune (G.)
Busaune (G.)
trombón (Sp.)

Trommel (G.)
drum
percussion
tabor
timpanum (Lat.)
cassa (It.)
tamburo (It.)
caisse (Fr.)
tambour (Fr.)
tambor (Sp.)
caja (Sp.)

Trommelschlag (G.)
drumbeat
beat of a drum
colpo di tamburo (It.)
coup de baguette (Fr.)
toque (Sp.)
redoble (Sp.)

Trommelwirbel (G.)
drum-roll
tremolo
rullo (It.)

roulement (Fr.)
Paukrnwirbel (G.)
redoble (Sp.)

trompa (Sp.)
horn
*French horn
corno (It., Sp.)
cor (Fr.)
Waldhorn (G.)
cuerno (Sp.)
corno francés (Sp.)

trompa de caza (Sp.)
natural horn
hunting horn
corno da caccia (It.)
cor de chasse (Fr.)
trompe (Fr.)
Jagdhorn (G.)
Waldhorn (G.)

trompa de París (Sp.)
*Jew's harp
jaw's harp
mouth organ
ribeba (It.)
spassapensieri (It.)
trompe de laquais (Fr.)
trompe de Béarn/Berne (Fr.)
Mundharmonika (G.)
Maultrommel (G.)
trompa gallega (Sp.)
trompa inglesa (Sp.)

Trompetenstoss (G.)
*fanfare
flourish
bugle call
trumpet call
fanfara (It.)
squillo di tromba (It.)
sonnerie (Fr.)
Tusch (G.)
sonada (Sp.)
fanfarria (Sp.)

toque de corneta (Sp.)

trompette thébaine (Fr.)
*Aïda trumpet
straight trumpet
herald's trumpet
state trumpet
ceremonial trumpet
buisine (Fr.)
chamade (Fr.)
Fanfarentrompete (G.)
trompeta egipcia (Sp.)

troparium (Lat.)
troper, troparium
*anthology
collection of tropes, sequence
etc.
tropario (It., Sp.)
tropaire (Fr.)
Tropar(ium) (G.)

trope
contrafactum (Lat.)
added text, music
prosa, prosula (Lat.)
sequence
sequentia (Lat.)
clausula (Lat.)
prose (Fr.)
motet

troppo (It.)
too much
overdone
trop (Fr.)
zu sehr (G.)
zu viel (G.)
demasiado (Sp.)

trou (Fr.)
fingerhole (on a wind instr.)
buco (It.)
foro (It.)
Griffloch (G.)
Tonloch (G.)

Fingerloch (G.)
orificio (Sp.)
agujera (Sp.)

trou de souffleur (Fr.)
prompt-box
prompt side
stage right
buca del suggeritore (It.)
Souffleurkasten (G.)
concha del apuntador (Sp.)

troubadour (Prov.)
balladeer
bard
minstrel
trouvère (Fr.)
trobairitz (Prov.)
trovatore, trov(i)ero (It.)
trovador (Sp.)
jongleur
scop
goliard
Spielmann (G.)
Minnesinger
Meistersinger

Troubadour, Trouvère song
formes fixes (Fr.)
lai
vers
canso, canzo
ballade
jeu-parti, joc-parti
sirventes
tenso
partimen
planh
descort
chanson avec refrains
alba
enueg
chanson de geste
chanson de toile
pastourelle
virelai

rondeau
reverdie
cantus coronatus

troupe
band of musicians, actors
ensemble
company
touring company
strolling players

trozo (Sp.)
piece
composition
opus
pezzo (It.)
morceau (Fr.)
pièce (Fr.)
Stück (G.)
pieza (Sp.)

true pitch
absolute pitch
perfect pitch
concert pitch

Trugschluss (G.)
*deceptive cadence
half-cadence
imperfect cadence
false cadence
interrupted cadence
suspended cadence
avoided cadence
surprize cadence
irregular cadence
broken cadence
cadenza evitata (It.)
cadence interrompue (Fr.)
Trugkadenz (G.)
cadencia evitada (Sp.)

trump
*trumpet

2. *Jew's harp

jaw's harp
Jew's trump
mouth-organ

trumpet
cornet
bugle
clarion
buisine, buzine
tuba (Lat.)
tromba (It.)
clarino (It.)
trompette (Fr.)
Trompete (G.)
trompete (Sp.)

trumpet call
*fanfare
military call
flourish
bugle call
signal call
reveille
taps
caccia (It.)
chiamata (It. 17c.)
chamade (Fr. 17c.)
chasse (Fr.)
toque de corneta (Sp.)

trumpet marine
marine trumpet
mock trumpet
*tromba marina (It.)

trumpet voluntary
solo piece for trumpet
trumpet tune

truncatio (Lat.)
hocket
broken note
interrupted melody
hoquetatio, hoquetus (Lat.)
occitatio (Lat.)
ochetto (It.)

tactée (Fr.)
ho(c)quet (Fr.)
Hoketus (G.)
hoquet (Sp.)

tryout
audition (E., Fr.)
hearing
screen test
audizione (It.)
Vorspiel (G.)
audición (Sp.)

tuba
bass horn
sousaphone
serpent
helicon
ophicleide

2. reciting tone (chant)
dominant
tenor

tuba (Lat.)
trumpet
straight trumpet
*Aïda trumpet
herald's trumpet
state trumpet
salpinx (Gr.)
lituus (Lat.)

tubular bells
chimes
orchestral chimes
clock chimes
campane tubolari (It.)
cloches tubulaires (Fr.)
tubes de cloches (Fr.)
Röhrenglocken (G.)
campanólogo (Sp.)

tuck, tucket (old E.)
*fanfare (E., Fr.)
flourish

squillo di tromba (It.)
fanfara (It.)
sonnerie (Fr.)
Tusch (G.)
Trompetenstoss (G.)
toque de trompeta (Sp.)
fanfarra (Sp.)
sonada (Sp.)

Tudor church music
*cathedral music
Anglican music
Episcopal music
musique de cathédrale (Fr.)
Kirchenmusik (G.)
música de las catedrales (Sp.)
música catedralícia (Sp.)

tune (n.)
melody
*song
air
ditty
jingle
aria
canto (It.)
chanson, chansonette (Fr.)
Lied (G.)
Gesang (G.)
Wiese (G.)
canción (Sp.)

tune (vb.)
adjust the pitch
tune up/down
accordare (It.)
intonare (It.)
intonare (It.)
accorder (Fr.)
abstimmen (G.)
einstimmen (G.)
stimmen (G.)
akkordieren (G.)
acordar (Sp.)
afinar (Sp.)

tune book
hymn collection
*hymnal
hymnary
psalter
songbook
*anthology
innario (It.)
hymnaire (Fr.)
Hymnar (G.)
hymnario (Sp.)

tunesmith
composer
song-writer
songsmith
tin-pan-alley
bard
minstrel
Troubadour
Trouvère
Minnesinger
Meistersinger

tuning (n.)
*intonation
temperament
accorditura (It.)
accord (Fr.)
Stimmung (G.)
afinación (Sp.)

tuning fork
diapason (It., Fr.)
corista (It.)
tonimetro (It.)
fourchette tonique (Fr.)
Stimmgabel (G.)
diapasón (Sp.)

tuning key/hammer/wrest
accordatoio (It.)
accordoir (Fr.)
clef d'accordeur (Fr.)
Stimmhammer (G.)
Stimmschlüssel (G.)

afinador (Sp.)
templador (Sp.)

tuning system
just intonation
equal temperament
mean-tone tuning
microtonal tuning

tuono (It.)
a tone
a pitch
musical sound
color
timbre
tono (It., Sp.)
*ton (Fr.)
Ton (G.)

2. key
mode
scale

tuono chorista (It.)
choir pitch
church pitch
ton de choeur (Fr.)
ton de chapelle (Fr.)
Chorton (G.)

turba (Lat.)
crowd (in a passion play)
mob
chorus
synagoga (Lat.)

ture-lure (Fr.)
refrain
chorus
fa-la-la
toure-loure (Fr.)

Turkish crescent
jingling Johnny
Chinese pavilion
Turkish pavilion

Turkish hat
Turkish music
bell tree
Janissary music
banda Turca (It.)
*chapeau Chinois (Fr.)
Schellenbaum (G.)
sombrero Chino (Sp.)

Turkish (military) style
alla Turca (It., Sp.)
à la Turk (Fr.)
nach Turkischer Art (G.)

turn
ornament
neighbor notes
groppo, gruppo (It.)
groupe (Fr.)
brisé (Fr.)
doublé (Fr.)
double cadence (Fr.)
tour de Gosier (Fr.)
noeud (Fr.)
Doppelschlag (G.)
Halbzirkel (G.)
grupeto, grupito (Sp.)

turnaround
bridge to a repeat (in a song)
turnback
segue (It.)

turntable
*phonograph
gramophone
record player
victrola
talking machine
giradischi (It.)
tourne-disques (Fr.)
Plattenspieler (G.)
Sprechsmaschine (G.)
tocadiscos (Sp.)

Tusch (G.)

*fanfare
flourish
bugle call
fanfara (It.)
squillo di tromba (It.)
sonnerie (Fr.)
Trompetenstoss (G.)
sonada (Sp.)
fanfarria (Sp.)

tutte (le) corde (It.)
release soft pedal
tre corde (It.)
toutes les cordes (Fr.)
alle Saiten (G.)
*ohne Dämpfer (G.)
todas las cuerdas (Sp.)

vs. una corda (It.)

tutti (It.)
full chorus/orchestra
all
omnes (Lat.)
concerto (It. 17c.)
ripieno (It.)

2. full organ
great chorus
organo pieno/pleno (It.)
*grand choeur (Fr.)
grand-jeu (Fr.)
volles Werk (G.)
grosses Spiel (G.)
gran juego (Sp.)

tuyau d'orgue (Fr.)
pipe (org.)
tube
canna d'organo (It.)
Pfeife (G.)
tubo (Sp.)
caño (Sp.)

twang
strum (guitar, etc.)

pluck
thrum
pick

twelfth (interval)
octave plus a fifth
duodecima (It.)
douzième (Fr.)
Duodezime (G.)
duodécima (Sp.)

2. quint (org.)
mutation stop (2 2/3)

twelve-tone music
serial music
dodecaphonic music
atonal music
musica dodecafonica (It.)
dodecafonia (It.)
musique dodécaphonique (Fr.)
dodécaphonique (Fr.)
Zwölftonmusik (G.)
Dodekaphonie (G.)
música dodecafónica (Sp.)
dodecafonía (Sp.)

twice
repeat
reprise
*bis (It., Fr.)
alta volta (It.)
noch Einmal (G.)
Zugabe (G.)
otra vez (Sp.)
encore

two-foot stop (org.)
fifteenth
piccolo
2 octaves above

two-handed octaves
blind octaves (piano)

two-part form

*binary form
AB form
bipartite form
bar form
bipartito (It.)
binario (It., Sp.)
biparti (Fr.)
binaire (Fr.)
zweiteilige Form (G.)
bipartido (Sp.)

tympanum (Lat.)
*drum
percussion
cassa (It.)
tamburo (It.)
caisse (Fr.)
tambour (Fr.)
Trommel (G.)
tambor (Sp.)
caja (Sp.)

Tyrolienne (Fr.)
Ländler (G.)
waltz
mazurka
Varsovienne (Fr.)
Schottische (G.)

tzigana (Sp.)
gypsy song
canzone gitana (It.)
chant tzigane (Fr.)
chant gitan (Fr.)
Zigeunerlied (G.)
canto gitano (Sp.)
canción gitana/tzigana (Sp.)

U

überblasen (G.)
overblow (wind instr.)
overtones
harmonics
ottavizzare (It.)
octavier (Fr.)
octavar (Sp.)

Übergang (G.)
transition (E., Fr.)
modulation
bridge
channel
release
transizione(It.)
Überleitung (G.)
transición (Sp.)

übergreifen (G.)
cross hands (piano)
incrociare ((It.)
croiser (Fr.)
cruzar (Sp.)

übermässig (G.)
augmented
aumentato (It.)
augmenté (Fr.)
aumentado (Sp.)

Übung (G.)
*etude
a study
practice piece
lesson
exercise
drill
studio (It.)
esercizio (It.)

exercice (Fr.)
estudio (Sp.)
ejercicio (Sp.)

Übungsapparat (G.)
dumb piano
dumb spinet
dumb organ
practice keyboard
digitorium
stummes Klavier (G.)

ufficio divino (It.)
*Divine Office
Opus Dei (Lat.)
monastic office
day hours
canonical hours
office divin (Fr.)
Stundenoffizium (G.)
hora canónica (Sp.)

uillean pipes
*bagpipes
union pipes
Irish bagpipes
Irish organ

ukulele
small guitar
banjo
banjo-ukulele

ultima prova (It.)
dress rehearsal
full rehearsal
open rehearsal
répétition générale (Fr.)
Generalprobe (G.)
ensayo general (Sp.)

Umfang (G.)
range
compass
tessitura
gamut

ambitus (Lat., Fr., E.)
estensione (It.)
étendue (Fr.)
ambito (It., Sp.)

Umkehrung (G.)
reversal
*inversion (chord, interval)
rivolto, rivoltato (It.)
renversement (Fr.)
invertido (Sp.)

umoresca (It.)
humoresque (E., Fr.)
caprice (E., Fr.)
fancy
toye
Humoreske (G.)
humoresca (Sp.)

una corda (It.)
soft pedal down
left pedal
muted
une corde (Fr.)
*pédale douce (Fr.)
eine Saite (G.)
linke Pedal (G.)
pedal sordina/suave (Sp.)
una cuerda (Sp.)

vs. tre corde (It.)

unaccompanied
*a cappella (It.)
alla Palestrina (It.)
stile antico (It.)
stile osservato (It.)
sans instruments (Fr.)
style de chapelle (Fr.)
à la Palestrienne (Fr.)
im Kapellstil (G.)
Palestrina-Stil (G.)
ohne Instrumente (G.)
unbegleitet (G.)
a capilla (Sp.)

música vocal (Sp.)

vs. accompanied

unanime (Fr.)
note-for-note style
homophonic
homorhythmic
*note-against-note
simple counterpoint
first species counterpoint

unca (Lat.)
hooked note
*eighth-note
quaver

unda maris (Lat. org.)
organ stop (detuned)
voix celeste (Fr.)
vox angelica (Lat.)
vox coelestis (Lat.)
vox humana (Lat.)

under one's breath
whispered
*aside
stage whisper
undertone
very soft
in a low voice
sotto voce (It.)
pianissimo (It.)
mezza voce (It.)
de coté (Fr.)
à part (Fr.)
beiseite (G.)
a parte (Sp.)
a sovoz (Sp.)

underlay (vocal music)
text underlay
placement of the words
accentuation

underscore

*incidental music
film music
*backround music
musique de scène (Fr.)

undicesima (It.)
eleventh interval
compound fourth
onzième (Fr.)
Undezime (G.)
oncena (Sp.)

undulzione (It.)
vibrato
tremolo

unequal voices
mixed voices
SATB
voci miste (It.)
voix mixtes (Fr.)
gemischte Stimmen (Gr.)
voces mixto (Sp.)

vs. equal voices

ungarischer Volktanz (G.)
*czardas, csardas
Hungarian dance
danza ungharesa (It.)
danse Hongroise (Fr.)
danza hungara (Sp.)

unichord
*monochord
unichordum (Lat.)
*tromba marina

unified organ
*extention organ
unit organ
unit orchestra
duplexing
cinema organ
theatre organ
organo da teatro (It.)

orgue de cinéma (Fr.)
Kinoorgel (G.)
órgano de cine (Sp.)

unione (It.)
coupler (org.)
piston
combination stop
copula (Lat.)
accoppiamento (It.)
accouplement (Fr.)
Koppel, Koppelung (G.)
acoplamiento (Sp.)

unison
monophonic
all perform same melody
unisonus (Lat.)
unisono (It., Sp.)
a due (It.)
unisson (Fr.)
Einklang (G.)

vs. in harmony

2. *prime (interval)

unstable
dissonant
unresolved
active (tonr, chord)

Unterdominante (G.)
subdominant
fourth degree
fa
sottodominante (It.)
sous-dominante (Fr.)
Subdominante (G.)
subdominante (Sp.)

Unterhaltung (G.)
*entertainment
show
spectacle
revue

442

variety show
floor show
musical
musicale
follies
minstrel show
light opera
masque
spettacolo (It.)
divertissement (Fr.)
entremés (Sp.)

Unterhaltungsmusik (G.)
light music
*backround music
dinner music
salon music
café music
cocktail music
easy listening
elevator music
dentist music
incidental music
Muzak
musica leggera (It.)
musique légère (Fr.)
leichte Musik (G.)
música ligera (Sp.)

Untermediante (G.)
submediant
6th degree
superdominant
la
sopraddominante (It.)
sus-dominante (Fr.)
sous-médiante (Fr.)
superdominante (Sp.)

Untersatz (G.)
sub-bass (org.)
pedal stop (16ft.)
bourdon
subbasso (It.)
soubasse, sous-basse (Fr.)
bajo mayor (Sp.)

Unterwerk (G.)
*choir division/manual (org.)
chair organ
positive organ
organo di coro (It.)
positif (Fr.)
Rückpositiv (G.)
órgano de coro (Sp.)

up-tempo
fast
quick tempo
*allegro (It.)

upbeat (n.)
pick-up
last beat of the measure
weak beat
off-beat
unaccented beat
anacrusis (Lat.)
arsis (Gr.)
anticipazione (It.)
anacrusi (It.)
levata (It.)
anacrouse (Fr.)
élévation (Fr.)
élan (Fr.)
levé (Fr.)
Auftakt (G.)
Anakrusis (G.)
Aufschlag (G.)
Hebung (G.)
anacrusa (Sp.)

upbow
with the point of the bow
arcata in su (It.)
arco in su (It.)
a punta d'arco/dell'arco (It.)
poussé (Fr.)
de la pointe (Fr.)
avec le pointe de l'archet (Fr.)
Aufstrich, Anstrich (G.)
Hinaufstrich (G.)
Gestossen (G.)

mit der Spitze (G.)
an der Bogenspitze (G.)
arcada hacia arriba (Sp.)
empujado (Sp.)
con la punta (Sp.)
arco por arriba (Sp.)
a la punta del arco (Sp.)

vs. downbow

upper partial
partial
*overtone
harmonic
aliquot tone

upright bass
*bass
doublebass
contrabass
string bass
bass viol
bass fiddle
bull fiddle
acoustic bass
contrabasso (It.)
contrebasse (Fr.)
Kontrabass (G.)
contrabajo (Sp.)

upright harpsichord
clavicytherium (Lat.)
cembalo verticale (It.)
claviciterio (It.)
clavecin vertical (Fr.)
Klavizitherium (G.)
claveciterio (Sp.)

upright piano
cabinet piano
spinet
pianette
console piano
vertical piano
studio piano
couched harp

giraffe piano
upright grand
pianoforte verticale (It.)
piano droit (Fr.)
piano à tavolins (Fr.)
Klavier (G.)
piano vertical (Sp.)

vs. grand piano

Urtext (G.)
original edition
authentic edition
first edition
autograph score

use
rite
*liturgy
ritual
ceremony

ut (Lat.)
do
first degree
tonic note
root
finalis (Lat.)

ut supra (Lat.)
as above
as before

V

valeur (Fr.)
rhythmic value
time value
length of a note/rest
duration
valor (Lat., Sp.)
valore (It.)
Wert (G.)
Notenwert (G.)

valse (Fr.)
*waltz
valser (It.)
Walzer (G.)
vals (Sp.)

valve
piston (E., Fr.)
pistone (It.)
valvola (It.)
Ventil (G.)
Pumpventil (G.)
Perinetventil (G.)
pistón (Sp.)

vamp
introduction
lead-in
cue
pick-up
vamp till ready

variant
alternate version
variation
alia modo (Lat.)

variations (on a theme)
theme and variations

partita
variazione (It.)
Variation (G.)
Veränderung (G.)
variación (Sp.)
folia
chaconne
passacaglia
change-ringing
diferencia (Sp. 16c.)
glosa (Sp. 16c.)
dump, dompe
heterophony

variety show
talent show
revue
vaudeville
minstrel show
follies
musical
cabaret
masque
entertainment
extravaganza
spectacle

varsovienne (Fr.)
Polish dance in triple time
mazurka
waltz
Ländler (G.)
Tyrolienne (Fr.)
varsoviana (It.)

Vaterunser (G.)
Lord's Prayer
Our Father
paternoster
Pater Noster (Lat.)
Pasternoster (It.)
Notre Père (Fr.)
Padre Nuestro (Sp.)

vaudeville (Fr., E.)
variety show

revue
*musical comedy
minstrel show
burlesque
burletta (It.)
follies

2. chanson
secular song
vau de ville (Fr.)
voix de ville (Fr.)

veloce (It.)
*fast
swift
rapid
allegro (It.)
presto (It.)
vite (Fr.)
schnell (G.)
veloz (Sp.)

vs. lento

Vêpres (Fr.)
Vespers
Evening Prayer
Evensong
canonical hour
day hour
*Divine Office
Vespro (It.)
Abendandacht (G.)
Visperas (Sp.)

Veränderung der Knaben-stistimme (G.)
voice-change
*changing voice
breaking of the voice
cambiata
mutazione della voce (It.)
mue de la voix (Fr.)
Stimmbruch (G.)
mudanza de la voz (Sp.)

verdeckte Quinten (G.)
parallel fifths
hidden fifths
covered fifths
consecutive fifths
quinte parallele (It.)
quinte seguito (It.)
succession de quintes (Fr.)
quintes parallèles (Fr.)
quintas paraleles (Sp.)

Vergrüsserung (G.)
augmentation (E., Fr.)
aumentazione (It.)
Augmentation (G.)
aumento, aumentación (Sp.)

vs. Diminutuin (G.)
Verkleinerung (G.)

verhallend (G.)
morendo (It.)
*decrescendo (It.)
fading out
die away
diminuendo (It.)
en perdant le son (Fr.)
sterbend (G.)
expirando (Sp.)

verismo (It., Sp.)
realism in 19c. opera
passion
opera
music drama
vérisme (Fr.)
Verismus (G.)

Verkehrung (G.)
*inversion (E., Fr.)
inversione (It.)
renversement (Fr.)
Umkehring (G.)
inversión (Sp.)

verkleinert (G.)

diminished (interval, chord)
diminuto (It.)
diminué (Fr.)
vermindert (G.)
diminuido (Sp.)

verrillon (Fr.)
*glass harmonica
musical glasses
glass harp
*hurdy-gurdy
armonica a vetro (It.)
Glasspiel (G.)
Glasharfe (G.)
copólogo (Sp.)

vers (Fr., Prov.)
song (12c.)
canso, canzo (Prov.)
*Troubadour song
bar (song)

vers mesuré (Fr. 16c.)
chanson mesurée (Fr.)
musique mesurée (Fr.)
polymetric
homophonic
free meter
irregular barring
uneven barring

Verschiebung (G.)
*soft pedal (piano)
left pedal
damper pedal
una corda (It.)
pédale gauche (Fr.)
linke Pedal (G.)
eine Saite (G.)
pedal sordina/suave (Sp.)

vs.Tonhaltungspedal (G.)

verse
stanza
strophe

couplet
distich
versus (Lat.)
verso (It., Sp.)
vers (Fr.)
Vers (G.)
copla (Sp.)

2. line of poetry/text

3. **versicle (liturgy)**
short prayer statement
short verse
versiculus (Lat.)
versetto, versicolo (It.)
versiculet (Fr.)
Versikel (G.)
versículo (Sp.)

2. introduction of a pop song
section before the chorus
solo section

verset (Fr.)
organ verse
organ hymn
alternatim (Lat.)
prelude
voluntary
interlude
verso, versetto (It.)
Versett, Versetl (G.)
versillo (Sp.)

verse anthem
anthem with solo sections
motet in English
cantata

vs. full anthem

Versetzen (G.)
*transpose
change key
transportare (It.)
transposer (Fr.)

446

transposieren (G.)
transportar (Sp.)

Versetzungszeichen (G.)
  *accidental sign
  chromatic sign
  accidente (It., Sp.)
  alterazione (It.)
  accident (Fr.)
  altération (Fr.)
  Vorzeichen (G.)
  alteración (Sp.)

version
  edition
  *arrangement
  rendition
  setting
  Fassung (G.)

verstimmt (G.)
  out of tune
  off pitch
  off-key
  tone-deaf
  monotone
  detuned
  stonare (It.)
  détonner (Fr.)
  detonieren (G.)
  desafinar (Sp.)

vertical aspect/dimension
  harmony
  chordal structure

vs. horizontal (melody)

vertical flute
  *recorder
  English flute
  duct flute
  fipple flute
  beak flute
  flauto a becco (It.)
  flauto diritto (It.)

flûte à bec (Fr.)
Blockflöte (G.)
flauta de pico (Sp.)
flauta dulce (Sp.)

vs. transverse flute

vertical harpsichord
  clavicytherium
  upright harpsichord

vertical piano
  *upright piano
  studio piano
  cottage piano
  spinet
  console piano
  upright grand
  giraffe piano
  pianoforte verticale (It.)
  piano droit (Fr.)
  Klavier (G.)
  piano vertical (Sp.)

vs. grand piano

verwandte Tonart (G.)
  relative key
  modo somigliante (It.)
  tono relativo (It., Sp.)
  mode relatif (Fr.)
  Paralleltonart (G.)
  Relativtonart (G.)
  clave paralela (Sp.)

vs. tonic major/minor
  parallel key

very
  much
  rather
  molto (It.)
  assai (It.)
  très (Fr.)
  beaucoup (Fr.)
  viel (G.)

mucho (Sp.)

Verzierung (G.)
  *ornament
  grace note
  embellishment
  adornamento (It.)
  abbellimento (It.)
  ornement (Fr.)
  agrément (Fr.)
  adorno (Sp.)

Vesperale (Lat.)
  *anthology
  collection of Vesper chants
  Vesperal

Vespers
  canonical hour
  prayer service
  *Divine Office
  Evensong
  Vesperae (Lat.)
  vespro (It.)
  vêpres (Fr.)
  Abendandacht (G.)
  visperas (Sp.)

vibraphone
  vibraharp
  vibes
  xylophone
  marimba

vibration
  sound, sound wave
  oscillation
  frequency
  cycle
  hertz
  acoustics
  musical tone
  vibrazione (It.)
  Schwingung (G.)
  vibración (Sp.)

vibrato
tremolo
wobble
flutter
vibré (Fr.)
Bebung (G.)
virado (Sp.)

victrola
*phonograph
turntable
gramophone
record player
record changer
talking machine
giradischi (It.)
tourne-disques (Fr.)
Plattenspieler (G.)
tocadiscos (Sp.)

vide, vi --- de (Lat.)
a *cut
deletion
abridgement
inciso (It.)
coupure (Fr.)
Schnitt (G.)
Einschnitt (G.)
corte (Sp.)

vido (Sp.)
sound-hole
F-hole
effe (It.)
ouïle (Fr.)
F-Loch (G.)
efe (Sp.)

vielle, vièle (Fr. 13-15c.)
fiddle, fidel
violin
viella (It.)
violon rustique (Fr.)
Fiedel (G.)
fidula (Sp.)
violin rústico (Sp.)

2. *hurdy-gurdy
viola da orbo (It.)
vielle à roue (Fr.)
viola de rueda (Sp.)

vielle organisée (Fr.)
hurdy-gurdy with organ
pipes
organized hurdy-gurdy
lira organizzata (It.)
Orgelleier (G.)

vielstimmig (G.)
polyphonic
multi-voiced
a più voci (It.)
à plusiers voix (Fr.)
a muchas voces (Sp.)
a varias voces (Sp.)

vs. einstimmig (G.)

vierhändig (G.)
four-handed (piano)
a quattro mani (It.)
à quatre mains (Fr.)
a cuatro manos (Sp.)

Viertel(note) (G.)
quarter note
crotchet
nera (It.)
semiminima (It.)
quarto (It.)
noire (Fr.)
schwarze Note (G.)
negra (Sp.)
semínima (Sp.)

Viertelpause (G.)
quarter rest
crotchet rest
pausa di semiminima (It.)
soupir (Fr.)
silencio de negra/semínima
(Sp.)

pausa de negra/semínima (Sp.)

Viertelton (G.)
quarter-tone
quarto di tono (It.)
quart de ton (Fr.)
cuarto de tono (Sp.)

Vierundsechzigstelnote (G.)
64th-note
hemidemisemiquaver
semibiscroma (It.)
sessantaquattresimo (It.)
quadruple-croche (Fr.)
semifusa (Sp.)

Vierundsechzigstelpause (G.)
64th rest
hemidemisemiquaver rest
pausa di semibiscroma (It.)
seizième de soupir (Fr.)
silencio de semifusa (Sp.)
pausa de semifusa (Sp.)

vihuela (Sp.)
guitar
Spanish guitar
lute
viol

villancico (Sp.)
song, part-song
madrigal
*Christmas carol/motet
natalizio (It.)
Quempas (G.)
chant de noël (Fr.)
zéjel (Sp.)
cantata

villanella (It.)
part-song
*madrigal
glee
canzona, canzonetta (It.)
frottola

villanesca (It.)
villotta (It.)

vinata, vinetto (It.)
*drinking song
tavern song
dithyramb
*bacchanal
brindisi (It.)
chanson à boire (Fr.)
Trinklied (G.)
canción baquica (Sp.)

viol, viola, violina (org.)
labial string stop
gamba (It.)
viole d'orchestre (Fr.)

viol (family)
consort viol
division viol
viola da gamba (It.)
viola da braccio (It.)
viola d'amore (It.)
viola bastarda (It.)
viola pomposa (It.)
viole (Fr.)
dessus de viole (Fr.)
taille de viole (Fr.)
basse de viole (Fr.)
pardessus de viole (Fr.)
contre-basse de viole (Fr.)
Gambe (G.)
viola de gamba (Sp.)

viola (E., It., Sp.)
alto (Fr.)
Bratsche (G.)
Viola, -e (G.)

viola clef
*C-clef
alto clef
chiave di do (It.)
clef d'ut/d'alto (Fr.)
C-Schlüssel (G.)

clave de viola (Sp.)
llave de do (Sp.)

viola da orbo (It.)
*hurdy-gurdy
viola de rueda (Sp.)

viole d'amour (Fr.)
violet, English violet
hardanger fiddle
viola d'amore (It.)
viola di bordone (It.)
viola di fagotto (It.)
Liebesgeige (G.)
Baryton (G.)

violin
devil's box
fiddle
violino (It.)
violetta (It.)
violon (Fr.)
Geige (G.)
violín (Sp.)
rebec
*kit

violin clef
*G-clef
soprano clef
treble clef
chiave di sol (It.)
clef de sol (Fr.)
G-Schlüssel (G.)
clave de sol (Sp.)
clave aguda (Sp.)

violin maker
luthier (Fr.)
liutaio (It.)
violinaio (It.)
Geigenbauer (G.)
Saiteninstrumentenmacher (G.)
violero (Sp.)

violinette

small violin
*kit
violino piccolo (It.)
Quartgeige (G.)
Terzgeige (G.)

violinist
fiddler
violinista (It., Sp.)
violoniste (Fr.)
Geiger, Geigerin (G.)

violino primo (It.)
first violin(ist)
concertmaster
principal violin
violino principale (It.)
chef d'attaque (Fr.)
Konzertmeister (G.)
Primgeiger (G.)
erste Geige (G.)

violón (Sp.)
*bass viol
double-bass viol

violoncello (It., E.)
'cello
bass violin
viola da gamba
violoncino (It.)
violoncelle (Fr.)
Violcell (G.)
violoncelo (Sp.)

violonar (Fr.)
*bass
double-bass
violone (It.)
violonaro (It.)
octobasse (Fr.)

virelai (Fr.)
chanson balladée (Fr.)
forme fixe (Fr.)
round dance

449

ballata (It.)
cantigas (Sp.)
Troubadour song

virginal(s)
*harpsichord
spinet
clavichord
clavecin (Fr.)
virginale (It., Fr.)
spinetta, spinettina (It.)
épinette (Fr.)
Virginal (G.)
Instrument (G.)
virginal (Sp.)

Virginia reel
duple dance
reel
*contredance
square dance

virgule (Fr.)
comma
breath mark
virgula (It.)
signo di respirazione (It.)
signe de respiration (Fr.)
Atemzeichen (G.)
Komma (G.)
coma (Sp.)

virtuoso, virtuosity
bravura (It.)
florid
difficult playing
cadenza (It.)

visigothic chant
Mozarabic chant
Grgorian chant
plainsong

vite, vitement (Fr.)
*fast
allegro (It.)

presto (It.)
schnell (G.)

vs. lent, lentement (Fr.)

vivace (It.)
lively
animated
*animato (It.)

vocal music
sung music
song
choral music
solo music
operatic music
art song
folk song

vs. instrumental music

vocal (n.)
pop song
tune
the sung part

vocal cords
larynx
voice box
pipes
vocal folds
vocal bands
corde vocali (It.)
cordes vocales (Fr.)
Stimmbänden (G.)
cuerdas vocales (Sp.)

vocal ensemble
*chamber choir/chorus
Kammerchor (G.)

vocal score
piano-vocal score
reduction
abridgement
condensed score

vs. full score

vocalise (n.)
excercize (vocal)
etude
warm-up
vocalizzi (It.)
vocalises (Fr.)
Vokalise (G.)
vocalización (Sp.)

vocalize (vb.)
warm up
practice singing
solfege
vocalizzare (It.)
vocaliser (Fr.)
vokalisieren (G.)
vocalizar (Sp.)

vocalist
singer
songster, songstress
crooner
artiste
folksinger
troubadour
minstrel
bard
balladeer
vocal artist
prima donna (It.)
diva (It.)
cantatrice (It.)
cantante (It., Sp.)
chanteuse (Fr.)
Sänger (G.)

voce (It.)
voice, vocal part
instrumental part
vox (Lat.)
parte (It., Sp.)
voix (Fr.)
partie (Fr.)
Stimme (G.)

voz (Sp.)

voce di petto (It.)
chest voice
full voice
voce piena (It.)
voix de poitrine (Fr.)
voix de gorge (Fr.)
Bruststimme (G.)
voz de pecho (Sp.)

voce di testa (It.)
head voice
high voice
falsetto
voix de tête (Fr.)
Kopfstimme (G.)
voz de cabeza (Sp.)

voce intermedia (It.)
inner voice/part
meane, mene
medius (Lat.)
voix intermédaire (Fr.)
voix moyenne (Fr.)
Mittelstimmen (G.)
Innenstimme (G.)
voz interior/intermedia (Sp.)
parte interior/intermedia (Sp.)

vs. parte estrema (It.)

voci miste (It.)
mixed voices
S.A.T.B.
unequal voices
voces inaequalis (Lat.)
voix mixtes (Fr.)
gemischte Stimmen (G.)
voces mixtas (Sp.)

voci pari (It.)
equal voices
S.S.A., T.T.B., etc.
voces aequales (Lat.)
voci equali (It.)

voix égales (Fr.)
gleiche Stimmen (G.)
voces iguales (Sp.)

Vogelorgel (G.)
bird organ
*barrel organ
serinetta (It.)
serinette (Fr., E., Sp.)

voice (n.)
pipes
vox (Lat.)
voce (It.)
voix (Fr.)
Stimme (G.)
voz (Sp.)

voice (vb.)
tune (org.)
regulate
adjust
scale
revoice
intonare (It.)
entonner (Fr.)
tönen (G.)
entonar (Sp.)

voice-crossing
incrosciemento (It.)
croisement (Fr.)
Kreuzung (G.)
cruzamiento (Sp.)

voice-change
changing voice
cambiata
alto-tenor
adolescence
mutazione della voce (It.)
mue de la voix (Fr.)
Veränderung der
Knabenstimme (G.)
Stimmbruch (G.)
mudanza de la voz (Sp.)

voice-leading
part-leading
movimento di voci (It.)
condotta delle voci/parti
conduite des voix (Fr.)
enchaînement (Fr.)
Stimmführung (G.)
conducción de las voces (Sp.)
dirigiendo la voz (Sp.)

voix (Fr.)
*voice

voix céleste (Fr.)
soft organ stop
labial reed stop
detuned stop
vox angelica (Lat.)
vox coelestis (Lat.)
vox humana (Lat.)
voce celeste (It.)
voix de céleste (Fr.)
Engelstimme (G.)
voz celeste (Sp.)

voix de fausset (Fr.)
falsetto (It.)
head voice
high voice/register
countertenor

volata (It.)
vocal run
scale passage
trill
passaggio (It.)
volatine (Fr.)
Volate (G.)

Volkslied (G.)
folk song
ethnic folk-song
national song
traditional song
canzone populare (It.)
chanson folklorique (Fr.)

chanson populaire (Fr.)
Volksweise (G.)
canto folklorico (Sp.)
canto popular (Sp.)

volles Werk (G.)
*full organ
great organ
great chorus
tutti (It.)
organo pieno (It.)
grand choeur/orgue (Fr.)
grand jeu (Fr.)
Hauptwerk (G.)
gran juego (Sp.)

vollkommene Kadenz (G.)
authentic cadence
full cadence
full close
*perfect cadence
cadenza perfetta (It.)
cadence parfaite (Fr.)
cadencia perfecta (Sp.)

volta (It.)
dance in 6/8 time (17c.)
galliard (Fr.)

2. *ballata (14c.)
piedi (It.)
ripresa (It.)

3. time (occasion)
repeat
fois (Fr.)
Mal (G.)
vez (Sp.)

volti subito (It.)
turn immediately/quickly
V.S.
tournez aussitôt (Fr.)
sofort umblättern (G.)
vuelve a prisa (Sp.)

volume (E., Fr., It.)
loudness
gain
amplitude (E., Fr.)
bel, decibel
ampiezza (It.)
Klangfülle (G.)
Tonstärke (G.)
amplitud (Sp.)

voluntary
prelude (org.)
postlude
interlude
praeludium (Lat.)
preludio (Lat., It., Sp.)
prélude (Fr.)
Vorspiel (G.)

vom Anfang (G.)
from the beginning
from the top
repeat section A
reprise
recapitulation
da capo (It.)
D.C.
ab initio (Lat.)
au début (Fr.)
von Vorn (G.)
desde el principio (Sp.)

vom Blatt (G.)
at (first) sight
a prima vista (It.)
à (premier) vue (Fr.)
a primera vista (Sp.)

vom Zeichen (G.)
go back to the sign
*dal segno (It.)
D. S.
dal segno al fine (It.)
du signe à la fin (Fr.)
vom Zeichen bis zu Schluss
(G.)

desde el signo hasta el fin (Sp.

Vorgeiger (G.)
first violin
*concertmaster
assistant conductor
first chair
principal violin
violino primo (It.)
chef d'attaque (Fr.)
Konzertmeister (G.)
concertino (Sp.)

Vorhalt (G.)
suspension
delayed cadential note
*appoggiatura (It.)
sospensione (It.)
retard (Fr.)
Verzögerung (G.)
retardo (Sp.)

Vorhang (G.)
curtain (theat.)
drop
traveler
scrim
sipario (It.)
rideau (Fr.)
telón (Sp.)

Vorsänger (G.)
*cantor
precentor
chanter
leader of song (chant)
accentor
cantore (It.)
chantre (Fr.)
Kantor (G.)
primicerio (It., Sp.)

Vorschlag (G.)
non-harmonic tone
accented dissonance
*appoggiatura (It.)

appogiature (Fr.)
apoyatura (Sp.)

Vorspiel (G.)
  prelude
  voluntary
  Nachspiel (G.)
  postlude
  overture

2. audition (E., Fr.)
  tryout
  hearing
  screen test
  audizione (It.)
  audición (Sp.)

Vortrag (G.)
  performance
  rendition
  interpretation (E., Fr.)
  delivery
  execution
  interpretazione (It.)
  interpretación (Sp.)

Vortragszeichen (G.)
  expression marks
  segno di espressione (It.)
  signe d'expression (Fr.)
  signo de expresión (Sp.)

Vorzeichen (G.)
  accidental sign
  chromatic sign
  accidente (It.)
  alterazione (It.)
  accident (Fr.)
  altération (Fr.)
  Versetzsungszeichen (G.)
  accidente (Sp.)
  alteración (Sp.)

Vorzeichnung (G.)
  key and time signatures

vox, voces (Lat.)
  pitch
  musical sound
  note

2. voice
  part

vox angelica (Lat.)
  labial reed stop (org.)
  detuned
vox coelestis (Lat.)
vox humana (Lat.)
  *voix céleste (Fr.)

vox organalis (Lat.)
  descant
  organum
  polyphony
  harmony part
  duplum (Lat.)
  discantus (Lat.)
  motetus (Lat.)

vox principalis (Lat.)
  chant part
  organum
  polyphony
  tenor
  cantus firmus (Lat.)

voz (Sp.)
  voice
  voce (It.)
  voix (Fr.)
  Stimme (G.)

voz de cabeza (Sp.)
  head voice
  high voice/range
  falsetto
  *voix de tête (Fr.)

voz de pecho (Sp.)
  chest voice
  full voice

low voice
  *voix de poitrine (Fr.)

voz extrema (Sp.)
  outer voice(s)
  parte estrema (It.)
  partie extrême (Fr.)
  Aussenstimmen (G.)

vs. voz intermediaria (Sp.)

vuoto (It.)
  *grand pause
  G. P.
  general pause
  measure rest
  empty bar/measure
  misura vuota (It.)
  silence générale (Fr.)
  Generalpause (G.)
  cesura (It., Sp.)

W

wa-wa, wah-wah
mute (brass instr.)
Harmon mute
plunger mute
swing
jazz

wachsend (G.)
growing
getting louder
*crescendo (It.)

Wächterlied (G.)
morning song
dawn song
*alba (Prov.)
albata (It.)
aube, aubade (Fr.)
Tagelied (G.)
albada (Sp.)

wait(s)
watchmen (15-16c.)
minstrel
scop
Stadtmusikanten (G.)

Waldhorn (G.)
*horn
natural horn
French horn
hunting horn
corno da caccia (It.)
corno naturale (It.)
cor naturel (Fr.)
cor d'harmonie (Fr.)
cor de chasse (Fr.)
Jagdhorn (G.)
Naturhorn (G.)

cuerno de caza (Sp.)
trompa natural (Sp.)

2. organ reed stop
horn stop

walk-on
extra
*super
supernumerary
bit part
minor role
Statist (G.)

walking bass
scale-wise bass line
jazz bass line
broken octaves
boogie-woogie
murky (18c.)
murky bass

waltz
dance in ¾ time
three-step
mazurka
Varsovienne (Fr.)
Tyrolienne (Fr.)
Ländler (G.)
valzer (It.)
valzer a tre passi (It.)
trois-temps (Fr.)
valse (Fr.)
Dreitritt (G.)
Walzer (G.)
vals (Sp.)

Walze (G.)
*crescendo pedal (org.)
swell pedal
crescendo rotativo (It.)
rouleau crescendo (Fr.)
Registerwalze (G.)
rodillo del crescendo (Sp.)

2. *Alberti-bass figure

2. 3. piano-player roll
cilindro (It.)
rouleau (Fr.)
cylindre (Fr.)
rollo (Sp.)
cilindro (Sp.)

warble
sing
croon
trill
intone

washboard
jug band
scraper
skiffleboard
tavola da lavare (It.)
planche à laver (Fr.)
Waschbrett (G.)
tabla de lavar (Sp.)
güiro (Sp.)

washtub bass
string bass
*bass
jug band
upright bass
stand-up bass
string bass
bass fiddle
bull fiddle

Wasserorgel (G.)
hydraulis
hydraulic organ
water organ
hydraulos (Gr.)
organum hydraulicum (Lat.)
organo idraulico (It.)
orgue hydraulique (Fr.)
órgano hidráulico (Sp.)

weak beat
second and last beat of a measure
feminine ending

Wechseldominante (G.)
dominant of the dominant
five of five
secondary dominant
dominante secondaria (It.)
dominante de passage (Fr.)
Zwischendominante (G.)
dominante de paseje/paso (Sp.)

Wechselgesang (G.)
*antiphonal singing
responsive singing
call and response
antiphonal choirs
double chorus

Wechselnote (G.)
*cambiata (It.)
escape note
non-harmonic tone
ornament
nota cambiata (It.)
note de rechange (Fr.)
nota cambiada (Sp.)

Wecksignal
*reveille
wake-up call
bugle call
diana (It., Sp.)
diane (Fr.)
Morgensignal (G.)
Weckdienst (G.)
toque de alborada (Sp.)

wedding march
bridal march
bridal chorus
marcia nuziale (It.)
marche nuptiale (Fr.)

Hochzeitsmarsch (G.)
marcha nupcial (Sp.)

wedding song
nuptual song
bridal song
epithalamy
epithalamium (Lat., E.)
epithalamion (Gr.)
epitalamio (It., Sp.)
canto nuziale (It.)
épithalame (Fr.)
chanson de noce (Fr.)
Brautlied (G.)
canto nupcial (Sp.)

Weinachtslied (G.)
Christmas carol/song
canzona di Natale (It.)
natalizio (It.)
chant de noël (Fr.)
cantique de noël (Fr.)
Quempas (G.)
villancico (Sp.)
zéjel (Sp.)
cántico de Navidad (Sp.)
kolenda, koloda (Pol.)

Weise (G.)
tune
*song
melody
ditty
cantus, cantio (Lat.)
canto (It.)
chant, chanson (Fr.)
Gesang (G.)
Lied (G.)
canción (Sp.)

well-tempered (keyboard instr.)
equal temperament
tempered tuning
Wohltemperirtes (Clavier) (G.)

vs. just intonation
mean-tone tuning

weltliche Musik(G.)
secular music
non-religious music
profane music
musica profana (It.)
musique profane (Fr.)
música profane (Sp.)

vs. geistliche Musik (G.)

Werk, Werck (G.)
organ division
partial organ
*manual, pedal

Wert (G.)
time value
duration
length of a note/rest
valor (Lat., Sp.)
valeur (Fr.)
valore (It.)
Notenwert (G.)

western music
occidental music

vs. oriental music
Eastern music

Wettbewerb (G.)
competition
contest
concorso (It.)
concours (Fr.)
concurso (Sp.)
puy (Fr. medieval)

Wetterharfe (G.)
Aeolian harp
wind harp
arpa eolia (It., Sp.)
harpe éoline (Fr.)

Windharfe (G.)
Äolsharfe (G.)
Geisterharfe (G.)

whip (percussion)
slapstick
horsewhip
frusta (It.)
fouet (Fr.)
Peitche (G.)
zurriaga (Sp.)
tralla (Sp.)
látigo (Sp.)

whiskey tenor
high tenor
Irish tenor
lyric tenor
countertenor
falsetto

whistle (vb.)
fischiare (It.)
siffler (Fr.)
pfeifen (G.)
silbar (Sp.)

whistle flute
fipple flute
flageolet
duct flute
penny whistle
fife
beaked flute
*recorder
tonette
flutophone
toy flute
flauto a becco (It.)
flûte à bec (Fr.)
Blockflöte (G.)
flauta de pico (Sp.)

Whit Sunday
Pentecost
Dominica Pentecostes (Lat.)

Pascha rosarum (Lat.)
Pentecoste (It.)
Pentecôte (Fr.)
Pfingsten (G.)
Pentecostés (Sp.)

white key(s) (keyboard)
diatonic keys
tasto bianco (It.)
touche blanche (Fr.)
Untertaste (G.)
weisse Taste (G.)
tecla blanca (Sp.)

vs. black keys (sharps/flats)

whittle and dub (old E.)
pipe and tabor
fife and drum
galoubet (Fr.)
Querpfeife-Trommel (G.)
Schwegel und Tamburin (G.)
fluviol y tambori(l) (Sp.)

whole consort
chest of viols, recorders, etc.
set of like instruments

vs. broken consort

whole note
semibreve (E., It.)
brevis (Lat.)
intero (It.)
ronde (Fr.)
carrée (Fr.)
Ganze, Ganzenote (G.)
redonda (Sp.)

whole rest
semibreve rest
pausa di semibreve (It.)
pause (Fr.)
ganze Pause (G.)
silencio de redonda (Sp.)
pausa de redonda (Sp.)

whole tone
major second
whole step
tone
seconda maggiore (It.)
seconde majeure (Fr.)
grosse Sekunde (G.)
segunda mayor (Sp.)

whole-tone scale
anhemitonic scale
pentatonic scale
scala esatonale (It.)
scala per toni interi (It.)
gamme par tons (Fr.)
gamme anhémitonique (Fr.)
Ganztonleiter (G.)
gama por tonos enteros (Sp.)
escala por tonos (Sp.)

wie oben (G.)
as above
repeat
come supra (It.)
comme plus haut (Fr.)
como arriba (Sp.)

wie vorher (G.)
as before
same
repeat
reprise
from the beginning
from the top
da capo (It.)
*come prima (It.)
simile (It.)
comme avant (Fr.)
como antes (Sp.)

Wiegenlied (G.)
cradle song
*lullaby
slumber song
by by
lullatio (Lat.)

nanna, ninna nanna (It.)
berceuse (Fr.)
Schlummerlied (G.)
nana (Sp.)

wind band
military band
brass band
*band
banda (It., Sp.)
orchestre fanfare (Fr.)
Blasorchester (G.)

wind chest (org.)
wind supply
air chamber
segreta (It.)
laye (Fr.)
Windkasten (G.)
camara de aire (Sp.)

wind instrument
horn (jazz)
brass and woods
strumento a fiato (It.)
instrument à vent (Fr.)
Blasinstrument (G.)
Windinstrument (G.)
instrumento de viento (Sp.)

wind machine
eolifono (It.)
machine à vent (Fr.)
éoliphone (Fr.)
Windmaschine (G.)
máquina de viento (Sp.)

Windharfe (G.)
Aeolian harp
*Wetterharfe

Wirbel (G.)
roll of a drum

2. drumstick
mallet

3. peg
tuning peg

Wirbeltrommel (G.)
*tenor drum
side drum
snare drum
military drum
cassa rullante (It.)
caisse roulante (Fr.)
Rolltrommel (G.)
redoblante (Sp.)

wire brushes (percussion)
brushes
steel brushes
spazzole (It.)
balais (de jazz) (Fr.)
Besen, Jazzbesen (G.)
Rute (G.)
escobillas (Sp.)

with abandon
free
unrestrained
con abbandono (It.)
avec abandon (Fr.)
abandoné (Fr.)
mit Hingabe (G.)
con abandono (Sp.)

with the point of the bow
*up-bow
a punta d'arco/dell'arco (It.)
à/de la pointe (Fr.)
mit der Spitze (G.)
a la punta del arco (Sp.)

vs. with the frog

with the wood (of the bow)
*col legno (It.)
avec le bois (Fr.)
mit dem Holz (G.)
mit der Bogenstange (G.)
con le madera (Sp.)

wobble (voice)
*tremolo
vibrato
shake
wide vibrato

wood block(s)
*Chinese wood blocks
Korean temple blocks
clog box
tap box
temple blocks
blochetto (It.)
cassa di legno (It.)
*caisse Chinoise (Fr.)
Holzblock (G.)
caja China (Sp.)

wood harmonica
xylophone
straw fiddle
marimba
vibraphone, vibraharp
gigelira (It.)
*claquebois (Fr.)
patouille (Fr.)
harmonica de bois (Fr.)
Strohfiedel (G.)
armonica de madera (Sp.)

woodwinds, woods
woodwind instruments
legni (It.)
bois (Fr.)
Holzbläser (G.)
maderas (Sp.)

word-painting
tone-painting
tone poem
symphonic poem
program symphony
descriptive music
program music
program chanson
eye music

vs. absolute music

words
   text
   lyric(s)
   libretto
   poem
   script
   testo (It.)
   paroles (Fr.)
   texte (Fr.)
   Text (G.)
   texto (Sp.)

work song
   sea shanty/chanty
   spiritual
   prison work song
   spinning song

world music
   pop music
   jazz
   rock
   hip-hop
   rap
   techno
   electronica
   reggae
   ska

wrest-pin
   tuning pin

wrong note
   bad note
   false note
   mistake
   nota falsa (It., Sp.)
   fausse note (Fr.)
   Misston (G.)
   falsche Note (G.)

Würfelspiel (G.)
   dice music
   chance music

aleatory music
indeterminacy
tone clusters
pitch aggregate

Würstfagott (G.)
   sausage bassoon
   *racket(t)
   cervellato (It.)
   cervelas (Fr.)

XYZ

xirimía (Sp.)
*shawm
oboe
cialamello (It.)
chalumeau (Fr.)
Shalmei (G.)
caramillo (Sp.)
chirimía (Sp.)

xota (Sp.)
jota (Sp.)
dance in triple time
Aragonaise (Fr.)
Aragonesa (Sp.)

xylophone (E., Fr.)
straw fiddle
wood harmonica
marimba
vibraharp, vibraphone
vibes
gigelira (It.)
organo di legno (It.)
sticcado pastorale (It.)
sticcato (It.)
xilofono (It.)
patouille (Fr.)
harmonica de bois (Fr.)
orgue de paille (Fr.)
échelettes (Fr.)
régale de bois (Fr.)
claquebois (Fr.)
Strohfiedel (G.)
Xylophon (G.)
xilófono (Sp.)
xilórgano (Sp.)
armonica de madera (Sp.)

yodel
folk song
voice-breaking
Jodel (G.)

yuletide song/carol
*Christmas song/carol
holiday song
nowell
natalizio (It.)
canzona di Natale (It.)
noël (Fr.)
chant/cantique de noël (Fr.)
Weinachtslied (G.)
Quempas (G.)
cántico de Navidad (Sp.)
villancico (Sp.)
zéjel (Sp.)

yunque (Sp.)
anvil
incudine (It.)
enclume (Fr.)
Amboss (G.)

zählen (G.)
count time
beat time
keep the beat
keep time
contare (It.)
compter (Fr.)
contar (Sp.)

Zählzeit (G.)
*beat
count
pulse
tactus (Lat.)
battuta (It.)
temps (Fr.)
Takt (G.)
tiempo (Sp.)
compás (Sp.)

zajal, zéjel (Sp.)

villancico (Sp.)
medieval song
Christmas carol/song
natalizia (It.)
cantiga (Sp.)
virelai (Fr.)
Weinachtslied (G.)

zampogna (It.)
*bagpipe
cornamusa (It., Sp.)
piva (It.)
musette (Fr.)
cornemuse (Fr.)
biniou (Fr.)
Dudey (G.)
Dudelsack (G.)
Sackpfeife (G.)
gaita (Sp.)
zampoña (Sp.)

zanfonía (Sp.)
*hurdy-gurdy
barrel organ
hand organ
ghironda (It.)
organetto (It.)
chifonie (Fr.)
orgue de Barbarie (Fr.)
Dreorgel (G.)
Leier, Leierkastel (G.)
cifonía (Sp.)
organillo (Sp.)

zarabanda (Sp.)
sarabande (E., Fr.)
suite movement in ¾
sarabanda (It.)

zarzuela (Sp.)
operetta
musical
seynète (Fr.)
Singspiel (G.)
masque
tonadilla (Sp.)

sainete (Sp.)

Zäsur (G.)
caesura
*breath mark
general pause
railroad tracks
break
cesura (It., Sp.)
césure (Fr.)
*Generalpause (G.)

zeitgenössische Musik (G.)
*contemporary music
modern music
20th-century music
new music
avant-garde (Fr.)
new-age music
new wave music

Zeitmass (G.)
tempo
time
speed
pace
movement
temps (Fr.)
mouvement (Fr.)
tiempo (Sp.)

Zeitmesser (G.)
metronome
mechanical beat, tempo
chronometer
metronomo (It., Sp.)
métronome (Fr.)
Metronom (G.)
Taktmesser (G.)

zéjel (Sp.)
villancico (Sp.)
*zajal

Zeremonie, -iell (G.)
ceremony

rite, ritual
religious service
*liturgy
rubrics
ordo (Lat.)
cerimonia (It.)
cérémonie (Fr.)
ceremonia (Sp.)

zibaldone (It.)
quodlibet
*medley
potpourri
olio
salmagundi, -y
musical miscellany
pasticcio (It.)
mélange (Fr.)
salmi(s) (Fr.)
salmigondis (Fr.)
Querschnitt (G.)
mezcla (Sp.)

ziehharmonika (G.)
*accordion
concertina
squeezebox
hand harmonica
fisarmonica (It.)
soufflet (Fr.)
Konzertina (G.)
fuelle (Sp.)
bandoneón (Sp.)

ziemlich (G.)
very
rather
*assai (It.)
molto (It.)
très (Fr.)
sehr (G.)
mucho (Sp.)

Zierrat, Ziernoten (G.)
ornaments
grace notes

embellishment
abbellimenti (It.)
petites-notes (Fr.)
ornements (Fr.)
Verzierung (G.)
adorno (Sp.)

Zigeunerlied (G.)
Gypsy song
zingana (It.)
zingaresca (It.)
canzone gitana (It.)
chant tzigane (Fr.)
chant gitan (Fr.)
canto gitano (Sp.)
canción gitana/tzigana (Sp.)

zilafone, zilofone (It.)
xylophone
*claquebois (Fr.)

zimbalon (It.)
cimbalon, cimbalom
*dulcimer
zither
cembalo ungherese (It.)
cymbalum (Fr.)
Hackbrett (G.)
cimbalón (Sp.)
zimbalón (Sp.)

Zimbel (G.)
high *mixture (org.)
compound stop
Scharff (G.)

2. antique cymbals
finger cymbals
*crotales (Fr.)

Zimbelstern (G.)
*bells (org.)
tinkling bells
Cymbelstern (G.)
Glockenstern (G.)
Zimbelrad (G.)

zinck
- cornett
- cornetto (It.)
- cornet (Fr.)
- **Zink (G.)**

zither
- *dulcimer
- psaltery
- cimbalom
- cetra da tavolo (It.)
- **zittera (It.)**
- cithare (Fr.)
- bûche (Fr.)
- Schlagzither (G.)
- **Zither (G.)**
- Hummel, Humle (G.)
- citara (Sp.)

zolfa (It.)
- sol-fa
- *solmization

zu zweit (G)
- in 2
- à 2
- a due (It.)

zufolo (It.)
- whistle flute
- duct flute
- flageolet
- ocarina
- *recorder
- shepherd's pipe

Zug (G.)
- slide (of a trombone)
- coulisse (Fr.)

2. stop (org.)
- draw knob
- draw stop
- tirante (It., Sp.)
- tirant (Fr.)
- registre (Fr.)

registro (Sp.)

Zugabe (G.)
- encore
- again, more
- repeat
- ancore (It.)
- bis (Lat., Fr., G.)
- altra volta (It.)
- noch einmal (G.)
- otra vez (Sp.)

Zunehmend (G.)
- crescendo (It.)
- getting louder
- en augmentant (Fr.)
- anschwellen (G.)
- **Zunahme (G.)**
- wachsend (G.)
- creciendo (Sp.)

zupfen (G.)
- to pluck
- strumm
- pick
- pizzicare (It.)
- pincer (Fr.)
- puntear (Sp.)

Zupfgeige (G.)
- *guitar
- chitarra (It.)
- guitare (Fr.)
- Gitarre (G.)
- guitarra (Sp.)

zurriaga (Sp.)
- whip
- slapstick
- horsewhip
- frusta (It.)
- fouet (Fr.)
- Pritche, Peitsche (G.)
- tralla (Sp.)
- látigo (Sp.)

zurückhaltend (G.)
- slowing down
- retarding
- *ritardando (It.)
- rallentando (It.)
- allargando (It.)
- en retardant (Fr.)
- retardando (Sp.)

Zusammenschlag (G.)
- ornament
- grace note
- *mordent
- neighbor note
- *acciaccatura (It.)
- battement (Fr.)
- Pralltriller (G.)
- quiebro (Sp.)

Zweitaktpause (G.)
- 2-measure rest
- breve rest
- pausa di breve (It.)
- demi-bâton (Fr.)
- pause de brève (Fr.)
- silence de brève (Fr.)
- Doppeltaktpause (G.)
- Zweiganzepause (G.)
- silencio de breve (Sp.)
- pausa de breve (Sp.)

Zweiunddreissigstelnote (G.)
- 32nd-note
- demisemiquaver
- biscroma (It.)
- trentaduesimo (It.)
- triple-croche (Fr.)
- fusa (Sp.)

Zweiunddreissigstelpause (G.)
- 32nd-rest
- demisemiquaver rest
- pausa di biscroma (It.)
- huitième de soupir (Fr.)
- silencio de fusa (Sp.)
- pausa de fusa (Sp.)

Zwickel (G.)
heel of a bow
frog
nut
tallone (It.)
talon (Fr.)
hausse (Fr.)
Frosch (G.)
talón (Sp.)

vs. Spitze (G.)
point

Zwillingsgesang (G.)
gymel, gimel, gemell
cantus gemellus (Lat.)
divided part
semel
singing in thirds

Zwischendominante (G.)
secondary dominant
dominant of the dominant
five of five
Wechseldominante (G.)

Zwischenraum (G.)
space on the staff
spazio (It.)
interligne (Fr.)
espacio (Sp.)

Zwischensatz (G.)
development section

2. middle section
B-section

Zwischenspiel (G.)
entr'acte (Fr.)
act-tune
curtain-tune
interlude
divertissement (Fr.)
intermezzo (It.)
Zwischenaktmusik (G.)

Zwölftonmusik (G.)
twelve-tone music
serial music
dodecaphonic music
musica dodecafonica (It.)
musique dodécaphonique (Fr.)
música dodecafónica (Sp.)

zydeco music
la-la music
cajun music

Zymbel (G.)
*cymbal (percussion)
piatti (It.)
cymbale (Fr.)
Becken (G.)
platillo (Sp.)

2. mixture (org.)
compound stop
cymbale (Fr.)
cimbel (G.)
Scharff (G.)
címbala (Sp.)